Please remember that this is a library book,
and that it belongs only temporarily to each
person who uses it. Be considerate. Do
not write in this, or any, library book.

**Readings in
Child Development
and
Relationships**

Russell C. Smart and Mollie S. Smart

Department of Child Development and Family Relations
University of Rhode Island

Readings in
CHILD
DEVELOPMENT
and
RELATIONSHIPS

The Macmillan Company, New York
Collier-Macmillan Limited, London

THE MACMILLAN COMPANY
866 Third Avenue, New York, New York 10022
COLLIER-MACMILLAN CANADA, LTD., Toronto, Ontario

Library of Congress catalog card number: 70–152819

PRINTING   456789   YEAR   456789

Preface

A sufficient reason for studying child development is a liberal one, the expansion of man's understanding of man. The practical value of such understanding is potentially great, in addition to the intrinsic reward of the liberal one. There is no conflict between the two. In order to understand man, we observe him in dynamic interaction, acting upon the physical and biological world, being influenced by it, and relating to other human beings. Man's most serious problem, the threat he poses to his own survival, stems from his actions upon the physical and biological world and from his relationships with his own species. His social and moral development have not kept pace with his intellectual growth. Child development research is focused upon the sources, early stages, and growth processes of all facets of man.

The child development movement in the United States and Canada began in the 1920's. Of course children had been studied before, but only from the point of view of the beholder. Educators, physicians, psychologists, and parents had studied children and had written about them. The philosophy of child development, however, was that the child is a whole person, living in relationship to other people who surround and support him in a widening series of inclusions. Although the study of growth had to be broken into manageable units, such as the growth of the mind and the growth of the body, students of child development recognized divisions as arbitrary and sought ways of studying the child as a whole and of putting the pieces back together after they had examined them. The child was recognized not only as a whole person, but as a person-in-relation. It was therefore essential to study parent–child relationships and to study the family. Because families are parts of communities, regions, and nations, these wider social networks are also pertinent to understanding the child.

The pioneer child development centers gathered together specialists from a wide variety of disciplines in order to study the child, a whole person-in-relation. The centers were located in the Merrill-Palmer School in Detroit and at the universities of California, Cornell, Georgia, Iowa, Minnesota, McGill, and Toronto. The staff of the centers came from the fields of anthropology, education, medicine, nutrition, nursing, physiology, psychology, social work, and sociology. While focusing on common problems these individuals educated each other, with the result that many professionals of varying backgrounds became specialists in child development. The first child development textbook, *Growth and Development of the Young Child* (Saunders, 1930), was written by a nurse and social worker, Winifred Rand, a nutritionist and former dean of home economics, Mary Sweeny, and a psychologist, Lee Vincent. Although Rand was primarily responsible for the parts on family and community, Sweeny for physical growth and nutrition, and Vincent for psychological development, the three authorities worked closely together to present an integrated account of living children interacting in human settings.

We had the privilege of beginning our professional lives at the Merrill-Palmer School. Although we were not there when it all began, we heard about it from those who started it. The first nursery school teachers had to be imported from England, because America had none. Mary Sweeny told about finding out how to feed young children. Nobody knew what was good for them and what they would eat. Miss Sweeny and her students worked in the kitchen, in the nursery school, and with parents to produce a body of knowledge which stands today. Longitudinal growth records were being collected. The Merrill-Palmer mental test for preschool children had just been standardized. The great people from other centers and other fields came often for meetings and speeches. Margaret Mead and Lawrence K. Frank were among them. The classwork was as integrated as the research and writing. Rarely was a class held with only one teacher. Even three or four might be present, each with a particular point of view and contribution to make. Students came with readings and observations. Class was a true sharing of knowledge and analysis of ideas and meanings. In staff meetings, the older and famous members taught us younger ones; they also listened to us.

Our field has grown enormously in terms of knowledge and personnel. During the past ten or fifteen years, psychologists have flocked to the child, recognizing early growth as a rich field for research. With the elaboration and sophistication of research in the many fields basic to child development, it is growing more and more difficult to keep the elements of mind, body, family, and community in focus. At the same time, it is growing more and more essential to educate child development specialists who can work to solve the human problems of today. Who will direct thousands of day care centers in which children will have the means for optimal health and growth and where parents will be strengthened? Who will help floundering adolescents to achieve identity and integrity? Who will influence local and national governments to pursue policies that support sound human values? Such problems require the efforts of caring individuals equipped with broad knowledge of human development and relationships.

The readings in this book represent a sampling of the field of child development and relationships. The level of difficulty varies considerably from one reading to another. "His Ancient Heritage" by N. J. Berrill is a masterful presentation, in nontechnical language, designed for the intelligent public served by the *Saturday Review*. In contrast, research reports from such professional journals as *Child Development* and *Developmental Psychology* are likely to be difficult in spots, especially for the student who has not studied statistics. Although content was the first consideration in our choice of articles, we have also tried to select a variety of sources and authors. The selection includes writings by specialists from most of the fields mentioned. With the exception of the concluding section, the readings are organized on an age-level basis in order to treat the child as a whole. The readings are supplementary to our textbook, *Children: Development and Relationships*, but of course they can be used with any text in child development.

The first four parts are concerned with the infant, the preschool child, the school-age child, and the adolescent. At each age level, the readings reflect concern with the child as a physical, intellectual, emotional, and social being interacting with his family, peers, and community and being influenced by wider social spheres. Although we stress the normal and try to provide concepts of what most children are like, we also hope to make clear the uniqueness of every individual. We also want to interest American students in children everywhere in the world. They will thus learn more about Americans, but what is more important, they will participate, we hope, to a greater degree as human beings in the human scene.

Part V is called "Summary" but it can be read before the other parts. It consists of one chapter titled "An Overview of Human Life and Growth." It takes a brief look at man in relation to his biological setting.

This book is the result of the labors of a great many people. Duwayne Keller and Claire Lehr made very helpful comments about an early draft. We thank the authors and publishers of the selections for their permission to reprint. Our very special gratitude goes to Elizabeth Lamberton who carried on the correspondence with the authors and publishers which resulted in the permissions. She also attended to many other details of preparing a book like this, cheerfully and carefully. Deborah Petterson and Mary Fields also helped in parts of the process. We thank them for their assistance.

R. C. S.
M. S. S.

Contents

Suggestions for the Student

Some of the readers of this book will be more familiar with textbooks than with research articles and reviews of research. Although some of our selections are as easy to read as textbooks, or even easier, we want to offer some suggestions. Some of our comments are general and some are specific as to how to study this book and how to learn from it.

Our personal conviction is that one cannot get the maximum amount out of a book like this by reading it and doing nothing more. Learning requires some kind of activity on the part of the learner. For most college students, reading is not a great effort. They quite easily get the general drift of what they read, but they do not grasp enough details in reading really to understand. However, when one takes notes concerning what one reads, the activity involved in phrasing the author's words means that, other things being equal, the note taker has made the ideas his own. Copying the words in the book is not what we mean by note taking. Although such copying is an active process, it exercises only the muscles used in writing and may not involve thinking or understanding. Note taking to us means thinking about what the words say, picking out and rephrasing the important ideas, making sure that the new words have not made any important changes in the ideas. Note taking becomes a highly personalized skill, and there are many ways of doing it. (The two of us do it quite differently.) All good methods of note taking are the result of an active thinking process.

TAKING NOTES ON DIFFERENT KINDS OF READING   Those articles in this book which are reviews of research and statements of theoretical positions require about the same kind of notes. There are usually not a great many main points, although some of them may have subsidiary points made in connection with them. Often these points are reiterated in a summary, which may come at the beginning or the end of the selection. If there is no summary, the author may have omitted it because he thought he made his points so clearly that they would not be missed. In any case, assume the author had a message and ask yourself, "What does the author want me to learn? Why does he think it important? What evidence does he present for accepting the truth of his statements?"

The selections which are research reports are more specialized kinds of writing and therefore require a different kind or form of note taking. Here is an outline that we have developed over our years of teaching and that students have found helpful.

HOW TO MAKE AN ABSTRACT OF RESEARCH ARTICLES

Author, name of   The complete title of the article, as stated in the journal. Name of journal, year, volume, inclusive pages. (Month). For the selections in this book add the bibliographic reference for this book also, in the same form. Note that so far you have been copying, exercising your writing muscles. You should not do much more copying.

Purpose   State the purpose in the author's words if he has not been too verbose. Do you see why copying may be a good idea here? But make an active decision to copy. Do not just keep on writing.

Subjects   Name, ages, sex, SE status, hereditary factors, environmental factors, all the important identifying material that the author gives. Put it in tabular form if possible.

Apparatus and procedure   A brief description of any special apparatus, tests, or techniques. If a standard test is used, be sure to mention any deviations from the usual method of presentation or scoring. If the length of time the test continued or the number of determinations is important, be sure to include these facts.

Results   What the investigator found, in terms of scores, etc. Put these in tabular form also if you can. Keep in mind you are writing a summary, but do not leave out any important items. Also remember that you usually make abstracts for use over a long period of time, and that later you may want to know the results of this study for a purpose different from your present one.

Conclusions   How the author interprets his findings. Does he think his hypothesis is substantiated? What does he think is the "next step"? Does he tie his results into the main body of knowledge in his field?

Remarks   This is the place, and the *only* place, for you to say what you think. Is it a good study? Are there any points on which you disagree? Can you offer any interpretations other than those given by the author? What are the theoretical implications? Are there implications for practice? What further studies does this suggest to you?

The following questions are some of the points you should investigate under each of the major headings. All of them, of course, are not applicable to any one study, and there may be others in some instances. A beginning student will not have the background for answering all of them.

Purpose   Does the author state the purpose clearly? Allowing for personal enthusiasms, was the purpose worthwhile?

Subjects   Is the number adequate? Is the sample clearly described as to age, sex, SE status, education, race, and so on? Remember that in different studies different things are important. The two criteria here are whether the sampling is good and whether the sample is reproducible. That is, if you wanted to check the experiment, has the author given you enough information so that you could reproduce the group in all important characteristics?

Apparatus and procedure   As far as you can tell, did the investigator set up his procedure so that his results are not biased by it? Are factors controlled that might invalidate the results? Is there a better way of testing the same hypothesis? If statistics were used, are they adequate? Why did the investigator use the ones he did? If statistics were not used, why did he handle the data as he did? Do you approve of his methods? Why?

Results   Are the results clearly stated? Are sufficient raw data given so that someone else could rework them? Would the results be different if better methods of handling the data had been used? What effect does the sampling have on the results? Do you know of any other studies which bear on this one, either substantiating it or contradicting it?

Conclusions   Do the author's conclusions follow from the results he has stated? Do they bear any relation to his stated purpose? Do the conclusions as stated take into account any limitations in the sampling or method?

This is not the only way of keeping track of research articles. This outline, however, is as exhaustive as most people will need for ordinary purposes. Only occasionally, when you are engaged in writing a minute analysis of the literature on one topic, will you want to keep a more inclusive record of the details in an article. More often you will want to record less material than this outline requires. It is a lot of work to make a complete abstract, but when you have done it, your thinking becomes clearer and your files are that much more well stocked. Complete abstracts should not be neglected.

A VERY SHORT COURSE IN STATISTICS   Many students who read this book will not have had a course in statistics. Usually the authors of research articles interpret the statistics they use and state the conclusions that follow from them. But because you should not get in the lazy habit of skipping over the statistics, we include this section in order to help you to understand some of the important kinds of statistics.

AVERAGES, OR MEASURES OF CENTRAL TENDENCY   What a non-statistician calls the average, a statistician calls the *mean* or the *arithmetic mean*. The average (mean) cost of your textbooks for this semester is the sum of what you paid for all the books divided by the number of books. A mean is a number that, mathematically, is most representative of a series of similar numbers.

Another kind of average is the *median*. A median is the middle number when a series of numbers is arranged from small to large. There are two conditions under which it is used. The median is used when some of the numbers are much larger or smaller than the others. If you were able to get four used textbooks for $4, $4.75, $5, and $7, but had to spend $15 for a new edition, the mean cost would be $7.15. The median cost of $5 is more representative of the series of numbers. The median is also used when the unit of measurement is not divisible into smaller units. The mean number of children per family is an incorrect use of the mean, although it is sometimes reported, because there can be no such thing as a fractional child, and means rarely come out as integers. Since a median can be an integer, the average number of children per family should always be stated as a median.

Occasionally you may find other measures of central tendency in research articles. A statistics textbook will explain them.

TESTS OF SIGNIFICANCE   In most research two or more groups are compared with each other. The important question is, "Are the differences due to chance, or to a real difference in condition or treatment of the groups?" The researcher sets up the hypothesis (called the null hypothesis) that there is no true difference. He applies an appropriate statistical test, on the basis of which he decides to accept or reject the null hypothesis. He would accept the null hypothesis if the test showed that a difference as large as the one discovered could have arisen by chance. If the test showed that the difference could have arisen by chance less than five times out of 100 repetitions of the samples, he rejects the null hypothesis and concludes there *is* a true, or significant, difference. The statistical notation for such a statement is $p < .05$, which is read, "the probability is less than five in 100." Occasionally a more stringent test of significance is used, which is written $p < .01$. This means that the result could be obtained by chance less than 1 per cent of the time. Note that a statistician does not say a difference could *never* occur by chance, but the probability of its occurring by chance is such and such.

There are many different kinds of tests of significance, depending on the kind of data being used. Some of the more usual are χ^2 (chi-squared), the t test, and the F test of analysis of variance. Always a test of significance gives the basis for deciding whether the difference could have arisen by chance.

CORRELATION   A coefficient of correlation measures the degree to which two measures (height and weight, for instance) vary together. Note carefully that correlation coefficients do not say anything about causation. Height and weight are positively correlated, but a person's weight does not cause his height, nor does his height cause his weight.

Coefficients of correlation range in size between $+1.00$ and -1.00. If the coefficient is .00, there is no relationship between the two measures. The closer it is to 1.00, either positive or negative, the closer is the relationship. If there was discovered to be a correlation of $+1.00$ between height and weight in a group of children, the tallest child would be the heaviest, the second tallest would be second heaviest, and so on to the shortest, the lightest. If you knew the height of one of these children in relation to the others, you could place him exactly in weight, in relation to the others. If a correlation coefficient is -1.00, the relationship is perfectly inverse. Suppose the coefficient between reading and arithmetic scores is .00 or not significantly different from .00. The best prediction of any child's reading test score, knowing what his arithmetic test score is, would be the mean reading score of the group of children. Such a prediction would not be very helpful, unless the score in arithmetic (the independent variable) is itself close to the mean.

Most often the correlation coefficient reported is the Pearson product-moment coefficient (r). Another one often used is the rank-order coefficient (rho, or ρ).

Part One

INFANCY

1

Prenatal Development and Birth

Between conception and birth the human being grows from a single cell to a mass of about 7 pounds. The single cell, although simple as compared with the myriad cells composing the newborn infant, is itself a complex organism. The factors operating to shape the nine-month growth are numerous; the interrelationships among the factors are subtle. It used to be generally agreed that the prenatal child was a tyrannical parasite, taking what it needed from the mother's bloodstream, at her expense, if need be. It is now apparent that deprivation of the mother deprives her unborn child.

Even the social settings of childbearing are significant for the baby and the mother. A Scottish sociologist, Raymond Illsley of the University of Aberdeen, traces the complicated interrelationships between social class and the performance of mothers in childbearing. In the process he uses data from large numbers of women and shows that, on the average, women from more deprived cultural settings produce more handicapped children than women from favored settings.

It is not the social setting itself which affects prenatal development, but factors within the social setting, such as nutrition and personal hygiene. Therefore inadequate nutrition and poor personal hygiene, if they occur in a wealthy, otherwise advantaged person, also will have an adverse effect.

Anthropologist Margaret Mead and psychologist Niles Newton discuss the varieties of family structures within which men and women develop as parents. The main focus of this article is on fatherhood. Biological fatherhood is only a brief episode in many animals' lives. The roles and responsibilities of human fatherhood, essential for the survival and development of the child, as developed in various cultures, are the subject matter in this article. (See also the article by Biller in Chapter 8, which reports research on American boys whose fathers were not present in the homes in which the boys were growing up.) What a man does for and with his children after they are born is subject to a great deal of variation.

In the next article Carlo Valenti, a research obstetrician, describes modern techniques for intrauterine diagnosis and treatment. He outlines the hereditary basis of Mongolism and gives the case history of a mother who was saved from producing a Mongoloid child. Valenti faces the reader with the new moral decisions and social adaptations required by recent progress in medicine.

In the last article, a series of excerpts from a longer article, Shank discusses the most recent knowledge regarding optimum nutrition in pregnancy. It is clear that although there are nutritional needs that are unique to pregnancy, optimum nutrition of pregnancy does not begin at conception, or end at birth. The woman's body needs to have good stores of the *nutritional elements before conception. Equally important are the eating habits which result in the woman's nutritional state. Because eating habits are resistant to change, it would be extremely difficult for a woman to improve poor eating patterns to the point of providing good nutrition during the short period of nine months.*

Significance of Class Differences to Childbearing

Raymond Illsley
UNIVERSITY OF ABERDEEN, SCOTLAND

Socio-economic status does not itself affect biological functioning. For purposes of epidemiological research, it is best regarded as an abstraction, a classificatory system designed to subdivide populations according to their social background, characteristics, behavior, and values. Class differences in reproductive behavior merely indicate the possible existence of environmental influences. As a research tool, social class is perhaps comparable to the physician's thermometer, which may indicate that a problem exists but cannot provide a diagnosis. Social classes differ in status origin, education, diet, housing, types of activity, age at marriage and childbirth, parity, physical health, etc.; the difficult but essential task is to identify which of these and many other social influences, acting singly or in combination, produce high obstetric risks.

There is no reason to assume that the same class-related factor is responsible for variations in each pregnancy complication or that for a specific complication the same social etiology applies at different times and places. The components of class reflect the culture of the time and place. This point is illustrated below in a discussion of the difficulties encountered in comparing class performance from decade to decade and from area to area.

The decrease in infant mortality since the beginning of the century has occurred most strikingly for causes of death associated with poor living conditions. One might therefore have expected a long-term tendency toward an equalization of rates. Yet, as reported above, class differentials have hardly changed in Britain (the only country for which data are available) over 40 years of great social, economic, and medical change. Various theories have been advanced to explain these surprising results. Most of these theories are based on the concept of time lag; methods of treatment, the availability of health services, even income, it was argued, could perhaps be changed suddenly, but other, less tangible influences changed slowly—e.g., housing conditions, the physical environment of large towns, habits of hygiene, methods of infant care, the actual use of health facilities, and so forth. Indeed, in the short run,

Reprinted from S. A. Richardson & A. F. Guttmacher (eds.), *Childbearing—Its Social and Psychological Aspects*. Baltimore: Williams and Wilkins, 1967, pp. 82–86, 105–108. By permission of the Association for the Aid of Crippled Children.

it might well be that the educated middle classes would benefit most because their education enabled them to take immediate advantage of improved medical and social services. Thus, decreasing death rates might initially be accompanied by wider class differences, followed, after an interval, by a gradual tendency toward equalization. The history of public health services and the results of health campaigns lend weight to this type of argument; in current campaigns for the early detection of cervical cancer, it is the middle-class woman with a low disease risk who receives the regular check-up.

Another, supplementary explanation has been advanced by Illsley (1955). He showed that women brought up in the lower socio-economic groups who married professional or skilled workers tended to be taller and of better physique than those who remained in the lower social classes at marriage. They also gave birth to heavier babies and had fewer perinatal deaths. Women who moved down the social scale at marriage had high prematurity and perinatal death rates. Illsley postulated a continuous process of social mobility which tended to concentrate healthy women in the upper social groups and the least healthy in the lower social groups, a process which would keep class mortality rates apart as long as social inequality existed. The decreasing size of the semiskilled and unskilled groups, combined with selective upward mobility would, more-over, increase the concentration of less healthy mothers in these groups, thus counteracting any tendency to improvement in their mortality rates.

This argument highlights a property of current methods of status classification which makes them inappropriate for certain types of investigation. If we compare, over time, the mortality rates of two groups, each of which marries entirely within itself (e.g., two castes), and the one with the higher mortality rate is given preferential social and medical care, the two rates should eventually move together. Comparisons over time between countries or regions, between white and colored, are of this kind. Such comparisons would be vitiated, however, if group boundaries were substantially loosened by intermarriage or migration so that the group receiving preferential treatment eventually lost its healthy members to the other group and received their least healthy in return. This is frequently the case in class comparisons, because those members of the lower class who receive preferential treatment as children tend simultaneously to grow into healthy adults and to rise in the social scale. Preferential treatment of one group, as children, results, 20 years later, in the superior health of adults in the other social group.

If we wish to know whether improved living conditions for low-status groups have produced women more capable of producing viable babies, we should classify perinatal or infant mortality rates not by the social status which women reach as adults (their husband's social class) but by their status in childhood (their father's social class). This argument applies to all status groups in a mobile society, to individual occupations as much as to general social classes, because the status reached in adult life reflects the conditions of upbringing which made that status possible.

Time comparisons are complicated by a further technical property of most social classifications. The range of social variation between upper- and lower-status groups depends on their size. Thus, if we compare the upper and lower 5 percent of a population, the range will be greater than if we compare the upper and lower quartiles. Unfortunately, the boundaries of status or class groups are usually fixed by external factors—the percentage of the population possessing certain defined social characteristics—and cannot be manipulated for analytical convenience. In the British example, the lowest social class is defined as "unskilled workers," who formed a considerable proportion of the population 50 years ago but are a relatively small category today. Thus, in comparing the mortality rates of the lowest social class in 1910 and 1960 we might be comparing the lowest quartile of the 1910 population with a highly concentrated 10 percent of the 1960 population. The upper class, on the other hand, will have increased its relative size. For purposes of time comparison, it would be more appropriate to use a "percentile" type of classification so that, for example, the highest and lowest ranking 10 percent could be compared with each other at each time point.

Parallel difficulties occur when we compare the meaning of class from one area to another. The problem is illustrated in Figure 1, derived from the British Perinatal Mortality Survey (Butler and Bonham, 1963). The same criteria of classification were applied to occupations of husbands in the Northern, Midland, and Southern regions of Britain to produce four class categories: professional and managerial, clerical, skilled manual workers, and semiskilled and unskilled workers. Perinatal death rates are expressed as a ratio of the

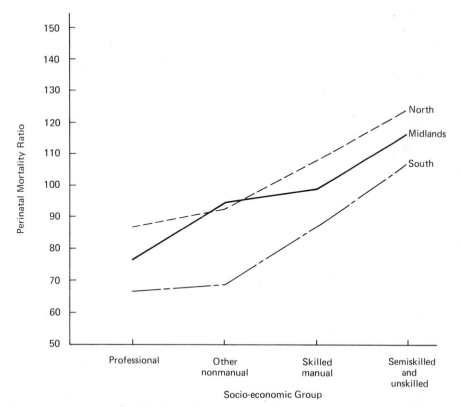

FIGURE 1.   *Perinatal death rates in each region and socio-economic group in Great Britain in 1958 expressed as a ratio of the national rate (Great Britain = 100).*

over-all British rate. It is clear that the rates of each class vary consistently with the region. Indeed, they vary so sharply that professional workers in the North are equivalent to skilled manual workers in the South. Thus, similarity of socio-economic status (as defined by our crude indices) is no guarantee of social identity. There are many reasons for this, some technical, some more truly sociological.

1. When we use classifications which distinguish individuals with a given characteristic—e.g., professional workers, or unskilled workers, people above or below a certain income level, etc.—we may select quite different proportions of the populations in two areas. We may, as in the time comparison discussed above, be comparing the lowest ranking 10 percent of one community with the lowest ranking 25 percent of another. This possibility is even more likely if we deal with selected clinic or hospital populations from different areas.

In most instances such disparity in relative size tends to obscure class differences. In the example given in Figure 1, semiskilled and unskilled workers constituted 31 percent of the population in the north of Great Britain compared with 21 percent in the south. If the Southern group were increased to 31 percent by the reclassification of the lowest ranking skilled workers as semiskilled, the regional differential in the perinatal death rates of semiskilled and unskilled workers would be even greater. On the other hand, in hospital populations, with their overt and hidden biases, class differentials may be obscured; where, for example, private hospital patients in a relatively poor community are compared with those in public hospitals in a richer community, real differences between classes in the two communities may easily be eliminated.

The use of a "percentile" approach avoids this problem but poses an alternative dilemma: equivalent ranks in two communities may have little in common other than their percentile position.

2. Groups with the same nominal class in two areas may, because of heterogeneity within a single class, be widely different in other respects. Thus "skilled workers" in one area may denote craftsmen, whereas in others the term may mean workers in heavy industry, miners, agricultural workers, etc.

3. Behind these technical problems of classification there lies a further sociological problem: within even a relatively small area, separate communities may exist which differ so much in their ways of life that the pooling together of nominally similar social classes from each community may be a meaningless operation. . . .

THE INTERRELATIONSHIP OF SOCIAL AND OBSTETRIC PROCESSES

Each of . . . these factors . . .—social class; country, region, and area; illegitimacy; age; parity; and maternal height—is clearly associated with many aspects of reproductive functioning. The range of differences along a single axis is in each case strongly marked. Although all these factors are interrelated, there is some reason to assume that each may exercise an "independent" effect or indicate the presence of a further causal factor so that when they occur together their impact is cumulative. The range of perinatal death rates occurring between tall wives of professional men in the south of England and short wives of manual workers in the north of Britain is itself large (mortality ratio of 58 compared to 140); if simultaneous data were available on age and parity and the analysis were extended over a wider geographic and ethnic range, these differences would be further widened (Illsley and Kincaid, 1963). It is clearly important to study the interrelationships among these factors and the social processes by which they become interrelated and through which they jointly relate to obstetric behavior. The intrinsic effect of other specific factors, such as nutrition in pregnancy, smoking, physical activity, etc., can then be viewed against the general socio-medical background.

The period of infancy, childhood, and adolescence may be regarded not only as one of growth and learning but also as one of differentiation. The child undergoes environmental experiences, both physical and cultural, which shape his physique and health and his emotional and intellectual growth and simultaneously implant the social values and habits which will characterize his behavior as an adult. The physical and cultural stimuli are not independent of one another: the socio-economic conditions which influence education, social values, aspirations, and opportunities also affect the child's material environment and nutrition; and the nutritional experience which influences his growth simultaneously patterns his later dietary habits.

In the highly diversified, mobile, changing society of the industrial West, this is a complex process; the increasingly technological nature of the economy demands the emergence from lower socio-economic strata of huge population groups with skills and values different from those of their parents, and the informal educational institutions of the family and the social group are systematically supplemented by the vast educational machinery of the modern state. This is a selective movement: persons move up into the higher socio-economic strata whose material and cultural environment has most fitted them to take advantage of increasing educational and occupational opportunities. There is a corresponding downward movement of individuals and groups who, for many reasons, have been unable to grasp these opportunities. The vast literature on the subject cannot be summarized here (see Glass, 1954; Lipset and Bendix, 1959) but its implications are important, for it leads to the existence of adult groups with characteristic patterns of social and biological inter-correlations. It is this process of socialization, selection, and acculturation that produces the tendency for certain biological characteristics and social habits and values to hang together. Thus each of the various socio-economic groups is characterized not only by similarity in wealth but also by broadly similar educational levels, nutritional habits, housing and work conditions, habits in relation to age at marriage, attitudes to family size, spacing and methods of birth control, access to and motivation to use health services, and also by their physical build and their basic health status.

In terms of the variables discussed above, the lower social classes tend to marry early, to have many children at short intervals, to be drawn from poorer regions and housing areas, and to be short in stature. Around these basic factors are clustered other typical characteristics: illegitimacy, prenuptial conception, poor diet, infectious environments; heavy manual work, late or inadequate antenatal care, lack of ready access to information and advice, poor motivation to seek such help, limited knowledge of biological functioning, lack of control over their environment and consequent anxiety, inadequate or ill-balanced dietary intakes, etc. These characteristics do not, of course, all occur uniformly in all members of lower socio-economic groups, and they may be modified by ethnic or religious influences in a heterogeneous society; each characteristic, however, occurs most frequently in these groups and there is an internal logic in their simultaneous manifestation.

Many implications flow from such patterns. In studying the etiology of a pregnancy condition, the simultaneous occurrence of many factors inevitably leads to accidental correlations. The term "young multipara," for example, connotes many factors besides youth and multiparity; depending on the culture in which it is applied, it may connote short, unhealthy women, poor antenatal and obstetric care, economic disadvantage (nonwhite, unskilled workers, unemployed, etc.), and a host of related factors. Its implications may not always lead in the same direction. As we have seen, youth appears to be a favorable factor in relation to stillbirth, and stillbirth rates are relatively low for young women and for second and third pregnancies, but youth and multiparity in combination are associated with high stillbirth and infant death rates. The "elderly primigravida" has the low infant mortality rates appropriate to her favorable social characteristics and the high stillbirth rates associated with age.

Systematic study of the specific influence of a biological variable seems to require, therefore, detailed knowledge of the operation and interrelation of social and biological factors as they apply in the culture being studied—a requirement very rarely met. This requirement becomes more important when (1) the sampling basis of the study population is unknown; and (2) smaller groups from different populations or institutions are being added together to form a large total sample.

These are the conditions under which research is normally conducted in most centers. A hospital located in one area of a large city is likely to draw its population from the surrounding neighborhood; this is likely to be socially selected. Certain socio-economic groups may already have been drawn off to be patients of private or specialized hospitals and, where home confinement is common, self-selection of another and biased kind may also have important effects. Valid conclusions may still be drawn from such studies, but the validity will depend on the nature of the population, the problem being studied, the strength of diagnostic tools, the clinical insight of the medical practitioner, etc. Some of the difficulties arising in such studies will be considered in more detail later.

A second series of implications affects those studies dealing with the consequences of the birth process for the functioning of the child. A low level of functioning in a child may result from a multiplicity of genetic, intrauterine, perinatal, and postnatal influence, some biological, some social and psychological. When the level of functioning of children whose birth was characterized by a particular condition (e.g., low birth weight) is below average, there is at least a prima facie case for arguing that the condition itself affected the child's functioning. This, however, is one of several possibilities which, in terms of low birth weight and infant I.Q., may be stated as follows:

1. A direct causal link exists (as stated above).

2. Women of low I.Q. may be prone to bear small babies, many of whom thus inherit a low intellectual potential.

3. Low birth weight and low infant I.Q. may both independently be resultants of maternal pregnancy pathology.

4. Low-birth-weight babies may be born into postnatal environments relatively unfavorable to intellectual growth.

A number of variations could be played on a combination of such hypotheses, either for premature babies in general or for clinical subcategories.

We are thus dealing with genetic, perinatal, and sociopsychological processes which may each have its own pathways but which may be and usually are interconnected. The association of birth weight with social status and maternal height, for example, already introduces the problem of genetic and social factors in the determination of stature, their joint effect on birth weight, the relationship of each to other aspects of maternal functioning, the genetic inheritance of intelligence, and the effect of parental socio-economic status on intellectual development. The problem is, of course, complicated if studies are based on partial and biased populations where one or all of the processes involved may be distorted by selection.

References

BUTLER, N. R., and BONHAM, D. G., 1963: *Perinatal Mortality*. Edinburgh: Livingstone.

GLASS, D. (ed.), 1954: *Social Mobility in Great Britain*. London: Routledge, Kegan and Paul.

ILLSLEY, R., 1955: Social class selection and class differences in relation to stillbirths and infant deaths, *Brit. Med. J.*, 2:1520–4.

———, and KINCAID, J. C., 1963: "Social Correlates of Perinatal Mortality," in *Perinatal Mortality*, N. R. Butler and D. G. Bonham (eds.). Edinburgh: Livingstone.

LIPSET, S. M., and BENDIX, R., 1959: *Social Mobility in Industrial Society*. London: Heineman.

Fatherhood

Margaret Mead
THE MUSEUM OF NATURAL HISTORY

Niles Newton
NORTHWESTERN UNIVERSITY

Mead (1949) has emphasized that human fatherhood is a fundamental social invention. In all human societies there is at least some help given by some men to childbearing women. "Which woman and which children are provided

Reprinted from S. A. Richardson and A. F. Guttmacher (Eds.), *Childbearing—Its Social and Psychological Aspects*. Baltimore: Williams and Wilkins, 1967, pp. 189–192. By permission of the Association for the Aid of Crippled Children.

for is entirely a matter of social arrangements although the central pattern seems to be that of a man's providing for the woman who is his sexual partner and whatever children she may happen to have.''

There are, of course, many variations on the basic theme reviewed by Mead. Some societies have brothers who help sisters with all aspects of childbearing except fertilization. In many societies some men do not help directly with childbearing, preferring instead the life of a monk or other nonfamily types of living. Some highly organized societies may substitute the state for some aspects of fatherly care by taxing men and other wage earners in order to provide allowances for mothers.

Mead (1949) points out also that fatherly behavior is disrupted by slavery and some forms of indentured labor and serfdom as well as during periods of extreme social unrest, such as wars, revolutions, famines, epidemics, or abrupt transition from one kind of economy to another. "Men may flounder badly in these periods, during which the primary unit may again become mother and child.''

Possibly because it is so easy under some conditions for men not to assume nurturing and assisting behavior toward childbearing women and children, many societies have developed ways of emphasizing the responsibilities of men. The Arapesh are an example of a society that begins to develop very active feelings of responsibility for women and children at a young age. The betrothed of an Arapesh boy, who should be about six years younger than he, moves into his house when she is seven or eight years old. The boy is required to grow yams, work sago, and hunt meat to feed his future wife (Mead, 1935).

Most societies emphasize responsibilities toward women and children somewhat later, through economic exchanges and rituals preceding cohabitation or during the first pregnancy. Whether the money is paid to the groom in the form of a dowry to ensure his feeling a moral obligation for future economic support of the woman and child, or whether the money is paid in the form of a bride price to the wife's family, or whether the economic exchange between families tends to be fairly equal does not matter so much as the fact that in all these cases the responsibility of men for women and their children is emphasized.

Many primitive cultures very directly stress the father's role during childbearing. The father feels personally responsible for the growth of the fetus because of the common belief that what the father does during pregnancy, as well as what the mother does, affects the health and development of the fetus. Food and activity restrictions involve not only the mother but the father also. The Ifugao of the Philippines do not permit the husband to cut or kill anything during his wife's pregnancy. Relatives must even cut wood for him, which he then carries home (Ford, 1945). The Pacific Ocean Easter Islander father gets a real sense of participation in birth by having his wife recline against him during labor and delivery (Métraux, 1940). The Kurtatchi father of the Pacific Islands is excluded from the labor, which takes place in another hut, but the importance of his impending fatherhood is emphasized by the fact that he must stop work and remain in seclusion. On no account may he lift anything heavy or touch a sharp instrument (Blackwood, 1935).

Very often the regulations cover both husband and wife, thus emphasizing the mutual nature of the undertaking. The Ila husband and wife avoid the flesh of a hartebeest, since the young of this animal are born blind and they fear the human infant will be born blind if hartebeest flesh is eaten by the parents (Smith and Dale, 1920).

Ceremonies involving husband as well as wife also emphasize fatherhood. Among the Lepcha, for example, both parents have a ceremonial cleansing in the fifth month of pregnancy (Gorer, 1938). The custom of couvade occurs in many parts of the world. Essentially it involves a period of activity restriction and "regulation" for the father as well as the mother for a time after birth. Ford's sample (1945) of 64 cultures contains records of the customs of 18 tribes in this regard. Seventeen tribes from Asia, North America, Oceania, and South America involved the father in couvade after delivery. In only one group was it definitely recorded that there was no couvade. There may be real survival value in this custom as it may particularly emphasize the father's role and responsibilities at the crucial time as each child is born. It may help him to identify with mother and baby.

In American middle-class culture, often particular emphasis is put on the wedding ceremony rather than on the later phases of fatherhood. A very elaborate wedding ceremony emphasizes man's assumption of economic responsibility for a woman and her future children. This ceremony involves name changing on the part of the woman and changes in the residence, tax status, and financial liability of both. This suitably expresses the American concept that the father's role is particularly concerned with monetary support. In fact, the American man is often actively discouraged from aiding his wife directly at the time of parturition, seldom being permitted in the delivery room and being restricted in the times he may visit with his wife in the post-delivery hospital phase. During this period, too, he may be permitted to see his baby for a few minutes behind nursery glass, but touching his baby is taboo in most hospitals. However, he is permitted to call attention to his new fatherhood by giving gifts of cigars to other men, and very recently participation in pregnancy has developed in some areas in the form of "parents' classes" which the husband as well as his expectant wife attend.

BIOLOGICAL PATERNITY AND ILLEGITIMACY

Social paternity is probably a very ancient custom, since some responsibility to nurture women and children by men is felt in all known societies, but biological paternity and concepts of illegitimacy are, in contrast, probably fairly recent. The Trobrianders, living near New Guinea, and the Aranda (Ford, 1945) believe that coitus exists merely for pleasure. They do not recognize its direct connection with conception and thus do not have the concept of physiological paternity.

Other societies know about biological paternity but regard it as a fact of minor significance. For example, the Ila young man is rather pleased if his bride has a fatherless child as thus he already has the start of a family (Smith and Dale, 1920). The Lepcha woman with an illegitimate child may be sought after and get a richer husband owing to her demonstrated fertility (Morris, 1938), although on her marriage her child usually stays with her family, the social father role being assumed by the grandfather rather than the husband of the woman. The Pukapuka (Beaglehole and Beaglehole, 1938) do not have a word for the physiological state of virginity; sexual experience takes place quite irrespective of marriage. A woman with an out-of-wedlock child is regarded as one who has proven herself fertile and thus able to carry on the patrilineal line.

In Antigua, in the West Indies, "the unmarried mother outnumbers the married mother by two to one, and there is no social or other stigma associated with this state of affairs." The teenager starting on her first pregnancy feels she will be treated better by her boy friend if she is not legally married to him. Here perhaps better social fathering occurs when marriage is not solemnized. It is interesting that under these conditions an extensive demographic study found no significant difference in the stillbirth rate between illegitimate and legitimate children (Uttley, 1961).

Other societies, however, have greatly emphasized the fact of physical paternity. In these societies the type of care the woman receives in pregnancy and the type of care her child receives are very definitely related to whether the child is the biological child of a duly wedded husband. If the child is illegitimate, its right to live is often jeopardized. Induced abortion of illegitimate conceptions occurs in many societies in which great shame is attached to illegitimacy. In some cultures even the mother may be killed. The custom in Jordan some years ago was to kill the unmarried mother; and even in 1925 no child born of an unmarried woman could be registered in the village. Granqvist (1950) comments: "Although the fellaheen fear punishment by Government, their ideas of morality still demand that the child and the mother must die."

Still other societies do not see legitimacy and illegitimacy in simple, dichotomous terms but have developed various degrees of legitimacy symbolizing different degrees of status. Among the Vietnamese, "children born of a second wife are not exactly illegitimate but do not have the same rights as children born of the first wife" (Dê, 1951). The Tupinamba had five categories of illegitimacy (d'Evreux, 1864), the highest status accruing to the offspring of the Tupinamba man and woman, and the lowest to the offspring of a Frenchman and slave of the Tupinamba.

On the other hand, low social status may make the illegitimate child more welcome. Thus the child of an unmarried Bambara mother may not live to cry more than once, but the child of an unmarried slave of the Bambara is welcome (Henry, 1910). In Goajiro, among very poor families, the illegitimately pregnant woman is merely ridiculed, whereas the woman of high class is nearly always abandoned by her relatives (Gutierrez de Pineda, 1948).

Thus in some cases illegitimacy is so construed as to deny the child any help or protection from any men, whereas in other cases the child is helped by the men of the mother's family rather than by the biological father. In still others the child is helped by the husband of his mother. In terms of outcome of the pregnancy, illegitimacy can mean death, negligent care, or care that is as good as that furnished to legitimate babies and their mothers in the same cultures, depending on social attitudes and customs. . . .

References

References originating from the Human Relations Area Files are marked with an asterisk. In cases where Human Relations Area Files foreign language texts have been quoted in this paper, the translations into English are those of the Human Relations Area Files.

*BEAGLEHOLE, E., and BEAGLEHOLE, P., 1938: "Ethnology of Pukapuka," *Bernice P. Bishop Museum Bulletin 150*, Honolulu.

*BLACKWOOD, B., 1935: *Both Sides of Buka Passage*. Oxford: Clarendon Press.

*Dê, T. D., 1951: "Notes on Birth and Reproduction in Vietnam," unpublished manuscript by Margaret Coughlin.

*GORER, G., 1938: *Himalayan Village: An Account of the Lepchas of Sikkim*. London: Michael Joseph.

*GRANQVIST, H., 1950: *Child Problems Among the Arabs*. Helsingfors: Söderström.

*GUTIERREZ DE PINEDA, V., 1948: "Organizacion social en la Guajira," *Rev. Inst Etnolog. Nac. (Bogota)*, 3.

*HENRY, J., 1910: "L'ame d'un peuple Africain," *Bibliotheque-Anthropos, 1*, No. 2.

*MEAD, M., 1935: *Sex and Temperament in Three Primitive Societies*. New York: William Morrow.

———, 1949: *Male and Female*. New York: William Morrow.

*MÉTRAUX, A., 1940: "Ethnology of Easter Island," *Bernice P. Bishop Museum Bulletin 160*. Honolulu.

*MORRIS, J., 1938: *Living with Lepchas: A Book about the Sikkim Himalayas*. London: William Heinemann.

*SMITH, E. W., and DALE, A. M., 1920: *The Ila-Speaking Peoples of Northern Rhodesia*. London: Macmillan.

UTTLEY, K. H., 1961: The birth, stillbirth, death and fertility rates in the coloured population of Antigua, West Indies, from 1857 to 1956, *Trans. Roy. Soc. Trop. Med. Hyg.*, 55:59–78.

The Child: His Right to Be Normal

Carlo Valenti

DOWNSTATE MEDICAL CENTER, STATE UNIVERSITY OF NEW YORK

In his new classic of modern biology, *The Person in the Womb*, Dr. N. J. Berrill makes this, among other, declarations:

> If a human right exists at all, it is the right to be born with normal body and mind, with the prospect of developing further to fulfillment. If this is to be denied, then life and conscience are mockery and a chance should be made for another throw of the ovarian dice.

Reprinted from *Saturday Review*, December 7, 1968, pp. 75–78. Copyright © 1968 Saturday Review, Inc. By permission.

In accord with this philosophy, I draw attention to some favorable prospects for "another throw."

About one in fifty babies is born with a greater or less degree of abnormality inherited from its parents. These weaknesses, more than 500 of them severe enough to be classified as diseases (diabetes, for example), are ordered by the genes carried on the chromosomes. No one has ever seen a gene, but we can identify chromosomes under the microscope. Every normal person has a complement of forty-six of them, paired in twenty-three sets. One of the twenty-three pairs determines sex. The determination is made by chance and occurs as follows (see Figure 1).

The female sex chromosomes are paired XX. In any division of the germ cell in preparation for mating with a male sperm, the female half of the marriage will therefore always be X.

The male sex chromosomes are paired XY. When the division of this germ cell occurs, the sperm may be X or it may be Y.

When a female egg is penetrated by an X sperm, the nuclei of the egg and the sperm will fuse XX and the offspring will be female.

When a female egg is penetrated by a Y sperm, the offspring will be XY, or male.

The choice is simple when everything goes well in the reproductive process. However, faulty working of the ovaries or testes sometimes produces fertilized XXX eggs (super-females, not always fertile), XXYs (outwardly male, but without sperm), XOs (outwardly female, but without ovaries and therefore without eggs), XXXXYs (typically defective mentally), and XYYs (typically defective mentally, often aggressive to a criminal extent).

The other twenty-two pairs of chromosomes suffer displacements when parents bring together certain genetic characteristics. The results can be very sad. For example, the chromosome pairs numbered 13-14-15 are catalogued by the letter D. Pairs No. 21 and 22 are catalogued by the letter G. Sometimes one chromosome of these two pairs is displaced in what is called a D/G translocation. What happens is that one of the No. 21 pair crosses over to and joins up with one of the No. 15 pair, riding piggyback as it were and giving that one No. 15 a lopsided appearance.

The person who bears this particular pattern of chromosomes is a balanced carrier, for Mongolism. We say "balanced" because the total amount of genetic material on the chromosomes is normal, although the number of chromosomes is only forty-five. But the chromosomal pattern is thrown off balance when the balanced carrier's offspring inherits the lopsided chromosome from the carrier along with a 21 from the carrier and a 21 from the other parent. The total inheritance then is three 21s, two in the normal position and one on the lopsided chromosome. The three 21s doom their possessor to Mongolism.

Why focus on the Mongoloid?

A Mongoloid child—in medical terms, he is a victim of "Down's syndrome"—has folded eyes and a flat-rooted nose (the Mongolian-like features from which the popular name of the anomaly derives), small head, fissured protruding tongue, peculiarities in the lines of the palms of the hands and the soles of the feet, retarded intellectual development ranging from idiocy to a maximum prospective mental age of seven years.

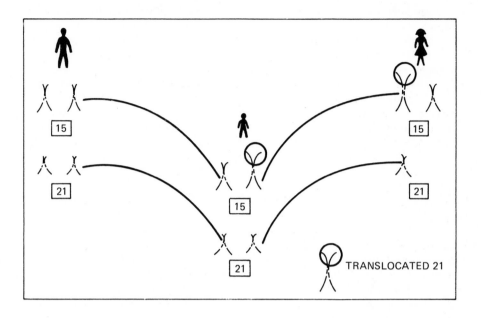

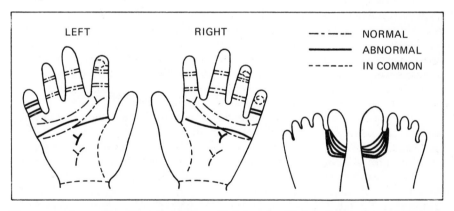

FIGURE 1.   *How Mongolism is transmitted through a "balanced carrier" to an offspring is demonstrated above. Only two of the twenty-three sets of chromosomes—the No. 15s and the No. 21s—are shown. Note that whereas the father has the normal 21 pair, the mother has one 21 in its normal place and the other upside down on the lopsided No. 15. When chance deals the child the lopsided 15, he has three 21s and is doomed. Palm prints and sole prints of Mongoloid child are below.*

Once given life, a Mongoloid is a poignant burden on its parents. For the Mongoloid appeals to all human instincts for companionship. He is cheerful, friendly, imitative, with a good memory for music and for details of situations he has experienced. A Mongoloid's life expectancy averages ten years—a decade of hopelessness, in most cases necessarily spent in a special institution.

Now it has been known for more than a dozen years that before a child is in finished form to leave his mother's womb the chromosomes of the prospective individual can be sampled and analyzed for aberrations. Dr. Fritz Fuchs, Danish-born chief of obstetrics and gynecology at Cornell University Medical College in New York, was able to pioneer such work in his native country because of the liberality of Denmark's laws governing therapeutic abortion.

The method developed by Dr. Fuchs and others is to obtain cells from the amniotic fluid, which is the stuff that every developing fetus floats in. Although the fetus derives almost all of its nourishment from rapidly pulsing blood fed from the placenta by way of the umbilical cord, the fetus before twelve weeks have passed by begins to swallow the amniotic fluid and excrete the fluid through its kidneys and bladder. In growing, the fetus sheds its skin gradually as we living persons shed ours, and other cells are dislodged from the mouth, bronchi, trachea, kidney, and bladder in the course of the swallowing and excreting. The fluid carrying all these cells must be sampled through the wall of the pregnant woman's abdomen by means of a hollow needle similar to those used to draw blood from a vein.

Where the needle enters the womb is of critical importance; if the wrong site were to be chosen, the placenta could be punctured or the fetus itself impaled. Either event could produce serious consequences.

To assure a safe choice, the exact location of the placenta and the floating head of the fetus is determined in the same way that submarines are located when afloat in sea water—that is, by sonar or echo-sounding. The method is feasible as early as the fourteenth week of pregnancy. A tiny portable gun that fires waves at very high speeds is moved across the prospective parent's abdomen in sweeps proceeding successively downward until the entire belly has been scanned. A pattern similar to that seen on a radar screen emerges. With it as a guide, the entry point of the amniocentesis needle is fixed.

After a sample of the amniotic fluid has been removed through the needle, the sample is spun in a centrifuge. The liquid part of the sample is then discarded. A pellet of cells remains. In this pellet is the knowledge we seek.

Two groups of investigators have reported varying success in culturing the cells on nutritive media they have independently developed. Their techniques, described in the medical literature, did not yield good results in our obstetrics and gynecology laboratory here at State University of New York's Downstate Medical Center in Brooklyn. So Edward J. Schutta, Tehila Kehaty, and myself have worked out a culturing method of our own and with it have obtained twenty successes in twenty-four trials. All our failures occurred where the amount of amniotic fluid used was below a certain level. The twenty successful cell cultures yielded seventeen chromosome analyses, or karyotypes. The three failures apparently were due to bacterial contamination.

Two to six weeks of growth are required before the culture is ready to be karyotyped—that is, placed on a glass laboratory slide, dried, stained, and examined microscopically to determine the chromosome pattern.

Last April, a Boston medical colleague familiar with our work referred to us a twenty-nine-year-old mother from Massachusetts who was sixteen weeks pregnant. She knew her grandfather, her mother, her brother, and herself to be balanced carriers of the D/G chromosomal translocation. That is, all four were outwardly normal and healthy, but each carried within himself only one No. 21 chromosome in its normal pairing, while the other 21 was grafted onto one of the No. 15 chromosome pair. In short, although not themselves Mongoloid, three generations of the family carried the genetic threat of Mongolism.

The young New Englander had already experienced a spontaneous abortion, borne a daughter who was also a balanced carrier of the D/G chromosomal translocation, and borne a Mongoloid son who had lived for five months. She wanted another child, and sought our assurance that it would be normal. With the support of her husband, an engineer by profession, she requested a cytogenetic diagnosis on the unborn baby.

Amniocentesis was performed after a sonar sounding on April 15. The amount of amniotic fluid obtained proved inadequate for optimum cell growth. Amniocentesis was performed again on April 29, luxuriant cell cultures were available within two weeks, and satisfactory chromosome preparations were ready for analysis on May 21. The karyotypes showed a male pattern with the D/G chromosomal translocation characteristic of Mongolism. Our hospital's abortion committee authorized a therapeutic interruption of pregnancy on the grounds that, since Mongolism was certain, failure to interrupt could subject the young mother to unjustifiable psychiatric trauma. Notice of the therapeutic abortion was posted routinely on the staff bulletin boards, and the abortion was done on May 31. Autopsy findings and palmprint and soleprint patterns were consistent with our cytogenetic diagnosis.

The young woman who volunteered for this experience recovered and returned to her New England home within forty-eight hours. She is still eager for another child if she can have a healthy one. She has requested application of amniocentesis to all future pregnancies.

This woman now has a chance for "another throw of the ovarian dice," as Dr. Berrill put it. The British medical journal, *Lancet*, last July published news of her case in the form of a letter from Schutta, Kehaty, and myself. The *Journal of the American Medical Association* has since notified us that it has accepted for publication a longer formal report of the case. So far as I know, it is the first piece of such news to appear in the medical literature anywhere. It may not be sensational news because D/G chromosomal translocations account for only 2 per cent of all Mongoloid children. But to the individual women involved, it is a promise of release from fear and guilt.

Furthermore, the potential benefits of amniocentesis and karyotyping are applicable to the much greater percentage of Mongolism caused by trisomies. In these there are forty-seven chromosomes, including three No. 21s which appear as triplets in the place of the normal 21 pair (as opposed to the pair of 21s and the 21 contained in the lopsided chromosome of the D/G Mongoloids).

Trisomies are related to aging. Human eggs spoil with time just as other eggs do. . . . Every woman's supply of eggs has been nested in her ovaries since well before she herself was born. All else being equal, she begins releasing them, at the rate of one a month (except during pregnancy and subsequent nursing), when she is about thirteen years old, and continues the process for the forty-odd years that intervene before menopause. Overall, the chance of an American woman giving birth to a Mongoloid child is one in 680. To age twenty-five, the chance is one in 2,000; after age forty-five, one in fifty.

Our laboratory has made cytogenetic diagnoses of two women who feared their pregnancies might produce Mongoloid infants. One of these women was thirty-six years old, the other thirty-seven. Amniocentesis and karyotyping showed no chromosomal aberrations.

The potential of prenatal study of fetal cells obtained by amniocentesis is far greater than we have yet been able to explore. Three broad areas are open to investigation. In the first, a smear of the fetal cells can be made immediately after the cells are collected from the amniotic fluid. The smear shows presence or absence of the sex chromatin body (a condensation of nuclear material), which only female cells possess. The sex of the unborn child can thus be identified and sex-linked hereditary diseases, such as hemophilia and muscular dystrophy, can be diagnosed in the fetus. More than ten years ago, Dr. Fuchs in Denmark demonstrated the value of the technique by screening hemophilic pregnancies and interrupting those that would have resulted in male babies. Only males actually develop hemophilia; females carry the disease without being afflicted by it.

The second field of study of cells obtained by amniocentesis is the analysis of their chromosome complement, as illustrated by the case of the young woman patient described above. Advanced maternal age can cause a number of chromosomal errors in addition to the error that results in Mongolism. Anguish for the mothers involved can be avoided in some cases by interruption of pregnancy. The number of such cases is at the moment still uncertain. The certainty is that in the present state of knowledge we cannot correct chromosomal errors. In the future, however, we may be able to correct the effect of the errors by refining our methods, by applying the principle that each effect is due to a particular enzyme and that each enzyme is ordered by a particular gene. One step in the refinement is to map the locations of the genes on the chromosomes of man, as has already been done with the mouse.

The third area of endeavor in intrauterine medicine (treatment of the fetus in the uterus) is analysis of enzymes produced by the fetal cells that are taken from the amniotic fluid. There are hereditary diseases in which deficiency of given enzymes is known in the adult. Detection of the same deficiencies in the fetal cells may permit diagnosis of diseases in the unborn baby and possibly correction of the deficiencies and thus prevention of the diseases.

For example, one of the signs of Mongolism is flaccid muscles at birth. If the body of a Mongoloid baby is laid prone on the palm of the hand, the baby's head and limbs will flop downward like those of a rag doll. The weakness of the muscles has been attributed to absence of a chemical which can be made only in the presence of a particular enzyme. According to prevailing genetic theory, this enzyme must be missing from Mongoloid cells and the absence must be related to the existence in the cells of three No. 21 chromosomes instead of the normal pair of 21s.

In an English experiment, a chemical named 5-hydroxytryptophan was administered to fourteen Mongoloid babies ranging from a few days to four months in age. Within one to seven weeks later, normal muscle tone was restored to thirteen of these babies, who became able to raise their heads, arms, and legs. Clearly, a missing something had been supplied and had counteracted at least some part of the effect of the abnormal set of three No. 21 chromosomes.

The English researchers were careful to point out that there is yet no evidence that their treatment will improve the mental development of Mongoloid babies. It is conceivable, however, that if Mongolism were diagnosed sufficiently early in the development of the fetus and if the missing chemical could be administered then, the effect on the child might be remarkable.

A great many scientists the world over are now studying enzyme deficiencies in hereditary diseases in the adult human. As their reservoir of knowledge grows, the potential of amniocentesis widens proportionately.

A major determinant of the ultimate effectiveness of intrauterine medicine will be the public attitude on abortion. At present, the laws of many states do not allow therapeutic abortion on genetic grounds. Genetic grounds are habitually construed as empirical statistical evaluations. Chromosomal analysis is not statistical but is direct and specific evidence of abnormality. As physicians, legislators, and the people come to understand the distinction, they will surely see that the law cannot be interpreted to exclude abortion based on chromosomal analysis. For a law that would compel a mother to give birth to a baby certain to be severely defective would be cruel and uncivilized.

A Chink in Our Armor

Robert E. Shank
WASHINGTON UNIVERSITY MEDICAL SCHOOL

In pregnancy, good nutrition can be a matter of life or death. And what is more, while this truism applies to pregnant women of all ages, the younger the mother, the greater the risk of poor diet.

Here is a chink in our medical armor that can be repaired.

This, briefly, is the conclusion of the Committee on Maternal Nutrition of the National Research Council. Its report, *Maternal Nutrition and the Course of Human Pregnancy*, the result of three years' study by thirteen scientists—including nine physicians—is being published this month. It provides an authoritative review of current evidence of the effect of food on the outcome of pregnancy. The report clearly shows the need for a significant change in the way physicians and others now view the pregnant woman's diet. It focuses on the need for a new approach to the dietary management of pregnancy, and suggests abandoning many current practices widely accepted as safe. Physicians, dietitians, and other health professionals will discover many practical suggestions for counseling pregnant women, prospective parents, and their families in the findings.

As Chairman of the Committee, I will try to summarize the important points of our findings, hoping that the results of our deliberations will thus

Reprinted from *Nutrition Today*, 5(2), 2–11. Copyright © 1970 Enloe, Stalvey and Associates. By permission.

become known to *Nutrition Today*'s wide audience of several hundred thousand health professionals. Everyone should avail himself of the wealth of information to be found in the complete report. (Available from the National Academy of Sciences, National Research Council, 2101 Constitution Avenue, N.W., Washington, D.C. 20418, price $7.50.)

GOSSIP THERAPY

In the most sophisticated society as well as among the most primitive tribes, gossip, old wives' tales, and ill-founded advice from physicians and others have often been the primary sources of dietary guidance for pregnant women. There are several reasons for this. Since nutrition is a very young science, it is only recently that we began to appraise the nutritive demands of the fetus. In the vacuum of this absence of scientific fact, gossip, superstition, and quaint ideas flew in—ideas that spawned faddism among professionals and laymen alike. It is hoped that we can now begin to rely less on mystery and more on fact.

It is little wonder that, for no one knows how long, pregnancy has been surrounded by mystery. Because of this, the woman has suffered all manner of proscriptions and deprivations, each calculated to shield her from the evils that might cause miscarriage or rob her body of vitality. In the absence of convincing scientific guidance, she has been the target of every fad and fancy the mind of man, aborigine or intellectual, could conjure.

The view that has been, and perhaps still is, most widely held by physicians is that, as long as the mother gets plenty of vitamins, the fetus will receive all the nourishment it needs regardless of her own nutritional status. The experience of women in Germany during World War I, who continued to give birth to viable, healthy babies despite the strictest food rationing, lent credence to this assumption. To medical educators this experience seemed to corroborate the view of Ludwig Prochownick, a German obstetrician who early in this century had contended that semistarvation of the mother was really a blessing in disguise. Keep the pregnant woman on a diet low in carbohydrates; restrict her fluid intake; and the result will be much less discomfort and difficulty for the mother at delivery time because the baby will be small and of light weight, he reasoned. This concept has been accepted and is practiced by many obstetricians today. Despite growing evidence—which, after the deliberations of the Committee on Maternal Nutrition, would seem to be overwhelming—the old argument continues to be offered that the maternal organism is somehow mysteriously endowed with an innate ability to produce a viable offspring regardless of the mother's own health or nutritional status. Anyway, it is said, the pregnant woman will instinctively act to meet the health needs of herself and her unborn infant. One argument is as fallacious as the other.

SWINGING PENDULUM

In the past thirty years, maternal nutrition has had its ups and downs. There have been times, as during World War II when food was rationed, when physicians in the United States and Canada thought it very important, and periods when what the pregnant woman ate was considered as one of those aspects of childbearing that pretty well took care of itself. Following the major advances in the science of nutrition during the period 1920–1940 when most of the vitamins were identified and their metabolic roles described, the 1940's became a decade of enthusiasm about the importance of diet in pregnancy outcome. This was followed by an era of disillusionment, even disinterest— attitudes due primarily to a series of reports in the 1950's which appeared to negate earlier claims that maternal nutrition could significantly affect the course of human pregnancy.

Now the pendulum is swinging back. The evidence, gained largely from more dispassionate appraisal of experience, indicates that maternal nutrition *is* critically important to both mother and fetus. Two things appear responsible for this development: rapidly expanding knowledge of the role of nutrition in prevention and treatment of disease; and second, realization that the numbers of stillbirths and infant deaths in the United States and Canada are considerably higher than one would expect.

The number of American women who die as a sequel to pregnancy has steadily decreased in the past three decades from 367.0 per 100,000 live births in 1940 to 83.3 in 1950 to 28.0 in 1967. This rate is more than three times as high in nonwhite as in white women, however. Proportionately, more nonwhite women bear children during adolescence and have higher parities, but these factors do not completely account for the observed differences in maternal mortality rates. In localities where mothers of both races receive comparably good maternity care, the difference is lessened. However, there is no reason to believe that fewer women and children die in pregnancy because of improved nutritional care alone. The improvement must be credited to the use of antibiotics and other forms of modern treatment. The statistics would be even better if physicians would adopt the routines for maternal nutrition now suggested.

As we have seen in so many other aspects of medical practice, when one cause of illness is overcome, another is unmasked. We are now aware of problems which appear to arise from a strange combination of malnutrition and the increasing number of younger and younger girls who become pregnant in America. Although the infant mortality rate reached a record low value of 22.4 per 1,000 live births in the United States in 1967, this rate is substantially higher than that prevailing in many other countries. This rate, which applies to the first year of life, includes babies who die during the first month of life; i.e., the first four weeks after delivery. The United States ranked thirteenth and Canada placed fourteenth in infant mortality in both 1966 and 1967. Under any circumstance, the importance of nutrition is hard to overestimate since low birth weight is now known to be associated with increased risk of neonatal death, i.e., within the first 28 days of life. Furthermore, malnutrition is one of the factors contributing to the relatively large group of infants with perinatal handicaps and congenital injuries, or who fail to grow and develop normally.

THE REASONS

Among the reasons a woman may give birth to a baby of less than normal weight, or what must now be considered as healthy weight, we can distinguish eleven causes, any one or a combination of which could be decisive. These, not in the order of importance, are: biologic immaturity (which is to say the mother is younger than seventeen), high parity, short stature, low prepregnancy weight for height, limited weight gain during pregnancy, poor nutritional status, smoking, chronic disease, certain infections, complications of pregnancy, and a history of prior reproductive loss.

In our studies, two causes of poor pregnancy outcome stand out above all others—poor nutrition and youth of the mother. Any research effort attempting to assess the relative importance of single factors, including poor nutrition, on outcome of pregnancy has been fraught with problems. And the results have been very difficult to interpret. This is true because many characteristics that thwart normal pregnancy tend to cluster in the same groups of women. For example, women in poor families are at the same time usually members of large families lacking good medical care, proper food, and education. Here we also find the greatest prevalence of infectious diseases, poor health, and bad food habits. This environment spawns the youngest mothers, who seldom grow and develop in childhood to their full genetic potential before they become pregnant. These are the young girls who enter pregnancy with suboptimal health and nutritional status. Every physician knows exceptions to this picture. While poverty is integral to this clustering of circumstances, there are, of course, women with adequate incomes who for other reasons, including the cult of slimness, approach childbearing with threatening health habits, poor health, and nutritional status which make them indistinguishable from their poorer sisters.

Why should this be so? Why should youth and suboptimal nourishment of the pregnant woman be so crucial to the outcome of this critical experience? The answer lies, so the Committee felt, in the essentials of the physiologic context of childbearing. From the first hours after fertilization, the maternal metabolic system begins a vast readjustment to efficiently provide the environment and sustenance necessary to support life and the normal growth of the fetus. Many physical and biochemical changes one sees in normal pregnancy resemble those associated with certain disease. For instance, blood volume expands, bringing with it reduction in concentrations of blood hemoglobin and plasma albumin. Amino acids may be excreted in the urine. The activity of certain enzymes in blood, such as alkaline phosphatase, increases markedly. The thyroid gland is often enlarged. Pulmonary and cardiovascular dynamics change. Edema is not infrequent. In short, clinical standards considered "normal" for the nonpregnant woman cannot always be used for the pregnant woman. The World Health Organization reminds us that

> from the standpoint of physiological function, pregnancy cannot be regarded as a process of foetal growth superimposed on the ordinary metabolism of the mother. Foetal development is accompanied by extensive changes in maternal body composition and metabolism.
>
> The (W.H.O.) Committee prefers to use the term "adjustment" rather than "adaptation" to describe the physiological changes occurring during pregnancy. Adaptation implies adjustment to an essentially undesirable situation, whereas pregnancy is neither abnormal nor undesirable. Many of the adjustments begin in early pregnancy before foetal growth is appreciable and, therefore, cannot be

interpreted as reactions to stress. Undoubtedly many of them are under hormonal control, although the precise mechanisms are poorly understood. . . .

CRUCIAL WEIGHT CHANGES

Weight gain reflects the overall physiologic consequences of pregnancy. Experience in the United States indicates that the average total weight gain in pregnancy is approximately 24 pounds, but weight gain varies greatly. Young women fed equally well tend to gain slightly more weight than older women, primigravidas more than multigravidas, and thin women more than fat women. In Western societies, the total additional calorie cost of a normal pregnancy is approximately 40,000 k calories more than that usually consumed by the same woman when not pregnant, or about 200 k calories more each day than she would usually eat. This is commensurate with total weight gain of 25 pounds.

Many observations demonstrate that malnourished girls deliver fragile babies, maternal physiology is readjusted in a fashion which would alter nutritional requirements, and women exhibit a characteristic increase in energy demand during pregnancy.

It is hardly surprising to conclude that diet during pregnancy may have important influences on the outcome. This may seem obvious now, but it was not always so. As the Committee's report points out, "One specific way in which diet during pregnancy affects the outcome of pregnancy is seen in the relationship between maternal gain in weight and the weight of infants at birth. A number of studies have shown that a strong positive association exists between the total gain in weight of the mother and the birth weight of her child. Similarly, there is an important positive association between the prepregnancy weight of the mother and the birth weight of her child. . . .

FETAL GROWTH

These conclusions are supported by studies in several species of experimental animals which have demonstrated that calorie and protein restrictions in the maternal diet profoundly affect litter size and survival, birth weight, growth patterns, and behavior of progeny. The timing and duration of dietary restriction influence the results, since fetal growth and development rates vary between species. The effects on cellular growth patterns are different between organs, and seem more extensive when the dietary restriction coincides with most rapid cell division. For example, dietary deprivation at the time of greatest rate of growth of the brain results in persistent modification and damage; deprivation at times of slower rates of cell division leads to changes which can later be corrected with improved diet. The greatest rates of cell division and of growth occur *in utero* in some species but in the postnatal period in others.

In man, birth occurs during the steepest part of the growth curve of the conceptus; in rodents, carnivores, and the pig, the event precedes maximal growth. Moreover, the relative severity of dietary restriction in animal experimentation is likely to be greater than that commonly encountered in human populations. Additional research in animals is necessary before we can achieve a sound understanding of these relationships. There is equal need for caution in extrapolating these findings to human reproduction. . . .

PREGNANCY TOXEMIAS

For years, the concept has persisted that nutrition is related in some way to the occurrence and course of toxemias of pregnancy. But little is known about the relative importance of the many etiological factors involved. Toxemia has been called "the disease of theories." Measures for prevention and treatment, including dietary procedures, have thus remained largely empirical. Lack of accepted criteria for diagnosis and absence of a suitable laboratory animal model have handicapped the study of these toxemias.

A variety of symptom complexes continues to be included under the term "toxemia." To facilitate discussions, the toxemias considered were those that could be divided into "preeclampsia" and "eclampsia." Preeclampsia was defined as an acute hypertensive disorder appearing after about the twentieth week of pregnancy, and accompanied by edema of hand and face and/or proteinuria. Eclampsia was defined as closely related to preeclampsia and, in most cases, its end result.

In the United States the maternal mortality rate from acute toxemia has dropped from 52.2 per 100,000 live births in 1940 to 6.2 in 1965. Mortality rates by states vary widely from one-third or less the national average in some states to four or five times the national average in others. The most striking association of these differences is with per capita income. The lower a state's per capita income, the higher the maternal mortality from toxemia, and vice versa. This same relation appears to hold with respect to incidence of the disease.

The relative importance of diet in the etiology of toxemia of pregnancy has been a controversial subject for many years during which calories, protein, and salt have each at one time or another been thought to be the cause of major concern. The concept of *caloric restrictions* to avoid large total weight gains and to protect against toxemia derived from the observed reduction in the incidence of toxemia in Europe during World War I, as mentioned earlier. Since the war was accompanied by a scarcity of food and pregnant women gained less, the restricted diet was considered the protective factor. During the 1920's and 1930's, caloric restriction to limit weight gain during pregnancy was widely advocated in the United States to prevent toxemia and other complications. The practice found its way into textbooks of obstetrics and has been widely followed by the medical profession—despite the fact that the practice has been subjected to little scientific scrutiny. That such caloric restriction may not be beneficial is suggested by recent university hospital studies on a large group of women who gained in excess of 30 pounds during pregnancy. Nine percent of these women developed toxemia, but 91 percent did not. Confusion has resulted from failure to distinguish between weight gained as a result of edema and that due to deposition of fat. There is no evidence that women with large total weight gain due to excessive accumulation of fat are more likely to develop toxemia than women with lesser accumulations.

The quantity of protein consumed has been held by some to influence both development of toxemia and the effectiveness of measures designed to prevent its appearance. For example, it has been widely suspected that changes in diet in the United States, particularly in the protein intake, may have contributed to the decreased national incidence of this complication. Although the proportion of total calories furnished by protein in the average diet in the United States has remained fairly constant at 11 to 13 percent, an increasing proportion has come from animal sources. The evidence is insufficient with respect to the influence of levels of protein intake of individual women to allow conclusions to be drawn concerning the influence of dietary protein levels *per se* on the development or prevention of toxemia.

Since edema is a characteristic feature of toxemia, routine salt limitation during pregnancy to avoid or reduce edema formation has gained wide acceptance in practice. Diuretics are also commonly prescribed to accomplish the same goal, often in conjunction with salt restriction. Recent experimental studies on pregnant rats demonstrated deleterious effects of salt depletion. The safety of routine salt restriction must be questioned, as well as the use of diuretics in prenatal care. The NRC report cautions against the routine use of these procedures in prenatal care.

GUIDELINES

Maternal Nutrition and the Course of Human Pregnancy contains much salient information to justify new and extended effort to utilize nutritional knowledge and services in prenatal care. The report demonstrates that reproductive efficiency is least in adolescents, the nonwhite, and those of lowest income. These are the highest-risk groups, but there are broad opportunities to improve the outcome of pregnancy for all women of all ages and strata by more careful attention to diet. Obstetricians and physicians who routinely prescribe diets restricted in calories and salt, and who feel that the routine use of diuretics is an integral part of prenatal care, are placing patients and their offspring at disadvantage and unnecessary risk.

This NRC study indicates several principles which the physician and his professional assistants will find useful in providing prenatal care which will assure the best possible outcome of pregnancy:

1. Weight gain in pregnancy should be closely monitored with the objective of achieving an average total gain of 24 pounds. This represents a gain of 1.5 to 3.0 pounds during the first trimester, followed by a gain of .8 pounds each week during the remainder of pregnancy. No scientific justification is found for routine limitations of weight gain to lesser amounts.

2. Severe restriction of calories is unphysiologic and potentially harmful to the developing fetus and the mother. Moreover, caloric limitation inevitably is accompanied by restriction of other nutrients essential for growth processes. Weight reduction of obese women should not be undertaken during pregnancy, but in interpartum periods.

3. The pattern and rate of weight gain is of particular importance. A sudden sharp increase in weight after the twentieth week of pregnancy may signal water retention and the possible onset of preeclampsia.

4. The occurrence of pregnancy in the adolescent, and girl under 17 years of age, poses special and important problems. Standardized diets which are

often used in prenatal clinics are not suited to the particular nutritional needs of the adolescent. To sustain and complete her own growth she requires a diet rich in calories, protein, and calcium. Calorie deprivation is poorly tolerated. Pregnancy, with its added nutritional requirements, demands that every effort must be made to encourage an enhanced and appropriate food intake.

5. The dietary intake and food habits of the pregnant woman should be carefully reviewed and appropriate counseling provided. Special attention should be paid to women who enter pregnancy in a poor state of nutrition and to those with poor dietary habits. Young adolescents, women who have been on slimming regimens, and those of low socioeconomic status are particularly apt to fail to meet the metabolic demands of pregnancy. When modification of the woman's usual diet is indicated during pregnancy, it should be undertaken in accordance with the principles of good nutrition. The planning or assessment of diets should be guided by the Recommended Dietary Allowances (1968) of the National Research Council.

6. The widespread practice of routinely restricting salt intake, and at the same time prescribing diuretics, is of doubtful value in preventing preeclampsia and is potentially dangerous. The routine use of diuretics without specific clinical indications is unsound and potentially harmful.

7. The provision of vitamin and mineral supplements should not be regarded as a solution for poor food habits. The supplements' cost, relative to the cost of enhancing the nutrient intake with foods, should be considered, especially in caring for pregnant women with inadequate incomes. Except for iron and folic acid, the routine augmentation with vitamin and mineral preparations is of uncertain value. When supplementation is considered necessary, the quantities of nutrients supplied should approximate the daily amounts suggested in the Recommended Dietary Allowances (1968).

8. In view of the apparent widespread incidence of nutritional anemia and the increased iron requirements of pregnancy, iron supplementation is needed during the second and third trimesters in amounts of 30 to 60 mg per day.

9. A daily supplement of .2 to .4 mg folate during pregnancy should prevent folic acid deficiency in all pregnant women.

10. In areas where the soil and water are deficient in iodine, the use of iodized salt should be encouraged.

This report is intended to call to the attention of physicians, nutritionists, and other health professionals the new emphasis on diet which pregnancy requires. Present knowledge and information indicate that the course and outcome of pregnancy can be more favorable for many women if nutritional practices are improved. A salient and not-to-be-forgotten fact is that such efforts should extend into childhood and adolescence. The woman who is likely to produce a healthy baby is one who has, through best health and nutritional practices, reached sexual maturity after completing her own growth and achieving the potentials for physical development provided by heredity.

2

Early Infancy

Erik H. Erikson's discussion of basic trust provides an orientation to infancy and to the infant's family and culture. Feelings as well as thoughts are likely to be aroused by this great philosopher-analyst who makes the infant's experience and achievements so real and so important.

Growth in early infancy is very rapid, especially in small babies. James M. Tanner, a specialist in human biology, explains the birth catch-up capacity, relating it to survival value and to genetic variability. The complicated subject of breast feeding is discussed thoroughly, from the standpoint of infant and mother, by Marian Breckenridge, a nutritionist and authority on child growth, and psychologist Margaret Murphy. This treatment has particular significance for the United States, where breast feeding is little understood. We do not know of research which proves that bottle feeding, well done, is less satisfactory than beast feeding. The student who is particularly interested in this topic is advised to read a monograph* which space does not permit our including here. In it, breast feeding is examined in the context of the mother's personality, the sex of the child, the length of nursing, and other factors, which shows the complexity of the psychological aspects of infant feeding.

The research of a psychiatrist, Peter Wolff, is the basis of "State and Behavior in the Neonate." Wolff describes the six basic states in which infants live and gives physiological and psychological information about them.

* M. I. Heinstein, Behavioral correlates of breast-bottle regimes under varying parent-infant Relationships. *Mono. Soc. Res. Child Devel.*, 1963, *28*, 4.

Basic Trust vs. Basic Mistrust

Erik H. Erikson
HARVARD UNIVERSITY

The first demonstration of social trust in the baby is the ease of his feeding, the depth of his sleep, the relaxation of his bowels. The experience of a mutual

Reprinted from *Childhood and Society*. Copyright © 1968 by W. W. Norton & Company, Inc., pp. 247–251. By permission.

regulation of his increasingly receptive capacities with the maternal techniques of provision gradually helps him to balance the discomfort caused by the immaturity of homeostasis with which he was born. In his gradually increasing waking hours he finds that more and more adventures of the senses arouse a feeling of familiarity, of having coincided with a feeling of inner goodness. Forms of comfort, and people associated with them, become as familiar as the gnawing discomfort of the bowels. The infant's first social achievement, then, is his willingness to let the mother out of sight without undue anxiety or rage, because she has become an inner certainty as well as an outer predictability. Such consistency, continuity, and sameness of experience provide a rudimentary sense of ego identity which depends, I think, on the recognition that there is an inner population of remembered and anticipated sensations and images which are firmly correlated with the outer population of familiar and predictable things and people.

What we here call trust coincides with what Therese Benedek has called confidence. If I prefer the word "trust," it is because there is more naïveté and more mutuality in it: an infant can be said to be trusting where it would go too far to say that he has confidence. The general state of trust, furthermore, implies not only that one has learned to rely on the sameness and continuity of the outer providers, but also that one may trust oneself and the capacity of one's own organs to cope with urges; and that one is able to consider oneself trustworthy enough so that the providers will not need to be on guard lest they be nipped.

The constant tasting and testing of the relationship between inside and outside meets its crucial test during the rages of the biting stage, when the teeth cause pain from within and when outer friends either prove of no avail or withdraw from the only action which promises relief: biting. Not that teething itself seems to cause all the dire consequences sometimes ascribed to it. As outlined earlier, the infant now is driven to "grasp" more, but he is apt to find desired presences elusive: nipple and breast, and the mother's focused attention and care. Teething seems to have a prototypal significance and may well be the model for the masochistic tendency to assure cruel comfort by enjoying one's hurt whenever one is unable to prevent a significant loss.

In psychopathology the absence of basic trust can best be studied in infantile schizophrenia, while lifelong underlying weakness of such trust is apparent in adult personalities in whom withdrawal into schizoid and depressive states is habitual. The re-establishment of a state of trust has been found to be the basic requirement for therapy in these cases. For no matter what conditions may have caused a psychotic break, the bizarreness and withdrawal in the behavior of many very sick individuals hides an attempt to recover social mutuality by a testing of the borderlines between senses and physical reality, between words and social meanings.

Psychoanalysis assumes the early process of differentiation between inside and outside to be the origin of projection and introjection which remain some of our deepest and most dangerous defense mechanisms. In introjection we feel and act as if an outer goodness had become an inner certainty. In projection, we experience an inner harm as an outer one: we endow significant people with the evil which actually is in us. These two mechanisms, then, projection and introjection, are assumed to be modeled after whatever goes on in infants when they would like to externalize pain and internalize pleasure, an intent which must yield to the testimony of the maturing senses and ultimately of reason. These mechanisms are, more or less normally, reinstated in acute crises of love, trust, and faith in adulthood and can characterize irrational attitudes toward adversaries and enemies in masses of "mature" individuals.

The firm establishment of enduring patterns for the solution of the nuclear conflict of basic trust versus basic mistrust in mere existence is the first task of the ego, and thus first of all a task for maternal care. But let it be said here that the amount of trust derived from earliest infantile experience does not seem to depend on absolute quantities of food or demonstrations of love, but rather on the quality of the maternal relationship. Mothers create a sense of trust in their children by that kind of administration which in its quality combines sensitive care of the baby's individual needs and a firm sense of personal trustworthiness within the trusted framework of their culture's life style. This forms the basis in the child for a sense of identity which will later combine a sense of being "all right," of being oneself, and of becoming what other people trust one will become. There are, therefore (within certain limits previously defined as the "musts" of child care), few frustrations in either this or the following stages which the growing child cannot endure if the frustration leads to the ever-renewed experience of greater sameness and stronger continuity of development, toward a final integration of the individual life cycle with some meaningful wider belongingness. Parents must not only have certain ways of guiding by prohibition and permission; they must also be able to represent to the child a deep, an almost somatic conviction that there is a meaning to what they are doing. Ultimately, children become neurotic not from frustrations, but from the lack or loss of societal meaning in these frustrations.

But even under the most favorable circumstances, this stage seems to introduce into psychic life (and become prototypical for) a sense of inner division and universal nostalgia for a paradise forfeited. It is against this powerful combination of a sense of having been deprived, of having been divided, and of having been abandoned—that basic trust must maintain itself throughout life.

Each successive stage and crisis has a special relation to one of the basic elements of society, and this for the simple reason that the human life cycle and man's institutions have evolved together. In this chapter we can do little more than mention, after the description of each stage, what basic element of social organization is related to it. This relation is twofold: man brings to these institutions the remnants of his infantile mentality and his youthful fervor, and he receives from them—as long as they manage to maintain their actuality—a reinforcement of his infantile gains.

The parental faith which supports the trust emerging in the newborn, has throughout history sought its institutional safeguard (and, on occasion, found its greatest enemy) in organized religion. Trust born of care is, in fact, the touchstone of the *actuality* of a given religion. All religions have in common the periodical childlike surrender to a Provider or providers who dispense earthly fortune as well as spiritual health; some demonstration of man's smallness by way of reduced posture and humble gesture; the admission in prayer and song of misdeeds, of misthoughts, and of evil intentions; fervent appeal for inner unification by divine guidance; and finally, the insight that individual trust must become a common faith, individual mistrust a commonly formulated evil, while the individual's restoration must become part of the ritual practice of many, and must become a sign of trustworthiness in the community.[1] We have illustrated how tribes dealing with one segment of nature develop a collective magic which seems to treat the Supernatural Providers of food and fortune as if they were angry and must be appeased by prayer and self-torture. Primitive religions, the most primitive layer in all religions, and the religious layer in each individual, abound with efforts at atonement which try to make up for vague deeds against a maternal matrix and try to restore faith in the goodness of one's strivings and in the kindness of the powers of the universe.

Each society and each age must find the institutionalized form of reverence which derives vitality from its world-image—from predestination to indeterminacy. The clinician can only observe that many are proud to be without religion whose children cannot afford their being without it. On the other hand, there are many who seem to derive a vital faith from social action or scientific pursuit. And again, there are many who profess faith, yet in practice breathe mistrust both of life and man.

[1] This is the communal and psychosocial side of religion. Its often paradoxical relation to the spirituality of the individual is a matter not to be treated briefly and in passing (see *Young Man Luther*). (E.H.E.)

The Birth Catch-Up

James M. Tanner
INSTITUTE OF CHILD HEALTH, LONDON

This capacity to catch up in growth seems to be used normally around the time of birth in man. There is evidence that the growth rate of the foetus at least in weight slows down during the last four weeks of pregnancy, as illustrated in Figure 1. The prenatal values are calculated from McKeown and Record's (2) data on birthweights of live children born after a shorter gestation than average. In using them we are assuming that these early-delivered children's weights are the same as the weights of foetuses of the same age as yet still in the uterus; in other words that amongst healthy singletons the early-born are not specially big or small children for their gestational age. Such an assumption may be challenged. But there is good evidence also of a catch-up occurring after birth, particularly in small babies. Figure 2, taken from the Ministry of Health (3) partially longitudinal survey of some 17 thousand babies shows this

Reprinted from "The Regulation of Human Growth," *Child Development*, *34*, 828–830. Copyright © 1963 by the Society for Research in Child Development, Inc. By permission.

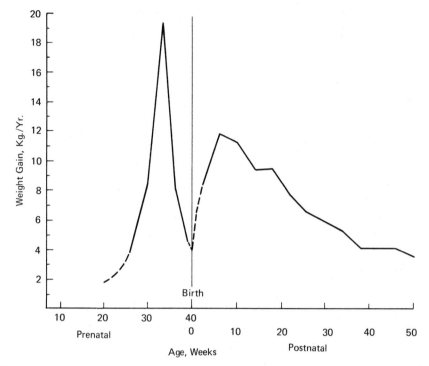

F I G U R E 1.   *Velocity of growth in weight of singleton children. Prenatal curve is derived from data of McKeown and Record (2) on birthweights of live-born children delivered before 40 weeks of gestation. Postnatal data from Ministry of Health (3) mixed longitudinal data (their Table VII). Dotted line shows estimate of velocity immediately before and after birth, showing catch-up.*

well. Babies below the average weight gained more than the others, thus reducing the range of weight in the whole group. The catch-up finishes by about 5 months in these data and is distinctly more marked in boys than in girls (see Ministry of Health [3], Figure III). Thus there is a negative correlation between birthweight and weight gain from birth to 3 months or from birth to 6 months of the order of about −.15 (7). The negative correlation is still present, though lower, by the time 1 year is reached. Norval, Kennedy, and Berkson (4) give figures for the correlation of birthweight with the birth-to-1-year increment of −.15 in boys and −.05 in girls. The catch-up occurs also in length, indeed probably to a greater extent than in weight. Simmons and Todd (6) found it in the longitudinal data of the Brush Foundation and in 1938 remarked that "of particular interest are the negative coefficients between birth length and the birth to one year increment in length (boys −.46, girls −.01) and of the three month length with the three month to one year increment in length (boys −.20, girls −.05). It appears that during the first post-natal year our short babies gain in length more than our long babies and that this reversal occurs to a greater extent in the male than in the female" (6, p. 126). Thomson (8) found correlations of the order of −.4 in both sexes between birth length and the length increment from birth to 6 months, in some four and a

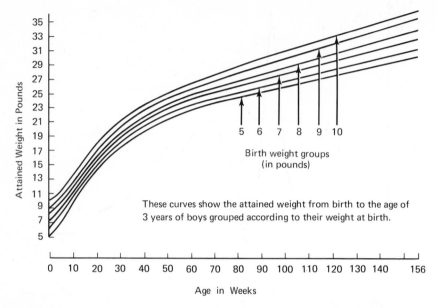

FIGURE 2. *Attained weight from birth to age 3 of boys grouped according to birthweight. From Ministry of Health (3).*

half thousand babies in Edinburgh. By 1 year the correlation had somewhat dropped, but was still appreciable (average correlation −.35).

The catch-up mechanism at birth is of much genetical importance. It seems to be the chief means by which variability in adult size is maintained in the population. Most of the adult size variability is established by 2 years after birth, since by then the individual's adult size is to a large extent fixed (presuming adequate environmental conditions). The correlation coefficients between length of child at 2 years and length of the same child when adult is nearly .8; it approaches .7 even at age 1. (Genetical differences in the time and intensity of the adolescent spurt account for the remainder of the adult variability.) Thus there would be many genetically large children developing in the uteri of small mothers and constituting a problem at the time of birth, unless selection for assortative mating were very strong, a solution which would produce other genetically undesirable effects. The problem is solved by birth size being controlled almost entirely by uterine factors (5), the correlation of birth length and adult length being only about .2. The catch-up after birth does the rest. Note that this is a true regulatory problem, for the form of Figure 2 makes it clear that only some of the small babies catch up. A proportion of them need little or no catch-up to reach and continue on their natural growth curves, since they are genetically small; it is those aimed, so to speak, at large-ness who catch up on to their proper track. The same phenomenon appears particularly clearly in cattle, where the size at birth of a calf born to a small-breed mother mated with a large-breed father is considerably smaller than a calf of large-breed mother and small-breed father. The two calves grow at different rates after birth so that by the time adult size is reached there is no longer any difference (1). . . .

References

1. DICKINSON, A. G. Some genetic implications of maternal effects: an hypothesis of mammalian growth. *J. agric. Sci.*, 1960, 54, 379–390.
2. McKEOWN, T., and RECORD, R. G. Observations on foetal growth in multiple pregnancy in man. *J. Endocrin.*, 1952, 8, 386–401.
3. Ministry of Health. Standards of normal weight in infancy. *Min. Hlth. Rep. Publ. Hlth. No. 99*, London: H.M.S.O., 1959.
4. NORVAL, M. A., KENNEDY, R. L. J., and BERKSON, J. Biometric studies of the growth of children of Rochester, Minnesota. The first year of life. *Hum. Biol.*, 1951, 23, 274–301.
5. PENROSE, L. S. *Recent advances in human genetics*. London: Churchill, 1961.
6. SIMMONS, K., and TODD, T. W. Growth of well children: analysis of stature and weight, 3 months to 13 years. *Growth*, 1938, 2, 93–134.
7. THOMSON, J. Observations on weight gain in infants. *Arch. Dis. Childh.*, 1955, 30, 322–327.
8. THOMSON, J. Infant growth. *Arch. Dis. Childh.*, 1956, 31, 382–389.

The Infant's First Food

Marian E. Breckenridge
LATE OF THE MERRILL-PALMER INSTITUTE

Margaret N. Murphy
PURDUE UNIVERSITY

THE INFANT'S FIRST FOOD

One of the adjustments the infant makes at birth is a change in the manner of nourishment. He now ingests appropriate food, namely, milk, orally through sucking, digests it and absorbs the necessary nutrients. A vital part of this adjustment is becoming accustomed to the feeding situation, that first intimate mother-child relation through which he obtains his food. In this situation both mother and child can gradually establish a satisfying venture which not only provides the infant with food, but also can be the beginning of a close relation between mother and child (Bakwin, 1964). The infant is believed to derive a sense of security and of belonging in this relation from the warmth of the mother's body and from the comfort of being held. These are different variables from those of the feeding process itself (Guthrie, 1967).

During the first few days the infant becomes proficient in finding the nipple and sucking, and the mother becomes adjusted to the pull on the nipple. At this time the nursing period may be limited to five to ten minutes to allow the mother time to adjust to the pull on the nipples and to help to prevent them from becoming sore. A short nursing time seems to satisfy the infant. During this transition period, colostrum is secreted by the mammary glands. This secretion is admirably adapted to the needs of the newborn. It contains less fat and more protein, ash and vitamin A than does milk secreted later when lactation is completely established. The colostrum period varies with individual women from one to five days. During the next five days the composition changes gradually to that of mature milk. Most authors agree that the principal changes from colostrum to mature milk are completed by the tenth day (Committee on Nutrition, 1960).

When the infant absorbs and digests breast milk or its substitute, he begins the third stage in his progress toward maturation of the nutriture. Human milk, if the supply is adequate, provides the essential nutrients for the early months except vitamin D. The adequacy of vitamins other than D depends upon the mother's diet. The amount of breast milk the infant receives depends on the ability of the mother to synthesize milk and the demands he makes in sucking. The usual amount is about 1 pint after the first week or two, and this increases to about 1 quart a day in the fifth month (Toverud, Stearns and Macy, 1950). The amount he needs at a feeding can be determined by the infant if he is fed when he is hungry (as indicated by rooting, sucking or crying) and permitted to nurse until he is satisfied. He will not necessarily take the same amount at each feeding.

Some infants have a sharp satiety reaction (Bakwin, 1964); when they are satisfied, further attempts at feeding are actively resisted. In others, satiety appears gradually and is preceded by playfulness toward the end of feeding. Bakwin pointed out that some infants do not seem to know when they have had enough food. These infants regurgitate and vomit frequently. Recognition of satiety was indicated as being especially difficult in infants with small appetites.

If the infant is not breast fed, a formula to meet his needs should be prescribed by a physician. Both the nutritional and emotional needs of the infant can be met in bottle-feeding. Standardized interviews with mothers of five-year-old children (Sears, Maccoby and Levin, 1957) showed that the early feeding experience, whether breast or bottle, had no consistent effect upon later behavior such as aggression in the home, "considerable" or "high" conscience, dependency, severe feeding problems, bed-wetting at age five or strong emotional reaction to toilet training. The authors point out that feeding as well as other experiences affect the child, but the effects are specific to each child.

The self-regulation type of feeding program can be followed with bottle-fed infants. One mother, whose baby was bottle-fed and varied his intake at different feedings, met the problem by dividing the milk unevenly among the bottles for the day. This baby was taking 35 ounces. She distributed this in two bottles of 6 ounces, three of 5 ounces, and two of 4 ounces. She found that the baby, after having been asleep, wanted to eat several times at $1\frac{1}{2}$- to 2-hour intervals and so took less at those times. When she anticipated that he would sleep four or five hours after a feeding, she gave him 6 ounces. Thus she was able to satisfy the baby without waste of formula or keeping him waiting in the middle of a feeding in order to warm another bottle.

LACTATION

Lactation consists of two processes: secretion and "let-down" or flow of milk. Secretion is strikingly increased after the birth of the infant and appears to be caused by a change in the balance of endocrines. The exact mechanisms have not been fully agreed upon (Turner, 1966). The inhibitory action of ovarian hormones is reduced, while the stimulating action of prolactin of the posterior pituitary gland is increased. Hormones of the thyroid and of the adrenal cortex also act in controlling lactation. The "let-down," or flow of milk, is effected by a complex psychosomatic mechanism by which, it is believed, sensory stimuli associated with suckling excite nerves of an afferent arc to the midbrain, which in turn acts to release the posterior pituitary hormone, oxytocin (Linzell, 1959; Lloyd, 1962).

The processes of lactation are influenced by a number of biologic, emotional and social factors which interact one with another. Heredity, size and anatomic structure of the breast (which has a strong hereditary component), food and environmental conditions such as the balance of rest and activity, which takes into account the amount and intensity of work, will affect lactation.

The potentiality for both the quantity of milk and the length of time lactation continues under normal conditions is inherent in the mother (Macy et al., 1930). Various conditions will determine how much of that potential will be utilized; one is the demand by the baby. A hungry baby nursing vigorously, as is likely to be the case of an infant on a self-regulatory schedule, is an aid to lactation. Illingworth and Stone (1952) found that 80 per cent of babies on self-demand feeding in Jessup Hospital for Women in Sheffield, England, were fully breast fed at one month, compared with 65 per cent of those on schedule. This difference was significant.

Food is another factor. Nutrition for lactation begins before the birth of the baby. A study in Australia (Woodhill et al., 1955) indicates a consistent correlation between the duration of lactation and the level of maternal diet before and during pregnancy. After the birth of the infant certain nutrient intakes should be increased above those during pregnancy in order to supply the nutrients required for the elaboration of milk. According to the Recommended Allowances of the Food and Nutrition Board (National Academy of Sciences—National Research Council, 1964), diet during lactation is increased over that of pregnancy about one half in calories, protein, calcium and vitamin A and about one third in thiamine, riboflavin and ascorbic acid. These additions to an adequate diet during the latter half of pregnancy will provide sufficient energy and nutrients (1) to maintain the mother's body and to meet her energy needs, and (2) to provide the essentials for milk and the activity of the mammary glands. The nursing mother will probably find that she desires the additional food. The need for extra calcium, riboflavin, vitamin A and protein indicates a liberal intake of milk. At least 1 quart a day is advisable. Liberal amounts of fruits and vegetables, including citrus fruits, are also indicated. Other foods providing protein and calories can be chosen according to the mother's needs and preferences. Vitamin D can be supplied by fortified milk or a concentrate. . . .

Physical rest and relaxation are also essential for successful lactation. The flow of milk can be stimulated or inhibited by the emotional state. A mother who dislikes breast feeding, is indifferent to it or has mixed feelings about it, or who is tense from concern about the care of the infant or feels uncomfortable about the nursing situation or is under some emotional strain is less likely to be successful than one who begins the experience with desire and determination to nurse her infant, who is calm and enjoying the experience (Call, 1959; Egli et al., 1961, Newton and Newton, 1950b).

The society in which a woman lives may influence her feelings about breast feeding and her willingness or hesitation to try it. The practice of breast feeding is closely bound to the culture of a society. In the United States the prevailing fashion for some time has been to feed infants by the bottle. This was shown in a survey (Meyer, 1958) in which 21 per cent of mothers were breast feeding their babies when they left the hospital, compared with 38 per cent in an earlier survey (Bain, 1948). American mothers nurse their infants less often and for a shorter time than do women in Europe, Asia or Africa. The practice of most European mothers falls between that of mothers in American and the Eastern countries (Aitken and Hytten, 1960),

The decline of breast feeding seems to accompany increasing sophistication of a community (Jelliffe, 1962). Salber et al. (1959) commented that lactation is certain to be affected when woman's role in society is not clearly defined and there is conflict between her ambitions and her biological make-up.

In spite of the low incidence of breast feeding among mothers in the United States, there is a slight revival among women of the middle and upper social classes (Salber et al., 1958, 1959; Yankhauer et al., 1958). Education seems to be an influencing factor. From a sample of mothers in the Boston area, Salber and Feinlieb (1966) found that only 22 per cent of the total group breast-fed, but that 70 per cent of those married to students, 40 per cent of those in the upper social class and only 14 per cent in the lower social class breast-fed. This difference between social classes in breast-feeding practices, which is the reverse of an earlier period, has also been reported in England (Douglas, 1950).

Many women, especially those having their first baby, will profit by some assistance in understanding the process of lactation and by suggestions of ways it can be promoted. A woman can learn that the reflex which releases milk from the breast is stimulated by the sucking of the infant and by associations with the nursing situation (sight of the baby, time for feeding, breast preparations for feeding) and inhibited by pain and distraction. The following suggestions for aiding this reflex to function, as offered by Newton and Newton (1950a), include (1) feeding the baby when he is hungry to afford more vigorous nursing; (2) no supplementary bottle if possible; (3) avoiding pain, emotional conflict and embarrassment; (4) conditioning the reflex by the use of pleasant stimuli, e.g., favorite food or music preceding nursing, nursing in the same quiet place, stroking the breast with clean tissue, or manual expression of a little milk.

A woman needs guidance while lactation is being established. She may need help in the techniques of nursing. The techniques necessary for successful management have been demonstrated by Barnes et al. (1953) and Waller (1946). Mothers sometimes become concerned because milk is slow to come after delivery. The child may receive almost no milk for the first few days. The mother needs to understand that his needs at this time are small. It is not until the fifth day that transitional or mature milk begins to flow. This may be a crucial time for the mother, since she may be leaving the hospital to return home on the fifth day, before lactation has become firmly established. At this time she faces the responsibilities of the care of the infant and of the home. Unless she has some assistance during this transitional period, lactation may suffer because of fatigue and anxieties. Some knowledge of what to expect in the behavior of the infant and some opportunity to care for babies before the birth of her own may strengthen her confidence in her ability to care for her child. Also, the provision of opportunities for her to become acquainted with her baby in the hospital so that he is no stranger when they arrive home may help. Jackson et al. (1956) found a significantly longer period of breast feeding (up to seven months) among mothers who had rooming-in, and thus had their babies with them, than among mothers whose babies were kept in the nursery. The husband can also be of assistance by giving support to the mother and seeing that she is relieved of some of the household responsibilities.

Although most women are able to breast-feed their babies, some cannot. For those who cannot there is ample evidence that babies can thrive on bottle feedings modified to approximate the composition of human milk. A good bottle feeding is preferable to inadequate breast feeding. Also these mothers can give their babies the essential mothering during feeding time and at other times of the day. No mother should feel inadequate or have any sense of self-reproach because of inability to nurse her child.

VARIATION IN QUANTITY OF MILK SECRETED   As lactation proceeds, the quantity of milk secreted from day to day and from week to week may vary considerably (Macy et al., 1931). The gradual increase in milk flow is evidently peculiar not only to the individual, but also to the particular lactation period. The average daily output of milk in three women from the sixth week through the fourteenth month of lactation was 2602 cc in one lactation period and 3134 cc in another period in the same subject, 2366 cc for one lactation period in another subject, and 1419 cc for the third subject (Macy and co-workers, 1931). These women produced especially large quantities of milk. The total quantity of breast milk produced during a lactation period was found to depend not only on the women's immediate capacity to produce, but also on the demands placed on the mammary glands and on the duration of the lactation period. The investigators showed that, if augmented milk production is to be secured, the milk should be removed from the breast at regular intervals and as completely as possible. These observations confirm the belief that excessive and heavy work tends to depress maximum output of milk and also that nervous factors such as excitement, fear and anxiety lessen the flow, and that severe shock may cause complete cessation.

DIFFERENCES BETWEEN BREAST AND BOTTLE FEEDING

There is wide agreement that breast feeding is preferable to bottle feeding, but most infants in this country are bottle-fed (Bakwin, 1964; Maternal and Child Health and Food and Nutrition Sections, 1966). This section presents the similarities and differences of human and cow's milk and the progress of infants receiving each.

When comparing the *content of human and cow's milk* and their relative value in promoting health and growth of an infant, it must be remembered that infants are generally fed not whole cow's milk, but formulas in which the cow's

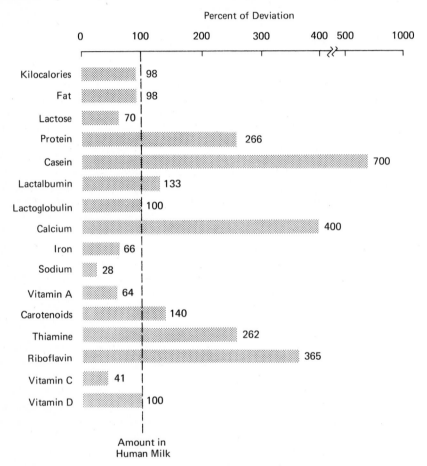

Comparison of Nutritive Value of Cow's
and Human Milk

FIGURE 1. *Relative amounts of various nutrients in human and cow's milk.* [Based on data from *Composition of Human Milk*, National Research Council Publication No. 254, Washington, D.C., 1953, National Research Council. (H. A. Guthrie: *Introductory Nutrition.* St. Louis, C. V. Mosby Company, 1967, p. 334.)]

milk is adapted by dilution, addition of carbohydrates, and treatment to soften the protein curd. When comparison of the progress of infants fed the two milks is made, it is important to note the composition of the formula. Grouping all bottle-fed infants as receiving the same food introduces an error which could lead to misinterpretations of observations.

Infants fed breast milk or cow's milk receive, ounce for ounce, different amounts and proportions of certain nutrients (Committee on Nutrition, 1960; Guthrie, 1967; Macy, Kelley and Sloan, 1950) (Fig. 1). Cow's milk contains about three times as much protein as human milk; the proteins of each milk have essentially the same biologic value (György, 1961) and similar ability to promote nitrogen retention (Fomon, 1960). The protein of cow's milk forms a heavy curd in the stomach, whereas human milk, having less casein and more lactalbumin, forms a finely divided, flocculent mass which is easily digested. Milk mixtures used in bottle feeding are treated, however, so that the protein curd is also soft, small and digestible. Cow's milk also contains about four times as much calcium and six times as much phosphorus as human milk. These and some other constituents, when absorbed in excess of bodily needs, must be excreted. Young infants excrete more water with them, since the kidney's function of concentrating urine is immature in the early months (Smith, 1959). When young infants are fed cow's milk in relatively large proportions, the resulting increase in certain minerals and the metabolic products of proteins to be excreted may tax the water reserve, whereas the breast-fed baby is not subjected to this strain (György, 1961).

Human milk contains three to four times more of the essential fatty acids (Williams, 1961). The significance of this difference is not known. Human milk is about one-third richer in iron than cow's milk. Dietary iron is apparently not utilized during the first four or five months (Smith et al., 1955). After this age the difference in iron of the two milks would be important if the infant were not fed other foods rich in iron.

Human milk is also about one-third richer in vitamin A and more than twice as rich in vitamin C. A quart of human milk contains about 41 mg. of vitamin C (Williams, 1961); a cow's milk formula prepared by boiling and diluting may contain almost none (Stevenson, 1947). Human milk, if the mother's diet is adequate in vitamin C, meets the recommended allowance for vitamin C, but a cow's milk formula falls far short of it. The niacin content of breast milk is about twice that of cow's milk, but both milks are a poor source of this vitamin, though a good source of tryptophan, precursor of niacin, which compensates for the relatively small amounts of niacin. Cow's milk is more than twice as high in thiamine. But when thiamine in human milk is compared with the amount an infant receives in bottle feeding, the amounts are similar, owing primarily to the loss of thiamine in the sterilization process. The riboflavin content of cow's milk is more than three times that in human milk, but the relative utilization of the two milks is not known (National Academy of Sciences—National Research Council, 1964). Cow's milk also is about five times richer in vitamin B_{12} and about four times richer in B_6. The amount in human milk appears to be ample, however. The water-soluble vitamins C and B in breast milk vary with the mother's diet, since these vitamins are not stored. Neither human nor cow's milk contains significant amounts of vitamin D.

The feces of breast-fed infants are acid in reaction; those of bottle-fed infants are neutral or alkaline. György (1961) stated that there is a prevalence of *Lactobacillus bifidus* in the intestinal flora of breast-fed infants and that these bacteria and the acidity in the intestine may be beneficial through the suppression of pathogenic or otherwise harmful bacteria. Human milk contains a fiftyfold greater supply of a factor which stimulates the growth of *L. bifidus* than cow's milk (Williams, 1961).

Weight and weight gains have been used chiefly in the *comparison of growth* of infants who have been breast-fed or bottle-fed. In the United States (Gross and Moses, 1956; Paiva, 1953), the United Kingdom (Levin et al., 1959; Stewart and Westropp, 1953; Thomson, 1955) and Sweden (Mellander et al., 1960) breast-fed infants gain about the same in weight or slightly more than bottle-fed infants from birth to one month or to three or four months. From three or four months on the gains are greater for the artificially fed. When the whole six-month period or the first year is considered, the bottle-fed infants' gains exceed those of the breast-fed. Aitken and Hytten (1960) remarked that the ability of bottle-fed infants to gain almost as well or equally well as the breast-fed in the early months and better in the later months implies a high standard of artificial feeding and hygiene and possibly other environmental conditions. In less favorable conditions results differ, as indicated by studies in a Stockholm children's home (Gyllenswärd, 1960) where the infants breast-fed for at least six months gained more than those bottle-fed, and in Singapore, where Millis (1956), comparing gains in weight of infants breast-fed for only twelve weeks and those breast-fed for more than twenty-four weeks, found that only in the well-to-do Chinese families was the first-year gain greater for infants weaned early.

Progress in weight is not the only criterion a physician uses in evaluating the feeding program of an infant. Gross and Moses (1956) commented that "it would be particularly undesirable to use weight gain alone as a measure of breast feeding." Just what measures physicians use which cause them to advocate breast feeding are not clearly defined. Jackson et al. (1964), studying 599 American infants through six months of age, used at least four length and weight measurements: one at birth, one at six months, and the others at intervals of not less than one month. They found that infants fed various cow's milk formulas and vitamin supplements grew at about the same rate as infants fed human milk with or without vitamin supplements.

Little information about skeletal development of breast- and bottle-fed infants is available. Stewart and Westropp (1953) noted no difference in skeletal maturity at one year. Mellander et al. (1960) observed that girls, but not boys, who were weaned early had significantly more ossification centers at seven or eight months than those weaned late.

Comparison of the incidence of disease in breast- and bottle-fed infants can easily be complicated by environmental conditions under which the infant is fed. The value of breast feeding as a protection against disease is greater in less developed countries (Welbourn, 1958) and in less favored economic classes (Aldrich, 1947) where lack of knowledge and facilities militates against carrying out adequate health measures, or where supervision of the infant's feeding by physicians and nurses is not available. A study of American Indians showed that

95 per cent of infants with severe diarrhea in a group requiring hospitalization were bottle-fed, although only 30 per cent of the infants in the area were being bottle-fed (Maternal and Child Health and Food and Nutrition Section, 1966). Stevenson (1947) found that in a series of carefully supervised infants who were given complements of vitamins considered adequate, there was no significant increase in the incidence of gastrointestinal and other infections in the bottle-fed group. Aitken and Hytten (1960) concluded that "it would appear that under modern standards of hygiene bottle-fed infants suffer no higher overall incidence of infections throughout infancy than breast-fed infants."

Breast-fed infants may have some advantages, however. Stevenson (1947) found that breast-fed babies had significantly fewer respiratory infections during the second half of the first year than those bottle-fed. Stewart and Westropp (1953) found that although the incidence of gastrointestinal and other infections in infancy was not related to the length of breast feeding, it was rare for an infant to have a gastrointestinal infection while receiving breast milk solely. Douglas (1950) found that the difference between breast-fed and bottle-fed infants was not in the number of infections, but in the timing of them. Bottle-fed infants had their peak of incidence earlier than breast-fed infants. The younger the child, the more immature he is and perhaps less well equipped to cope with infections. Whether these differences between breast- and bottle-fed infants can be attributed to qualities in the milk or to conditions associated with the feeding procedure remains to be ascertained.

The existence of viral antibodies in human milk has been known for some time (Valquist, 1958). These antibodies have been considered relatively unimportant in the immune system of the human infant because the quantity is usually low and the absorption slight (Smith, 1959). Recent studies (Gonzaga et al., 1963, Warren et al., 1964; Review, 1965) indicate that breast-fed infants are more resistant to infection with poliomyelitis virus. This was attributed to the inhibition of virus replication within the intestinal tract by the antibodies in human milk. The incidence of measles has also been reported to be lower in breast-fed than in bottle-fed infants (Review, 1958). These findings raise the question whether antibodies in human milk may not have some immunologic value and offer some degree of immunity to intestinal infections during early infancy.

The feeding of breast milk virtually eliminates the possibility of a milk allergy. Heiner et al. (1964) reported that clinical sensitivity to cow's milk occurs in 0.3 to 7 per cent of all infants. During the first few months these infants become hyperallergic to proteins of cow's milk. The sensitivity ranges from immediate, anaphylactoid reactions to markedly delayed reactions from chronic low-grade gastrointestinal blood loss. Milk-induced hypochromic microcytic anemia is the best example of the latter.

There are certain psychological components in breast and bottle feeding. Psychologically, both infant and mother gain something in the nursing situation. The infant gains comfort in his close physical contact with another person. He may profit indirectly by the effect of nursing upon the mother. There is some feeling that the greatest psychological advantage accrues to the mother who feels that she is involved in a unique relation with the child and is fulfilling her true maternal role (Guthrie, 1967). Spock (1950) suggested that breast feeding gives a woman confidence in herself as a mother and that as a result she is more relaxed and effective in her relations with and care of her child.

The bottle-fed infant need not be deprived of close mother-child contacts. Such contacts can be provided in a bottle-feeding situation.

Mothers have various reasons for not breast feeding their infants. Sometimes they are unable to nurse their infants because they cannot produce sufficient milk to satisfy the infant's needs. For many mothers the freedom and flexibility of social life that bottle feeding allows are an important consideration in the choice of the type of feeding. Among fifty-five mothers who had had a satisfying breast-feeding experience, the loss and restriction of their social life were considered disadvantages by twenty-nine of them (Guthrie, 1967). Some mothers cannot breast-feed because they must work; still others may have strong feelings against it (Sears, Maccoby and Levin, 1957). In this event, even if the mother could nurse her infant, the experience would satisfy neither mother nor child. In any case, the mother should have no sense of inadequacy or self-reproach (Levine, 1951).

Although knowledge of the excretion of drugs in milk is limited, nearly all products ingested by the mother are believed to be excreted in her milk in some form. Knowles (1965) recommends curtailment of unnecessary medication during lactation, but does not discourage breast feeding.

Bibliography

AITKEN, F. C., and HYTTEN, F. E. 1960. Infant feeding: comparison of breast and artificial feeding. *Nutrition Abst. and Rev.*, *30*:341–371.

ALDRICH, C. A., 1947. Advisability of breast feeding. *J.A.M.A.*, *135*:915–916.

BAIN, K. 1948. The incidence of breast feeding in hospitals in the United States. *Pediatrics*, *2*:313–320.

BAKWIN, H. 1964. Feeding programs for infants. *Fed. Proc.*, *23*:66–68.

BARNES, G. R., Jr., et al. 1953. Management of breast feeding. *J.A.M.A.*, *151*:192–199.

CALL, J. D. 1959. Emotional factors favoring successful breast feeding of infants. *J. Pediat.*, *55*:485–496.

Committee on Nutrition. 1960. Composition of milks. *Pediatrics*, *26*:1039–1047.

DOUGLAS, J. W. B. 1950. The extent of breast feeding in Great Britain in 1946, with special reference to health and survival of children. *J. Obst. Gynaec. Brit. Emp.*, *57*:335–361.

EGLI, G. E., et al. 1961. The influence of the number of breast feedings on milk production. *Pediatrics*, *27*:314–317.

FOMON, S. J., YOUNOSZAI, M. K., and THOMAS, L. N. 1966. Influence of Vitamin D on linear growth of normal full-term infants. *J. Nutrition*, *88*:345–350.

GONZAGA, A. J., WARREN, R. J., and ROBBINS, F. C. 1963. Attenuated poliovirus infections in infants fed colostrum from poliomyelitis immune cows. *Pediatrics*, *32*:1039–1045.

GROSS, R. T., and MOSES, L. E. 1956. Weight gains in the first four weeks of infancy: A comparison of three diets. *Pediatrics*, *18*:362–368.

GUTHRIE, H. A. 1967. *Introductory Nutrition*. St. Louis, C. V. Mosby Company.

GYLLENSWÄRD, C. 1960. Reported in F. C. Aitken and F. E. Hytten: Infant feeding: comparison of breast and artificial feeding. *Nutrition Abst. & Rev.*, *30*:341–371.

GYÖRGY, P. 1961. Orientation in infant feeding. *Proc. 5th International Congress of Nutrition.* Fed. Proc. 20 Part III: 169–176.

HEINER, D. C., WILSON, J. F., and LAHEY, M. E. 1964. Sensitivity to cow's milk. *J.A.M.A.*, *189*:563–567.

ILLINGWORTH, R. S., and STONE, D. G. H. 1952. Self-demand feeding in a maternity unit. *Lancet*, *262*:683–687.

JACKSON, E. B., et al. 1956. Statistical report on incidence and duration of breast feeding in relation to personal-social and hospital maternity factors. *Pediatrics*, *17*:700–715.

JACKSON, R. L., WESTERFIELD, R., FLYNN, M. A., KIMBALL, E. R., and LEWIS, R. B. 1964. Growth of "well-born" American infants fed human and cow's milk. *Pediatrics*, *33*:642–652.

JELLIFFE, D. B. 1962. Culture, social changes and infant feeding. Current trends in tropical regions. *Am J. Clin. Nutrition*, *10*:19–45.

KNOWLES, J. A. 1965. Excretion of drugs in milk. A review. *J. Pediat.*, *66*:1068–1082.

LEVIN, B., et al. 1959. Weight Gains, Serum Protein Levels and Health of Breast Fed and Artificially Fed Infants. *Med. Res. Council Spec. Rep.* Ser. No. 296. London, Her Majesty's Stationary Office.

LEVINE, M. 1951. A modern concept of breast feeding. *J. Pediat.*, *38*:472–475.

LINZELL, J. L. 1959. Physiology of the mammary glands. *Physiol. Rev.*, *39*:534–576.

LLOYD, C. W. 1962. The Ovaries. Chap. 7 in R. H. Williams (Ed.): *Textbook of Endocrinology.* 3rd ed. Philadelphia, W. B. Saunders Company.

MACY, I. G., et al., 1930. Human milk flow. *Am. J. Dis. Child.*, *39*:1186–1204.

MACY, I. G., et al. 1931. Human milk studies. *Am. J. Dis. Child.*, *42*:569–589.

MACY, I. G., KELLEY, H., and SLOAN, R. 1950. Composition of Milks. Bulletin No. 119. Washington, D.C., National Academy of Science—National Research Council.

Maternal and Child Health and Food and Nutrition Section 1966. Economy in nutrition and feeding of infants. *Am. J. Pub. Health*, *56*:1756–1784.

MELLANDER, O., et al. 1960. Reported in The Nornbotten Study. *Nutrition Rev.*, *18*:6–8.

MEYER, H. F. 1958. Breast feeding in the U.S.: extent and possible trend. *Pediatrics*, *22*:116–121.

MILLIS, J. 1956. The influence of breast feeding on weight gain in infants in the first year. *J. Pediat.*, *48*:770–775.

National Academy of Sciences—National Research Council. 1964. Recommended Dietary Allowances. Report of the Food and Nutrition Board. Revised 1964. Publication 1146. Washington, D.C., National Academy of Sciences—National Research Council.

NEWTON, N. R. and NEWTON, M. 1950a. Relation of let-down reflex to ability to breast feed. *Pediatrics*, *5*:726–733.

———, 1950b. Relationship of ability to breast feed and maternal attitudes toward breast feeding. *Pediatrics*, *5*:869–875.

PAIVA, S. L. 1953. Pattern of growth of selected groups of breast fed infants in Iowa City. *Pediatrics*, *11*:38–47.

Review. 1958. The role of breast-feeding in immunity. *Nutrition Rev.*, *16*:261–263.

Review. 1965. Breast-feeding and polio susceptibility. *Nutrition Rev.*, *23*:131–133.

SALBER, E. J., et al. 1958. Patterns of breast feeding. I. Factors affecting the frequency of breast feeding and reasons for weaning. *N. Eng. J. Med.*, *259*:707–713.

SALBER, E. J., et al. 1959. Patterns of breast feeding in a family health clinic. II. Duration of feeding and reasons for weaning. *N. Eng. J. Med.*, *260*:310–315.

SALBER, E. J., and FERNLEIB, M. 1966. Breast-feeding in Boston. *Pediatrics*, *37*:299–303.

SEARS, R. R., MACCOBY, E., and LEVIN, H. 1957. Patterns of Child Rearing. New York, Harper and Row.

SMITH, C. A. 1959. Physiology of the Newborn Infant, 3rd ed. Springfield, Ill., Charles C Thomas.

SMITH, C. A., et al. 1955. Persistence and utilization of maternal iron for blood formation during infancy. *J. Clin. Invest.*, *34*:1391–1402.

SPOCK, B. 1950. Round table discussion on present day attitudes toward breast feeding. (Smith, C. A., Chairman) *Pediatrics*, *6*:656–659.

STEVENSON, S. S. 1947. Adequacy of artificial feeding in infancy. *J. Pediat.*, *31*:616–630.

STEWART, A., and WESTROPP, C. 1953. Breast-feeding in the Oxford Child Health Survey. 2. Comparison of bottle-fed and breast-fed babies. *Brit. Med. J. 2*:305–308.

THOMSON, J. 1955. Observations on weight gain in infants. *Arch. Dis. Childhood*, *30*:322–327.

TOVERUD, K. U., STEARNS, G., and MACY, I. G. 1950. Maternal Nutrition and Child Health; Interpretative Review. Bulletin No. 123, Washington, D.C. National Academy of Science—National Research Council.

TURNER, C. D. 1966. *General Endocrinology*. 4th ed. Philadelphia, W. B. Saunders Company.

VALQUIST, B. 1958. The transfer of antibodies from mother to offspring. *Advances Pediat.*, *10*:305–310.

WALLER, H. 1946. The early failure of breast feeding; clinical study of its causes and their prevention. *Arch. Dis. Child.*, *21*:1–12.

WARREN, R. J., LEPOW, M. L., BARTSCH, G. E., and ROBBIN, F. C. 1964. The relationship of maternal antibody, breast feeding, and age to the susceptibility of newborn infants to infection with attenuated polioviruses. *Pediatrics*, *34*:4–13.

WELBOURN, H. F. 1958. Bottle feeding: A problem of civilization. *J. Trop. Pediat.*, *3*:157–170.

WILLIAMS, H. H. 1961. Differences between cow's and human milk. *J.A.M.A.*, *175*:104–107.

WOODHILL, L. M., et al. 1955. Nutrition studies of pregnant Australian women. Part II. Maternal diet and the duration of lactation. *Am. J. Obst. & Gynec.*, *70*:997–1003.

YANKHAUER, A., et al. 1958. Social stratification and health practices in child-bearing and child-rearing. *Am. J. Pub. Health*, *48*:448–463.

State and Behavior in the Neonate

Peter H. Wolff

HARVARD UNIVERSITY, MEDICAL SCHOOL

The following excerpt is part of Wolff's discussion of the results of his study of neonates. The "raw data" that he mentions in the first sentence are his reports of observations of behavior made during the babies' four days in the hospital following birth, for a total of twenty-four hours of observation. Some of the behavior was spontaneous; some was the result of stimuli systematically applied by Wolff. During the observations the babies were in various "states." The description of these states is the content of the excerpt.

Reprinted from "The causes, controls and organization of behavior in the newborn," *Psychological Issues*, 1966, *5*:1, 80–86. By Peter H. Wolff. By permission of International Universities Press, Inc. Copyright 1966 by International Universities Press, Inc.

The state concept was useful for grouping the raw data and interpreting the results, but it was never precisely defined. At times it referred to a quantitative continuum in levels of excitation, at other times to unconnected descriptive categories identified by discontinuous criteria such as the appearance of the eyes and the pattern of vocalization. By the first definition, state might have been equated with level of reticular activation, and in this sense called *arousal state*. Properly, however, "arousal" refers to a functional change rather than to a stable condition or a state. Moreover, "arousal" would have been inappropriate since the term implies some knowledge about the functional status of the nervous system, but no electroencephalographic recordings were used in this study for independent corroboration. According to the second definition, the concept of state was meant to imply *stable structures of the whole* which in practice were identified by selected behavioral indices, but signified a semistable organization of action patterns.

Terminological difficulties in defining state are not entirely of my own making, and come up in all infant studies which take heed of the great variability and instability of infantile response patterns. I would like to propose that both conceptions of "state" are meaningful and both can be useful at different levels of discourse as long as the distinction between, and the functional interdependence of, the two dimensions are kept in mind.

The theoretical limitations of state as an arousal continuum in isolation from organismic considerations become evident when we compare highly aroused "colicky" infants with infants who are frantic because they have been teased by repeated presentation and withdrawal of the nipple, or infants who cry because they are hungry with infants who cry because they are left alone. On the electroencephalogram these infants might all show the same degree of arousal, but behaviorally they would be clearly differentiated according to their motor activity and their selective responses to environmental intervention. The limitations of state as an arousal continuum become even clearer in the case of older individuals, for example, who may be excited for a great variety of physical and psychological reasons that cannot be adequately categorized on a quantitative continuum.

Since both dimensions of state are nevertheless important in the study of infant development, I will first review the findings in terms of the arousal dimension in order to tie them in with findings reported by others, and then interpret the results in terms of state as a "structure of the whole," in order to put them into a developmental framework for more extensive studies.

REGULAR SLEEP

Regular sleep may now be defined as a state which obtains when internal or external stimulations are absent or subliminal; when, with the exception of spontaneous discharges, motor activity is minimal; and when thresholds to sensory stimulations are high. I have assumed that this combination of factors fosters a disposition of neural activity in low-frequency, high-amplitude pulses which instigate periodic motor discharges. Intense external or visceral stimuli can break into regular sleep at any time, but the infant is usually immune to mild arousal stimuli during regular sleep until an inherent cycling biological clock alters the state automatically. At that point the infant becomes more susceptible to both internal and external stimulations.

Sleep induced by white noise is a special state, probably analogous to but certainly not identical with regular sleep. The onset of continuous white noise may elicit a transient arousal but the infant rapidly habituates to the stimulus, and, depending on his previous history, either goes back to sleep or gradually goes into a state analogous to regular sleep. While exposed to white noise, the infant is less susceptible to external stimulation than during natural sleep, presumably because white noise raises the threshold to external stimulations. When random noise is turned off the infant may revert to a higher arousal state—thus the disturbing effects of visceral stimuli are suppressed by the white noise. Finally, the noise may redistribute spontaneous discharge behaviors—thus white noise damps the trigger effect of physiological stimuli.

Regular sleep was classified as the low point on the arousal continuum, or as the condition when the infant is least susceptible to external stimulations. Jouvet has described a phase of sleep in animals which appears to be more profound than synchronous sleep, and which is called "rhombencephalic," or "activated," or "paradoxical" because it can be induced by the experimental stimulation of brain-stem centers, and because the organism shows intermittent twitching movements and irregular respirations although the thresholds to external stimulations are higher than during synchronous sleep (Jouvet et al., 1959, Jouvet, 1963). It has also been called "archisleep" because it is the prevalent form in premature infants and newborn kittens (Parmalee et al., 1964).

Since respirations were my only defining criterion for depth of sleep, I could not distinguish what I have called irregular, and assumed to be light, sleep from what Jouvet calls profound desynchronized sleep, and therefore cannot assess the implications of Jouvet's findings for sleep in the full-term human neonate.

IRREGULAR SLEEP

One probable cause for the transition from regular to irregular sleep was the intrusion of intense external or visceral stimulations; since no systematic experiments were conducted to convert regular to irregular sleep by external stimulation, my only evidence for the disruptive effects of extrinsic stimulation is the observation that the ratio of regular to irregular sleep becomes smaller as the time for feeding comes closer.

Another mechanism for the transition from regular to irregular sleep was inferred from the retrospective analysis of sleep records which indicated that the cycles of alternating deep and light sleep described by Aserinsky and Kleitman (1955) are present at birth, and that even the powerful sleep-inducing effects of white noise do not override these cycles.

As the infant passes from regular to irregular sleep he becomes more susceptible to pre-existing visceral or external stimulation. Disturbing stimuli which were subthreshold during regular sleep now become sufficient to initiate diffuse motor activity; the sensory feedback from this activity in turn raises the level of reticular activation, further reduces sensory thresholds to external stimulation, and desynchronizes autochthonous neural pulses so that spontaneous discharges are rare.

DROWSINESS

Drowsiness is a "paradoxical" state in which the infant is almost immobile yet sensitive to external stimuli, while the incidence of spontaneous discharges is high at certain times, low at others.

According to the stated assumptions, a combination of immobility, regular respirations, and absence of focused attention (which by analogy from electroencephalographic studies on adults might be expected to desynchronize large-amplitude pulses) should predispose the organism to paroxysmal discharges during drowsiness, but spontaneous discharges in drowsiness were frequent only at the time of falling asleep. At least in some respects, therefore, drowsiness while falling asleep and while waking up are not identical conditions, even though the infant's clinical appearance may be the same. The observed difference raises a larger question: whether it is ever sufficient to define the organism's state according to static criteria alone or whether one must also consider the sequence of steps leading to the state in question as one of its defining properties. The infant who is alert-inactive after a period of drowsiness may well behave in quite a different manner from the baby who becomes alert-inactive after a period of crying. Comparisons of this kind were not made in the present study but deserve further attention, since they add the temporal to the spatial dimension in our conceptions about the hierarchic integration of states.

ALERT INACTIVITY

Although Kleitman (1963) modified his original genetic theory of sleep and wakefulness (Kleitman, 1939) to assimilate the neurophysiological findings of the intervening period, his classification of the sleep-waking continuum remains the only one based on ontogenetic principles. Rejecting the conception of a biological instinct for sleep (as well as other partial explanations), Kleitman proposed that a *wakefulness of necessity* provoked by disturbing internal or external stimulations is the only form of wakefulness in the infant and that as soon as the disturbing stimuli are removed the infant returns to sleep. Sleep is considered as the ontogenetically "basic" condition on which a voluntary waking state is superimposed in the course of cortical maturation.

Stating a contrary point of view, I proposed (Wolff, 1965) that the full-term infant may be awake for brief periods even while he is free from distressing internal or external stimuli. Naturalistic observations indicate that newborn infants are alert and inactive for limited periods of time after all controllable visceral and external irritations have been alleviated by the mother, and that the first developmental increases in the duration of alertness occur *after* the infant has been fed, diapered, and burped—in other words, after all distressing circumstances under the mother's control have been eliminated.

What then "causes" the newborn infant to be alert and inactive? There is now evidence to support the assertion that newborn infants can selectively attend to their immediate environment for brief periods of time (Fantz, 1958, 1961; Wolff, 1959; B. L. White, 1963; Wolff and White, 1965; Salapatek and Kessen, 1965). It is also possible to maintain the infant in a state of alert inactivity by focusing his attention on a specific visual task, but the state evaporates as soon as the "interesting spectacle" is removed, while the drowsy or fussy baby can be repeatedly brought back to a state of alert inactivity by environmental distractions which have no peremptory qualities since the infant has a "choice" of responding or not responding (Wolff, 1965). Periods of alert inactivity induced in this way last for a considerably longer time (10–40 minutes) than the "orienting investigatory reflex" (Sokolov, 1963; Berlyne, 1960), and cannot be considered homologues of such a "reflex."

This is not to say that the infant intends to wake in order to act, as might be the case for an adult who wakes up by habit or because he has a job to do. The need to function (Piaget, 1936), the driving force of manipulatory or exploratory behavior (Harlow, Blazek, and McClearn, 1956), or competence motivation (R. W. White, 1963) can hardly be invoked as mechanisms for arousal from sleep in the infant. But once the infant wakes to the point of drowsiness for other reasons, a provocative or "interesting" environment may initiate and then maintain the quiet alert state. The greater the number of pathways for attending to the environment, and the more diverse the structures for organizing the perceived events, the longer we would expect the infant to remain awake and attentive. In this way we could account for the finding that discontinuous jumps in total time of alertness occur at those points in motor development when the infant acquires new ways of exploring his environment and of expanding his range of "interesting spectacles," for example with the inception of hand-eye coordination or turning over (see B. L. White, 1963).

The proposed arousal continuum can now be extended to include the alert states: inherent biological clocks as well as visceral or external stimulations contribute to the transition from regular to irregular sleep; once the infant is in light sleep he becomes more sensitive to stimulations which have been subliminal during regular sleep. Depending on the intensity of such stimuli he may remain in irregular sleep and eventually return to regular sleep, or he may become drowsy. When the eyes open while he is still drowsy, his attention may be drawn to novelties in the environment and direct his action to objects. The act of attending itself will desynchronize large-amplitude pulses and inhibit spontaneous discharge even while the infant is immobile and breathing regularly, and as long as he is occupied with directed motor actions, diffuse activity is inhibited. Sooner or later the intensity of visceral stimulations breaks through, and then neither the influx of nonspecific external excitations (e.g., visual and tactile events that do not draw the infant's attention) nor the attending to external events will be sufficient to keep diffuse motility in check.

WAKING ACTIVITY AND CRYING

The conditions of heightened arousal classified here as waking activity and crying, can be described in terms of the concepts already at our disposal. When internal or external stimuli are sufficiently intense to overcome the "defensive" aspects of attending, a cycle is set in motion which only fatigue or the mother's intervention will interrupt: diffuse activity provoked by noxious stimuli presumably increases the level of reticular activation and further sensitizes the organism to the offending stimuli; the infant enters a state in which motility itself promotes his response to noxious stimulation, and the more sensitive he becomes, the more vigorously he struggles. Such a cycle may be compared to the tantrum of a young child, or the hysterical attack of an adult, both of which seem to feed themselves once the person has given way to motility.

The cycle starts with soft whimpering and gentle movements, and these gradually lengthen to become a rhythmical pattern of crying and kicking. If allowed to persist they eventually break down into uncoordinated thrashing and spasmodic screeching, flooding the infant with proprioceptive and tactile stimuli to which he cannot habituate since their intensity and locus varies constantly. A high influx of nonspecific but variable stimulations renders him insensitive to those additional "test" stimuli which might have evoked a noticeable response during sleep, drowsiness, or alert inactivity.

While the primary causes of heightened arousal that interrupt the stable state of alert inactivity in the neonate are probably physical and physiological stimulations, the borderline between physical and psychological causes at this stage is indistinct. During the early days after birth, stimulations of some "psychological" significance which are not painful in the physiological sense can provoke excitement and crying. For example, infants respond with outrage to partial body restraint (e.g., when they are "badly" swaddled), but with calmness and drowsiness to total body restraint or "good" swaddling; even well-fed infants react with excitement and crying when a pacifier is repeatedly offered and taken away. Global "psychological" provocations therefore act side by side with physiological distress and physical pain as sufficient causes of heightened arousal and must be included among the instigations of high arousal states in the neonate.

References

ASERINSKY, E., and KLEITMAN, N. (1955). A Motility Cycle in Sleeping Infants as Manifested by Ocular and Gross Body Activity. *J. Applied Physiol.* 8:11–19.

BERLYNE, D. E. (1960). *Conflict, Arousal and Curiosity.* New York: McGraw-Hill.

FANTZ, R. L. (1958). Pattern Vision in Young Infants. *Psychological Reports* 8:43–47.

———(1961). The Origin of Form Perception, *Scientific American, 204*:66–72.

HARLOW, H. F., BLAZEK, W. C., and McCLEARN, G. E. (1956). Manipulatory Motivation in the Infant Rhesus Monkey. *J. Comp. Physiol. Psychol.,* 49:444–448.

JOUVET, M., MICHEL, F., and COURJON, J. (1959). Sur un Stade d'Activité Électrique Cérébrale Rapide au Cours du Sommeil Physiologique. *C. F. Soc. Biol.,* 1953:1024.

———(1963). The Rhombencephalis Phase of Sleep. In *Brain Mechanisms*, Vol. 1, ed. G. Moruzzi, A. Fessard, and H. H. Jasper. New York: Elsevier, pp. 406–424.

KLEITMAN, N. (1939). *Sleep and Wakefulness.* Chicago: University of Chicago Press.

———(1963). *Sleep and Wakefulness*, 2nd. edition, revised and enlarged. Chicago: University of Chicago Press.

PARMALEE, A. H., AKIYAMA, Y., WENNER, W., and FLESCHER, J. (1964). Activated Sleep in Premature Infants. Address to Assoc. Psychophysiol. Study of Sleep, March.

PIAGET, J. (1936). *The Origins of Intelligence.* New York: International Universities Press, 1952.

SALAPATEK, P., and KESSEN, W. (1965). Visual Scanning of Triangles by the Human Newborn. Paper presented at the Eastern Psychological Association Meetings, April.

SOKOLOV, Y. N. (1963). *Perception and the Conditioned Reflex.* New York: Macmillan.

WHITE, B. L. (1963). The Development of Perception During the First Six months of Life. Address to the American Association for the Advancement of Science, Cleveland, Ohio, December.

WHITE, R. W. (1963). Ego and Reality in Psychoanalytic Theory. *Psychological Issues, III* (3). New York: International Universities Press.

WOLFF, P. H. (1959). Observations on Newborn Infants. *Psychosom. Med., 21* : 110–118.

———(1965). The Development of Attention in Young Infants. *Ann. N.Y. Acad. Sci. 118* : 815–830.

———and WHITE, B. L. (1965). Visual Pursuit and Attention in Young Infants. *J. Amer. Acad. Child Psychiat., 4* : 473–484.

3

Emerging Resources for Coping with the World

American values with regard to children are compared with Soviet values by the first author, psychologist David Rosenhan. He maintains that the Soviets are eager to have their infants and children develop just as fast as they can. Americans, on the other hand, are concerned with health, and although they believe that the child should be allowed to grow at his own rate, they have some ambivalence about precocity. The Soviets believe more strongly in environmental influence than do Americans. The reader can judge for himself how closely the next article is consistent with the American values described by Dr. Rosenhan.

The focus of an article by Lois B. Murphy, well known for her research on personality development and her long-standing concern for the well-being of children, is on what young children need for optimal development. Dr. Murphy summarizes and clarifies what is known about meeting children's needs and what needs to be learned through research.

The synchronization between motor development and language development is shown in an excerpt from Biological Foundations of Language, *by Eric Lenneberg. His emphasis on maturation as a basis for speech and other learning makes an interesting contrast to the Soviet beliefs described by Dr. Rosenhan. Lenneberg's chart of developmental milestones is very impressive.*

Preface to *Soviet Preschool Education*

David Rosenhan
SWARTHMORE COLLEGE

Not long ago, but long after I had completed my formal undergraduate and graduate training, I attended a seminar that proved to be one of the strangest and most stimulating in my career. Entitled: "What shall the values in

Preface, by David Rosenhan, to *Soviet Preschool Education*, Volume II: *Teacher's Commentary*, edited by Henry Chauncey. Preface by David Rosenhan. Copyright © 1969 by Holt, Rinehart and Winston, Inc. Reprinted by permission of Holt, Rinehart and Winston, Inc.

American education be?", it was convened by William Kessen of Yale University for more than thirty people, all deeply committed to quality education through their disciplines, mainly psychology and education. Kessen made only one stipulation at the outset: that it would be a true seminar in that he would neither prime the meeting with his own ideas nor otherwise goad the participants to action, but would rather listen for the ideas that came from them.

A strange seminar indeed. Forty-five minutes passed, as I recall, in absolute silence, punctuated only by an occasional self-conscious giggle, enshrouded by anxious glances as one member looked to his peer for salvation from intellectual helplessness. The seminar terminated silently, profoundly. We went our ways.

What was it that sealed our mouths, fogged our wits? Lord knows we cared, for the issue of values goes right to the heart of educational programs, curricula and goals. We who were the planners, preachers and implementers in American education, had nothing to say about the premises that underlay our work. Sad, indeed. Was it that we feared to speak openly lest we offend the sensibilities of an illustrious colleague? Was it that the present turmoil in American education has shaken our values to the roots, to such a degree that the entire matter needs to be reconsidered and that the first approach to reconsideration is silence? Was it, perhaps, that no value consensus can be arrived at in a democracy such as our own that stresses individualism and the right of each man to have his own values? Was it, worst of all, that we had no values, that we traveled the American educational scene by the pragmatic seat of our pants, that we were carpenters rather than creators, implementers and not ideators?

This seminar (for it was truly that) was discussed heatedly for months to come. We never did answer these questions, nor did we finally come up with an educational Magna Carta upon which all could agree. We were, however, brought in that silence more poignantly than by words to examine the central issue of education: What shall our values be?

Our Soviet counterparts apparently have none of our problems in this regard. *Soviet Preschool Education: Teacher's Commentary* not only communicates clearly and in considerable detail the ways and means of proper education for children aged two months through seven years, but also the philosophies that should guide that education. I will not dilute your pleasure by describing at length those values here: they are amply and well interspersed among the educational instructions that are found in the volume. There are, however, tacit value metaphors hidden beneath the explicit philosophies and it will serve us some considerable gain to explicate some of these. Two that are most striking are what I would call the values of *precocity* and *intentional environmentalism*. They are, in many ways, overlapping categories and they emerge as forceful premises on the Soviet educational scene. Let us examine them in quite some detail.

It will surprise you, I am sure, as you peruse the first thirty pages of this volume, to find that the Soviets teach everything as early as they can. At four months, the rudiments of vocalization and sound discrimination are introduced: at eight months, the beginnings of toilet training. Play itself is ordered and designed to the child's capacity with a view to serving as the basis for what will come later. At one year of age, a full educational program is in swing: Esthetics—yes, esthetics!—through music appreciation; speech training;

neatness and toilet training; obedience and self-control; active stimulation of interest in the environment—these and many others constitute the core curriculum for infants. It is a sensible program, tailored to the infant's capacities with considerable leeway given to individual differences. But its most striking hallmark is its emphasis on precocity: that which will be learned inevitably ought to be learned early.

It is not automatically evident why earlier is better, and extreme precocity best. Perhaps for the Soviets it is simply a matter of insurance. Soviet preschools, by our standards, seem understaffed and overworked (teachers and their assistants put in a twelve hour day with only a 30 minute break). A mandate for precocity may serve to assure society that Soviet children will be functioning as they should be functioning when the appropriate time arrives. A more interesting view, however, holds that the Soviet imagination, like our own, is captured by the notion that precocity augurs future achievement, that the earlier we start the further we go. On this matter, the evidence is ambiguous at best, and the measure of that ambiguity is amply reflected in our own society. On the one hand, we do have a vigorous nursery school movement and a Headstart program (albeit one whose merit and future are, at this writing, clouded). There is, moreover, a privately held norm of precocity, especially in the middle class, that permits us to take great pleasure in the child who walks, talks or tumbles before these are expected, and encourages us to teach him at home before he is taught in school.

Yet we are ambivalent about the virtues of precocity; this is seen mainly in the laissez-faire theories of development that are tacitly and overtly held in our public school systems. In these theories cognitive development is linked to age and physical development, these latter held to be immutable, and therefore cognitive development immutable also. Such thinking is buttressed from several sources. First are the normative studies, such as by Gesell and Ilg, which dominate the common mind such that it thinks only of that which is ordinarily achieved and turns away from that which is potentially achievable. Second are the oversimplified views of Piagetian psychology which see cognitive growth as a naturally unfolding process that cannot be hastened. Finally, there is fear, most evident in the writings of Dr. Spock, that appears to originate in the presumed fragility of the child and leads us to feel that in attempting anything we may attempt too much, and by attempting too much the child might be harmed. (Not to speak of parental aspiration: better not to aspire than to risk failure.) The sum of the matter is that while we take joy on the occasion of precocity, we are hesitant to facilitate it, and herein lies our first tacit value contrast with the Soviets.

The norm of precocity is linked in Soviet thinking to intentional environmentalism. This is to say that on the question of the relative contribution of nature and nurture to cognitive social and personality development, they opt strongly for nurture. But nurture is not a random thing: environments don't simply happen. They are created, willy-nilly, or intentionally, by those who live in them. The Soviets prefer to intentionally create their environments, to leave as little as possible to chance happening. One senses throughout this volume that they have not only a fair image of the kind of person they would have at each stage of development, but also of the manner in which he might be created. Correctly or incorrectly, they believe that for a child to be sociable, he needs to spend his infancy in a crib with other infants: for him to have an appreciation of music at eight years, he needs to be systematically exposed to melody at age eight months; for language to blossom, its elements need to be inculcated early. Toilet training, speech, moral behavior, muscular development, independence, curiosity, cognition and conformity are all analyzed into their elemental components, graded for their difficulty, and systematically fed to the child just as early as possible.

The American system, by contrast, is more casual. Of course, we have no nurseries for our infants: until they are three years old (and commonly until five), our children are raised at home. That fact alone guarantees a greater diversity of child-rearing approaches, if only because there are no systematic social controls and mothers are not usually professionally-trained infant teachers. These facts notwithstanding, there *are* manuals for mothers, one of the most widely used being Spock's *Baby and Child Care*. And even taking into consideration that Spock speaks to parents and this volume to teachers, the diversity of approach is remarkable. Confronted by a child whose development is irregular in some respects, the Soviet teacher is urged to concentrate on the weaknesses with a view to bringing them up to par. Compare this to Spock's advice to the American mother confronted with the same dilemma: "Enjoy him as he is . . . that's how he'll grow up best . . . enjoy your child for what he is . . . and forget about the qualities he doesn't have." (pp. 43–44) Indeed, the very notion of facilitating or encouraging development, particularly in a formal way during the early years, is anathema, the mark of an overly pushy parent. Hear Spock again: "A child becomes interested in dressing dolls properly, coloring carefully, playing trains realistically, each at a certain stage of his development. You can't hurry him. When you try, you only make him feel incompetent. This does more harm than good . . . let *him* show *you* how [to play]." (pp. 306–307) Compare this now to the Russian mandate, here in connection with language development: "Every moment in which the nurse and her assistant are in close contact with the child must be utilized: during care, feeding, independent games and outdoor play. . . . Name objects at the moment children seem to take a particular interest in them; name actions and movements while the child is performing them. . . . Develop in the child the ability to imitate sounds and words used by adults and create the necessary conditions to stimulate the children to pronounce various sounds as often as possible." (p. 48) Clearly the Soviet approach is one of active intervention, while ours is mainly one of appreciative watching.

Perhaps the critical difference between the Soviet approach and ours lies herein: that we are concerned to avoid pathology and they to promote development; that our manual for child-rearing is authored by a physician whose main concern is to interpret and prevent illness and harm (. . . "and when you try, you only make him feel incompetent. This does more harm than good.") while theirs is compiled by educators whose central mission is the promotion of talent (. . . "Create the necessary conditions to stimulate the child . . ."). My own judgment and that of many of my colleagues is increasingly on the side of educational intervention from the earliest years. Much as the absence of vice is no guarantor of virtue, the absence of illness in no way signifies the maximal development of educational potential. If we believe (and the scientific evidence is now too large to ignore) that early experience is critical for subsequent development, we may need to become intentional environmentalists ourselves, leaving development not to fortuitous chance (too many children are under-privileged in that regard), not even to avoidance of injury, but to the careful and orderly elaboration of ability.

There is a close and sensible relationship between the practices recommended in this book and psychological theory and practice. Not that *all* psychological research is translated into practice, nor that only matters that have been clearly researched are recommended. Far from it: scientific psychology and scientific education are not so advanced that we can rely on them fully, but neither are they so retarded that they can teach us nothing. This volume, you will find, is a delightful blend of good sense and good science.

Take language development as a case in point. The common view, strongly buttressed by many normative studies, holds that language "develops": that at a certain age, the infant babbles "da-da," that somewhat later he acquires a more descriptive word or two, that by age two his vocabulary is larger, and by four, larger still. A moment's reflection, however, reminds us that language does not "develop," certainly not as second-year molars develop. It is acquired, learned, by exposure to speakers. And exposure to speakers is by no means equal for all children, as recent explorations into the language of under-privileged children have dramatically demonstrated. And if the child actively *learns* language (rather than passively developing it), language should be *teachable*, with better methods or with worse. The Soviets offer some concrete suggestions for language education.

For the infant, the words we speak have no meaning unless they are associated with things he somehow knows. Otherwise, words are quickly assimilated into the noisy and meaningless surroundings. Language teaching begins, reasonably enough, with precise pairing of familiar things with words. (Even before that, by training vocalization and sound discrimination.) "Mommy has arrived," the nurse says to the five-month-old. "Let's go to Mommy." By nine months the nurse is pointing to familiar toys and naming them; hiding the toy and asking the infant to find it; giving commands ("bring me the rattle"). Subsequently, a program for naming actions and abstractions is implemented and finally, as the child approaches the time to learn reading and writing (about seven years old), consciousness of phonics and word structure is developed. The stress is not only on active teaching, but on *programmatic* teaching of language, such that the steps constitute a sensible progression from the simple to the complex.

Readers familiar with the works of Vygotsky or Piaget, or the more recent efforts of Roger Brown, George Miller and John Flavell, will easily understand the relations between language and thought, and abstract learning itself. Some of the relevant research in this area is, in fact, presented in Volume I of *Soviet Preschool Education*. Clearly, the simple message of all research in this area is that language is too important a matter for its acquisition to be left to chance or passive "development." The foundations of thought and facilitators of interpersonal relationship must be taught actively, sensibly, relentlessly.

Neither is moral development left to the accident of growing up, to chance learning. Concern for others, moral judgment and behavior, thoughtfulness, respect and courtesy are taught, again at early ages. There will be some disagreement about how far moral education can proceed at age three, but clearly the rudiments are inculcated then, to be developed later. The Soviet program is specific about how this is done. Not by preachments alone, but by *actions* performed by adults jointly with children. Adults influence children by their behavior, by their personal approach to other people around them, toward traditions, and toward the homeland. Such personal moral qualities as humility, modesty, truthfulness, diligence, sociability, goodwill, cooperativeness, thoughtfulness and cheerfulness form the foundation of a child's moral being. The evaluation and development of these qualities is aided by the example set by the teacher, by the consistent and fair attitude she maintains towards all the children of the group. Many of the techniques recommended here are supported by and consistent with research findings that have been available both in America and abroad. Many other techniques seem to be based more on good sense, or at least on good intentions, and will require further verification.

The matter of verification is critical for those who would propose educational procedures as for those who would borrow them. If education is too important a matter to be left to chance, it is also too important to be left to good intentions, however well those seem founded in common sense. What is critical is what works, and how and why it works. For determining these there are no easy substitutes for research. One cannot really assess from these volumes the degree to which a substantial research effort in education is ongoing in the Soviet Union. Clearly some progress is being made, as is evident in Volume I: how much and how successful are the questions. In any event, for those who would utilize these promising Soviet techniques for the solution of educational problems elsewhere, the message is clear and urgent: a program of evaluation, no less substantial in commitment and fiscal magnitude than that of the educational program itself, is required.

There is not, to my knowledge, a manual quite like this one presently available. For older children there is, of course, Marie Montessori's *The Montessori Method*, which describes her work in the *Casa dei Bambini* in the slums of Rome. Even earlier, there is the writing of Pestalozzi, who apparently greatly influenced Soviet thinking on education, and of Froebel. Readers familiar with those writings will immediately sense important commonalities and differences. All of these writers, along with authors of these volumes, hold that development is an unfolding process, and that education consists simply of not hindering that process, and of providing the child with precisely what it requires from the environment at each stage of development. There are differences in view about what the environment needs to supply and how it should do so. Montessori, you will recall, opts for structure, carefully designing all manner of educational apparatus to the presumed needs of the children. This volume suggests no special equipment, relying rather on what society naturally provides: a ball, a doll, a flower. Soviet conceptualization, on the other hand, stresses a matter that is considerably muted, if it is present at all, in these other writings: the critical importance of a warm teacher-child relationship. Throughout this volume where the Soviets criticize their teachers, it is entirely for neglect and abuse of this relationship: for their rudeness, their ordinary tendency to make

invidious comparisons between children, their confusion of curiosity with dis-
obedience, their failure to sustain a loving, caring relationship. It is no small
mission that they assign their teachers, to retain and encourage that which is
personal and facilitating midst that which is systematically required and
anomic. It does us well to recall, as we revise our own curricula for young
children, that care precedes technique, that positive regard is a necessary
ingredient for intellectual maturation.

If there has been a central message in education during the past century,
it is that the child is father to the man, that what is acquired early determines
in good measure what will be learned later. How early is "early"? For us,
education in kindergarten begins around age five. Is that early enough?
Perhaps it is for privileged children, though I doubt it. But it is patently not
early enough for underprivileged ones for whom enrichment programs such as
Headstart now begin at age three, and even at this age show no real pattern of
merit. Clearly we shall have to begin earlier, for the underprivileged as perhaps
for the privileged, at home or in formal institutions. For such a program. *Soviet
Preschool Education* is unique and will provide an excellent first approximation
for a general program.

Children Under Three: Finding Ways to Stimulate Development*

Lois Barclay Murphy
MENNINGER FOUNDATION

I. ISSUES IN RESEARCH

Since the beginning of World War II, the U.S. gross national product
(GNP)—the aggregate of its agricultural and industrial output—has steadily
increased. Unfortunately, the Nation has not proportionately increased its
resources for protecting its human products. Neglect of prenatal care, birth
defects, nutritional needs, and appropriate infant care lies behind our poor
standing among the nations in infant mortality rates—13 highly developed
nations have reported rates lower than the United States.[1] It also underlies
much of the distorted development of children as reflected in mental retardation, delinquency, and mental illness. This neglect has been paralleled by the

Reprinted from *Children*, 1969, *6*, 46–51. By permission.

* The observations on which this article is based were made during work under two grants
from the Public Health Service—MH10421 to the Children's Hospital of the District of Columbia
and 5 R12 MH9236–02 to the Menninger Foundation, Topeka, Kans.
[1] United Nations, Department of Economic and Social Affairs, Statistical Office: Demographic
yearbook, 1966. United Nations, N.Y. 1967.

country's failure to provide employment for the thousands of workers abandoned by employers as technology has superseded human labor on farms, in mines, and in factories.

As a result of such neglect of human needs, today large numbers of children throughout the Nation are unable to make use of the learning opportunities provided by the schools. Discouraged, depressed, undernourished parents become apathetic and so rear their children for passive tolerance of frustration rather than for active mastery of a skill. Too many children in lower socio-economic groups do not learn to learn; their speech, concepts, experience, and drive to achieve are inadequate for learning. Their normal aggression is not directed into socially constructive channels, and they have little help in dealing with emotional problems, which arise more often among the disadvantaged than among other segments of the population.[2] In the past decade, however, many pressures—the space race, a personal concern about retardation on the part of persons in high office, and research reporting school failure among millions of poor children, white, black, and Mexican-American—have brought about efforts to do something about their faltering intellectual development.

The first response was legislation to provide some Federal aid to the schools, but this could do little to help the child who arrived at kindergarten or the first grade with an irreversible intellectual handicap. Then came Project Head Start to ready the preschool child for school and also some exhilarating experiments in the cognitive stimulation of preschool children, sometimes reinforced by candy rewards. But it was discovered that "Head Start was too late" and candy was not enough. Some children's IQ's did increase as they participated in these experiments, but their scores tended to lapse back again or even to get lower after they entered school. As this tendency became apparent, there came a push for cognitive stimulation of babies, based on the research efforts of learning theorists. Some of these theorists, however, were operating from their own conceptual islands, ignoring the forces of drive, motivation, affective response, constitutional factors, individual personality, and subculture values that could thwart or attenuate the effects of learning techniques and gastric rewards. Nevertheless, some cognitive stimulators even asserted that the prevention of delinquency, emotional disturbance, and a negative self-image could all be achieved through early cognitive stimulation.

Meantime, other forces were at work. The stultifying and distorting effects of sterile institutional life on children without families had led to the widespread avoidance of institutional care. Foster families were to provide the nearest equivalent to a natural family for the children who had no "real" mother or father, or no adequate parents. In some cases this goal was achieved. But in the large cities, the limited space in most families' homes and the many parentless, neglected, or mistreated children defeated efforts to find foster homes for all who needed them; moreover, the stress experienced by families who attempted to bring up foster children in a crowded urban setting led in many instances to shifts from one home to another,[3] which defeated the aim of a stable family life for these children. After a series of acceptances and rejections,

[2] Srole, L., et al.: Mental health in the metropolis. McGraw-Hill, New York, N.Y. 1962.
[3] Mass, H. S.; Engler, R. E., Jr.: Children in need of parents. Columbia University Press, New York, N.Y. 1959.

many children became disturbed and alienated and as a result they had difficulties in school and the community.

In response to these problems, the pendulum has swung back to a revived interest in group care, at least in the form of supplementary care during the day. This interest has become more intense as a result of the view that mothers who passively receive public assistance might better go to work and let their children be cared for in adequate day-care centers. Because of the simultaneous concern about school failures, the thinking about day care has tended to focus on cognitive stimulation, as if this were the only need to be met.

Most of the discussion of cognitive stimulation has been oriented toward children from 3 to 5 years old, but in the past 5 years children under 3 have also begun to receive attention. Under the impression that "Head Start is too late," research workers have been exploring the effects of cognitive stimulation on babies.

AN UNDERLYING ERROR   One major error underlies many failures to provide for adequate development: the notion that "We have *the* answer." There was a time when the central concern of administrators of child-care programs was to prevent infection; they thought that if the children were kept clean they would grow well. At other times, "the" answer was thought to be good nutrition, or fresh air, or activity, or freedom. And now it is cognitive stimulation. But disappointments have followed each one-track attempt to follow "the" one important prescription, as Skeels,[4] Spitz,[5] and others have shown in studying clean, but sterile, institutions. We now know that institutionalized children who are merely kept clean and well fed lack most of the ingredients for healthy personality, social, and cognitive development; and that these lacks contribute to varying degrees and kinds of deficiency and distortion—mental retardation, social inadequacy, disorganized behavior, delinquency, failure to grow, and at worst marasmus and death.

In Israeli kibbutzim and in the best day-care centers in the United States, the multiple needs of the child are met: warm, mothering caretakers provide stimulation, space for activity, time for free play, response to the child's efforts, along with lots of fresh air and good food—and a chance to experience joy. It seems paradoxical that so many recent investigators are again following a single track—cognitive stimulation through specific teaching programs—and overlooking many other aspects of development, despite evidence that nutrition, activity, emotions, and human relationships affect a child's learning.

Moreover, in many instances the idea of what learning is has been shaped by a narrow range of concepts such as vocabulary, memory, reasoning, and comprehension and by Piaget's insights regarding the child's development of time and space concepts and the conservation of objects. But the growth of a child's mind involves many cognitive functions (including complex sensory-motor and coping efforts) not measured in intelligence tests. These include, for example: differentiation between the familiar and the strange; the process of

[4] Skeels, Harold M.: Effects of adoption on children from institutions. *Children*, January–February 1965.
[5] Spitz, René: Hospitalism—an inquiry into the genesis of psychiatric conditions in early childhood. *In* The psychoanalytic study of the child, vol. I. International Universities Press, New York, N.Y. 1945.

familiarization (visual and auditory examination, manual manipulation, and so forth); movement-in-space problems; combining objects; solving problems requiring manipulation; use of tools, such as the door knob, screen hook, faucet knob; self-dressing—pulling off and putting on socks; finding or creating substitutes; and clarification of relationships and experience by rehearsing them in fantasy.

Ability to do such things develops in children who are growing up in an environment where they are exposed to a variety of objects, challenges, and opportunities to use their minds and bodies and can observe the everyday problem solving of their parents and brothers and sisters. As with all aspects of mental development, development of these skills needs the support of varied experience.

CRITERIA FOR EVALUATION   How then shall we formulate what is needed to foster good physical, emotional, social, and cognitive development? And what criteria should guide research for evaluating programs for children under 3?

Here I list seven basic areas to consider in evaluating proposals for early child care:

1. *Adequate nutrition*—proteins, vitamins, minerals, and other nutrients required for the physical development of the child. In many parts of the world, where infants receive insufficient protein and other nutrients, the mortality rates among children are high. A large proportion of those who manage to live are malnourished, vulnerable to infection, and retarded. Similar conditions are reported to exist among infants and small children in "hunger areas" of the United States.

2. *Ability to deal with the baby in distress.* How to handle the baby who has poor digestion, colic, diarrhea or constipation, or susceptibility to infection is still inadequately understood by many child-care workers. That there are *emotional and mental consequences of distress in early infancy* is even less appreciated. Such babies need help with gastrointestinal and other aspects of basic functioning. Marked or prolonged infantile distress, or both, can contribute to anxiety, hostile reactions, withdrawal, and disturbances of perception and cognition.

3. *Stimulation designed to meet the infants' needs, tolerance level, and capacity for enjoyment* at different stages of sensory-motor development, emotional response, and resources for self-management. What is too much for one infant may not be enough for another. The kind and amount of stimulation provided each infant have to be based on intelligent observations made by his mother or mother-surrogate. Sensitive mothers report such observations as: "He likes bright colors"; "He minds soft noises more than loud ones"; "His bath has to be just the right temperature"; or "He can sleep in the midst of noise." One baby likes to be jounced vigorously while another likes gentle, rhythmic rocking. Visual, auditory, kinesthetic, rhythmic stimulation are each important. The proper amount of stimulation implies both protection from excessive or overwhelming stimuli, which the baby cannot manage or which disrupt his functioning, and provision of enough stimulation of satisfying kinds to encourage response.

4. *Talking to the baby.* This provides important support for the baby's own vocalizing efforts that are a precursor of language.

5. *Opportunities for exercise of emerging sensory-motor functions,* through handling toys and other objects. Such activities as touching, feeling, banging, throwing, or combining teach the baby the qualities of things and also help him develop awareness of himself, the different parts of his body and what he can do. Being played with by older children and adults helps him become accustomed to different people, to distinguish his mother or caretaker from others, and to develop flexibility in responding to and interacting with others. In addition, the adult's or older child's delight, pride, and surprise at the baby's reaction provide an important feedback to the infant and, by enhancing the importance to him of his own achievements, stimulate further efforts on his part.

6. *Encouragement of the baby's efforts* to make himself comfortable, amuse himself, feed himself, and master new skills. Such efforts can help the baby develop independence and an ability to cope with problems.

7. *Continuity in a few basic, warm relationships,* as with a mother, father, brothers, sisters, and other relatives. Such continuity contributes to the development of a stable core of self, a sense of being valued, a capacity for dependable relationships, a sense of trust, and identification with motherly and fatherly adults.

INTERRELATED FACTORS   The child's emotional and affective development seems to go hand in hand with his social responsiveness. And, according to studies made among children of higher socioeconomic status, relationships also exist between social behavior and the level of language development.[6] Both superior language development and superior social and emotional development have been found to reflect the quality of family interaction. Some studies of family life that describe conversation between parents and children at mealtimes suggest that the higher level of verbal exchange found in middle- and upper-middle-class families is an integral part of the social atmosphere in families that enjoy their children and communicate with them regularly. In such families, the social and emotional interaction itself provides cognitive stimulation and contributes substantially to language development as well as to the development of perception and other cognitive faculties. Our studies at the Menninger Foundation found positive correlations between the mother's talking to the baby and the baby's vocalization, as well as between the baby's vocalization and his later IQ.[7] These findings probably reflect the mother's affective response to communication initiated by the baby as well as the baby's response to the mother.

It is astonishing that in current efforts to stimulate the intellectual development of deprived children, so little detailed analysis has been made of the day-to-day communication between parents and children in well-functioning families as compared with parent-child communication in depressed families of any specific socioeconomic, racial, or other subcultural group. Aspects of

[6] Murphy, G.; Murphy, L. B.; Newcomb, T. M.: Experimental social psychology. Harper & Row, New York, N.Y. 1937.
[7] Murphy, L. B.; Moriarty, A. M.: Development, vulnerability, and resilience. In preparation.

cognition stimulated by such communication also need to be studied. There is no lack of research methods. For example, Barker and Wright have provided detailed, moment-by-moment records of a child's life through one day:[8] Escalona and Leitch have provided even more detailed records on infants;[9] Leon Yarrow and his team have recorded in detail a baby's response to environment.[10]

Much recent research on cognitive development as such and ways of stimulating it in young children has been carried out without a sufficiently broad orientation to the total context of mental development. The procedure of some investigators might be compared to that of a man who in order to fly to Samoa equipped himself with the best airplane and took off with a plan to fly southwest without studying all the relevant factors such as headwinds, tailwinds, climatic variations at different longitudes and latitudes, or visual landmarks. The need is for a full analysis of the *total* development context in which learning takes place, both in formal stimulation situations (which always include factors not mentioned in the records) and within families of various socioeconomic backgrounds.

SOME QUESTIONS   A host of questions cry for answers: What was the atmosphere in the learning situation in which marked success occurred as compared with the situation that produced only limited success? Did the first situation involve a day-care teacher who enjoyed children and made their daily experiences happier, more fun, and thereby, perhaps, more stimulating? Is it possible that some caretakers who take a personal interest in each child evoke in the child a deeper identification with the teacher and a deeper investment in the learning process? Do some children through identification with the teacher or through other as yet unrecognized processes acquire a "drive to learn" that furthers their progress?

The lack of curiosity and drive to explore, of capacity for organization, planning, and creativity, and of the resourcefulness that these traits utilize and develop has been characteristic of many children in Head Start programs. A child needs such tendencies and capacities to clarify potential uses of his cognitive resources and to find new satisfactions in putting them to work in interesting ways. But the roots of such cognitive activity have not been adequately studied. Could it be that the relative emptiness and monotony of the environment in economically deprived homes automatically prevent the child from making comparisons, finding interesting similarities and differences, organizing experiences in exciting new ways, or trying to make an increasingly detailed and expanding "cognitive map," as children in middle-class homes must do to cope with the variety of experiences in their richer environment?

There is an urgent need to compare the effects of different experimental methods with the effects of the methods used in good "traditional" nursery schools as described in the literature.[11,12] Such a comparison, ideally, would

[8] Barker, R.; Wright, H.: One boy's day. Harper & Row, New York, N.Y. 1951.
[9] Escalona, S. R.: Leitch, M. E., et al.: Earliest phases of personality development. Child Research Monograph No. 17, 1953.
[10] Yarrow, Leon: Conceptualizing the early environment. *In* Early child care (Laura L. Dittmann, ed.). Atherton Press, New York, N.Y. 1968.
[11] Beyer, E.: Teaching young children. Pegasus Press, New York, N.Y. 1968.
[12] Read, K.: The nursery school. W. B. Saunders Co., Philadelphia, Pa. 1966.

involve a careful, comprehensive analysis of the cognitive aspects of all the activities of children in nursery school. An analysis of this kind would require fresh study of the complex processes through which the child integrates and reconstructs his observations of objects, parts of the environment, and adult roles and rehearses for future activity. These mental processes and others are involved in activities typical of good nursery school programs—for example, block construction, puzzle-solving, painting and drawing, storytelling and description of discoveries by the child, and group imaginative play. Cognitive aspects of social experience should also be studied. Such processes as learning to take turns, to work together on joint tasks, to explain feelings of anger instead of beating up or biting the offender, to plan a joint block-building project all involve cognitive efforts of varying degrees of complexity of understanding, verbal skill, sequential ideation, organization of objects and people, and useful fantasy.

Complex preschool activities like these have significance for many aspects of development in the young child, among others: (a) putting cognitive skills to work in activity the child cares a great deal about; (b) developing skills, insight, and values important as foundations for socialization; and (c) enhancing the sense of autonomy, the capacity to cope with varied life situations, and the drive to continue in the social use of cognitive resources. The child becomes self-propelling in his cognitive, affective, and social use of the environment. These beginnings imply possible next steps in research, which are foreshadowed in the discriminating reports of Herbert Zimiles.[13]

INDIVIDUAL DIFFERENCES   Another point needs emphasis. Most results of experiments in cognitive stimulation have been reported in terms of averages or means on the assumption that the only adequate measurement of change is a summary of the change in a group as a whole. Such a statistical approach has been sharply criticized by some of the world's most outstanding statisticians. One of these, C. R. Rao,[14] urges that subgroups be looked at separately to avoid the confusion of results when two contrary tendencies are represented in the same group. For instance, when we find that in a given group the level of cognitive functioning has decreased in some children and dramatically increased in others, we need to consider the factors behind these opposite responses. What was going on in the lives of those children whose level of functioning has decreased? Did the child become ill? Was there some severe trauma at home? Was the child disturbed by separation from home and mother? Did the child have special needs that were not met? Similarly we need to learn more about the children who made the greatest progress. Were these the children whom the teacher particularly appreciated or enjoyed, tuned in with, or felt she understood?

In other words, we need to consider the individual physiological, social, and emotional context of both negative and positive changes in cognitive

[13] Zimiles, Herbert: An analysis of current issues in the evaluation of educational programs. In The disadvantaged child, vol. 2 (J. Hellmuth, ed.). Special Child Publications, Seattle, Wash. 1969.
[14] U.S. Department of Health, Education, and Welfare, National Institute of Mental Health: Proceedings of a conference on classification in psychiatry and psychopathology, Chevy Chase, Md., 1965, p. 559.

development. At the same time we need more study of the differences in individual children's responses to whatever is offered or withheld—differences in what evokes interest and drive as contrasted with withdrawal, in vulnerability to deprivation, separation, and strangeness, and in capacity to cope with the stresses of life.

Research on the early years, then, must ask: What physical, emotional, and cognitive support does each child need for optimal all-round development?

A project that will attempt to answer these questions is just getting underway at the Children's Hospital of the District of Columbia. It is aimed at demonstrating the advantages for infants and young children of group care in settings that emphasize warm relationships and careful attention to the individual needs of each child. Still in a pilot stage, the project is designed on the theory that only comprehensive support for the infant's physical, mental, and personality development will be adequate.

The project will attempt to provide the baby with a foundation for developing a strong healthy body and emotional stability, a trusting but independent outlook, curiosity and drive to learn, responsiveness to and considerateness of other people, and a capacity for participating in social endeavors. In one group each child's mother or mother substitute will receive help closely related to the needs of her child in the belief that if the gains from a good beginning are to be maintained, the child's mother must be helped to understand his needs and to use the community resources to strengthen her family life. She will also receive training and education that will develop her own potentialities, confidence, and determination to further support her children's development. The program is bound to be expensive, but its potentialities are great, especially since attention to each child's individual maturational tempo, areas of sensitivity, and range of interest is rarely included in experimental programs. . . .

The Regularity of Onset of Speech and Language

Eric H. Lenneberg
HARVARD UNIVERSITY, MEDICAL SCHOOL

The onset of speech consists of a gradual unfolding of capacities; it is a series of generally well-circumscribed events which take place between the second and third year of life. Certain important speech milestones are reached in a fixed sequence and at a relatively constant chronological age. Just as impressive as the age constancy is the remarkable synchronization of speech milestones with motor-developmental milestones, summarized in Table 1.

Reprinted from *Biological Foundations of Language.* Copyright © 1967 by John Wiley & Sons, Inc. By permission. Pp. 127–135.

TABLE 1.

Developmental Milestones in Motor and Language Development

AT THE COMPLETION OF:	MOTOR DEVELOPMENT	VOCALIZATION AND LANGUAGE
12 weeks	Supports head when in prone position; weight is on elbows; hands mostly open; no grasp reflex.	Markedly less crying than at 8 weeks; when talked to and nodded at, smiles, followed by squealing-gurgling sounds usually called *cooing*, which is vowel-like in character and pitch-modulated; sustains cooing for 15–20 seconds
16 weeks	Plays with a rattle placed in his hands (by shaking it and staring at it), head self-supported; tonic neck reflex subsiding.	Responds to human sounds more definitely; turns head; eyes seem to search for speaker; occasionally some chuckling sounds
20 weeks	Sits with props	The vowel-like cooing sounds begin to be interspersed with more consonantal-sounds; labial fricatives, spirants and nasals are common; acoustically, all vocalizations are very different from the sounds of the mature language of the environment
6 months	Sitting: bends forward and uses hands for support; can bear weight when put into standing position, but cannot yet stand with holding on; reaching: unilateral; grasp: no thumb apposition yet; releases cube when given another	Cooing changing into babbling resembling one-syllable utterances; neither vowels nor consonants have very fixed recurrences; most common utterances sound somewhat like ma, mu, da, or di
8 months	Stands holding on; grasps with thumb apposition; picks up pellet with thumb and finger tips	Reduplication (or more continuous repetitions) becomes frequent; intonation patterns become distinct; utterances can signal emphasis and emotions
10 months	Creeps efficiently; takes side-steps, holding on; pulls to standing position	Vocalizations are mixed with sound-play such as gurgling or bubble-blowing; appears to wish to imitate sounds, but the imitations are never quite

(continued)

TABLE 1 *Continued*

AT THE COMPLETION OF:	MOTOR DEVELOPMENT	VOCALIZATION AND LANGUAGE
		successful; beginning to differentiate between words heard by making differential adjustment
12 months	Walks when held by one hand; walks on feet and hands— knees in air; mouthing of objects almost stopped; seats self on floor	Identical sound sequences are replicated with higher relative frequency of occurrence and words (mamma or dadda) are emerging; definite signs of understanding some words and simple commands (show me your eyes)
18 months	Grasp, prehension and release fully developed; gait stiff, propulsive and precipitated; sits on child's chair with only fair aim; creeps downstairs backwards; has difficulty building tower of 3 cubes	Has a definite repertoire of words —more than three, but less than fifty; still much babbling but now of several syllables with intricate intonation pattern; no attempt at communicating information and no frustration for not being understood; words may include items such as thank you or come here, but there is little ability to join any of the lexical items into spontaneous two-item phrases; understanding is progressing rapidly
24 months	Runs, but falls in sudden turns; can quickly alternate between sitting and stance; walks stairs up or down, one foot forward only	Vocabulary of more than 50 items (some children seem to be able to name everything in environment); begins spontaneously to join vocabulary items into two-word phrases; all phrases appear to be own creations; definite increase in communicative behavior and interest in language
30 months	Jumps up into air with both feet; stands on one foot for about two seconds; takes few steps on tip-toe; jumps from chair; good hand and finger coordination; can move digits independently; manipulation	Fastest increase in vocabulary with many new additions every day; no babbling at all; utterances have communicative intent; frustrated if not understood by adults; utterances consist of at least two

TABLE 1 *Continued*

AT THE COMPLETION OF:	MOTOR DEVELOPMENT	VOCALIZATION AND LANGUAGE
	of objects much improved; builds tower of six cubes	words, many have three or even five words; sentences and phrases have characteristic child grammar, that is, they are rarely verbatim repetitions of an adult utterance; intelligibility is not very good yet, though there is great variation among children; seems to understand everything that is said to him
3 years	Tiptoes three yards; runs smoothly with acceleration and deceleration; negotiates sharp and fast curves without difficulty; walks stairs by alternating feet; jumps 12 inches; can operate tricycle	Vocabulary of some 1000 words; about 80% of utterances are intelligible even to strangers; grammatical complexity of utterances is roughly that of colloquial adult language, although mistakes still occur
4 years	Jumps over rope; hops on right foot; catches ball in arms; walks line	Language is well-established; deviations from the adult norm tend to be more in style than in grammar

The temporal interlocking of speech milestones and motor milestones is not a logical necessity. There are reasons to believe that the onset of language is not simply the consequence of motor control. The development of language is quite independent of articulatory skills (Lenneberg, 1962); and the perfection of articulation cannot be predicted simply on the basis of general motor development. There are certain indications for the existence of a peculiar, language-specific maturational schedule. Many children have learned a word or two before they start to toddle, and thus must be assumed to possess a sufficient degree of motor skill to articulate, however primitive; yet the expansion of their vocabulary is still an extremely slow process. Why could they not rapidly increase their lexicon with "sloppy" sound-symbols much the way a child with a cleft palate does at age three? Similarly, parents' inability to train their children at this stage to join the words *daddy* and *by-by* into a single utterance cannot be explained on the grounds of motor incompetence, because at the same age children babble for periods as long as the duration of a sentence. In fact, the babbled "sentence" may be produced complete with intonation patterns. The retarding factor for language acquisition here must be a psychological one, or perhaps better, a cognitive one and not mechanical skill. About age three manual skills show improved coordination over earlier periods, but dexterity is still very immature on an absolute scale. Speech, which requires infinitely precise and swift movements of tongue and lips, all well-coordinated with laryngeal and respiratory motor systems, is all but fully developed when most other mechanical skills are far below their levels of future accomplishment. The evolvement of various motor skills and motor coordinations also has specific maturational histories; but the specific history for speech control stands apart dramatically from histories of finger and hand control.

The independence of language development from motor coordination is also underscored by the priority of language comprehension over language production. Ordinarily the former precedes the latter by a matter of a few months (especially between the ages of 18 to 36 months). In certain cases this gap may be magnified by many years (Lenneberg, 1964). Careful and detailed investigations of the development of understanding by itself have been undertaken only in more recent years (Brown and Bellugi, 1964; Ervin, 1964; Ervin and Miller, 1963). The evidence collected so far leaves little doubt that there is also an orderly and constant progression in this aspect of language development.

The development of children with various abnormalities provides the most convincing demonstration that the onset of language is regulated by a maturational process, much the way the onset of gait is dependent upon such a process, but at the same time the language-maturational process is independent of motor-skeletal maturation. In hypotonic children, for instance, the musculature in general is weak, and tendon reflexes are less active than normal. Hypotonia may be an isolated phenomenon that is quickly outgrown or a sign of a disease such as muscular atrophy, which would have unfortunate effects on the child's future motor development. Whatever the cause, the muscular development alone may be lagging behind other developmental aspects and thus disarrange the normal intercalation of the various processes. Here, then, speech and language emerge at their usual time while motor development lags behind.

On the other hand, there are some children with normal intelligence and normal skeletal and motor development whose speech development alone is markedly delayed. We are not referring here to children who never learn to speak adequately because of acquired or congenital abnormalities in the brain, but rather of those who are simply late speakers, who do not begin to speak in phrases until after age four, who have no neurological or psychiatric symptoms which can explain the delay, and whose environment appears to be adequate. The incidence of such cases is small (less than one in a hundred), but their very existence underscores the independence of language-maturational processes from other processes.

There are also conditions that affect all developmental processes simultaneously. These are diseases in which growth and maturation are retarded or stunted through a variety of factors (for instance, of an endocrine nature as in hypothyroidism); or retardation may be due to an intracellular abnormality such as the chromosomal disorder causing mongolism. In these cases all processes suffer alike, resulting in general "stretching" of the developmental time scale, but leaving the intercalation of motor and speech milestones intact (Lenneberg, Nichols, and Rosenberger, 1964). The preservation of synchrony between motor and speech or language milestones in cases of general retardation is, I believe, the most cogent evidence that language acquisition is regulated by maturational phenomena.

The evidence presented rules out the possibility of a direct, causal relationship between motor and speech development. Normally, growth and maturation proceed at characteristic rates for each developmental aspect. In the absence of specific retardations affecting skills or organs differentially, a picture of consistency evolves such as represented in Table 1 or in the many accounts of normal human development (McGraw, 1963; Gesell and Amatruda, 1947).

The use of the word *skill* brings out another interesting aspect of the emergence of speech. With proper training probably everybody could attain some proficiency in such diverse skills as roller-skating, sketching, or piano playing. However, there are also vast individual differences in native endowment and considerable variation with respect to the age at which training is most effective. Perfection can rarely be expected before the teens. The establishment of speech and language is quite different; a much larger number of individuals show equal aptitude, absence of the skill is rare, and onset and fluency occur much earlier, with no particular training required.

Nevertheless, individual differences in time of onset and reaching of various milestones exist and must be accounted for. The rate of development is not constant during the formative years, and there may be transient slowing in the rate of maturation, with subsequent hastening. This is hardly surprising in view of the complex interrelation of intrinsic and extrinsic factors that affect development. Nevertheless, there is a remarkable degree of regularity in the emergence of language. Figure 1 illustrates the regularity in the attainment of three major language-developmental levels and Figure 2 illustrates the sudden increase in vocabulary size, particularly around the third birthday.

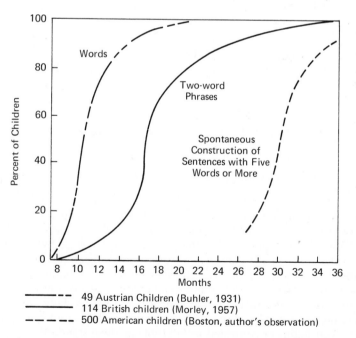

FIGURE 1.   *Emergence of various developmental milestones in the acquisition of language*

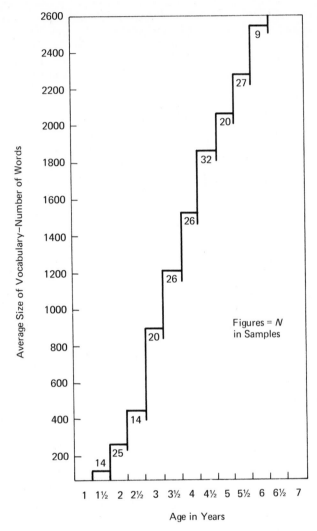

F I G U R E 2. *Average vocabulary size of ten samples of children at various ages.* (Data based on Smith, 1926.)

In a survey of 500 middle and lower-class children in the Boston area, examined in connection with an epidemiological study, we found that nine out of ten children had acquired all of the following verbal skills by the time they reached their 39th month; ability to name most objects in the home, fair intelligibility, ability to comprehend spoken instructions, spontaneous utterance of syntactically complex sentences and spontaneity in oral communication. The field observations were made in the child's home by specially trained social workers who worked with a screening test and a schedule of questions. Any child who was found or suspected to fall short of these standards was referred by the social worker, to my office where he was examined by a speech therapist, an audiologist, and by myself. Fifty-four children were thus referred and found to fall into the classifications shown in Table 2.

T A B L E 2.
Distribution of Causes for Failing Language Screening Test
(Given to 500 children at about the third birthday)

	NUMBER
(1) Uncooperative child but, upon more intense examination, apparently normal speech development (health good, environment adequate)	7
(2) Poor articulation, but otherwise normal onset of language milestones (health good, environment adequate)	29
(3) Various types of speech defects associated with psychiatric conditions	9
(4) Speech defects associated with other behavioral disorders due to gross environmental abnormalities	2
(5) Speech defects associated with central nervous system disease	3
(6) Delayed onset of speech, unexplained (health good, environment adequate)	4

Differences in age at onset becomes much less dramatic if we scrutinize these statistics. Of 486 children who were free from nervous or mental disease and were raised in an adequate environment (all children in the sample except those of groups 3, 4, and 5) only 33 (less than 7%) were below the norm of attainment. . . .

References

BROWN, R. W. and BELLUGI, U. (1964), Three processes in the child's acquisition of syntax, in *New Directions in the Study of Language*, E. H. Lenneberg (ed.), M.I.T. Press, Cambridge, Massachusetts.

BÜHLER, C. (1931), *Kindheit und Jugend* (3rd ed.) Hirzel, Leipzig.

ERVIN, S. M. (1964), Imitation and structural change in children's language, in *New Directions in the Study of Language*, E. H. Lenneberg (ed.), M.I.T. Press, Cambridge, Mass.

—— and MILLER, W. R. (1963), Language development, *Child Psychology*, 62nd Yearbook, National Society for the Study of Education. Univ. of Chicago Press, Chicago, Ill.

GESELL, A. and AMATRUDA, C. S. (1947), *Developmental Diagnosis; normal and abnormal child development, clinical methods and pediatric applications* (2nd ed.), Hoeber, New York.

LENNEBERG, E. H. (1962), Understanding language without ability to speak: a case report, *J. abnorm. soc. Psychol.* **65**:419–425.

—— (1964), Speech as a motor skill with special reference to nonaphasic disorders, in *The Acquisition of Language*, Monograph of the Society for Research in Child Development. U. Bellugi and R. Brown (eds.), Serial No. 92, Vol. 29, No. 1.

——, NICHOLS, I. A., and ROSENBERGER, E. F. (1964), Primitive stages of language development in mongolism, in *Disorders of Communication Vol. XLII: Research Publications*, A.R.N.M.D. Williams and Wilkins, Baltimore, Maryland.

McGRAW, M. B. (1963), *The Neuromuscular Maturation of the Human Infant.* Hafner, New York.

MORLEY, M. (1957), *The Development and Disorders of Speech in Childhood.* Livingstone, London.

SMITH, M. E. (1926), An investigation of the development of the sentence and the extent of vocabulary in young children, *Univ. Iowa Stud. Child Welfare*, Vol. 3, No. 5.

4
Relationships with People

This section is an unusually long one because research in the area of relationships with people is prolific. Consideration of positive social and emotional development is especially relevant to problems in today's world. How do people come to love one another and what can go wrong? The study of social relationships in infancy gives some information about the foundations of feeling, caring, and giving. Although experimentations with human beings in these areas is usually unacceptable, additional insights and clues are contributed by animal research and by comparisons with other cultures.

The first article, by John Paul Scott, reviews facts known about animals other than man in order to give the background for his message about the social development of human beings. The subject of imprinting, first observed in birds, is introduced by Scott in this article. Later articles in this chapter will develop the topic further. The concept of critical periods is also used by other authors, not only in this chapter but throughout this book, because it is one of the important child development concepts. Among the applications to human existence that Scott makes is the timing of the adoption of children by foster parents.

Mary D. Salter Ainsworth has investigated the attachment of the infant to his mother and has written extensively on this topic. Here, with Silvia M. Bell, she shows that it is possible to experiment with babies and mothers without harming them. Using a miniature sample of a real-life situation Ainsworth and Bell studied the relation between attachment and exploratory behavior.

Michael Lewis and Susan Goldberg found a difference in the way mothers treated boys and girls when they studied sex differences in play behavior of one-year-olds.

Peer relationships in infancy have not been studied very much in the United States, because until recently, babies have not often come together in groups. In the kibbutzim of Israel, however, infants live closely together. A famous psychiatrist, Bruno Bettleheim, describes infant–infant relationships in "Crib Mates," an excerpt from his book The Children of the Dream.

The last article is included as a balance for the others. Although personality development is greatly influenced by the people with whom the child interacts, the individual also has his own unique characteristics, from the beginning. A pediatrician, Herbert Birch, and two psychiatrists, Stella Chess and Alexander Thomas, have collaborated on a longitudinal study of temperament or behavioral style. Their dimensions of temperament are helpful in understanding individuals, in appreciating individuality, and in realizing that parent–child interaction is the product of the child just as much as it is of the parent.

Critical Periods of Social Development

John Paul Scott

BOWLING GREEN STATE UNIVERSITY

Among animals living under natural conditions, the social environment is often the most stable feature of the surroundings. A lamb living in a flock of mountain sheep experiences changing weather conditions from day to day, and even from hour to hour as rain ceases and the sun comes out. Predators may be present one day and gone the next, and even the food supply varies enormously with the seasons. However, other members of the flock are always present. Individuals die and are replaced by younger ones, but reproduction always takes place in the same way year after year, and behavior develops in a very consistent fashion in succeeding generations.

Because of its stability, the important effects of the early social environment do not become apparent until experimenters interfere with it by drastic methods. For example, the behavior of domestic sheep develops in ways very similar to those of mountain sheep, generation after generation; but the simple act of taking a young lamb from its mother at birth and rearing it on a bottle away from the flock produces a radically different animal, one that stays apart from the flock and attempts to follow people everywhere like Mary's little lamb in the nursery rhyme.

Two general methods are used in this kind of experiment. One is to take a young mammal or bird from its parents at birth or hatching and rear it by hand away from its own kind. The second method is to take young animals and rear them in isolation, providing the equivalent of parental care by mechanical means. By these methods the important phenomenon of primary socialization, or imprinting, was discovered.

PRIMARY SOCIALIZATION (IMPRINTING)

One of the major functions of most highly developed animal societies is the care and protection of the young. In order for this to work efficiently the young animal must become attached to the members of its own species. It will not suffice for the newborn animal to have a generalized positive reaction to all members of its own species, for efficient care depends on its staying with particular individuals who are ready and equipped to give that care. Therefore, it must become attached to particular individuals and be able to discriminate between these and others. We call this process primary socialization, implying that this is the first way in which the behavior of the young animal becomes modified in relation to the rest of society, and we can define it as the formation of the first social relationships, and particularly the formation of emotional attachments. All the highly social animals which have been so far studied have a short period early in life when this process takes place.

Imprinting in Birds   Birds are characteristically flying animals, but all are flightless as they emerge from the egg. Characteristically, most of them develop very rapidly so that they can reach the relative safety of the air as soon as possible. Some of the small perching birds are able to fly twelve or fourteen days after hatching, and even large birds like ducks and geese are very nearly full grown in about six weeks. The Japanese quail, a domestic bird noted for rapid development, may produce eggs as soon as eight weeks after its own egg was originally laid.

Some birds, like chickens and ducks, are born in a precocious state and are able to walk as soon as they are hatched. If eggs of these species are hatched in an incubator and the newly emerging young are shown only a model of a parent bird, they will soon begin to follow it. The model need not have any great resemblance to a bird, as young chicks will readily become attached to square boxes or round balloons. They will also become attached to almost any other living thing, from white rats to human beings. Using the right technique, it is easy to produce the comical effect of a chick following a person as if he were its mother. The peak of the imprinting effect occurs about seventeen hours after hatching and declines rapidly thereafter. By three or four days of age, young chicks become quite fearful of strange objects, and getting them to form an attachment becomes increasingly difficult (Hess, 1962).

Other birds are born in a very immature state. Most people are familiar with the blind and naked nestlings of the perching birds. These birds also form emotional attachments, but at a much later date and in a much more gradual way, with the result that hand rearing has little effect until a week or so after hatching. In doves and pigeons, whose newly hatched young are also helpless, the degree of attachment to a human being varies inversely with the age at which the young squab is removed from its parents' nest. Klinghammer (1967) found that mourning doves taken before 8 days never developed fears of human handlers, but those taken a day or two later showed fears as adults.

When begun at the proper time, hand-rearing has drastic effects on a bird's later behavior. A hand-reared male turkey, for example, may be able to mate with his own kind as an adult, but if he has a choice between another turkey and a human being, he will go to the human being—and perseveringly repeat the behavior patterns of courtship in spite of the fact that these do not produce any response. The result of primary socialization, or imprinting, has been to transfer the development of social relationships from one species to another. Because experience in the early period of primary socialization not only determines the nature of primary relationships but also indirectly determines the later ones, the period of primary socialization is a critical period for later development.

Primary Socialization in Mammals.   Like birds, some mammals are precocious and others are born in various stages of immaturity. The large herd animals are all precocious, and the effects of hand rearing such animals are well known. Bottle-raised fawns become extremely tame and attached to people and lose so many of their "instinctive" fears that they are seldom able to survive if turned loose in the wilds afterwards.

Of all the herd animals we know most about domestic sheep and goats. If a young lamb is taken from its mother at birth and reared on a bottle, it becomes a most unsheeplike sheep, following people everywhere, unafraid of dogs, and independent of its own kind. It is unresponsive to other sheep even if raised in the same field with the flock, but the behavior which prevents its becoming attached to other sheep is that of the adult females rather than its own. The young lamb will approach the females but they always butt it away and reject it as they would any strange lamb. The young orphan lamb soon learns to stay away from them and develops its relationships only with people.

The length of the critical period for primary socialization in the young lamb has never been determined, but it must begin soon after birth and last for at least a week. On the other hand, the critical period for a mother forming an attachment to her own lamb is a matter of hours. If a mother has her lamb taken away at birth, she will accept it if it is brought back again within two to four hours and will "own" it during a somewhat longer period if she is kept isolated from other sheep in the meantime (Hersher et al., 1963). This emphasizes the fact that the relationship between mother and offspring is a dual one and that the mother forms an attachment to her offspring as well as the reverse.

The situation in slowly developing animals like the dog is quite different. The young puppy is born in a very immature state with respect to its sense organs, being both blind and deaf. Even the sense of smell is poorly developed. This means that the newborn puppy is unable to discriminate between one individual and another, and the process of forming an emotional attachment does not begin until the puppy is about three weeks of age.

By this time the sense organs have matured, and for the next several weeks the young puppy is able to form new relationships rapidly with any strange dog or human being. Although the first reaction to a stranger of a young puppy between three and seven weeks of age is to crouch down or escape, this response is only momentary. Within a few seconds or minutes it will approach and investigate, nosing the stranger's clothes, and wagging its tail. In one experiment, Freedman, King, and Elliot (1961) raised puppies in a one-acre field that was surrounded by a high board fence so that the animals could not see people. They were fed through a hole in the fence, and their only human contact came when they were removed for a week's socialization in the laboratory at different ages. By fourteen weeks of age, those pups which had no human contact were acting like little wild animals, but those with previous contact showed different degrees of positive attraction. This experiment showed that the peak of the ability to rapidly form a new social relationship occurs between six and eight weeks of age, declining thereafter with the increasingly prolonged fear responses to strangers. It is perhaps no accident that the peak of this capacity occurs very close to the time when a mother normally weans her puppies completely from the breast. At this age neither dogs nor their wild ancestors, the wolves, are truly self-sufficient, and wolf cubs continue to be fed by their elders, including other members of the pack as well as parents. It is therefore highly adaptive for the puppy to be able to form new relationships readily at this time. Whether similar timing occurs in other species is a matter for investigation.

Duration and Nature of the Critical Period   As we have seen from these various examples, the critical period for primary socialization can be as short as a few hours in a rapidly developing animal like the chicken, or it can extend over a period of several weeks in a slowly developing mammal like the dog. All of the animals in which this phenomenon has been studied are alike in that they can form social attachments quite rapidly during the critical period.

In the dog, lasting effects can be produced by daily contacts extending over a period of as little as a week. Puppies reared in isolation during the critical period will develop normal relationships with people if allowed as little as two twenty-minute periods of contact per week throughout the whole period of several weeks. All animals in which primary socialization has been studied are also alike in that the critical period comes early in life, although not necessarily at the point immediately after hatching or birth.

What determines the length of the critical period and what brings it to a close? These questions raise the problem of the basic nature of the process involved. What exactly happens to an animal forming a strong social attachment? One clue comes from the fact that the attachments are made before the animal develops a strong fear response to strangers. A young chick or puppy does not quickly form a social relationship with a stranger after the critical period because its first response is to run away and stay away, thus effectively preventing any prolonged contact. Furthermore the fact of becoming attached to one individual and staying with it, as a chick stays with its mother, will keep it out of contact with other hens, not to mention other species of animals and particularly predators such as foxes.

Although this still does not answer the question of the nature of the positive mechanism of forming an attachment, all evidence indicates that emotional responses are involved. A young puppy will exhibit distress vocalization as soon as it is removed from the familiar objects and individuals to which it becomes attached during the critical period. At six or eight weeks of age, a temporarily isolated puppy may average 140 vocalizations per minute and keep up this rate for hours. This obvious emotional distress is relieved by the presence of another individual or by familiar surroundings. Thus the puppy experiences an uncomfortable emotion which is relieved by staying with its own kind. The emotional reaction itself appears to be a very simple primary response that has the effect of maintaining an attachment between the animal and another member of its own species. Furthermore, the effect of artificially producing other unpleasant emotions, such as fear responses to noise or electric shock, is to intensify the reaction of staying with its own kind and to speed up the general process of attachment. The young animal must learn very quickly that being separated from familiar individuals is unpleasant and that being with them relieves this unpleasantness. In terms of learning theory, staying with familiar animals and persons is reinforced by the punishing effect of separation and the relief afforded by reunion (Scott, 1967).

General Theory of Critical Periods   The concept of a critical period may be examined on several levels of complexity. Most superficially, a critical period is based on time, and within this dimension a critical period can be defined as a time when a large effect can be produced by a smaller change in conditions than in any later or earlier period in life. From this viewpoint, critical periods have enormous practical importance for the modification of behavior through

training and education. In the case of the critical period for primary socialization, a small amount of contact at an early period in life will determine which
individuals will be the close social relatives of the animal in its infancy and often
for the rest of its life. A similar period of contact in adult life may produce only
momentary reactions to passing strangers.

Considered more deeply, critical periods must depend on internal processes. There must be changes taking place within the animal which are correlated with time and hence account for the existence of critical periods. Time
itself is a term of description and measurement rather than an explanatory
concept. A fundamental question is: what changes go on within the individual
which make a critical period in life different from any other? The most general
answer is that a critical period is one in which rapid organization of some kind
is taking place. While this is going on, it is easy to change the nature of the
organization. However, organization in itself has a tendency to produce
stability. *Therefore, any period in life when rapid organization is taking place is a critical
period,* since the changes which are easily and often accidentally produced at that
time become a fixed and relatively permanent feature of the stabilized organization (Scott, 1962). In the case of primary socialization, the young animal is
organizing its first social relationships.

By extension we can reason that *any period in life when a major new relationship
is being formed is a critical one for determining the nature of that relationship.* Such a
period would occur in later life during courtship and mating and the resulting
formation of the first sexual relationship, and we have already seen an example
of a critical period in the formation of a relationship by the mother sheep for
her offspring. Such a period should occur in any mammal when the young are
born. The period of primary socialization is an unusually critical one in that it
may indirectly affect the formation of these later relationships.

Periods and Processes From what has been said above it is obvious that
the important thing about the process of primary socialization is not time,
although this permits us to easily describe and predict events, but the actual
process itself. Therefore, the things to look for in development are times at which
organizational processes are proceeding at a maximum speed.

Primary Socialization in Human Infants . . . There appears to be a definite
neonatal period in human infants, extending from birth to about five or six
weeks of age. During this period all behavior is organized around the problems
of neonatal life, particularly that of neonatal nutrition, which is accomplished
by suckling. Marked by the appearance of the smiling response to human
faces, there is a period of rapid improvement in the capacity for visual perception. By six months of age, the decrease in rate of smiling to strangers indicates that the infant readily distinguishes between familiar and unfamiliar
faces. The period from approximately five or six weeks to six or seven months
of age is thus the period during which the process of primary socialization, or
the formation of the first social relationships, takes place (Gray, 1958). One
consequence of the timing of this period is that a young baby will usually form
its first social relationships with its own parents. Since it usually has more
contact with its mother than any other individual, the earliest, and presum-

ably strongest, relationship will be formed with her, although under other conditions of child rearing it would be possible for a baby to form a strong relationship with any individual who took care of it. We have no data on how long a baby takes to form a lasting social relationship, but if results with other animals are any guide, it probably needs very little time. The baby's reactions are consistent with those of other animals in that its positive responses to a stranger during this period are easily and quickly evoked. The puppy during the critical period of socialization wags its tail at strangers, and the human infant smiles.

THE EFFECTS OF ISOLATION

Drastic experiments with social isolation of human infants are never performed for obvious reasons, and what evidence we have is confined to accidental cases in which children have been hidden from the outside world for criminal or emotional reasons. The most famous case is that of the "Nuremberg boy," Kaspar Hauser, who was discovered wandering in the streets as a young adult in the year 1828. He could at first speak little more than his own name but later reported that he had been kept in a dungeon without companions and that his only playthings were a toy dog and two hobbyhorses. He was therefore not only a social isolate but also the product of rearing in a barren environment. No information was available as to how early he was placed in isolation, and all that can be said is that he showed a considerable degree of recovery from its effects.

Results of Animal Experiments on Isolation   Rearing a young bird or mammal in isolation from its own kind (and from any other species with which it might associate) produces bizarre and striking effects on behavior. The longer the isolation is continued the more drastic are the results. An isolated male Indian jungle fowl will as an adult attempt to go through the usual motions of courtship to a female but direct these toward his own body so that he spins and whirls in behavior never seen in ordinary roosters (Kruijt, 1964). A puppy isolated during the critical period will often show bizarre postures such as standing still in the corner of a room with one paw raised above its head and forced into the angle of the walls (Fuller and Clark, 1966a, 1966b).

From our understanding of the process of primary socialization, we would predict that the isolated animal would become attached to whatever was available in the environment during the critical period. The only living thing present is the animal itself. We would therefore predict that a chicken reared in isolation would become imprinted upon its own body and, indeed, the reaction of the isolated adult is consistent with this expectation. From experiments with attachments to inanimate models we would also predict that the isolated animal would become attached to anything present in the physical surroundings, such as food dishes or even the walls of the confining chamber. Thus isolated puppies after their release from confinement will sometimes play for hours with food and water dishes each in a solitary fashion. More than this, the effects of isolation upon the subsequent behavior of a puppy are bound up with the development of the capacity of fear. During isolation there is very little to frighten the young animal, but it nevertheless develops a capacity for a complete fear response. The result is that the release from isolation produces a strong fearful reaction which becomes associated with the entire outside world. The puppy standing in the corner is probably attempting to escape as far as possible from all the strange stimulation around it, or perhaps it is trying to draw some comfort from contact similar to the walls of its box.

Results of Semi-isolation on Human Behavior   As indicated above, drastic isolation experiments are never done on children, but isolation occurs commonly enough in normal experience for us to know something of its effects. Short periods of isolation produce crying and a strongly unpleasant emotional reaction; in fact, temporary isolation was formerly often used as a method of punishment for young children, just as solitary confinement is still occasionally used as a drastic punishment for adult prisoners.

Children's lives differ a great deal with respect to the number and closeness of social contacts that are permitted during early development. Some children grow up in remote rural areas with a limited group of family acquaintances, and others are deliberately exposed to a large number outside the family, as in the case of those who are sent to nursery school. We would predict that the result of semi-isolation would be the development of shyness with strangers, and this seems to be the case with children brought up in isolated rural environments where they may never see anyone except members of their immediate families during their early years. However, there is undoubtedly wide variation in emotional responses among children, and some should have a much greater hereditary capacity for the development of shyness than others. Effects of rearing in such an environment should therefore vary among individuals.

A much more serious disturbance of behavior is the development of autism. An autistic child tends to play entirely by himself and to be unresponsive to others. The symptoms, at least, are very similar to those of young animals raised in isolation, but the circumstances are different. Such children usually live in what seem to be normal family surroundings. Some evidence indicates that their parents are not warmly emotional, but this explanation hardly seems adequate, especially in view of the tendency of animals to become attached to completely unresponsive objects. The autistic child behaves as if he had become socialized only to himself. We can hypothesize that there has been some derangement of the whole process of socialization, that the derangement is definitely connected with the development of emotional reactions, and that it may have a partially hereditary basis.

RESULTS OF BREAKING A SOCIAL RELATIONSHIP

Unlike rearing in isolation, the breaking off of a social relationship is something which frequently happens in human development as a result of death, illness, financial misfortunes, and other disruptions of family life. The practical problems of replacing such relationships through adoption, together with its frequently unfavorable results, have inspired a considerable amount of observational work. The psychiatrist John Bowlby (1951) became interested in the results of broken relationships when he studied the case histories of a group of juvenile thieves and discovered that a large number of them had been separated from their mothers for long periods during infancy. He and his associates then made first-hand studies of children as they were separated from their parents, particularly in cases of hospitalization, which can necessitate an abrupt, drastic and long-lasting separation from familiar surroundings. They found that children are indeed seriously upset by these experiences, and their results have prompted many children's hospitals to change their practices through encouraging frequent visits by parents and by decreasing the time of separation as much as possible.

Primary Results of Separation in Infants   As we saw in Chapter 2, Schaffer (1958) found two kinds of reactions in babies returned to their homes after a period of separation in hospitals. Before seven months such babies show what he calls a "global syndrome," becoming depressed and staring anxiously at everything in the room, living and non-living. After seven months, the babies show an "overdependency syndrome." They cry a great deal and try to avoid being separated from anyone who is caring for them. The earlier reaction is related to change in the physical environment and indicates that the babies have become attached to their surroundings and are disturbed by leaving them. This reaction is undoubtedly related to the process of localization, or becoming attached to a particular place. . . . The changed reaction after seven months indicates that the baby is now reacting primarily to the separation from people, which is equivalent to the temporary breaking of a social relationship.

Permanent separation produces more drastic effects. Yarrow (1964) studied a group of seventy-five infants that were transferred to a foster mother sometime during their first year. A few showed distress when transferred as early as three months, but by six months 86 per cent showed serious emotional disturbances, and all infants over seven months showed reactions severe enough to be called emotional trauma.

Bowlby (1960) and his colleagues have also studied the degree of emotional disturbance produced by separation at various ages. During the second half of the first year, the emotional reaction to separation may appear after only a few hours. As a child grows older, he becomes more and more capable of managing separation for long periods, particularly after he has learned to talk and begins to have some concept of the time at which his parents may return.

Most parents are familiar with the emotional symptoms of separation when they leave their children for a few days to travel or take a vacation. The baby-sitter or caretaker of course finds that the children are emotionally disturbed and hard to handle, being given to frequent crying and periods of depression. An experienced baby-sitter soon learns to try to keep the children amused and stimulated and thus counteracts the emotion of depression in her charges. On their return, the parents find the children tearful, demanding, and sometimes antagonistic. They often conclude that this behavior is the result of the baby-sitter's "spoiling" them. Actually, the children have been emotionally hurt by their parents and react in various ways. Some of these seem to be simple attempts to punish the parents. If the separation has been unusually long, a child may react with real coldness, as if reluctant to enter into a close social relationship again and thus run the risk of future separations and the resulting emotional pain. Obviously, breaking a social relationship, even temporarily, is a serious matter for a child. Although separation can never be completely avoided, and perhaps should not be, parents should manage it as carefully as possible, especially in the case of younger children.

Adoption From a theoretical viewpoint, any emotional damage which might result from adoption should be the effect not of forming a new relationship but of breaking off an old one. The more well established the original relationship, the more the child should be disturbed by breaking it, but this principle is limited by the fact that as a child becomes older he can understand the circumstances better and protect himself against their emotional consequences. We shall discuss here only the effects of breaking a relation in infancy.

The theoretically ideal time for an adoption is, of course, soon after birth and no later than the end of the neonatal period. At this age the baby should react to its adopted parents just as it would to its real ones, and their only concern should be to give it the good physical care that any baby should have. If adoption takes place during the period of socialization, extending from five or six weeks to approximately six or seven months, a new relationship should be formed with ease, but most easily toward the beginning of the period rather than the end. Some immediate emotional upset would be expected, in accordance with Schaffer's observations, but this should be as much the result of the change in locality as the break in a primary social relationship.

Once the primary social relationship has been strongly established and the fear reaction to strangers has begun to appear, a much more severe emotional upset should result. Indeed, such objective evidence as is available indicates that children who have been separated from familiar persons and surroundings and adopted in the second half of the first year are more likely to show later difficulties of personal adjustment than those adopted in the first. It is, however, difficult to tell how much of this maladjustment is due to permanent emotional damage suffered by the infant at the time, and how much is due to the pattern of parent-child relationships which is being organized for the first time immediately after adoption and whose effects continue long into the future. Any continuing social relationship is a two-way affair, and unless foster parents are aware of the problems of adoption and are able to make emotional readjustments of their own, the habits and attitudes that they set up during their own critical period of emotional adjustment and behavioral organization will almost certainly be different toward a fearful, emotionally disturbed infant than toward a normally clinging and welcoming one.

Various circumstances such as death or lack of foster parents available to take an orphan at the most suitable time may make adoption necessary at various periods later than the optimum. If such an unavoidable situation arises care should be taken to make the transition as smooth as possible. For example, the prospective parents can be introduced to their new child in his own familiar environment and their visits repeated over a period of several hours or even days in such a way that the child can overcome his fear of strange people without having to contend with the fear of strange surroundings at the same time. Second, the transition can be made in such a way that the child is taken into his new environment for a few hours only and then returned to his original home before being taken away for good. Returning the child more often might also be desirable in order to preserve some continuity between his former and future existences.

To summarize: All evidence from both human development and that of other social mammals indicates that even temporarily breaking contact with individuals and surroundings to which a primary attachment has taken place is a strongly disturbing emotional experience. This reaction has undoubtedly evolved as an adaptation to being lost or separated from the familiar. For a young and dependent social mammal, such a situation is often extremely dangerous. Unless the infant gives an immediate emotional reaction and starts signaling its whereabouts, its life may be lost within a few hours. Hence the distress vocalization of young puppies and the crying responses of human babies when left alone in strange places have strong survival value.

The results of permanent separation and the consequent complete break in a strongly developed social relationship are serious at any time in life, as anyone knows who has experienced the death of a close relative or the breakup of a marriage. For a young infant, the problem of permanent separation is usually settled by adoption, and here we can learn much from experiments with dogs, whose adoption (by the human species) is a normal occurrence. Much can be done to alleviate the painful emotions produced by separation, but the adopted puppy almost inevitably becomes more sensitive to separation and, consequently, more dependent on its human foster parents. These characteristics are desirable in a dog, as few people want a completely independent pet, but less so in a child, who should eventually develop into an independent and responsible adult. The answer seems to be to manage the child's separation in such a way as to decrease the painful emotional reactions as much as possible and to allow him an opportunity to integrate and organize the two portions of his existence.

References

BOWLBY, J. Maternal Care and Mental Health. Geneva: World Health Organization, 1951. Review of effects of disrupting maternal care.

———. Separation anxiety. *International Journal of Psychoanalysis*, 1960, *41*, 1–25. Summary of observations of infants' emotional reactions to separation from their mothers.

FREEDMAN, D. G., KING, J. A., and ELLIOTT, O. Critical period in the social development of dogs. *Science*, 1961, *133*, 1016–1017. The best experimental study of the critical period for primary socialization in this species.

FULLER, J. L., and CLARK, L. D. Genetic and treatment factors modifying the post-isolation syndrome in dogs. *Journal of Comparative and Physiological Psychology*, 1966a, *61*, 251–257. Some dog breeds are more severely affected by isolation than others; results of attempted therapy.

———, Effects of rearing with specific stimuli upon post-isolation syndrome in dogs. *Journal of Comparative and Physiological Psychology*, 1966b, *61*, 258–263. Visual isolation has more severe effects than restriction of space alone.

GRAY, P. H. Theory and evidence of imprinting in human infants. *Journal of Psychology*, 1958, *46*, 155–166. Review of the evidence concerning the effects of adoption at different ages.

HERSHER, L., RICHMOND, J. B., and MOORE, U. A. Maternal behavior in sheep and goats. In H. L. Rheingold (Ed.), *Maternal behavior in mammals*. New York: Wiley, 1963. Pp. 203–232. The herd animals rapidly form an exclusive bond with their young, as well as the young becoming attached to their mothers.

HESS, E. H. Imprinting and the critical period concept. In E. L. Bliss (Ed.) *Roots of behavior*. New York: Harper, 1962. Pp. 254–263. The primary socialization process in the domestic chick.

KLINGHAMMER, E. Factors influencing choice of mate in altricial birds. In H. W. Stevenson, E. H. Hess, and H. L. Rheingold (Eds.), *Early behavior: Comparative and developmental approaches*. New York: Wiley, 1967. Pp. 5–42. Experiments with imprinting in ring doves and mourning doves with a review of work on other altricial species.

KRUIJT, J. P. *Ontogeny of social behavior in Burmese red jungle fowl*. Leiden: Brill, 1964. Descriptive and experimental studies of behavioral development in the wild ancestor of the domestic chicken.

SCHAFFER, H. F. Objective observations of personality development in early infancy. *British Journal of Medical Psychology*, 1958, *31*, 174–183. Age changes in emotional reactions to separation from relatives.

SCOTT, J. P. Critical periods in behavioral development. *Science*, 1962, *138*, 949–958. General review of facts and theory relating to critical periods.

———. The process of primary socialization in the dog. In G. Newton and S. Levine (Eds.), *Early experience and behavior*. Springfield, Ill.: Thomas, 1967. Summarizes experiments with this process in the dog.

YARROW, L. J. Separation from parents during early childhood. In M. L. Hoffman and L. W. Hoffman (Eds.), *Review of child development research*. New York: Russell Sage Foundation, 1964. Pp. 89–136. Good critical review of the literature on this topic.

Attachment, Exploration, and Separation: Illustrated by the Behavior of One-Year-Olds in a Strange Situation*

Mary D. Salter Ainsworth and Silvia M. Bell
JOHNS HOPKINS UNIVERSITY

The concepts of attachment and attachment behavior are considered from an ethological-evolutionary viewpoint. Attachment behavior and exploration are viewed in balance, and the biological functions of each are discussed. As an illustration of these concepts, a study is

Reprinted from *Child Development*, *41*, 50–67. Copyright © 1970 by The Society for Research in Child Development, Inc. By permission.

* An earlier version of this paper was prepared while the first author was a fellow of the Center for Advanced Study in the Behavioral Sciences. It was presented at the annual meeting of the American Psychological Association, at San Francisco, September 1968, in a symposium, "Attachment Behaviors in Humans and Animals." The extended project which yielded the data has been supported by grant 62-244 of the Foundations' Fund for Research in Psychiatry, and by USPHS grant RO1 and HD 01712; this support is gratefully acknowledged. We are also appreciative of help given by the following in various aspects of the "strange situation" study: George D. Allyn, John Conklin, Elizabeth A. Eikenberg, Edwin E. Ellis, William C. Hamilton, Mary B. Main, Robert S. Marvin II, Eleanor S. McCulloch, and especially Barbara A. Wittig who helped in the original planning of the strange situation.

reported of 56 white, middle-class infants, 49–51 weeks of age, in a strange situation. The presence of the mother was found to encourage exploratory behavior, her absence to depress exploration and to heighten attachment behaviors. In separation episodes such behaviors as crying and search increased. In reunion episodes proximity-seeking and contact-maintaining behaviors were heightened. In a substantial proportion of Ss, contact-resisting behaviors were also heightened in the reunion episodes, usually in conjunction with contact-maintaining behaviors, thus suggesting ambivalence. Some Ss also displayed proximity-avoiding behavior in relation to the mother in the reunion episodes. These findings are discussed in the context of relevant observational, clinical, and experimental studies of human and nonhuman primates, including studies of mother-child separation. In conclusion, it is urged that the concepts of attachment and attachment behavior be kept broad enough to comprehend the spectrum of the findings of this range of studies.

. . . It is the purpose of this paper to highlight some distinctive features of the ethological-evolutionary concept of attachment, by citing reports of the interactions between the infant's attachment behavior and other behaviors mentioned above; to illustrate these interactions by a report of the behavior of 1-year-olds in a strange situation; and to note parallels between strange-situation behavior and behavior reported in other relevant observational, clinical, and experimental contexts.

Let us begin with some definitions and key concepts distinctive of the ethological-evolutionary viewpoint, as proposed by Bowlby (1958, 1969) and Ainsworth (1964, 1967, 1969). *An attachment* may be defined as an affectional tie that one person or animal forms between himself and another specific one— a tie that binds them together in space and endures over time. The behavioral hallmark of attachment is seeking to gain and to maintain a certain degree of proximity to the object of attachment, which ranges from close physical contact under some circumstances to interaction or communication across some distance under other circumstances. *Attachment behaviors* are behaviors which promote proximity or contact. In the human infant these include active proximity- and contact-seeking behaviors such as approaching, following, and clinging, and signaling behaviors such as smiling, crying, and calling.

The very young infant displays attachment (proximity-promoting) behaviors such as crying, sucking, rooting, and smiling, despite the fact that he is insufficiently discriminating to direct them differentially to a specific person. These initial behaviors indicate a genetic bias toward becoming attached, since they can be demonstrated to be either activated or terminated most effectively by stimuli which, in the environment of evolutionary adaptedness, are most likely to stem from human sources. When these behaviors, supplemented by other active proximity-seeking behaviors which emerge later—presumably through a process of learning in the course of mother-infant interaction— become organized hierarchically and directed actively and specifically toward the mother, the infant may be described as having become attached to her.

The intensity of attachment behavior may be heightened or diminished by situational conditions, but, once an attachment has been formed, it cannot be viewed as vanishing during periods when attachment behavior is not evident. Therefore, it seems necessary to view attachment as an organization of behavioral systems which has an internal, structural portion that endures throughout periods when none of the component attachment behaviors have been activated.

Viewed in the context of evolutionary theory, infant-mother attachment may be seen to fulfill significant biological functions, that is, functions that promote species survival. The long, helpless infancy of the human species occasions grave risks. For the species to have survived, the infant has required protection during this period of defenselessness. It is inferred, therefore, that the genetic code makes provision for infant behaviors which have the usual (although not necessarily invariable) outcome of bringing infant and mother together.

Exploratory behavior is equally significant from an evolutionary point of view. As Hamburg (1968) has pointed out, a prolonged infancy would miss its adaptive mark if there were not also provisions in the genetic code which lead the infant to be interested in the novel features of his environment—to venture forth, to explore, and to learn. The implication is that the genetic biases in a species which can adapt to a wide range of environmental variations provide for a balance in infant behaviors (and in reciprocal maternal behaviors) between those which lead the infant away from the mother and promote exploration and acquisition of knowledge of the properties of the physical and social environment, and those which draw mother and infant together and promote the protection and nurturance that the mother can provide.

The interaction between exploratory and attachment behaviors has been highlighted in field studies of ground-living nonhuman primates (e.g., South-wick, Beg, & Siddiqi, 1965; DeVore, 1963; Goodall, 1965; Schaller, 1965) as well as studies of such species in captive colonies (see Hinde, Rowell, & Spencer-Booth, 1964, 1967) and in laboratories (e.g., Harlow, 1961; Harlow & Harlow, 1965; Mason, 1965.) Although at first infant and mother are in almost continuous close contact, soon they are in collusion to make more elastic the bonds that unite them. The infant ventures forth to investigate his environment and to play with other infants, and gradually spends more and more time "off" his mother. His expeditions take him further and further away from her, and she becomes increasingly permissive and retrieves him less promptly and less frequently. Alarm or threat of separation, however, quickly brings mother and infant together again.

Naturalistic studies of the attachment-exploration balance are very time consuming; the interaction between the two sets of behaviors must be observed over a wide range of situations. A short-cut alternative is to utilize a controlled strange or unfamiliar situation in which the child, with and without his mother, is exposed to stressful episodes of different kinds. So powerful is this technique in evoking behavioral changes that it is likely to be used with increasing frequency in studies of mother-infant interaction. The ethological-evolutionary view of the attachment-exploration balance is a useful model to use when planning and when interpreting the findings of strange-situation studies.

Of strange-situation studies already reported in the literature, only two have been guided by an ethological-evolutionary point of view. Harlow (1961) used a strange situation to demonstrate the security function of surrogate cloth mothers for infant rhesus macaques. Ainsworth and Wittig (1969) made a preliminary report of the attachment-exploration balance in human 1 year olds. Other studies—Arsenian (1943), Cox and Campbell (1968), Rheingold

(1969)—focused on exploratory behavior and reported that the presence of the mother supports it, but paid scant attention to attachment behavior and its hierarchical manifestations in reunion episodes as well as during separation.

The strange-situation procedure provides more than an opportunity to observe how exploratory behavior is affected by mother-present, mother-absent, or other conditions. It is a laboratory microcosm in which a wide range of behaviors pertinent to attachment and to its balance with exploratory behavior may be elicited. Attachment behaviors may be seen as complicated by "negative" behaviors, such as avoidance and aggression. And yet, since the laboratory situation provides but a very small sample of mother-infant interaction, strange-situation findings are not self-interpreting. Perception of the implications of the behaviors that occur in it is facilitated by reference to the findings of other studies—naturalistic, clinical, and experimental. For this reason the ensuing report of a strange-situation study is presented as a useful *illustration* of the shifting balance between exploratory and attachment behavior implicit in the ethological-evolutionary view of attachment. The discussion which follows the presentation refers to relevant findings of other studies. The propositions offered in conclusion comprehend these other relevant considerations as well as the findings of the illustrative strange-situation study.

THE STRANGE SITUATION

In the course of a longitudinal, naturalistic investigation of infant-mother attachment during the first year of life, there was little opportunity in the home environment to observe the balance of attachment and exploratory behaviors under conditions of novelty and alarm. Therefore, a laboratory situation was devised as a test situation to which the Ss were introduced when nearly 1 year old. It was desired to observe the extent to which the infant could use his mother as a secure base from which he could explore a strange environment, with fear of the strange kept in abeyance by her presence. It was also intended to observe the extent to which attachment behavior might gain ascendancy over exploratory behavior under conditions of alarm introduced by the entrance of a stranger and under conditions of separation from and reunion with the mother.

METHOD   *Subjects*   The 56 Ss were family-reared infants of white, middle-class parents, who were originally contacted through pediatricians in private practice. One subsample of 23 Ss, who had been observed longitudinally from birth onward, were observed in the strange situation when 51 weeks old. The second subsample of 33 Ss, studied in the context of an independent project (Bell, 1970), were observed when 49 weeks old.

Procedure   The strange situation was comprised of eight episodes which followed in a standard order for all subjects. The situation was designed to be novel enough to elicit exploratory behavior, and yet not so strange that it would evoke fear and heighten attachment behavior at the outset. The approach of the stranger was gradual, so that any fear of her could be attributed to unfamiliarity rather than to abrupt, alarming behavior. The episodes were arranged so that the less disturbing ones came first. Finally, the situation as a whole was intended to be no more disturbing than those an infant was likely to encounter in his ordinary life experience. A summarized account of the procedure has been given elsewhere (Ainsworth & Wittig, 1969) but will be reviewed here.

The experimental room was furnished—not bare—but so arranged that there was a 9 × 9-foot square of clear floor space, marked off into 16 squares to facilitate recording of location and locomotion. At one end of the room was a child's chair heaped with and surrounded by toys. Near the other end of the room on one side was a chair for the mother, and on the opposite side, near the door, a chair for the stranger. The baby was put down in the middle of the base of the triangle by the three chairs and left free to move where he wished. Both the mother and the female stranger were instructed in advance as to the roles they were to play.

> *Episode 1* (M, B, O). Mother (M), accompanied by an observer (O), carried the baby (B) into the room, and then O left.
>
> *Episode 2* (M, B). M put B down in the specified place, then sat quietly in her chair, participating only if B sought her attention. Duration 3 minutes.
>
> *Episode 3* (S, M, B). A stranger (S) entered, sat quietly for 1 minute, conversed with M for 1 minute, and then gradually approached B, showing him a toy. At the end of the third minute M left the room unobtrusively.
>
> *Episode 4* (S, B). If B was happily engaged in play, S was nonparticipant. If he was inactive, she tried to interest him in the toys. If he was distressed, she tried to distract him or to comfort him. If he could not be comforted, the episode was curtailed—otherwise it lasted 3 minutes.
>
> *Episode 5* (M, B). M entered, paused in the doorway to give B an opportunity to mobilize a spontaneous response to her. S then left unobtrusively. What M did next was not specified—except that she was told that after B was again settled in play with the toys she was to leave again, after pausing to say "bye-bye." (Duration of episode undetermined.)
>
> *Episode 6* (B alone). The baby was left alone for 3 minutes, unless he was so distressed that the episode had to be curtailed.
>
> *Episode 7* (S, B). S entered and behaved as in episode 4 for 3 minutes, unless distress prompted curtailment. (Ainsworth & Wittig 1969, planned a somewhat different procedure for episode 7, which was attempted for the first 14 *S*s but, as it turned out, approximated the simpler procedure reported here, which was used for the remaining *S*s.)
>
> *Episode 8* (M, B). M returned, S left, and after the reunion had been observed, the situation was terminated.

The behavior of the *S*s was observed from an adjoining room through a one-way vision window. Two observers dictated continuous narrative accounts into a dual channel tape recorder which also picked up the click of a timer every 15 seconds. (This represents the procedure we now consider standard. For the first 14 *S*s, however, the dual channel recorder was not available, so one observer dictated, while the other made written notes. For the second subsample of 33 Ss, author Bell was the sole observer.) The protocols were subsequently transcribed and consolidated, then coded. Reliability of observation was checked by separate codings of the dictated reports made by the two authors in four cases observed by both. Product-moment coefficients of .99 were found for each of locomotor, manipulatory and visual exploration, and one of .98 for crying.

The narrative record yielded two types of measure. A frequency measure was used for three forms of exploratory behavior—locomotor, manipulatory, and visual—and for crying. A score of 1 was given for each 15-second time interval in which the behavior occurred. The maximum was 12 for an episode, since the standard length of an episode was 3 minutes, and longer or shorter episodes were prorated. Frequency measures were obtained for episodes 2 through 7. Product-moment reliability coefficients for two independent coders for eight randomly selected cases were as follows: exploratory locomotion, .99; exploratory manipulation, .93; visual exploration, .98; crying, .99.

The second measure was based upon detailed coding of behaviors in which the contingencies of the mother's or stranger's behavior had to be taken into consideration. The codings were then ordered into 7-point scales on the assumption that not only could the same behavior be manifested in different degrees of intensity, but that different behaviors could serve the same end under different intensities of activation. There were five classes of behavior thus scored.

Proximity- and contact-seeking behaviors include active, effective behaviors such as approaching and clambering up, active gestures such as reaching or leaning, intention movements such as partial approaches, and vocal signals including "directed" cries.

Contact-maintaining behaviors pertain to the situation after the baby has gained contact, either through his own initiative or otherwise. They include: clinging, embracing, clutching, and holding on; resisting release by intensified clinging or, if contact is lost, by turning back and reaching, or clambering back up; and protesting release vocally.

Proximity- and interaction-avoiding behaviors pertain to a situation which ordinarily elicits approach, greeting, or at least watching or interaction across a distance, as when an adult entered, or tried to engage the baby's attention. Such behaviors include ignoring the adult, pointedly avoiding looking at her, looking away, turning away, or moving away.

Contact- and interaction-resisting behaviors including angry, ambivalent attempts to push away, hit, or kick the adult who seeks to make contact, squirming to get down having been picked up, or throwing away or pushing away the toys through which the adult attempts to mediate her interventions. More diffuse manifestations are angry screaming, throwing self about, throwing self down, kicking the floor, pouting, cranky fussing, or petulance.

These four classes of behavior were scored for interaction with the mother in episodes 2, 3, 5, and 8, and for interaction with the stranger in episodes 3, 4, and 7.

Search behavior was scored for the separation episodes 4, 6, and 7. These behaviors include: following the mother to the door, trying to open the door, banging on the door, remaining oriented to the door or glancing at it, going to the mother's empty chair or simply looking at it. Such behaviors imply that the infant is searching for the absent mother either actively or by orienting to the last place in which she was seen (the door in most cases) or the place associated with her in the strange situation (her chair.)

In scoring these five classes of behavior, the score was influenced by the following features: the strength of the behavior, its frequency, duration, and latency, and by the type of behavior itself—with active behavior being considered stronger than signaling. Detailed instructions for scoring these behaviors as well as for coding the frequency measures are provided elsewhere.[1]

Reliability coefficients (rho) for two independent scorers for 14 randomly selected cases were, for behaviors directed to the mother, as follows: proximity- and contact-seeking, .93; contact-maintaining, .97; proximity- and interaction-avoiding, .93; contact-resisting, .96; search, .94.

FINDINGS   The findings to be reported here are of behaviors characteristic of the sample as a whole. Individual differences were conspicuous, instructive, and significantly correlated with other variables. Some of these have been reported elsewhere (Ainsworth & Wittig, 1969; Ainsworth & Bell, 1970; Bell, 1970) but they cannot be considered here.

Exploratory Behavior   Figure 1 shows how three forms of exploratory behavior vary in successive episodes from 2 through 7. There is a sharp decline in all forms of exploratory behavior from episode 2 when the baby was alone with his mother to episode 3 when the stranger was present also. (This and all other interepisode differences reported here are significant at the .01 level or better, as tested by the binomial test, unless noted otherwise.) Exploration remains depressed through episode 4 when the baby was left with the stranger. Visual and manipulatory exploration (visual at the .02 level) recover significantly in episode 5, aided by the mother's attempts to interest the baby again in play, although similar efforts by the stranger in episodes 4 and 7 were ineffective. Visual and manipulatory exploration decline again in episode 6 after the mother departs for a second time, leaving the baby alone. All forms of exploratory behavior decline to their lowest point in episode 7 after the stranger had returned but while the mother was still absent.

To supplement the visual exploration score, which measured visual orientation to the physical environment, visual orientation to the mother and to the stranger were also coded. The only noteworthy findings may be summarized as follows: In episode 2, the baby looked at the toys and other aspects of the physical environment much more frequently than at the mother, at whom he glanced only now and then, keeping visual tabs on her; in episode 3, the stranger, the most novel feature of the environment, was looked at more than the toys, and the mother was looked at no more frequently than before.

---

[1] The following materials have been deposited with the National Auxiliary Publications Service: instructions for conducting the strange situation procedure, instructions to the mother, instructions for coding behaviors for frequency measures, and instructions for coding socially interactive behaviors. Orders NAPS Document 00762 from ASIS National Auxiliary Publications Service, c/o CMM Information Sciences, Inc., 22 West 34th Street, New York, New York 10001; remitting $3.00 for microfiche or $1.00 for photocopies.

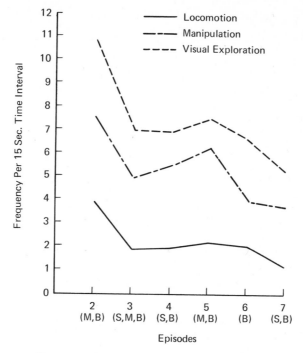

F IGURE 1. *Incidence of exploratory behavior.*

Crying   Figure 2 suggests that the strange situation does not in itself cause alarm or distress, for crying is minimal in episode 2. Crying does not increase significantly in episode 3 ($p = .068$), which suggests that the stranger was not in herself alarming for most Ss, at least not when the mother was also present. The incidence of crying rises in episode 4 with the mother's first departure; it declines upon her return in episode 5, only to increase sharply in episode 6 when she departs a second time, leaving the baby alone. It does not decrease significantly when the stranger returns in episode 7, which suggests that it is the mother's absence rather than mere aloneness that was distressing to most of the babies, and that the greater incidence of crying in episode 6 than in episode 4 is largely due to a cumulative effect.

Search Behavior During Separation   The mean strength of search behavior was moderate in episode 4 (3.0), significantly stronger in episode 6 (4.6), and moderate again in episode 7 (2.5). Although this might suggest that search behavior is especially activated by being left alone and reduced in the presence of the stranger, this interpretation is not advanced because of the contingencies of the stranger's behavior and her location near the door. Some infants (37 percent) cried minimally if at all in episode 6, and yet searched strongly. Some (20 percent) cried desperately, but searched weakly or not at all. Some (32 percent) both cried and searched. All but four Ss reacted to being left alone with either one or other of these attachment behaviors.

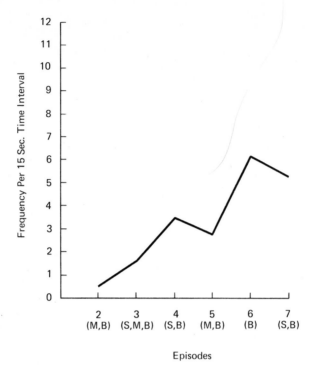

Episodes

FIGURE 2.   *Incidence of crying.*

Proximity-Seeking and Contact-Maintaining Behaviors   Figure 3 shows that efforts to regain contact, proximity or interaction with the mother occur only weakly in episodes 2 and 3 but are greatly intensified by brief separation experiences. Contact-maintaining behavior is negligible in episodes 2 and 3, rises in the first reunion episode (5), and rises even more sharply in the second reunion episode (8). In the case of both classes of behavior the increase from episodes 2 through 5 to 8 is highly significant ($p < .001$). Some Ss showed these behaviors in relation to the stranger also. Thus, for example, a few infants approached the stranger in each of the episodes in which the stranger was present, but substantially fewer than those who approached the mother. Some infants were picked up by the stranger in episodes 4 and 7—in an attempt to comfort them—and some of these did cling to her and/or resist being put down again. Nevertheless proximity-seeking and contact-maintaining behaviors were displayed much less frequently and less strongly to the stranger than to the mother.

Contact-Resisting and Proximity-Avoiding Behaviors   Table 1 shows the incidence of contact-resisting and proximity-avoiding behaviors directed to both mother and stranger. Contact-resisting behavior directed toward the mother occurred very rarely in the preseparation episodes because the mother had been instructed not to intervene except in response to the baby's demands, and therefore episodes 2 and 3 are omitted from the table. In the reunion episodes,

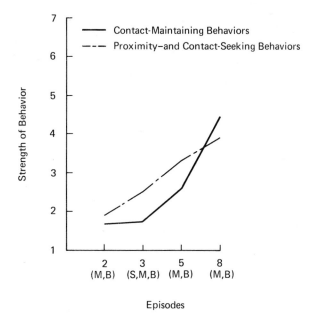

FIGURE 3.   *Strength of proximity-seeking and contact-maintaining behaviors directed toward the mother.*

some Ss resisted contact with the mother, but many did not. Therefore Table 1 shows the incidence of this behavior rather than its mean strength.

About one third of the sample showed contact-resisting behavior to the mother in episode 5, at least to some degree, and about one half showed it in episode 8. All but one infant who scored relatively high (4 or higher) in contact-resisting behavior received a comparably high score on contact-maintaining behavior. Thus, at least when directed to the mother, contact-resisting behavior seems to represent classic ambivalence—wanting to be held, wanting to be close, and at the same time angrily resisting contact.

Contact and interaction with the stranger were also resisted but somewhat less frequently than with the mother. Six Ss showed fairly strong contact- or interaction-resisting behavior (scores of 4 or higher) with both stranger in episode 7 and with mother in episode 8, but, for the most part, babies who tended to resist the mother did not resist the stranger and vice versa.

Proximity- and interaction-avoiding behavior did not occur in relation to the mother in the preseparation episodes, for the mother's nonparticipant role made no claim on the baby's attention. But, as shown in Table 1, it occurred to some degree in about half the sample in each of the reunion episodes, 5 and 8. About one third of the sample avoided the stranger at some time in episode 3 —ignoring her, avoiding meeting her eyes, or moving further away from her. The incidence of these behaviors declined in episode 4, and even in episode 7 remained less than in episode 3. About half the sample avoided neither mother nor stranger, but those who showed this behavior in any strength (score of 4 or over) to one did not show it to the other.

Table 1

Incidence of Contact-Resisting and Proximity-Avoiding Behavior to Mother and Stranger

Strength of Behavior	Behavior to Mother		Behavior to Stranger		
	Episode 5	Episode 8	Episode 3	Episode 4	Episode 7
Resist Contact					
6–7	4	6	0	6	7
4–5	5	8	5	3	12
2–3	9	13	2	3	3
1	38	29	49	44	34
Avoid Proximity					
6–7	7	5	4	1	1
4–5	17	13	7	3	6
2–3	3	7	7	1	2
1	29	31	38	51	45

DISCUSSION

These findings illustrate the complex interaction between attachment behavior, response to novel or unfamiliar stimulus objects and situations, and responses to separation from the attachment object and to subsequent reunion. First, let us consider response to novelty. It is now commonly accepted that novelty may elicit either fear and avoidance or approach and exploration, depending both on the degree of novelty and upon circumstances. One of the conditions which facilitates approach and exploration of the novel is the presence, in reasonable but not necessarily close proximity, of the mother—the object of attachment. The infants of the present sample showed little alarm in the preseparation episodes of the strange situation. Their attachment behavior was not activated; they tended not to cling to the mother or even to approach her. They used her as a secure base from which to explore the strange situation. This finding is not new. Similar observations have been reported by Arsenian (1943), Cox and Campbell (1968), Ainsworth and Wittig (1969), and Rheingold (1969) for human subjects, and by Harlow (1961) for rhesus macaque infants. The presence of the mother can tip the balance in favor of exploring the novel rather than avoiding it or withdrawing from it.

Absence of the mother tends to tip the balance in the opposite direction with a substantial heightening of attachment behavior and concomitant lessening of exploration. During the mother's absence, proximity-promoting behaviors (crying and search) are evident. The mother's return in the reunion episodes did not serve to redress the balance to its previous level. Attachment behaviors—proximity- and contact-seeking and contact-maintaining behaviors

—remained heightened. Crying did not immediately subside in many cases and, despite the mother's attempts to evoke a renewed interest in exploring the properties of the toys, exploration remained depressed below its initial level.

It was assumed that separation episodes totaling 9 minutes at most would not have any lasting effect on the balance between attachment and exploratory behavior, and indeed the posttest behavior of the infants tended to confirm this assumption. Nevertheless these minuscule separations evoke behaviors which are similar in kind to those provoked by longer separations, although differing in duration and intensity. The behavior of these 1-year-old humans in response to separations lasting only a few minutes bears remarkable resemblance to the behavior of infant monkeys in response to separation for longer periods—a week (Spencer-Booth & Hinde, 1966) or a month (Kaufman & Rosenblum, 1967). In these experiments the mother was removed, and the infant left in his familiar social group. Attachment behavior, including distress calling and search for the mother, was heightened, and exploratory and play behavior was depressed during the separation. The infants responded more intensely to frightening stimuli during separation than when the mother was present. As separation continued there was some lessening of the intensity of distress and search, and some recovery of exploration and play—a recovery not manifest by the human infants in this sample in their very brief separations. When the mother was restored, however, the infant monkeys clung to her more and explored less than they had before separation—differing in this from nonseparated controls—and these effects lasted for three months or more.

The response of infant monkeys to experimental separations strongly resembles the behavior of young children, aged from 8 months to 3 years, when they undergo separations of several days, weeks, or even months away from home in hospitals or residential nurseries. Robertson and Bowlby (1952), Bowlby (1953), Schaffer (1958), and Heinicke and Westheimer (1965) have shown that the child is at first acutely distressed, protests the separation, and attempts to regain the mother by all means at his disposal. This initial phase of response tends to give way to despair, which in turn may give way—if the separation endures long enough—to a brightening of affect and renewed responsiveness to companions and to things in the environment. Attachment behavior directed toward the mother may have disappeared, but reunion with the mother tends to reactivate it and indeed to intensify it beyond its pre-separation level. This heightened level tends to persist for a more or less prolonged period, usually much longer than the separation itself. During the period after reunion when the child's attachment behavior is heightened, he is focused on his mother, attends less to other people and to things in his environment, explores less, and presumably learns less. An unduly prolonged heightening of attachment behavior may be viewed as a distortion of the attachment-exploration balance. Some long-term follow-up studies (e.g., Bowlby, Ainsworth, Boston, & Rosenbluth, 1956) suggest that this kind of behavior, often described as overdependent, may in some instances be a lasting effect of long, depriving separations.

Let us turn from attachment behavior to consider those behaviors that work against contact- and proximity-seeking, namely, contact-resisting and proximity- and interaction-avoiding behaviors. Contact-resisting behavior, as directed toward the mother, usually occurred in conjunction with contact-seeking behavior, and hence, as suggested earlier, implies an ambivalent response. Ambivalent or rejecting and angry responses are reported as common in young children returning home after brief separations (e.g., Heinicke & Westheimer, 1965.) Separation heightens aggressive behavior of this kind as well as attachment behavior, and predisposes the child toward angry outbursts upon minimal provocation. Spencer-Booth and Hinde (1966) report similar increase of aggression in monkeys: Unusually intense tantrums occur in response to any discouragement of contact-seeking behavior during the period of reunion after separation. Some of our strange-situation Ss showed contact-resisting behavior toward the stranger. Although in some cases this may indicate fear of the strange person, it seems likely that in some, perhaps most, it is a manifestation of aggression evoked by the mother's departure.

Proximity-avoiding behavior, on the other hand, seems likely to stem from different sources in the case of the stranger than in the case of the mother, even though the overt behavior seems the same in both cases. Ignoring the stranger, and looking, turning, or moving away from her probably imply an avoidance of the unfamiliar and fear-evoking person. This is suggested by the fact that these responses are more frequent (as directed toward the stranger) in episode 3, when the stranger has first appeared, than in later episodes. Similar avoidance of the mother cannot be due to unfamiliarity, and seems unlikely to be caused by fear. Such behavior occurs in the reunion episodes, and is more frequent than avoidance of the stranger.

Proximity- and interaction-avoiding behavior in relation to the mother is shown in striking form by some young children upon reunion after separations lasting for weeks or months. Robertson and Bowlby (1952) and Heinicke and Westheimer (1965) report that some children do not seem to recognize their mothers upon reunion, and that for a longer or shorter time they remain distant from her and treat her like a stranger. Bowlby (1960) has termed this kind of distanciation "detachment." During a prolonged separation, detachment tends to succeed protest and despair reactions, and after reunion it may persist for a long time—even indefinitely in cases in which separations have been very long and depriving. Such behavior has not yet been reported in nonhuman primates—perhaps because their experimental separations have been brief, perhaps because of species differences.

Avoidance responses of the kind observed in the strange situation in relation to the mother—looking away, turning away—may be detachment in the making and so constitute a primitive kind of defense. The constellation of individual differences in the strange-situation sample supports this hypothesis, although it is impossible here to present detailed evidence.

It may be pertinent, however, to refer to a similar looking-away response found in two experiments on the conditioning and extinction of attachment behaviors. Brackbill (1958) worked with the smiling response. During the conditioning period she provided contingent reinforcement for smiling by responding socially to the baby each time he smiled—and smiling increased in frequency. During the extinction period she met the baby's smile with an impassive face. Not only did the frequency of smiling decrease, but when the experimenter failed to respond to a smile, the baby fussed and looked away. It became increasingly difficult to catch the baby's eye. He looked away from the person who had previously reinforced his attachment behavior but who no longer did so. Similar results are reported for an experiment on babbling by Rheingold, Gewirtz, and Ross (1959).

These findings highlight the fact that in extinction—as indeed learning theorists have often themselves emphasized—there is an active process of blocking the response by another, antithetical behavior, rather than or in addition to the weakening of the strength of smiling (or babbling) behavior itself. This suggests that detached behavior may consist of responses, incompatible with attachment behavior, which have, often temporarily, gained the greater strength. That attachment can endure despite a period of detachment is shown by the strength with which attachment behavior can break through into overt expression in the case of young children who do not at reunion seem to recognize their mothers, but who subsequently manifest much heightened proximity-seeking and contact-maintaining behavior.

In summary, continuities have been noted between attachment and exploratory behavior and their activating and terminating conditions, observed in the microcosm of the laboratory strange-situation, and similar behaviors and conditions as reported by field studies, clinical studies, and experimental studies for both humans and nonhuman primate subjects. It is urged that the concept of attachment and attachment behavior employed as a guide in future studies be given a broad enough perspective to comprehend the spectrum of findings relevant to attachment which have been sampled in this discussion.

PROPOSITIONS FOR A COMPREHENSIVE CONCEPT OF ATTACHMENT

The following propositions are suggested as essential to a comprehensive concept of attachment. They are based on an ethological-evolutionary point of view, and have been formulated on the basis of reports of a broad range of investigations, including naturalistic studies of mother-infant interaction, and studies of mother-child separation and reunion in both human and nonhuman primates, as well as the illustrative strange-situation study reported here.

1. Attachment is not coincident with attachment behavior. Attachment behavior may be heightened or diminished by conditions—environmental and intraorganismic—which may be specified empirically. Despite situationally determined waxing and waning of attachment behavior, the individual is nevertheless predisposed intermittently to seek proximity to the object of attachment. It is this predisposition—which may be conceived as having an inner, structural basis—that is the attachment. Its manifestations are accessible to observation over time; a short time-sample may, however, be misleading.

2. Attachment behavior is heightened in situations perceived as threatening, whether it is an external danger or an actual or impending separation from the attachment object that constitutes the threat.

3. When strongly activated, attachment behavior is incompatible with exploratory behavior. On the other hand, the state of being attached, together

with the presence of the attachment object, may support and facilitate exploratory behaviors. Provided that there is no threat of separation, the infant is
likely to be able to use his mother as a secure base from which to explore,
manifesting no alarm in even a strange situation as long as she is present. Under
these circumstances the relative absence of attachment behavior—of proximity-
promoting behavior—cannot be considered an index of a weak attachment.

4. Although attachment behavior may diminish or even disappear in the
course of a prolonged absence from the object of attachment, the attachment
is not necessarily diminished; attachment behavior is likely to reemerge in full
or heightened strength upon reunion, with or without delay.

5. Although individual differences have not been stressed in this discussion,
the incidence of ambivalent (contact-resisting) and probably defensive
(proximity-avoiding) patterns of behavior in the reunion episodes of the strange
situation are a reflection of the fact that attachment relations are qualitatively
different from one attached pair to another. These qualitative differences,
together with the sensitivity of attachment behavior to situational determinants,
make it very difficult to assess the strength or intensity of an attachment. It is
suggested that, in the present state of our knowledge, it is wiser to explore
qualitative differences, and their correlates and antecedents, than to attempt
premature quantifications of strength of attachment.

References

AINSWORTH, M. D. The development of infant-mother interaction among the Ganda.
In B. M. Foss (Ed.), *Determinants of infant behaviour II*. London: Methuen, 1963.
Pp. 67–112.

———. Patterns of attachment behavior shown by the infant in interaction with his
mother. *Merrill-Palmer Quarterly*, 1964, **10**, 51–58.

———. *Infancy in Uganda: infant care and the growth of love*. Baltimore: Johns Hopkins
University Press, 1967.

———. Object relations, dependency and attachment: a theoretical review of the
infant-mother relationship. *Child Development*, 1969, **40**, 969–1025.

———, & BELL, S. M. Some contemporary patterns of mother-infant interaction in
the feeding situation. In J. A. Ambrose (Ed.), *The functions of stimulation in early
post-natal development*. London: Academic, 1970.

———, & WITTIG, B. A. Attachment and exploratory behavior of one-year-olds in a
strange situation. In B. M. Foss (Ed.), *Determinants of infant behaviour IV*. London:
Methuen, 1969. Pp. 111–136.

ARSENIAN, J. M. Young children in an insecure situation. *Journal of Abnormal and Social
Psychology*, 1943, **38**, 225–249.

BELL, S. M. The development of the concept of the object as related to infant-mother
attachment. *Child Development*, 1970, **41**, 291–311.

BOWLBY, J. Psychopathological processes set in train by early mother-child separation.
Journal of Mental Science, 1953, **99**, 265–272.

———. The nature of the child's tie to his mother. *International Journal of Psychoanalysis*,
1958, **39**, 350–373.

———. Separation anxiety. *International Journal of Psychoanalysis*, 1960, **41**, 69–113.

———. *Attachment and loss*. Vol. 1. *Attachment*. London: Hogarth, 1969; New York:
Basic Books, 1969.

————; AINSWORTH, M. D.; BOSTON, M.; & ROSENBLUTH, D. The effects of mother-child separation: a follow-up study. *British Journal of Medical Psychology*, 1956, **29**, 211–247.

BRACKBILL, Y. Extinction of the smiling response in infants as a function of reinforcement schedule. *Child Development*, 1958, **29**, 115–124.

CAIRNS, R. B. Attachment behavior of mammals. *Psychological Review*, 1966, **73**, 409–426.

COX, F. N., & CAMPBELL, D. Young children in a new situation with and without their mothers. *Child Development*, 1968, **39**, 123–131.

DEVORE, I. Mother-infant relations in free-ranging baboons. In H. L. Rheingold (Ed.), *Maternal behavior in mammals*. New York: Wiley, 1963. Pp. 305–335.

GEWIRTZ, J. L. A learning analysis of the effects of normal stimulation, privation and deprivation on the acquisition of social motivation and attachment. In B. M. Foss (Ed.), *Determinants of infant behaviour*. London: Methuen, 1961. Pp. 213–299.

————. Mechanisms of social learning: some roles of stimulation and behavior in early human development. In D. A. Goslin (Ed.), *Handbook of socialization theory and research*. Chicago: Rand McNally, 1969. Pp. 57–212.

GOODALL, J. Chimpanzees of the Gombe Stream Reserve. In I. DeVore (Ed.), *Primate behavior: field studies of monkeys and apes*. New York: Holt, Rinehart & Winston, 1965. Pp. 425–473.

HAMBURG, D. A. Evolution of emotional responses: evidence from recent research on non-human primates. In J. Masserman (Ed.), *Science and psychoanalysis*. Vol. **12**. New York: Grune & Stratton, 1968. Pp. 39–52.

HARLOW, H. F. The development of affectional patterns in infant monkeys. In B. M. Foss (Ed.), *Determinants of infant behaviour*. London: Methuen, 1961. Pp. 75–97.

————, & HARLOW, M. K. The affectional systems. In A. M. Schrier, H. F. Harlow, & F. Stollnitz (Eds.), *Behavior of nonhuman primates*. Vol. **2**. New York: Academic, 1965. Pp. 287–334.

HEINICKE, C. M., & WESTHEIMER, I. *Brief separations*. New York: International Universities Press, 1965.

HINDE, R. A., ROWELL, T. E.; & SPENCER-BOOTH, Y. Behaviour of socially living rhesus monkeys in their first six months. *Proceedings of the Zoological Society of London*, 1964, **143**, 609–649.

————. The behaviour of socially living rhesus monkeys in their first two and a half years. *Animal Behaviour*, 1967, **15**, 169–196.

KAUFMAN, I. C., & ROSENBLUM, L. A. Depression in infant monkeys separated from their mothers. *Science*, 1967, **155**, 1030–1031.

MACCOBY, E. E., & MASTERS, J. C. Attachment and dependency. In P. Mussen (Ed.), *Carmichael's manual of child psychology*, New York: Wiley, 1970.

MASON, W. A. Determinants of social behavior in young chimpanzees. In A. M. Schrier, H. F. Harlow, & F. Stollnitz (Eds.), *Behavior of nonhuman primates*. Vol. **2**. New York: Academic, 1965. Pp. 287–334.

MORGAN, G. A., & RICCIUTI, H. N. Infants' responses to strangers during the first year. In B. M. Foss (Ed.), *Determinants of infant behaviour IV*. London: Methuen, 1969. Pp. 253–272.

RHEINGOLD, H. L. The effect of a strange environment on the behavior of infants. In B. M. Foss (Ed.), *Determinants of infant behavior IV*. London: Methuen, 1969. Pp. 137–166.

————; GEWIRTZ, J. L.; & ROSS, H. W. Social conditioning of vocalizations in the infant. *Journal of Comparative and Physiological Psychology*, 1959, **52**, 68–73.

ROBERTSON, J., & BOWLBY, J. Responses of young children to separation from their mothers. II. Observations of the sequences of response of children aged 16 to 24 months during the course of separation. *Courrier Centre International de l'Enfance*, 1952, **2**, 131–142.

ROBSON, K. S. The role of eye-to-eye contact in maternal-infant attachment. *Journal of Child Psychology and Psychiatry*, 1967, **8**, 13–25.

SCHAFFER, H. R. Objective observations of personality development in early infancy. *British Journal of Medical Psychology*, 1958, **31**, 174–183.

———. The onset of fear of strangers and the incongruity hypothesis. *Journal of Child Psychology and Psychiatry*, 1966, **7**, 95–106.

———, & EMERSON, P. E. The development of social attachments in infancy. *Monographs of the Society for Research in Child Development*, 1964, **29**, (3, Serial No. 94).

SCHALLER, G. B. The behavior of the mountain gorilla. In I. DeVore (Ed.), *Primate behavior: field studies of monkeys and apes*. New York: Holt, Rinehart & Winston, 1965. Pp. 324–367.

SCHWARZ, J. C. Fear and attachment in young children. *Merrill-Palmer Quarterly*, 1968, **14**, 313–322.

SOUTHWICK, C. H.; BEG, M. A.; & SIDDIQI, M. R. Rhesus monkeys in North India. In I. DeVore (Ed.), *Primate behavior: field studies of monkeys and apes*. New York: Holt, Rinehart & Winston, 1965. Pp. 111–159.

SPENCER-BOOTH, Y., & HINDE, R. A. The effects of separating rhesus monkey infants from their mothers for six days. *Journal of Child Psychology and Psychiatry*, 1966, **7**, 179–198.

WALTERS, R. H., & PARKE, R. D. The role of the distance receptors in the development of social responsiveness. In L. P. Lipsitt & C. C. Spiker (Eds.), *Advances in child development and behavior*. Vol. **2**. New York: Academic, 1965. Pp. 59–96.

Play Behavior in the Year-Old Infant: Early Sex Differences*

Susan Goldberg
UNIVERSITY OF ZAMBIA

Michael Lewis
EDUCATIONAL TESTING SERVICE

32 boys and 32 girls, 13 months old, were observed with their mothers in a standardized free play situation. There were striking sex differences in the infants' behavior toward their mothers and in their play. Earlier observation of the mothers' behavior toward the infants at 6 months indicates that some of these sex differences were related to the mothers' behavior toward the infants. It was suggested that parents behave differently toward girls and boys,

* This research was conducted at the Fels Research Institute and was supported in part by grants HD-00868, FR-00222, and FR-05537 from the National Institute of Mental Health, U. S. Public Health Service. Editorial assistance was supported by research grant 1 P01 HD01762 from the National Institute of Child Health and Human Development. Portions of this paper were presented at the 1967 meeting of the Society for Research in Child Development, New York. We would like to thank Lynn Godfrey, Cornelia Dodd, and Helen Campbell for their aid in data analysis.

even as infants, reinforcing sex-appropriate behavior. This study emphasizes the importance of observing the freely emitted behavior of the very young child.

Until recently, the largest proportion of studies in child development gave attention to nursery and early grade school children. The literature on sex differences is no exception. A recent book on development of sex differences which includes an annotated bibliography (Maccoby, 1966) lists fewer than 10 studies using infants, in spite of the fact that theoretical discussions (e.g., Freud, 1938 [originally published in 1905]; Piaget, 1951) emphasize the importance of early experience. Theoretical work predicts and experimental work confirms the existence of sex differences in behavior by age 3. There has been little evidence to demonstrate earlier differentiation of sex-appropriate behavior, although it would not be unreasonable to assume this occurs.

Recently, there has been increased interest in infancy, including some work which has shown early sex differences in attentive behavior (Kagan & Lewis, 1965; Lewis, in press). The bulk of this work has been primarily experimental studying specific responses to specific stimuli or experimental conditions. Moreover, it has dealt with perceptual-cognitive differences rather than personality variables. There has been little observation of freely emitted behavior. Such observations are of importance in supplying researchers with the classes of naturally occurring behaviors, the conditions under which responses normally occur, and the natural preference ordering of behaviors. Knowledge of this repertoire of behaviors provides a background against which behavior under experimental conditions can be evaluated.

The present study utilized a free play situation to observe sex differences in children's behavior toward mother, toys, and a frustration situation at 13 months of age. Because the Ss were participants in a longitudinal study, information on the mother-child relationship at 6 months was also available. This made it possible to assess possible relations between behavior patterns at 6 months and at 13 months.

METHOD

SUBJECTS   Two samples of 16 girls and 16 boys each, or a total of 64 infants, were seen at 6 and 13 months of age (± 6 days). All Ss were born to families residing in southwestern Ohio at the time of the study. All were Caucasian. The mothers had an average of 13.5 years of schooling (range of 10–18 years) and the fathers had an average of 14.5 years of schooling (range of 8–20 years). The occupations of the fathers ranged from laborer to scientist. Of the 64 infants, 9 girls and 10 boys were first-born and the remaining infants had from 1 to 6 siblings.

THE 6-MONTH VISIT   The procedure of the 6-month visit, presented in detail in Kagan and Lewis (1965), included two visual episodes and an auditory episode where a variety of behavioral responses were recorded. The infant's mother was present during these procedures. At the end of the experimental procedure, the mother was interviewed by one of the experimenters, who had been able to observe both mother and infant for the duration of the session.

The interviewer also rated both mother and infant on a rating scale. The items rated for the infant included: amount of activity, irritability, response to mother's behavior, and amount of affect. For the mother, the observer rated such factors as nature of handling, amount of playing with the baby, type of comforting behavior, and amount of vocalization to the baby. Each item was rated on a 7-point scale, with 1 indicating the most activity and 7 the least. For the purpose of this study, it was necessary to obtain a measure of the amount of physical contact the mother initiated with the child. Since scores on the individual scales did not result in sufficient variance in the population, a composite score was obtained by taking the mean score for each mother over all three of the touching-the-infant scales. These included: amount of touching, amount of comforting, and amount of play. The composite touch scores (now called the amount of physical contact) resulted in a sufficiently variable distribution to be used for comparison with the 13-month touch data.

THE 13-MONTH VISIT   Kagan and Lewis (1965), who employed the same 64 infants for their study, described the procedures used at 6 months, which were similar to those of the present (13-month) study. The only addition was a free play procedure, which will be discussed in detail below.

The playroom, 9 by 12 feet, contained nine simple toys: a set of blocks, a pail, a "lawnmower," a stuffed dog, an inflated plastic cat, a set of quoits (graduated plastic doughnuts stacked on a wooden rod), a wooden mallet, a pegboard, and a wooden bug (a pull toy). Also included as toys were any permanent objects in the room, such as the doorknob, latch on the wall, tape on the electrical outlets, and so forth. The mother's chair was located in one corner of the room.

PROCEDURE   Each *S*, accompanied by his mother, was placed in the obser- vation room. The mother was instructed to watch his play and respond in any way she desired. Most mothers simply watched and responded only when asked for something. The mother was also told that we would be observing from the next room. She held the child on her lap, the door to the playroom was closed, and observation began. At the beginning of the 15 minutes of play, the mother was instructed to place the child on the floor.

MEASUREMENT   Two observers recorded the *S*'s behavior. One dictated a continuous behavioral account into a tape recorder. The second operated an event recorder, which recorded the location of the child in the room and the duration of each contact with the mother.

Dictated Recording   During the initial dictation, a buzzer sounded at regular time intervals, automatically placing a marker on the dictated tape. The dictated behavioral account was typed and each minute divided into 15-second units, each including about three typewritten lines. The typed material was further divided into three 5-second units, each unit being one typed line. Independent experimenters analyzed this typed material. For each minute, the number of toys played with and amount of time spent with each toy was recorded.

Event Recorder   To facilitate recording the activity and location of the child, the floor of the room was divided into 12 squares. For each square, the observer depressed a key on the event recorder for the duration of time the child occupied that square. From this record it was possible to obtain such measures as the amount of time spent in each square and the number of squares traversed. A thirteenth key was depressed each time the child touched the mother. From this record, measures of (a) initial latency in leaving the mother, (b) total amount of time touching the mother, (c) number of times touching the mother, and (d) longest period touching the mother were obtained.

The data analysis presented in this report provides information only on sex differences (a) in response to the mother and (b) in choice and style of play with toys. Other data from this situation are presented elsewhere (Lewis, 1967).

RESULTS

RESPONSE TO MOTHER (13 MONTHS)   *Open Field*   Boys and girls showed striking differences in their behavior toward their mothers (see Table 1). First, upon being removed from their mothers' laps, girls were reluctant to leave their mothers. When Ss were placed on the floor by their mothers, significantly more girls than boys returned immediately—in less than 5 seconds ($p < .05$ for both samples by Fisher Exact Probability Test). This reluctance to leave their mothers is further indicated by the time it took the children to first return to their mothers. Girls, in both samples, showed significantly shorter latencies than boys. Out of a possible 900 seconds (15 minutes), girls returned after an average of 273.5 seconds, while boys' average latency was nearly twice as long, 519.5 seconds. This difference was highly significant ($p < .002$, Mann-Whitney U test). All significance tests are two-tailed unless otherwise specified.

TABLE 1

Summary of Infant Behavior to Mother in Free Play Session

BEHAVIOR	GIRLS	BOYS	p
Touching mother:			
$\bar{x}$ latency in seconds to return to mother	273.5	519.5	< .002
$\bar{x}$ number of returns	8.4	3.9	< .001
$\bar{x}$ number of seconds touching mother	84.6	58.8	< .03
Vocalization to mother:			
$\bar{x}$ number of seconds vocalizing to mother	169.8	106.9	< .04
Looking at mother:			
$\bar{x}$ number of seconds looking at mother	57.3	47.0	< .09
$\bar{x}$ number of times looking at mother	10.8	9.2	NS
Proximity to mother:			
$\bar{x}$ time in squares closest to mother	464.1	351.4	< .05
$\bar{x}$ time in squares farthest from mother	43.8	44.3	NS

Once the children left their mothers, girls made significantly more returns, both physical and visual. Girls touched their mothers for an average of 84.6 seconds, while boys touched their mothers for only 58.8 seconds ($p < .03$, Mann-Whitney U test). Girls returned to touch their mothers on an average of 8.4 times, and boys 3.9 times ($p < .001$, Mann-Whitney U test). For the visual returns, the number of times the child looked at the mother and the total amount of time spent looking at the mother were obtained from the dictated material. The mean number of times girls looked at the mother was 10.8 (as compared with 9.2 for boys), a difference which was not significant. The total amount of time looking at the mother was 57.3 seconds for girls and 47.0 seconds for boys ($p < .09$, Mann-Whitney U test).

Finally, vocalization data were also available from the dictated material. The mean time vocalizing to the mother was 169.8 seconds for girls and 106.9 seconds for boys ($p < .04$, Mann-Whitney U test).

Another measure of the child's response to his mother was the amount of physical distance the child allowed between himself and his mother. Because the observers recorded which squares the child played in, it was possible to obtain the amount of time Ss spent in the four squares closest to the mother. The mean time in these squares for girls was 464.1 seconds; for boys, it was 351.4 seconds ($p < .05$, Mann-Whitney U test). Moreover, boys spent more time in the square farthest from the mother, although the differences were not significant.

Barrier Frustration   At the end of the 15 minutes of free play, a barrier of mesh on a wood frame was placed in such a way as to divide the room in half. The mother placed the child on one side and remained on the opposite side along with the toys. Thus, the child's response to stress was observed.

TABLE 2

Summary of Infant Behavior During Barrier Frustration

BEHAVIOR	GIRLS	BOYS	p
$\bar{x}$ number of seconds crying	123.5	76.7	$< .05$
$\bar{x}$ number of seconds at ends of barrier	106.1	171.0	$< .001$
$\bar{x}$ number of seconds at center	157.7	95.1	$< .01$

Sex differences were again prominent, with girls crying and motioning for help consistently more than boys (see Table 2 and Fig. 1). For both samples, amount of time crying was available from the dictated record. Girls' mean time crying was 123.5 seconds, compared with 76.7 seconds for boys ($p < .05$, Mann-Whitney U test). Boys, on the other hand, appeared to make a more active attempt to get around the barrier. That is, they spent significantly more time at the ends of the barrier than girls, while girls spent significantly more time in the centre of the barrier—near the position where they were placed ($p < .01$, Mann-Whitney U test).

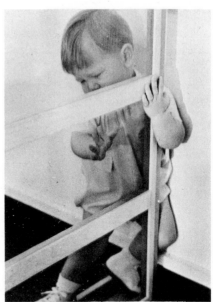

FIGURE 1.   *These two pictures illustrate typical sex differences in children responding to a frustration situation. The girl, at the left, is standing at the middle of the barrier and crying helplessly, while the boy, at the right, though showing signs of distress, is making an active attempt to get around the barrier.*

TOY PREFERENCE (13 MONTHS)   A second area of experimental interest was toy preference. When the nine toys were ranked in order of the total amount of time they were played with, girls and boys showed similar patterns of preference.

Table 3 presents each toy and the amount of time it was played with. Play with the dog and cat were combined into one category. The toys which were used most were the lawnmower, blocks, and quoits, and those that were used least were the stuffed dog and cat. On a *post hoc* basis, it seems as if the toys which received the most attention were those that offered the most varied possibilities for manipulation.

Although there were no sex differences in overall toy preference, there were significant sex differences in the amount of time spent with individual toys and in the ways toys were used. Girls played with blocks, pegboard, and with the dog and cat (the only toys with faces) more than boys did ($p < .03, p < .03, p < .01$, respectively, Mann-Whitney U test).

In terms of style of play, there were also sex differences (see Fig. 2). Observation of girls' play indicates that girls chose toys which involved more fine than gross muscle coordination, while for boys, the reverse was true—building blocks and playing with dog and cat versus playing with mallet and rolling the lawnmower over other toys. Moreover, boys spent more time playing with the nontoys (doorknob, covered outlets, lights, etc.; $p < .005$, Mann-Whitney U test).

In terms of overall activity level, boys were more active than girls. Girls

TABLE 3

Mean Time Playing with Toys, by Sex

	GIRLS	BOYS	*p*
Total time with:			
Mallet	51.7	60.8	–
Bug	50.2	45.3	–
Pail	34.6	22.9	–
Blocks	126.5	77.5	<.03
Lawnmower	220.3	235.6	–
Cat plus dog (combined)	31.0	9.1	<.01
Quoits	122.7	130.3	–
Pegboard	37.2	28.7	<.05
Nontoys	6.9	31.0	<.005
Putting toys in pail	28.2	43.0	–
Banging toys	19.7	34.8	<.05
Lawnmowing on other toys	2.8	9.8	–
Other manipulation of two toys	28.2	10.3	<.05

tended to sit and play with combinations of toys ($p < .05$, Mann-Whitney U test), while boys tended to be more active and bang the toys significantly more than girls ($p < .05$, Mann-Whitney U test). In addition, the children were rated by two observers on the vigor of their play behavior; a rating of 1 was given for high vigor, 2 was given for medium vigor, and 3 for low vigor. These ratings were made from the dictated material for each minute, so that the final

FIGURE 2.   *These pictures illustrate some of the sex differences observed in play behavior. The little girl, at the left, is squatting in one place, cuddling a soft animal. In contrast, the little boy, right, is actively swinging and banging the lawnmower over other toys.*

score for each S represented a mean of 15 vigor ratings. The interobserver reliability was $\rho = .78$. The boys played significantly more vigorously than girls (mean for boys was 2.45, varying from 1.2 to 3.0; for girls, the mean was 2.65, varying from 1.9 to 3.0 [$p < .05$, Mann-Whitney U test]). This vigor difference was also seen in the style of boys' play; for example, boys banged with the mallet and mowed over other toys. Thus, there were not only significant differences in the choice of toys, but also in the way the toys were manipulated. The data indicate that there are important and significant sex differences in very young children's response to their mothers, to frustration, and in play behavior.

Mother-Infant Touch (6 Months)   One possible determinant of the child's behavior toward the mother in the playroom is the mother's behavior toward the child at an earlier age. The 6-month data indicated that mothers of girls touched their infants more than mothers of boys. On the composite score, where 1 indicated most touching and 7 least, there were twice as many girls as boys whose mothers were rated 1–3 and twice as many boys as girls whose mothers were rated 5–7 ($p < .05$, χ^2 test). Moreover, mothers vocalized to girls significantly more than to boys ($p < .001$, Mann-Whitney U test), and significantly more girls than boys were breast-fed rather than bottle-fed ($p < .02$, Mann-Whitney U test). Thus, when the children were 6 months old, mothers touched, talked to, and handled their daughters more than their sons, and when they were 13 months old, girls touched and talked to their mothers more than boys did. To explore this relationship further, mothers were divided into high, medium, and low mother-touch-infant groups (at 6 months), with the extreme groups consisting of the upper and lower 25 per cent of the sample. For the boys at 13 months, the mean number of seconds of physical contact with the mother indicated a linear relation to amount of mother touching (14, 37, and 47 seconds for the low, medium, and high mother-touch groups, respectively; Kruskal-Wallis, $p < .10$). Thus, the more physical contact the mother made with a boy at 6 months, the more he touched the mother at 13 months. For the girls, the relation appeared to be curvilinear. The mean number of seconds of touching the mother for the low, medium, and high mother-touch groups was 101, 55, and 88 seconds, respectively (Kruskal-Wallis, $p < .10$). The comparable distribution for number of seconds close to the mother was 589, 397, and 475 seconds (Kruskal-Wallis, $p < .03$). A girl whose mother initiated very much or very little contact with her at 6 months was more likely to seek a great deal of physical contact with the mother in the playroom than one whose mother was in the medium-touch infant group.

Observation of the mothers' behavior when their infants were 6 months old revealed that five of the seven mothers of girls who showed little physical contact were considered by the staff to be severely rejecting mothers. The data suggest that the child of a rejecting mother continues to seek contact despite the mother's behavior. This result is consistent with Harlow's work with rejected monkeys (Seay, Alexander, & Harlow, 1964) and Provence's work with institutionalized children (Provence, 1965; Provence & Lipton, 1962) and suggests that the child's need for contact with his mother is a powerful motive.

DISCUSSION

Observation of the children's behavior indicated that girls were more dependent, showed less exploratory behavior, and their play behavior reflected a more quiet style. Boys were independent, showed more exploratory behavior, played with toys requiring gross motor activity, were more vigorous, and tended to run and bang in their play. Obviously, these behavior differences approximate those usually found between the sexes at later ages. The data demonstrate that these behavior patterns are already present in the first year of life and that some of them suggest a relation to the mother's response to the infant in the first 6 months. It is possible that at 6 months, differential behavior on the part of the mother is already a response to differential behavior on the part of the infant. Moss (1967) has found behavioral sex differences as early as 3 weeks. In interpreting mother-infant interaction data, Moss suggests that maternal behavior is initially a response to the infant's behavior. As the infant becomes older, if the mother responds contingently to his signals, her behavior acquires reinforcement value which enables her to influence and regulate the infant's behavior. Thus, parents can be active promulgators of sex-role behavior through reinforcement of sex-role-appropriate responses within the first year of life.

The following is offered as a hypothesis concerning sex-role learning. In the first year or two, the parents reinforce those behaviors they consider sex-role appropriate and the child learns these sex-role behaviors independent of any internal motive, that is, in the same way he learns any appropriate response rewarded by his parents. The young child has little idea as to the rules governing this reinforcement. It is suggested, however, that as the child becomes older (above age 3), the rules for this class of reinforced behavior become clearer and he develops internal guides to follow these earlier reinforced rules. In the past, these internalized rules, motivating without apparent reinforcement, have been called modeling behavior. Thus, modeling behavior might be considered an extension or internalization of the earlier reinforced sex-role behavior. However, it is clear that the young child, before seeking to model his behavior, is already knowledgeable in some appropriate sex-role behavior. In that the hypothesis utilizes both early reinforcement as well as subsequent cognitive elaboration, it would seem to bridge the reinforcement notion of Gewirtz (1967) and Kohlberg's cognitive theory (1966) of identification.

The fact that parents are concerned with early display of sex-role-appropriate behavior is reflected in an interesting clinical observation. On some occasions, staff members have incorrectly identified the sex of an infant. Mothers are often clearly irritated by this error. Since the sex of a fully clothed infant is difficult to determine, the mistake seems understandable and the mother's displeasure uncalled for. If, however, she views the infant and behaves toward him in a sex-appropriate way, our mistake is more serious. That is, the magnitude of her displeasure reveals to us the magnitude of her cognitive commitment to this infant as a child of given sex.

Regardless of the interpretation of the observed sex differences, the free play procedure provides a standardized situation in which young children can be observed without interference from experimental manipulation. While behavior under these conditions may be somewhat different from the young child's typical daily behavior, our data indicate that behavior in the play situation is related to other variables, that behavior can be predicted from earlier events, and that it is indicative of later sex-role behavior. The results of the present investigation as well as the work of Bell and Costello (1964), Kagan and Lewis (1965), and Lewis (in press) indicate sex differences within the first year over a wide variety of infant behaviors. The fact that sex differences do appear in the first year has important methodological implications for infant research. These findings emphasize the importance of checking sex differences before pooling data and, most important, of considering sex as a variable in any infant study.

References

BELL, R. Q., & COSTELLO, N. S. Three tests for sex differences in tactile sensitivity in the newborn. *Biologia Neonatorum*, 1964, **1**, 335–347.

FREUD, S. Three contributions to the theory of sex. Reprinted in *The basic writings of Sigmund Freud*. New York: Random House, 1938.

GEWIRTZ, J. The learning of generalized imitation and its implications for identification. Paper presented at the Society for Research in Child Development Meeting, New York, March, 1967.

KAGAN, J., & LEWIS, M. Studies of attention in the human infant. *Merrill-Palmer Quarterly*, 1965, **11**, 95–127.

KOHLBERG, L. A cognitive-developmental analysis of children's sex role concepts and attitudes. In E. Maccoby (Ed.), *The development of sex differences*. Stanford, Calif.: Stanford University Press, 1966.

LEWIS, M. Infant attention: response decrement as a measure of cognitive processes, or what's new, Baby Jane? Paper presented at the Society for Research in Child Development Meeting, symposium on "The Role of Attention in Cognitive Development," New York, March, 1967.

———. Infants' responses to facial stimuli during the first year of life. *Developmental Psychology*, in press.

MACCOBY, E. (Ed.) *The development of sex differences*. Stanford, Calif.: Stanford University Press, 1966.

MOSS, H. Sex, age and state as determinants of mother-infant interaction. *Merrill-Palmer Quarterly*, 1967, **13** (1), 19–36.

PIAGET, J. *Play, dreams and imitation in childhood*. New York: Norton, 1951.

PROVENCE, S. Disturbed personality development in infancy: a comparison of two inadequately nurtured infants. *Merrill-Palmer Quarterly*, 1965, **2**, 149–170.

———, & LIPTON, R. C. *Infants in institutions*. New York: International Universities Press, 1962.

SEAY, B., ALEXANDER, B. K., & HARLOW, H. F. Maternal behavior of socially deprived rhesus monkeys. *Journal of Abnormal and Social Psychology*, 1964, **69**(4), 345–354.

Crib Mates

Bruno Bettelheim
UNIVERSITY OF CHICAGO

This importance of the peer group begins in the very first days of life. We do not know whether, in the human being, something akin to the imprinting of animals takes place. But there is no doubt that the earliest experiences make a deep impact and are hence apt to shape all later ones in some measure.

Imprinting is thus nothing but an extremely important early experience. And in our own culture, at this most impressionable age, it is only or mainly the mother's image that is scanned by the infant as he nurses. In the kibbutz, by comparison, what greets the infant who wakens to feed, and looks around at his world? As likely as not, and from the very beginning, he sees just as much of the metapelets and other mothers tending their babies, as he does his own mother. She only emerges as separate and special when she puts him to breast.

Much more important in time and emotional impact are the constant companions who live in his room. Them he always sees and reacts to. Much of the waking time spent by the middle-class infant watching his parents, the kibbutz infant spends watching his roommates. As a matter of fact, so important may be the infant in the crib next to him, for example, that if his crib mate is moved to another room he may lose his appetite and get run down, a condition that improves when his "friend" or "twin" is returned.

Separation anxiety in the kibbutz is thus very typically experienced around the absence of a peer. And it can never be felt as acutely as by the middle-class infant whose mother leaves him, because however important the infant in the next crib, he is not the only one in the room, nor the only one life revolves around. At least two others are still left for companionship. And while the positive attachment to one person (the mother) seems diluted, when compared to our settings, separation anxiety is much less acute because of the continuing presence of several important others (metapelet, other infants). Thus again if we consider only the positive attachments, things seem to favor the middle-class child. But if we consider the ratio between security gained from positive attachment versus separation anxiety, it may very well be that kibbutz infants again enjoy the advantage.

While all children are "children of the kibbutz," and feel essentially like siblings, this is not just a matter of semantics. Those children who, from birth on, live together as an age-group, experience each other not only as siblings but as twins, since they were nurslings together and close crib companions. True, they do not share identical parents, and their heredity is radically different. But because of their otherwise "twinlike" existence they show some of the psychological features that characterize twins: the deep dependence and reliance on each other, the feeling that no one but their twin can ever fully understand them or share their innermost being. Only instead of one twin they have several, and of both sexes.

Because of this, though for other reasons too, the polarization, through which one twin often asserts his identity by being as different as possible from the other twin, I did not find in the kibbutz. I got to know one set of twins rather well. From all appearances (and from what I was told) they were identical twins, and by that time quite grown up. While extremely close to each other, they showed few of the characteristics I observe among identical twins in our setting. They were neither "half" a person without the other, nor did they show any need to develop in opposite ways to feel secure in their personal identity. My guess is that, having lived "like twins" from birth on with several others, and not just their own twin, they did not feel as dependent on each other as seems true of twins in our families.

Perhaps the difference in parentage and natural endowment gives enough real differentiation to those who from birth on grow up like twins so that there is no need to strive for any more on their own. It is not enough, though, to cancel out the strange situation that four or more infants share all vital steps in growing up and developing, as would be true with us only of twins or of infants growing up in institutions.

This is why the kibbutz child, in his relatedness to other children, feels closest to his very own age-group, in many ways more so than to his natural siblings, who come next, and third, to all other kibbutz children.

What does this collective life look like, for the older infant from the time he can crawl? These infants, when they wake, are placed in large playpens; then, as soon as they can walk, in rather large, fenced-in play spaces. For many periods of the day, even when the metapelets are supposedly taking care of a group of infants or toddlers, they are left to their own devices. Often this is for hours at a stretch, while the metapelets clean the house, fetch the food, sort the laundry, do the mending. During this time the infant, and later the small child, is never alone, as an infant raised at home might be even if the mother is just busy in another room.

In playpen and play yard the children crawl over each other, push each other down, and while at first the pushed down child may wail, he soon learns his place in the pecking order and adjusts accordingly. But life is not just bad times and getting pushed down; most of the time the children play successfully together. Since no parent interferes with the pecking order, and even the metapelet does so only rarely, each child stays in his given place and soon learns to play according to the hierarchy established. As long as he does, and soon they all learn to do it for most of the time, there is always someone to play with; they are never alone.

American readers will wonder what happens to the low man on the totem pole, to the weak child or the meek one who—were this a society based on nothing but the pecking order—would always come last, would never come into his own except by withdrawing or submitting. And this might well happen in our competitive society where winning is so highly valued. But things are not so in the kibbutz.

I did not see a single case of a bully or of bullying. I did see the weaker infants pushed over by stronger ones, but never deliberately—if one can speak of being deliberate in such things before the age of two—nor gloatingly. And thereafter such a child was usually picked up and comforted by another child, sometimes by the one who pushed him down. Depending, of course, on the relative maturity of the child, this stage may be reached anywhere between age two and two-and-a-half.

By toddler age, then, life is truly with the group; the children are comrades, not competitors. If one is stronger, he will use and occasionally misuse his strength, but not for long. Very soon the group spirit asserts itself, and he feels the disapproval and desists. The spirit of helpfulness among them is much more evident than the desire for dominance. Since there are no parents around for whom to vie, and since the competitive spirit is frowned on, the push is toward acting like brothers and sisters, where the stronger one exerts some controlling influence, but also feels called on to use it in the interests of his brothers and sisters. And this is well established by the toddler age. But even before then, they have all learned to be self-reliant to a degree most uncommon in our middle-class settings.

How early they are forced by the arrangements to learn self-reliance may be illustrated by two observations made in one of the oldest and wealthiest of left-wing kibbutzim. The first one concerns babies and occurred while I was interviewing an elderly metapelet, in charge of the infants' house there for many years. I was asking how many babies she had in her care, and she told me there were sixteen in the nursery, but that each metapelet was only responsible for four. "I work four hours in the morning," she said, "from 7:00 to 11:00, and then I return again at 12:30."

I wondered what happens then, between 11:00 and 12:30? (The time, then, was shortly after 11:00, and the babies were in a playpen on the porch, just outside the room where we spoke.) The answer was: "They don't need anybody, they're in the playpen during that time." Nevertheless, we could hardly hear each other at times because the wailing of the babies was so loud. So I said I could hear them crying right now so they seemed to need someone to look after them, and the metapelet told me: "If they cry too long, some other metapelet will look to see what's the matter. There is always one metapelet in the house serving all four groups."

The crying continued, and I went out to see what went on. I found seven babies in a large playpen out in the sun, with some nice toys in it. Two bigger babies crawled all over a little one and took a toy away from him. He cried for a long time while the one metapelet on duty was occupied with washing furniture. Finally she came out on the porch and picked up the crying one for a moment but without comforting him. He continued to cry, but more quietly now. So she put him down at another spot in the playpen and left. And soon he stopped crying and went about his business.

As soon as the being picked up may have raised some hopeful expectations in the baby, he was returned to the old situation to fend for himself as best he could. If many such experiences are repeated, as they are, it may force the infant (and all other infants who watch it) to give up hoping for comfort from a mother figure, or any desire for her presence.

It was not that the metapelet was insensitive. She was merely convinced

that the baby had to learn to get along in his group, and not to rely on the inter-
cession of someone outside it; that her comforting would only retard a piece of
learning that was more important than temporary discomfort.

And a year or two later, when they are toddlers, they have indeed learned
much: how to fend for themselves, how to get along with the group, how to find
comfort there and satisfaction. One day, for example, I observed an entire
toddlers-house group who had been playing for quite a while in the large play
space in front of their house while the metapelet was away fetching their lunch
from the communal kitchen and her adolescent helper was inside setting the
table. On her return the metapelet called to the children to come in for lunch.

Scrambling to get there, one little boy fell and started to cry; he had
obviously hurt himself. The metapelet very nicely went over to him, picked
him up, but then set him down a moment later, before she had really discovered what was wrong, and long before he had quieted down or been
reassured. She then went indoors because she had to, since there were now some
fourteen children inside to be taken care of and fed by her and her helper.

Eventually after some hard inner struggle the boy fought down his crying.
The others were too busy with their meal and each other to offer comfort at
this moment, so the best thing was to join them as soon as he could. But first
he took a knife from the table and went back outside where he sat down to
scrape the dirt off his slightly bleeding knee. This took some time, and quite a
few minutes later, he was still there and had not yet come to the table.

The metapelet could not have returned to him easily, even had she wished.
Her other duties forbade it. But after some ten minutes the boy had got complete
hold of himself and rejoined the group. He really had no true choice in the
matter. Had he stayed behind, he would have gotten no comfort for his hurt
and would not only have missed out on lunch but also the companionship of
the children and metapelet.

During this same toddler age, though, the peer group also comes to be a
source of comfort in lieu of adults. It was charming, for example, to see a three-
year-old come up to an age-mate who was upset about something, inviting him
to play, cheering him up, leading him back to the group. But because of it,
the small child is more and more relieved of having to struggle by himself with
an inner experience. Because even (or especially) if no other comfort is available.
the group and its doings are always there to divert his attention to an external
experience with them, and away from the one with himself.

At critical times, such as at night, small children have only their mutual
comforting to rely on, since it may take quite a while for the single night watch
to hear a child who wakes up crying, and a bit longer till he or she comes
around. Though no one in the small community is entirely a stranger, the night
watch rotates among members from day to day, or week to week. So even
when the night watch is finally summoned by the child's anxious cry, the person
who comes when the child thus awakens from a nightmare, deeply shaken, is
more or less a stranger and can therefore give only small comfort. But as likely
as not, when the night watch finally gets there, he finds that some other child
has already soothed the anxious one.

Thus when in deep emotional distress, the kibbutz child soon learns to rely
on the help of another child for comfort and security. Later on, too, it will more

likely be a more advanced or a bit older child in his peer group and not the metapelet who will help him on the toilet, with getting dressed, and at all other times when he cannot manage by himself.

Behavior Problems Revisited:
Findings of an Anterospective Study*

Stella Chess and Alexander Thomas
NEW YORK UNIVERSITY SCHOOL OF MEDICINE

Herbert G. Birch
ALBERT EINSTEIN COLLEGE OF MEDICINE

A number of theoretical formulations have been advanced to explain the origin and nature of behavior problems in childhood. These have included the constitutionalist view in which the symptoms of disturbance are considered to be the direct expression of a predetermined constitutional pattern in the child, the psychoanalytic view in which disturbance is seen as the outcome of conflicts between instinctual drive seeking expression and satisfaction and repressing forces seeking to inhibit or contain them, the learning theory approach in which symptoms are viewed as conditioned maladaptive learned patterns based on conditioned reflex formations, and the culturist view in which symptoms are considered to be the more or less direct expression of sociocultural influences.

A unique opportunity to investigate the genesis and evolution of behavior problems and to test the validity of these theories has presented itself during the course of our New York longitudinal study of individuality in behavioral development. In this study, in progress since 1956, 39 of the 136 children who have been followed from the earliest months of life onward by a variety of data-gathering techniques have developed behavior disturbances of various types and varying degrees of severity.

Until now, none of the numerous studies in the field has provided a body of evidence sufficient to validate one or another of the extant theoretical formulations. Aside from any other questions as to the adequacy of the data offered as evidence, the approaches have relied primarily on data gathered retrospectively. A number of recent studies, including several from our own center, have revealed significant distortions in retrospective parental reports on the early developmental histories of their children (Robbins, 1963; Wenar, 1963; Chess et al., 1966). It has become clear that retrospective data are insufficient for the study of the genesis of behavior disorders and that anterospective data gathered by longitudinal developmental studies are essential.

Reprinted from *The Journal of the American Academy of Child Psychiatry*, 1967, 6, 321–331. Copyright © 1967 by International Universities Press, Inc. By permission.

* This investigation was supported by Grant MH-03614 from the National Institute of Mental Health.

Previous longitudinal studies—at Berkeley (MacFarlane et al., 1954), the Fels Institute (Kagan and Moss, 1962), Yale (Kris, 1957), and Topeka (Murphy et al., 1962)—have made certain contributions to the understanding of the evolution of behavior disorders. The possible significance of temperamental characteristics of the child in interaction with parental functioning has been indicated. A lack of correlation between the child's patterns of psychodynamic defenses and the occurrence of behavioral dysfunction has been found. Symptoms typical of various age-periods have been tabulated, their vicissitudes over time traced, and correlations among different symptoms determined. However, each of these studies has been limited either by small sample size, which has not permitted generalization of the findings, or by the absence of systematic psychiatric evaluation of the children, which has severely restricted the possibility of categorizing the behavior disturbance and of making meaningful correlations with the longitudinal behavioral data.

Our New York longitudinal study has had available, by contrast, both a total sample of substantial size and the data resulting from independent clinical psychiatric evaluation in all of the children with behavior problems. The data on the total sample include information gathered longitudinally and anterospectively at sequential age levels from early infancy onward on the nature of the child's own individual characteristics of functioning at home, in school, and in standard test situations; on parental attitudes and child care practices; on special environmental events and the child's reactions to such events; and on intellectual functioning. In addition, psychiatric evaluation has been done in each child presenting symptoms by the staff child psychiatrist. Wherever necessary, neurological examination or special testing, such as perceptual tests, have been done. Clinical follow-up of each child with a problem has also been carried out systematically.

Details of the data-gathering procedures and of the techniques of data analysis have been reported elsewhere (Chess et al., 1962; Thomas et al., 1963). Since the developmental data were gathered before the child was viewed as a problem by either the parent or the psychiatrist, they were uncontaminated by the distortions which inevitably attend retrospective histories obtained after the appearance of the behavioral disturbance. Data as to environmental influences, such as parental practices and attitudes, changes in family structure, illnesses and hospitalization, and the character of the school situation, were also obtained in advance of the behavioral disturbance and so were also not distorted by the fact of pathology.

The size of the sample and the nature of the data have made possible various quantitative analyses comparing children with and without behavior problems as well as individual longitudinal case studies. In all our analyses we have been concerned with tracing the ontogenesis and development of each behavioral disturbance in terms of the interaction of temperament and environment, as well as the influence of additional factors in specific cases, such as brain damage, physical abnormalities, and characteristics of intellectual functioning. *Temperament*, in our usage, refers to the behavioral style of the individual child and contains no inferences as to genetic, endocrine, somatologic or environmental etiologies. It is a phenomenological term used to describe the characteristic tempo, energy expenditure, focus, mood, and rhythmicity typifying the behaviors of the individual child, independently of their contents. We have used nine categories of reactivity within which to subsume temperamental attributes. They are activity level, rhythmicity, adaptability, approach withdrawal, intensity of reaction, quality of mood, sensory threshold, distractibility, and persistence and attention span.[1] A child's temperamental organization, therefore, represents his characteristic mode of functioning with respect to these features of behavioral organization. It refers to the *how* rather than to the *what* or the *why* of behavior. No implications of permanence or immutability attach to such a conception.

The prevalence rate of behavior problems in our study population approximates that found in other studies (Lapouse and Monk, 1958; Glidewell et al., 1963). The types of symptoms were typical of those usually coming to notice in preschool and early school age children of middle-class highly educated parents.

In each of the thirty-nine children with behavior problems the psychiatric assessment has been followed by a detailed culling of all the anterospective data from early infancy onward for pertinent information on temperament, environmental influences, and the sequences of symptom appearance and development. It has been possible in each case to trace the ontogenesis of the behavioral disturbances in terms of the interaction of temperament and environment. Temperament alone did not produce behavioral disturbance. Instances of children of closely similar temperamental structure to the children with behavior problems were found in the normally functioning group. Rather, it appeared that both behavioral disturbance as well as behavioral normality were the result of the interaction between the child with a given patterning of temperament and significant features of his developmental environment. Among these environmental features intrafamilial as well as extrafamilial circumstances such as school and peer group were influential. In several cases, additional special factors such as brain damage or physical abnormality were also operative in interaction with temperament and environment to produce symptoms of disturbed development.

A number of case summaries illustrating typical interactive patterns of development in children with and without behavior problems have been presented in several previous publications (Chess et al., 1963; Birch et al., 1964). At this time we would like to present some of the characteristic temperamental patterns found among the children, the environmental demands which are typically stressful for children with each of these temperamental constellations, and the parental and other environmental approaches which intensify such stressful demands to the point of symptom formation. Symptoms manifested by the children included tantrums, aggressive behavior, habit disorders, fears, learning difficulties, nonparticipation in play activities with other children, and lack of normal assertiveness.

A temperamental pattern which produced the greatest risk of behavior problem development comprises the combination of irregularity in biological functions, predominantly negative (withdrawal) responses to new stimuli, nonadaptability or slow adaptability to change, frequent negative mood, and

---

[1] See Thomas et al. (1963) for criteria of each of the nine categories and for details of the scoring method.

predominantly intense reactions. As infants, children with this pattern show irregular sleep and feeding patterns, slow acceptance of new foods, prolonged adjustment periods to new routines, and frequent periods of loud crying. Their laughter, too, is characteristically loud. Mothers find them difficult to care for, and pediatricians frequently refer to them as the "difficult infants." They are not easy to feed, to put to sleep, to bathe, or to dress. New places, new activities, strange faces—all may produce initial responses of loud protest or crying. Frustration characteristically produces a violent tantrum. These children approximate 10 percent of the total study population but comprise a significantly higher proportion of the behavior problem group (Rutter et al., 1964). The stressful demands for these children are typically those of socialization, namely, the demands for alteration of spontaneous responses and patterns to conform to the rules of living of the family, the school, the peer group, etc. It is also characteristic of these children that once they do learn the rules, they function easily, consistently, and energetically.

We have found no evidence that the parents of the difficult infants are essentially different from the other parents. Nor do our studies suggest that the temperamental characteristics of the children are caused by the parents. The issue is rather that the care of these infants makes special requirements upon their parents for unusually firm, patient, consistent, and tolerant handling. Such handling is necessary if the difficult infant is to learn to adapt to new demands with a minimum of stress. If the new demand is presented inconsistently, impatiently or punitively effective change in behavior becomes stressful and even impossible. Negativism is a not infrequent outcome of such suboptimal parental functioning.

The problems of managing a difficult child not infrequently highlight a parent's individual reaction to stress. The same parents who are relaxed and consistent with an easy child may become resentful, guilty, or helpless with a difficult child, depending on their own personality structures. Other parents, by contrast, who do not feel guilty or put upon by the child's behavior may learn to enjoy the vigor, lustiness, and "stubbornness" of a difficult infant.

At the opposite end of the temperamental spectrum from the difficult infant is the child who is regular, responds positively to new stimuli (approaches), adapts quickly and easily to change, and shows a predominantly positive mood of mild or moderate intensity. These are the infants who develop regular sleep and feeding schedules easily, take to most new foods at once, smile at strangers, adapt quickly to a new school, accept most frustrations with a minimum of fuss, and learn the rules of new games quickly. They are aptly called "easy babies" and are usually a joy to their parents, pediatricians, and teachers. By contrast to the difficult infant, the easy child adapts to the demands for socialization with little or no stress and confronts his parents with few if any problems in handling. However, although these children do as a group develop significantly fewer behavior problems proportionately than do the difficult infants, their very ease of adaptability may under certain circumstances be the basis for problem behavior development. Most typically we have seen this occur when there is a severe dissonance between the expectations and demands of the intra- and extrafamilial environments. The child first adapts easily to the standards and behavioral expectations of the parent in the first few years of life. When he moves actively into functional situations outside the home, such as in peer play groups and school, stress and malfunctioning will develop if the extrafamilial standard and demands conflict sharply with the patterns learned in the home. As a typical example, the parents of one such child had a high regard for individuality of expression and disapproval of any behavior or attitude in their child which they identified as stereotypical or lacking in imagination. Self-expression was encouraged and conformity and attentiveness to rules imposed by others discouraged even when this resulted in ill manners and a disregard of the desires of others. As the child grew older she became increasingly isolated from her peer group because of continuous insistence on her own preferences. In school her progress was grossly unsatisfactory because of difficulty in listening to directions. The parents were advised to restructure their approach, to place less emphasis on individuality and instead to teach her to be responsive to the needs of others and to conform constructively in behavior in class and in activities with her peers. The parents, acutely aware of the child's growing social isolation and the potential seriousness of her educational problem, carried out this plan consistently. At follow-up, six months later, the child had adapted to the new rules easily, the conflict between standards within and without the home had become minimal, and she had become an active member of a peer group and had caught up to grade level in academic work.

It is certainly true that a severe dissonance between intra- and extra-familial environment demands and expectations may produce stress and disturbance in psychological development for many types of youngsters, including the difficult child. In our case series, however, it has been most readily apparent as a dominant pathogenic factor in these easy children.

Another important temperamental constellation comprises the combination of negative responses of mild intensity to new stimuli with slow adaptability after repeated contact. Children with this pattern differ from the difficult infants in that their withdrawal from the new is quiet rather than loud. They also usually do not have the irregularity of function, frequent negative mood expression, and intense reactions of the difficult infants. The mildly expressed withdrawal from the new is typically seen with the first encounter with the bath, a new person, a stranger, or a new place. With the first bath the child lies still and fusses mildly, with a new food he turns his head away quietly and lets it dribble out of his mouth, with a stranger who greets him loudly he clings to his mother. If given the opportunity to re-experience new situations without pressure, such a child gradually comes to show quiet and positive interest and involvement. This characteristic sequence of response has suggested the appellation the "Slow to Warm Up" as an apt if inelegant designation for these children. A key issue in their development is whether parents and teachers allow them to make an adaptation to the new at their own tempo or insist on the immediate positive involvement which is difficult or impossible for the slow-to-warm-up children. If the adult recognizes that the slow adaptation to a new school, new peer group or new academic subject reflects the child's normal temperamental style, patient encouragement is likely. If, on the contrary, the child's slow warm-up is interpreted as timidity or lack of interest, adult impatience and pressure on the child for quick adaptation may occur. The child's reaction to this stressful pressure is typically an intensification of his withdrawal tendency. If this increased holding back in turn stimulates increased impatience and pressure on the part of the parent or teacher, a destructive child-environment interactive process will be set in motion.

In several other instances in our study population, nursery school teachers have interpreted the child's slow initial adaptation as evidence of underlying anxiety. In still another case, an elementary school teacher estimated that a child's slow initial mastery of a new accelerated academic program indicated inadequate intellectual capacity. In these cases, the longitudinal behavioral records documented a slow warm-up temperamental style and made possible the recommendation that judgment be suspended until the child could have a longer period of contact with the new situation. The subsequent successful mastery of the demands of the new situation clarified the issue as one of temperamental style and not psychopathology or lack of intellectual capacity.

A contrast to the slow-to-warm-up child is the very persistent child who is most likely to experience stress not with his initial contact with a situation but during the course of his ongoing activity after the first positive adaptation has been made. His quality of persistence leads him to resist interference or attempts to divert him from an activity in which he is absorbed. If the adult interference is arbitrary and forcible, tension and frustration tend to mount quickly in these children and may reach explosive proportions.

Type-specific stress and maladaptive child-environment patterns can be identified for other temperamental patterns, such as the very distractible or highly active child, but the scope of this presentation does not permit their description.

Currently influential psychoanalytic theories of the ontogenesis of behavior problems place primary emphasis on the role of anxiety, intrapsychic conflict, and psychodynamic defenses. Our findings do not support these concepts. Our data suggest that anxiety, intrapsychic conflict, and psychodynamic defenses, when they do appear in the course of behavior problem development, are secondary phenomena which result from the stressful, maladaptive character of an unhealthy temperament-environment interaction. Once any or all of these secondary factors appear they can add a new dimension to the dynamics of the child-environment interaction and substantially influence the subsequent course of the behavior problem. It is not surprising that in retrospective studies which begin when the child already presents an extensively elaborated psychological disturbance the prominent phenomena of anxiety and conflict should be labeled as primary rather than secondary influences. Also, if the fact of temperamental individuality is not given serious attention, certain temperamental patterns, such as those of the difficult child or the child with a slow warm-up, are easily misinterpreted as the result of anxiety or as defenses against anxiety.

Our findings also challenge the validity of the currently prevalent assumption that a child's problem is a direct reaction of a one-to-one kind to unhealthy maternal influences. The slogan "To meet Johnny's mother is to understand his problem" expresses an all too frequent approach in which a study of the mother is substituted for a study of the complex factors which may have produced a child's disturbed development, of which parental influences are only one. Elsewhere we have described this unidirectional preoccupation of psychologists and psychiatrists with the pathogenic role of the mother as the "Mal de

Mere" syndrome (Chess, 1964). The harm done by this preoccupation has been enormous. Innumerable mothers have been unjustly burdened with deep feelings of guilt and inadequacy as a result of being incorrectly held exclusively or even primarily responsible for their children's problems. Diagnostic procedures have tended to be restricted to a study of the mother's assumed noxious attitudes and practices, with investigations in other directions conducted in a most cursory fashion, or not at all. Treatment plans have focused on methods of changing maternal attitudes and ameliorating the effects of presumed pathogenic maternal attitudes on the child and have ignored other significant etiological factors.

Our data on the origin and development of behavior problems in children emphasize the necessity to study the child—his temperamental characteristics, neurological status, intellectual capacities, and physical handicaps. The parents should also be studied rather than given global labels such as rejecting, overprotective, anxious, etc. Parental attitudes and practices are usually selective and not global, with differentiated characteristics in different areas of the child's life and with marked variability from child to child. Parent-child interaction should be analyzed not only for parental influences on the child but just as much for the influence of the child's individual characteristics on the parent. The influence of other intra- and extrafamilial environmental factors should be estimated in relation to the interactive pattern with each specific child with his individual characteristics rather than in terms of sweeping generalizations.

Our finding that an excessively stressful maladaptive temperament-environment interaction constitutes a decisive element in the development of behavior problems suggests that treatment should emphasize the modification of the interactive process so that it is less stressful and more adaptive. This requires first of all an identification of the pertinent temperamental and environmental issues. Parents can then be armed with this knowledge in the service of modifying their interactive pattern with the child in a healthy direction. Parent guidance rather than parent treatment should be the first aim. If the parent cannot learn to understand his child and utilize this understanding effectively, it then becomes pertinent to inquire into the factors which may be responsible for such a failure of parent guidance. In our experience such failures are in a minority. Most parents do appear able to cooperate in a parent guidance program. When this is accomplished, the parent and psychiatrist can truly become allies in the treatment of the child's problem.

References

BIRCH, H. G., THOMAS, A., & CHESS, S. (1964), Behavioral development in brain-damaged children: three case studies. *Arch. Gen. Psychiat.*, 11:596–603.

CHESS, S. (1964), Mal de Mere. *Amer. J. Orthopsychiat.*, 34:613–614.

———, HERTZIG, M., BIRCH, H. G., & THOMAS, A. (1962), Methodology of a study of adaptive functions of the preschool child. *This Journal*, 1:236–245.

———, THOMAS, A., & BIRCH, H. G. (1966), Distortions in developmental reporting made by parents of behaviorally disturbed children. *This Journal*, 5:226–234.

———, THOMAS, A., RUTTER, M., & BIRCH, H. G. (1963), Interaction of temperament and environment in the production of behavioral disturbances in children. *Amer. J. Psychiat.*, 120:142–148.

GLIDEWELL, J. C., DOMKE, H. R., & KANTOR, M. B. (1963), Screening in schools for behavior disorders: use of mother's report of symptoms. *J. Educ. Res.*, 56:508–515.

KAGAN, J. & MOSS, H. A. (1962), *Birth to Maturity: A Study in Psychological Development*. New York: Wiley.

KRIS, M. (1957), The use of prediction in a longitudinal study. *The Psychoanalytic Study of the Child*, 12:175–189. New York: International Universities Press.

LAPOUSE, R. & MONK, M. A. (1958), An epidemiologic study of behavior characteristics in children. *Amer. J. Pub. Hlth.*, 48:1134–1144.

MACFARLANE, J. W., ALLEN, L., & HONZIK, M. P. (1954), *A Developmental Study of the Behavior Problems of Normal Children between Twenty-one Months and Fourteen Years* [University of California Publications in Child Development, Vol. II]. Berkeley: University of California Press.

MURPHY, L. B. et al. (1962), *The Widening World of Childhood*. New York: Basic Books.

ROBBINS, L. C. (1963), The accuracy of parental recall of aspects of child development and of child-rearing practices. *J. Abnorm. Soc. Psychol.*, 66:261–270.

RUTTER, M., BIRCH, H. G., THOMAS, A., & CHESS, S. (1964), Temperamental characteristics in infancy and the later development of behavioral disorders. *Brit. J. Psychiat.*, 110:651–661.

THOMAS, A., CHESS, S., BIRCH, H. G., HERTZIG, M., & KORN, S. (1963), *Behavioral Individuality in Early Childhood*. New York: New York University Press.

WENAR, C. (1963), The reliability of developmental histories: summary and evaluation of evidence. *Psychosom. Med.*, 25:505–509.

Part Two

THE PRESCHOOL
CHILD

5

Personality and Body

The section on the preschool child begins with Erik H. Erikson's description of the two stages pertinent to this period. Although the critical period for development of the sense of autonomy begins in late infancy, it continues into the early preschool stage, the second and third years of life. The development of the sense of initiative then becomes crucial.

Because the student of child development needs a perspective on growth through childhood, the next selection is not confined to the preschool period. Pediatrician Dorothy V. Whipple writes on the nature of human growth and how it is measured, evaluated, and influenced. The term ages *in the title refers not only to stages of an individual's growth but also to historical ages. The measurement not only of height and weight, but of body build, the configuration of the human body, are dealt with here. We particularly wish to draw the reader's attention to Whipple's conclusions.*

One article relates physical development to behavior. The relationship between mildly deviant behavior and minor physical anomalies is explored in a study by Mary F. Waldrop and Charles F. Halverson, Jr.

Autonomy vs. Shame and Doubt
Initiative vs. Guilt

Erik H. Erikson
HARVARD UNIVERSITY

AUTONOMY VS. SHAME AND DOUBT

In describing the growth and the crises of the human person as a series of alternative basic attitudes such as trust vs. mistrust, we take recourse to the term a "sense of," although, like a "sense of health," or a "sense of being unwell," such "senses" pervade surface and depth, consciousness and the unconscious. They are, then, at the same time, ways of *experiencing* accessible to introspection; ways of *behaving*, observable by others; and unconscious *inner states* determinable by test and analysis. It is important to keep these three dimensions in mind, as we proceed.

Muscular maturation sets the stage for experimentation with two simultaneous sets of social modalities: holding on and letting go. As is the case with all of these modalities, their basic conflicts can lead in the end to either hostile or benign expectations and attitudes. Thus, to hold can become a destructive and cruel retaining or restraining, and it can become a pattern of care: to have and to hold. To let go, too, can turn into an inimical letting loose of destructive forces, or it can become a relaxed "to let pass" and "to let be."

Outer control at this stage, therefore, must be firmly reassuring. The infant must come to feel that the basic faith in existence, which is the lasting treasure saved from the rages of the oral stage, will not be jeopardized by this about-face of his, this sudden violent wish to have a choice, to appropriate demandingly, and to eliminate stubbornly. Firmness must protect him against the potential anarchy of his as yet untrained sense of discrimination, his inability to hold on and to let go with discretion. As his environment encourages him to "stand on his own feet," it must protect him against meaningless and arbitrary experiences of shame and of early doubt.

The latter danger is the one best known to us. For if denied the gradual and well-guided experience of the autonomy of free choice (or if, indeed, weakened by an initial loss of trust) the child will turn against himself all his urge to discriminate and to manipulate. He will overmanipulate himself, he will develop a precocious conscience. Instead of taking possession of things in order to test them by purposeful repetition, he will become obsessed by his own repetitiveness. By such obsessiveness, of course, he then learns to repossess the environment and to gain power by stubborn and minute control, where he could not find large-scale mutual regulation. Such hollow victory is the infantile model for a compulsion neurosis. It is also the infantile source of later attempts in adult life to govern by the letter, rather than by the spirit.

Shame is an emotion insufficiently studied, because in our civilization it is so early and easily absorbed by guilt. Shame supposes that one is completely exposed and conscious of being looked at: in one word, self-conscious. One is visible and not ready to be visible; which is why we dream of shame as a situation in which we are stared at in a condition of incomplete dress, in night attire, "with one's pants down." Shame is early expressed in an impulse to bury one's face, or to sink, right then and there, into the ground. But this, I think, is essentially rage turned against the self. He who is ashamed would like to force the world not to look at him, not to notice his exposure. He would like to destroy the eyes of the world. Instead he must wish for his own invisibility. This potentiality is abundantly used in the educational method of "shaming" used so exclusively by some primitive peoples. Visual shame precedes auditory guilt, which is a sense of badness to be had all by oneself when nobody watches and when everything is quiet—except the voice of the superego. Such shaming exploits an increasing sense of being small, which can develop only as the child stands up and as his awareness permits him to note the relative measures of size and power.

Too much shaming does not lead to genuine propriety but to a secret determination to try to get away with things, unseen—if, indeed, it does not result in defiant shamelessness. There is an impressive American ballad in which a murderer to be hanged on the gallows before the eyes of the community, instead of feeling duly chastened, begins to berate the onlookers, ending every salvo of defiance with the words, "God damn your eyes." Many a small child, shamed beyond endurance, may be in a chronic mood (although not in possession of either the courage or the words) to express defiance in similar terms. What I mean by this sinister reference is that there is a limit to a child's and an adult's endurance in the face of demands to consider himself, his body, and his wishes as evil and dirty, and to his belief in the infallibility of those who pass such judgment. He may be apt to turn things around, and to consider as evil only the fact that they exist: his chance will come when they are gone, or when he will go from them.

Doubt is the brother of shame. Where shame is dependent on the consciousness of being upright and exposed, doubt, so clinical observation leads me to believe, has much to do with a consciousness of having a front and a back—and especially a "behind." For this reverse area of the body, with its aggressive and libidinal focus in the sphincters and in the buttocks, cannot be seen by the child, and yet it can be dominated by the will of others. The "behind" is the small being's dark continent, an area of the body which can be magically dominated and effectively invaded by those who would attack one's power of autonomy and who would designate as evil those products of the bowels which were felt to be all right when they were being passed. This basic sense of doubt in whatever one has left behind forms a substratum for later and more verbal forms of compulsive doubting; this finds its adult expression in paranoiac fears concerning hidden persecutors and secret persecutions threatening from behind (and from within the behind).

This stage, therefore, becomes decisive for the ratio of love and hate, cooperation and willfulness, freedom of self-expression and its suppression. From a sense of self-control without loss of self-esteem comes a lasting sense of good will and pride; from a sense of loss of self-control and of foreign overcontrol comes a lasting propensity for doubt and shame.

If, to some reader, the "negative" potentialities of our stages seem overstated throughout, we must remind him that this is not only the result of a preoccupation with clinical data. Adults, and seemingly mature and unneurotic ones, display a sensitivity concerning a possible shameful "loss of face" and fear of being attacked "from behind" which is not only highly irrational and in contrast to the knowledge available to them, but can be of fateful import if related sentiments influence, for example, interracial and international policies.

We have related basic trust to the institution of religion. The lasting need of the individual to have his will reaffirmed and delineated within an adult order of things which at the same time reaffirms and delineates the will of others has an institutional safeguard in the *principle of law and order*. In daily life as well as in the high courts of law—domestic and international—this principle apportions to each his privileges and his limitations, his obligations and his rights. A sense of rightful dignity and lawful independence on the part of adults around him gives to the child of good will the confident expectation that the kind of autonomy fostered in childhood will not lead to undue doubt or shame in later life. Thus the sense of autonomy fostered in the child and modified as life progresses, serves (and is served by) the preservation in economic and political life of a sense of justice.

INITIATIVE VS. GUILT

There is in every child at every stage a new miracle of vigorous unfolding, which constitutes a new hope and a new responsibility for all. Such is the sense and the pervading quality of initiative. The criteria for all these senses and qualities are the same: a crisis, more or less beset with fumbling and fear, is resolved, in that the child suddenly seems to "grow together" both in his person and in his body. He appears "more himself," more loving, relaxed and brighter in his judgment, more activated and activating. He is in free possession of a surplus of energy which permits him to forget failures quickly and to approach what seems desirable (even if it also seems uncertain and even dangerous) with undiminished and more accurate direction. Initiative adds to autonomy the quality of undertaking, planning and "attacking" a task for the sake of being active and on the move, where before self-will, more often than not, inspired acts of defiance or, at any rate, protested independence.

I know that the very word "initative" to many, has an American, and industrial connotation. Yet, initiative is a necessary part of every act, and man needs a sense of initiative for whatever he learns and does, from fruit-gathering to a system of enterprise.

The ambulatory stage and that of infantile genitality add to the inventory of basic social modalities that of "making," first in the sense of "being on the make." There is no simpler, stronger word for it; it suggests pleasure in attack and conquest. In the boy, the emphasis remains on phallic-intrusive modes; in the girl it turns to modes of "catching" in more aggressive forms of snatching or in the milder form of making oneself attractive and endearing.

The danger of this stage is a sense of guilt over the goals contemplated and the acts initiated in one's exuberant enjoyment of new locomotor and mental power: acts of aggressive manipulation and coercion which soon go far beyond the executive capacity of organism and mind and therefore call for an energetic halt on one's contemplated initiative. While autonomy concentrates on keeping rivals out, and therefore can lead to jealous rage most often directed against encroachments by younger siblings, initiative brings with it anticipatory rivalry with those who have been there first and may, therefore, occupy with their superior equipment the field toward which one's initiative is directed. Infantile jealousy and rivalry, those often embittered and yet essentially futile attempts at demarcating a sphere of unquestioned privilege, now come to a climax in a final context for a favored position with the mother; the usual failure leads to resignation, guilt, and anxiety. The child indulges in fantasies of being a giant and a tiger, but in his dreams he runs in terror for dear life. This, then, is the stage of the "castration complex," the intensified fear of finding the (now energetically erotized) genitals harmed as a punishment for the fantasies attached to their excitement.

Infantile sexuality and incest taboo, castration complex and superego all unite here to bring about that specifically human crisis during which the child must turn from an exclusive, pregenital attachment to his parents to the slow process of becoming a parent, a carrier of tradition. Here the most fateful split and transformation in the emotional powerhouse occurs, a split between potential human glory and potential total destruction. For here the child becomes forever divided in himself. The instinct fragments which before had enhanced the growth of his infantile body and mind now become divided into an infantile set which perpetuates the exuberance of growth potentials, and a parental set which supports and increases self-observation, self-guidance, and self-punishment.

The problem, again, is one of mutual regulation. Where the child, now so ready to overmanipulate himself, can gradually develop a sense of moral responsibility, where he can gain some insight into the institutions, functions, and roles which will permit his responsible participation, he will find pleasurable accomplishment in wielding tools and weapons, in manipulating meaningful toys—and in caring for younger children.

Naturally, the parental set is at first infantile in nature: the fact that human conscience remains partially infantile throughout life is the core of human tragedy. For the superego of the child can be primitive, cruel, and uncompromising, as may be observed in instances where children overcontrol and overconstrict themselves to the point of self-obliteration; where they develop an over-obedience more literal than the one the parent has wished to exact; or where they develop deep regressions and lasting resentments because the parents themselves do not seem to live up to the new conscience. One of the deepest conflicts in life is the hate for a parent who served as the model and the executor of the superego, but who (in some form) was found trying to get away with the very transgressions which the child can no longer tolerate in himself. The suspiciousness and evasiveness which is thus mixed in with the all-or-nothing quality of the superego, this organ of moral tradition, makes moral (in the sense of moralistic) man a great potential danger to his own ego—and to that of his fellow men.

In adult pathology, the residual conflict over initiative is expressed either in hysterical denial, which causes the repression of the wish or the abrogation of its executive organ by paralysis, inhibition, or impotence; or in overcompensatory showing off, in which the scared individual, so eager to "duck," instead "sticks his neck out." Then also a plunge into psychosomatic disease is now common. It is as if the culture had made a man over-advertise himself and so identify with his own advertisement that only disease can offer him escape.

But here, again, we must not think only of individual psychopathology, but of the inner powerhouse of rage which must be submerged at this stage, as some of the fondest hopes and the wildest phantasies are repressed and inhibited. The resulting self-righteousness—often the principal reward for goodness—can later be most intolerantly turned against others in the form of persistent moralistic surveillance, so that the prohibition rather than the guidance of initiative becomes the dominant endeavor. On the other hand, even moral man's initiative is apt to burst the boundaries of self-restriction, permitting him to do to others, in his or in other lands, what he would neither do nor tolerate being done in his own home.

In view of the dangerous potentials of man's long childhood, it is well to look back at the blueprint of the life-stages and to the possibilities of guiding the young of the race while they are young. And here we note that according to the wisdom of the ground plan the child is at no time more ready to learn quickly and avidly, to become bigger in the sense of sharing obligation and performance than during this period of his development. He is eager and able to make things cooperatively, to combine with other children for the purpose of constructing and planning, and he is willing to profit from teachers and to emulate ideal prototypes. He remains, of course, identified with the parent of the same sex, but for the present he looks for opportunities where work-identification seems to promise a field of initiative without too much infantile conflict or oedipal guilt and a more realistic identification based on a spirit of equality experienced in doing things together. At any rate, the "oedipal" stage results not only in the oppressive establishment of a moral sense restricting the horizon of the permissible; it also sets the direction toward the possible and the tangible which permits the dreams of early childhood to be attached to the goals of an active adult life. Social institutions, therefore, offer children of this age an *economic ethos*, in the form of ideal adults recognizable by their uniforms and their functions, and fascinating enough to replace, the heroes of picture book and fairy tale.

Human Growth Through the Ages

Dorothy V. Whipple
GEORGETOWN UNIVERSITY SCHOOL OF MEDICINE

A human being starts being himself as a single cell. In 9 months he becomes a 6- or 7-lb baby; in less than 20 years he achieves 5 to 6 ft in height and 100 to 200 lb in weight. During this time there is a great temptation to evaluate how well he is doing by how big he has become. While in general there *is* a correlation between his size at any given time and his general well-being, the use of height/weight data as a measure of health is fraught with danger. However, although it is not possible to construct absolute standards of growth, enough is known to justify the cautious use of height/weight data.

THE NATURE OF GROWTH

Each animal species has a growth pattern characteristic of itself. Birds do not grow as do cows, but all birds follow a bird pattern. A hummingbird and an eagle follow similar patterns, even though the absolute values of their weights at any age are very different. In the same way a Jersey cow and a Holstein cow

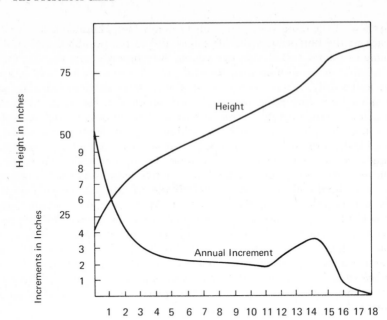

FIGURE 1.   *Human growth pattern.*

have in common a cow pattern. This is as true of the human species as it is of the other animal species. A pigmy baby in Africa grows in the same way as a baby in Scandinavia or a baby in a Park Avenue apartment in New York (Figure 1).

Mammals below the human being (except the primate group to which human beings belong biologically) grow rapidly in early life and soon reach their mature size. They do not pass through the long, slow growing period of middle childhood, nor do they show a pubescent spurt in growth. In most mammals puberty comes soon after weaning and is not accompanied by an increase in the rate of somatic growth.

The long postponement of puberty in the human being is an evolutionary trait. The development of the brain is the distinguishing factor that separates man from lower species, and it takes time for this elaborate mechanism to complete its development. The hypothalamus controls the onset of puberty. When this part of the brain reaches maturity, it triggers an endocrine mechanism that initiates the maturation of reproductive function. The long childhood of the human being allows time not only for somatic growth but also for the development of the qualities of humanness. During the early years the child is prepared for adulthood in all areas of development; his body increases in size and develops increasingly intricate motor capacities, his personality emerges, he absorbs his culture. Under optimal conditions he becomes not only a full-sized adult competent in motor activities but an adult mature on the human level. The changes are so profound that it is not surprising that optimal development on all fronts is not always achieved. While development takes place in all areas simultaneously, the rate of development varies from area to area. Somatic growth and development will be considered in this section.

The greatest increments in human growth take place prior to birth; in children in the United States this is roughly 20 in. During the first year another 10 in. is added, and during the second year another 5 in. The human child achieves approximately half his ultimate height by the age of 2 years. During the third year the annual increment slows down to 3 to 4 in. and thereafter to 2 to 3 in. per year, until the growth spurt of puberty begins to makes its appearance.

During intrauterine life nourishment is absorbed and body substances that did not exist before are created. The increase in size of the fetus is due to creation of nervous tissue, of bone, of muscle, of connective tissue, and of all the multitudinous tissues which compose the animal organism. Later in life, new-cell creation slows down in most tissues, and most of the further increase in size is due to enlargement of the already created cells.

The early growth of the fetus and the infant appears to be primarily under control of the genes (Goldberg, 1955). Retardation of growth prior to the age of 2 years is usually attributed to primordial dwarfism (Kogut et al., 1963) or intrauterine growth retardation (Szalay, 1964). The anterior pituitary hormones, especially the growth hormone, are thought to be responsible for the steady growth through the years of middle childhood. Thyroxin initiates the development of centers of ossification in the long bones. In the period immediately preceding puberty, androgens from the adrenal cortex and the testes and estrogens from the ovary begin to make their appearance, stimulated probably by gonadotropins from the hypophysis.

In the girl, the estrogens stimulate both the growth of the long bones and finally maturational changes in the epiphyses followed by their closure; simultaneously the estrogens stimulate reproductive maturing. In the boy, androgens stimulate growth of the long bones more than estrogen does in the girl, both in duration of effect and in magnitude of increments. Ultimately androgens bring about closure of the epiphyses in the male, and growth in height comes to an end. It is the androgens which are responsible for maturation of the male reproductive system and the male secondary sexual characteristics.

The controlling factors of human growth inherent in the organism are thus seen to be the genes and the endocrines. Since it is, in the last analysis, the genes which control the endocrines, the growth potential of any individual human being can be thought of as lying within his genes. The actual growth of an individual, however, is determined both by his genetic potential and by the environmental stresses and strains to which he is subjected. The assumption that there is an optimal growth for each individual predetermined in his genes leads logically to a second assumption, namely, that deviants from this optimum reflect environmental hazards.

There are mountains of figures on human growth; nevertheless, what is optimum for any individual is still difficult to determine. It is possible, however, to cull from the available data some information that is useful in helping children attain their maximum well-being.

All growth studies fall into one of two categories: cross-sectional and longitudinal. Confusion between these categories is responsible for much of the prevalent misinformation about growth.

CROSS-SECTIONAL STUDIES

In a cross-sectional study all the children are measured once. Data are obtained, for example, from a school population of children varying in age from 6 to 18 years. The end result of such a study gives information on a group of 6-year-olds, a group of 7-year-olds, and so on for each age group. When all the data on the 6-year-olds are averaged, a figure of what the "average 6-year-old" has accomplished in 6 years is obtained. The meaning of this figure depends upon how homogeneous the group of 6-year-olds is. Size at age 6 varies with genetic background, with socioeconomic level, with physical and emotional health, and probably with other factors as well. If the population measured contains children who fall in many of these different categories, the average figure is not of much value as a standard against which to compare the accomplishments of any given child in 6 years. Average figures from a cross-sectional study are useful in comparing groups. The average size of 6-year-olds in a New York City public school can be compared with the average size of the 6-year-olds in a Japanese school or a French school or a Mississippi school or in an English school in 1850.

In a cross-sectional study the figures represent a static phenomenon. They are not a continuum, because no child moved from one group to the next. In many cross-sectional "growth" studies the data are used as though they were a continuum. The average figures of distance attained at the various ages are put together, and the resulting curve is called a "growth" curve (though nothing grew—all was static). In using cross-sectional data in this way the assumption is made that all children of age 6, when the study was made, will be of the same size 1 year hence as those age 7 at the time of measurement. This assumption is not valid; children do not progress at the same rate at different ages. Differences in the rate of progression exist at all ages, but during the spurt of growth at puberty the differences are very marked indeed. Each child grows rapidly for 1 or 2 years during his period of sexual maturation. However, there is about an 8-year span during which individual children pass through this growth spurt. Girls mature earlier than boys, but even within the same sex there is a range of several years during which maturation may take place.

A girl who has not started to mature may grow 1 in. in height between 11 and 12 years of age; another girl in early puberty at this age may grow 5 in. in this same chronological time. The difference obtained in a cross-sectional study of height between the average 11-year-old girl and the average 12-year-old girl gives a figure which distorts the amount of gain of the early- and late-maturing girls.

In Figure 2a the growth of girls maturing at different ages is plotted in individual increments. The dotted line represents the average figure, which bears little resemblance to the individual curves. In Figure 2b these data are replotted in such a way that peak growth in height of all the girls is placed at a single point. Again the dotted lines represent the average, which comes much

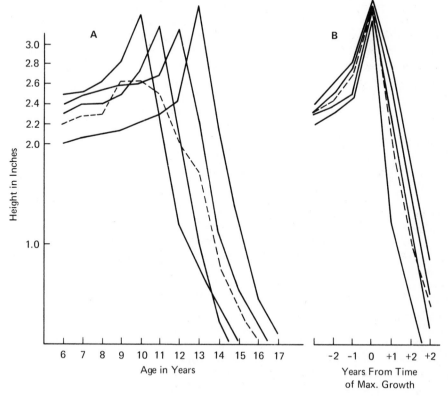

A—Plotted Against Age   B—Plotted Against Time of Maximum Growth
Solid lines are increments of individual girls ● Dotted lines are averages of all four girls.

FIGURE 2.   *Height increments of girls maturing at different ages.*

closer to demonstrating the magnitude of the pubertal growth spurt than did the first average.

Valuable information can be obtained from cross-sectional studies, but such studies are of relatively little value in studying the velocity of growth—the increment per unit of time.

LONGITUDINAL STUDIES

In a longitudinal study a group of children is followed over a period of time. The same children are measured at successive periods. *Growing*, not merely growth accomplishment, is measured. Data from individual children can be combined and recombined in many ways. For example all the girls who reach the menarche at age 12 can be put in one group and their growth compared with girls who reach the menarche at age 13. It is soon seen that age of menarche has far more significance for growth than chronological age.

Longitudinal studies are more difficult to conduct than cross-sectional ones. It takes years to complete a study in which the investigator is waiting for his subjects to grow up; families move about, so it is difficult to maintain a group of children for a long span of years; longitudinal studies are expensive; and investigators as well as children grow older with the years!

At the present time in the United States there are a number of large-scale longitudinal studies, some under way, others completed. The Brush Foundation Study of Child Health and Development in Cleveland, the Fels Research Institute Study of Prenatal and Postnatal Environment at Antioch, Longitudinal Studies of Child Health and Development of the Harvard School of Public Health in Boston, Studies of the Institute of Human Development in Berkeley, California, are some of the most outstanding studies.

GENETIC INFLUENCES

There are many genes which influence growth. Since it is of course impossible to identify them individually, the problem is to relate observable and measurable qualities of a child with his growth potential. Growth in childhood is correlated with (1) size at birth, (2) sex, (3) speed of maturation, and (4) body build, and perhaps with other factors, too.

Of these four factors sex, with only rare exceptions, is readily observable at birth. It is certainly genetically determined, and there is no conceivable environmental factor which can change this basic fact about the individual.[1]

Birth weight is information easy enough to come by, but by itself it does not offer enough information to warrant prediction of growth.

Body build and rate of maturing are probably genetically determined. Rate of maturing, while not determinable at birth, shows itself during the early years. Combined with sex and birth weight, it offers the best information for predicting what a given child should accomplish under good conditions.

There is considerable evidence to suggest that although both body build and rate of maturing are genetically determined, they, unlike sex, may both be subject to change by environmental forces (see below).

SIZE AT BIRTH   The size at birth after full-term pregnancy is an index, although a rough one, of the ultimate size of the mature man. While dependent upon the genetic growth potential operating since conception, birth weight is influenced by many other factors. It is only a first step in estimating the growth potential of any given child.

First-born infants are usually smaller by some ounces than later-born infants (Meredith, 1950). Why this should be so is unknown, and there seems to be no correlation between this small difference and growth potential.

Infants born to small women and fathered by large men are often smaller at birth than would be expected as judged by their ultimate growth (Tanner, 1956). Apparently some dampening effect from the mother keeps an infant in utero from becoming too large to pass through her small birth canal.

Birth weight is related to duration of gestation. Lubchenco, Hansman, Dressler, and Boyd related birth weight to gestational age in a large series of

---

[1] Some of the new work on chromosomal patterns has cast doubt upon the absolute quality of sex. However, even for these infinitesimally few individuals with atypical chromosomal patterns, sex can still be considered a gene-determined absolute.

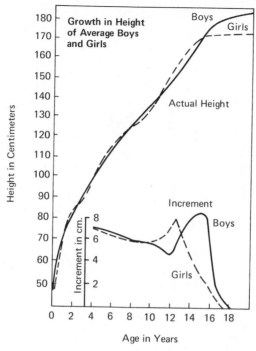

F I G U R E 3.   *Growth of average boys and girls.*

premature and full-term infants. Their data suggest that infants destined to be large are already large by the end of 24 weeks of gestational age.

Sex   Boys and girls have different growth patterns. At birth boys are slightly bigger (between 1 and 4 per cent) than girls in both height and weight. During the first year of life boys grow slightly faster than girls, but between the ages of 1 and 9 the growth rate differences between boys and girls are almost nonexistent.

At puberty the first significant differences in height and weight between the sexes become evident. It is at this time that the different endocrines exercise their effects—androgens in the male and estrogens in the female. Girls mature earlier than boys, so that for a few years the girls in any population group are larger than the boys in almost all dimensions. Then the boys begin their pubertal spurt; they catch up and pass the girls and end up roughly 10 per cent bigger (Figure 3).

Speed of Maturing   Some children progress along their predetermined growth pattern at a faster rate than others. The age at which a child matures sexually is a milestone that is convenient to use as a peg. Some girls accomplish sexual maturity in eleven years from birth; others take 16 or even 17 years to reach the same level of maturity. Boys are not so speedy as girls. The speediest can reach manhood in 12 years; the slow ones may take 18 years.

FIGURE 4.   *Classic body builds: Uncle Sam, John Bull, and Hercules.*

Early maturers are early in all their physiologic accomplishments (Reed and Stuart, 1959). In general, during childhood they are taller and heavier than later maturers. Their skeletons grow faster, they get their teeth earlier, they develop muscular capacity and coordination a little sooner than the late maturers. The speed of maturation is a gene-determined phenomenon. The early maturers become adults who have more weight for height than late maturers.

BODY BUILD   Adult human bodies vary in all their external dimensions. Almost all classifications consist of two extreme types and one intermediate one. At one extreme human beings are tall and thin, the typical Uncle Sam; at the other extreme they are short and fat, the John Bull. In between there is the strong muscular athlete, the Hercules (Figure 4).

Sheldon uses the terms *endomorph, mesomorph,* and *ectomorph* to describe the three types (Figure 5). The endomorph has a round head and large, fat abdomen predominating over this thorax. His arms and legs are short, with considerable fat in the upper arm and thigh but with slender wrists and ankles. He has a great deal of subcutaneous fat. His body is thick, his skeleton large. The endomorph is plump as a child and tends to put on weight as he gets older.

The mesomorph is the strong athlete. Bone and muscle predominate, but he has much less fat than the endomorph. He has broad shoulders and chest and heavily muscled arms and legs with the lower segment strong in relation to the upper.

The endomorph is the linear man; he has a thin, peaked face with a receding forehead, a thin, narrow chest and abdomen, spindly arms and legs.

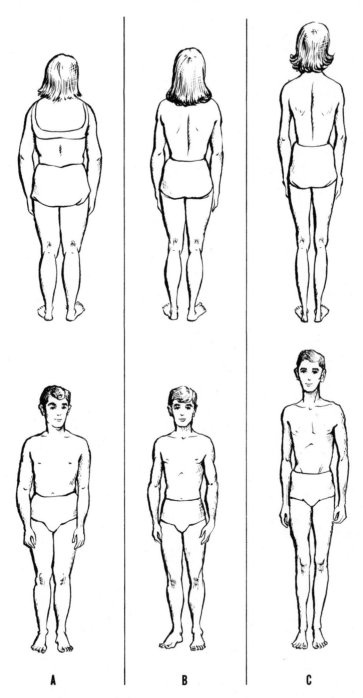

FIGURE 5.   *Somatypes: (A) endomorph, (B) mesomorph, (C) ectomorph.*

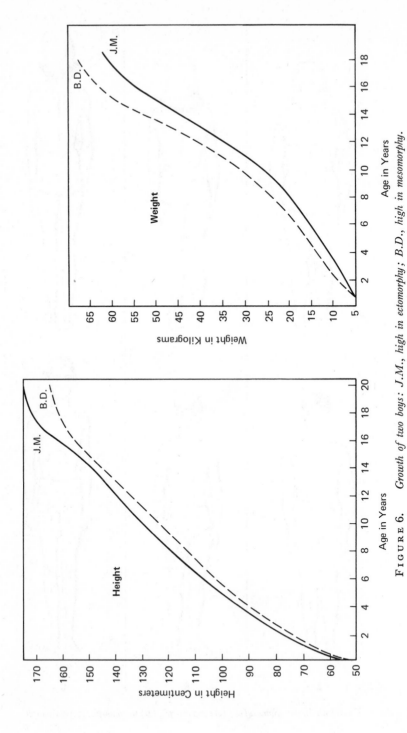

FIGURE 6. *Growth of two boys: J.M., high in ectomorphy; B.D., high in mesomorphy.*

His muscles are neither large nor strong. He has very little subcutaneous fat. He seldom becomes obese.

The majority of people have a moderate amount of each component in their somatotype. Virtually all somatotyping has been done on adults. In the Brush Foundation Growth Study a group that had been followed since childhood was somatotyped in early adult life. With the knowledge of their adult somatotypes their growth records were sorted out and recombined into groups of homogeneous somatotypes. The ectomorphs were taller than the mesomorphs at all ages from 4 onward, but the mesomorphs were heavier from age 2 onward. From the age of 2 the mesomorphs had more weight for height than the ectomorphs. (Figure 6 shows the growth of two boys, one high in ectomorphy, the other high in mesomorphy.)

Unfortunately somatotyping at the early ages has not at present been worked out. From longitudinal growth studies it was obvious, after the subjects reached adult size and could be somatotyped, that their growth in childhood varied according to the body build they finally achieved. This is important, but at present data are lacking with which to predict growth based on somatotype at birth (Dupertuis and Michael).

Bayley and Bayer (1946) have suggested another way of classifying body builds. They describe androgyny, the degree of masculinity in the female and femininity in the male. Androgyny emphasizes the fact that every individual has some characteristics of the opposite sex. Bayley and Bayer describe an undifferentiated pattern of body build characteristic of the neuter gender quality of early childhood. At puberty the pattern fans out either toward the hyperfeminine or the hypermasculine or remains intermediate (asexual). Some individuals travel all the way to the extreme of their sex; others stop part way, retaining elements of the undifferentiated pattern of childhood (Figure 7).

While the final measurement of androgyny cannot be made until maturity is reached, nevertheless, like the somatotypes of Sheldon, the androgyny type is, Bayley and Bayer believe, an innate trait uniquely characteristic of the individual and possessed by him all his life. By means of certain anthropometric

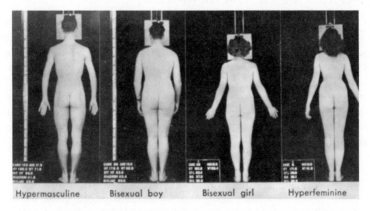

Hypermasculine   Bisexual boy   Bisexual girl   Hyperfeminine

FIGURE 7.   *Androgynic patterns.* (From Bayley and Bayer, Photos of Cases 5, 45, 66 and 168 in The Assessment of Somatic Androgyny, *Am. J. Phy. Anthrop.* 4:433, 1946. Courtesy of the Wistar Institute of Anatomy and Biology, Philadelphia.)

measurements during childhood these investigators have been able, at least roughly, to categorize children before puberty with respect to their androgyny scores.

In the androgyny score considerable emphasis is placed on the distribution of subcutaneous fat and muscles. Women on the whole deposit more fat than men, and men develop larger muscle mass than women. Amount of muscle and of fat are also factors in the somatotyping system of Sheldon.

These two different methods of describing body build overlap. The meso-morph of Sheldon is the muscular type and is closely related to the hyper-masculine on the androgyny scale. As a male this type tends to mature early. The endomorph deposits an abundance of fat and is related to the hyper-feminine on the scale of Bayley and Bayer. As a female this type tends to mature early. The ectomorph of Sheldon, the linear person, is the asexual person of Bayley and Bayer; in both sexes they are late maturers. The muscular girl is high in mesomorphy on Sheldon's scale, high in masculinity on that of Bayley and Bayer. Unlike the muscular boy, she tends to be a later maturer. The fat boy is high in endomorphy and high in femininity. He does not follow the early-maturing pattern of the endomorphic girl, he tends to be a late maturer (Bayer, 1940).

Brozek raises the question of how stable the body type of an individual remains through the life span. He feels that while there are stable (genetic) aspects to body build, the variable (environmental) aspects have been confused in most of the attempts to categorize body build.

It is doubtless true that body build is not a simple, single, gene-directed characteristic. Body build is the result of the growth and development of the skeletal structure, the muscles, and the adipose tissue. Each of these parts of the organism is acted upon by many things, both intrinsic and extrinsic. Neverthe-less there are measurable tendencies toward one or another of the recognized body types which are useful clinically.

ENVIRONMENTAL INFLUENCES

There is good reason to believe that nutrition is a factor not only in the rate of growth but also in the speed of growth and the ultimate stature achieved. Children known to be on poor diets can be stimulated to grow at a more rapid rate by improvements in their diets. Where the optimum is reached in relation to diet is not so clear. Can children on adequate diets (adequate to the best of our present-day knowledge) be stimulated to grow more by supplements of protein, minerals, vitamins, or anything else? Opinion is divided on this matter. There is also this question, by no means answerable at present: Is more necessarily better?

It is also obvious that physical health has an effect on growth. Children with serious organic disease such as congenital heart disease, nephritis, or some of the inborn errors of metabolism do not grow as do normal children. The decreased incidence of serious acute disease in children since the introduction of antibiotics and improved immunization procedures may play a role in the larger size of today's children. Emotional factors also affect growth. Infants deprived of maternal care fail to gain weight adequately even on excellent diets.

But here, as in so many places in human development, the resultant growth depends not only upon the amount and kind of emotional deprivation but also upon the inherent traits of the child reacting to the deprivation.

An interesting trend in growth over the last hundred years is thought probably to be related to nutrition. The data on heights and weights of school children indicate that the whole process of growth has been undergoing a speeding-up process. Children born in the 1930s are appreciably larger at age 5 (and probably before) than children born at the beginning of the century (Meredith, 1941). The amount of this secular change is quite considerable. . . .

American (Meredith, 1941), British (Clements, 1953) and Swedish (Broman et al., 1942) data all give similar trends. The average gain between 1880 and 1950 is about $1\frac{1}{2}$ cm and $\frac{1}{4}$ kg per decade at ages 5 to 7 and about 2 cm and $\frac{1}{2}$ kg per decade during puberty. The fully grown adult (Tanner, 1956) has increased in height about 1 cm per decade for the past century.

Hathaway compared the figures obtained by various American investigators from 1902 to 1952 (Figure 8). The data from Hathaway's compilations are averages based on cross-sectional studies. Data from Bayley's longitudinal study of California children showed a similar increase in size of the children over their parents. The range of heights and weights at all ages has been unaffected over the years. There have been, and still are, big children and adults and little ones. But big and little alike are all a little bigger than they used to be.

How long has the secular trend been in operation? There is very little reliable data before 1880; however, Robert, in 1876 made a significant comment in discussing the physical requirements of factory children: "A factory child of the present day at the age of 7 years weighs as much as one of 8 did in 1833—each age has gained one year in 40 years" (Tanner, 1955); and Clements comments on the small size of the armor worn in the Middle Ages.

In this connection it should be pointed out that uniformly a high socioeconomic level is reflected in greater weight gains. Every study made the world over has shown that those children from the more privileged groups gain more and gain it sooner than the less privileged in any society. . . .

The effect of socioeconomic levels has been demonstrated in many studies (Meredith, 1941). Chinese girls of upper class in Hong Kong grow larger and mature earlier than girls of similar genetic background but of a less favored economic level (Lee, Chang, and Chan, 1963). That economic level makes a difference is a clearly established fact. Why it should be so is not so clear. Probably, like the secular trend, nutrition is a factor, but so too may be other factors, like regularity of sleep and meals, more outdoor exercise, better medical care—factors that go along with a higher level of education and greater ease of life in the more prosperous groups in any society.

Does climate have an effect on growth? Mills has made a case for the gradual change in the world temperature to be at least partly responsible for the secular trend. He suggests that difficulty in heat loss may retard human growth as it does in experimental animals. However, current studies on children in the tropics and in temperate and cold regions do not seem to bear out this hypothesis. Race and climate are difficult factors to disentangle from nutrition and socioeconomic level. West African children (Mackay, 1952) are a good deal retarded in relation to American children, but Whites and Negroes in New York

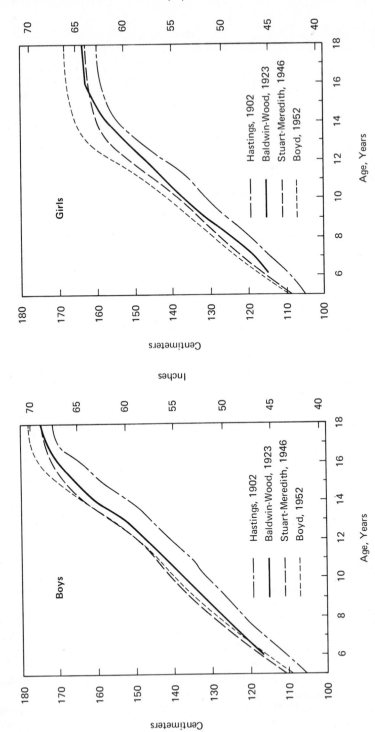

F I G U R E 8. *Average heights of American children by various investigators.* (From Hathaway, *Height and Weights in Children and Youths in the U.S.,* U.S, Dept. Agric., 1957.)

City in similar economic circumstances showed no appreciable differences (Michelson, 1944), indicating that race was not a significant factor here. But how about climate? Using age of menarche (see below) as a criterion, Ellis gives 14.3 years as the mean age at menarche in Nigerian school girls of upper socioeconomic level and Levine 14.4 years as that of Eskimo girls. Wilson and Sutherland found the expected class difference in school girls in Colombo, Ceylon, to range from 12.8 years for the menarche in the upper group to 14.4 years in the lower, about the same class differential as found in the temperate zone.

Japanese children (Ito, 1942) born and reared in California were taller and heavier than children of similar parentage who remained in Japan. The California-reared Japanese children were also more advanced in skeletal development than the children who remained in Japan. This difference is usually attributed to better food and generally better living conditions, although the possible effect of climate cannot be ignored.

The effect of climate, if any, on growth is difficult to distinguish from the other variables affecting the children measured; however, it is clear that season has a definite influence on growth (Palmer, 1933; Reynolds and Sontag, 1944). In the Northern Hemisphere, October, November, and December are the months of greatest weight gain, and it may be five or six times as much as during the months of April, May, and June, when weight gain is at a minimum. . . . About two-thirds of the annual gain in weight is made in the fall (the 6 months from September to February) and only one-third in the remaining 6 months of the year. Height gains are maximum in April, May, and June, and minimal in September, October, and November. The reason for the seasonal variation is quite unknown. It appears in well-nourished children as well as in poorly nourished ones. Suggestions have been made that hormone secretions are involved or that environmental temperatures or length of day are factors.

The age at which the changes of puberty take place is basically a genetically determined phenomenon; nevertheless, malnutrition can delay the events of puberty. In the secular trend the age of puberty is most pronounced. Maturation occurs earlier now than it did a century ago. Kiil found the average age of menarche of Norwegian girls in 1850 to be 17.0 years and in 1950 13.5 years. In the United States the average age of menarche has dropped from 14.2 years in 1900 to 12.9 years in 1950 (Mills, 1950). The effect of the economic depression as measured in Hagerstown, Maryland, was not sufficient to affect the growth of children measured. Nevertheless there was a demonstrable retardation of the age at which both boys and girls matured. Similar data were obtained both in France and in Belgium during World War II.

It would appear that the human body has to grow a certain amount before puberty can take place. If growth takes place rapidly, puberty comes early; if growth is slow, puberty must wait until the body has reached the requisite size, or more likely, maturity level.

The speed with which the human body *can* grow is doubtless genetically determined, but the actual speed is the resultant of the genetic potential and the opportunity afforded by the environment.

CONCLUSIONS

The following conclusions on the nature of human growth seem reasonably substantiated:

1. All children possess the potential for a pattern of growth characteristically human; every child (barring those with gross defects) passes through the same stages as every other child. These stages are related to most of the measurable aspects of growth, such as physical measurements, development of organs, and maturation of function and behavior.

2. The differences among normal children, within the range of the human pattern, are large. These differences are reflected not only in the magnitude of the measurements but in the tempo of growth itself.

3. Correlations exist between various aspects of growth. A child who deviates from the mean with respect to one type of growth is apt to deviate proportionately in other aspects. While correlations between the various aspects of growth are frequent, they are by no means universal; in some children progression is less uniform than in others.

4. Genetic and endocrine factors are responsible for the basic patterns of growth and maturation. These patterns tend to persist through the life span, contributing to the uniformity of individual growth.

5. Genetic patterns can be modified by environmental factors, such as disease, nutrition, emotions. The effect of quantitatively similar environmental factors varies, depending both on the time in the life cycle when specific deprivations occur and, probably, on the genetic makeup of the individual on whom they are acting.

References

BAYER, LEONA M.: Weight and Menses in Adolescent Girls with Special Reference to Build, *J. Pediat.*, *17*:345, 1940.

BAYLEY, NANCY, and LEONA M. BAYER: The Assessment of Somatic Androgyny, *Am. J. Phys. Anthropol.*, N.S. *4*:433, 1946.

BROZEK, JOSEPH: *Body Measurement and Human Nutrition*, Wayne State University Press, Detroit, Mich., 1956.

CLEMENTS, E. M. B.: Changes in the Mean Stature and Weight of British Children over the Past 70 Years, *Brit. M. J.*, *2*:897, 1953.

DUPERTUIS, C. W., and N. B. MICHAEL: Comparison of Growth in Height and Weight Between Ectomorphic and Mesomorphic Boys, *Child Development*, *24*:203, 1953.

ELLIS, R. W. B.: Age of Puberty in the Tropics, *Brit. M. J.*, *1*:85, 1950.

GOLDBERG, MINNIE B.: What Makes Us Grow As We Do, *J. Am. M. Women's A.*, *10*:110, 1955.

HATHAWAY, MILLICENT L.: Heights and Weights of Children and Youths in the U.S., Home Economics Research Report 2, U.S. Department of Agriculture, 1957.

ITO, P. K. Comparative Biometrical Study of Physique of Japanese Women Born and Reared Under Different Environments, *Human Biol.*, *14*:279, 1942.

KIIL, V.: (Quoted by J. M. Tanner) in *Growth at Adolescence*, Charles C Thomas, Publisher, Springfield, Ill., 1955.

KOGUT, MAURICE D., S. A. KAPLAN, and S. N. S. SHIMIZU: Growth Retardation, Use of Sulfation Factor as Bioassay for Growth Hormone, *Pediatrics*, *31*:538, 1963.

LEE, MARJORIE M. C., K. S. F. CHANG, and MARY M. C. CHAN: Sexual Maturation of Chinese Girls in Hong Kong, *Pediatrics*, *32*:389, 1963.

LEVINE, V. E.: Studies in Physiological Anthropology: III. The Age of Onset of Menstruation of the Alaska Eskimos, *Am. J. Phys. Anthropol.*, N.S. *2*:252, 1953.

LUBCHENCO, LULA O., CHARLOTTE HANSMAN, MARIAN DRESSLER, and EDITH BOYD: Intrauterine Growth as Estimated from Liveborn Birth Weight Data at 24–42 Weeks of Gestation, *Pediatrics*, *32*:793, 1963.

MACKAY, D. H.: Skeletal Maturation of the Hand: A Study of Development in East African Children, *Tr. Roy. Soc. Trop. Med. & Hyg.*, *46*:135, 1952.

MATTHEWS, C. A., and M. H. FOHRMAN: *Beltsville Standards for Growth of Jersey and Holstein Cattle*, U.S. Department of Agriculture Technical Bulletin, Nos. 1098 and 1099, 1954.

MEREDITH, H. V.: Stature and Weight of Children of the U.S. with Reference to Influence of Racial, Regional, Socio-Economic and Secular Trends, *Am. J. Dis. Child.*, *62*:909, 1941.

———: Stature and Weights of Private School Children in Two Successive Decades, *Am. J. Phys. Anthropol.*, *28*:1, 1941.

———: Birth Order and Body Size, *Am. J. Phys. Anthropol.*, *8*:195, 1950.

MICHELSON, N.: Studies in Physical Development of Negroes: IV. Onset of Puberty, *Am. J. Phys. Anthropol.*, N.S. *2*:151, 1944.

MILLS, C. A.: Temperature Influence on Human Growth and Development, *Human Biol.*, *22*:71, 1950.

PALMER, C. E.: Seasonal Variations of Average Growth in Weight and Height of Elementary School Children, *Pub. Health Rep.*, *48*:211, 1933.

REED, R. B., and H. C. STUART: Patterns of Growth in Height and Weight from Birth to 18 Years of Age, *Pediatrics*, 24 (supp.):904, 1959.

REYNOLDS, E. L., and L. W. SONTAG: Seasonal Variations in Weight, Height, and Appearance of Ossification Centers, *J. Pediat.*, *24*:524, 1944.

SHELDON, W. H.: *The Varieties of Human Physique*, Harper & Row, Publishers, Incorporated, New York, 1940.

SZALAY, GLENN C.: Intrauterine Growth Retardation versus Silver's Syndrome, *J. Pediat.*, *64*:234, 1964.

TANNER, J. M.: *Growth at Adolescence*, Charles C Thomas, Publisher, Springfield, Ill., 1955.

———: Adult Body Measurements, *Arch. Dis. Childhood*, *31*:372, 1956.

WILSON, D. C., and I. SUTHERLAND: The Age of Menarche in the Tropics, *Brit. M. J.*, *2*:607, 1953.

Minor Physical Anomalies:
Their Incidence and Relation to Behavior
in a Normal and a Deviant Sample*

Mary F. Waldrop and Charles F. Halverson, Jr.

NATIONAL INSTITUTE OF MENTAL HEALTH

The cumulative incidence of certain minor physical anomalies was related to impulsive, fast-moving behavior in samples of normal preschool children (Waldrop, Pedersen, & Bell, 1968). These anomalies, which are typically associated with Down's Syndrome and other congenital defects have been thought to result from chromosomal irregularities or noxious agents which affect fetal development during the first weeks of pregnancy (Achs, Harper, & Siegel, 1966; Gustavson, K., 1964). Each anomaly does occur, however, in the normal population (Benda, 1960; Smith & Bostian, 1964).

The relation of the occurrence of these physical characteristics to behavior was interpreted as evidence for congenital contributors to poorly controlled, hyperactive behavior. The same factors which probably operated sometime during the first trimester of pregnancy could have influenced *both* the occurrence of the slight morphological aberrations and the hyperactive behavior so that where one was found the other tended to be present.

To extend and amplify the meaning of the findings from the original study (Waldrop et al., 1968) we will report here three additional studies involving the incidence of minor anatomical anomalies and their relation to hyperactive, uncontrolled behavior. First, we replicated the original study, again using normal two-and-a-half-year-old boys and girls who attended our research nursery school. Second, we extended the original study by evaluating the stability of the findings over five years for 84 per cent of the children in the original study. Third, we observed children with congenital defects in hearing and in speech production to provide further evidence on probable etiologies of these anomalies.

In all three of these studies, just as in the original study, each child was examined for the presence of the 18 minor physical anomalies and was given two scores—one was the total count of anomalies, the other was a sum of the weighted scores.[1] The original list (Waldrop et al., 1968) was revised as follows: (a) "Index finger longer than middle finger" was eliminated from the list

Reprinted from paper presented at meetings of The Society for Research in Child Development, Inc., Santa Monica, Calif., March, 1969. By permission.

* We wish to thank Mrs. Gerda Schoenfeld (teacher), Miss Beverly Whitlock (Director), and others at the Easter Seal Treatment Center, Rockville, Maryland, for their interest, expert assistance, and cooperation in part of this study.

[1] Weights of one or two, depending on severity, were given to the nine anomalies which Goldfarb and Botstein (unpublished manuscript) found were significantly more frequent among their sample of schizophrenic children than among their sample of normal children. Weights of one were given to the six anomalies which they found were more frequent, though not significantly so, among their deviant sample. No weights were given to the three anomalies which they found either to be nonexistant in their samples or more frequent—not significant—among their sample of normal children.

because of lack of incidence, (b) "Head circumference outside normal range" was added to the list, with a circumference deviating more than 1.5 standard deviations from the reported mean for that age and sex being weighted 2, and one deviating between 1.0 and 1.5 such standard deviations being weighted 1 (Vickers & Stuart, 1943) and, (c) other anomalies were defined more precisely.

TABLE 1

List of Anomalies and Scoring Weights

ANOMALY	WEIGHT
Head	
Fine electric hair:	
Very fine hair that will not comb down	2
Fine hair that is soon awry after combing	1
Two or more hair whorls	0
Head circumference outside normal range:	
$> 1.5\,\sigma$	2
$> 1.0 \leqslant 1.5\,\sigma$	1
Eyes	
Epicanthus:	
Where upper and lower lids join the nose, point of union is:	
Deeply covered	2
Partly covered	1
Hypertelorism:	
Approximate distance between tear ducts:	
$> 1.5\,\sigma$	2
$> 1.0 \leqslant 1.5\,\sigma$	1
Ears	
Low-seated ears:	
Point where ear joins the head not in line with corner of eye and nose bridge:	
Lower by > 0.5 cm	2
Lower by $\leqslant 0.5$ cm	1
Adherent ear lobes:	
Lower edge of ears extend:	
Upward and back toward crown of head	2
Straight back toward rear of neck	1
Malformed ears	1
Asymmetrical ears	1
Soft and pliable ears	0
Mouth	
High-steepled palate:	
Roof of mouth:	
Definitely steepled	2
Flat and narrow at the top	1
Furrowed tongue (one with deep ridges)	1
Tongue with smooth-rough spots	0

(continued)

TABLE 1   (*Continued*)

ANOMALY	WEIGHT
Hands	
Curved fifth finger:	
Markedly curved inward toward other fingers	2
Slightly curved inward toward other fingers	1
Single transverse palmar crease	1
Feet	
Third toe longer than second:	
Definitely longer than second toe	2
Appears equal in length to second toe	1
Partial syndactylia of two middle toes	1
Big gap between first and second toes	1

Table 1 is the revised list of the 18 minor physical anomalies along with the epitomical descriptions and scoring weights.

Because individual anomalies occurred with low frequency, only a cumulative score showed sufficient range for correlational analyses. Because the total score and the weighted score correlated greater than .85 in every sample, only the results using the weighted scores will be reported here. Inter-rater reliabilities for judging the anomalies was satisfactory for all samples (mean $r = .83$).

REPLICATION STUDY

The two-and-a-half-year-olds in the Replication Study were like the subjects in the original study except that they were not selected as newborns having hospital records free from complications of pregnancy and delivery. Twenty-six of the children who participated in the Replication Study were selected because their parents, when newlyweds, had participated in another phase of the longitudinal research program at the Child Research Branch, National Institute of Mental Health. The other 32 children lived in neighborhoods near our research nursery school. The procedures and measures, however, that were used to evaluate the 33 boys and 25 girls as they attended our research nursery school in groups of five for five weeks were the same as those used in the original study. In the original study all preschool behavior measures relating significantly to the anomaly score were factor-analyzed for both males and females, with the result that measures reflecting fast-acting, impulsive, uncontrolled behavior were loaded heavily on the first factor for males and the first factor for females. These two first factors, one for males and one for females, were labeled hyperactivity. The second factor for males represented a tractability factor, but the second factor for females represented intractability and inhibition. The measures included some ratings done independently by two teachers and some observations based on behavioral counts or times.

The mean anomaly score for the replication sample of 33 males was 4.09, standard deviation was 2.08, and the range was from 1 to 9. Since the correlates of the anomaly score in the replication sample of males were very similar to the correlates in the original sample, we obtained for each of the boys in the replication sample a factor score based on the weights from the previous hyperactivity factor. (For this replication sample of males, the reliabilities for the ratings and observations ranged from .72 to .92.) This hyperactivity factor score for the males in the replication sample was found to be significantly correlated with the anomaly score ($r = .49, p < .01$). That is, the boys in the Replication Study who had high anomaly scores tended to be high on the hyperactivity factor. Further substantiation of this relation was obtained by correlating the anomaly score with an objective count of times the child was restrained by the teachers during "resting" time ($r = .46, p < .01$). Frenetic, impulsive, poorly controlled behavior was again found to characterize preschool boys who had more than an average number of minor anomalies.

The mean anomaly score for the replication sample of 25 females was 3.56, standard deviation was 2.20, and the range was from 0 to 7. Relations to the cluster of variables making up the hyperactivity factor in the original sample of females were not found again in the replication sample of females. Instead, variables making up the intractability-inhibition factor seemed to characterize the replication sample of females with the high anomaly scores. A score for each girl based on the weighted measures from this previously obtained second factor was significantly related to the anomaly score ($r = .42, p < .05$). That is, girls with the greater number of minor anomalies moved about less, opposed peers more, and were more perseverative than girls with fewer anomalies. For this replication sample of females the inter-rater and split-half reliabilities for the ratings and observations ranged from .53 to .92. Also, during the five weeks of nursery school, the girls with high anomaly scores were rated by the teachers as showing more fearfulness ($r = .48, p < .01$) and more vacant staring ($r = .63, p < .001$), and as staying closer to an adult ($r = .44, p < .01$), than those with low anomaly scores. These three measures (Fearfulness, Vacant staring, Closeness to an adult base) were based on 11-point rating scales which had inter-rater reliabilities greater than .80. A child high on "Fearfulness" was described as characteristically appearing to be guarded, wary, defensive, apprehensive, frightened, or panicky. A child high on "Closeness to an adult base" was described as spending an unusually large amount of time clinging tightly to teacher, hiding her eyes, not exploring the situation either visually or otherwise. A child high on "Vacant staring" was described as being immobile and staring without apparent focus much more than other children did. Since these three measures were significantly interrelated, a composite was formed by summing her standard scores on the three ratings. This composite was significantly related to the anomaly score ($r = .59, p < .01$). Thus, girls with high anomaly scores in this sample were overcontrolled, inhibited, stubborn, and perseverative rather than hyperactive.

The higher incidence of these minor physical anomalies in the Replication Study when compared to the original study is due to having more precise norms making it possible to set a smaller deviation from the normal as a criterion for an anomaly. Also, we included in the Replication Study the anomaly "Head circumference outside normal range" that was not reported in the original study.

STABILITY STUDY

Other investigators have reported on the stability of hyperactivity between the preschool years and early adolescence. For example, Kagan and Moss (1962), using the term *hyperkinesis* to mean the inability to inhibit impulses to action, found that hyperkinetic behavior showed a high degree of stability over the years three to fourteen for both sexes. MacFarlane, Allen, and Honzik (1962) reported almost the same percentage of cases that showed "overactivity" at three showed "overactivity" at seven. They also reported an inter-age correlation of .42 between age five and ten years.

In the present investigation, the interest was in seeing if this stability of hyperactive behavior held true for the original sample over a period of five years, as well as in seeing if the anomaly scores were stable. In addition, it was expected that (a) hyperactivity at seven and a half would relate to the anomaly score at seven and a half and to the anomaly score at two and a half, and (b) hyperactivity at two and a half would relate to the anomaly score at seven and a half.

The stability data for the anomalies and hyperactive behavior were obtained from a follow-up study at age seven and a half of 35 males and 27 females who had been among the two-and-a-half-year-olds studied in the original sample. A person who had not known the children at age two and a half, and had no knowledge of their previous anomaly score or their nursery school behavior, assessed each child for the presence of the minor physical anomalies.

Impulsive, fast-moving behavior at age seven and a half was evaluated by one objective measure and two reliable ratings made of the child in free play and testing situations. Two ratings, "Frenetic behavior" and "Inability to delay," were made with no previous knowledge of the child. A child rated high on "Frenetic behavior" was one who much more than the others showed impulsive, fast-moving, ineffective, incomplete, and hyperactive play. A child rated high on "Inability to delay" was one who when required to wait to take part in any activity seemed unusually unable to wait for gratification. The objective measure of hyperactive free play was the distance (in 9 × 9 in. square floor units) traversed during free play divided by time, for each shift in location during 20 minutes of free play. The setting was a nursery school playroom very similar to the one used when the children were age two and a half. Data were obtained from a continuous narrative spoken by an observer into a tape recorder and subsequently scored for a number of shifts in location and rate of each shift.

In addition to evaluating minor physical anomalies and impulsive, fast-moving behavior, we tested each child for IQ and motor coordination. The IQ measure (WISC) was part of a larger assessment package concerned with longitudinal correlates of cognitive behavior. We plan to report this aspect of the study elsewhere. Our thinking regarding individual differences in motor coordination was that "clumsiness" might be correlated with the anomaly score since poor gross and fine motor coordination has often been found associated with an aggregate of symptoms defining hyperactivity. Both "hyperactivity," or "acting out," and motoric involvements such as athetoid movements and lack of balance have been considered "soft signs" of some minimal cerebral dysfunction. In order to measure individual differences in both fine and gross motor coordination we constructed a scale which combined adaptations of the Lincoln Oseretsky test of motor development (Sloan, 1955) and a neurological examination developed by Ozer (1968; unpublished manuscript). From the Oseretsky test we deleted a number of items that were either too easy or too difficult for our age range, and then added some of the tasks from the Ozer neurological examination.

The final version of the scale consisted of 34 items, most of which were scored on a simple pass-fail criterion. Typical tasks the child was asked to perform were balancing on each leg for at least ten seconds, touching each finger tip with the thumb in rapid succession, and sorting matchsticks into boxes as rapidly as possible. Inter-coder agreement for the motor scale was quite high ($r = .97$).

TABLE 2

Correlates of the Anomaly Score at Age 7½
(Stability Study)

VARIABLES	MALES N = 35 $\bar{X} = 4.91, \sigma = 2.66,$ RANGE: 1–11	FEMALES N = 27 $\bar{X} = 3.74, \sigma = 2.33,$ RANGE: 0–10
Anomaly score at 2½	.71**	.70**
Rate of shifts during free play at 7½	.30†	.36†
Inability to delay at 7½	.39‡	.63**
Frenetic behavior at 7½	.34†	.52‡
Motor coordination at 7½	−.41‡	−.48‡
Full scale IQ at 7½*	−.34†	−.46‡
Verbal IQ at 7½	−.35†	−.33†
Hyperactivity factor at 2½	.47‡	.69**
Inability to delay at 2½	.49‡	.41†
Frenetic behavior at 2½	.45‡	.43†

* Correlates with IQ measures based on total anomaly scores and other correlates based on weighted anomaly scores.
† $p < .05$
‡ $p < .01$
** $p < .001$

The results of the Stability Study are summarized in Table 2. This table shows the correlation of the anomaly score at age seven and a half with the following: (a) the anomaly score at age two and a half, (b) the three measures of impulsive, fast-moving behavior, (c) the motor coordination scale, (d) IQ measures, (e) a factor score based on the weighted measures included in the hyperactivity factor for males and hyperactivity factor for females in the original study, and (f) ratings of "Frenetic play" and "Inability to delay" when the children were two and a half. Of interest, too, is the fact that "Frenetic play" at seven and a half correlated significantly with the same rating done independently at two and a half: males, .34 ($p < .05$) and females,

.64 (p < .001). For "Inability to delay" the across-age correlates were: males, .50 (p < .01) and females, .40 (p < .05).

These data demonstrate that: (a) the weighted anomaly score tended to be stable over the five years, (b) children with high anomaly scores still tended to be more frenetic and have less behavioral control than children with few anomalies, (c) children at age seven and a half with high anomaly scores tended to be clumsy, (d) children at age seven and a half with more than an average number of minor physical anomalies tended to have lower than average IQ scores, (e) frenetic, fast-moving behavior showed continuity over five years, and (f) the children at age seven and a half with high anomaly scores tended to have been hyperactive as two-and-a-half-year-olds. In other words, generally speaking both the anomaly score and the associated hyperactive behavior were stable over the five-year period. Also, children at age seven and a half with high anomaly scores were likely to be poorly coordinated and to have lower than average verbal ability.

STUDY OF CHILDREN DEFICIENT IN SPEECH AND/OR HEARING

If minor anomalies do result from variations in embryological development, it is reasonable to expect that there would be a higher incidence of the anomalies in a sample of children selected for congenital deficiencies than there would be in a sample of normal children. To test this hypothesis we examined 31 boys and 10 girls who had been referred by physicians to an Easter Seal Treatment Center Nursery School because of deficiencies in speech and/or hearing. Mothers of 4 of the 31 boys and 7 of the 10 girls were thought to have had rubella while they were pregnant with these children.

The mean anomaly score for the Easter Seal samples was compared with the mean anomaly score for the replication samples of boys and girls. See Table 3. The replication samples were chosen for this analysis because we had used exactly the same method of scoring anomalies in these samples as in the Easter Seal samples.

TABLE 3

Comparison of Anomalies in Easter Seal and Replication Samples

SAMPLE	MALES				FEMALES			
	N	$\bar{X}$	σ	RANGE	N	$\bar{X}$	σ	RANGE
Replication Study	33	4.1	2.1	1–9	25	3.6	2.2	0–7
Easter Seal	31	7.6	2.3	3–12	10	8.3	2.3	4–11
Rubella Subsample	4	7.2	2.3	5–11	7	9.0	1.8	6–11

A t value of 6.35 (p < .001) was obtained when the means of the anomaly scores for males in the Easter Seal sample were compared with the means for males in the Replication Study. For females this t value was 5.39 (p < .001).

In the small subsample of four boys and seven girls from the Easter Seal samples where there was direct evidence of a teratogenic agent (rubella) present during early prenatal development, the mean anomaly scores were also significantly higher than the mean anomaly scores in the replication samples. For males the t was 2.32 ($p < .05$), for females the t was 6.48 ($p < .001$), and for the combined sample the t was 5.96 ($p < .001$).

From Table 4 we can make interesting comparisons across two male samples (replication and Easter Seal) of the percentage of children having each of the observed anomalies. Indeed, it was surprising to find that close to three-fourths of the boys in the Easter Seal Center sample had curved fifth fingers, high-steepled palates, partial syndactylia of the second and third toes, and epicanthus.

TABLE 4

Incidence of Anomalies

ANOMALIES	EASTER SEAL MALES (%)	REPLICATION STUDY MALES (%)
Curved 5th finger	88	21
High steepled palate	72	48
Partial syndactylia	68	30
Epicanthus	68	42
Asymmetrical ears	64	27
Abnormal head circumference	56	30
Hyperteliorism	56	15
Soft pliable ears	48	21
Big gap between 1st and 2nd toes	48	9
Two or more hair whorls	44	27
Third toe longer than 2nd	32	39
Low seated ears	28	21
Electric hair	16	12
Malformed ears	16	6
Adherent ear lobes	12	27
Single palmar crease	4	12

No behavior measures were collected on the Easter Seal children. Their teachers, however, characterized at least 32 of the 41 children as hyperactive, and used phrases such as "destructive," "overactive," "management problem," "unable to wait," "constantly demanding attention," "jumpy," "very aggressive," "a behavior problem," "swings from the rafters" to describe them.

The results from the Easter Seal samples are evidence that there is a higher incidence of these *minor* physical anomalies among children with *major* congenital problems. This finding, plus the well-known fact that an even higher incidence of these minor anomalies is found among children with gross chromosomal defects (Down's Syndrome), argues for the congenital etiology of the anomalies. Thus it would seem that the higher the incidence of multiple minor physical anomalies the greater the severity of the congenital problem.

DISCUSSION

These analyses have not been directed to the location of cut-off points where the presence of a certain number of minor physical anomalies might indicate impulse-control problems; but some suggestions based on clinical observations can be offered. Consistently across samples, boys with some of these anomalies (4–8) seemed to have trouble with inner controls—they were active, frenetic, unable to wait, intractable, and had poor motor control. Girls with the same number of anomalies (4–8) were variable across samples. In one sample they were very similar to the boys, that is, they were fast-moving, frenetic, and intractable; in another sample they were still intractable, but instead of being fast-moving and having poor motor control they tended to be immobile, to stare vacantly, and to have excessive motor control. Both boys and girls seemed to have difficulties with control, whether too much or too little. The children who had a major deficiency typically considered congenital (i.e., impaired speech and/or hearing) had on the average four more of these anomalies than the "normal." It is well known that those children with a great many anomalies tend to have major, specifically congenital defects, such as Down's Syndrome. Thus it seems that the higher the incidence of multiple minor physical anomalies the greater the severity of a congenital problem or vice versa.

It is plausible to think in terms of the neurological substrate for control of impulsive behavior as developing at the same time as these minor anomalies develop. The same insult (about which we can only speculate at this time) most likely results in *both* the occurrence of the anomalies and the relatively poor control over behavior which was seen in children with high anomaly scores.

The causes for the anomalies and the predisposition to fast-moving behavior in boys and to either fast-moving or immobile behavior in girls could be genetic, such as some chromosomal irregularity; or the cause could be the result of a noxious agent affecting embryological development, such as the rubella virus; or the cause could be subtle variations in early embryological development. At this time we can only speculate about which of these alternatives may be true.

References

ACHS, R., HARPER, R., & SIEGEL, M. Unusual dermatoglyphic findings associated with rubella embryopathy. *New England Journal of Medicine*, 1966, *274*, 148–150.

BENDA, C. E. *The child with mongolism*. New York: Grune & Stratton, 1960.

GOLDFARB, W., & BOTSTEIN, A. Physical stigmata in schizophrenic children. Unpublished manuscript, Henry Ittleson Center for Child Research, Brooklyn, N.Y.

GUSTAVSON, K. *Down's syndrome: a clinical and cytogenetical investigation*. Uppsala: Institute for Medical Genetics of the University of Uppsala, 1964.

KAGAN, J., & Moss, H. A. *Birth to maturity*. New York: Wiley, 1962.

MACFARLANE, J. W., ALLEN, L., & HONZIK, M. A developmental study of the behavior problems of normal children between 21 months and 14 years. Berkeley & Los Angeles: University of California Press, 1962.

OZER, M. N. The neurological evaluation of school-age children. *Journal of Learning Disabilities*, 1968, *1*, 84–87.

——, & MILGRAM, N. A. The effects of neurological and environmental factors on the language development of Head Start Children: an evaluation of the Head Start Program. Unpublished manuscript.

SLOAN, W. The Lincoln-Oseretsky motor development scale. *Genetic Psychology Monograph*, 1955, *51*, 183–252.

SMITH, E. W., & BOSTIAN, K. E. Congenital anomalies associated with idiopathic mental retardation. *Journal of Pediatrics*, 1964, *65*, 189–196.

VICKERS, V. S., & STUART, H. C. Anthropometry in the pediatrician's office. Norms for selected body measurements based on studies of children of North European stock. *Journal of Pediatrics*, 1943, *22*, 155–170.

WALDROP, M. F., PEDERSEN, F. A., & BELL, R. Q. Minor physical anomalies and behavior in preschool children. *Child Development*, 1968, *39*, 391–400.

6

Intellectual Development

The first two authors, psychologists Lawrence Kohlberg and Edward Chittenden, discuss the process of cognitive development according to Piaget. Kohlberg describes what traditional intelligence tests measure and compares them with what Piagetian tests measure, giving some insights into what aspects of intelligence are inherited, what are modifiable by training and what can be depressed by a very impoverished environment. Chittenden illustrates Piaget's theory with practical examples, stressing the major role of the child's own activity and the minor but supporting role of the teacher.

Children differ in their patterns of inhibiting action while planning and considering information. Such differences in reflectivity were found in two-year-olds by N. Dickon Repucci, who related these measures to sustaining of involvement in play. Results suggest a biological component in reflectivity which is modified by experience as the child matures.

Bilingualism is the topic of the last two articles. Carol Feldman and Michael Shen show that there are advantages to speaking two languages. Bilingual Head Start children did better than monolinguals in tests of appreciation of object constancy, naming and using labels in sentences. Knowing that the same thing is called by two different names is probably helpful to the young child in coming to realize that names are arbitrary, rather than attributes of objects. The short article by kindergarten-training-instructor Maebah Becenti is a poignant description of what the non-English-speaking child encounters when he enters a school where only English is spoken. The author knows from firsthand experience as a Navajo child.

Psychometric and Piagetian Measures of Preschool Intellectual Growth

Lawrence Kohlberg
HARVARD UNIVERSITY

I. PSYCHOMETRIC GENERAL INTELLIGENCE IN THE PRESCHOOL PERIOD

The claim that early stimulus deprivation leads to irreversible cognitive deficit must be viewed with great caution. As increasingly careful work has been done in the effects of early deprivation in infants, the impressionistic conclusions of

Reprinted from "Early Education: A Cognitive-Developmental View," *Child Development*, *39*, 1048–1055. Copyright © 1968 by The Society for Research in Child Development, Inc. By permission.

Spitz and Bowlby as to massive irreversible cognitive and developmental retardation due to maternal and stimulus deprivation in infancy have come increasingly under question (Robinson, 1968; Yarrow, 1964). A number of studies (Dennis & Najarian, 1957; Rheingold & Bayley, 1965) indicate that some observed retardation due to infant institutional deprivation, and some observed compensation by infant enrichment programs, wash out in later development.

The major factual considerations leading to the notion of a preschool critical period in cognition derive from neither animal nor institutionalization studies. The real basis for stressing preschool cognitive programs comes from the belated recognition by educators that differences in the child's educational achievement are primarily due to the characteristics of the child and of his home environment rather than to the child's elementary schooling as such. This point has been ably documented by Bloom (1964). According to Bloom, longitudinal studies indicate that about 50 per cent of the child's final intelligence and about 33 per cent of his performance on school achievement tests is predictable from measures of his intelligence before he enters school. While the fact that later achievement is quite predictable from intelligence test functioning at school entrance is unquestionable, the implication that the preschool era is a "critical period" for the environmental stimulation of intellectual development and that raising the IQ in this period is a practical and feasible goal for preschool programs is questionable.

The critical-period interpretation of test stabilization data starts from the finding that tests administered in the first year of life do not predict adult intelligence scores, that tests administered at school entrance sizably do predict these scores, and that there is only a small increase in predictability found if tests are administered later than school entrance. The critical-period interpretation of this large increase in predictability from age 1 to age 6 is due to the fact that environmental stimulation has "fixed" intellectual growth and functioning during this period. This interpretation, as elaborated by Bloom (1964), is based on two assumptions. The first is that the degree of predictability from a childhood test to an adult ability test is a function of the proportion of the pool of adult knowledge and skills tested which has developed at the childhood age. The second assumption is that the filling in of the ability pool between the two time points is largely a function of differential environment. Neither assumption seems tenable in light of other known findings concerning intelligence. The stability of intelligence tests after age 6 is not necessarily due to the completion of development at age 6 of half the elements composing adult ability but may be due to the continuing stable influence of both heredity and environment after this age. With regard to stabilization due to the environment, it should be recognized that the stimulation potential of home and neighborhood are more or less constant throughout childhood. The fact that low IQ of 6-year-olds from culturally deprived homes predicts to low IQ in adolescence does not necessarily indicate that the effect of environment on adult intelligence occurred primarily in the preschool years. The deprivation of the environment is fairly constant and continues to operate throughout the childhood years and accordingly contributes to the predictability of the preschool IQ to later intelligence.

With regard to stabilization due to heredity, there is also no reason to assume that this factor is completely manifest in early infancy or in the preschool years. With regard to the hereditary, no new evidence has accumulated in the last 25 years to modify earlier conclusions as to massive genetic components of general intellectual ability. It is not meaningful to specify definite quantitative estimates of hereditary and environmental contributions to intelligence, because such estimates depend upon the range of variation of heredity and of environments considered. If all the children considered grow up in middle-class suburban homes and schools, then most of the variation in their intelligence will be due to hereditary variability. If environments vary tremendously, so that some children are raised in orphanages without stimulation and some in a rich environment, then environment will account for much more of the variability in intelligence. In spite of these qualifications, it is safe to say that the twin studies suggest that at least 50 per cent of the reliable variation in general intelligence test scores (if reliably or repeatedly measured) at the school-age level among a "normally" reared, medically normal group of American children is contributed by hereditary factors. A very large portion of the predictability of later intelligence and achievement scores from scores on intelligence tests given at entrance to school, then, is the product of hereditary factors.

The major reason the hereditary contribution to stability of intelligence scores has been questioned recently is that infant tests do not predict to adult status, and it has been assumed that a hereditary factor should be manifested at birth. In fact, however, baby tests simply do not measure the same dispositions as do later intelligence tests, whether these dispositions be viewed as due to hereditary or to environment. Baby tests were not constructed to measure cognition (i.e., eduction of relations and categories) but to record the age of appearance of sensory and motor responses.[1] Factor analytic studies indicate very little overlap between the content of baby tests and the content of intelligence tests, whereas they indicate something like a general cognitive factor in intelligence tests given after age 4.

Accordingly, the hereditary components of adult intelligence are not manifested in baby tests, which represent hereditary (and environmental) factors quite different than those influencing school-age or adult intelligence test functioning. Because of this, much of the difference between the adult predictive power of infant tests and of school entrance tests is due to the fact that only the latter tap the hereditary contribution to adult intellectual status. This is demonstrated by the studies of Skodak, Skeels, and Honzik, reviewed by Jones (1954), which indicate a regular rise up until age 5 in the correlations between the IQ of children in foster homes and the education of their real mothers; this almost exactly parallels the rise in infant-mother correlations found for home-reared children. These correlations, then, cannot be attributed to stimulation by the real parents themselves. Rather, they indicate that the cognitive abilities of the adults (reflected in educational status or test per-

---

[1] This assumption is not clearly implausible, however, for the cognitive baby tests patterned after Piaget's baby observations, developed by Uzgiris and Hunt (1964) and by this writer (Kohlberg, 1961).

formance) represent hereditary factors, which influence later cognitive performance of their children and are quite different from the hereditary factors influencing baby test performance.

The increase of predictability between infant tests and tests at school entrance is, then, largely the result of the fact that infant tests do not reflect the hereditary contribution to adult intelligence and is only in part the result of the filling in of intellectual skills by environment in these years. The weakness of the alternative "critical period" interpretation may be indicated by imagining findings in which baby tests at 1 month did not predict to adult intelligence, but baby tests at 7 months predicted 40 per cent of the variance of adult intelligence. The critical-period interpretive model would then require one to say: first, that 40 per cent of adult intellectual abilities were acquired in the first 6 months and, second, that their acquisition was primarily due to environment. In fact, the only plausible interpretation of the finding would be that the 1-month test was invalid as an intelligence test and that the 7-month test was a good indicator of the hereditary components of adult intellectual functioning.

We have claimed that neither cognitive-developmental theory nor empirical findings support the notion that the preschool period is a specially open period for stimulating general intelligence or general cognitive development. These conclusions are strengthened by the rather disappointing findings concerning the actual effects of preschool cognitive stimulation upon performance on psychometric tests of general intelligence. Morrisett (1966) summarizes reviews of the literature (Fowler, 1968; Robinson, 1968) as well as unpublished work suggesting "that there is no compelling evidence for the long-term effectiveness of short-term educational intervention at the preschool level. Many preschool programs for disadvantaged children have shown that they make relatively large gains in intelligence test performance during the first year of the program; but this characteristic acceleration in intellectual growth is not always maintained during a second preschool year or when the children enter first grade." As one of many examples of such findings, we may cite a study of our own (Kohlberg, 1968). An integrated Montessori program for Head Start children aged 3 and 4 led to a mean 14-point increase in Stanford-Binet IQ in the first 6 months. No significant further increase in IQ was found during the remaining $1\frac{1}{2}$ years in which the children were in the program. The initial IQ increases could not be considered actual increases in general cognitive-structural development, since they were not paralleled by any significant increases in performance upon Piaget cognitive-structural tasks. The primary cause of the IQ increase was an improvement in attention and rapport with adults. Increases in rated attention in the classroom (as well as in the test situation) were marked during the first 6 months, and individual improvement in rated attention correlated .63 with improvement in Stanford-Binet IQ's during this period. In addition to attention, verbalization showed a sharp initial spurt related to improvement on IQ performance. In summary, then, it appears that the IQ changes were more a result of changes in cognitive motivation than a change in cognitive capacity. These changes in turn had a ceiling rather than moving continuously upward, and the motivational changes themselves did not lead to a later increase in cognitive capacity because of increased general learning.

II. PIAGET CONCEPTS AND MEASURES OF PRESCHOOL INTELLECTUAL GROWTH

In the preceding section, we concluded that studies using psychometric tests indicate a heavy hereditary determination of intelligence and suggests that the effects of programs of preschool stimulation upon intelligence are rather minor and transient. We must now consider Hunt's (1961) suggestion that these conclusions may be specific to the concepts and methods employed by psychometric tests and might be revised by work with the newer concepts of methods of studying intelligence developed by Piaget.

It is not surprising to find that psychometric tests include a core of performance due to general cognitive ability of a partially hereditary nature, when this core constituted the rationale for their construction. The rationale of the general intelligence test of Binet, Spearman, and Wechsler (Spearman, 1930) is that of measuring a fixed biological capacity, as is implied in the division of performance into "g" (general ability) and "s" (specific experience) factors. Experience factors are largely consigned to "specificity" rather than to general intelligence. This rationale led to the construction of tests designed to wash out experience effects, partly by providing novel tasks and partly by providing a random and heterogeneous sample of tasks. Such tests lead to a sum score in which individual differences in experience with specific tasks might be expected to balance out. Stated differently, the Binet-Spearman approach has avoided defining basic cognitive achievements except in highly general terms ("eduction of relations and correlates") applicable to any task. Any item or achievement is a good intelligence test item if it elicits individual differences relating to other ability items. The more the item fails to correlate generally with all other items the worse or the more "specific experience loaded" the item is assumed to be.

There can be no question that this approach has yielded longitudinally stable and situationally general measures, which predict to all sorts of good outcomes in personality adjustment and in general problem solving as well as in scholastic achievement. However, the Spearman-Binet-Wechsler approach is not the only approach to yielding longitudinally stable and situationally general measures of cognitive development. In contrast to the psychometric approach to intelligence, the Piaget approach attempts to specify the basic concepts or operations characterizing each developmental era. It does not range over a wide variety of developmental items in order to wash out specific experience effects and leave a general rate of learning or development factor. Instead, it attempts to theoretically define some general cognitive operations and restricts items to those which may elicit such operations.

In a sense, then, Piaget's definition of intelligence or intellectual development is an a priori theoretical one, and it is irrelevant to him whether or not it leads to measures of situationally general and longitudinally stable individual differences. However, it is obvious that cognitive age-development as defined by Piaget's conceptions and cognitive age-development as defined by the Binet sampling approach must have some relation to one another. In fact the correlations between summed scores on Piaget tests and Binet scores are in the .70's for children of a given age (Kohlberg, 1966; DeVries, in preparation). These findings seem to accord with Piaget's view that psychometric tests of intelligence get at the same thing as his tests, but in less pure and conceptually understandable form (1947, p. 154):

> It is indisputable that these tests of mental age have on the whole lived up to what was expected of them: a rapid and convenient estimation of an individual's general level. But it is no less obvious that they simply measure a "yield," without reaching constructive operations themselves. As Pieron rightly pointed out, intelligence conceived in these terms is essentially a value-judgment applied to complex behavior. Inhelder was able to distinguish moronism from imbecility by the presence of concrete groupings and slight backwardness by an inability to reason formally. This is one of the first applications of a method which could be developed further for determining level of intelligence in general.

In this spirit, Pinard and Laurendeau (1964) have been developing a standardized method of assessing general intelligence or mental age with the Piaget procedures.

The writer's own view on this problem is somewhat different than that expressed by Piaget. My interpretation is that there is a hereditary general ability component of psychometric tests, a general "eduction of relations and correlates" or "rate of information-processing" factor, which contributes, along with other factors, to general cognitive-structural development as defined by Piaget. As I stressed earlier, the insistence of Piaget that *universal cognitive structures* are the result of interaction and are not pre-formed or maturational does not constitute a denial of the quantitative influence of heredity upon *individual differences in rate* of formation of these structures. It might be found that the rate at which experience was assimilated to create new cognitive structures was largely a function of genetic factors, and yet these structures would still be said to depend upon experiences as long as it was found that every child who developed the structures had had certain universal physical or social experiences.

While hereditary factors may enter into Piaget level, Piaget's theory also provides a definite rationale for the existence of item-general and longitudinally predictive differences in cognitive level based on differential amounts of general experience. The Piaget approach allows experiential effects to define general rather than specific differences in performance. General effects of experience are revealed in manner of handling a familiar object, specific effects in familiarity with the object itself. As an example, the dream experience is familiar to all children at every age, and the dream scale attempts to assess the qualitative mode of thought-response to the dream, not familiarity with it. It assumes that the structural level of the concept involves the general effects of experience and is not much affected by highly specific experience with the object in question. This focus is supported by the assessment of presence or absence of a level of thought or an intellectual operation, not assessment of speed and facility in its use. Piaget procedures treat the high school boy and Einstein as alike in possession of formal operations, though they differ greatly in their use. The generality of intellectual level in the Piaget view results from the fact that cognitive stages are structured wholes rather than from an innate rate factor. Intellectual performance is general because it rests on general operations which develop as total structures, not because it represents a general biological factor intersecting with specific experience or learnings (Smedslund, 1964).

In similar fashion, Piaget's theory may be used to account for the stability of intelligence without postulating an innate rate of growth factor. Longitudinal stability of cognitive level is implied by the existence of invariant sequences in cognitive development which has been found for many Piaget-type tasks (Sigel, 1964; Sigel & Hooper, 1968). Attainment of a given level of development implies successive attainment of all the preceding levels of development. Accordingly, relative cognitive maturity at a later age should be predictable from maturity at an earlier age without the assumption of an innate rate factor. If all children must go through an invariant sequence in cognitive development, children at a lower level at an earlier time point must go through more intervening stages and therefore will be relatively low at a later time point.

The writer and his colleagues (DeVries, in preparation; Kohlberg, 1963; Kohn, in preparation) have been engaged in research comparing psychometric and Piaget intellectual measures at ages 4 to 7 with regard to the following hypotheses derived from the framework just stated:

1. There should be a "general factor" among Piaget tests greater than that found among general psychometric items, but largely accounting for the general factor in the psychometric items.

2. Relative level on the Piaget tasks should be more longitudinally stable in the years 4 to 7 than would be expected from the stability of psychometric intelligence in this period.

3. Piaget items should depend more on general experience, and hence chronological age, than psychometric items. Accordingly older average children should be more advanced on Piaget tasks than younger bright children matched for psychometric mental age.

4. Mere chronological aging should not, however, lead to greater development on Piaget items if the environment is very deprived. Culturally disadvantaged children, then, should show more retardation on nonverbal Piaget tasks than control children matched for psychometric mental age.

While much of the data from this research program has not yet been processed, some preliminary findings are available. While correlating with the Binet, Piaget tasks also hang together after Binet and other psychometric intellectual factors are removed. Presumably the intertask consistency of Piaget level represents a "general factor" independent of any innate rate factors entering into the Binet. The fact that chronological age correlates with the Piaget factor, with Binet mental age controlled, but that this correlation does not hold under conditions of cultural deprivation, gives additional support to the notion that the Piaget "factor" represents a general and longitudinally predictive residue of effects of experience upon cognitive development.

The logic and preliminary findings just mentioned suggest a number of reasons why Piaget measures might reflect general increments in cognitive development due to natural or educational experience better than do psychometric measures. In principle they resolve the paradox of the Binet, which almost forces us to view any educational increments as specific contents or as motivational sets not truly reflecting cognitive-structural development.[2] Insofar as Piaget measures of intelligence define general and sequential (longitudinally predictive) structural effects of general experience, they should be valuable in assessing the effects of various types of general cognitive-stimulation programs, whether or not these programs define accelerating Piagetian intellectual development as explicit objectives.

The possibility that Piagetian measures will detect some general and stable effects of preschool cognitive-stimulation programs more clearly than do psychometric measures does not, however, change the fundamental caution about preschool stimulation of general intelligence or cognitive development reflected in the previous section. The findings on acceleration of Piaget concrete operations indicate that such acceleration is neither easy nor does it typically generalize, either to other Piaget tasks or to Binet mental age tasks. With regard to the critical-period issue, it also does not appear that a wave of longitudinal, twin, and experimental studies using Piagetian measures would lead to radically different conclusions than those of the psychometric studies as to the role of heredity and of preschool experience upon long-range intellectual development. The fact that Piagetian and psychometric measures correlate as well as they do seems to preclude this possibility.

References

BLOOM, B. *Stability and change in human characteristics.* New York: Wiley, 1964.

DENNIS, W. and NAJARIAN, P. Infant development under environmental handicap. *Physchological Monographs,* 1957, *71* (7, Whole No. 436).

DEVRIES, R. Performance of bright, average, and retarded children on Piagetian concrete operation tasks. Unpublished monograph, University of Chicago, Early Educational Research Center, in preparation.

FOWLER, W. The early stimulation of cognitive development. In R. Hess and R. Bear (Eds.), *Preschool education: Theory, research and action.* Chicago: Aldine, 1968.

HUNT, J. McV. *Intelligence and experience.* New York: Ronald, 1961.

JONES, H. Environmental influences in the development of intelligence. In L. Carmichael (Ed.), *Manual of child psychology.* New York: Wiley, 1954.

KOHLBERG, L. A schedule for assessing Piaget's stages of sensorimotor development in infancy. Unpublished schedule, Yale University, 1961, mimeographed.

———. Stages in children's conceptions of physical and social objects in the years 4 to 8—a study of developmental theory. Unpublished monograph, 1963, multigraphed (in preparation for publication).

———. The Montessori approach to cultural deprivation. A cognitive-development

---

[2] This was our interpretation of Binet increments in the Montessori program. We claimed they were due to attentional and verbalization factors rather than to general or cognitive-structural development, since the changes were not reflected in increments in Piaget performance. The study also suggested that this was not due to any failure of the Piaget tasks to assess general cognitive level. It was found that Piaget tests were more stable than the Binet tests, i.e., they yielded test-retest reliabilities between a 2- to 4-month period in the 90's. It was also found that when a child was initially high on the Piaget tests and low on the Binet tests, he would increase markedly on the Binet test at the later period. In other words, the Piaget tests were more situation-free measures of cognitive capacity. Using nonverbal techniques (choice of lengths of gum, glasses of Coca Cola) to indicate possession of the conservation concept, the Piaget tasks elicited evidence of cognitive maturity masked by distractibility or shyness in the Binet situation. The Piaget tests, then, seemed to eliminate some "noncognitive" situational and verbal factors due to experience.

interpretation and some research findings. In R. Hess and R. Bear (Eds.), *Preschool education, theory, research and action.* Chicago: Aldine, 1968.

――――. Cognitive stages and preschool education. *Human Development*, 1966, *9*, 5–19.

――――, and LESSER, G. *What preschools can do: theories and programs.* Chicago: Scott, Foresman, in press.

KOHN, N. The development of culturally disadvantaged and middle class Negro children on Piagetian tests of concrete operational thought. Doctoral dissertation, University of Chicago, in preparation.

MORRISETT, L. Report of a conference on preschool education in *Items of the Social Science Research Council*, June, 1966.

PIAGET, J. *The psychology of intelligence.* London: Routledge, Kegan, 1947.

PINARD, A. and LAURENDEAU, M. *Causal thinking in children.* New York: International University Press, 1964.

RHEINGOLD, H., and BAYLEY, N. The later effects of an experimental modification of mothering. In C. B. Stendler (Ed.), *Readings in child behavior and development.* New York: Harcourt, Brace & World. 1965.

ROBINSON, H. The problem of timing in preschool education. In R. Hess and R. Bear (Eds.), *Preschool education: theory, research and action.* Chicago: Aldine, 1968.

SIGEL, I. The attainment of concepts. In M. Hoffman and L. Hoffman (Eds.), *Review of child development research.* Vol. 1. New York: Russell Sage, 1964.

――――, and HOOPER F. (Eds.), *Logical thinking in children: research based on Piaget's theory.* New York: Holt, Rinehart and Winston, 1968.

SMEDSLUND, J. Concrete reasoning: a study of intellectual development. *Monographs of the Society for Research in Child Development*, 1964, *29* (2, Serial No. 93), 3–39.

SPEARMAN, C. The psychology of "g." In C. Murchison (Ed.), *Psychologies of 1930.* Worcester, Mass.: Clark University Press, 1930.

UZGIRIS, I., and HUNT, J. McV. A scale of infant psychological development. Unpublished manuscript, University of Illinois, 1964.

YARROW, L. Separation from parents during early childhood. In M. L. Hoffman (Ed.), *Review of child development research.* Vol. 1. New York: Russell Sage, 1964.

What Is Learned and What Is Taught

Edward A. Chittenden

EDUCATIONAL TESTING SERVICE

Much of the knowledge children absorb is best acquired by exploration in the real world where they may freely, actively construct their vision of reality, rather than be passively instructed about it. Such is the view of Piaget and other advocates of a "natural" approach to child development.

What is the place of planned instruction in programs for young children, and in what ways does such instruction contribute to the child's cognitive development? When is a highly structured approach in teaching young children

Reprinted with permission from *Young Children*, Vol. XXV, No. 1, October, 1969. Copyright © 1969, National Association for the Education of Young Children, 1834 Connecticut Ave., Washington, D.C. 20009.

appropriate, and when does a more supportive, less directive role seem called for? These questions have been discussed and debated by teachers for many years; they are important questions which raise complex issues and defy simple answers.

In this article, some of these issues are looked at in the light of two quite different, but complementary, sources of evidence. One source stems mainly from the investigations of Piaget and his colleagues on the development of intellectual processes. The other source stems from the many educational studies which have failed, in one way or another, to obtain clear evidence of differential effects of instruction.

Research workers in education have long been aware of the uncomfortable fact that a great many educational "experiments" fail to produce any objective, quantifiable evidence indicating that one approach in instruction is any better (or worse) than the next in terms of the child's intellectual growth. Whether the outcomes in these experiments are measured by IQ change, reading readiness tests or by teacher ratings, children seem to be remarkably impervious to most experimental efforts of the educator. The reasons offered for such findings of "no-effects" are complex and varied, and they range from problems of statistical inference to the question of appropriate criterion measures. In a recent review of this "no-effect" question, Stephens (1967) argues that the number of studies, at all levels of education, reporting negative findings of this sort is now so substantial that educators should stop trying to explain the result away, and should instead examine the result for what it may really represent.

A current study directed by Dr. Millie Almy of Teachers College provides the opportunity to look at the question of instruction and its effects (or lack of effects) on cognitive development, from the point of view of developmental psychology. In carrying out her earlier research (Almy, Chittenden & Miller, 1966), Dr. Almy had become interested in the apparent relationship between the developmental theory of Piaget and the new curricula for teaching science and math. New math, for example, with its emphasis on ways of thinking was much closer to Piaget's studies than was the older, traditional arithmetic. The new science curricula were quite compatible with Piaget's emphasis on abilities to order, to classify, etc. Moreover, it seemed that the new curricula which stressed discovery and exploration on the part of the learner, expressed an orientation toward teaching which resembled instructional implications of Piaget's theory.

The curricula involved in Dr. Almy's current research are: Karplus's Science Curriculum Improvement Study (SCIS), the AAAS Science programs, and the Greater Cleveland Mathematics Program. Schools on the east and west coasts were identified in which the Math and one of the science programs, or Math only, had been introduced in the kindergarten and first grades. Children in these schools, and a control group of children with no special programs, were followed longitudinally from kindergarten to second grade. In all, over 600 children were studied.

The cognitive measures used by Dr. Almy were directly adapted from Piaget's work. The measures included: conservation tasks, class inclusion problems, serial ordering items, tests of the understanding of transitive relations $(A > B, B > C, A ? C)$, and matrices. The tasks were selected for the purpose of distinguishing between responses which Piaget would classify as "logical operations" and responses which would be classified as "pre-operational." In addition to examining the effects of instruction upon cognition, Dr. Almy also undertook a content analysis of the programs and an investigation of teachers' reactions to curricular innovation.

An analysis of her results shows that there is little evidence that the new programs had any acceleratory effect on the development of logical operations. The children with no special instructional programs performed as well on the Piagetian tasks as did children who had had these programs for two years. This result appears to hold regardless of verbal abilities.

In some ways, these could be considered surprising results. The tests appear to be appropriate measures of the kinds of abilities supposedly fostered by the new instructional programs, yet no major difference between the groups of children is evident. On the other hand, such no-effects findings might well be anticipated on the basis of previous instructional studies, and also on the basis of Piaget's research on intellectual development.

PIAGET: A DEVELOPMENTAL PERSPECTIVE OF LEARNING

During the past 10 years, the work of Jean Piaget and his colleagues has moved from a status of relative obscurity in this country, to a status of relative fame. Perhaps the most widely cited aspect of his work relates to his accounts of the major stages in the development of human intelligence. In particular, much of the research in this country, including the many studies of conservation, has centered on the characteristics of the preoperational stage (ages two to seven) and the stage of concrete logical operations (ages seven to eleven).

While Piaget's analysis of stages is becoming well known, his ideas regarding the factors which bring about cognitive change are less widely discussed. What stimulates cognitive growth during the course of a stage of development? What factors contribute to the change from one level of thought to another?

ASSIMILATION/ACCOMMODATION

The central assumption in Piaget's (1967) analysis of cognitive change is his belief that development depends upon a continuous interaction between organism and environment—an interaction which involves, on the one hand, environmental forces (objects, people, events) acting upon the child and, on the other hand, the child acting selectively upon the environment. The two-way exchange is given form by the two complementary processes of "assimilation" and "accommodation." Simply stated, assimilation represents the organism acting upon the environment, and accommodation represents the influence of environmental constraints upon the organism.

The process of assimilation is perhaps most clearly illustrated with reference to observations of infant behavior. At a certain age, give a baby something new and what does he do with it? He probably puts it into his mouth. He may then take it out of his mouth and go through a little shaking routine, with movements resembling those used on his rattles. If he's about one year of age, his repertoire may include throwing it on the floor, banging it on the table, and looking or listening with interest at the result. Each of these means for exploring an object may be thought of as representing assimilatory actions for they are the baby's way of acting on his environment. They are his means of trying to assimilate objects or events of his world. Very young infants may exhibit only staring or sucking "schemas" while older ones exhibit more variety and complexity in assimilatory schemas. Children in nursery school have even richer and more elaborate ways of exploring and investigating their world.

In the very attempt to assimilate and to act upon the environment, the environment brings about changes in the assimilatory structures. The baby encounters objects that don't fit into his mouth, or objects that don't make a banging noise, and gradually he begins to differentiate between objects to suck, ones to bang, ones to squeeze, etc. The nursery school child may have the idea (the assimilatory expectation) that all big things are heavy—too heavy for him to lift—a generally accurate expectation that is built upon considerable experience. Now he is given a large block of styrofoam and finds he can lift it! His expectations are not met, and he encounters an exception which along with other exceptions will eventually lead to differentiation between the physical properties of size and weight.

These changes in concepts of size and weight, and changes in the baby's reactions to objects, are the kinds of changes which reflect the process of accommodation. Through accommodation, the realities of the environment act upon the organism and force changes in the assimilatory patterns, and thus gradually contribute to the formation of new and more elaborate ways of exploring the world.

It is important to emphasize the fact that attempts at assimilation and cognitive exploration on the part of the baby, the child, or the adult, will occur only when the object in question is perceived as familiar to some extent, and hence can activate assimilatory action. As an everyday illustration, perhaps you have noted an episode resembling the following. At the zoo, a father, mother and older child will be staring in awe at a giraffe or some other exotic creature. The three-year-old, however, is tugging at his mother's hand, not intrigued with the giraffe but wanting her to come with him while he feeds the pigeons—common, ordinary park pigeons. Pigeons are familiar to him, and their tameness in the situation intrigues him much more than the bizarre animals behind bars. For the adults, pigeons are too familiar to be interesting. For the baby in the stroller, pigeons are too distant and he spends most of his time batting at a plastic disc which hangs on the stroller and shines in an interesting way in the sun.

These common observations simply illustrate the point that curiosity and assimilatory action are aroused by the new or the novel in the context of the familiar. It is an obvious point, but a valuable one for educators to remember. In classrooms, in order to stimulate interest we sometimes devote too much effort to stressing what is new or novel and neglect the importance of familiarity.

Through assimilation and accommodation, the constraints of the environment force change in the cognitive system and thus lead to the development of new and more comprehensive assimilatory patterns. This spiral of action and reaction, described as an "equilibration" process, is central to Piaget's analysis of cognitive change.

From the teacher's point of view, Piaget's theoretical analysis of the assimilation/accommodation processes suggests several other important characteristics of learning and cognitive change.

Action   First, there is a stress on the role of action on the part of the learner. Children do not learn new ways of thinking through passive absorption of events, and Piaget's model does not depict them as sponges, soaking up wisdom. Instead, Piaget stresses the central role of active exploration. The baby is active in his carriage as he scratches the sides, stares at objects, studies his hands. The toddler lifts things, carries them about, and arranges them. Nursery school and kindergarten children are continually on the go. Of course, some of this activity can be rather aimless or frivolous, but most of it in normal settings is activity with purpose. Piaget states: "Knowledge is not a copy of reality. To know an object, to know an event, is not simply to look at it and make a mental copy, or image, of it. To know an object is to act on it" (1964, p. 8).

Repetition   Not only is action an important part of the Piagetian model, but it appears to be an action of a somewhat repetitious sort. The observant parent or teacher can give many illustrations of what appear to be repetitious behaviors associated with cognitive development. A three-year-old for several days in a row may elect to complete one puzzle. Each day he appears to go through the same sequence, but probably if we had complete movie records we would find evidence of slight, purposeful variations. The toddler laboriously piles his blocks in one chair, then transports them to another—one by one—then when finished, starts all over again. A five-year-old may spend several successive days in pouring water into various containers, mixing in color, etc.

Assimilation and accommodation are gradual processes and the child's actions upon the environment are repeated again and again with slight modifications each time. The young child who begins to differentiate the properties of size and weight has learned to do so on the basis of many liftings and pushings of objects, and only several years later will the distinction between the two be formally recognized. Concepts of weight (as an attribute separable from size) are not suddenly or quickly learned. Rather, Piaget's work implies that these and other concepts are the product of a long history of actions upon the world. It seems that Piaget differs on this point from Bruner in that Piaget depicts the child as somewhat slower and methodical, somewhat more systematic in acquisition of new ideas, while Bruner tends to depict moments of discovery and cognitive leaps.

Variation   Size and weight concepts come not only from experiences with styrofoam blocks, but they stem from experiences in all kinds of situations with all kinds of objects. Basic abilities to handle quantity and number come not just from manipulating counting cubes, but from a variety of interactions which range from block construction to handing out cookies, one to a customer. The modification of assimilatory schemas requires a variety of experiences as well as repetition and time.

Objects   Finally, we should note in Piaget's model the emphasis which is placed on the role of the object world, or the physical environment, in contrast to the adult and social world. The role of the physical world appears to be especially critical in relation to the development of logic, science and math concepts.

Piaget has described two distinct kinds of experiences with objects. First, there is physical experience which "consists of acting upon objects in order to find out something from the objects themselves" (1966, p. v.). Experiences of weighing, mixing things in water and modeling clay, would be of this type.

Secondly, there are "logicomathematical" experiences. Here, the child is also manipulating objects, but attention is not directed to the *properties* of the objects but rather to the *actions* of manipulating them. If a child counts 10 stones, if he arranges them in some way, the weight or other physical properties of the stones are in this case quite unimportant. Instead, what is important are the actions of counting, whether stones, beads or blocks are counted. Objects are essential here, but the child is learning from the actions he performs on them (the act of counting; the act of grouping, etc.) and not from the properties of the objects. Around the ages of seven or eight, these actions of ordering, enumerating and grouping, become "internalized" as concrete logical operations.

In summary, the following educational implications can be drawn from Piaget's theory.

- The theory points up the importance of exploration and activity.
- The theory stresses the important function of real events and concrete objects in children's learning. For areas of science and math, it implies that what is learned from the physical environment, through actions upon that environment, may be more important than what is learned from people, books, or TV.
- Finally, equilibration and the process of assimilation/accommodation stress the significance of self-directed and self-regulated learning. On this third point, Piaget has been rather clear: "In the area of logico-mathematical structures, children have real understanding only of that which they invent themselves, and each time that we try to teach them something too quickly, we keep them from reinventing it themselves" (1966, p. vi).

These ideas are not new to educational thought. What is new is that they are stated in the context of a comprehensive theory of intellectual development —a theory based on a half century of research.

The actions and operations of comparing objects constituted the basis for one of the tasks which Dr. Almy used to assess the cognitive development of her subjects. The task, which is intended to appraise the child's understanding of transitive relations, is posed in the following way: using three wooden rods, A is demonstrated to be longer than B, and B demonstrated to be longer than C; the subject is then asked about A and C. Since the problem, in its several variations, is set up in a way which prevents the subject from making an easy perceptual comparison of A and C, correct responses indicate the use of concrete logic. On such a task, older children will readily respond that A is longer than C, and when asked "Why?" they may assert "This (A) was bigger than that (B) and that (B) was bigger than that (C); so the first one *has* to be longer!" Their explanations and their tone of voice denote a conviction about the accuracy of their logical answer. In Piaget's terms, this would be considered an "operational" response, since the actions of comparing (A greater than B, etc.) have become internalized and are coordinated into a group of logical operations.

Younger children of five or six behave differently on such a task. They may say that C is longer, because "I can tell!", "I can see it." Or, they may say that they do not know which is longer, and will ask to compare A and C directly by placing them close together. This is a preoperational response, characterized by a dependence on intuition and perception, rather than by a reliance on logic.

Piaget has argued that the kind of ability required in the transitivity problem is an ability which is not readily taught. Most children learn eventually to handle this problem, but the ability to do so rests upon an extensive developmental history of action on objects, over time, in a variety of settings. It is not directly taught by parents or teachers. Piaget believes that similar complex histories underlie the related operational abilities tested on such other tasks as serial ordering, class inclusion, conservation. In a recent review, Kohlberg (1968) suggests that we might distinguish between the basic concepts and abilities of Piaget's studies ("natural" or "spontaneous" concepts) and the concepts or abilities that are products of specific learning situations. Most Piagetian tasks would measure abilities at the "natural" end of this spectrum while the traditional achievement tests, for example, might primarily measure the outcomes of specific instruction.

The curricula studied by Dr. Almy undoubtedly led to learning of specific concepts, but contrary to what might be anticipated from the manuals for these curricular programs, there was little evidence that they appreciably affected the development of more basic or "natural" thought processes. The growth of concrete logical operations was not markedly influenced by these programs.

Such a finding, while disappointing to some, can nevertheless be interpreted as supporting Piaget's theory. If we accept Piaget's model, we would assume that the abilities tested in Dr. Almy's posttest require a developmental background so broad and varied that it would extend well beyond the boundaries of any instructional program. We would also assume that the condition of self-regulated equilibration, through assimilation and accommodation, could not be met in the confines of an instructional program, even a loosely structured program which permits considerable individual exploration.

Her results and the theory of Piaget would also support a proposal set forth by Stephens in his intriguing book, *Process of Schooling* (1967). Stephens proposes that to understand the effectiveness or apparent lack of effectiveness of schools and instruction, we should adopt the model of agriculture rather than the model of the factory. The factory educator, he says, looks at schooling as an assembly line and expects that for every innovation on the instructional assembly line of the classroom you should get some measurable effects on the product— on the pupils coming out. The agricultural model, on the other hand, views schooling differently.

> In agriculture we do not start from scratch, and we do not direct our efforts to inert and passive materials. We start, on the contrary, with a complex and ancient process, and we organize our efforts around what seeds, plants, and

insects are likely to do anyway ... we do not supplant or ignore these older organic forces. We always work through them [1967, p. 11].

In this way, Stephens reminds us to look at all the forces at work in education, at developmental and cultural factors as well as at the instructional variables.

By adopting this view, we do not fall into the trap that has snared a number of researchers, particularly those in educational technology who tend toward the factory model and expect a revolutionary product as a result of their revolutionary hardware. ("Revolution" is a favorite word.) If Stephens is correct, they are headed for some major disappointments in this regard. The agriculture model, while less neat and precise, appears to be a more realistic one and does not mislead teachers, or pupils, or parents of pupils into expecting revolutionary results from important, but humanly limited, innovations in education.

In conclusion, Piaget's work and the kind of evidence reported by Almy and by Stephens gives us a clearer picture of the course of cognitive growth and the function of instruction. For Piaget, the distinguishing quality of human intelligence is the fact that man creatively acts upon his environment and *constructs* a reality; ideas of conservation, understanding of transitive relations, are but examples of such constructions. If the early years of childhood are given over to the business of *constructing*, then it is not surprising that *in*struction, in the more formal sense of the word, would sometimes seem out of place. From the teacher's point of view, then, the young child embodies two puzzling qualities— while he readily learns a great deal, he is, paradoxically, rather difficult to teach.

While such evidence may moderate our expectations regarding the effects of instruction on cognitive development, it should also give us a better understanding of the positive contributions of instruction. Piaget's work and the related studies suggest at least two important functions of instruction, or "directive" teaching. First, instruction in the classroom can serve the function of setting into motion the processes of assimilation and accommodation for a particular area of exploration. The teacher can arouse curiosity by introducing the novel in the context of the familiar, and through planned discussions and activities can encourage the child's subsequent investigations. Secondly, instruction can serve an equally important function of helping the child consolidate what he has been learning. The child can be taught what he already "knows." Some of the best (although unnoticed) teaching at any level of education is probably of this consolidating type.

Teachers of young children are often observed to proceed in precisely these ways. When a good teacher is observed to instruct, in a directive sense, she is either involved in getting a child or children "launched" or in helping a child consolidate or "digest" what he has lately been learning. But for the central period of self-directed exploration between the "start" and the "finish" these teachers often adopt a much less directive, but supporting role.

In our programs for young children, whether in fields of math and science or in art, we should ask whether we focus too much on the "middle," prolonged period of learning and equilibration, where instruction may be of least value, to the neglect of the initial and the consolidation phases where the teacher's efforts might be of very great value.

References

ALMY, M., CHITTENDEN, E. & MILLER, P. *Young Children's Thinking.* New York: Teachers College Press, 1966.

KOHLBERG, L. Early education: a cognitive-developmental view. *Child Develpm.*, 1968, 39, 1013–1062.

PIAGET, J. In R. E. Ripple & V. N. Rockcastle, (Eds.). *Piaget rediscovered: a report of the Conference on Cognitive Studies and Curriculum Development.* School of Education, Cornell University, March, 1964.

————. Introduction to Almy, M., *et al. Young Children's Thinking.* New York: Teachers College Press, 1966.

————. *Six Psychological Studies.* New York: Random House, 1967.

STEPHENS, J. M. *The Process of Schooling: A Psychological Examination.* New York: Holt, Rinehart & Winston, 1967.

Individual Differences in the Consideration of Information Among Two-Year-Old Children*

N. Dickon Reppucci
YALE UNIVERSITY

One central aspect of children's behavior in play and in situations of response uncertainty may involve the degree to which the child considers available information and forms a plan to guide behavior. Twenty-five boys and 25 girls, aged 27 months, were observed in a 30-minute free-play session in which mobility and time spent in sustained involvement with toys were coded. In addition, the response times on an embedded figures task and on a two-choice discrimination task which induced conflict were obtained. Sustained involvement with toys was positively related to response times in conflict situations, and negatively related to motor activity.

Reflection-impulsivity refers to individual differences among school-age children in their decision time in a problem situation containing a number of simultaneously available solutions (Kagan, 1964, 1965b). Reflection is the tendency to respond slowly and consider the alternatives; while impulsivity is the tendency to respond quickly without evaluating adequately the alternative

Reprinted from *Developmental Psychology*, 1970, 2, 240–246, by permission of The American Psychological Association.

* This article is based on a dissertation submitted to the faculty of the Graduate School of Harvard University in partial fulfillment of the requirements for the PhD degree. The author wishes to thank Jerome Kagan, Michael Novey, and all those members of Jerome Kagan's staff who contributed to this project. This research was supported in part by a Predoctoral Research Fellowship MH-15, 206 OIAI from the National Institute of Mental Health and from research Grant MH-8792, from the National Institute of Mental Health, United States Public Health Service, to Jerome Kagan.

hypotheses. Match-to-sample tests, for example, the Matching Familiar Figures (MFF) and the Haptic Visual Matching test (HVM), typically have been used to assess reflection-impulsivity (Kagan, 1965a, 1965b, 1965c). In these tests, the child is asked to select from an array of similar stimuli the one which is identical to a standard stimulus. Decision time is the operational measure of reflection-impulsivity. This dimension has been shown to be stable across varied tasks (Kagan, 1965b), reliable over time (Kagan, 1966), and modifiable (Kagan, Pearson, & Welch, 1966).

Recently, Pedersen and Wender (1968) reported a relation between a style of play behavior at $2\frac{1}{2}$ years of age and test performance at 6 years that may be related to reflection-impulsivity. The behavior of thirty $2\frac{1}{2}$-year-old boys was rated over 4 weeks in a nursery school situation. Four years later, each subject was administered the Sigel Sorting Test and a shortened form of the Wechsler Intelligence Scale for Children (WISC). Verbal ability at 6 years was independent of the earlier behavior ratings but children who frequently sought physical contact and attention from adults and spent little time in sustained directed activity (SDA) with toys did poorly on the performance scales of the WISC and used a relational strategy of classification on the Sigel Sorting Test. These subjects behaved as if they were impulsive (Kagan, Rosman, Day, Albert, & Phillips, 1964). In comparison, subjects who had long periods of sustained play did well on the performance scales and used categorical sorts which is more typical of reflective children. A negative correlation between attention-seeking behavior and sustained directed activity affirmed the independence of these two groups of children. Thus, it appears that $2\frac{1}{2}$-year-old children who display long periods of sustained involvement with toys are more likely to be reflective than those who have short epochs of play.

One central aspect of children's behavior in play and in situations of response uncertainty seems to involve the degree to which the child considers available information and forms a plan. The tendency to form a plan to guide behavior may increase sustained involvement in play and prolong response time in ambiguous situations. For example, one child in a room with toys immediately begins playing with blocks and does so for a few seconds before going to another toy; another child in the same situation looks over the toys and then plays with the blocks for 60 seconds or more. Correspondingly, in a situation of choice between alternatives, the child who played with blocks for a few seconds makes a decision almost immediately; in comparison, the long-playing child makes a choice after considering the alternatives. In both situations, the fast responding child seems to act on impulse with no plan to guide his behavior; whereas the slow-responding child appears to reflect on the available alternatives in a more thoughtful fashion before acting. This example is not meant to imply that one child has more information than another but rather that the second child considered the available information in both situations more deliberately than the first child and then made use of it.

In a study related to information processing in a conflict situation, Maher, Weisstein, and Sylva (1964) found a wide range of oscillation responses among young children when confronted with a choice between different goal objectives; some never oscillated and others did so with great frequency. The stability of the response was demonstrated in a correlation of .94 between children's oscillations on a risk of no reward condition and those on a certainty of some reward condition. The children who oscillated the least seemed to consider the alternatives and then responded, whereas children who oscillated the most did not seem to form a plan before responding. The former may have a more reflective attitude and the latter a more impulsive one.

In another study, Scarr (1966) devised a task directly analogous to those used to assess reflection-impulsivity. Each of 61 pairs of monozygotic and dizygotic twin girls, aged 6–10 years, had to choose between a hidden toy which she had not seen and a second toy which she had seen and which was placed in a box identical to the one containing the hidden toy. On the variable of decision time, the identical twins demonstrated greater within-pair similarity than the fraternal twins. This finding may constitute evidence for a hereditary component in the reflection–impulsivity dimension.

Finally, there is evidence to indicate that motorically active children are more impulsive and less likely to consider information for any sustained time period. Heider (1966) found that highly active infants were often characterized by minimum delay in response as preschool children. Kagan (1965a) found that preschool children who engaged in vigorous activities were impulsive in their responses to MFF and HVM tests administered between the ages of 7 and 13 years. Shaefer and Bayley (1963) found that very active 10-month old boys were rated as low on attentiveness during the period 27–96 months of age.

The purpose of the present investigation is to demonstrate a correlation between indexes of reflection–impulsivity in tasks of uncertainty and indexes of sustained involvement in play among 2-year-old children. It is expected that these two dimensions share variance because they are both influenced by the tendency to consider available information and to form a plan to guide behavior. Moreover, a measure of motor activity is expected to be negatively related to both sustained involvement with toys and longer decision times because motorically active children are less likely to sustain involvement and consider information.

METHOD

SUBJECTS

The subjects for this study were 50 white children, 25 boys and 25 girls, aged 27 months who were originally recruited by advertisements in one of the local newspapers as part of an extensive longitudinal study being conducted by Jerome Kagan.[1] The children were seen as close to 27 months from their date of birth as possible within 14 days. With the exception of 1 child who was accompanied by her older sister (the child's chief caretaker because of the mother's paralytic condition), all children came to the laboratory with their mothers. Social class was indexed by parents' educational level[2] and children from varied educational levels were represented in the sample.

[1] J. Kagan, R. McCall, N. D. Reppucci, J. Jordan, and C. Minton, unpublished study entitled "Change and Continuity in the First Two Years: An Inquiry into Early Cognitive Development," 1969.
[2] Social class was indexed by parent's educational level using the following metric: 6 = post-college, 5 = college degree, 4 = part college, 3 = high school diploma, 2 = ninth grade completed, and 1 = ninth grade not completed.

PROCEDURE

Free Play   The experimenter escorted the mother and child into a large
(21 × 15 feet) furnished playroom. Brown masking tape on the floor divided the
room into 35 equal squares, 3 × 3 feet. The experimenter offered the mother a seat
on the end of the couch, but gave her no explicit instructions. The mother and
child were left in the room alone for a 5-minute adaptation period in order to
alleviate any fears which the child might have regarding this new environment.
At the end of this adaptation period, the experimenter returned and arranged
10 toys (bell-boys, mallet, playdough, pixie doll, wagon, colored wooden blocks,
large clear plastic box, flutterball, riding train, and toy rule) in a standard pattern
on the rug. The experimenter gave the mother two magazines and asked her not
to initiate any interaction with the child, not to encourage him to act in any
particular way, and not to prohibit any activity unless she considered his safety
at stake; but, within the context of these restrictions, to be as natural as possible.
The experimenter then left the room and the child was allowed to play with the
toys for 30 minutes.

During the 30-minute free-play session, the major variable coded was length
of involvement in SDA with toys. The SDA was defined as a single uninterrupted
behavioral involvement with toys that might include one or more act changes,
for example, ringing the bell on the train, sitting on the train, loading blocks into
the train, riding the train around the room, ringing the bell, and then loading
blocks into the train again; this behavior would be scored as one SDA, even though
there were six act changes and four different acts. Two assistants independently
coded SDA on an Esterline Angus event recorder for all 50 children. The mean
of these two recordings was used unless the difference between the coders was
more than 5 seconds. In such cases, SDAs were corrected by listening to a tape-
recorded description of the session. If any questions of accuracy remained, a
permanent television tape of the session was used. The initial reliability coefficients
for uncorrected SDA for 20 children ranged .72–1.00, with a mean reliability coefficient of .97. Since these figures seemed inflated by a very high agreement between
the coders on SDAs 100 seconds in length or longer, reliability coefficients were
obtained for uncorrected SDAs less than 100 seconds in length. The range was
.64–1.00 and the mean reliability coefficient was .88.

A record of the child's locomotor movement (the number of squares traversed)
was also obtained. The mean reliability coefficient for five children was .97.

Embedded Figures Task (EFT)   The experimenter presented the child with a
figure of a girl and taught him to touch the figure. Next, while keeping this
model within the child's view, she presented him with a series of backgrounds with
the figure embedded in them. The child's task was to find and touch the figure.
Following the initial learning, the experimenter showed the child six sets of embedded figures, each consisting of a model and three embeddings of the model.
The first three sets were relatively easy discrimination tasks consisting of a dog,
horse, and bird in backgrounds containing a number of colored figures that
looked progressively more like the model as the difficulty increased. The final three
sets were schematic drawings of a cat, car, and flower, embedded in black and
white line backgrounds. If possible, at least one response to each embedding was
obtained. Only two children refused to play at all, and only two others failed to
complete at least the first four sets. Length of fixation time to the stimulus before
making a response was recorded. The mean reliability coefficient for three children
was .99.

Conflict Situation Task (CST)   The experimenter told the child they were going to play a game with candy (M&Ms). The conflict apparatus had two cups in the front below two white plastic encasements. Each encasement contained both a red and yellow light which were invisible unless turned on. The experimenter controlled the lighting and could turn on any single light or any combination of one light on each side. Each time the child touched the yellow light first, he was rewarded with an M&M which was delivered in the cup below the correct light. Once the experimenter felt confident that the child had learned the discrimination she used a fixed schedule for alternative stimuli, in which the most probable chance score would be 50% correct (Gellermann, 1933). After the child had five *consecutively* correct trials in this schedule, two red lights were presented, producing a negative conflict situation in which there was no correct answer (negative). After receiving two more red and yellow light discrimination trials, the child was presented with two yellow lights, a positive conflict situation in which both choices were correct (positive). Seventy percent of the children learned the task and were presented with the conflict situation. Length of fixation time before making a choice was recorded and mean reliability coefficient for three children was .99.

RESULTS

The hypothesis that a conflict had been induced in the child had to be demonstrated. Berlyne (1960) stated that "situations in which uncertainty is of importance are situations of conflict [p. 29]" and showed that increased reaction time in a two-choice discrimination situation is a measurable index of conflict (Berlyne, 1957, 1960, 1965). Therefore, if conflict had been successfully induced,

TABLE 1

t *Test for Matched Decision Times of the Conflict Situation Task*

VARIABLE	DIFFERENCE BETWEEN MEANS	df	t
Girls			
Neg-Pre tr	2.12	16	2.88†
Pos-Pre tr	0.69	15	2.06
Neg-Cri	2.46	16	3.91‡
Pos-Cri	0.58	15	1.95
Boys			
Neg-Pre tr	3.15	17	4.60‡
Pos-Pre tr	1.04	15	2.41*
Neg-Cri	3.24	17	4.58‡
Pos-Cri	1.04	16	3.29†

NOTE.—Neg-Pre tr = decision time to the negative conflict trial minus decision time to the immediately preceding trial; Pos-Pre tr = decision time to the positive conflict trial minus decision time to the immediately preceding trial; Neg-Cri = decision time to the negative conflict trial minus the mean decision time to the five criterion trials; Pos-Cri = decision time to the positive conflict trial minus the mean decision time to the five criterion trials.

* $p < .05$, two-tailed test.
† $p < .01$, two-tailed test.
‡ $p < .001$, two-tailed test.

the response time to the conflict trials should have increased over the response times to the mean of the five criterion trials and to the trials immediately preceding each conflict trial, regardless of individual differences among the children. The t tests were performed and the p values are presented in Table 1. The results clearly indicate that conflict was induced.

Seven variables from the three tasks—free play, EFT, and CST—were investigated. The measures of sustained involvement in the free play were the length of the median and 75th percentile SDAs. The measures of reflection-impulsivity were the mean first response times (length of fixation time before

TABLE 2
Product-Moment Correlations Between All Variables

VARIABLE	MEDIAN SDA	75th PERCENTILE SDA	RESPONSE TIME TO DHB	RESPONSE TIME TO CCF	DECISION TIME TO NEGATIVE CONFLICT	DECISION TIME TO NEGATIVE CONFLICT	MOBILITY
Girls							
Social class	−.13	.06	−.06	.09	.34	.35	.18
Median SDA		.68†	−.01	.33	.51†	.52†	−.39†
75th percentile SDA			.09	.21	.17	.29	−.42†
Response time to DHB[a]				.33	.02	.29	−.23
Response time to CCF[b]					.32	.23	−.44†
Decision time to negative conflict						.73‡	−.17
Decision time to positive conflict							−.06
Boys							
Social class	.34	.50†	.23	.31	−.13	−.06	−.02
Median SDA		.78‡	.08	.31	.35	.38	−.36*
75th percentile SDA			.09	.25	.44*	.71‡	−.42†
Response time to DHB				.67‡	.08	.20	−.24
Response time to CCF					.05	.34	−.38†
Decision time to negative conflict						.75‡	−.29
Decision time to positive conflict							−.48†

NOTE.—SDA = sustained directly activity; DHB = dog, horse, bird; CCF = cat, car, flower.
[a] Mean first fixation time before response to the dog, horse, bird series of the embedded figures task (EFT).
[b] Mean first fixation time before response to the cat, car, flower series of the EFT.

* $p < .10$, two-tailed test.
† $p < .05$, two-tailed test.
‡ $p < .01$, two-tailed test.

making a response) to the dog, horse, bird (DHB) series and to the cat, car, flower (CCF) series of EFT, and the decision times (length of fixation time before making a response) to the negative and positive conflicts of CST. The measure of mobility was the number of squares traversed during the free play. The correlation matrix for these variables plus social class is presented in Table 2.

The indexes of sustained involvement were correlated with a tendency toward longer decision times in the conflict situations. The relations between the decision times in the conflict situations and the length of sustained directed activity were striking. The correlations between response times to EFT, especially the CCF series, and sustained directed activity were generally in the expected direction but were not statistically significant. Social class was positively related to the 75th percentile SDA for boys but was not related to any of the other variables for either sex. Moreover, as predicted, mobility was negatively related to the other measures.

DISCUSSION

The establishment of a relation between long epochs of sustained involvement in play and long response times in situations of conflict among 2-year-old children provides support for the hypothesis that a dimension involving the tendency to consider available information and to form a plan to guide behavior is operative during the third year of life. This finding, in conjunction with that of Pedersen and Wender (1968), strengthens the belief that a dimension influencing reflection–impulsivity in grade-school children might be detected during the preschool years. The lack of relation between response times to either of the EFT series and the other variables suggests that in relatively easy situations of response uncertainty the influence of the reflection–impulsivity dimension is less than in more difficult ones. The pattern of increasing correlation between response time to the CCF series and the other variables adds credence to this argument, since the CCF series were more difficult than the DHB series (the mean first response time to the DHB series for all children was 3.0 seconds; for the CCF series, it was 5.2 seconds).

It is expected that the 2-year-old children who had long decision times and long involvements with toys are reflective on tests like MFF and HVM at 5 and 6 years of age. Observation of six of the children at 3 years of age revealed remarkable stability over the 9-month period from 27 to 36 months. In a 20-minute free-play session in which there were three toys in the play-room, three children, who spent long periods of time involved with toys at 27 months, had very long SDAs (75th percentile SDAs were 408, 565, and 1,194 seconds) at 36 months; whereas three children, who had short periods of involvement at 27 months had short SDAs (75th percentile SDAs were 62, 71, and 92 seconds) 9 months later. In addition, on a revised and more difficult version of the EFT, the three children with long SDAs had longer response times (mean of 15 trials = 12.9 seconds) and fewer errors (mean of 15 trials = .20) than the three children with short SDAs who had shorter response times (M = 6.2 seconds) and increased errors (M = .53). The children with long SDAs performed in a manner similar to reflective grade-school children while children with short SDAs resembled impulsive older children.

The moderate relation between social class and sustained involvement in play among boys indicates that level of cognitive development may influence the dimension, but the lack of relation between educational level and any of the other measures for either sex argues against this as the major explanation of the results. The inverse relation between mobility and both sustained involvement and decision time suggests a possible biological influence. The explanation which is favored is that a child's tendency to consider information and to form a plan to guide behavior is a basic variable which is modified by the environment as the child matures. This notion implies that the tendency to consider information is not dependent on existing cognitive structures—all children have the tools to consider information before responding but this is not the preferred mode of functioning for many of them. With age, of course, consideration of information increases for all children (Kagan, Rosman, Day, Albert, & Phillips, 1964). Flavell, Beach, and Chinsky (1966) have shown that while the 5-year-old child has learned words for familiar objects, he may not have learned to use these words in a problem context. That is, a child may "have" a language but not "use" it. Impulsive children *have* information but do not use it as extensively as reflective children do.

If the assumption that part of the variance in the reflection–impulsivity dimension is the result of a biological predisposition, then one should be able to find antecedents of this dimension during the first year of life. In conjunction with Jerome Kagan and others, the author is currently in the process of analyzing data collected as early as age 4 months with this goal in mind.

References

BERLYNE, D. E. Conflict and choice time. *British Journal of Psychology*, 1957, **48**, 196–118.

———. *Conflict, arousal and curiosity*. New York: McGraw-Hill, 1960.

———. Uncertainty and conflict: A point of contact between information-theory and behavior-theory concepts. In R. J. C. Hayser, C. C. Anderson, C. M. Christensen, & S. M. Hanka (Eds.), *The cognitive processes readings*. Englewood Cliffs, N. J.: Prentice-Hall, 1965.

FLAVELL, J. H., BEACH, D. R., & CHINSKY, J. M. Spontaneous verbal rehearsal in a memory task as a function of age. *Child Development*, 1966 **37**, 283–299.

GELLERMANN, L. W. Change orders of alternating stimuli in visual discrimination experiments. *Journal of Genetic Psychology*, 1933, **42**, 206–208.

HEIDER, G. M. Vulnerability in infants and young children: A pilot study. *Genetic Psychology Monographs*, 1966, **73**, 1–216.

KAGAN, J. Developmental studies in reflection and analysis. In A. H. Kidd & J. L. Rivinori (Eds.), *Perceptual and conceptual development in the child*. New York: International Universities Press, 1964.

———. Impulsive and reflective children: Significance of conceptual tempo. In J. Krumboltz (Ed.), *Learning and the educational process*. Chicago: Rand McNally, 1965. (a).

———. Individual differences in the resolution of response uncertainty. *Journal of Personality and Social Psychology*, 1965, **2**, 154–160. (b).

KAGAN, J. Reflection-impulsivity and reading ability in primary grade children. *Child Development*, 1965, **36**, 609–628. (c).

———. Reflection-impulsivity: The generality and dynamics of conceptual tempo. *Journal of Abnormal Psychology*, 1966, **71**, 12–24.

———, PEARSON, L., & WELCH. L. The modifiability of an impulsive tempo. *Journal of Educational Psychology*, 1966, **57**, 359–365.

———, ROSMAN, B., DAY, D., ALBERT, J., & PHILLIPS, W. Information processing in the child: Significance of analytic and reflective attitudes. *Psychological Monographs*, 1964, **78** (1, Whole No. 578).

MAHER, B. A., WEISSTEIN, N., & SYLVIA, K. The determinants of oscillation points in a temporal decision conflict. *Psychonomic Science*, 1964, **1**, 13–14.

PEDERSEN, F. A., & WENDER, P. H. Early social correlates of cognitive functioning in six-year-old boys. *Child Development*, 1968, **39**, 185–194.

SCARR, S. Genetic factors in activity motivation. *Child Development*, 1966, **37**, 663–673.

SCHAEFER, E. S., & BAYLEY, N. Maternal behavior, child behavior and their intercorrelations from infancy through adolescence. *Monographs of the Society for Research in Child Development*, 1963, **28**(87, Serial No. 3).

Some Language-Related Cognitive Advantages of Bilingual Five-Year-Olds*†

Carol Feldman
UNIVERSITY OF CHICAGO

Michael Shen
UNIVERSITY OF PENNSYLVANIA

It was an accepted notion for many years that bilingual children had serious deficits in contrast with their monolingual peers (3). But recent research has shown that some bilingual children do *not* do worse than monolinguals on

Reprinted from a paper presented at meetings of The Society for Research in Child Development, Inc., Santa Monica, California, March, 1969. By permission.

* The research or work reported herein was performed pursuant to a contract with the Office of Education, U.S. Department of Health, Education, and Welfare through the Chicago Early Education Research Center, a component of the National Laboratory on Early Childhood Education. Contractors undertaking such work under Government sponsorship are encouraged to express freely their professional judgment in the conduct of the work. Points of view or opinions stated do not, therefore, necessarily represent official Office of Education position or policy.
† The claims made in this paper are limited by the following considerations:
  (1) The bilingual subjects must speak enough English to understand the test questions.
  (2) The results only apply to lower-class subjects, since middle-class monolinguals may do much better.
  (3) The advantages as discerned here are temporary, applying only to five-year-old subjects. By six or seven years, most subjects get close to 100% of the test items correct.

general measures of intellectual development (5). Fishman (4) argues that disadvantages commonly associated with bilingualism would not appear in bilinguals whose languages were situation specific. In fact one might expect that in some cognitive areas, the bilinguals' knowledge of two languages might be advantageous. In particular one might expect that functions related to labelling would be advanced by having two languages, for the child would thus be facilitated in his acquisition of a mature notion of the nature of labels.

Piaget (6) argues that object constancy must be established before the child can learn to use verbal labels as names for objects. And the ability to use labels alone as names for objects ought to be a precursor to more elaborate cognitive skills involving the use of labels in sentences. Object constancy, naming, and the use of names in sentences ought to emerge in that order in development and the order ought to be apparent in the five-year-old child for whom object constancy is almost an accomplished fact and for whom the use of sentences is just beginning to emerge. One might expect that all three of these skills would be better in bilingual than monolingual children.

Inasmuch as I expect this advantage to be apparent simply because the bilinguals have two languages, one might expect that the advantages of the middle class child [who, according to Bernstein (2), has two language codes] over the lower class child could be looked at in the same way. The middle class child is said to have both an elaborated and a restricted language code while the lower class child is said to have only a restricted code. Bernstein has attributed the middle class child's advantage to special properties of the elaborated code. The more elaborate syntax of this code is said to be suited to a facilitation of the encoding of abstract and complex ideas. However at the age of five none of these subtle syntactic aspects of the elaborated code would be apparent as syntactic development is not sufficiently advanced. I suggest that at five years the middle class child may have an advantage nonetheless, because he has two codes rather than one. For either the bilingual or the middle class child having two codes may facilitate his awareness that there are different ways to say the same thing. This is turn may facilitate a decline in seeing names as a part of the things which they name, a characteristic of thought which Piaget (7) attributes to childhood egocentrism.

The notion that the two codes of a middle class child are similar to the two languages of a bilingual lower class child is supported by Fishman (4) who argues that bilingualism which is situation specific (bilingualism with diglossia) may appear in "speech communities whose linguistic diversity is realized through varieties not yet recognized as constituting separate languages." This is much like arguing that Bernstein's middle class children were actually bilinguals with diglossia and suggests that there might be comparable advantages from the two sorts of codes found in the lower class bilingual and in the middle class monolingual child.

The present study attempts to show that in bilingual five year olds there are advantages that would be expected from their having two languages: in object constancy, in naming, and in the use of names in sentences. Secondarily, it is suggested that object constancy should be in advance of naming, as Piaget suggests, and that naming should be in advance of using names in sentences.

METHOD

SUBJECTS   The subjects were fifteen bilingual and fifteen monolingual Head Start children. The bilinguals were primarily of Mexican origin. Approximately half of the monolinguals were Negro and half of them of Mexican origin. The children lived in the same neighborhood and were enrolled in the same classes.

The bilinguals were selected by asking classroom teachers and a special language teacher to identify bilinguals. To be classified as bilingual children had to demonstrate understanding of several simple Spanish questions and to speak Spanish at home. These criteria meant that several children whom the teachers classified as bilingual on the basis of Spanish surnames were here considered to be monolingual.

The children were four, five and six years of age with a mean age of five years. There were the same number of male and female children at each age in each group.

PROCEDURE   The children were taken to a room removed from the classroom and were told that they were going to play a "candy game." They were given candy non-contingently at the beginning of the session, during breaks between the main sections, and at the end of the experiment. The experimenter was seated in front of a table on which he variously placed the toys that were being named.

1. *Object Constancy*   In the first part of the procedure each of several objects (cup, plate, sponge, etc.) was physically transformed. The transformations were that a cup was crushed, a paper plate was spray painted, a sponge was dirtied, a match was burned, and a suction cup soap holder was adhered to a wall so that the child saw it sideways and straight on. The transformations were done in view of the child and then the transformed object was placed with a second object identical to the pre-transformed object. The child was asked, "Which was the one that I showed you before?" and was required to pick one object from the pair.

2. *Naming*   In the second part of the procedure the child was told that he was going to play the "name game." The experimenter pointed out that objects, just like people, have names. The purpose of this section was to test the child's ability to use verbal labels to name familiar objects which were present. Three kinds of labelling ability were tested: The ability to use common names (i.e., call a cup "cup"), the ability to learn nonsense names (i.e., call a cup "wug"). and the ability to switch common names (i.e., call a cup "plate"). For each of these the subject was required in some cases to demonstrate his knowledge by speaking (production) and in other cases by pointing (comprehension).

The subject was presented with pairs of familiar toy objects (car, airplane; frog, lamb; monkey, squirrel). The experimenter switched the names of the objects in the pair (e.g., by holding up the car and saying "The name of this is 'airplane'"). The subject was asked both which object was called an "airplane," and which one was really an airplane. A similar procedure was followed in relabelling objects with nonsense syllables [e.g., "wug," "niss," (1)] and asking which one was called a "wug" and what it really was.

3. *Sentences*   In the third part of the experiment the child was required to demonstrate his ability to use the three sorts of labels described in part two (common, switched common, and nonsense labels) in simple relational sentences like "The cup is on the plate," by placing objects in a relationship stated by E and in other cases by describing the relationship in which E placed them. The labels used in the sentences were "cup," "plate," "can," "car," and "airplane" and the objects that were named were presented.

The rationale for using simple relational sentences was that referential word meaning, which can account for most of the meaning in these sentences, is the simplest sort of meaning and earliest to emerge. The notion is that such words as "table," "cup" get their meaning by standing for or referring to a thing. Simple relational sentences are syntactically simple and semantically simple since most of the meaning of the sentence can be conceived of as lying in the referential meaning of the component words. Words like "cup," "plate," and even the verb part of the predicate "on" can all be thought of as referring to things or states of the world.

RESULTS

The results were analyzed in terms of the number of correct responses. The results were first analyzed by looking at performance of the two groups of subjects in the three sections of the experiment (Table 1). The range of performance on the three tasks (bilingual: 94–54 per cent, monolingual: 84–35 per cent) suggests the appropriateness of the tasks for the age tested. The three tasks: object constancy, naming, using labels in sentences were increasingly difficult in the order expected. That is, both bilinguals and monolinguals found object constancy easier than naming, and naming easier than the use of names in a sentence.

Bilinguals did significantly better than monolinguals at all three tasks. The apparently uniform advantage that appears in this analysis will be seen in later analyses not to actually exist, but it would otherwise raise serious questions about the legitimacy of comparing the two groups.

As a post-hoc analysis the results in Table 1 were split for both subject groups within each task into verbal or production and pointing or comprehension responses (Table 2). I call the pointing responses comprehension measures because the subject had to understand what E asked him to point to. I chose this terminology because it implies that the underlying knowledge is the same in the two procedures and only the nature of the performance is different. There were only comprehension measures in the object constancy task, which was intended to be as purely cognitive as possible. Performance in equivalent tasks was broken down into comprehension and production for parts two and three of the experiment. In every case bilinguals did better than monolinguals on the comprehension measures. However in parts two and three where there were also production measures bilinguals did better one time (part three) but not the other (part two). It appears that the bilinguals' advantage in these tasks is most evident in comprehension measures.

In general, comprehension scores were superior to production scores for both groups (bilinguals: 80 per cent vs. 63.7 per cent; monolinguals: 65 per cent vs. 54 per cent; Table 3). This is interesting because it corroborates a notion common in the psycholinguistic literature; namely, that comprehension tends to be in advance of production in language development. Comprehension may be more reliable for looking at these processes largely because the subjects are so young.

Table 1 shows that we found the tasks appropriate for five year olds, tasks one through three increasingly difficult for both groups, and bilinguals better than monolinguals at all three tasks. In Table 2 we found that the bilinguals' advantage over the monolinguals was more apparent in compre-

TABLE 1

The Percent of Correct Responses on Three Tasks:
Object Constancy, Naming and Use of Names in Sentences
in the Monolingual vs. Bilingual Subjects

		BILINGUALS % CORRECT	MONOLINGUALS % CORRECT	t	p
1. Object constancy		94.7	84.0	1.71	$<.05$
2. Object relabelling		80.7	69.1	1.93	$<.05$
	t	1.81	1.74		
	p	$<.05$	$<.056$		
2. Object relabelling		80.7	69.1	1.93	$<.05$
3. Relations		54.1	35.6	2.42	$<.025$
	t	6.59	6.46		
	p	$<.001$	.001		

TABLE 2

The Mean Number of Correct Comprehension and Production Responses for Each of the Three
Tasks and the Two Groups in Table 3

	BILINGUALS $\bar{X}$	MONOLINGUALS $\bar{X}$	t	p
1. Object constancy				
A. Comprehension	4.73	4.20	1.71	$<.05$
B. Production	–	–	–	–
2. Object relabelling				
A. Comprehension	12.20	10.07	2.39	$<.025$
B. Production	3.13	3.07	–	N.S.
3. Relations				
A. Comprehension	2.27	1.33	1.81	$<.05$
B. Production	2.60	1.87	2.21	$<.025$

TABLE 3

Percentage of Correct Responses of Monolinguals vs. Bilinguals on Questions Requiring Verbal and Non-verbal Responses

	BILINGUAL (%)	MONOLINGUAL (%)
Comprehension	80.0	65.0
Production	63.7	54.8

hension than production measures, and that comprehension was generally better than production (Table 3).

It is not until well past the age of five that children understand sentence meaning, but there may well be precursors to their understanding sentence meaning. These might logically emerge around five years. I suggest that the precursor state to the adult concept of sentence meaning would be the child's understanding that meaning is a function of use. A child could clearly demonstrate this understanding by his use of words in a sentence. He could also demonstrate it by his ability to switch names. While he might be able to learn common labels, and still think that names are parts of things, his willingness to rename things implies that he knows that the meaning of a word is just what a person uses it to mean.

In parts two and three there were three kinds of labelling tasks which we will now separate (Table 4): (1) switched common labels; (2) common, correct labels; and (3) nonsense labels, which were used in two sorts of situations: (A) alone as a label, and (B) in a sentence. As would be expected from

TABLE 4

Percentages of Correct Responses with Three Kinds of Labels (1, 2, and 3) Used Alone (A) and in Sentences (B) in Bilingual and Monolingual Subjects

		BILINGUAL (%)	MONOLINGUAL (%)	t	p
1. Switched common label					
A. Used alone		68.8	31.1	3.37	< .005
B. In a sentence		6.7	13.3	–	N.S.
	t	7.29	1.89		
	p	< .001	< .05		
2. Regular common label					
A. Used alone		85.9	85.2	–	N.S.
B. In a sentence		73.3	52.0	2.18	< .025
	t	3.42	4.23		
	p	< .005	< .001		
3. Nonsense label					
A. Used alone		91.1	93.3	–	N.S.
B. In a sentence		53.3	16.7	3.22	< .005
	t	3.45	10.69		
	p	< .005	< .001		

Table 1, the ability to use names as labels (A) is in advance of the ability to use the names in relational statements (B) in both bilinguals and monolinguals. Further it is found that task 1 is harder than 2 and 1 is harder than 3. That is, in general switching names is harder than either using ordinary names or learning new nonsense names (Table 5). This is true for both the monolingual and bilingual subjects and for both task types A and B with a single exception: monolinguals do so poorly at using both switched names (13 per cent) and nonsense names (16 per cent) in sentences that there is no difference between the two measures.

TABLE 5

Percentage of Correct Responses of Bilingual and Monolingual Subjects Comparing Three Kinds of Labels: (1, 2, and 3) Used in Two Kinds of Tasks: Alone (A) and in Sentences (B)

	A		B	
	BILINGUAL (%)	MONOLINGUAL (%)	BILINGUAL (%)	MONOLINGUAL (%)
1. Switched common label	68.8	31.1	6.7	13.3
2. Regular common label	85.9	85.2	73.3	52.0
t	2.36	6.35	9.85	5.06
p	$<.025$	$<.001$	$<.001$	$<.001$
1. Switched common label	68.8	31.1	6.7	13.3
3. Nonsense label	91.1	93.3	53.3	16.7
t	3.88	4.77	5.11	.23
p	$<.001$	$<.001$	$<.001$	N.S.

The most interesting findings lie in the contrast between the bilingual and monolingual groups (Table 4). Here it is clear that the bilinguals are not just generally superior to the monolinguals. In tasks 2A, the use of common names alone, and 3A, the use of nonsense names alone, the subject groups are equally competent. However, the bilinguals are better than the monolinguals in the use of these same names in relational statements (2B and 3B). Task 1, switching names, was found to be generally more difficult for both groups than tasks 2 or 3. The use of switched names as labels was superior in the bilinguals but the use of these names in a sentence was so poor in both groups there was no difference between them.

DISCUSSION

First, why should the ability for both monolinguals and bilinguals to use names as labels be in advance of the ability to use them in statements? It seems intuitively reasonable that one has to learn how to use the labels as such before one can use them in a more complex structure like a statement. Although this is consistent with Piaget's notion, there is a twist obtained here. It appears that the ability to use names as labels has to reach some threshold level before the child is able to use them correctly in relations any significant percentage of time. Hence, in task 1 where labelling is correct only about 60 per cent (bilinguals) and 30 per cent (monolinguals) of the time, the use of labels in relations is correct close to 0 per cent of the time. Whereas in tasks 2 and 3 where labelling is correct around and above 85 per cent of the time, in three out of four cases (except in 3B) labels are used correctly in relations a significant percentage of time (around 50 per cent). It appears tentatively that labelling has to consolidate before use in sentences of those labels can occur and not simply that labelling is a precursor function.

It may not be the case that labelling is important because it is a basic and paradigmatic function but because until it occurs and consolidates, other language functions, which are different in kind from labelling, cannot occur at all. The fact that there is an apparent ceiling effect rather than co-variation supports the notion that labelling may be necessary for later language functions but different in kind from them.

The second set of findings involves the difference for both groups obtained between task 1 and tasks 2 and 3. Changing a label is harder than knowing a correct one, or learning a new one. One can argue that around this age children are rapidly acquiring new words and hence are receptive to learning nonsense words which may be perceived as new labels by the child. However, five-year-old children are rigid in being unwilling to give up what they have already learned as it is such a recent and tenuous acquisition. On another level one may suggest the unwillingness to switch names represents an inability to see language meaning as a function of the speaker's use of the word, an inability to see that the name of a thing is just what a speech community chooses to call it.

Bilinguals then are superior in their ability to switch names used alone and also in the use of common names and nonsense names in relational statements. The ability to use names in statements clearly involves some ability to see language as usable by people in linguistic contexts. Similarly an ability to switch names may be said to require a notion of meaning as use; whereas, the ability to know names and to learn new ones is possible for a child who thinks names are a part of things and has no notion of use.

Naming is subject to two possible interpretations. The first is that names get their meaning by standing for or referring to objects. The second is that they are like all other language functions in depending for their meaning on use.

Hence I am proposing that naming is important because it is the first place that the child learns that language meaning is related to use. Until he has naming mastered at a fairly high level he cannot switch from the first gear of name meaning as reference to a second gear of name meaning as a function of use. Naming is nonetheless important because it appears that a certain threshold level of success at naming is required before the child can develop his first true language function, a notion of meaning as use.

The advantage of the bilingual child in switching names and using labels in sentences can be taken as evidence for a notion of meaning as a function of use. This advantage is not identical to an ability to use names as labels for in their acquisition of common names and their ability to learn new nonsense names, the bilinguals and monolinguals are equal. The threshold effect observed further suggests a difference in kind between naming ability and a notion of meaning as use. I am suggesting then that the mere presence of two language codes as in the case of a lower class bilingual, or perhaps a middle class mono-lingual, facilitates the shift from a notion of meaning as word reference into seeing meaning as a function of use which I believe to be the precursor to an adult meaning system.

SUMMARY

Monolingual and bilingual five-year-old Head Start children were com-pared in their ability at tasks involving object constancy, naming, and the use of names in sentences. The three tasks constitute a natural sequence of language skills. They were all found easier for bilinguals than monolinguals, and this was clearest on non-verbal measures. In a further analysis it was found that switching names and using names in sentences was better in bilinguals but the knowledge of names and facility for acquiring new names was equivalent in the two groups. It was suggested that young children might first perceive names as attributes of things they name. With such a notion they might nonetheless easily learn new words. However they later learn that names refer to the things they name because someone so uses them. Having a notion of meaning as a function of use might facilitate acquisition of the ability to use labels in sentences.

References

1. Berko, J. The child's learning of English morphology. *Word*, 1958, 14, 150–177.
2. Bernstein, B. Social class and linguistic development: A theory of social learning. In A. Halsey, J. Floyd, & A. Anderson (Eds.), *Society, Economy, and Education*. Glencoe: Free Press, 1961.
3. Darcy, N. A review of the literature on the effects of bilingualism upon the measure-ment of intelligence. *J. Genet. Psych.*, 1953, 82, 21–58.
4. Fishman, J. A. Bilingualism with and without diglossia; diglossia with and without bilingualism. *J. Soc. Issues*, 1967, 23, 29–38.
5. Peal, E. & Lambert, W. E. The relation of bilingualism to intelligence. *Psychol. Monogr.*, 1962, 76(27), 1–23.
6. Piaget, J. *The Construction of Reality in the Child*. New York: Basic Books, 1954.
7. ———. *The Child's Conception of the World*. Totowa, New Jersey: Littlefield, Adams, and Co., 1967.
8. ———. *Six Psychological Studies*. New York: Random House, 1967.

Children Who Speak Navajo

Maebah Becenti

TOADLENA BOARDING SCHOOL, NEW MEXICO

Navajo families do not speak English among themselves. Thus, when a Navajo child begins school, he has difficulty learning English, much as the English-speaking child encounters when learning Spanish, French, or any other foreign language.

Have you ever tried to correct a foot fault in tennis, to stop biting your fingernails or to stop smoking? It wasn't easy, was it? Modifying your speech habits can be just as difficult. I have chosen to write on the problems of the child who speaks Navajo to make teachers of Navajo children aware of the problems of the bilingual child, and to attempt to answer some of the questions commonly raised by those interested in Navajo education. I believe that similar difficulties are faced by any child who must be educated in a second language.

Experiences and skills that are taken for granted by the teachers of first-grade white children cannot be expected of the Navajo children. Many Navajo children come to school the first day lacking a familiarity with the English language or much of the background experience which is common to the lives and environment of most white children. The teachers are confronted with students who have been speaking and thinking only in their native tongue.

One of the difficulties encountered by the child is his inability to make correctly all of the sounds in the new language. In most cases he is unaware that his speech differs from that of the teacher. His ear has not been trained to note the distinction. It seems more appropriate to correct a child when he is young, less sensitive, and more easily changed than to wait until he is older and less receptive.

Sounds that cause trouble are the ones not found in the child's own language. For example, the Navajo children substitute "d" for "th" because the Navajo language has no "th" sound. They substitute "b" for "v" for the same reason. The Navajos have trouble pronouncing endings on words such as ing, k, s and t. Glottal stops are the most common consonantal sound in Navajo. An example of this is "ha' a' aah," which means the word *east*. The features of the Navajo vowels are nasality, tone and length.

Some of our parents do not speak English. Therefore, whenever we go home we cannot help but speak the native language to make communication possible. I believe this is one of the bad influences on those of us who are trying to improve our English.

Even though a child learns to speak by imitation, he is handicapped for some time because he does not think in the second language. When an English-speaking person first learns to say "adios," for example, he thinks "goodbye." The translation process slows up the pace for the bilingual child because he

Reprinted with permission from *Young Children*, Vol. XXV, No. 3, January, 1970. Copyright © 1970, National Association for the Education of Young Children, 1834 Connecticut Ave., N. W., Washington, D.C. 20009.

is trying to think how he can best translate a certain word or sentence. Sometimes, the word needed does not exist. For instance, we do not have a word for "sorry" and therefore have to describe a situation similar to the word.

A Navajo child is often confused with negative questions, such as, "You are not hurt, are you?" Instead of answering "No" he will answer "Yes," the way he would answer that question in his native language. It requires drilling and practice to correct this problem.

Teachers of Navajo children frequently ask why Navajos are shy and reluctant to speak. As a Navajo, I know that this problem exists and wonder how we can solve it. One solution might be simply to make it possible for the Navajos to mingle with the English-speaking children more. By this method, we may be able to overcome the inferiority and inadequacy that the Navajo children feel. But as far as I know, shyness is not a custom of the Navajo people or anything of the like. One of the reasons Navajo children are reluctant to respond orally may be fear. A certain child may know the answer to a specific question, and he wants to answer that question. But he is afraid and embarrassed that he will be ridiculed by his fellow classmates. The Navajo students tend to ridicule students who recite in class a great deal. This reason may also explain low voice volume in class. Sometimes, a child is not sure whether he will say the right thing(s).

Some Navajo students write English better than they speak it. This may come about because the bilingual child has more time to think while writing than while speaking.

As teachers of these bilingual students, let us make every effort and use every opportunity for the Navajo children to become proficient in communication skills. It is my sincere hope that someday we will speak as fluently as the English-speaking people.

7

The Role of Play in Development

Play is the young child's chief mode of interaction and development. Although there seems to be a growing appreciation of the fact that children learn through play, there are also increases in efforts to program and control young children's learning. In the traditional nursery school, play is respected and facilitated. Compensatory education for young children is a new field in which many approaches to children's learning are being tried by professionals from a variety of disciplines. Some of these programs include play as a mode of learning, others do not.

The value of play is emphasized by David Elkind in his analysis of the contribution that the traditional nursery school makes to middle-class children and to education in general. Elkind is convinced that a structured nursery school can be worthwhile for deprived children and can help them catch up with the development that the middle-class child achieves at home, in interaction with his family. He is very convincing in arguing that the remedial program for the deprived child should not be inflicted on the well-developed child. Social play in the nursery school is the setting of a study by Rosalind Charlesworth and Willard Hartup. This study is part of a series dealing with the reinforcements that children give each other during play.

Of the many reports of research on compensatory education, only one is reprinted here. Susan W. Gray and Rupert A. Klaus report on The Early Training Project, seven years after its beginning. In addition to its age and the careful controls used, the project is noteworthy for its parent program and research methods which permit accurate estimates of its results.

The Case for the Academic Preschool: Fact or Fiction?

David Elkind
UNIVERSITY OF ROCHESTER

The advantages an academic preschool offers to an underprivileged child are considerable. The school can provide kinds of stimuli he would probably not otherwise receive and help him acquire the skills and knowledge needed to cope effectively with later learning. But

Reprinted with permission from Young Children, Vol. XXV, No. 3, January, 1970. Copyright © 1970, National Association for the Education of Young Children, 1834 Connecticut Ave., N.W., Washington, D.C. 20009.

what about the privileged middle-class child? What has the academic preschool to offer him?

Over the past few years there has been a remarkable growth of professional interest in young children and in the preschool education they receive. In part, this new interest in young children derives from research (some of which is reviewed by Scott, 1968, and by Stevenson, Hess & Rheingold, 1967), which suggests that the preschool years are of great importance not only for social and emotional but also for intellectual growth. While the research findings came as no surprise to nursery school teachers, they seem to have come as something of a revelation to many educators and psychologists (e.g., Bruner, 1960; Fowler, 1962; Hunt, 1961).

This "new" recognition of the importance of the preschool years for mental growth has had two major consequences. One of these is a movement (that has succeeded or will soon succeed in states such as California, Massachusetts and New York) to provide preschool education for all children whose parents desire it. The second major consequence of this new focus upon the preschool child is a growing sentiment towards changing the character of preschool education. While the advocates of change in preschool education (e.g., Berlyne, 1965; Fowler, 1962; Hunt, 1961; Sava, 1968) are somewhat vague in their specifications, it seems fair to say that they appear to advocate more formal, academic types of instruction. In the present essay, I want to deal primarily with this second consequence and to examine some of the arguments for the formalization of preschool education.

Those who advocate more structured nursery school instruction (e.g., Sava, 1968) seem to base their position on four types of arguments: (a) The earlier we start a child in the formal academic path, the earlier he will finish and the cheaper the total educational cost; (b) learning comes easy to the young child and we should take advantage of the preschooler's learning facility and eagerness to learn; (c) intellectual growth is rapid in the preschool years and instruction will help to maximize that growth while failure to provide appropriate intellectual stimulation may curtail the child's ultimate level of achievement and (d) traditional preschool experience is too soft, too directed towards emotional well-being and too little concerned with cognitive stimulation. Let us take up each of these arguments in turn.

IS THE ACADEMIC PRESCHOOL ECONOMICAL?

There is certainly a sense in which preschool instruction may be more economical than later educational interventions. In the case of disadvantaged children who do not profit from what Strodtbeck (1964) called "the hidden curriculum of the middle-class home," there is a real need for more structured learning experiences such as those provided by Bereiter and Englemann (1966); Kami and Radin (1967) and Blank and Solomon (1968). To the child who comes from the often chaotic stimuli of the ghetto, the structure of a formal instructional program is a needed counterpoise to his experience at home. The structured preschool experience offered to the disadvantaged child helps compensate for the cognitive and linguistic preparation that the middle-class child receives in the home. In the case of disadvantaged children, then, preparation is certainly cheaper in the long run than reparation or remedial education later.

The advocates of preschool instruction have not, however, limited their sights to the disadvantaged child only, but aim their arguments at the middle-class child as well. There is so much to learn these days, it is argued, that we need to start children earlier if they are to complete their education while still young. Besides it is more economical to educate at the preschool than at the college level. While these arguments seem to have merit, they do not really hold up under careful scrutiny.

It is true of course that we are living in an era of explosive increases in knowledge and that our highly technical civilization will require ever more highly trained individuals. Our task is thus to speed up the educational process. Such a speedup, however, can be accomplished in several ways just as it can be done in industry. If a manufacturer wishes to speed up his production, he can either get his workers to work longer hours or make his production facilities operate more rapidly and efficiently. In most cases, the latter solution results in a more economical manufacture and a better product. The same probably holds true in education.

Our educational system today is really not geared to the needs of young people growing up in today's world. Too much of it is geared to the acquisition and storing of information and too little to teaching young people how to retrieve information. By the time we are adults most of us have forgotten about four-fifths of what we learned in school. That, after all, is a pretty poor yield. Our educational system, thus, has a lot of dead wood and could be streamlined so there would be no need to start children at the preschool level in order to complete their education in a reasonable time. Children in Western Europe often do not begin school until age six or seven but are better educated than our young people when they complete high school. In any case, if we taught children to read and write at the preschool level there would still have to be a total change and reorganization at all educational levels. It might be more profitable in the long run to streamline our existing instructional institutions before creating new ones.

Formal instruction of the middle-class child does not appear, then, to have any economic advantages. Nor does it have the necessary preparatory quality it has for the disadvantaged child. The typical middle-class home provides a good deal of structure and instruction. Middle-class parents are constantly conversing with their children, labeling things for them, answering their questions, providing them with "educational" toys and instilling them with the idea that they, the parents, look favorably upon academic achievement. In the context of this structured tutelage in the home, additional instruction in the preschool would merely gild the lily. We shall, at a later point, return to the role of the preschool for middle-class children. At this point, it is only necessary to say that formal instruction of the middle-class preschool child is probably a less effective procedure than streamlining the educational system as a whole.

IS THE ACADEMIC PRESCHOOL EFFICIENT?

Those who advocate preschool instruction for the middle-class child argue that the preschool youngster is an eager and facile learner. While both of these contentions are true, they do not necessarily imply the efficacy of preschool instruction in the formal sense. Let us look first at the young child's eagerness to learn. This eagerness is present in his constant questions, his curiosity and exploratory behavior. Actually, this eagerness is present at the kindergarten and first grade levels as well. But by the time children reach the fifth and sixth grade, more than 50 percent of the children once eager to learn dislike school, the prime agency of instruction. *It is at least possible that the dislike of school and of learning is a direct result of our lock step instructional processes which kill spontaneous interest.* The introduction of formal instruction at the preschool level could thus well have the effect of bringing children's eagerness to learn to an earlier grave than heretofore.

If we look now at the young child's facility in learning, it too offers no direct invitation for formal instruction. The young child learns quickly but what he learns, he learns by rote—not by reason and thought. Read a story to him several times and he will know it by heart. But in problem solving and in other types of learning situations, he has great difficulty and uses trial and error. In all but rote situations he is a terribly inefficient learner. This observation has now been substantiated by evidence from many different kinds of studies (White, 1965), which strongly suggest that something happens between the ages of four and seven which transforms the young child who learns merely on the basis of association to an older one who learns with the aid of language mediation and with deductive reasoning.

These data are important because as the writer has argued elsewhere (Elkind, 1969a), most of the tool skills required of the young child, such as reading and arithmetic, require the logical and linguistic structures that usually do not emerge until age six or seven. Accordingly, if we try to teach children to "read" and "do math" while still at the preschool level, they may learn by different means than they will at a later time. Such training could actually produce difficulties later and interfere with the successful mastery of these tasks at the cognitive level. Moreover, since such skills cannot be easily learned by rote means, children will have to invest much more time in the preschool learning to read than they would have to invest had they waited until they were older before learning this tool skill.

This is not to say—I want to emphasize—that the preschool period is not a very important one in preparing children for formal instruction in tool subjects. Listening to stories, learning the alphabet and familiarity with numbers and quantitative relations are all important preparatory education for formal instruction. Preparing children for reading and mathematics is, however, different from teaching them reading and arithmetic, which should be delayed until the child gives evidence of having attained mediational learning—the ability to learn with the aid of rational and linguistic formulae. Of course, no blocks should be placed in the path of the exceptional child who learns to read and do math through his own efforts and interest. Accordingly, while it is true that the young child is an eager and facile learner, this does not imply that he be given formal instruction in tool subjects. Such instruction could well stifle his spontaneous interest in learning because the skills themselves call for learning abilities the young child does not yet possess. His facility in rote learning is of little help in learning skills such as math and reading that require rational learning processes. In view of these considerations, it makes more sense for preschool education to focus upon preparation for formal instruction than upon formal instruction itself.

DOES THE ACADEMIC PRESCHOOL MAXIMIZE MENTAL GROWTH?

Those who argue for an academic preschool suggest that early childhood is a "critical period" in mental growth. The idea of critical periods in human development derives from analogies with animal studies. Such studies show that during certain periods in their development, animals are particularly susceptible to environmental influence. Young chicks, to illustrate, become attached to the prominent object about them approximately 17 hours after birth. Thereafter, the chick responds to this object as if it were his "mother," whether it is a box, balloon or graduate student (Scott, 1968). In humans, the period of primary socialization appears at the last quarter of the first year, when the infant gives evidence of fear of strangers and anxiety over the mother's departure (Schaffer & Callender, 1959).

While there is thus some evidence for a critical period for human socialization, there is no unequivocal evidence for such periods in *mental* development. The evidence adduced by those who favor the critical period hypothesis is of three sorts: (a) mental growth curves, (b) case histories and (c) data from academic preschools. Let us examine the evidence.

The argument for critical periods based on mental growth curves derives from the writings of psychometricians such as Bloom (1964). Bloom suggests that half the child's intellectual capacity is attained by age four and another 30 percent by age eight. There is, therefore, evidence that early childhood is a period of very rapid intellectual growth. This evidence, however, does not necessarily imply that the period is critical in the sense that if stimulation is not received during this epoch, later stimulation will not be able to accomplish the same result. Let us look at the mental growth curves in more detail since they appear to be the primary basis for the critical period notion with respect to mental growth.

Unlike growth curves for height and weight, which involve merely recording the successive measurements on the same individuals across time, mental growth curves involve the correlations between test scores at successive age levels. What mental growth curves really tell us is not how much of a child's total mental capacity he has at any given time, but only how much of his total intellectual ability we can predict at any age. To illustrate, from a child's IQ score at age four, we can predict with 50 percent accuracy what his IQ will be at age 17. That is the *only* straightforward interpretation of the mental growth curves report by Bloom (1964).

Suppose, however, that we accept the interpretation that ability to predict is related to total ability, and that a child does attain half his total mental ability by age four and 80 percent by age eight. Does this imply we ought to start academic instruction early to capitalize on this rapid growth period? Not at all! In the first place, the rate of mental growth appears to decline as the rate of formal instruction increases. That is, almost 75 percent of a child's mental growth takes place before he receives formal schooling and the rate of mental growth declines as the amount of formal schooling increases—only 20 percent growth between eight and 17. There is, in effect, *a negative correlation between mental growth and formal instruction!* Looked at in this way, one could legitimately argue that formal schooling ought to be *delayed* rather than introduced early to maximize mental growth.

Another argument for the criticalness of early childhood for mental growth comes from the writings of Fowler (1968), who states:

"The unvarying coincidence of extensive early stimulation with cognitive precocity and subsequent superior competence in adulthood suggest that stimulation is a necessary if not sufficient condition for the development of his abilities" (p. 17). What Fowler forgets, however, is that correlation is *not* causation. It is true that many great scientists and artists received early instruction, but it is also true that they had gifted parents and were genetically well endowed. Furthermore, and more importantly, what of all those children whose parents stimulated and instructed them almost from the day of their birth and who did not achieve later eminence? In science, it is necessary to acknowledge negative as well as positive instances, and my guess is that the negative instances far exceed the positive. I have seen one such product of early stimulation, an autistic (schizophrenic) boy who believed he was a tape recorder. When he was an infant, his mother bathed him in a sea of tape-recorded sound to stimulate his musical talents. In arguing about the benefits of early instruction, it is only fair to report the possible costs of intense instructional pressure at home and at school.

Finally, a third argument for the criticalness of the preschool period comes from those who cite the effects of preschool instructional programs, such as those of Head Start, Bereiter and Englemann (1966), and so on. To the extent that these programs are directed at disadvantaged children, the gains may be very real indeed but are probably of smaller magnitude than they appear (Jensen, 1969). This is because when the children take the initial pretest before the training, they are strange to the situation and examiners, whereas afterwards they feel at home and their test performance reflects that fact (Zigler & Butterfield, 1968). As I indicated earlier, however, there may be real benefits for disadvantaged children in an academically oriented preschool.

The question I wish to raise is whether such instructional programs would equally benefit middle-class children. Recently, Gottesman (1968) reviewed some of the animal and human research relevant to this issue. In general, the studies show that enriched environments benefit disadvantaged or deprived subjects to a much greater extent than they do advantaged or non-deprived subjects. As Jensen (1969) suggests, there seems to be a minimum level of stimulation necessary for children to realize their abilities. If the actual level is below that minimum, they do not realize their full potential. If, however, the environment is richer than necessary, it does not further implement their growth. If this view is correct, mental growth would have to be regarded as analogous to physical growth. Poor diet can stunt a child's height, but an abundantly rich one will not increase his ultimate height beyond a certain limit. If this analogy holds true, the level of stimulation children need to maximize their intellectual growth may be far less than we imagine and excessive enrichment wasteful.

Indeed, most middle-class preschool children are probably over- rather than understimulated. Such overstimulation occurs because we frequently overestimate the young child's ability to assimilate new experience. Most parents have had the experience of taking their preschoolers to the circus, carnival or zoo. Children are usually more interested in the food than other attractions. Usually it is not until weeks later that the youngster will begin to talk about or draw the events which transpired at the event. Children cannot assimilate new experiences in as large a dose or as rapidly as adults, and protect themselves by tuning out the stimulation they cannot process.

In summary, we have reviewed three arguments for the criticalness of early childhood intellectual stimulation and have not found any one of them entirely satisfactory. I do not wish, however, to deny the importance of the early childhood period for intellectual growth. The preschool period is important, even critical, but not because growth is most rapid at the time, or because great men received early stimulation, or because there is evidence to show the lastingness of early instruction. No, the preschool period is important for a simple reason, namely, mental growth is cumulative and depends upon what has gone before.

Whether we are talking about Piagetian stages, the acquisition of a skill such as playing the piano or knowledge in a particular area, there is a cumulative learning aspect. What the child learns in the preschool period must adequately prepare him for what he is to learn later. It is in this sense, and this sense only, that early childhood is a critical period in intellectual development. In the next section, we will deal in more detail with the preparatory role of the preschool.

IS THE ACADEMIC PRESCHOOL SUPERIOR TO THE TRADITIONAL PRESCHOOL?

The advocates of an academic preschool see little of intellectual value in traditional preschool education perpetuated by, as Sava (1968) derogatorily put it, the "child lovers." Such attitudes seem to reflect a boundless ignorance of what is accomplished in the traditional preschool and of the skill required to run such a school effectively. What the supporters of the academic preschool fail to realize is that the preschool child is a very different psychosocial being than the school-age child, and that the traditional preschool is well suited to his intellectual and emotional needs.

In the first place, emotions and intellect are not as separate at ages three and four as they will be later and an emotionally distraught preschooler is cognitively disorganized as well. The preschool teacher's concern with and response to the young child's feelings have cognitive as well as emotional benefits. Then too, preschool represents the child's first separation from home, his first experience with a peer group and a substitute mother figure. The preschool child still has a lot of social learning to do, and the traditional preschool provides the opportunity, security and structure for such learning.

Secondly, and more importantly, the traditional preschool does provide for cognitive stimulation and instruction in the most general and significant sense of that term. Play is, after all, the child's work and much of his motor play is preparatory to later cognitive developments. In stacking and building with blocks, the child learns about spatial relations, balance, weight and gravity. Likewise in large motor play such as climbing, swinging, running, he learns the motor and perceptual coordinations that are essential to later fine motor coordinations involved in reading and writing. Those who deride play in the preschool ignore the fact that all play has a cognitive component and role in all creative endeavor, whether it be intellectual or artistic.

Finally, the traditional preschool program has incorporated for many years some of the most innovative ideas in educational practice today. The traditional nursery school has, to illustrate, always sought to *individualize instruction* and allow each child, in today's lexicon, to do "his thing" whether it be carpentry, doll play, painting or block building. Also, *discovery learning* is built into many preschool activities, such as dramatic play. When a child play-acts roles with other children, he is learning about adult roles and reciprocal rules of behavior. He is, moreover, engaging in the social interchanges with peers that Piaget (1948) regards as so important to the overcoming of egocentrism. Finally, in providing a range of materials and allowing the child to engage in those which send him at the moment, the traditional preschool capitalizes upon *intrinsic motivation* to learn in the best sense of that term (Elkind, 1969b).

The traditional preschool, thus, does much more than the advocates of the academic preschool credit. Indeed, the traditional preschool already embodies ideas that are only now beginning to appear at higher education levels, such as individualized instruction, discovery learning, peer group stimulation and use of intrinsic motivation. This is not to say, of course, that the traditional preschool is perfect and that there is no room for improvement. For one thing, the value of the preschool will vary with the quality of the teacher. Teacher variability at the preschool level is as great as at every other level of education and can always stand improvement. For another thing, traditional preschools may have too little material for spontaneous practice in logical and mathematical thinking and teachers might benefit from our new knowledge about the thinking capacities of preschool children (Inhelder & Piaget, 1969).

In short, with respect to middle-class children, the traditional preschool still appears to be consonant with the maximum benefit to intellectual and emotional growth of the preschool child. While the traditional preschool can probably increase considerably its effectiveness in preparing children for academic instruction, there is no strong evidence for exposing young, middle-class children to academic instruction itself. Indeed, it would be ironic if, in the name of progress, preschools were forced to adopt the lock step curricula already being given up at higher levels of education.

SUMMARY AND CONCLUSIONS

In this essay I have discussed four of the arguments for introducing an academic curriculum into preschool education. These arguments are that academic instruction is: (a) more economical; (b) more efficient; (c) more necessary and (d) more cognitively stimulating than the traditional preschool. I have tried to show that each of these arguments is weak at best and that there are stronger arguments for not having an academic preschool, at least for the middle-class child. There is no preponderance of evidence that formal instruction is more efficient, more economical, more necessary or more cognitively stimulating than the traditional preschool program. Indeed, while there is room for improvement in the traditional preschool, it already embodies some of the most innovative educational practices extant today. It would, in fact, be foolish to pattern the vastly expanded preschool programs planned for the future upon an instructional format that is rapidly being given up at higher educational levels. Indeed, it is becoming more and more apparent that formal instructional programs are as inappropriate at the primary and secondary levels of education as they are at the preschool level.

References

BEREITER, C. & ENGLEMANN, S. *Teaching Disadvantaged Children in the Preschool*. Engelwood Cliffs, N.J.: Prentice Hall, 1966.

BERLYNE, D. E. Curiosity and education. In J. D. Krumboltz (Ed.), *Learning and the Educational Process*. Chicago: Rand McNally, 1965, 67–89.

BLANK, MARION & SOLOMON, FRANCES. A tutorial language program to develop abstract thinking in socially disadvantaged preschool children. *Child Develpm.*, 1968, 39, 379–390.

BLOOM, B. S. *Stability and Change in Human Characteristics*. New York: Wiley, 1964.

BRUNER, J. S. *The Process of Education*. Cambridge, Mass.: Harvard Univ. Press, 1960.

ELKIND, D. Developmental studies of figurative perception. In L. P. Lipsitt & H. W. Reese (Eds.), *Advances in Child Development and Behavior*. New York: Academic Press, 1969, 1–28a.

———. Piagetian and psychometric approaches to intelligence. *Harvard educ. Rev.*, 1969, 39, 319–337b.

FOWLER, W. Cognitive learning in infancy and early childhood. *Psycholog. Bull.*, 1962, 59, 116–152.

GOTTESMAN, I. I. Biogenetics of race and class. In M. Deutsch, I. Katz & A. Jensen (Eds.), *Social Class, Race, and Psychological Development*. New York: Holt, Rinehart & Winston, 1968, 11–51.

HUNT, J. McV. *Intelligence and Experience*. New York: Ronald Press, 1961.

JENSEN, A. R. How much can we boost IQ and scholastic achievement? *Harvard educ. Rev.*, 1969, 39, 1–123.

KAMI, C. & RADIN, N. A framework for a preschool curriculum based on some Piagetian concepts. *J. creative Behav.*, 1967, 1, 314–324.

PIAGET, J. *The Moral Judgment of the Child*. Glencoe, Ill.: The Free Press, 1948.

———. *The Early Growth of Logic in the Child*. New York: Norton, 1969.

SAVA, SAMUEL G. When learning comes easy. *Saturday Rev.*, Nov. 16, 1968, 102–119.

SCHAFFER, H. R. & CALLENDER, W. M. Psychologic effects of hospitalization in infancy. *Pediatrics*, 1959, 24, 528–539.

SCOTT, J. P. *Early Experience and the Organization of Behavior*. Belmont Calif.: Wadsworth, 1968.

STEVENSON, H. W., HESS, E. H. & RHEINGOLD, HARRIET L. (Eds.). *Early Behavior*. New York: Wiley, 1967.

STRODTBECK, F. L. The hidden curriculum of the middle-class home. In C. W. Hunnicutt (Ed.), *Urban Education and Cultural Deprivation*. Syracuse: Syracuse Univ. Press, 1964, 15–31.

WHITE, S. H. Evidence for a hierarchical arrangement of learning processes. In L. P. Lipsitt & C. C. Spiker (Eds.), *Advances in Child Development and Behavior*, Vol. 2. New York: Academic Press, 1965, 187–220.

ZIGLER, E. & BUTTERFIELD, E. C. Motivational aspects of changes in IQ test performance of culturally deprived school children. *Child Develpm.*, 1968, 39, 1–14.

Positive Social Reinforcement in the Nursery School Peer Group*

Rosalind Charlesworth
ANN ARBOR PUBLIC SCHOOLS

Willard W. Hartup
UNIVERSITY OF MINNESOTA

An observational method was devised for obtaining normative information on the amount and kinds of positive social reinforcement dispensed by preschool-age children to each other in nursery school. Data were collected in 4 preschool classes. It was found that children in the older groups reinforced their peers at a significantly higher rate than those in the younger groups and that the amount of reinforcement given was positively related to the amount received. Reinforcement was dispensed in a higher proportion when a child was engaged in dramatic play activity than when he was engaged in other pursuits (such as art, music, or table games). About half the reinforcements were given in response to overtures from the recipients and half spontaneously. The consequence of reinforcement was, in largest proportion, the continuation of the recipient's activity at the time of reinforcement.

Numerous attempts are currently being made to study patterns of young children's social behavior within the conceptual framework of reinforcement theory. Only a few studies (Floyd, 1964; Hartup, 1964; Patterson, Bricker, & Greene, 1964), however, have dealt particularly with preschool-age peers as agents of reinforcement. The results of the Patterson et al. (1964) study strongly support the utility of applying reinforcement theory to the observational study of aggressive behavior as it occurs in the nursery school. The present study investigated patterns of positive social behavior in the nursery school peer group considered in terms of this theory. Previous studies of positive social behavior have used more molecular descriptive concepts (Swift, 1964), such as "cooperation," "leadership," "sympathy," and "social participation."

Skinner's rubric "generalized reinforcer" was chosen as the basis for defining positive social reinforcement. Skinner (1953) postulates that reinforcement from people gives rise to several important forms of generalized social reinforcers: attention (attending to another), approval (praise or acceptance), affection (physical gestures or verbal statements), submissiveness (following a request or suggestion), and tokens (giving tangible physical objects). Gewirtz (1961) has elaborated further the processes by which these stimuli acquire reinforcing properties in early infancy and become the prime

Reprinted from *Child Development*, *38*, 993–1002. Copyright © 1967, by The Society for Research in Child Development, Inc. By permission.

* The authors wish to acknowledge the assistance of Elizabeth Konen, Nancy Mann, and Marilyn Rausch in carrying out this study. They also extend thanks to the staff of the University of Minnesota Laboratory Preschool for their cooperation, and to Sandra Cohen and James Bryan for their helpful reviews of an earlier manuscript. This project was carried out while the first author was supported by NICHD grant No. T1-HD-105-01.

maintainers of social life. For the present study, Skinner's conceptualization was used as a guide for defining categories of social behavior, and an observational method was then designed for obtaining information concerning reinforcement frequencies occurring in the nursery school peer group.

METHOD

SUBJECTS   The children observed were enrolled in a laboratory preschool. They were, for the most part, children of university faculty members and other professional people. The subjects for the principal investigation consisted of two groups of children between the ages of 4–1 and 4–9 and two groups between 3–4 and 4–0. The total sample included 35 boys and 35 girls, divided into preschool classes of 16, 17, 18, and 19 children each. The major portion of the children in the two older groups had had previous nursery school experience. One group of 3-year-olds consisted of children with no previous experience, while the other group was about equally divided between new children and nursery school veterans. One of the older and one of the younger groups met five mornings per week, while the other two groups met three afternoons per week.

THE OBSERVATIONAL TECHNIQUE   *Procedure*[1]   The observer arrived in the room before the children. Prior to collecting any data, the observer spent time sitting in the room practicing the observational technique, learning the children's names, and allowing the children to become accustomed to her presence. The observations began during the fourth week of the school year and continued for 5 weeks. Each day the observer began as soon as half the children had arrived and continued until cleanup was announced. The children were observed in random order for 3-minute periods. A child was never observed more than twice on the same day. Twelve 3-minute time segments were recorded for each child in each of the older groups, ten segments for one of the younger groups, and eight for the other. For purposes of statistical analysis, the scores for the younger groups were extrapolated to 12 observation periods. Tally was made of the location of the observers during each observation period.

The following information was recorded: the child's name and the names of the other children and adults engaged in the same activity or in parallel activity; the activity in which the child was engaged; a detailed running account of the child's behavior and the behavior of any child with whom he interacted.

There were two observers. Two of the groups (one 3-year-old and one 4-year old) were observed exclusively by O_1 and one (4-year-old) by O_2. In the fourth group (3-year-old), half of the observations were carried out by the O_1 alone and half by both observers simultaneously. A comparison of the

[1] An observation and Coding Manual containing a description of the conditions for observation, instructions for recording observations, the coding procedure, and sample protocols has been deposited as Document No. 9617 with the ADI Auxiliary Publications Project, Photoduplication Service, Library of Congress, Washington, D.C. 20540. A copy may be secured by citing the Document No. and by remitting $2.50 for photoprints or $1.75 for 35 mm. microfilm. Advance payment is required. Make checks or money orders payable to: Chief, Photoduplication Service, Library of Congress.

number of codeable incidents recorded by each observer showed that O_1 recorded 16 per cent more codeable incidents than did O_2.

The observation protocols were coded using the following group of categories:

I. *Giving positive attention and approval:* attending, offering praise and approval, offering instrumental help, smiling and laughing, verbal help, informing another of a third person's needs, general conversation.

II. *Giving affection and personal acceptance:* physical and verbal.

III. *Submission:* passive acceptance, imitation, sharing, accepting another's idea or help, allowing another child to play, compromise, following an order or request with pleasure and cooperation.

IV. *Token giving:* giving tangible physical objects, such as toys or food, spontaneously.

These categories coincide with those listed by Skinner (1953) as possessing widely shared reinforcing value in humans, It is not argued that the ratings covered all classes of social stimuli having reinforcing value. Crying, for example, can be positively reinforcing in peer interaction but was not tabulated in this study. Judgments concerning the frequency of social reinforcers were made using the following considerations: (a) the occurrence of a reinforcement was defined in terms of the kind of action involved, rather than in the effects the action had upon the child perceiving it; and (b) the record needed to contain evidence that the recipient perceived the potentially reinforcing activity of his peer. The reinforcements were also coded as to whether they were accepted, rejected, or ignored. In the data analysis, the frequencies of reinforcements *given* are those positive social reinforcements which were followed by positive behavior on the part of the recipient. Also tabulated were instances for each child in which he received reinforcement from other children as recorded in the other children's protocols.

The observations were coded by one of the observers and a naïve coder in order to obtain information on the reliability of the coding procedure. Two ratios were computed. The first, .77, is a ratio of agreement/agreement + disagreement in which agreement concerns the presence of positive social reinforcement (even though there might be disagreement as to the category of the reinforcement). A second ratio, in which agreement concerned the presence of a particular category of reinforcement, was .64, These reliability checks were based on 20 per cent (161) of the 3-minute protocols. A third coder tallied information on location, presence or absence of an overture, and consequences of reinforcement.

RESULTS AND DISCUSSION

GIVING POSITIVE SOCIAL REINFORCEMENT   *Findings*   Age and sex differences in frequency of giving positive social reinforcement were revealed by means of a series of two-way analyses of variance for unequal cell frequencies (Table 1). For total frequencies (the sum of all reinforcements regardless of category), there was a significant age difference, with the 4-year-olds giving more reinforcement than 3-year-olds ($F = 9.30$, $p < .01$). Most of this difference is accounted for by Category I: Giving Attention and Approval ($F = 15.03$, $p < .01$). For Category II, a significant age by sex interaction was found ($F = 5.68$, $p < .025$). When the means are examined (Table 2), it can be seen that younger and older boys gave affection and personal acceptance in almost

TABLE 1

Summary of Analyses of Variance for Positive Social Reinforcement Scores for Two Age Groups

		REINFORCEMENT SCORE				
SOURCE	df	TOTAL FREQUENCY (F)	CATEGORY I (F)	CATEGORY II (F)	CATEGORY III (F)	TOTAL N DIFFERENT PEERS (F)
Age	1	9.30†	15.03†	3.29	1.51	21.25†
Sex	1	3.31	1.03	1.30	6.03*	2.73
A × S	1	1.35	< 1.00	5.68*	< 1.00	3.53
Within	66	–	–	–	–	–

* $p < .02$.
† $p < .01$.

TABLE 2

Means and Ranges of Positive Social Reinforcement Scores for Four Sex and Age Groups

			REINFORCEMENT SCORE									
			TOTAL FREQUENCY		CATEGORY I		CATEGORY II		CATEGORY III		TOTAL N DIFFERENT PEERS	
SEX	AGE	N	$\bar{X}$	R	$\bar{X}$	R	$\bar{X}$	R	$\bar{X}$	R	$\bar{X}$	R
M	4	17	22.82	6–49	10.29	2–24	3.18	0–10	8.47	0–23	5.76	2–11
F	4	16	21.06	2–54	9.56	1–24	4.06	0–14	6.19	0–18	5.88	2–9
M	3	18	17.77	4–35	6.09	1–15	3.58	0–16	7.74	3–25	4.44	2–8
F	3	19	9.79	0–33	4.36	0–14	1.07	0–5	3.82	0–15	2.74	0–7

equal amounts, while younger girls gave much less frequent affection than older girls or either group of boys. Boys were found to give submissive types of reinforcements (Category III) significantly more frequently than girls ($F = 6.03$, $p < .025$).[2] It was also found that older children reinforced a significantly greater number of other children than did the younger children ($F = 21.25$, $p < .01$).

Another set of analyses was conducted in order to test classroom and sex

[2] No separate analysis of Category IV was completed due to the small frequencies obtained.

TABLE 3

Summary of Analyses of Variance of Positive Social Reinforcement Scores for Two 4-Year-Old Classes

		REINFORCEMENT SCORE				
SOURCE	DF	TOTAL FREQUENCY (F)	CATEGORY I (F)	CATEGORY II (F)	CATEGORY III (F)	TOTAL N DIFFERENT PEERS (F)
Class	1	5.91†	8.01‡	4.50*	2.25	10.14‡
Sex	1	< 1.00	< 1.00	< 1.00	1.54	< 1.00
C × S	1	< 1.00	< 1.00	< 1.00	< 1.00	< 1.00
Within	29	–	–	–	–	–

* $p < .05.$
† $p < .02.$
‡ $p < .01.$

TABLE 4

Summary of Analyses of Variance of Positive Social Reinforcement Scores for Two 3-Year-Old Classes

		REINFORCEMENT SCORE				
SOURCE	DF	TOTAL FREQUENCY (F)	CATEGORY I (F)	CATEGORY II (F)	CATEGORY III (F)	TOTAL N DIFFERENT PEERS (F)
Class	1	< 1.00	< 1.00	< 1.00	< 1.00	5.52†
Sex	1	6.74†	1.69	7.79‡	5.12*	10.16‡
C × S	1	< 1.00	< 1.00	< 1.00	< 1.00	1.01
Within	33	–	–	–	–	–

* $p < .05.$
† $p < .02.$
‡ $p < .01.$

differences in giving reinforcements within the two age groups separately (Table 3 and Table 4). For the 4-year-olds. there were significant classroom differences on four of the five variables tested; only the frequency of submissive reinforcers did not differ significantly between the two classes for 4-year-olds. For the younger children, there were significant sex differences in favor of the boys in four of the five categories, with only attention and approval not reaching a significant level. There was also one significant classroom difference for the younger children. Subjects in one classroom reinforced a larger number of children than those in the other ($F = 5.52$, $p < .025$).

Differences in the mean number of positive reinforcements given were also analyzed according to the sex of the recipient. Boys gave significantly more reinforcements to other boys than they gave to girls ($t = 4.43, p < .002$), and girls gave more reinforcements to other girls than to boys ($t = 2.18, p < .05$).

The proportions of each type of reinforcement given were tabulated. Most frequently given by the 4-year-olds was attention and approval (46 per cent), followed by submission (35 per cent), affection and personal acceptance (16.8 per cent), and token giving (2.27 per cent). The proportions of two categories of reinforcers show a slight age shift: the 3-year-olds used a larger proportion of attention and approval (37 per cent) than the 4's. The 3-year-olds give almost exactly the same proportion (16.5 per cent) of affection and personal acceptance and more (5.5 per cent) tokens.

Discussion   The findings presented above show that considerably more positive social reinforcement was given by 4-year-olds than by 3-year-olds. Also, the older children distributed their reinforcements to a larger number of other children than did the younger children. These findings parallel the classic findings of Parten (1932) and others concerning the association between chronological age and social participation. The present findings, however, document the fact that the preschool years encompass a period of marked increases in the child's use of generalized social reinforcers in his interactions with peers.

The findings also reveal early differences between boys and girls with respect to certain aspects of peer interaction and utilization of social reinforcers. Boys participated in more give-and-take play in the nursery school than did girls; that is, they gave more submissive reinforcements generally, and they gave more reinforcements during dramatic play. The finding that younger girls gave considerably less affection and personal acceptance than boys and that 82 per cent of this type of reinforcement was given spontaneously indicates that when girls are placed in a group setting at age 3 they are less socially active than boys. Further, the younger girls gave less total reinforcement than younger boys. Thus, sex differences in use of social reinforcers, particularly by younger nursery school children, are clearly revealed by the data. On the other hand, measures of what might be called "social activity level" or "general social participation" were not procured. Therefore, it cannot be argued, without further study, that the sex differences (or the age differences discussed in the preceding paragraph) are independent of differences in general activity or participation.

The differences between the older classes in the number of reinforcements given may be related to two factors. The teacher of the group in which the most reinforcements were given felt that this was an unusually socially active group. In contrast to the other older group, these children not only gave more reinforcements but also had a lower frequency of rejected reinforcements (these were not included in the totals given). There was also a significant difference in the number of different individual children reinforced in each of these two groups. The group in which more reinforcements were given was the 3-day-per-week group.

Evidence for the early formation of a sex schism is apparent in the data on object choice. Boys tended to reinforce boys and girls to reinforce girls. These data indicate that the relative deprivation of reinforcing stimuli from persons of the opposite sex cited by Stevenson (1965) extends from early in the preschool years in the interaction of the child with his peers.

GIVING AND RECEIVING OF REINFORCEMENT   *Findings*   The relationship between giving and receiving of positive social reinforcement was tested by the use of the within-groups correlation coefficient (Walker & Lev, 1958). The correlation between the total numbers of reinforcements given and the total number received was large ($r = .79$) and highly significant ($p < .01$). Each separate category of giving reinforcement was significantly related to each category of receiving it, with correlations ranging from $r = .38$ ($p < .01$) to $r = .64$ ($p < .01$) (Table 5). Also highly related were the number of individual

TABLE 5

Within-Groups Correlations Between Frequencies of Giving and Receiving
Positive Social Reinforcement for Four Classrooms

	GIVING POSITIVE SOCIAL REINFORCEMENT		
RECEIVING POSITIVE SOCIAL REINFORCEMENT	CATEGORY I (r)	CATEGORY II (r)	CATEGORY III (r)
Category I	.39	.45	.64
Category II	.51	.38	.65
Category III	.69	.54	.58

Note. All correlations are significant beyond .01 ($N = 70$).

children reinforced by a child and the number of individuals he received reinforcements from ($r = .46$, $p < .01$). The total frequency of reinforcements given and the number of people to whom they were distributed were correlated $r = .62$ ($p < .01$), and the total number of reinforcements received and the number of people they were received from were correlated .70 ($p < .01$).

Discussion   The results on the giving and the receiving of reinforcement indicate that these are reciprocal activities. Those who give the most get the most, and vice versa. Since precaution was taken to base the measures of giving and receiving on different events, this finding is of substantial interest. For one thing, it suggests that reinforcement giving is an operant which comes under the control of generalized social reinforcers of other children at very early ages. This finding also is reminiscent of the commonality between dependency behavior and nurturance giving found by Hartup and Keller (1960) and Eininger (1965).

LOCATION, OVERTURES, AND CONSEQUENCES   *Findings*   Each reinforcing incident was categorized as to the type of play occurring at the time the child was reinforcing the "other." The type of play (or location of the child) was categorized: (a) dramatic play—housekeeping area, blocks, trucks, puppet play, and so forth; (b) table activities—puzzles or other manipulative table toys, art activities, stories or flannel board, and so forth; (c) wandering—going from place to place without engaging in the available activities or standing on the sidelines observing. Overall, 65 per cent of the reinforcement was given during dramatic play activities. The following proportions of specific kinds of reinforcement occurred during dramatic play: Category I, 59 per cent; Category II, 70 per cent; Category III, 67 per cent; and Category IV, 77 per cent. Boys gave a larger proportion of their reinforcements (74 per cent) during dramatic play than did girls (51 per cent).

A tally was made of the types of activity in which children were engaged when no reinforcements were given during the 3-minute observation period. During these observation periods, children were usually engaged in table activities (60 per cent) or wandering about the room (19 per cent), while only 21 per cent of these observations found the child in a play area where dramatic play was in progress or was a possibility.

Each reinforcement was also coded as to whether an overture had been made by the recipient, that is, whether an indication was given that reinforcement was desired. Overtures, overall, were present almost half (47 per cent) of the time but the proportions differed for each category of reinforcement. For attention and approval, the proportion was 49 per cent; for submission, 67 per cent; for affection and personal acceptance, 18 per cent; and for tokens, 4 per cent. There were no age or sex differences in proportion of overture present for total frequencies.

The coder found it somewhat difficult to code the consequences of reinforcement, and thus, the following results are tentative. For the most part (58 per cent), reinforcement was followed by the recipient continuing the activity in which he was engaged at the time of reinforcement. Sixteen per cent of the reinforcements were followed by a change in behavior, 6 per cent were rejected, 8 per cent were ignored, and 12 per cent could not be rated.

Discussion   The data on location of reinforcement show that opportunities for dramatic play activities are particularly conducive to the child's acquisition of positive social skills with peers. It is clear from the results of this study that, as would be expected, activities which involve attending to a project or to an adult do not elicit as large quantities of social reinforcement from peers as do dramatic play activities. It is also interesting that boys, who are usually characterized as being more active than girls in the nursery school play group, do indeed engage in a larger proportion of social reinforcing peer interaction during dramatic play than girls, who divide their reinforcements almost equally between dramatic play and more sedentary activities.

The data on overture present or absent suggest that different stimuli elicit the giving of different kinds of social reinforcers. Attention, approval, and submission seem to require a prior social response from another child. On the other hand, affection, personal acceptance, and tokens appear to function as instrumental actions used to initiate an interaction sequence. The data concerning the consequences of peer reinforcement are particularly important, although in need of replication. It appears that reinforcement (as defined by the actions observed in the present study) usually sustains ongoing behavior and that very few reinforcements are rejected.

CONCLUSIONS

The observational method used, although time consuming and comparatively subjective, yielded promising results concerning the positive social reinforcement behavior of preschool children. The results indicated that children of this age manifest a wide variety of positive behaviors, and developmental changes are apparent. The ultimate value of the present observational method will depend on the predictive value of the information obtained. As is reported elsewhere (Hartup & Coates, 1967; Hartup, Glazer, & Charlesworth, 1967), the present measures of classroom behavior have been found to be predictive of behavior in two other situations. Consequently, further work utilizing this approach to the study of peer reinforcement seems warranted.

References

EININGER, MARY ANN. Dependency behavior as related to two kinds of nurturance in young children. Unpublished M.A. thesis, University of Minnesota, 1965.

FLOYD, JOANNE. Effects of the amount of reward and friendship status of the other on the frequency of sharing in children. Unpublished doctoral dissertation, University of Minnesota, 1964.

GEWIRTZ, J. L. A learning analysis of the effects of normal stimulation, privation and deprivation on the acquisition of social motivation and attachment. In B. Foss (Ed.), *Determinants of infant behavior*. New York: Wiley, 1961.

HARTUP, W. W. Friendship status and the effectiveness of peers as reinforcing agents. *Journal of experimental child Psychology*, 1964, **1**, 154–162.

———, & COATES, B. Imitation of a peer as a function of reinforcement from the peer group and rewardingness of the model. *Child Development*, 1967, **38**, 1003–1016.

———, GLAZER, JANE, & CHARLESWORTH, ROSALIND. Peer reinforcement and sociometric status. *Child Development*, 1967, 38, 1017–1024.

———, & KELLER, E. D. Nurturance in preschool children and its relation to dependency *Child Development*, 1960, **31**, 681–689.

PARTEN, MILDRED B. Social participation among preschool children. *Journal of abnormal and social Psychology*, 1932, **27**, 243–269.

PATTERSON, G. E., BRICKER, W., & GREEN, M. Peer group reactions as a determinant of aggressive behavior in nursery school children. Paper presented at the meetings of the American Psychological Association, 1964.

SKINNER, B. F. *Science and human behavior*. New York: Macmillan, 1953.

STEVENSON, H. W. Social reinforcement of children's behavior. In L. P. Lipsitt and C. C. Spiker (Eds.), *Advances in child development and behavior*. Vol. 2. New York: Academic Press, 1965. Pp. 97–126.

SWIFT, JOAN. Effects of early group experience: the nursery school and day nursery. In M. Hoffman and L. Hoffman (Eds.), *Review of child development research*. Vol. 1. New York: Russell Sage Found., 1964. Pp. 249–288.

WALKER, HELEN, & LEV, J. *Elementary statistical methods*. New York: Holt, 1958.

The Early Training Project: A Seventh Year Report*

Susan W. Gray and Rupert A. Klaus

GEORGE PEABODY COLLEGE FOR TEACHERS

This is a report at the end of fourth grade of a preschool intervention project for children from low income homes. Its purpose was to investigate whether one could offset progressive retardation in elementary school. Special experiences provided for the 44 experimental children were based upon variables associated with attitudes and aptitudes conducive to school achievement. Intensive work was done for three summers; in the remaining months there were weekly home visits. Over the years the experimental children remained significantly superior to control children on intelligence tests. On measures of language and achievement trends still remained, but differences were no longer significant by the end of fourth grade. There is a slight but parallel decline across groups. Evidence is presented on younger siblings.

The Early Training Project has been a field research study concerned with the development and testing over time of procedures for improving the educability of young children from low income homes. The rationale, the general design and methodology, and findings through the second year of schooling have been reported in some detail in *The early training project for disadvantaged children, a report after five years*, by Klaus and Gray (1968). A briefer report, up to school entrance, is given in Gray and Klaus (1965). The purpose of this report is to present the findings at the end of the fourth grade, three years after all experimental intervention had ceased.

The major concern of the Early Training Project was to study whether it was possible to offset the progressive retardation observed in the public schooling careers of children living in deprived circumstances. In addition, the writers undertook to study the spillover effect upon other children in the community and upon other family members.

The general research strategy was one of attempting to design a research "package" consisting of variables which—on the basis of research upon social class, cognitive development, and motivation—might be assumed to be relevant to the school retardation which is observed in deprived groups and which at the same time might be subject to the effects of manipulation. Because this was a problem with major social implications, we also tried to design a general treatment approach which it would be feasible to repeat on a large scale, in the event that the procedures proved successful.

Subjects were 88 children born in 1958. Sixty-one of these lived in a city of 25,000 in the upper South. The remaining 27, who served as a distal control

Reprinted from *Child Development*, *41*, 909–924. Copyright © 1970, by The Society for Research in Child Development. Inc., By permission.

* Major financial support for this study was received from the National Institute of Mental Health, under Mental Health Project Grant 5-R11-MH-765. Additional support for research staff during the later phases of the study was made possible through Grant HD-00973 from the National Institute of Child Health and Human Development, from the Office of Education, Contract OEC 3-7-070706-3118, and Grant 9174 from the Office of Economic Opportunity.

209

group, resided in a similar city 65 miles away. The children were all Negro.
When we initiated the study the schools of the city were still segregated; we
chose to work with Negro children because in this particular setting we had
reason to believe that our chances of success were greater with this group.

The children were selected on the basis of parent's occupation, parent's
education, income, and housing conditions. At the beginning of the study
incomes were considerably below the approximate $3,000 used as the poverty
line for a family of four. Occupations were either unskilled or semi-skilled; the
educational level was eighth grade or below; housing conditions were poor.
The median number of children per family at the beginning of the study was
five; in about one-third of the homes there was no father present.

From the 61 children in the first city three groups were constituted by
random assignment. The first group (T1) attended, over a period of three
summers, a ten-week preschool designed to offset the deficits usually observed
in the performance of children from disadvantaged homes. In addition, this

TABLE 1
Layout of General Research Design

TREATMENTS	T1 THREE SUMMER SCHOOLS	T2 TWO SUMMER SCHOOLS	T3 LOCAL CONTROLS	T4 DISTAL CONTROLS
First winter 1961–62	(Criterion development, curriculum planning, general tooling up)			
First summer 1962	Pre-test Summer school Post-test	Pre-test Post-test	Pre-test Post-test	Pre-test Post-test
Second winter 1962–63	Home visitor contacts			
Second summer 1963	Pre-test Summer school Post-test	Pre-test Summer school Post-test	Pre-test Post-test	Pre-test Post-test
Third winter 1963–64	Home visitor contacts	Home visitor contacts		
Third summer 1964	Pre-test Summer school Post-test	Pre-test Summer school Post-test	Pre-test Post-test	Pre-test Post-test
Fourth winter 1964–65	Home visitor contacts	Home visitor contacts		
Fourth summer 1965	Follow-up tests	Follow-up tests	Follow-up tests	Follow-up tests
Fifth summer 1966	Follow-up tests	Follow-up tests	Follow-up tests	Follow-up tests
Seventh summer 1968	Follow-up tests	Follow-up tests	Follow-up tests	Follow-up tests

group had three years of weekly meetings with a specially trained home visitor during those months in which the preschool was not in session. The second group (T2) had a similar treatment, except that it began a year later; the children received two summers of the special preschool and two years of home visits. The third group (T3) became the local control group, which received all tests but no intervention treatment. The fourth group (T4), the distal control group, was added to the design because of the somewhat ghetto-type concentration of Negroes in the first city. The local and distal control groups also made possible the study of spillover effects upon children and parents living in proximity to the experimental children. The general layout of the experimental design is given in Table 1.

By reading down the columns, one may see the particular treatment and testing sequence followed for each of the four groups. Periodic testing is continuing for the children through elementary school.

THE INTERVENTION PROGRAM

The overall rationale for the intervention program grew out of the literature on child-rearing patterns in different social classes, plus the writers' own observations in low income homes. On the basis of this study, the intervention program for children was organized around two broad classes of variables: attitudes relating to achievement, and aptitudes relating to achievement. Under attitudes we were particularly interested in achievement motivation, especially as it concerns school-type activities, in persistence, in ability to delay gratification; and in general interest in typical school materials, such as books, crayons, puzzles, and the like. We were also concerned with the parent's attitude toward achievement, particularly in their aspirations for their children, especially as they related to schooling.

In the broad class of aptitude variables relating to achievement we were particularly interested in perceptual and cognitive development and in language. Children from low income homes have been shown to have deficits in these areas, all of which appear closely related to school success in the primary grades.

In the summer months, for 10 weeks the children met in assembled groups. Each of the two experimental groups had a head teacher, who was an experienced Negro first grade teacher. There were in addition three or four teaching assistants. These assistants were divided about equally as to race and sex.

The work with the parents in the project was carried on largely through a home visitor program in which a specially trained preschool teacher made weekly visits to each mother and child. Both the home program and the school program are described in considerable detail in *Before first grade* (Gray, Klaus, Miller, and Forrester, 1966) and in Klaus and Gray (1968).

Prior to and after each summer session children in all four groups were tested on several instruments. From the first summer certain standardized tests of intelligence and language were used, along with a number of less formal instruments. At the end of first grade, achievement tests were added. This testing schedule is shown in Table 1. In general the .05 level of significance was used.

RESULTS

The detailed results of the testing program through May, 1966, the end of the second grade for the children, are given in Klaus and Gray (1968). This paper gives the results as they relate to the spring and summer testings of 1968 with some additional information on performance of younger siblings. The same kinds of analyses were used for the 1968 data as were used in the earlier paper.

In 1968 the following tests were administered to all children still residing in middle Tennessee: the Binet, the Peabody Picture Vocabulary Test, and the Metropolitan Achievement Test. The analyses here reported are based only upon those children available for testing with the exception of one child in the distal control group.

TABLE 2

Mean Stanford-Binet MA and IQ Scores for the Four Treatment Groups at Each Administration

	T1(N = 19)		T2(N = 19)		T3(N = 18)		T4(N = 23)	
DATE OF ADMINISTRATION	MA (MO.)	IQ	MA (MO.)	IQ	MA (MO.)	IQ	MA (MO.)	IQ
May 1962	40.7	87.6	43.8	92.5	40.3	85.4	40.3	86.7
Aug. 1962	50.7	102.0	46.9	92.3	44.3	88.2	43.4	87.4
May 1963	55.6	96.4	56.0	94.8	53.2	89.6	50.4	86.7
Aug. 1963	59.3	97.1	60.6	97.5	55.0	87.6	52.3	84.7
Aug. 1964	68.0	95.8	71.6	96.6	62.3	82.9	59.4	80.2
Aug. 1965	83.8	98.1	86.3	99.7	79.4	91.4	77.0	89.0
June 1966	88.7	91.2	93.4	96.0	86.8	87.9	82.9	84.6
July 1968	106.0	86.7	111.4	90.2	104.7	84.9	96.2	77.7

The Stanford-Binet scores are given in Table 2, and are portrayed graphically in Figure 1. A Lindquist (1953) Type 1 analysis of the results of 1962–1968, in terms of IQ, gave a significant F of 4.45 for the four groups, and F of 16.81 for repeated measures, and F for interaction of groups over time of 3.51. All of these were significant at the .01 level or beyond. Next an analysis was made by the use of orthogonal comparisons. These are given in Table 3. Here it may be seen that the two experimental groups remained significantly superior to the two control groups.

The comparison of the first and the second experimental groups for 1968 showed an F of less than 1.00. The comparison of the two control groups, however, yielded an F that, although not conventionally significant, was still large enough (3.52 where $F_{.95}$ = 3.96) to be suggestive of a sharper decline in the distal than in the local control group. As was true of earlier analyses the larger part of the variance appeared to be carried by the second experimental group and the distal control group.

The scores across the ten administrations of the Peabody Picture Vocabulary Test are given in Table 4 in MA and IQ form. A Lindquist (1953) Type 1 analysis of variance was performed for the MA scores.

TABLE 3

Orthogonal Comparisons of Treatment Group Sums for Binet IQ Scores for the Eight Administrations

DATE OF ADMINISTRATION	HO: T1 = T2 + T3 + T4		HO: T2 = T3 + T4		HO: T3 = T4	
	F RATIO	CONCLUSION	F RATIO	CONCLUSION	F RATIO	CONCLUSION
Aug. 1962	12.67*	T1 > T2 + T3 + T4	1.44	T2 = T3 + T4	<1.00	T3 = T4
May 1963	2.91	T1 = T2 + T3 + T4	3.36	T2 = T3 + T4	<1.00	T3 = T4

DATE OF ADMINISTRATION	HO: T1 + T2 = T3 + T4		HO: T1 = T2		HO: T3 = T4	
	F RATIO	CONCLUSION	F RATIO	CONCLUSION	F RATIO	CONCLUSION
May 1962	2.07	T1 + T2 = T3 + T4	1.53	T1 = T2	<1.00	T3 = T4
Aug. 1963	18.53*	T1 + T2 > T3 + T4	<1.00	T1 = T2	<1.00	T3 = T4
Aug. 1964	29.94*	T1 + T2 > T3 + T4	<1.00	T1 = T2	<1.00	T3 = T4
Aug. 1965	11.12*	T1 + T2 > T3 + T4	<1.00	T1 = T2	<1.00	T3 = T4
June 1966	5.99*	T1 + T2 > T3 + T4	1.18	T1 = T2	<1.00	T3 = T4
July 1968	7.50*	T1 + T2 > T3 + T4	<1.00	T1 = T2	3.53	T3 = T4

* $p < .05$; $F_{.95} = 3.97$.

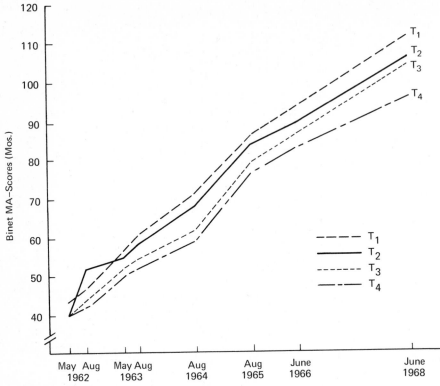

FIGURE I. Mental ages for experimental and control groups on the Stanford-Binet.

TABLE 4

Mean PPVT Mental Age Scores and IQ Equivalents for the Four Treatment Groups for the Ten Administrations

DATE OF ADMINIS-TRATION	TEST FORM	T1(N = 19) MA (MO.)	IQ	T2(N = 19) MA (MO.)	IQ	T3(N = 18) MA (MO.)	IQ	T4(N = 23) MA (MO.)	IQ
May 1962	A	30.0	69.5	30.6	70.1	29.4	66.4	32.2	74.0
Aug. 1962	B	36.8	75.3	33.1	63.9	32.7	65.8	30.7	62.8
May 1963	A	44.8	79.0	40.7	69.6	39.1	69.3	39.5	69.8
Aug. 1963	B	45.0	78.4	50.7	83.6	38.4	64.0	37.6	63.8
May 1964	B	55.6	81.2	60.1	85.5	45.8	65.4	48.7	70.9
Aug. 1964	A	59.1	83.0	62.0	87.0	50.6	72.4	48.7	69.6
June 1965	B	74.2	89.0	76.2	90.3	67.6	83.0	67.3	84.0
Aug. 1965	A	70.6	86.2	76.5	91.8	65.4	80.2	66.3	83.4
June 1966	A	78.1	86.7	81.9	89.3	75.4	83.9	71.2	80.7
July 1968	A	96.4	84.5	100.3	86.7	91.7	81.8	89.3	78.7

F for groups was 5.16, indicating a significant effect of the experimental treatment upon the children's performance. F for repeated testings was 376.73, an effect that would be clearly expected when MA scores were used. These were selected in preference to IQ scores on this particular test since the IQ scores appear to lack discrimination at certain levels. The interaction between groups and time was non-significant. Orthogonals were next used. Here was found that T1 + T2 was significantly greater than T3 + T4 up until 1968, in which year differences were not significant. As may be seen from Table 4, differences in mean scores were still apparent. Heterogeneity had increased over time, however, so that differences were no longer significant. In no analysis at any point of time was either experimental group significantly superior to the other. Nor did either control group show itself to be significantly superior to the other one.

TABLE 5

Metropolitan Achievement Test Grade Equivalent Mean Scores for the Various Subtests for the Three Administrations

Subtest and Year	T1	T2	T3	T4
Word knowledge:				
1965	1.69	1.73	1.79	1.37
1966	2.32	2.47	2.29	1.98
1968	3.58	3.90	3.54	3.27
Word discrimination:				
1965	1.68	1.81	1.82	1.37
1966	2.64	2.73	2.65	2.20
1968	3.73	3.95	3.76	3.47
Reading:				
1965	1.72	1.82	1.84	1.46
1966	2.52	2.75	2.56	2.11
1968	3.52	3.89	3.72	3.10
Arithmetic computation:				
1965	1.52	1.62	1.54	1.43
1966	2.41	2.55	2.49	2.05
1968	3.92	4.07	4.06	3.79
Spelling:				
1966	2.42	2.85	2.60	1.99
1968	4.26	4.69	4.24	3.67
Language:				
1968	3.52	4.00	3.63	3.17
Arithmetic problem-solving and concepts:				
1968	3.31	3.54	3.75	3.26

The results for the Metropolitan Achievement Test are given in Table 5. A Lindquist (1953) Type 1 analysis was performed on each subtest, and orthogonal comparisons made. In the interest of brevity a table of orthogonal comparisons is not given. In 1965, at the end of first grade, the experimental children were significantly superior on three of the four tests used at that time: word knowledge, word discrimination, and reading. For arithmetic computation scores, F was less than 1.00. The local controls were also somewhat superior to the distal controls on these tests, an indication possibly of horizontal diffusion or, either in interaction or independently, a somewhat better instructional program. In 1966 five subtests were given. This time only two were significant, word knowledge and reading. On the other three tests, however, the F's ranged from 2.69 to 2.84, suggesting probabilities at about the .10 level. In neither year was T1 significantly superior to T2. The highest F was 1.16, where $F_{.95}$ is 3.97. In the comparisons of T3 and T4, T3 was superior to T4 on reading and arithmetic computation. On word knowledge, word discrimination, and spelling the F's ranged from 3.19 to 3.85, suggesting probabilities beyond the .10 level ($F_{.90} = 2.77$). At the end of the fourth year no significant effects were found with the single exception of reading, on which T3 was superior to T4. There is some suggestion of residual effect since in six of the seven possible comparisons of experimental and controls, the experimentals were superior. Also on all seven possible comparisons the local control group was superior to the distal control group.

The Binet was administered in all four groups to those younger siblings who were of testable age. This was first done in 1964 and again in 1966. Since

TABLE 6

Initial Binet Scores of Treatment Group Children and Younger Siblings in Two Testings

Testing	Groups	Mean Scores (First Testing, 1962) for Treatment Group Children with Younger Siblings			Mean Scores for Younger Siblings		
		N	CA	IQ	N	CA	IQ
1964 testing of	T1	12	47	82	13	54	82
younger siblings	T2	16	46	89	21	53	83
born in 1959	T3	7	50	84	9	54	71
and 1960	T4	12	48	88	14	62	74
1966 retesting of	T1	12	47	82	13	78	85
younger siblings	T2	14	46	92	19	76	85
initially tested	T3	5	46	82	7	76	78
in 1964	T4	11	48	86	13	77	75
1966 testing of	T1	10	44	87	11	58	84
younger siblings	T2	9	47	91	10	52	87
born in 1961	T3	7	48	83	9	56	76
and 1962	T4	12	47	88	15	55	84
1966 testing of	T1	15	50	84	24	69	84
all younger	T2	17	46	91	29	68	86
siblings	T3	8	47	84	16	65	77
	T4	15	47	86	28	63	80

TABLE 7
Orthogonal Comparisons of Binet Scores of Younger Siblings

	HO: T1 + T2 = T3 + T4		HO: T1 = T2		HO: T3 = T4	
	F RATIO	CONCLUSION	F RATIO	CONCLUSION	F RATIO	CONCLUSION
All younger siblings 1966	3.48	T1 + T2 = T3 + T4	.75	T1 = Y2	.00	T3 = T4
Younger siblings first tested in 1966	.77	T1 + T2 = T3 + T4	.04	T1 = T2	.80	T3 = T4
Younger siblings retested in 1966						
1964 results	8.13*	T1 + T2 > T3 + T4	.74	T1 = T2	.01	T3 = T4
1966 results	4.72*	T1 + T2 > T3 + T4	5.11*	T1 > T2	2.07	T3 = T4

* $p < .05$; $F_{.95} = 3.97$.

the 1966 findings have not been previously reported they are presented here in Table 6. In 1964, 57 children were tested. Fifty of these same children were tested again in 1966, along with 43 additional siblings who were too young to test in 1964.

An analysis of co-variance was performed on these scores, with the IQ's at first testing of the target-age children used as the covariable. Also, where there were two younger siblings in the same family, one was dropped, so that the analysis was based on 87 children. Separate analyses were also performed for the 1964 and the 1966 results of all children who were retested. In addition, an analysis was performed on the 1966 results for those children who were being tested for the first time.

On all younger siblings tested in 1966 the F between groups was not significant at the .05 level ($F = 3.97$). It was significant beyond the .10 level, and therefore we made further analyses. Orthogonal comparisons were used, with the hypotheses shown in Table 7. This is the same general approach as used with the target children. All orthogonal comparisons showed significant differences for the testing of all younger siblings in 1966: the combined experimental group siblings were superior to the combined control group siblings; the T1 siblings were superior to the T2 siblings; and the T3 siblings were superior to the T4 siblings. When the children who were tested for the first time are separated out, it is clear, both in the 1966 and the 1964 data, that most of the variance was being carried by younger siblings closer in age to the target age children. There are some interesting implications of these general results on younger siblings which will be examined in more detail in the discussion section.

DISCUSSION

The results on the one test of intelligence which was used consistently from the initiation of the program in 1962 until the testing at the end of the fourth grade, in 1968, are very much in line with what might be expected, for this was an intervention program that used a broad gauge approach and which was relatively successful in terms of improving the educability of young children from low income homes. Intervention caused a rise in intelligence which was fairly sharp at first, then leveled off, and finally began to show decline once intervention ceased. The control groups on the other hand tended to show a slight but consistent decline with the single exception of a jump between entrance into public school and the end of first grade. Differences between experimentals and controls on Binet IQ were still significant at the end of the third year after intervention ceased. All four groups have shown a decline in IQ after the first grade but the decline, as shown in Figure 1, tended to be relatively parallel. Perhaps the remarkable thing is, with the relatively small amount of impact over time that differences should still be significant. After all, the child experienced only five mornings of school a week for ten weeks for two or three summers, plus weekly home visits during the other nine months for two or three years. This suggests that the impact was not lost. It was not sufficient however, to offset the massive effects of a low income home in which the child had lived since birth onward.

The results on the PPVT showed a pattern that is not dissimilar. There was a rise during intervention, including the first grade, then a leveling-off and a slight decline. Here, however, differences between groups, although consistent were no longer significant.

The importance of the school situation for the maintenance or loss of a gain should be weighed. The children for the most part remained in schools in which the entire population was Negro. Eight of the local children at the end of first grade did enroll in schools that had previously been all white. Four more changed during the next two years. None of the distal children attended schools with white children. Since in this area, as in many places, race tends to be confounded with social class, the children in the study did not in general have the advantage of classmates with relatively high expectancies. There is some evidence that in both of the all-Negro schools the general teaching-learning situation, although fair, was less adequate than in the schools that have formerly been all white. This, plus the continuing effect of the home situation and the immediate community, took its toll. There are some data on achievement test scores to be presented later which suggest the impact of the two all-Negro schools which most of the children attended.

On the one achievement battery administered from first to fourth grade, the Metropolitan Achievement Test (Table 5), significant differences did not appear in 1968 on any of the subtests with sole exception of the reading score, in which the local control group was superior to the distant control group. The experimentals had been superior to the controls on three tests in 1965 and on two tests in 1966. One might interpret this as showing that the intervention program did have measurable effects upon test performance at the end of first grade, but that by the end of fourth grade, the school program had failed to sustain at any substantial level the initial superiority. Although disappointing, this is perhaps not surprising in a test battery so dependent upon specific school instruction.

An interesting sidelight is thrown on this matter by looking at the performance on the Metropolitan Achievement Test of the eight children from the local school who at the end of first grade enrolled in previously all-white schools.

TABLE 8

Mean Gains on the MAT over a 3-Year Period for 8 ETP Children in Integrated Schools and Matches in Negro Schools

	MEAN GAINS 1965–68			
	WORD KNOWL.	WORD DISC.	READ.	ARITH.
ETP *S*s in integrated schools beginning fall 1965	3.1	2.8	2.7	2.9
ETP *S*s in negro schools matched to the first group on spring 1965 *MAT* and on verbal rating by home visitor	1.7	2.0	1.6	1.7
Difference	1.4	.8	1.1	1.2

An attempt was made, on the basis of first grade achievement tests and home ratings of educational aspirations, to match these eight children with eight who remained in the Negro school. Admittedly, this is a chancy business, and one which should not be taken too seriously. Table 8 presents the gains in grade equivalents on the Metropolitan Achievement Tests from the end of first grade to the end of fourth grade.

On the four subtests common to both grade levels the picture is a clear one of more gain in the children who changed schools, varying from .8 to 1.4 years' greater gain. These data did not seem appropriate for subjection to statistical analysis. They do suggest however, the fairly obvious: that performance on achievement tests is directly related to school experience. The children who changed schools have made approximately "normal" gains for their three years; the children who did not change have gained two years or less during the three years from first through fourth grade.

The results on the younger siblings are to the writers among the most interesting findings of the study. We have termed the process by which such results are achieved and the product of that process as vertical diffusion, to suggest that this is a spread of effect down the family from the mother and possibly the target-age child to a younger child. In this study the effects of the older sibling and the mother upon the younger child were confounded. Some research currently being carried on under the direction of one of the writers has made possible the separation of the influence of mother and older siblings. Results so far indicate that most of the effect is coming from the mother. It is plausible to assume that the role of the mother was the more influential since considerable effort was expended by the home visitor over a period of three years with the first experimental group and over two years with the second experimental group. The emphasis of the home intervention was on making the mother a more effective teacher, or more generally, an effective educational change agent for her target-age child. Also worthy of note is the finding that vertical diffusion appeared more clearly in the younger siblings born in 1959 and 1960, who were within one to two and a half years in age of the older siblings. The siblings born in 1961 and 1962, when pulled out for separate analysis, did not show an effect which approached statistical significance. Vertical diffusion also appeared more operative in the first than in the second experimental group. A plausible explanation is that intervention lasted a year longer with the first group and began a year earlier. There is also in the data some suggestion of a process we have examined in more detail elsewhere (Klaus and Gray, 1968), one that may be termed horizontal diffusion, the spread of effect from one family to another. This we have in general analyzed by comparing the local and distal control groups. Here we found that the younger siblings in the local control group showed themselves to be superior to the distal control group.

To the extent that the findings on vertical diffusion have generality, they seem to point to the efficacy of a powerful process in the homes, presumably mediated by the parent, which may serve to improve the educability of young children. Before a second conclusion is reached by the reader, however, to the effect that "parent education" is the answer, we would like to point out that our procedure was clearly parent education with a difference. It was conducted in the home; it was done by skilled preschool teachers with some experience in working in the homes; it was highly concrete and specific to a given mother's life situation; it was continuous over a long period of time. Indeed, parent education probably is the answer, but in low income homes a very different kind of parent education from that usually provided may be needed.

Seven years after the Early Training Project began, in 1969, intervention programs for young children from low income homes are nationwide. These programs differ tremendously in the length and timing of the intervention, in the objectives and consistency with which they are followed, in the degree of specificity of the program, and in the length and extent of follow-up study of the sample.

It is hardly surprising, with the wild heterogeneity of such programs, that nationwide assessment of programs, such as the Westinghouse Survey of Project Head Start (1969), would find relatively small evidence of positive effects upon the child's achievement and personal adequacy. Leaving aside all the problems of measuring personal adequacy and even achievement in young children, such lack of results is only to be expected in situations where the bad or inappropriate so cancels out the good that little positive effect can be found, especially if the evaluation is somewhat premature.

At this point in time it seems appropriate to look more closely at those programs which have clearly followed an adequate research design, specified and carefully monitored their treatments, and conducted adequate follow-up study of the sample. Such programs are relatively few in number, for their history is short.

In the Early Training Project we have been more fortunate than most. The study was initiated nearly four years before the tidal wave of interests in such early intervention that came about through such nationwide programs as Project Head Start and Title I and III of the Elementary and Secondary Education Act. We have worked in a setting in which we have been free from administrative pressures either to change our procedures or to make premature conclusions from our data. The two communities in which families live have had little outward mobility; even at the end of seven years attrition is only a minor problem. For these reasons we believe the data collected over seven years with our four groups of children do shed some light upon the problem of progressive retardation and the possibility that it can be offset.

Our answer as to whether such retardation can be offset is one of cautious optimism. The effects of our intervention program are clearly evidenced through the second year of public schooling, one year after intervention ceased. There is still an effect, most apparent in the Binet, after two more years of non-intervention. Our data on horizontal and vertical diffusion, especially the latter, gives us some hope that intervention programs can have a lasting effect that goes beyond the children that were the target of that intervention program.

Still, it is clear from our data, with a parallel decline across the four groups in the second through fourth grades, that an intervention program before school entrance, such as ours, cannot carry the entire burden of offsetting progressive retardation. By some standards the Early Training Project might be seen as one of relatively massive intervention. And yet a colleague of ours (Miller, 1969) has estimated that in the years prior to school entrance the maximum amount of time that the children in the project could have spent with the Early Training Project staff was approximately 600 hours, less than two percent of their waking hours from birth to six years. Perhaps the remarkable thing is that the effect lasted as well and as long as it did. In a similar vein, we have estimated the amount of these contacts which was in the home as a maximum of 110 hours, are about 0.3 percent of the waking hours of the child from birth to six years. Surely it would be foolish not to realize that, without massive changes in the life situation of the child, home circumstances will continue to have their adversive effect upon the child's performance.

In 1968 the authors wrote:

> The most effective intervention programs for preschool children that could possibly be conceived cannot be considered a form of inoculation whereby the child forever after is immune to the effects of a low income home and of a school inappropriate to his needs. Certainly, the evidence on human performance is overwhelming in indicating that such performance results from the continual interaction of the organism with its environment. Intervention programs, well conceived and executed, may be expected to make some relatively lasting changes. Such programs, however, cannot be expected to carry the whole burden of providing adequate schooling for children from deprived circumstances; they can provide only a basis for future progress in schools and homes that can build upon that early intervention.

In 1969 we see no reason to alter this statement. Our seventh year results only serve to underscore its truth.

References

GRAY, S. W., & KLAUS, R. A. An experimental preschool program for culturally deprived children. *Child Development*, 1965, **36**, 887–898.

————, KLAUS, R. A., MILLER, J. O., & FORRESTER, N. J. *Before first grade*. New York: Teachers College Press, Columbia University, 1966.

KLAUS, R. A., & GRAY, S. W. The early training project for disadvantaged children: A report after five years. *Monograph of the Society for Research in Child Development*, 1968, *33* (4, Serial No. 120).

LINDQUIST, E. R. *The design and analysis of experiments in psychology and education*. Boston: Houghton Mifflin, 1953.

MILLER, J. O. Cultural deprivation and its modification; effects of intervention. In Haywood, C. H. (Ed.) *Social-cultural aspects of mental retardation*. New York: Appleton-Century-Crofts, Inc., 1970.

Westinghouse Learning Corporation. *The impact of Head Start: An evaluation of the Head Start experience on children's cognitive and affective development*. Westinghouse Learning Corporation, Ohio University, 1969.

8

Socialization:
Interactions and Results

Through his interactions with people, most of all parents, but also peers, other family members, and perhaps teachers, the young child develops patterns of social behavior and attitudes toward himself. Feelings as well as actions constitute his behavior in relation to himself and others. An abundance of research in this field reflects the great interest that it provokes. In light of the problem delineated by William Ballard in the last section of this book, it is heartening to notice a new emphasis in the area of socialization. Until quite recently, very little had been published on prosocial behavior and positive emotions. At present many psychologists are studying attachment, affection, generosity, kindness, and so on. We begin with a scholarly but tender and warming review, " The Kindnesses of Children," by David Rosenhan, in which he explores links between children's kindly behavior and other aspects of their development.

Henry B. Biller's study of sex role development in boys was based on boys' behavior and mothers' responses to questionnaires. Biller found differences between boys with fathers living in the family and boys whose fathers were absent. The masculinity of father-absent boys was affected by the mothers' behavior. Sex role preference in white and black children shows some significant race and sex differences in a study by Norman L. Thompson, Jr. and Boyd R. McCandless. Highly dependent and nondependent preschool children were compared as to performance on a puzzle task, given under two different conditions. Russell DiBartolo and W. Edgar Vinacke were the experimenters in this exploration of the effect of nurturance on performance of children who varied as to dependency.

The Kindnesses of Children*

David Rosenhan
SWARTHMORE COLLEGE

That we are occasionally deeply moved by the kindnesses of children needs no documentation here. One child's generosity to another, his spontaneous helpfulness to a needy adult, his willingness to forego his own pleasure without

Reprinted with permission from *Young Children*, Vol. XXV, No. 1, October, 1969. Copyright © 1969, National Association for the Education of Young Children, 1834 Connecticut Avenue, N.W., Washington, D.C. 20009.

* Some of the research reported here was conducted at the Center for Psychological Studies, Educational Testing Service, and was supported by Grant 1 PO 1 HD-01762 from the National Institute of Child Health and Human Development. Other research, and the writing of this report, was supported by MH-HD 13862 and MH-16462, both from the National Institute of Mental Health.

urging so that another may enjoy—these are the kinds of behaviors that make us feel that all is well in the world, however much our senses tell us otherwise. We are concerned in this paper with the origins of such behaviors, not only for their own sake but also because they appear to be progenitors of such behaviors in adults. And in adults they are not only moving but critically important, least of all, perhaps, for adult well-being, but mainly for society. Consider: the capacity of people to give much more than they apparently receive (and this is how we define altruistic or generous behavior)—as parents do for children, teachers for students, lovers for each other—forms one of the likely bases of socialization, education, patriotism, love, social order and cooperative cohesion. These capacities and social structures do not arise *de novo* in the adult, but rather spring from childhood antecedents.

Although rumor (buttressed by naive psychological theory) has it that man is selfish and concerned only with himself and his own gratifications, that is hardly the case. Indeed evidence for altruistic behavior can be found throughout the animal kingdom, and in large measure, too. After summarizing some of that evidence, Hebb and Thompson observe:

> The evidence indicates . . . that a disinterested concern for others can be found in mammalian development. Although it reaches its greatest potential only in man, it is not foreign to any higher animal, and is not something that is imposed only by reward and punishment on the growing child. It can, of course, be stultified or fostered during growth, but by his intellectual and emotional characteristics man has a greater *aptitude* for altruistic attitudes than any other animal, and it is of great importance to gain a more precise knowledge of the conditions of its development [Hebb & Thompson, 1968, p. 746].

My concern here is to describe some of what is known about altruism in children. In a developmental context, I want to explore the roles of (1) affect, (2) observational learning and (3) moral preachings. I shall also want to speculate on the interrelations between these variables and others from the cognitive and social domains.

THE ROLE OF AFFECT

Common sense tells us that affect is involved in some forms of altruistic behavior. When the Actor assists the Recipient, presumably the latter experiences pleasure and the former empathizes that pleasure. This is likely to be particularly true for the initial acquisition of prosocial behaviors, and somewhat less so for their later maintenance. For lack of a better term I call this *acquisition affect*, to denote the close proximity of special affective states to the learning of prosocial behaviors.

There is a second kind of role for affect, one that predisposes a child to be kind to others. *Predisposing affects*, like acquisition affects, tend mainly (though, as we shall see, not always) to be positive. Anger, for example, does not predispose to kindness, but joy may. We shall consider these two roles for affect in turn.

ACQUISITION AFFECT   In 1963 and 1964 we interviewed intensively a group of people who had been active in the Civil Rights movement through

1961, with a view to determining whether they shared common psychological characteristics (Rosenhan, in press). We located two groups. Members of the first had been active participants in Civil Rights actions for a year or longer at the time of interview. We called this group the Fully Committed, mainly because they had given up their homes, occupations and educations to participate in these activities. The second group consisted of people who had been occasional activists, and whom we called the Partially Committed. They had limited their participation to one or two Freedom Rides, without relinquishing their other pursuits.

There were no population differences between the Fully and Partially Committed, except for income where, as one might expect, the Fully Committed were poorer. Nor were there differences in attitudes towards Civil Rights. Indeed, if one were to judge by their verbal behavior, the Partially Committed were greater believers in the equality of blacks and whites than were the Fully Committed. Only two really striking differences emerged between these groups, and both of these differences referred to events that took place in childhood. First, the Fully Committed had parents who were themselves active altruists. Second, our respondents had maintained a positive relationship with their parents during their childhood and through the time of interview.

Let us examine the first finding, for which data are presented in Table 1. The parents themselves were prosocial activists in the events of an earlier era, in such matters as the Spanish Civil War, the Second World War or religious education. So it was possible that our respondents learned by doing, or at least learned by seeing their parents do. One respondent observed that "my father carried me on his shoulders during the Sacco-Vanzetti parades" while another remarked that his mother "felt close to Jesus and was warmed by His teachings. She devoted her entire life to Christian education."

TABLE 1

Evidence for Discrepancy Between Teaching and Practice by the Socializers of Fully Committed and Partially Committed Civil Rights Workers

DISCREPANCY	FULLY COMMITTED	PARTIALLY COMMITTED
Present	2	13
Absent	11	3
Evidence unclear or absent	2	5

$\chi^2 = 13.29$; df $= 2$; $p < .01$.

By contrast, the Partially Committed had parents who were at best mere verbal supporters of prosocial moralities, and at worst, hypocritical about those moralities. It was common for our Partially Committed to report that their parents preached one thing and practiced another. Moreover, our Partially Committed were so angered by the discrepancy between parental posture and action that we had reason to believe that our respondents had undergone nothing less than a "crisis of hypocrisy" during their childhood which resulted in their inability to make enduring commitments to prosocial (as to other) matters later on.

These data are amenable to a variety of interpretations, and I shall return to them later when I consider the role of observational learning in the development of altruism. For the present, however, it is useful to examine them in light of current theories of emotion. Schachter and Singer (1962) have observed that emotion results from the joint action of physiological arousal and cognitions appropriate to that arousal. In order to obtain arousal in the laboratory, Schachter and Singer injected their subjects with adrenaline (though they did not tell their subjects that). Aroused subjects subsequently observed a model go through a series of either joyful or angry antics. On a variety of measures, the subjects themselves subsequently manifested either joy or anger.

We speculate that our Fully Committed respondents were also aroused, not by injection, but by being family participants in what must have been very exciting events. Having been thus aroused, and having observed their parents participate in prosocial behavior (which is to say, serve as models) they, too, experienced emotion. Which emotion? Perhaps sympathy for the oppressed. Perhaps empathy. Perhaps affection for their parents. At this level our data are vague—they merely suggest that emotions of a prosocial kind play a significant role in the acquisition of altruistic behavior.

Data bearing more specifically on the role of affect in altruism were obtained in an experiment by Aronfreed and Paskal (1965). Six- to eight-year-old girls played a game involving two levers. If the child pressed one lever, she would often (60 percent of the time) get a piece of candy. If she pressed the other lever, a red light would go on with similar frequency. During the training phase of the experiment, a female experimenter sat close to the child and behaved in one of three ways each time the light went on. Either she exclaimed "there's the light," smiled at the child and gave her a warm hug; or she hugged the child without saying anything; or she said "there's the light" but did not hug the child. During the test phase of the experiment, the light on the front of the child's game was disconnected and the experimenter moved across from the child, facing the rear of the apparatus where there was an operative red light which she could see but the child could not. For this phase, each time the child pressed the lever that produced the light (for the experimenter), the experimenter exclaimed "there's the light."

It is clear that the red light, and the lever that activated it, are innocent or neutral stimuli: they have no special meaning. Paired with the experimenter's behavior, however, it should acquire meaning by classical conditioning, that is, it should come to mean "pleasure for the experimenter." The question is: Which of the three training experiences will most powerfully connect the red light to the experimenter's pleasure, such that the child will be most willing to press that lever and, at the same time deprive himself of candy?

The data from this experiment indicated that the *combination* of expressive cues ("there's the light") with affection (smiles and hugs) was so powerful that children in this condition pressed the red light lever more often than the candy lever! Children from the remaining two groups chose the candy-producing lever more often. Thus the combined effects of verbal expression and affection were more successful than either alone in conditioning pleasant affect to a neutral stimulus.

Midlarsky and Bryan (1967) repeated and elaborated this study in several significant ways. For half of their subjects, the experimenter remained impassive during the final testing. Even these children pressed the red-light lever more often than did children who had not witnessed expressive cues or experienced affection.

Midlarsky and Bryan (1967) also added an experimental condition which allowed them to assess the impact of the three treatment conditions upon charitability under conditions of anonymity. After they completed the task, the children were given some additional candies so that all children had an equal supply. They were then asked to donate candy to "needy children, whose parents can't afford to buy them any candy." Each child was told that the amount of the donation was her decision and that she need not donate at all if she did not choose to do so. In order to underscore the apparent privacy of her actions, the experimenter led her to the donation box and then waited outside of the room while she made (or failed to make) her contribution. Here, too, the combined effects of expressive cues ("there's the light") and affection (a smile and a hug) were greater than either alone in eliciting charitability.

PREDISPOSING AFFECTS   In the interview study of Civil Rights workers mentioned earlier, Fully Committed altruists appeared to have maintained a positive, cordial, warm and respecting relationship with their parent(s). That relationship extended far into childhood and continued through the time of the interview. True, there had been disagreements. True also, these disagreements sometimes extended to matters of considerable importance to both the respondent and his parent, including the matter of whether the respondent should be active in Civil Rights. Despite these differences, one sensed easily considerable fondness between parent and child.

The Partially Committed described their parents in negative or ambivalent terms. A substantial proportion described their relations with the socializing parent as downright hostile during the formative years and cool and avoidant at the time they were interviewed. One sensed discomfort, often anxiety and hostility, flowing from child to parent and perhaps vice-versa. These data are summarized in Table 2.

TABLE 2

Affective Reactions to the Primary Socializer by Fully Committed and Partially Committed Civil Rights Workers

VALENCE	FULLY COMMITTED	PARTIALLY COMMITTED
Positive	12	3
Negative or distinctly ambivalent	3	18

$\chi^2 = 15.55$; df $= 1$; $p < .001$.

Similar findings, this time in connection with student activists have been reported by Smith, Block and Haan.[1] Activists who participated in both protest and constructive volunteer activity contrasted clearly with "dissenters" who engaged only in protest. The former tended to report good relations with parents who were seen as humanistic but firm toward their children; the latter reported rather bad or ambivalent relations with parents, who were seen as inconsistent, lax and permissive.

The view that a positive affective relationship with a socializing agent facilitates altruism is supported not only by our naturalistic data but also by findings obtained by Rutherford and Mussen (1968). In their experiment, nursery school boys were given 18 identical pieces of candy which they could either keep for themselves or divide among themselves and two children in the class whom they liked best. Generous children (i.e., those who donated 15 or more candies to others) tended to see their fathers (though not their mothers) as nurturant in a doll play situation. Since the perception of parental nurturance is highly correlated with actual parental behavior in an interview situation (Mussen & Distler, 1960; Mussen & Rutherford, 1963), and since generous boys differentiated their parents in the imputation of nurturance, Rutherford and Mussen found it more plausible to view paternal nurturance as an antecedent rather than a consequence, of generosity.

It should be noted, however, that experimental attempts to manipulate directly the child's relationship to an altruistic socializer have *not* yet been successful. For example, children who had had a pleasant prior relationship with a charitable model were not subsequently more charitable than those who had a negative one (Rosenhan & White, 1967). Similar findings were obtained by Grusec and Skubiski (1969). Moreover, attempts by this writer to deepen the prior relationship by extending the period of exposure to the model have also been unsuccessful.

Success and Failure   Not only do long-term positive relationships predispose one to altruistic behavior, but brief bursts of positive affect seem to have similar effects. A series of experiments by Isen (1968) and Berkowitz and Connor (1966) have shown that the experience of success on a task generates significantly greater generosity in adults than does failure. Isen has interpreted her findings in terms of a "warm glow of success," suggesting that when people succeed, they experience positive affect which in turn expresses itself in increased willingness to be kind to others.

In an extension of these findings, Isen and Rosenhan (1969) gave fourth-grade children 25 cents for helping them test and give their opinions about newly manufactured toys. These children played a bowling game on which they either obtained many high scores (success) or many low ones (failure). Control children played a similar game which, however, lacked a score indicator. The experimenter (E_1) absented herself during these games on a pretext of having work to do. When the game was completed, E_1 returned and, shortly thereafter, a second experimenter (E_2), ostensibly a stranger, knocked on the door and was admitted. Speaking directly to E_1, she said that she was collecting money for children who had no toys, and asked permission to leave her charity

---

[1] Personal communication from M. B. Smith, May 1969.

box in the laboratory. After ascertaining that "anyone can give—even the children who help us here," E_1 led E_2 to a second room in the laboratory ostensibly to take her name and address, closing the door of the room firmly behind her. During the 60 seconds that E_1 and E_2 conferred together, the child was alone in the laboratory, supposedly unobserved with regard to whether or not he contributed.

Children who had experienced positive affect through the success induction contributed far more than children in either the failure or control conditions. Moreover, the number of children who had contributed was greater in the success than in the other conditions.

It was important that the procedures of this experiment be described in detail in order to communicate its salient feature: that a third party, ostensibly unassociated with the toy company, was requesting a donation. Under that condition, children who had experienced positive affect contributed more than those who had experienced negative affect, or none at all. A second experiment was conducted which differed from the first experiment in an apparently trivial respect. Instead of having someone bring in the charity box, the children's attention was now directed to a box that was already in the laboratory. They were simply told that *we* had been asked to collect for the Toy Fund, that we ourselves were going to contribute and they could contribute too, if they so desired. A 60-second period, during which children were alone, was allowed to permit them to contribute.

Under these conditions, no significant differences were obtained between failure and success. Both contributed more than controls. Boys, however, contributed significantly more after they had *failed* than after they had succeeded.

We have then, an instance where negative affect has an impact on generosity that is even greater than that of positive affect. And it is not the only one. Staub (1968) exposed fourth- and fifth-grade children to success, failure and intermediate scores on a bowling game. After they had finished playing, and by way of thanking the children for their efforts, the experimenter brought out a bowl of candy and gave it to the children. She then remarked that "actually we don't have enough candy and you should share some with another child. Why don't you take out your own candy and put it in this bag; whatever you want to leave for this other child you may leave in this bag." Under these conditions, fourth-grade children who experienced failure "shared" significantly *more* than children in the success condition.

How shall we reconcile these differences? Our present view, which remains to be tested, is that the crucial differences between these experiments lie in whether, in the subject's mind, generosity was directed to the primary experimenter (through whom he had either succeeded or failed) or to vaguely identified needy others. The "warm glow of success" hypothesis predicts that the positive affect generated by success will express itself in a desire to be helpful. Failure will not. Failure, however, does generate a desire to improve one's image in the eyes of another (Schneider, 1966). Thus, children who have failed will be generous if they feel that the experimenter might find out about it, but not otherwise. In Staub's (1968) experiment, as in the second experiment by Isen and myself, there were numerous cues which pointed to the possibility that we would know that the subject had contributed and would therefore think more highly of him. We shall return to the issues of "who knows whether I have been generous" in our discussion of the role of observational learning.

In summary, the evidence points strongly to the fact that positive affect is implicated in the acquisition of generous impulses and in the predisposition to behave generously. Similar observations have been made in regard to the acquisition of sympathy and empathy among children (Aronfreed, 1968; Lenrow, 1965). Negative affect becomes a factor in generous behavior only when the child is concerned with rectifying his negative self-image.

THE ROLE OF OBSERVATIONAL LEARNING

In a recent paper (Rosenhan, in press) we distinguished between two kinds of altruism: *normative altruism* and *autonomous altruism*. The first engenders a concern for others and is elicited and supported by a vast social network of relatively immediate rewards and punishments. Often characterized by low personal risk and cost to the actor, its central feature is the actor's concern for himself: whether *he* will be rewarded for engaging in an altruistic act, or *he* will be punished for failing to do so. In contrast, autonomous altruism is not legitimated by a visible system of reward and punishment but rather appears to derive its impetus from internalized cognitions and behavioral examples. Indeed, autonomous altruists quite often appear to disregard the external system of reward and punishment by sacrificing personal rewards to needy others for no visible immediate or future gain. In short, normative altruism seems characterized by the cluster of variables we associate with *social conformity*, while autonomous altruism reflects what we often call *commitment*.

Some evidence for this view was obtained in our study of Civil Rights activists. Fully Committed activists, you will recall, had parents who were themselves activists, who were exemplars of altruistic behavior. They had learned the altruistic norm by example as well as precept. Partially Committed activists were socialized by parents whose altruism was limited to preaching, and whose preaching was often violated in practice. Lacking a directly learned basis for altruism, the Partially Committed relied on more immediate (and, it might be added, transient) stimuli, such as group esprit and camaraderie and short-term personal rewards.

On the basis of the interview study, then, we concluded that the behavioral example provided by other altruists was a critical component of full altruistic commitment. We next sought to confirm this observation under controlled laboratory conditions. In an experiment conducted by Professor Glenn White and myself, children in the fourth and fifth grades alternated turns on a bowling game with an adult model. Each time the model obtained a winning score of 20, he took two 5 cent gift certificates from a large pile on a nearby table. These gift certificates served as money surrogates and were redeemable at a nearby candy store known to all the children. The model then deposited one of the gift certificates into a container labelled "Trenton Orphan's Fund." While the subject played, the model looked away, ostensibly waiting for his turn. This was done in order to minimize the possibility that the attention of the adult model might influence whether the child gave.

Model and child each had 10 turns, during which the model won and contributed twice. At the end of the game, the model pretended to have work to do elsewhere. After ascertaining that the child would like to play again by himself, the model departed, telling the child to return to his class when he was finished. The child then played 20 trials and obtained winning scores on four of them.

We had three concerns in this experiment. First, would children who were not exposed to a charitable model also contribute? After all, these children were 10 and 11 years old, old enough to understand who orphans were and what their needs might be. Moreover, they were likely to be aware that charitability was important and "good." For all of this, however, not a single child in this control condition contributed to the Orphans' Fund.

Our second question was concerned with whether the child would contribute in the presence of the charitable model. That a child contributes in the presence of an adult model would not really be surprising, since however much the model attempted to ignore the child's behavior, the model was still present in the room and the child knew it. Children are socialized to please adults, and certainly not to offend them. So we had little doubt that many children would contribute in the model's presence, and we were not surprised: 63 percent of the children contributed when the model was in the room.

Our final concern was the critical one: How would they behave in the model's absence? In a very broad sense, many of us are not concerned with the way a child behaves in our presence; it is his behavior when he is out of sight that concerns us. In this instance, the child had nothing to gain by contributing, and gift certificates to lose. Ostensibly no one would know if he had contributed (and we have considerable evidence to indicate that the children did not know they were being observed). Nevertheless, nearly 50 percent of the subjects contributed.

Clearly then, observation of a charitable model facilitates charitability (cf. Bandura, 1969), not only of the *normative* kind—as indexed by behavior in the presence of the model—but also of the autonomous sort that occurs in the absence of the model. Moreover, as Table 3 makes clear, autonomous and normative altruism are not unrelated, at least among children. Those who

TABLE 3

Relationship Between Giving in the Presence of the Model and Giving in His Absence

(Adapted from Rosenhan & White, 1967)

GAVE IN THE MODEL'S ABSENCE (AUTONOMOUS ALTRUISM)	GAVE IN THE MODEL'S PRESENCE (NORMATIVE ALTRUISM)		
	Yes	No	Total
Yes	51	6	57
No	25	38	63
Total	76	34	120

$\chi^2 = 29.84$; df $= 1$; $p < .001$.

contributed in the model's presence were far more likely than those who did not to contribute in his absence. And conversely, those who did not contribute in the model's presence, failed to contribute in his absence. Apparently, observation of an altruistic model *and* rehearsal in his presence greatly increase the likelihood that the model's charitability will be internalized by the child (Rosenhan & White, 1967).

The effects of models on altruistic behavior have been found in several other studies (Bryan & Walbek, 1969; Grusec & Skubiski, 1969; Harris, 1968; Rosenhan, 1969b; White, 1967). An experiment that is especially illuminating in this regard was conducted by Hartup and Coates (1967). Nursery school children individually observed a peer model who, on each of 10 trials, allocated only one of his earned trinkets to himself and five of these trinkets to "Alec" or "Kathy" (other nursery school children). The subjects were either relatively "popular" or "unpopular" as determined by the amount of positive reinforcement they had been observed to receive during sampled observations that were taken over a five-week period. Moreover, the model had either been quite rewarding to the child (i.e., had given him considerable positive reinforcement) or had not rewarded him at all. Subsequently, the experimenter and model went to an adjoining room while the subject played the game and earned trinkets.

As Table 4 indicates, there is no question that the observation of a peer model facilitates charitability. But what is of considerable interest is the manner in which the popularity of the child interacts with the rewardingness of the

TABLE 4
Mean "Giving to Other" Scores as a Function of Popularity of Child and Rewardingness of Model
(Adapted from Hartup and Coates, 1967)

Group	First Five Trials	Second Five Trials
Relatively popular children:		
Rewarding models	21.00	19.25
Nonrewarding models	13.42	13.83
Relatively unpopular children:		
Rewarding models	17.50	17.08
Nonrewarding models	22.83	18.58
No model	5.63	3.75

model, particularly during the first five trials. Popular children were more influenced by models who had been kind to them (i.e., been rewarding) than those who had not. Unpopular children, on the other hand, tended to imitate those who have not been kind to them more than those who have. Clearly, the socialization history of the child and his relation to the model are critical here as they were in the naturalistic study cited earlier (Rosenhan, in press).

THE ROLE OF MORAL PREACHINGS

There is no question but that, in our socialization of children, we spend much of our time telling them what is right and what is wrong, what is moral and what is immoral. Such preachments are heard from parents and teachers and, indeed, from children to each other. Surprisingly, very little is known about the impact of these teachings on behavior, nor is much known about the comparative effects of preaching versus behavioral example. Clearly, preaching has its effects at the verbal level: Children are able, with increasing age, to *tell* you what is right and wrong, and even why (cf. Kohlberg, 1963). But what are the effects on behavior?

In a recent study, White (1967) compared the effects of telling children that they should contribute to a particular charity, with observing a charitable model and with observing and rehearsing with such a model. Not surprisingly, many more of the children who had been told to give, subsequently gave anonymously (and gave more) than those who had been in the two modeling conditions. In fact, nearly all of the verbally instructed children contributed. This, however, occurred only when the groups were tested immediately after they had been trained. Wisely, White tested three groups again after a one-week delay, and found that the impact of preaching had deteriorated to the point where there was no difference between children who had been verbally instructed and those who had observed charitable models. Indeed, the stability of behavior—whether children were consistent contributors or noncontributors across the two testings—was markedly lower for the children who had been instructed than for those who had learned by observation. Thus, it is possible to argue that relative to observing a model, prosocial instruction has powerful short-run effects producing nearly uniform obedience, but considerably weaker delayed effects. Long-term effects, as indexed by test behavior which is separated from training by, say, a month, remain to be explored but would likely show even further weakness for prosocial preaching.

PREACHING AND PRACTICING   In children's experience, moral preachings are as likely to be paired with practices as not. And moral practices may be consistent with the preachings or inconsistent with them. It has already been shown that the consistency of preaching and practice among altruistic parents seems to be a critical determinant of altruistic commitment in the child, now himself become a man. Fully Committed Civil Rights activists reported parents who were themselves activists, whose preachings were consistent with their behaviors. Partially Committed activists appeared to have been socialized by inconsistent or hypocritical parents who preached a morality which they violated in practice. As indicated earlier, these data were obtained through retrospective interviews. We turn now to experiments that have sought to examine the effects of consistency and inconsistency between preachings and practices.

There are really two kinds of inconsistencies that can occur between preaching and practice. In one, the model sets a *higher* standard for himself than for the child. We call this a *child-indulgent* pattern and, in a study concerned with the internalization of norms for self-reward (Rosenhan, Frederick & Burrowes, 1968), we found that this pattern yielded a high degree of norm internalization (and little norm violation). There is, however, a second kind of discrepancy which occurs when the model sets a *lower* standard for himself than for the child. It is to this kind of discrepancy that notions of hypocrisy are addressed. Studies by Mischel and Liebert (1966) and Rosenhan, *et al.* (1968) indicate that experience with *self-indulgent* models produces considerably more norm violation than consistent or child-indulgent conditions. The central message of these studies is that where the verbal and behavioral modes are in competition, children will be mainly guided by behavioral example and only secondarily by verbal preachments.

These studies, however, have concentrated on internalization of norms for self-reward. What of rewarding others? What, in particular, is the impact of consistency and discrepancy in preaching and practice on the charitable behavior of children? Bryan and his colleagues have examined these issues in detail (Bryan, 1968, in press; Bryan & Walbeck, 1968, 1969). Their basic procedure utilizes a model who, in the presence of the child, behaves charitably or greedily, while preaching either charity or greed. The model's preachings consist of general exhortations on the value of charity ("It is good to give to poor children"); these statements simulate the elements of moral training as given by parents or teachers. Occasionally, the procedure includes an attempt to alert the subject to the potentially rewarding consequences of charitability, such as reminding him that charitable children are liked by others. Regardless of the variation employed, these experiments have produced one consistent outcome: moral preachings have no effect on behavior.

If the model behaves charitably, so will the child—even if the model has preached greed. And conversely, if the model preaches charity, but practices greed (Bryan and his colleagues call this the Young Republican condition!), the child will follow the model's precept and will not contribute to the charity. Behavior in the prosocial area is influenced by behavior, not by words.

If this is the case, why is it that we place so much tacit and explicit emphasis on moral adjuration and moral precept? Several of these studies suggest a possible reason. In addition to being given an opportunity to contribute to the charity, children were asked to rate the attractiveness of the model. Here the model's verbalizations were found to have profound impact. Models who preached charity were much more attractive to children than those who preached greed, regardless of what the model practiced. Indeed, much as the model's preaching had little impact on the child's behavior, so his practice had minimal impact on the child's *evaluation* of him. Thus, it is conceivable that since children tend to value more highly people who say the right things, such people are thereby encouraged to go right on saying them!

DEVELOPMENTAL AND OTHER VARIABLES ASSOCIATED WITH PROSOCIAL BEHAVIOR IN CHILDREN

Prosocial behavior, in both children and adults, has been a relatively new topic for researchers. Except for some early, classic work by Hartshorne, May and Maller (1929) and Beatrice Wright (1942), most of the work in this area has been undertaken in the past decade. It may therefore be somewhat premature to generalize about the relationship of prosocial behavior to other aspects of the child's functioning. Yet, some of the existing evidence is of considerable interest, and it is useful to speculate on the meaning of this material.

DEVELOPMENT OF PROSOCIAL BEHAVIOR

The evidence is now strong indeed that the acquisition and elicitation of generous behavior increases with age (Handlon & Gross, 1959; Midlarsky & Bryan, 1967; Wright, 1942; Ugerul-Semin, 1952; Rosenhan, 1969a). Just when generous behavior begins to be displayed is not clear. Our own studies (Rosenhan, 1969a) had led us to believe that generosity is rare indeed in the six-year-old, but the work of Hartup and Coates (1967) made it quite evident that generosity could be elicited in nursery school children. Clearly, variations in findings are to be expected, depending on the manner in which the charitable situation is structured; others may reflect differences in the underlying psychological makeup of the child. What might some of these variables be?

Cognitive Development　　Our experiments have required that the children contribute to the Trenton Orphans' Fund, a fund that we established for these experiments. While we ascertained that our subjects knew what orphans are, we cannot be certain that all of them possessed the cognitive maturity to understand the needs of orphans. Younger children in particular would likely have difficulty putting themselves in the role of a needy other (Piaget, 1926; Flavell, 1968), however much they might know that orphans have no parents. Moreover, the concept of abstract charity might well elude them. "Giving to Alec," as used in the Hartup and Coates (1967) experiment, is considerably more concrete and does not tax a young child's empathic abilities.

Our own experiments and those of other workers have been predicated on the view that observational learning greatly facilitates the elicitation, if not the initial acquisition, of generosity in children. But capacities for observational learning are not themselves unrelated to cognitive development. Complex capacities for imitation and symbolic play do not really emerge until a child is two (Piaget, 1962), and consequently there is no reason to believe that the observational learning of this capacity can occur before then. Evidence that cognitive development is related to observational learning has recently been offered by Coates and Hartup (1969).

Autonomous vs. *Normative Altruism: The Potential Role of Prosocial Moral Development*　　Earlier, I distinguished two kinds of altruism, autonomous and normative. The latter appears to be controlled by the forces of social reward and punishment, the former (about which we know less) by internalized norms that direct a person to be helpful, with less regard to consequences. It would appear that normative altruism emerges earlier, that autonomous altruism develops later, and possibly from it. In all of our experiments we have been able to elicit considerably more normative altruism (i.e., generosity in the presence of the model) than autonomous altruism (i.e., generosity in his absence), at whatever age. It is possible to believe that the generosity obtained with very young children by Hartup and Coates (1967) was of the normative sort, since their subjects were separated from the experimenter and the model by an open door, which may have encouraged them to believe they were being observed.

The distinction between normative and autonomous altruism brings to mind Kohlberg's (1963) developmental stages of morality. Kohlberg's first level of morality is dominated by obedience and fear of punishment, while his highest levels reflect the operation of moral principles. It may be that generous impulses can be similarly characterized and undergo similar processes of development from lower to higher stages.

Social Comfort   It is an error to assume that all children are comfortable in experimental situations. Quite likely, the younger they are the less at home they feel, and the more frightened they are by the novelty of the experimental context and the strangeness of the experimenter. On the other hand, the older they are, the more sensitive children become to nuances of social rules, and these may restrict or inappropriately cue their behavior.

The sensitivity of older children to social rules, and their fear of engaging in behaviors lest they make a social error is illustrated in studies by Staub and his colleagues (Staub & Feagens, 1969). Kindergarten through sixth-grade children heard sounds of another child's severe distress from another room. Attempts to help the child, or to get an adult to help, increased markedly from kindergarten to second grade, but then dropped in the fourth and sixth grades. Staub speculated that the older children may simply have feared adult disapproval for leaving the room and therefore were unwilling to take action. In a subsequent experiment, Staub (1969) tacitly communicated to some of his older children that it was permissible to go into the adjoining room, and found that those children aided the "distressed" child significantly more than those who did not have this information.

CORRELATES OF KINDNESS   Beyond Hartshorne, May and Maller's (1929) observation that "service" behaviors correlate with few other variables, there has been relatively little work done on correlates of kindness. What does exist, however, is illuminating. Rutherford and Mussen (1968) found that generosity in nursery school boys was negatively correlated with competitiveness in a laboratory game, and negatively correlated with teachers' ratings of gregariousness. Staub and Sherk (1968) found need for social approval *negatively* correlated with sharing in fourth-grade children. In a similar (and surprising) vein, both normative and autonomous altruism were positively related to teachers' ratings of obedience among eight-year-olds. Among 10-year-olds, however, the situation was drastically changed. Normative altruism was *negatively* correlated with obedience, and autonomous altruism not at all correlated with it (Rosenhan, 1969a). These data again suggest that at younger ages, kindness may be a matter of social conformity, but among older children it clearly is not.

SUMMARY

Evidence is accumulating that kindness is pervasive in the behavior of young children; it can easily be elicited in a variety of experimental or naturalistic settings. While we have learned a good deal about the development of altruistic propensities and how such propensities can be amplified, we have yet to learn just how they originate.

Positive affect and observational learning have both been shown to facilitate the occurrence of kindness, and both are likely to be implicated in its acquisition. One senses, too, that cognitive development, particularly the capacity to take the role of others and to engage in symbolic play, are very much implicated in kindness just as these same factors are involved in moral development.

Preaching about prosocial behavior, as opposed to providing examples of such behavior, appears to have little impact on the behavior of children. Nevertheless, the type of preaching affects the manner in which children evaluate the preacher.

Developmental studies, with rare exceptions, indicate that the incidence of generosity increases with age, and that the patterns of correlation between generosity and other variables undergo dramatic and meaningful changes with age.

References

ARONFREED, J. *Conduct and Conscience: The Socialization of Internalized Control over Behavior.* New York: Academic Press, 1968.

———— & PASKAL, V. Altruism, empathy and the conditioning of positive affect. Unpubl. mss., Univ. of Pennsylvania, 1965.

BANDURA, A. Social-learning theory of identificatory processes. In D. A. Goslin (Ed.), *Handbook of Socialization Theory and Research.* Chicago: Rand McNally, 1969.

BERKOWITZ, L. & CONNOR, W. H. Success, failure and social responsibility. *J. Pers. soc. Psychol.,* 1966, 4, 664–669.

BRYAN, J. H. Actions speak louder than words: Model inconsistency and its effect on self-sacrifice. Res. Bull. 68-16, Princeton: Educational Testing Service, 1968.

————. Children's reactions to helpers. In J. R. Macaulay & L. Berkowitz (Eds.), *Altruism and Helping.* New York: Academic Press, in press.

————. & WALBEK, N. Preaching and practicing self-sacrifice: Children's actions and reactions. Unpubl. mss., Northwestern Univ., 1968.

————. Determinants of conformity: The impact of words, deeds and power upon children's altruistic behavior. Unpubl. mss., Northwestern Univ., 1969.

COATES, B. & HARTUP, W. W. Age and verbalization in observational learning. *Develpml. Psychol.,* in press.

FLAVELL, J. H. *The Development of Communication and Role-Taking Skills in Children.* New York: John Wiley, 1968.

GRUSEC, J. & SKUBISKI, S. L. Model nurturance, demand characteristics of the modeling experiment, and altruism. Unpubl. mss., Univ. of Toronto, 1969.

HANDLON, B. J. & GROSS, P. The development of sharing behavior. *J. abnorm. soc. Psychol.,* 1959, 59, 425–428.

HARRIS, M. Some determinants of sharing behavior. Unpubl. doctoral dissertation, Stanford Univ., 1968.

HARTSHORNE, H., MAY, M. A. & MALLER, J. B. *Studies in Service and Self Control.* New York: Macmillan, 1929.

HARTUP, W. W. & COATES, B. Imitation of a peer as a function of reinforcement from the peer group and rewardingness of the model. *Child Develpm.,* 1967, 38, 1003–1016.

HEBB, D. O. & THOMPSON, W. R. The social significance of animal studies. In G.

Lindzey & E. Aronson (Eds.), *The Handbook of Social Psychology* Reading, Mass.: Addison-Wesley, 1968, 729–774.

ISEN, A. M. Success, failure, attention and reaction to others: The warm glow of success. Unpubl. doctoral dissertation, Stanford Univ., 1968.

———— & ROSENHAN, D. L. Success, failure and altruistic behavior. Unpubl. mss., Swarthmore College, 1969.

KOHLBERG, L. Moral development and identification. In H. Stevenson (Ed.), *Child Psychology: The 62nd Yearbook of the National Society for the Study of Education.* Chicago: Univ. of Chicago Press, 1963.

LENROW, P. B. Studies in sympathy. In S. S. Tomkins & C. E. Izard (Eds.), *Affect, Cognition and Personality.* New York: Springer, 1965.

MIDLARSKY, E. & BRYAN, J. H. Training charity in children. *J. Pers. soc. Psychol.*, 1967, 5, 408–415.

MISCHEL, W. & LIEBERT, R. M. Effects of discrepancies between observed and imposed reward criteria on their acquisition and transmission. *J. Pers. soc. Psychol.*, 1966, 3, 45–53.

MUSSEN, P. & DISTLER, L. Child-rearing antecedents of masculine identification in kindergarten boys. *Child Develpm.*, 1960, 31, 89–100.

———— & RUTHERFORD, E. Parent-child relations and parental personality in relation to young children's sex-role preferences. *Child Develpm.*, 1963, 34, 589–607.

PIAGET, J. *The Language and Thought of the Child.* New York: Harcourt Brace, 1926.

————. *Play, Dreams and Imitation in Childhood.* New York: Norton, 1962.

ROSENHAN, D. L. Studies in altruistic behavior: Developmental and naturalistic variables associated with charitability. Paper presented at meeting of Soc. Res. Child Develpm., 1969 (a).

————. Some origins of concern for others. In P. Mussen, M. Covington & J. Langer (Eds.), *Trends and Issues in Developmental Psychology.* New York: Holt, Rinehart & Winston, 1969, 134–153 (b).

————. The natural socialization of altruistic autonomy. In J. Macaulay & L. Berkowitz (Eds.), *Altruism and Helping.* New York: Academic Press, in press.

————, FREDERICK, F. & BURROWES, A. Preaching and practicing: Effects of channel discrepancy on norm internalization. *Child Develpm.*, 1968, 39, 291–302.

———— & WHITE, G. M. Observation and rehearsal as determinants of prosocial behavior. *J. Pers. soc. Psychol.*, 1967, 5, 424–431.

RUTHERFORD, E. & MUSSEN, P. Generosity in nursery school boys. *Child Develpm.*, 1968, 39, 755–765.

SCHACHTER, S. & SINGER, J. E. Cognitive, social, and psychological determinants of emotional state. *Psycholgl. Rev.*, 1962, 69, 379–399.

SCHNEIDER, D. J. Self-presentation as a function of prior success or failure and expectation of feedback of created impression. Unpubl. doctoral dissertation, Stanford Univ., 1966.

STAUB, E. The effects of success and failure on children's sharing behavior. Paper presented at meeting of Eastern Psycholgl. Assn., 1968.

————. The effects of variation in permissibility of movement on children helping another child in distress. Paper presented at meeting of Amer. Psycholgl. Assn., 1969.

———— & FEAGANS, L. A child in distress: The influence of age and number of witnesses on children's attempts to help. Paper presented at meeting of Eastern Psycholgl. Assn., 1969.

———— & SHERK, L. Need for approval, children's sharing behavior and reciprocity in sharing. Unpubl. mss., Harvard Univ., 1968.

UGUREL-SEMIN, R. Moral behavior and moral judgment of children. *J. Abnorm. soc. Psychol.*, 1952, 47, 463–474.

White, G. M. The elicitation and durability of altruistic behavior in children. Res. Bull. 67-27, Princeton: Educational Testing Service, 1967.

Wright, B. Altruism in children and perceived conduct of others. *J. abnorm. soc. Psychol.*, 1942, 37, 218–233.

Father Absence, Maternal Encouragement, and Sex Role Development in Kindergarten-Age Boys*

Henry B. Biller

UNIVERSITY OF RHODE ISLAND

In order to ascertain the effects of father absence and degree of maternal encouragement of masculine behavior on boys' sex role development, matched father-absent and father-present kindergarten-age boys were studied. Compared to father-absent boys, father-present boys were found to be much more masculine in projective sex role orientation and slightly more masculine in game preference but were not significantly different in terms of a rating scale measure of overt masculinity. For father-absent boys, but not for father-present boys, degree of maternal encouragement of masculine behavior was related to masculinity of game preference and the rating scale measure of overt masculinity.

A review of studies dealing with father absence and sex role development suggests that the possible effects of differences in maternal encouragement of masculine behavior among father-absent boys has been overlooked (Biller & Borstelmann, 1967). Because most fathers are very critical of having their sons overprotected and because fathers generally serve as models for masculine-independent behavior, when the father is absent the probability of maternal overprotection seems increased. There is some evidence that father absence during the preschool years is associated with overdependency of the child on the mother (Stolz et al., 1954), but the results of a recent study (Pederson, 1966) seem to suggest that the mother-son relationship can have either a positive or a negative effect on the father-absent boy's personality development. It would seem that a mother might be able to facilitate at least some aspects of her father-absent son's masculine development.

It is also quite possible that father absence and maternal encouragement of masculine behavior have different effects on the various aspects of sex role.

Reprinted from *Child Development.* 40, 539–546. Copyright © 1969 by The Society for Research in Child Development, Inc. By permission.

* This study was supported by Public Health Service Predoctoral Research Fellowship 1-F1-MH-32, 808-01, from the National Institute of Mental Health. Appreciation is expressed to the kindergarten directors, teachers, children, and parents who cooperated in this study, and to Drs. Lloyd J. Borstelmann and Darwyn E. Linder, of Duke University, and David L. Singer, of Teachers' College, Columbia University, who gave valuable suggestions. A less-detailed version of this paper was presented at the meeting of the Eastern Psychological Association, Philadelpia, April, 1969.

Biller and Borstelmann (1967) consider three aspects of sex role: sex role orientation (the perception and evaluation of the maleness or femaleness of the self), sex role preference (the individual's preferential set toward symbols and representations of sex role that are socially defined), and sex role adoption (how masculine or feminine the individual's behavior seems to others). Because of deprivation effects, father-absent boys often seem to have strong motivation toward a father figure and, similarly, a desire to act masculine. A father-absent boy may become aware of the higher valuation of the male role in our society, especially if his mother encourages him to do so; and he may develop a masculine preference. Although motivation to be with a father figure and to be masculine may be very strong, such motivation may not be sufficient to promote a masculine orientation or adoption in the absence of a masculine model.

METHOD

SUBJECTS   There are many potential differences (e.g., IQ and SES) between father-absent and father-present children that might contribute extraneously to differences in sex role development. For this reason it was decided to match father-absent and father-present Ss as closely as possible. The Ss in this study were 34 5-year-old Caucasian boys attending kindergarten classes in the Durham, North Carolina, area and their mothers; 17 of the boys were father absent and 17 father present. (There was a total of 159 father-present boys from among whom the matched father-present group was selected. In terms of matching criteria, no match was available for one of the father-absent boys; and there was incomplete information on two other father-absent and seven father-present boys.) Matched Ss did not differ more than 4 months in age, one SES level in terms of a five-level scale of parent occupation, and 10 IQ points on the Peabody Picture Vocabulary Test (PPVT) (Dunn, 1965); and they were identical in terms of sibling distribution (number and sex of siblings and whether older or younger than the Ss). The father-present and father-absent groups were essentially identical in age, IQ, and SES; the Ss had a mean age of 65 months, were mostly from working-class and lower-middle class backgrounds, and had a mean PPVT IQ of 105. Father-absent boys had not had fathers or father surrogates living in their homes for at least a year. Father absence was due to divorce or separation. Eleven of the boys had been father absent for more than 2 years, and the mean length of absence was 3 years, 2 months. In contrast, father-present fathers were reported to be home on a regular basis, usually 2 or more hours per weekday (when the boy was home and awake) and most of the weekend. (Part of the maternal questionnaire included items concerning how much time the boy spent with various members of his family, the boy's and the parents' schedules, and details of any parental absence from the home).

GENERAL PROCEDURE   The investigation was initially described to kindergarten directors, teachers, and parents as a study of different types of boys' play. Information concerning age, SES, and sibling distribution was ascertained from school files. Children were seen individually for sex role orientation, sex role preference, and IQ assessments; and teachers' ratings were used to estimate sex role adoption. Mothers were sent questionnaires assessing father availability and maternal encouragement of masculine behavior. The questionnaires were sent along with letters signed by the investigator and the appropriate kindergarten director. Another letter and questionnaire (after 1 month) and then a telephone call (after 2 months) followed if the questionnaires were not returned. Based on data in school files, 18 of 20 mothers of father-absent boys and 159 of 166 mothers of father-present boys returned completed questionnaires.

MEASUREMENT OF MATERNAL ENCOURAGEMENT   An earlier pilot study involved the interviewing of a dozen mothers of kindergarten-age boys to determine what kinds of questions might reveal their reactions when their sons exhibited masculine or unmasculine behavior. From the interview data multiple-choice questions were constructed to assess degree of maternal encouragement for masculine behavior. Excluding the buffer items, there were seven questions to elicit the mother's reactions to her son's behavior. Questions pertained to such situations as the boy picking up a heavy chair, wrestling with another boy, playing in the mud, climbing a tree, falling off his tricycle, painting boxes, and responding to being pushed by a boy of his own size. For each question, choice of the alternative indicating strong encouragement of assertive, aggressive, or independent behavior was scored 3 points; the alternative indicating acceptance of such behavior, 2 points; the alternative indicating interference, but not the stopping of the behavior, 1 point; and the alternative indicating strong discouragement of the behavior, 0 points. Split-half reliability computed by the Spearman-Brown formula was .84.

MEASUREMENT OF MASCULINITY   An extensively modified version of Brown's IT Scale was used to measure sex role orientation. In order to make the IT figure more sexually neutral in appearance, following a suggestion by Hall (Brown, 1962), only the face was presented. The IT figure was described to the S as "a child playing a make-believe game," a game in which "the child can be anybody or do anything in the whole world." The S was then asked to designate who IT was being and what IT was wearing and doing from among various pairs of pictures including people (Indian Chief or Indian Princess; man or woman), wearing apparel (men's clothes or women's clothes; men's shoes or women's shoes), and tasks (working with building tools or cooking utensils; fixing broken objects or washing and ironing). Each masculine designation was given 1 point, and 2 additional points (1 each) were given if the boy, when questioned, gave the child a boy's name and said the child would become a father. (The possible range of IT scores was from 0 to 11.) Split-half reliability computed by the Spearman-Brown formula was .83.

A game-preference task was used to assess sex role preference. Pictures of the same two boys playing four masculine games (archery, baseball, basketball, and football) and four feminine games (hopscotch, jacks, dancing, and jump rope) were drawn on 3 × 5-inch cards. These games had been found to be highly sex-typed by Rosenberg and Sutton-Smith (1964). The S was shown two games at a time and asked to select which game he would like to play the most. There were 16 comparisons: every masculine game was paired with every feminine game, and 1 point was given for every masculine choice. Split-half reliability computed by the Spearman-Brown formula was .79.

A rating scale of sex role adoption was used to estimate relative assertiveness aggressiveness, competitiveness, independence, and activity directed toward physical prowess and mastery of the environment. Items relating to lack of masculinity in terms of the boy's relative passivity, dependency, and timidity were also included. There were 16 items in all, 9 assumed to be representative of high masculinity, 7 of low masculinity. Concrete definitions were given of each behavior to be rated (e.g., "is active and energetic, on the move, plays hard"; "leads other children, organizes play activities, assigns tasks to others"; "is timid around others, is fearful when introduced to new adults and children, fears physical contact"). Each S was rated on each item in terms of a 5-point scale; very frequently, frequently, sometimes, seldom, and never. Each item was scored either 0, 1, 2, 3, or 4. For example, for the nine items assumed to relate to high masculinity, 4 points were scored when the behavior was checked as very frequent, 0 points when it was checked as never occurring. Two teachers' ratings were available for 31 of the 34 Ss, and the correlation between total scores derived from the two teachers' ratings was .82.

RESULTS

One-tailed tests of significance are reported because specific predictions (e.g., father absence negatively related to masculinity and degree of maternal encouragement positively related to masculinity) were decided upon before data collection. Comparisons made by use of t tests for matched pairs (Bruning & Kintz, 1968) revealed that the father-present boys had much more masculine IT scores ($t = 4.33$, df $= 16$, $p < .01$) and slightly more masculine game-preference scores ($t = 1.92$, df $= 16$, $p < .05$) but did not differ significantly from the father-absent boys in their rating scale scores ($t = 1.21$, df $= 16$, N.S.). In terms of t tests for uncorrelated means, the boys who had been father absent 2 or more years ($N = 11$) had significantly lower mean IT scores ($t = 2.82$, df $= 15$, $p < .01$) than the boys who had been father absent for 1 to 2 years, but there was no significant difference between the game-preference scores of the two father-absent groups ($t = .76$, df $= 15$, N.S.).

TABLE 1

Means of Masculinity Scores for Father-Availability Groups

Group	N	IT	Game	Rating Scale
Father-present (FP)*	17	8.89	11.61	39.22
Father-absent (FA)	17	5.71	9.06	37.94
Father-absent (FA1)† (1 to 2 years)	6	6.78	9.46	38.15
Father-absent (FA2) (more than 2 years)	11	4.39	9.15	37.60

* FP's had significantly higher IT scores ($p < .01$) and game scores ($p < .05$) than FA's.
† FA1's had significantly higher IT scores ($p < .01$) than FA2's.

The mean scores of the father-present and father-absent boys can be described in relation to the possible range in scores of the different sex role measures: IT scores, 0 to 11; game-preference scores, 0 to 16; rating scale scores, 0 to 64. The mean IT score (see Table 1) seemed relatively masculine for boys who were father present, relatively neutral for boys father absent 1 to 2 years, and somewhat feminine for boys father absent more than 2 years. The mean game-preference score was relatively masculine for father-present boys and relatively neutral for father-absent boys. In terms of mean rating scale scores, the boys as a group appeared relatively masculine. The mean sex role scores of the father-present boys were similar to those obtained from a larger sample of 5-year-old boys (Biller, 1968a).

With respect to a t test for matched pairs, the mothers of the father-present boys appeared to be slightly more encouraging of masculine behavior than did the mothers of the father-absent boys ($t = 1.89$, df $= 16$, $p < .05$). An examination of group means suggests that the mothers of father-present boys were generally accepting of masculine behavior in their sons (mean score $= 11.52$), while the mothers of father-absent boys appeared more ambivalent concerning masculine behavior in their sons (mean score $= 9.31$). For father-absent boys, degree of maternal encouragement of masculine behavior was positively related to game-preference scores ($r = .49$, df $= 16$, $p < .05$) and to rating scale scores ($r = .42$, df $= 16$, $p < .05$) but not to IT scores ($r = .12$, df $= 16$, N.S.). There were no significant relationships for father-present boys concerning maternal encouragement and masculine behavior (IT scores: $r = .08$, df $= 16$, N.S.; game-preference scores: $r = .21$, df $= 16$, N.S.; rating scale scores: $r = .11$, df $= 16$, N.S.).

Age, sibling distribution, SES, maternal employment, IQ, and reason for father absence were not significantly related to any of the sex role measures or to maternal encouragement for masculine behavior. (It should be noted that there was a restricted range of S variability in all these variables). For both the father-absent and father-present boys the different measures of masculinity showed positive but nonsignificant relationships to each other; for the total group of Ss the interrelationships reached low levels of significance (IT and game preference: $r = .25$, df $= 33$, $p < .10$; IT and rating scale: $r = .23$, df $= 33$, $p < .10$; game preference and rating scale: $r = .31$, df $= 33$, p $< .05$).

DISCUSSION

The seemingly greater effect of father absence on boys' sex role orientation than on more manifest aspects of their sex role development was consistent with previous investigations (Barclay & Cusumano, 1967; Biller, 1968b), as was the suggestion that father absence beginning before age 4 has more of a retarding effect on the development of a masculine sex role orientation than does father absence beginning after age 4 (Hetherington, 1966). It is possible that the effects of father absence on sex role preference and sex role adoption may also be quite dependent on the length and timing of father absence. For instance, the impact of father absence on sex role adoption may be more noticeable in 3- and 4-year-old boys than in 5- and 6-year-old boys, who may have more opportunity to interact with same-sex peers, especially if they are in kindergarten.

Mothers of father-absent boys seem to be, as a group, slightly less encouraging of masculine behavior in their sons than are mothers of father-present boys. However, degree of maternal encouragement for masculine behavior appears more important for father-absent boys than it does for father-present boys, at least with respect to sex role preference and sex role adoption development. It seems that a mother of a father-absent boy can influence her son's cognitive awareness of the incentive value of the masculine role and her son's motivation to imitate other males and act masculine. The sex role development of the father-present boys seems very much influenced by the father-son relationship (Biller & Borstelmann, 1967), but the mother-son relationship may assume critical importance in the sex role development of the father-absent boy. The presence of an interested and masculine father may mitigate the influence of an overprotective mother in the father-present home, or, on the other hand, an encouraging mother may find it difficult to facilitate her son's sex role development if he has a passive-dependent father who is frequently present as an example of masculine behavior. The mother of the father-absent boy may have more potential for either encouraging or discouraging her son's masculine development.

This study supports the value of distinguishing among different aspects of sex role. Father absence, particularly if it occurs early, appears to affect sex role orientation most. In father-absent boys maternal encouragement of masculine behavior appears to affect more manifest aspects of sex role, such as sex role preference and sex role adoption. These results are consistent with a developmental conception in which orientation development precedes preference and adoption development and, possibly is more resistant to change.

References

BARCLAY, A., & CUSUMANO, D. R. Father absence, cross-sex identity, and field-dependent behavior in male adolescents. *Child Development,* 1967, **38**, 243–250.

BILLER, H. B. A multiaspect investigation of masculine development in kindergarten age boys. *Genetic Psychology Monographs,* 1968, **78**, 89–138, (a)

————. A note on father-absence, socio-cultural backgrounds, and sex role development in young lower-class Negro and White boys. *Child Development,* 1968, **39**, 1003–1006. (b)

————, & BORSTELMANN, L. J. Masculine development: an integrative review. *Merrill-Palmer Quarterly,* 1967, **13**, 253–294.

BROWN, D. G. Sex role preference in children: methodological problems. *Psychological Reports,* 1962, **11**, 477–478.

BRUNING, J. L., & KINTZ, B. L. *Computational handbook of statistics.* Glenview, Ill.: Scott, Foresman, 1968.

DUNN, L. M. *Expanded manual for the Peabody Picture Vocabulary Test.* Minneapolis: American Guidance Service, 1965.

HETHERINGTON, E. M. Effects of paternal absence on sex-typed behaviors in Negro and White preadolescent males. *Journal of Personality and Social Psychology,* 1966, 4, 87–91.

PEDERSON, F. A. Relationships between father-absence and emotional disturbance in male military dependents. *Merrill-Palmer Quarterly,* 1966, 12, 321–331.

Rosenberg, B. G., & Sutton-Smith, B. The measurement of masculinity and femininity in children: an extension and revalidation. *Journal of Genetic Psychology*, 1964, 104, 259–264.

Stolz, L. M., et al. *Father relations of war born children.* Stanford, Calif.: Stanford University Press, 1954.

IT Score Variations by Instructional Style*

Norman L. Thompson, Jr. and Boyd R. McCandless
EMORY UNIVERSITY

Brown's It Scale for Children (ITSC) is an instrument widely used with young children for measuring sex-role preference. Evidence exists that many children may respond to masculine cues in It rather than projecting their own choices. In this study, the effects of three different instructions on the performance of Negro and white children were examined. These instructions were (a) projective, (b) semiprojective, and (c) objective. Each instruction was given to 72 lower-class prekindergarten children, 18 Negro boys, 18 white boys, 18 Negro girls, and 18 white girls. Race was an important variable in the responses to the test, many white girls apparently respond to masculine cues in the It figure; however, this was not true among Negro girls. This may be due to differences in sex-role prestige in these two subcultures. Lower-class Negro boys show greater preference for the feminine role as measured under the semiprojective and objective instructions. The relation of the ITSC scores and teacher ratings of the children's behavior supports the hypothesis that the development of sex-role preference precedes the development of sex-role adoption, suggesting that the rate of development may be faster among white boys.

The concept of sex-role identification occupies an important position in the attempt to understand personality development. A major research problem in the area concerns measurement. Thus, the authors of the present study have focused on Brown's (1956) It Scale for Children (ITSC), a widely used instrument for assessing sex-role development in children. This technique purports to measure sex-role preference, defined by Brown (1956) as "behavior associated with one sex or the other that the individual would like to adopt, or that he perceives as the preferred or more desirable behavior" (p. 3).

In the standard procedure, the child is presented with a modified stick figure, "It," which is assumed to be sexless. The task for the child is to choose

Reprinted from *Child Development*, 1970, *41*, 425–436, Copyright © 1970 by The Society for Research in Child Development, Inc. By permission.

* This research was supported in part by a U.S. Office of Education Small Grant to the Emory Division of Educational Studies, and by the Atlanta Education Improvement Program, Ford Foundation. Miss Elizabeth Perry of the Atlanta Education Improvement Program assisted centrally in data collection. This paper was presented March 1, 1969, at the meeting of the Southeastern Psychological Association, New Orleans.

what "It" likes in a series of pictures of various sex-typed items. The assumption behind the test is that the child considers himself as "It" and that the activities he chooses for "It" are actually those he would choose for himself (McCandless, 1967).

The major criticism leveled against the instrument is that "It" actually looks like a boy, rather than a neuter figure. Therefore, many children make choices for a boy figure rather than projecting their own choices onto "It" (Brown, 1962). There is considerable evidence to support such a criticism. Sher and Lansky (1968) found that girls as well as boys tended to see "It" as a male when asked the sex of the figure. They also found that boys tended to say "boy" and girls tended to say "girl" when asked the sex of the "It" figure while it was concealed in an envelope. When these children were then shown "It," more girls changed their attributions to "boy" than boys changed their attributions to "girl." Additional support for the hypothesis that "It" possesses masculine cues comes from the results of a study by Hartup and Zook (1960).

Lansky and McKay (1963) eliminated the possible masculine stimulus effect of "It" by testing kindergarten children with the figure concealed in an envelope. They found that boys were more variable than girls in this situation. Endsley (1967) obtained different results in a study in which he tested half the 3- to 5-year-old children with the standard instructions and half with "It" concealed in an envelope. He found that boys were less variable than girls under both conditions. There were no differences in the mean scores between the two conditions for the boys or girls. He thus found no support for the contention that "It" possesses a masculine bias.

Sher and Lansky (1968) tested kindergarten children randomly assigned to one of three different sequences. The first sequence began with the standard instructions. The second sequence began with "It" concealed in an envelope. In the third sequence, the children were first asked to attribute a sex to the picture of "It." The task for these latter children was to respond to the choices for an "It" of the sex they attributed to the figure. The results indicated that there were no differences among the three conditions for boys. However, the girls were more feminine on the concealed condition than on the other two conditions. As girls and boys also tended to see "It" as a boy when asked the figure's sex, Sher and Lansky concluded that it it is likely the "It" figure contains predominantly masculine cues. ITSC scores may reflect the child's attempt to match a sex-typed figure with its appropriate objects. Thus it appears the test may measure sex-role knowledge rather than sex-role preferences.

The present study was designed to explore further the effects of the instructions used with the ITSC. Three different sets of instructions were employed in the study. These instructions were designed to produce variations in the test situation ranging from projective to semiprojective to objective.

A second purpose was to explore the effects of the examiner's sex on the children's performance. It is possible that the examiner's sex has a systematic effect on the children's performance. However, this had not been previously tested.

The third purpose of this study was to add normative data for the ITSC for lower-class Negro and white children. Hartup and Zook (1960) found no social class differences among their preschool-aged Ss. In a study of older children, Hall and Keith (1964) found socioeconomic class differences, largely among the boys. Thomas (1966) tested deprived and non-deprived Negro and nondeprived white children. The results indicated that sex-role preferences mature more slowly among deprived Negro children than among nondeprived Negro and white youngsters. The feminine role had greater prestige among the deprived Negroes, while the masculine role had greater prestige among the non-deprived whites. The relative prestige of the two roles among the nondeprived Negroes was in transition but closer to that found among the whites. The present study is an extension of such work.

The final purpose was to explore the relationship between sex-role preference as measured by the ITSC and sex-role adoption as measured by teacher ratings.

Six hypotheses can be formally tested in connection with the four main objectives of the study:

1. When boys are compared with girls in ITSC (a) the boys' mean scores for all three instructions will be significantly higher (more masculine) than the girls'; (b) the boys' variances for the three instructions will be significantly smaller than the girls', except for condition C. This double hypothesis comes directly from Brown's results (1956, 1957).

2. Data do not permit a directional hypothesis about the effect of the sex of the examiner on Ss' performance. However, information is needed.

3. This set of hypotheses concerns the performance of the girls on the ITSC. (a) There will be a significant difference between the mean scores of instructions A (standard instructions) and B ("It" is concealed). The A score will be higher (more masculine). (b) There will be a significant difference between the mean scores of instructions A and C ("It-is-you"). The A score will be higher. (c) There will be a significant difference between the mean scores of instructions B and C. The B mean score will be higher.

Hypothesis 3b is based on Hartup and Zook's (1960) results; hypotheses 3a and 3c, on those of Sher and Lansky (1968).

4. The fourth set of hypotheses relates to the performance of the boys on the ITSC. (a) There will be no significant difference between the mean scores of instructions A (standard) and B (concealed). (b) There will be no significant difference between the mean scores of instructions A and C ("It-is-you"). (c) There will be no significant difference between the mean scores of instructions B and C.

Hypothesis 4b comes from Hartup and Zook (1960), while hypotheses 4a and 4c are based on Sher and Lansky's (1968) findings.

5. This set of hypotheses pertains to racial differences in performance on the ITSC. (a) Negro boys will score significantly more feminine than white boys on instructions A and B. (b) Negro girls will score significantly more feminine than white girls on instructions A and B. (c) Negro boys will be significantly more variable than white boys.

This set of hypotheses is based on Thomas's (1966) results.

6. There will not be a significant relation between sex-role preference as measured by the ITSC and sex-role adoption as measured by teacher ratings. This hypothesis is based on Ward's (1969) results. He found that sex-role preference develops before the age of five, while sex-role adoption comes later.

METHOD

SUBJECTS   The Ss were 72 kindergarten children, 36 boys and 36 girls, ranging from 51 to 66 months with a mean age of 57.50 months. The mean ages in months and standard deviations, respectively, for the four racial and sex groups were as follows: Negro boys, 55.94 and 2.68; Negro girls, 56.56 and 3.75; white boys, 58.33 and 3.61; and white girls, 59.17 and 3.09. Although the children were born at approximately the same time, the testing schedule necessitated testing each school at different times during the late winter and spring of the year. Fifty-eight of the Ss were enrolled in a special prekindergarten program for deprived children in three schools of the Atlanta, Georgia, public school system. Two of the schools were entirely Negro, while the third was predominantly white. The remaining 14 Ss were enrolled in Project Head Start classes in the same neighborhoods as the Ss in the special prekindergarten program. These classes were racially mixed. All Ss were deprived, lower-class children (McCandless, 1968).

Subjects from each school were assigned to each of the treatment groups. Assignment was random except that the groups were matched for race and sex. Only one S refused to be tested, and she was replaced by a classmate. Two Ss refused to be tested by a male examiner and were consequently tested by a female examiner.

PROCEDURE   The ITSC was administered individually in private rooms of the schools. Half of the Ss were tested by a male examiner and half by a female examiner. Each S was given the ITSC three times in one day according to his assigned sequence. Due to the sporadic attendance of many of the Ss, it was not feasible to lengthen the time between testings. One-third of the Ss were randomly assigned to the ABC sequence, one-third to the BCA sequence, and one-third to the CAB sequence. The instructions were:

> A (*standard instructions*).—These instructions were the same as Brown's (1956). The figure was called "It" and was visible to the child throughout this portion of the test.
> B (*concealed instructions*).—This technique was developed by Lansky and McKay (1963). The figure remained in the envelope, and the child was told, "There is a child named 'It' in the envelope."
> C ("*It-is-you*" *instructions*).—These instructions were developed by Hartup and Zook (1960). The figure was identified as the same sex as the child throughout this portion of the test.

The sections of the ITSC were administered according to Brown's manual (1956). However, the 16 pictured toys were presented in two groups of eight rather than one group of 16 pictures. Each group contained four boys' toys and four girls' toys arranged in the numbered order of the cards. Each S was instructed to choose four from each of the two groups.

The weighted scoring method developed by Brown (1956) was employed. Each masculine choice receives a positive score, and a feminine choice receives a 0. The possible scores range from 0 (most feminine) to 84 (most masculine).

TEACHER RATINGS   Sex-role adoption was measured by ratings of the *S*s'
behavior by the head and assistant teachers. The ratings were based on the
teacher's observations of the *S*s' behavior throughout the school year, or the
entire summer Head Start program. The masculine rating scale was developed
by Biller (1969). The feminine scale was constructed by McCandless and
Thompson for this study and was based on Biller's masculine scale.

Each scale contains 16 items describing various behaviors. The masculine
scale has nine items characteristic of masculine behavior in young children and
seven items characteristic of feminine behavior. The feminine scale contains
10 items characteristic of feminine behavior in young children and six items
characteristic of masculine behavior. The teacher is asked to rate the child on
a scale ranging from *very frequently* to *never* for each item of behavior. The masculine scale is scored so that a high score indicates masculine behavior and a
low score indicates nonmasculine behavior. The feminine scale is scored in such
a manner that a low score indicates feminine and a high score indicates non-
feminine behavior. This scoring procedure was employed so that the scoring
direction on these scales corresponded to the scoring direction of the ITSC.

The percentages of agreement between the two teachers was computed by
comparing the teachers' responses on each item. A disagreement of one step
gave a score of 75 percent agreement on that item, a disagreement of two steps
gave a score of 50 percent agreement, etc. The overall percentages of agreement
between the pairs of teachers ranged from 72.5 to 89.3 for the masculine scale
and from 76.6 to 86.7 for the feminine scale.

RESULTS

The age differences among the various racial and sex groups were examined. The difference between boys and girls for both Negro and white was not
significant (black, $t = .554$, df $= 34$; white, $t = .730$, df $= 34$). The difference
between Negro and white girls was significant at the .05 level of confidence
($t = 2.212$, df $= 34$). The difference between Negro and white boys was also
significant at the .05 level of confidence ($t = 2.176$, df $= 34$). Although these
mean differences are significant, the differences of 2.66 months between the
two groups of girls and 2.39 months between the boys are small for the overall
age of the children. Correlations between age and the various instructions of the
ITSC are given in Table 1. The only significant correlations work *against* the
hypothesis regarding racial differences between boys, and *for* the hypothesis
concerning girls.

An analysis of variance was performed on the order effect of the various
instructional conditions for boys and girls. A nonsignificant F of .580 (df $= 2$)
was obtained among the orders for boys, and a nonsignificant F of .348 (df $= 2$)
was obtained for the girls. The order in which the children received the ITSC
does not affect the scores significantly.

A separate analysis of variance that involved four factors—sex of child,
sex of examiner, race, and instructions revealed that the effects of the child's
sex were significant (F for 1 df $= 70.85$). This result, bearing on the validity
of the ITSC, supports hypothesis 1*a*: Boys will score higher than girls. As
shown in Table 2, the boys' mean scores were consistently higher than the

TABLE 1

Correlations Between Age and Instructional Conditions of the ITSC

GROUP	A (STANDARD)	B (CONCEALED)	C ("IT-IS-YOU")
Negro boys	−.68†	.32	−.13
White boys	.16	.13	.03
Negro girls	−.51*	.16	.09
White girls	.06	.00	.07

* $p < .05$.
† $p < .01$.

girls' for all instructional conditions. The various combinations of variances were examined by F tests for each subgroup. Hypothesis 1b (boys less variable than girls) was not supported, nor were there between-race differences in variance.

TABLE 2

Means and Standard Deviations of Subjects on the ITSC

	A		B		C	
GROUP	MEAN	SD	MEAN	SD	MEAN	SD
Males	54.22	17.60	56.67	16.13	61.50	15.28
Negro	46.78	14.73	53.33	13.03	56.56	14.76
White	61.67	17.08	60.00	18.12	66.44	14.15
Females	40.58	18.19	36.11	13.25	27.81	15.98
Negro	35.56	14.84	37.61	13.08	26.72	14.46
White	45.61	19.76	34.61	13.25	28.89	17.30

No hypothesis was made concerning the effect of the examiner's sex on the performance of the Ss. The results of the analysis of variance indicate that it produced no effect ($F = .188$).

The sex of child by instruction interaction was significant at less than the .01 level (F was 9.891 for 2 df). The effects of instructions were examined by means of t tests for correlated means. The results of these tests for boys and girls, separated by race, are shown in Table 3. Hypothesis 3a, which states that the girls' mean scores under A (standard instructions) will be higher (more masculine) than those under B (concealed instructions) is not supported for the total group. Hypothesis 3b, that the girls will score higher on A than on C ("It-is-you"), was supported for the total group and for white girls. Hypothesis 3c, which states that the girls will score higher on B and C, was supported for the total group and for black girls. The hypothesis was not supported for white girls. The hypothesis about effects of instructions on boys' performance, 4a ($A = B$), 4b ($A = C$), and 4c ($B = C$), were all supported for the total group and for the

TABLE 3

t Tests between the Instructional Conditions for Negro and White Subjects

GROUP	A–B	A–C	B–C
Males	.935	.826	1.404
Negro	2.408*	2.843*	.944
White	.390	1.000	1.322
Females	1.149	3.803‡	2.726*
Negro	.522	1.898	2.201
White	2.080	3.611‡	1.677

* p < .05.
† p < .01.
‡ p < .002.

white boys. However, the Negro boys were more masculine on both B and C than on A.

The analysis of variance indicated that race is a significant factor in ITSC scores. The data, which are summarized in Table 4, show that the Negro

TABLE 4

t Tests between Negro and White Subjects

GROUP	A	B	C	TOTAL
Males	2.722†	1.233	1.992*	2.673†
Females	1.678*	.664	.397	.858

* p < .10.
† p < .02.

boys were more feminine than white boys on the three instructional conditions combined.[1] On the individual instructions the Negro boys were significantly more feminine than white boys on A, with condition C ("It-is-you") reaching borderline significance. It is doubtful that the age difference between Negro and white boys produced these results. There were no significant correlations for boys between age and ITSC score except −.68 on A for the Negro boys (see Table 1). This indicates that the older the Negro boy, the more feminine he is likely to score under the standard instructions. If there had been no age

[1] This difference cannot be accounted for by different father-absent ratios for the ethnic groups. For Negro boys, 14 fathers were living at home and four were absent, while the white boys had 12 present and six absent. The Negro girls had 10 fathers present with eight absent, and the white girls had 14 present with four absent. In addition, one father-absent Negro girl had a grandfather living at home. An analysis was done to see if there were any differences in ITSC performances between father-absent and father-present children. Due to the small N's for children separated by sex and race, the data were collapsed over race. There were no significant differences between father-absent and father-present children for any instructional condition. The full data may be obtained from the authors.

difference between the two groups of boys, the difference on A might have been larger. There was no difference between the Negro and white girls on the combined instructional conditions. On the individual instructions, only A (standard) approaches significance. The differences on B and C are not significant. Therefore, hypothesis 5a was partially supported, while 5b was not supported. Nor was hypothesis 5c supported; it states that the Negro boys will be significantly more variable than white boys.

Hypothesis 6 states that there will be no significant relationship between sex-role preference as measured by the ITSC and sex-role adoption as measured by the teacher ratings. The results (Table 5) support the hypothesis, except for

TABLE 5
Correlation for Teachers' Ratings with ITSC

GROUP	A	B	C
Males:			
Negro	−.029	−.216	.004
White	.512*	.301	.479*
Females:			
Negro	.134	−.489*	.355
White	−.017	.247	.001

* $p < .05$.

the white boys. It may be that sex-role preference and sex-role adoption are coming into congruence by the approximate age of 5 years for lower-class white boys but not for the other groups.

The correlations among the treatments are reported in table 6. These indicate that the Negro boys were consistent across instructions, with the correlation between B and C reaching borderline significance ($p < .10$). The white boys were only consistent between conditions A and B. There was no consistency among the Negro girls across instructions; the white girls were consistent between B and C, with the correlation between A and C reaching borderline significance ($p < .10$).

TABLE 6
Correlations among Treatments

GROUP	A–B	A–C	B–C
Negro boys	.662‡	.510*	.458
White boys	.475*	.170	−.198
Negro girls	.286	.093	−.163
White girls	.121	.440	.576†

* $p < .05$.
† $p < .02$.
‡ $p < .01$.

DISCUSSION

The data from this study clearly suggest that race is an important variable in the responding to the ITSC. The type of instructions used did not affect the performance of the white boys, but the Negro boys were significantly more feminine on the standard instructions than on the concealed or "It-is-you" conditions. It is possible that the white boys' attitudes concerning their own sex role have developed consistently with their knowledge of the masculine sex role. The Negro boys made more feminine choices when the "It" figure was shown but not identified as being one sex or the other. Perhaps they see "It" as feminine. Such a conclusion is reasonable if, as has been suggested, the feminine role is preferred in lower-class black culture (Rainwater, 1966).

There is some support for the hypothesis that white girls respond to masculine cues in the "It" figure when, as in standard instructions, the figure is not identified by sex. This was not true for Negro girls. This difference could be due to the relative prestige of the sex roles in the two subcultures. For lower-class white girls, a neutral figure may be seen as masculine because the masculine role is more favored. Lower-class Negro girls may be similar to white boys, in that their sex-role attitudes have developed consistently with their knowledge of cultural advantage for their sex. However, the patterning of the Negro girls' scores suggests an additional possibility. The mothers of these girls may be more assertive and engage in more "masculine" activities than mothers in many other groups in the United States. These daughters are probably reinforced for imitating these activities. Although on the one hand the Negro girls may be learning what is typically the feminine role in our society, on the other they are learning the attitudes associated with the assertive role lower-class black women are forced to play.

The evidence from this study, in conjunction with previous studies (Hartup & Zook, 1960; Lansky & McKay, 1963; Sher & Lansky, 1968), supports the conclusion that standard "It" instructions measure variables in addition to sex-role preference, at least for white girls and Negro boys. Use of these instructions to measure which sex role a child prefers may thus be suspect.

The Negro boys in this study scored more feminine than white boys on the ITSC, while the Negro girls were more feminine than white girls only under standard instructions. Only the Negro boys and white girls were consistent across instructions. (The only exception to this was the correlation between standard and concealed instructions for the white girls.)

These results fall into a reasonable pattern if we look at the possible meaning of each instructional condition. The standard instructions are semi-projective in the sense that they reflect an interaction between the "projective" or "true" self and social expectations. These expectations vary according to whether the child sees "It" as a boy or girl. "It" under concealed instructions is most likely a projective test. The "It-is-you" instructions induce clear social expectations which are overridden only for high-autonomy children with inappropriate sex preference.

Regardless of the stimulus conditions, the Negro boys in the sample did not vary their response pattern. This may be because they have few adequate male models in their coculture. This, plus possible reinforcement for feminine "good behavior" activities, may account for their rather feminine scores. The white girls may be exposed to similar social dynamics. They live in a coculture which provides unattractive feminine models, and where males are clearly dominant and more highly valued. The nonsignificant AB correlation for these girls may be due to the small N and random variation; it may be due to mixed perceptions of "It" by the Ss, some seeing "It" as male and responding according to social expectations, while others respond projectively.

The relationship between ITSC performance and teachers' ratings of behavior supports hypotheses about the deleterious affects of a predominantly feminine-dominated subculture on the Negro boys and a masculine-dominated subculture on the white girls. For neither group is there a translation into behavior, as seen by teachers, of either their "true" preference or their social expectations. It is possible that they do not perceive the social expectations, or that they perceive these expectations but do not have adequate models. In contrast, it appears that white boys perceive appropriate sex-role behavior and exhibit it.

The Negro girls seem to see that femininity for "true" selves (as measured by the projective condition) calls for a strong male social posture. This fits with the model of a matriarchal society in which a true woman has to be strong. There is no relationship between the behavior of these girls and the standard instructions, since the scores represent an interaction between responses shaped projectively, by expectations, or both. The correlation obtained between behavior and condition C (knowledge of social expectations) suggests that they may perceive the social expectations of the general society and translate them into action that is perceived as appropriately feminine by the teachers.

This study indicates the importance of racial socially mediated factors in the development of sex-role attitudes and behaviors in lower class children. Gewirtz and Stinel (1968) believe that their generalized imitation paradigm can account for the attitudes and behaviors that are usually subsumed under identification. This suggests that research is needed in the lower-class Negro and white communities to determine the types of models available to the children, and especially the types of behaviors reinforced by adults in these groups.

References

BILLER, H. B. Father dominance and sex-role development in kindergarten age boys. *Developmental Psychology*, 1969, **1**, 87–94.

BROWN, D. G. Sex-role preference in young children. *Psychological Monographs*, 1956, **70** (14, Whole No. 421).

———. Masculinity-femininity development in children. *Journal of Consulting Psychology*, 1957, **21**, 197–202.

———. Sex-role preference in children: methodological problems. *Psychological Reports*, 1962, **11**, 477–478.

ENDSLEY, R. C. Effects of concealing "It" on sex-role preferences of preschool children. *Perceptual and Motor Skills*, 1967, **24**, 998.

GEWIRTZ, J. J., & STINGLE, K. G. Learning of generalized imitations as the basis for identification. *Psychological Review*, 1968, **75**, 374–397.

HALL, M., & KEITH, R. A. Sex-role preference among children of upper and lower social class. *Journal of Social Psychology*, 1964, 62, 101–110.

HARTUP, W. W., & ZOOK, E. A. Sex-role preferences in three- and four-year-old children. *Journal of Consulting Psychology*, 1960, **24**, 420–426.

LANSKY, L. M., & McKAY, G. Sex-role preferences of kindergarten boys and girls: some contradictory results. *Psychological Reports*, 1963, **13**, 415–421.

McCANDLESS, B. R. Children: behavior and development. (2d. ed) New York: Holt, Rinehart & Winston, 1967.

———. Predictor variable of school success of slum children. Paper presented at the meeting of the American Psychological Association, San Francisco, August, 1968.

RAINWATER, L. Crucible of identity: the Negro lower class family. *Daedalus*, 1966, **95**, 172–217. (Republished in T. Parsons and K. B. Clark (Eds.), *The Negro American*. Boston: Beacon, 1967. Pp. 166–204).

SHER, M. A., & LANSKY, L. M. The It scale for children: effects of variations in the sex-specificity of the It figure. *Merrill-Palmer Quarterly*, 1968, **14**, 323–330.

THOMAS, P. J. Sub-cultural differences in sex-role preference patterns. *Dissertation Abstracts*, 1966, **26**, 6894–6895.

WARD, W. D. The process of sex-role development. *Developmental Psychology*, 1969, **1**, 163–168.

Relationship Between Adult Nurturance and Dependency and Performance of the Preschool Child*

Russell DiBartolo and W. Edgar Vinacke†
STATE UNIVERSITY OF NEW YORK AT BUFFALO

This study determined the relationships between adult nurturance and child dependency and performance in a complex task. Sex differences were also investigated. Hypothesis 1 was that performance of preschool children on a complex task is more efficient under nurturant conditions than under nurturance-deprivation conditions. Hypothesis 2 stated that under nurturance deprivation children high in dependency will perform less efficiently than children low in dependency. Sex differences were expected in performance and dependency behavior as a function of level of nurturance and nurturant versus nurturant-deprivation conditions. The subjects were twenty-four 4-year-old children, 12 of each sex, in a federally supported preschool program. They were divided into high- and low-dependency groups, and assigned randomly within each group to either a nurturant or nurturance-deprivation condition. A puzzle task was administered to assess performance. Both Hypotheses 1 and 2 received significant support. No sex differences were found.

* This investigation was supported by Public Health Service Training Grant No. CA 5016 from the National Institutes of Health.

† The authors are indebted to Joyce DiBartolo for her services as experimenter. The assistance of Robert Barcikowski, State University of New York at Buffalo, in the statistical portion of this investigation is gratefully acknowledged.

This study is concerned with relationships among adult nurturance, child dependency, and performance of 4-year-old children in a prekindergarten school situation. It is also intended to ascertain whether sex differences appear in these relationships.

Investigators (Beller, 1955, 1959; Heathers, 1955; Moustakos, Sigel, & Schalock, 1956; Sears, 1963) who have examined conditions antecedent to dependency have presented arguments that describe dependency as either an acquired motive or as operant activity beginning in the infant's striving for physical gratification from the adult.

After dependency motivation has developed, it may be argued that the nurturant behavior of an adult acts as a secondary reinforcer associated with satisfaction of needs for security or reassurance. Subsequently, either the loss or a threat of the loss of gratifying adult behavior signals that satisfactions of these kinds cannot be obtained, thus activating fear or anxiety. As development continues, this anxiety becomes less and less overt. As a result, deprivation of nurturance instigates internal dependency responses which lead to a heightened level of dependency responses. In this framework, a situation in which dependency gratification is withheld by an adult may be considered as stressful, especially for the highly dependent child who will be more sensitive to this deprivation than will a low-dependent child. Thus, it is reasonable to expect that highly dependent children, with their heightened perception of nurturance deprivation, should become even more dependent and at a faster rate than children low in dependency (Beller, 1959).

Although the development of dependency may be much the same process for boys and girls, it is possible that parent-daughter and parent-son relationships may produce latent differences which may be reflected under controlled experimental conditions. Here, the manipulation of nurturance behavior and the observation of its effect on dependency may systematically be introduced free from interference from extraneous variables which may be found in the usual home or school situation.

Hartup (1958) concluded that nurturance withdrawal has the effect of enhancing the learning of simple tasks eliciting adult approval. This is interpreted as an attempt by the child to restore the relationship previously available in the nurturant situation because of anxiety-produced dependency behaviors. It is possible, however, that heightened dependency may be manifested in decreased efficiency on a more complex task. Following Hartup's general line of approach, this study uses a complex task to determine the effect of change in dependency in a nurturant situation as compared to a condition of deprivation of nurturance.

In pursuing this problem, the following hypotheses may be stated:

1. Performance of preschool children on a complex task is more efficient under nurturant conditions than under conditions of deprivation of nurturance.
2. Under deprivation of nurturance, children high in dependency will perform less efficiently than children low in dependency.

It was also hypothesized that sex differences would be evident.

METHOD

Nurturance was defined in accordance with Murray's (1938) formulation, as the need to aid the helpless. More fully, it signifies,

to give sympathy and gratify needs of a helpless object: an infant or any object that is weak, disabled, tired, inexperienced, etc.; to assist an object in danger; to feed, help, support, console, protect, comfort, nurse, heal, etc.

Nurturant Situation To establish the required conditions, the experimenter carried out the following behavior: (a) permissiveness—each subject was told that he could walk around the experimental room if he wished, get a drink of water, and partake in the task only if he wished to; (b) praise—before the subject began the task, the experimenter (female) told him that he was a very nice boy (or girl), a good helper; during the task, the experimenter told the subject that he was doing a very good job—this behavior was carried out at 10-second intervals or whenever the subject looked up. No instrumental help or clues[1] were offered by the experimenter; (c) affection—the experimenter told the child that she liked him very much, smiling as she explained the task in a soft tone of voice; (d) verbal reward—the experimenter verbally praised the child after completion of each task on the basis of speed, dexterity, attention to the task, and helpfulness of the child; (e) nearness—during the task, the experimenter sat immediately next to the subject (within 1 foot); (f) attention—the experimenter kept her undivided attention on the subject and his work on the task.

Nurturant-Deprivation Situation In contrast, the experimenter acted in a manner intended to remove the components of nurturance. Each of the dimensions of the nurturant situation was absent. At the start of the second task, the experimenter went to the rear of the experimental room out of sight of the subject, saying that she had to look at some books or arrange some cards.

Dependency This variable was defined according to Beller's (1957) dimensions of seeking help, physical contact, proximity, attention, and recognition. To measure these responses, Beller's 7-point behavior rating scale based on the frequency and persistence of these behaviors in the classroom situation was used. The composite score has been shown to be an indicator of a general dependency motive in young children (Beller, 1957).

Dependency Rating For 1 month prior to the experimental sessions, two classroom teachers independently rated the children for dependency by use of Beller's scale as described above. Each teacher selected two 10-minute periods each day in which to make the observations. Each child was observed at least three times weekly. The usual total observation time for each child was 12–16 minutes by each teacher for the 4-week period.

The mean score for girls was 18.7 ($SD = 3.78$) and for boys, 19.7 ($SD = 3.86$) The mean difference was not significant.

Rank order interjudge correlations were .43 for the girls' ratings and .70 for the boys' ratings. The overall interjudge coefficient was .54.

Task The experimental setting was puzzle solving. One of four jig-saw puzzles, each with 12 pieces, was used to assess the effects of the variables on performance.[2]

[1] No help was given on the test puzzle under any condition.
[2] These puzzles are produced by the Judy Company, Minneapolis, Minnesota.

Subjects   Twelve males and 12 females in a federally supported, pre-kindergarten school situation (Early Push Program) were used as subjects. Ages ranged 4 years–4 years, 11 months with mean ages of 4 years, 5 months for the males and 4 years, 4 months for the females. All the subjects were from low-income urban families and all were within the normal range of intelligence. Each had been in the same class with the same teachers from the beginning of the school year in late September to the time of the study in late April. The ethnic breakdown of the subjects was as follows: nine of Italian descent, including five males and four females; six of Irish descent, three males and three females; eight of Puerto Rican descent, three males and five females; and one Afro-American male.

Procedure: Familiarization Period   In order to counteract differential puzzle-solving abilities and practice effects during the experimental situation, a 2-week period of familiarization with puzzles was held prior to the study. This consisted of ten 20-minute periods, under both directed and free-play classroom conditions, using four puzzles, each with 12 pieces. The puzzle used in the performance task was chosen at random from these four puzzles just prior to the beginning of the experiment. During the familiarization period, the experimenter was present in the classroom.

Division into Groups   The behavior ratings were pooled for each child with the mean score adopted as the indication of dependency level. Based on these scores, within each sex, the subjects were divided into high- and low-dependency groups. Further subdivision into groups receiving experimental nurturance and nurturance deprivation was made at random from within the dependency levels. This assignment yielded 12 boys and 12 girls, 3 of each sex in each combination of high- and low-dependency under nurturance or nurturance-deprivation conditions.

Performance Task   Since the situation is an important variable in the induction of dependent behavior (Beller, 1959), the most relevant setting for the present study was considered to be one readily identified as usual and meaningful for the child. For this reason, the experimental sessions took place in an 8 × 12 foot room adjacent to the classroom and employed objects familiar to the children. A female experimenter, similar in age, physical stature, and temperament to the classroom teachers was used. During the course of the experiment, this person was unaware of the dependency level of each child and was told only which treatments to administer.

Each subject was brought individually to the experimental room and allowed to look around for 1 minute. After that, the subject was seated at a table on which the puzzle was placed. The experimenter then asked the subject to solve the puzzle, adopting the nurturant pattern of behavior. Time spent in puzzle solving during this period ranged 35–330 seconds. After a 3-minute rest period which consisted of talking with the experimenter about things other than the puzzle, the subjects solved the puzzle again, either under the condition of nurturance deprivation or under conditions of continued nurturance. Second-session performance times ranged 65–380 seconds.

RESULTS

The hypotheses were tested by a three-way analysis of covariance of second situation performance times with first task performance times taken as the covariate. The Scheffé method of post hoc comparisons was used for further analysis (Guenther, 1964). The dependency scores were considered independent of the performance scores. Tables 1 and 2 show the results of this analysis.

TABLE 1

Analysis of Covariance of the Effects of Nurturance, Dependency, Sex, and Their Interactions on Performance Times on the Test Puzzle

SOURCE OF VARIATION	DF	MS	F
Sex (A)	1	2865.120	1.29
Dependency (B)	1	19511.495	8.76*
A × B	1	.056	.00
Nurturance (C)	1	18944.888	8.51*
B × C	1	17931.349	8.05*
A × C	1	101.481	.05
A × B × C	1	1.817	.00
Error	16	2226.625	

*$p < .01$.

TABLE 2

Adjusted Cell Means, in Seconds, for the Test Puzzle

GROUP	HIGH DEPENDENT	LOW DEPENDENT	NURTURANCE TOTALS
Nurturance			
Boys	122.870	119.536	
Girls	141.266	136.649	
Total	264.136	256.185	520.321
Nurturance deprivation			
Boys	230.756	115.838	
Girls	256.863	142.888	
Total	487.619	258.726	746.345
Dependency totals	751.755	514.911	

NOTE. Equality of cell variances is assumed in the analysis. Since there are equal n's in each cell any inequality would be overcome by the robustness of the F test. Total variance for the test is the mean square error term in Table 1.

Hypothesis 1 is supported by the significant overall effect of nurturance. Further, a comparison between cell means of high-dependent children under nurturance and nurturance deprivation (Table 2) shows that this is a function of the interaction between nurturance deprivation and high dependency. A similar comparison for low-dependent children (Table 2) reveals a nonsignificant nurturance effect.

Evidence for Hypothesis 2 is provided by comparing the total mean for the high-dependent subjects with that of the low-dependent subjects under nurturance deprivation (Table 2). The significant difference between these groups again reveals a notable interaction between high dependency and nurturance deprivation but not between low dependency and nurturance deprivation. Moreover, a nonsignificant difference between high- and low-dependency groups within the nurturant condition (Table 2) points out the similarity of negligible interactive effects between the nurturance condition and high or low dependency.

No significant main effect of sex was evident from the main analysis. A look at Table 2, however, shows slightly better efficiency for the boys under each of the four dependency-nurturance situations.

DISCUSSION

The findings sustain the hypothesis that there is a close correspondence between adult nurturant behavior and child dependency, with children high in dependency keenly sensitive to changes in nurturance level. This awareness may be attributable to the highly dependent child's response to nurturance as a rewarding state of affairs, the removal of which results in a stressful, anxiety-producing situation. Thus, any setting in which dependency-gratifying behaviors are absent may be defined as stressful for a highly dependent child. Such stress may well interfere with efficient performance on a complex task. Further, the higher the child's dependency level, the more stressful the situation may seem and the more heightened his dependency behavior may become, with concomitant decreasing efficiency in performance. That such changes may be inferred from a performance measure is indicated by the results obtained from the dependency and performance analysis. This effect appears to be a general one, since no significant differences between sexes were found.

In the case of children low in dependency, adult nurturance may have only minimal reward effects and its deprivation may not be stressful. The behavior of such children may reflect either a quick adjustment merely to the event of a situational difference or, in fact, show no change at all.

The inefficient performance of highly dependent children under deprivation of nurturance and the lack of a significant effect for children low in dependency are consistent with the above notion of situational stress.

Although stress may enhance performance on a simple task, as seen in Hartup's (1958) study, it is reasonable to assume that it serves as an interference in the more complex task used in this study. Thus, both the present findings and those of Hartup provide explicit behavioral evidence for differential changes in dependency as shown by Beller's (1959) perceptual studies.

The finding of no sex differences is open to a number of interpretations. It was expected that the presence of a female experimenter might possibly bring about interactive effects. For example, it is reasonable to expect that under both nurturance and nurturance-deprivation conditions the performance of the females would be positively affected by the female experimenter. This result did not appear in the analysis. To further substantiate this, it is necessary that a similar study with a larger number of subjects be carried out using experimenters of both sexes.

On the other hand, the slight superiority in efficiency of the boys may also be a function of task relevance rather than sex differences. (The puzzle depicted a male television repairman at work.) Kagan and Moss (1962) have shown that dependency behavior in children between the ages 3–6 shows little resemblance to that of adult behavior or even to that of the later childhood years. (It is not until later childhood that a reliable relationship to adult dependency behavior is seen.) Such instability can account for the lack of a clear-cut difference in dependency ratings between sexes in this investigation.

Whatever reason is cited for failure to find sex differences in dependency, it appears that in studies of child dependency at the preschool level, no distinction on the basis of sex is necessary. Except for the possibility (not tested here) that a male experimenter might produce different effects on the two sexes, in contrast to the lack of such a difference for a female experimenter, boys and girls at the preschool level are similar in response to variations in adult nurturance.

Although a study such as this can give some explicit cues to the nature of the relationships of nurturance and dependency to performance, it is quite another matter to reach a full understanding of dependency changes under varied nurturant conditions. A short-term study, where it is possible to measure confidently only such discrete variables as performance, can, at best, serve as a basis for discussion of inferred dependency change and as a preliminary step in the longitudinal type of investigation needed for a truly sufficient study of dependency. Such an investigation might be carried out in a classroom situation over a period of a year using specific times within the normal routine for the manipulation of nurturance and securing definitive ratings of dependency. With extraneous factors, such as performance and sex (and perhaps others) partialed out by studies such as the present one, this long-term approach could finally bring to light the true relationship between the motives of nurturance and dependency.

References

Beller, E. K. Dependence and independence in young children. *Journal of Genetic Psychology*, 1955, **87**, 25–35.

———. Dependency and autonomous achievement striving related to orality and anality in early childhood. *Child Development*, 1957, **28**, 287–315.

———. Exploratory studies of dependency. *Transactions of the New York Academy of Sciences*, 1959, **21**, 414–425.

Guenther, W. C. *Analysis of variance.* Englewood Cliffs, N. J.: Prentice-Hall, 1964.

Hartup, W. W. Nurturance and nurturance withdrawal in relation to the dependency behavior of pre-school children. *Child Development*, 1958, **29**, 191–201.

Heathers, G. Emotional dependence and independence in nursery school play. *Journal of Genetic Psychology*, 1955, **87**, 37–57.

Kagan, J., & Moss, H. A. *Birth to maturity: A study in psychological development.* New York: Wiley, 1962.

Moustakos, C. E., Sigel, I., & Schalock, H. An objective method for the measurement and analysis of child-adult interaction. *Child Development*, 1956, **27**, 109–134.

Murray, H. *Explorations in personality.* New York: Oxford University Press, 1938.

Sears, R. R. Dependency motivation. *Nebraska Symposium on Motivation*, 1963, **11**, 25–64.

Part Three

THE SCHOOL-AGE
CHILD

9

Physical Characteristic.
and Skill.

Children grow taller, wider, and heavier. Some children change more rapidly in these dimensions than others. Children move their bodies, and parts of their bodies, some more skillfully than others. These statements hardly need formal proof. Even though physical and motor growth are obvious, it does not follow that they can be taken for granted. To understand child development fully, one needs to know the antecedents and consequences of physical and motor growth. This chapter contains two reviews of literature and two studies, one of each from each of the two related areas.

Tables of average heights and weights of children are useful not because they show what any given child should weigh, although they are sometimes misused in that way, but because they make it possible to see a child in relation to a group of children. To be of greatest use the averages should be of a group composed of children like the child whose growth is being assessed, but such norms are only occasionally available.

In the article reprinted from a longer article by Stanley M. Garn are given "Parent-specific Size Standards." These are the average heights of sons and daughters of short, average, and tall parents. Genetic factors for stature are therefore controlled, at least roughly. Other factors which influence children's heights are not controlled for in these tables. Elsewhere in the same article Garn reviews research on other antecedents and consequences of body size in children.

Anna Espenschade, in the second article, reviews some of the research that has been done on children's motor development. The figures quoted by Espenschade show the increasing skill which school children show in basic motor skills. The leveling off of girls' performance in adolescence may be due, at least in part, to a decrease in girls' motivation to perform well in these kinds of tasks, as Espenschade points out.

The third article, by Harben Young and Robert Knapp, is an interesting piece of research into the effects of making left-handed children use their right hands. Young and Knapp make use of culturally defined attitudes toward left-handedness by comparing boys of similar racial stock brought up in Italy and in the United States. The tests of lateral dominance are ones which beginning students of child development can use if they are interested in determining lateral dominance in children. The personality measures used by Young and Knapp are not so easily duplicated.

The Correlates of Body Size

Stanley M. Garn
THE FELS RESEARCH INSTITUTE

Body size from infancy through adolescence carries with it a variety of physiological, developmental, and behavioral correlates. For constant age, taller individuals have a larger basal oxygen consumption and in consequence they eat more because they need more. Taller children, like taller adults, have larger bones and in consequence their needs for calcium and phosphorous during growth must be proportionately larger. Taller children are also slightly but consistently advanced in a variety of developmental measures. Skeletal age tends to be advanced in taller children. Taller children are also slightly but consistently advanced in the number of teeth present at a given age (Cattell, 1928) and in the extent of calcification of the teeth as radiographically determined (Garn, Lewis, and Kerewsky, 1965).

Why the developmental correlates of size exist is not totally clear. To some extent they are a function of social stratification and socioeconomic group differences such that the more favored are both taller and developmentally advanced. To some extent, even within family lines, it can be shown that the physiologically more mature children are taller *because* they are more mature. Further, the mechanisms connecting tallness to dental development are by no means clear, particularly since the formation and eruption of the permanent dentition are to the very largest extent unrelated to most environmental influences.

THE CAUSE OF VARIATIONS IN SIZE   It should be pointed out here that there is no consistent explanation for variations in size in adulthood, nor is there as yet a satisfactory explanation for the mechanisms responsible for size variations in childhood. Granting that superior nutrition results in greater growth, the *mechanisms* by which this occurs are not known. Granting the genetic nature of stature, the mechanisms by which the genes make for variations in the length of the body and the size of its individual components are still not known.

One theory is that bigness is achieved through greater secretion of the growth-stimulating hormone (GSH) of the anterior pituitary. This is a reasonable theory, and it is in partial accordance with observational data. Hypopituitary children, lacking or partially lacking the growth stimulating hormone, do fail to grow. Hyperpituitary children do in fact achieve giantism. At the present time, however, there is no adequate measure of normal variations in growth hormone levels, either in the blood or in the urine nor are indirect indicators as alkaline phosphatase adequate for the purpose. With progress in the immunological approach to the measurement of growth-stimulating hormone, the possible relationship between variations in growth-stimulating

Reprinted from Stanley M. Garn, "Body Size and Its Implications," in L. W. Hoffman and M. L. Hoffman (Eds.), *Review of Child Development Research*, Vol. II, pp. 540–561. Published by Russell Sage Foundation, 1966. By permission.

hormone and statural differences may become clearer (Rimoin, Merimee, and McKusick, 1966).

Alternatively, differences both in size and in rate of growth may be a function of the bones *themselves* rather than in the amount of stimulating or trophic hormone. This is technically referred to as the target-organ theory. It refers to the notion (supported by observations on certain kinds of dwarfism) that variations in response of the target-organ, or end-organ, rather than the stimulating hormone are involved. Clearly, there is a pressing need for an understanding of the mechanisms through which variations in size are attained and through which ultimate size attainment is determined.

BODY SIZE AND BEHAVIORAL CORRELATES   In addition to the more obvious developmental, metabolic, and endocrine correlates of body size during the growing period, a large number of mental and behavioral correlates have also been reported (Abernethy, 1936; Ljung, 1965; Tanner, 1960, 1962). Though the magnitude of the correlations is generally low, for the most part they are systematically in the expected direction. Taller children tend to walk earlier (Norval, 1947). Boys and girls with a larger lean body mass tend to be advanced in gross motor development. A variety of studies report that "reading readiness" is positively correlated with stature. And most measures of "intelligence" appear to be loosely associated with body size during the growing period. Differences in nursery school behavior similarly relate in part to variations in the fat-free or lean body mass. (See Douglas, Ross, and Simpson, 1965; Ljung, 1965.)

Explanations for the behavioral correlations with body size are both numerous and varied and it is unlikely that all of the reported behavioral correlations have a common causal basis. A random sample of children represents a wide range of socioeconomic classes involving variations in caloric adequacy, medical care, parental attention, and parental encouragement. In the more complex behaviors, as represented by the introversion-extroversion continuum or dominance-submission scales, it is not improbable that larger body size gives a child initial advantage that he may then capitalize upon. Typed as a strong man, or leader, the large child may incorporate such successes into the system of devices he utilizes to deal with the world.

Nevertheless, there is reason to believe that some of the size-behavior correlates are in fact developmental in nature, representing a faster rate of behavioral development in those children who are ahead physically. More recent studies show a residual correlation between stature and test scores of children in Great Britain even among children of the same sex, age, stage of sexual development, social class, and size of family. However, to quote Douglas and his associates (1965), ". . . the correlation is not simply explained by an advancement in physical development being associated with an advancement in intellectual development."

THE PUBERTAL SPURT IN SIZE AND INTELLIGENCE   As long ago as 1922, Murdock and Sullivan advanced the notion of an adolescent "spurt" in the rate of mental growth, analogous to the well-known adolescent spurt in stature. In more recent years, this idea has been advanced by Tanner (1962) and investigated in England, Scotland, Canada, and Sweden. Boyne and Clark (1959) have reported secular changes in *both* stature and intelligence; and their British data are in accordance with Canadian reports (Binning, 1958) and a recent Swedish monograph by Ljung (1965) who studied "practically all the pupils in their respective year group in Sweden."

The rationale behind an adolescent spurt in "intelligence" paralleling the spurt in stature is not clear. The fact that there is a spurt in stature in almost all boys and in the majority of girls does not of itself indicate that the brain must behave like the bones. Indeed, it may be observed that intellective potential is not diminished in the panhypopituitary dwarf, nor is there any present evidence that intellectual activity is increased in the hyperpituitary child, or in the sexual precocities.

Granting that there is an adolescent spurt in intelligence, paralleling the spurt in stature and possibly involving changes in the brain itself, there remains to be seen whether this has a steroidal basis or not. Testosterone-treated boys and estrogen-treated girls would help to answer this question.

MUSCLE MASS AND AGE AT WALKING   As an example of the complexity of relationships between physical and behavioral variables, one may report a relationship between leg muscle mass and age at walking. Infants with large leg muscle masses (as determined radiographically) stand up and walk earlier. Infants with small leg muscle masses stand up and walk later (Garn, 1962b, 1963). This overall relationship is partially independent of body size per se as it is also independent of other Gesellian parameters at the same age level. While it might be argued that the relationship between leg muscle mass and walking or standing is the simple result of physical activity, the fact that muscle mass at six months is *predictive* of walking versus nonwalking or standing versus nonstanding at one year suggests that the relationship is developmental rather than directly causal in nature.

TWO-GENERATIONAL STUDIES OF SIZE AND BEHAVIOR   Most relationships between size and behavior in infancy and childhood pose the inevitable cart-or-horse problem, the same problem that attends relationships between size and maturation. Are more muscular boys bigger simply because they are more mature (hence, developmentally older) or do genes for earlier maturation also make for bigger size? Are correlations between size and behavior purely developmental, or are genes for size actually involved? Would parents of different sizes, within the same socioeconomic class, produce progeny who differ in the rates of psychomotor or intellective development?

It is possible to circumvent this problem by going back one full generation, categorizing the parents in terms of various parameters of size, and then examining the behavioral progress of the children so sorted. This is a classic approach in the genetics of animal behavior as extensively reviewed by Fuller and Thompson (1960). It can be applied to numerous parental size parameters, among them the familiar measurement of stature and the less familiar measurement of the bony chest breadth (representing the lean body mass).

Considering parental stature first, there is evidence for a relationship between parental stature and the psychomotor behavior of their progeny at six, twelve, and eighteen months. Taking fathers and mothers first separately, and then together (the combined-parent or "midparental" stature) and some 91 items in the total of the Gesell spectrum, the number of significant point biserial correlations is close to twice expectancy. There is some evidence, therefore, that taller parents, within a particular socioeconomic group, have infants who are slightly advanced in specific Gesell items (Hull, 1966).

Alternatively, taking the bony chest breadth of the parents (as measured on postero-anterior chest radiographs), it is clear that the parental bony chest breadth relates to Gesell, Merrill-Palmer, and even early Binet performance. Where both parents are above average in bony chest breadth, the progeny are not only notably larger from birth on, as characterized by greater body weight and far larger lean body mass, but they are systematically advanced in psychomotor, form board, and even language proficiency (Garn et al., 1960; Kagan and Garn, 1963).

It is not implied that the children of taller parents are "smarter" at six, twelve, or eighteen months; nor is it to be claimed that the progeny of parents with large fat-free masses are inherently more "intelligent" as reflected by their Gesell, eighteen-month Merrill-Palmer, or thirty-six-month Binet scores. The indication simply is that greater body size in either the horizontal or the vertical direction is attained through a faster rate of growth, and this faster rate of physical growth is associated with more rapid acquisition of the skills and abilities measured by the tests in question. So apart from nutrition, social experience, and parental stimulation, size per se does relate to behavioral development, in part because greater body size is attained by a higher rate of growth.

PARENT-SPECIFIC SIZE STANDARDS

Returning to size per se, it should be obvious that all massed-data "average" size standards, whether group-specific or not, or contemporary or not, suffer from the same major disadvantage. They are scarcely child-specific, that is, they do not apply well to individual children. Children come from a variety of parental mating types, and it is obvious that the children of tall parents and the children of short parents will be but poorly fitted by average values that fail to take parental size into account.

Though this statement is self-evident, it is best given substance by picturing two children from the Fels Longitudinal Studies. One, a girl (subject 356), is the child of very tall parents. Father and mother taken together average 181 cm —well above the nationwide male average of 175 cm. The other child (subject 371) is a boy, the child of very short parents. Together they average 164 cm— below the nationwide average for women alone. One might expect the girl to exceed the female norm and the boy to fall well below the age-size norm for the boys.

As shown in Figure 1, these children grow exactly as might be expected. The daughter of tall parents (subject 356) greatly exceeds the normative median for girls at all ages. Parent-specific size values are clearly needed for her. The boy, subject 371, the son of short parents, is well below the average for boys. His size has been a source of some concern to his physician since he was a

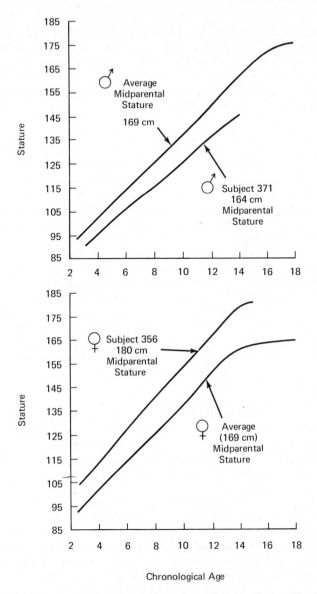

FIGURE 1. *Statural growth of the children of extreme parental size. The boy, shown in the upper part of Figure 1, is the progeny of two parents of short stature, with a midparental average of 164 cm. This subject (Fels No. 371) is short for his age, far below the average. On the other hand, subject No. 356, the daughter of tall parents, is well above the age-size average for girls. These two cases exemplify the need for parent-specific age-size standards. Where parental size is known, such standards are a vast improvement over the conventional average approach. See also Garn and Rohmann (1966).*

tot, even though the physician is himself an outstanding authority on child growth, and an early contributor to *Child Development*. For subject 371, parent-specific size standards for statural growth would have been distinctly useful. Clearly, there is a large proportion of children, the progeny of tall parents and the progeny of short parents, for whom conventional age-size standards are inappropriate and, in fact, deceptive.

PRELIMINARY PARENT-SPECIFIC AGE-SIZE STANDARDS   Despite the obvious need for parent-specific age-size standards for boys and girls, such have not been previously available. A parent-specific age-size table broken down into but two or three parental size categories would require a minimum of 200–300 boys and girls measured at each age, and 400–600 parents measured too. Given two sexes, 36 half-year age intervals, and the above minimum sample size at each age, at least 14,400 boys and girls would have to be measured and 28,800 mothers and fathers. Since the task of collecting and measuring over 14,000 boys and girls and the nearly 29,000 parents would be formidable in a purely cross-sectional context, the nonexistence of parent-specific age-size standards for children up to now is rather readily understood.

However, the longitudinal approach in this instance comes to our rescue. Having stature data on children taken at exact age intervals within narrow tolerance limits (Garn and Shamir, 1958), and having parental size data as well, it is a comparatively simple matter to sort the prepunched size data of children categorized according to parental size, and so to produce parent-specific age-size standards for growing children.

A part of such a table, newly constructed for the purposes of this review, is given in Table 1. Parental size here refers to the midparent value (the average of the paternal and maternal statures) as originally suggested by Galton eighty years ago. Parental stature here refers to stature measured early in the fourth decade; only three midparent size categories are tabulated, for reasons of simplicity. These are the 163 cm (short) midparent value, the 169 cm (median) midparent value, and the 175 cm (tall) midparent value.

As shown in Table 1, the use of parental size adds an important new parameter to age-size standards for children. Even at one year of age, the children so categorized are a centimeter or more apart. At age eighteen the difference is 2.4 cm (approximately one inch) or more. Were extreme parental size categories included as in the original tabulation from which this table is abridged, the differences would be even more dramatic. But the sample size is insufficient to justify including the extreme parental size categories here.

FURTHER APPLICATIONS OF PARENT-SPECIFIC SIZE STANDARDS While the parent-specific size standards for children given in Table 1 are applicable to American-born children of the middle socioeconomic classes (lower middle to upper middle) of Northwestern European ancestry and well nourished, as judged from subcutaneous fat measurements, the applicability of these standards is potentially wider. In field situations, as in nutritional surveys, where stature standards do not yet exist, the values given in Table 1 offer the possibility of being child-appropriate to a degree not conventionally possible. They have been applied, retrospectively, to several groups, including

TABLE 1

Parent-Specific Age-Size Tables for Boys and Girls of Three Selected Midparent Values

	BOYS PARENTAL MIDPOINT				GIRLS PARENTAL MIDPOINT		
AGE	163 CM	169 CM	175 CM	AGE	163 CM	169 CM	175 CM
1–0	73.1	75.1	77.1	1–0	73.0	74.0	74.6
2–0	85.4	87.4	88.9	2–0	84.0	85.5	88.2
3–0	93.2	96.0	98.3	3–0	90.4	93.8	96.5
4–0	99.5	103.1	106.3	4–0	96.8	103.9	103.8
5–0	105.6	110.0	112.7	5–0	103.5	109.1	111.0
6–0	110.9	115.4	118.7	6–0	110.2	115.0	117.3
7–0	116.2	121.3	124.6	7–0	116.5	120.2	124.0
8–0	121.6	126.8	130.4	8–0	122.4	125.8	130.2
9–0	126.9	131.9	136.0	9–0	128.6	131.4	136.6
10–0	132.5	137.4	141.5	10–0	135.1	136.9	143.1
11–0	138.5	143.0	146.8	11–0	141.6	143.4	149.6
12–0	144.7	148.4	152.4	12–0	147.8	150.3	155.8
13–0	151.0	154.9	159.6	13–0	154.2	157.0	161.7
14–0	158.8	161.6	167.8	14–0	158.8	160.4	165.9
15–0	165.8	167.9	174.7	15–0	159.8	162.2	168.4
16–0	169.4	172.8	176.6	16–0	160.5	163.4	169.7
17–0	170.9	175.4	177.8	17–0	160.8	164.0	170.9
18–0	171.5	176.2	178.6	18–0	161.0	164.3	171.8

The values shown are based on fully longitudinal analyses of the statural growth of more than 500 children representing in excess of 12,000 observations in all. The midparent value, here the average of paternal and maternal statures, refers to parental size at age thirty. To use, determine the midparent stature and present age of the child in question, reading out in the sex-appropriate column.

SOURCE: Fels Parent-Specific Size Tables for Midparent Categories shown smoothed and arranged by James Eagen. See Garn and Rohmann (1966).

the Aleut of Umnak and Atka in the Aleutians, for whom parental stature is individually available. For the Aleut children stature estimates based on parental size and using the appropriate Fels midparental size categories came remarkably close to observed individual size data.

New parent-specific size standards for children based on contemporary cross-sectional data and with parental size carefully measured (not reported) would be the ideal solution. It would be an immense undertaking, however, as mentioned above. A practical expedient might be to combine data from extant longitudinal studies (Harvard, Fels, Denver).

SIZE, CHROMOSOMES, AND SEX

At nearly all ages, as shown in Table 1, the human male is taller than the female, a point misconstrued in some elementary texts. At equal maturity levels, holding physiological age constant, sex difference in stature is even greater. Males are considerably taller than females at comparable levels of maturation and the fat-free weight is then far greater in the male (Fomon, 1966;

Owen et al., 1966). The 7 per cent sexual dimorphism in body size that may be seen after sexual maturity, the 3 per cent to 5 per cent sex difference in tooth size, and the 30 per cent sexual dimorphism in the adult lean body mass have their beginnings well before birth.

Final differences in size have their origin in pituitary timing and in the type and amount of steroid mediation. The male continues to grow for a longer time than the female, and the magnitude of the steroid-mediated adolescent growth spurt is generally larger. The total muscle mass and particularly the muscles of the upper back and shoulders are disproportionately responsive to androgenic (masculinizing) steroids. But many size differences, such as those in the size of the permanent teeth, which form in the jaws prepubertally, owe nothing to the later mechanisms of hormonal differentiation.

The sexual dimorphism in body size prior to puberty most likely has its origin in the Y chromosome, that small chromosome which apparently contains little but genes affecting size and sex. Y-containing chromosomal types, the normal XY and XXY, and to some extent the XXXY, appear to be taller than the non-Y chromosomal types, the XO, the normal XX, the XXX, and so on. Thus it is reasonable to believe that the difference between the normal XY (male) and the normal XX (female) has to do with genes on the Y chromosome. However, it also may be observed that the XO chromosomal type (Turner's syndrome) is generally smaller than the normal XX even in prepubertal life. To some extent, as suggested by a recent paper of Gorlin, Redman, and Shapiro (1965), early maturation and abnormalities of development increase with the number of chromosomes (XXX, XXXY, etc.).

Contrasting the long legs, narrow shoulders, and broad hips of subjects with Klinefelter's syndrome (XXY) with the short legs, broad shoulders, and narrow hips of Turner's syndrome (XO), Shimaguchi and associates (1964) suggest that the X chromosome includes genes affecting body build and body length. Tanner and his colleagues (1959) comment on the role of the X and Y chromosomes in skeletal maturation and therefore final size. However, the haploid XO is more than just a subject who never matures. There are multiple developmental defects wherever the number of sex chromosomes is less than or greater than two. So the extent of X and Y determination of the sexual dimorphism in size and development can only partially be ascertained by comparing the haploid XO with the XX and XY and those diploid chromosomal types with the polyploid XXY, XXXY, etc.

PARENT–CHILD SIZE SIMILARITIES AND THEIR CHROMOSOMAL BASES   Apart from the sexual dimorphism in size, which currently may be attributed to the Y chromosome in part, it is possible to estimate the extent to which sex chromosomes are involved in the determination of normal body size from various parent-child and sibling size correlations. Father–son and brother–brother stature correlations represent a test of Y-linkage. Father–daughter and sister–sister correlations provide a test of X-linkage (for fathers and daughters have the paternal X chromosome in common).

However, viewing complete parent–child size correlations, such as are given in Table 2, it would appear that the bulk of variance in stature is determined by autosomal genes, that is, genes on the 22 pairs of chromosomes that

TABLE 2
Parent–Child Stature Correlations

	Fa–Da		Fa–So		Mo–Da		Mo–So		M–P–Da		M–P–So	
	N	r	N	r	N	r	N	r	N	r	N	r
Birth	115	.14	135	.14	128	−.06	146	.15	114	.05	134	.18
0.12	147	.12	163	.17	162	−.01	176	.13	146	.07	161	.19
0.25	151	.24	169	.05	171	.16	184	.08	150	.25	167	.07
0.50	161	.29	171	.33	181	.14	187	.26	160	.28	170	.38
0.75	160	.32	169	.07	182	.29	185	−.02	159	.38	168	.04
1.00	165	.34	177	.36	186	.23	194	.27	164	.34	175	.42
1.50	161	.36	173	.09	180	.22	188	.15	161	.37	170	.14
2.00	158	.36	168	.37	179	.28	183	.30	158	.40	166	.45
2.50	158	.42	161	.39	175	.35	175	.33	158	.49	160	.47
3.00	153	.20	167	.37	172	.13	182	.32	152	.21	166	.45
3.50	149	.38	162	.41	165	.34	173	.37	149	.46	161	.51
4.00	150	.38	163	.36	166	.30	172	.36	150	.44	162	.48
4.50	143	.38	166	.40	157	.35	172	.36	143	.47	165	.50
5.00	141	.35	163	.38	158	.33	172	.35	141	.44	162	.48
5.50	135	.38	160	.37	150	.36	167	.37	135	.47	158	.49
6.00	136	.36	162	.36	150	.32	169	.36	136	.44	160	.49
6.50	126	.37	158	.36	141	.32	163	.40	128	.45	156	.51
7.00	127	.39	155	.34	140	.28	161	.34	127	.43	153	.47
7.50	121	.38	152	.38	134	.29	155	.36	121	.43	150	.50
8.00	116	.39	146	.39	129	.27	151	.35	116	.42	145	.50
8.50	107	.40	146	.37	119	.25	151	.34	107	.42	145	.48
9.00	108	.40	142	.37	119	.24	148	.34	108	.42	141	.48
9.50	106	.36	134	.36	116	.22	138	.33	106	.38	133	.46
10.00	105	.34	130	.36	114	.19	134	.35	105	.35	129	.47
10.50	106	.30	121	.38	113	.16	126	.35	106	.34	121	.48
11.00	100	.30	115	.39	107	.11	118	.33	100	.28	114	.48
11.50	99	.31	112	.40	104	.10	116	.35	99	.29	112	.49
12.00	95	.33	110	.40	100	.15	144	.31	95	.32	110	.46
12.50	91	.35	110	.38	95	.20	114	.29	91	.35	110	.45
13.00	91	.37	105	.36	96	.21	109	.28	91	.38	105	.42
13.50	87	.40	102	.35	91	.32	106	.25	87	.45	102	.40
14.00	85	.37	100	.34	89	.34	104	.27	85	.45	100	.41
14.50	82	.40	95	.31	86	.40	99	.34	82	.50	95	.42
15.00	80	.40	94	.32	84	.43	99	.36	80	.51	94	.43
15.50	74	.49	87	.33	77	.48	91	.33	74	.59	87	.41
16.00	76	.46	84	.34	79	.48	87	.36	76	.58	84	.45
16.50	69	.48	85	.37	73	.49	89	.45	69	.59	85	.50
17.00	69	.47	80	.33	73	.49	83	.41	69	.58	80	.46
17.50	64	.48	75	.35	67	.50	79	.46	64	.60	75	.47
18.00	65	.49	77	.33	69	.51	80	.38	65	.61	77	.46

This table which summarizes like-sexed and unlike-sexed parent-child correlations at half-year intervals through eighteen years is based upon complete serial-longitudinal size data from the Fels studies. The fact that father-son correlations do not exceed mother-son correlations argues against Y-linked inheritance, and the fact that father-son correlations are of the magnitude that they are represents evidence against X-linkage. Taken together, it appears that size is largely determined by autosomal genes and that somewhat less than 50 per cent of size variance is accounted for by genes held in common by the child and both parents. For details, see text. See also Fisher (1918) and Hewitt (1957).

have nothing to do with sex. Father–son correlations are not uniformly higher than mother–son correlations, and so on. There is a suggestion, in the shifting magnitude of correlations after puberty, that X-mediation may perhaps be involved in part but autosomal inheritance is still largely indicated. (See also Garn and Rohmann, 1966.)

In other parameters of human physical development, notably ossification timing and tooth calcification, the X chromosome seems to be disproportionately involved (Garn et al., 1965; Garn and Rohmann, 1962). Tanner and associates (1959) have compared normal males (XY), Turner's syndrome (XO), and Kleinfelter's syndrome (XXY) in an attempt to ascertain the role of the X and Y chromosomes in maturational timing.

However, the data newly presented in detail in Table 3 show the difficulty of demonstrating other than autosomal mediation of normal variations in stature at the present time. While the fact that father–daughter correlations exceed father–son correlations after age thirteen would implicate the X chromosome in part, exactly the same trend holds for the mother. That is, the mother–daughter correlations also exceed the mother–son correlations after age thirteen, and here the maternal contribution (an X chromosome in either case) is presumably equal. Accordingly, then, it is reasonable to say that the bulk of genes affecting stature within a sex are located on the autosomes, but that some measure of X-mediation appears to be superimposed. (See also Fisher, 1918; Hewitt, 1957.)

THE NUTRITIONAL MODIFICATION OF BODY SIZE

The proposition that body size can be modified by nutrition during growth needs scarce qualification today. It can be documented from the prenatal period through the completion of epiphyseal union. It can be shown experimentally in laboratory animals (Dickerson and McCance, 1961; Platt and Stewart, 1962) and it can be shown by a multitude of natural experiments, including famines, in man. It can be shown in relation to nutritional status, rating separately the caloric intake, the protein intake, and intake of fat-soluble vitamins. It can be shown in relation to socioeconomic status, where such status reflects the caloric reserve. The nutritional modification of stature and body size can also be demonstrated in malabsorption syndromes, where available nutrients are unable to pass through the gut. Regulating the amount of food available, within broad limits, regulates body size (Acheson, 1960).

Prenatally, body size can be modified by maternal nutrition up to a point. In famine situations, the body size of the newborn is reduced if the maternal caloric intake falls below 1,500 calories per day (Antonov, 1947; Smith, 1947a,b). Neonates in starvation areas and where protein-calorie malnutrition is common are smaller than are the newborn in Northwest Europe, the United States, New Zealand, and Australia. Still, depriving the mother has relatively less effect on her baby than might be suspected because of the peculiarly "parasitic" nature of the maternal-fetal relationship (Smith, 1947b).

Knowing this, the inability to control fetal size by adjusting the maternal caloric intake during pregnancy is better understood. There was a time when we tried to prevent overly large babies by dietary control measures. We established the twenty-pound rule, which is, that the mother should not gain more than twenty pounds during any single pregnancy. We now know that the twenty-pound rule has a cosmetic effect (keeping the mother from gaining excess fat during pregnancy) but it does not materially reduce the size of the infant at birth.

But if limited dietary attempts to manipulate birth size are relatively ineffective, intrauterine control of prenatal nutrition can still be demonstrated. Twins, particularly those monozygotic (single-egg) twins sharing a common placenta, are individually smaller than might be expected for their gestation length. Both monozygotic and dizygotic (separate-egg) twins compete for nutrients prenatally: in one sense twins are "starved" newborn. The same may be shown in some developmentally mature but extremely small full-term infants whose placental growth has been restricted and thus incapable of providing a full flow of nutrients. That such prenatal nutritional limitations may have a permanent effect is suggested when the smaller monozygotic twin at birth remains the smaller twin throughout life, i.e., the "runt" effect.

After birth and through the time of weaning there are numerous limitations on body size. In underdeveloped areas undergoing acculturation, the bottle-fed baby may be at a major disadvantage, for the "milk" is often highly diluted reconstituted milk and sanitary measures are nonexistent. The infant may thus be deprived nutritionally and subject to multiple diarrheas. In overdeveloped nations, on the other hand, the bottle-fed baby may become bigger than the breast-fed baby, the milkman having an endless supply compared with the mother. Now the point here is not bottle feeding versus breast feeding, but rather that the nutritional quality of the infant's diet affects the rate of growth. At the same time, we must consider the complex interaction of nutrition and infection (Scrimshaw and Béhar, 1961; Scrimshaw, Taylor, and Gordon, 1959). Growth of infants in many countries today is inhibited by diarrheas and other infections. At the same time, infants with suboptimal nutrition, particularly infants deprived of good quality protein, are more subject to diarrheas and other infections. So size in infancy is both directly influenced by nutrition and indirectly influenced by the diseases that malnutrition breeds.

Today, malnutrition and especially protein-calorie malnutrition (PCM) inhibit the growth of millions of preschool children in Central Asia, South America, Africa, Asia, India, and the Middle East (May, 1965). It is not infrequent in nutrition surveys to discover that such children in protein-calorie malnutrition areas average below the fifth percentile by recent American or English size standards or even below the first percentile. Such malnutrition has an economic basis, where calories and especially quality protein are in short supply. However, the problem is cultural as well. There may be excessive dependence upon a single cereal or root crop such as corn, manioc, or rice, each with its own characteristic limiting amino acids. Or, even where legumes and other crops abound, nutritional knowledge may be defective so that children are not given readily available foods that are necessary for their growth. In making the transition from the agricultural village to the industrial town, weaning may be premature, depriving the infant of good quality human milk protein and substituting a thin gruel of corn or a highly diluted watered "milk" with sugar added for calories. Vitamin-rich and protein-rich foods may be withheld from the preschool child under the mistaken notion that such "strong" foods are harmful. Small wonder that in such cultures and subcultures infant mortality is excessively high, those who survive are stunted and small, and both infants and children are particularly prone to infection, as described in the recent National Academy of Sciences conference on malnutrition in the preschool child (1966) and in the earlier conference volume on tropical health (National Academy of Sciences, 1962).

MALNUTRITION, SIZE, AND BEHAVIORAL DELAY   Recent studies on protein-calorie malnutrition (PCM) have suggested behavioral delay as well as delayed maturation and inadequate size attainment as a consequence. Children from protein-malnutrition areas of Central and South Africa are comparable to American children in psychomotor development during their first six months of life, or even ahead, but they tend to fall behind thereafter (Dean, 1954; Geber and Dean, 1957). Such behavioral delay is particularly pronounced in acute protein-calorie malnutrition, in the diseases known as *kwashiorkor* and *marasmus*. As studied in Mexico City and in Guatemala City, the degree of psychomotor delay is proportional to the degree of retardation in size. Some authorities have viewed this delay in the motoric, manipulative, and language development as indicative of major central nervous system impairment (Brown, 1965; Dean, 1954; Geber and Dean, 1957; Scrimshaw and Béhar, 1961; Stoch and Smythe, 1963).

Now behavioral abnormalities may be produced in experimental animals by giving them a diet deficient in quality protein (Moore et al., 1964). So the facts are clear enough. Attainment of various items on the Gesell schedule—creeping, crawling, standing, walking, drawing, using three words, pointing to parts of the body, and following the geometrical forms—may be delayed in geographical areas where protein malnutrition is common. Viewing a ward full of children hospitalized with kwashiorkor, one is impressed with their lethargy and their behavioral retardation. But the question is whether the behavioral delay is a simple function of the lethargy and malaise associated with acute illness, where the child has no real interest in his environment. Or it may be possible that the children with protein-calorie malnutrition are suffering from very real brain damage. It is possible that there is delayed cerebral growth in early kwashiorkor and marasmus. It is suggested, though by no means proven, that the consequences of protein-calorie malnutrition are both statural and psychological retardation, even persisting through adulthood (Stoch and Smythe, 1963) and involving deficient brain growth (Brown, 1965).

NUTRITION AND SIZE AT MATURITY

There is a jump in years from the preschool infant to the adolescent, and from malnutrition to overnutrition, but the same general principles apply. The poorer the state of nutrition, the smaller the size, the later the onset of sexual maturity, and the later the completion of growth. Thus, size and sexual maturity tend to be advanced in the higher socioeconomic groups and delayed in the lower. Similarly, menarche is earlier in fatter girls, in some cases by two or three years or more. Demonstrably, overnutrition as measured by obesity results in acceleration of the maturational process in both sexes. Fat children are more mature and bigger earlier (Garn and Haskell, 1960; Quaade, 1955; Wolff, 1955). While children can be stuffed into early maturity, as they can be starved into late maturity, it is not known how broadly these generalizations apply. Early maturing children are certainly bigger earlier, but they stop growing sooner. Starved children are late to mature but obviously may grow for a longer period of time. While there is compensatory growth, it has its limits; otherwise well-nourished and starved populations would tend to be alike in adult stature (Howe and Schiller, 1952).

The effects of nutrition on size are complicated. In man, malnutrition is rarely just a restriction in calories. Many of the malnourished populations of the world are short on fats and especially short on animal protein. In the several Guatemalan villages we have studied in conjunction with INCAP, the caloric intake in four-year-old children is approximately a third less than that of age-matched children in the Fels Longitudinal series. (See Figure 2.) On the other hand, protein intake in these Guatemalan villages ranges below 50 per cent of what comparable children in Ohio have to eat. And finally, as shown in Figure 2, the intake of *animal protein* is particularly restricted in these Guatemalan Indian villages so that the children from the villages of Santa Maria and

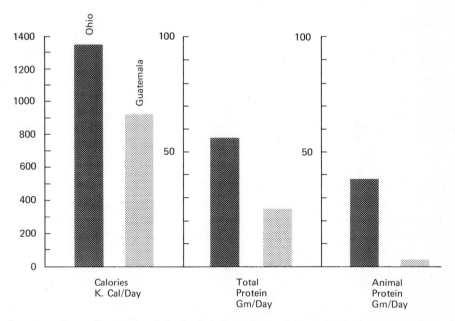

FIGURE 2.   *Comparative daily intakes of calories, protein, and animal protein in four-year-old children from southwestern Ohio and from two Mayan villages in Guatemala. The Mayan Indian children consume 30 per cent fewer calories, 50 to 60 per cent less protein, and 90 to 95 per cent less animal protein. These data, abridged from cooperative studies by the Institute of Nutrition of Central America and Panama (INCAP) and the Fels Research Institute, provide a dramatic example of how nutritional parameters restrict body size. Here animal protein becomes the limiting factor, not just for growth but for actual survival (see text).*

Santa Cruz average less than 10 per cent as much animal protein as do the children from Southwestern Ohio. It is the quality protein of animal origin much more than the caloric intake as a whole that appears to be the growth-limiting factor, and, along with being growth-restricting, protein deficiency predisposes the children in these areas of malnutrition per se. A program of protein-calorie supplementation now being carried out in the village of Santa Catarina promises to effect a "secular trend" in short order. (See *Federation Proceedings*, 1964, p. 338.)

NUTRITION AND SIZE   While it is dangerous to overgeneralize about growth mechanisms and the mechanisms that control body size, limited generalizations can be made. Caloric deficiency on the part of the mother, below levels we ordinarily find in our country, can reduce the size of newborn. Even with an adequate supply of mother's milk, infections during the nursing period can limit growth. Limited quantity and poor quality of the post-weaning diet, combined with parasitic infestations and recurrent infections thereafter, limit growth through the adolescent period and beyond. On the other hand, supernutrition certainly promotes maximum body size and early sexual maturation. Our children have virtually unlimited access to calories; their avenues for caloric expenditure have become limited; and childhood diseases and infections have far less impact because of immunizations, antibiotics, and superior medical care.

So in man we are now able to view both nutritional extremes as they affect body size. We can measure the impact of undernutrition and consequent infection on size in much of the world. In exploring the effects of malnutrition, and in the analysis of growth improvement following nutritional supplementation, we have a partial understanding of the mechanism of secular change in size. At the same time, we can document the auxogenic or growth-promoting effects of overnutrition and of supernutrition on our own children and adolescents, and we have begun to wonder whether greater body size and earlier maturation has been purchased at the expense of predisposition to cardiovascular and atherosclerotic diseases.

SUMMARY AND CONCLUSIONS

Despite methodological considerations, which favor recumbent length, and theoretical considerations (which view stature as a complex of independent axial and appendicular segments), stature—standing height—continues to be the most used measure of body size. In infancy and childhood, as in adolescence, stature has multiple correlates with physiological, metabolic, psychomotor, and intellective performances not all of which are simply "developmental" in nature.

Over the past century, excepting wartime and depression periods, stature has increased, the more so for the least favored groups. As shown by nutritional experiments, this "secular" trend may be attributed to an increase in caloric intake, an improvement in nutritional quality, and a decrease in childhood diseases, including those associated with malnutrition. Today, areas of protein-calorie malnutrition are areas of statural stunting, apparent developmental delay, and (possibly) permanent brain damage.

The use of stature as a reference parameter is predicated upon the availability of appropriate norms or standards. Unfortunately, many such standards are twenty to fifty years out of date, and (for much of the world) rarely group-specific. In stature prediction, the use of "bone age" rather than chronological age greatly improves results. For individuals, parent-specific stature standards constitute a methodological advancement, especially for the children of tall parents and the children of short parents. A new parent-specific age-size table is given in this paper.

Apart from nutritional modifications, stature has an obvious genetic parameter, as shown from midparent versus child correlations approximating .5. Present data suggest that most of the genes affecting stature are located on the autosomes. The Y chromosome, however, appears to be responsible for the sex difference in stature and the far larger sex difference in the lean body mass. The mechanism of genetic mediation of stature is not known, though a timing effect (regulating the duration of growth) can be isolated as one determinant.

Of major interest to the behavioral sciences is the extent to which genetic and nongenetic factors affecting stature attainment directly and indirectly affect behavior.

References

ABERNETHY, E. M. Relationships between mental and physical growth. *Monogr. Soc. Res. Child Develpm.*, 1936, 1, No. 7.
ACHESON, R. M. Effects of nutrition and disease on human growth. In J. M. Tanner (Ed.), *Human growth*. Oxford: Pergamon Press, 1960.
ANTONOV, A. N. Children born during the siege of Leningrad in 1942. *J. Pediat.*, 1947, 30, 250–259.
BINNING, G. Earlier physical and mental maturity among Saskatoon public school children. *Canad. J. Publ. Hlth.*, 1958, 49, 9–17.
BOYNE, A. W. & CLARK, J. R. Secular change in the intelligence of 11-year-old Aberdeen schoolchildren. *Hum. Biol.*, 1959, 31, 325–333.
BROWN, R. E. Organ weight in malnutrition, with special reference to brain weight. Paper read at International Congress of Pediatrics, Tokyo, November 7–13, 1965.
CATTELL, P. Dentition as a measure of maturity. *Harvard Monogr. Educ.* Cambridge: Harvard Univ. Press, 1928, No. 9.
DEAN, R. F. A. Standards for African children and the influence of nutrition. *J. Trop. Med.*, 1954, 57, 283–289.
DICKERSON, J. W. T. & McCANCE, R. A. Severe undernutrition in growing and adult animals: 8. The dimensions and chemistry of the long bones. *Brit. J. Nutr.*, 1961, 15, 567–576.
DOUGLAS, J. W. B., ROSS, J. M., & SIMPSON, H. R. The relation between height and measured educational ability in school children of the same social class, family size and stage of physical development. *Hum. Biol.*, 1965, 37, 178–186.
Federation Proceedings, 1964, 24, No. 2, Part I.
FISHER, R. A. The correlation between relatives on the supposition of Mendelian inheritance. *Trans. Roy. Soc. Edinb.*, 1918, 52, 399–433.
FOMON, S. Body composition of the infant. Part I: The male reference infant. In F. Falkner (Ed.), *Human Development*. Philadelphia: W. B. Saunders, 1966.
FULLER, J. L. & THOMPSON, W. L. *Behavior genetics*. New York: Wiley, 1960.

GARN, S. M. Determinants of size and growth during the first three years. *Mod. Prob. Pediat.*, 1962, **7**, 50–54.

———. Human biology and research in body composition. *Ann. N. Y. Acad. Sci.*, 1963, **110**, 429–446.

———. The applicability of North American growth standards in developing countries. *Canad. med. Ass. J.*, 1965, **93**, 914–919.

———. Malnutrition and skeletal development in the pre-school child. In *Pre-school child malnutrition—primary deterrent to human progress.* Washington: National Research Council—National Academy of Sciences, 1966.

———, CLARK, A., LANDKOF, L., & NEWELL, L. Parental body-build and developmental progress in their offspring. *Science*, 1960, **132**, 1555–1556.

——— & HASKELL, J. A. Fat thickness and developmental status in childhood and adolescence. *Amer. J. Dis. Child.*, 1960, **99**, 746–751.

———, LEWIS, A. B., & KEREWSKY, R. S. Genetic, nutritional, and maturational correlates of dental development. *J. dent. Res.*, 1965, **44**, 228–242.

——— & ROHMANN, C. G. X-linked inheritance of developmental timing in man. *Nature*, 1962, **196**, 695–696.

——— & ROHMANN, C. G. Interaction of nutrition and genetics in the timing of growth and development. *Pediat. Clin. N. Amer.*, 1966, **13**, 353–379.

——— & SHAMIR, Z. *Methods for research in human growth.* Springfield, Ill.: Charles C Thomas, 1958.

GEBER, M. & DEAN, R. F. A. Gesell test on African children. *Pediatrics*, 1957, **20**, 1055–1065.

GORLIN, R. J. REDMAN, R. S., & SHAPIRO, B. L. Effect of X-chromosome aneuploidy on jaw growth. *J. dent. Res.*, 1965, **44**, 269–282.

HEWITT, D. Some familial correlations in height, weight and skeletal maturity. *Ann. Hum. Genet.*, 1957, **22**, 26–35.

HOWE, P. E. & SCHILLER, M. Growth responses of the school child to changes in diet and environmental factors. *J. Appl. Physiol.*, 1952, **5**, 51–61.

HULL, E. I. Unpublished data on Fels subject material, 1966.

KAGAN, J. & GARN, S. M. A constitutional correlate of early intellective functioning. *J. genet. Psychol.*, 1963, **102**, 83–89.

LJUNG, B.-O. The adolescent spurt in mental growth. *Stockholm Stud. in Educ. Psych.* Uppsala: Almquist & Wiksell, 1965.

MOORE, A. U., BARNES, R. H., POND, W. G., MACLEOD, R. B., RICCIUTI, H. N., & KROOK, L. Behavioral abnormality associated with a kwashiorkor-like syndrome in pigs. *Fed. Proc.*, 1964, **23**, 397.

MURDOCK, K. & SULLIVAN, L. R. Some evidence of an adolescent increase in the rate of mental growth. *J. educ. Psychol.*, 1922, **13**, 350–356.

National Academy of Sciences-National Research Council. *Tropical health: Publication 996.* Washington: NAS-NRC, 1962.

National Academy of Sciences-National Research Council. *Pre-school child malnutrition—primary deterrent to human progress.* Washington: NAS-NRC, 1966.

NORVAL, M. A. Relationship of weight and length of infants at birth to the age at which they begin to walk alone. *J. Pediat.*, 1947, **30**, 676–678.

OWEN, G. M., FILER, L. J., JR., MARESH, M., & FOMON, S. J. Body composition of the infant. II. Sex-related difference in body composition in infancy. In F. Falkner (Ed.), *Human Development.* Philadelphia: W. B. Saunders, 1966.

PLATT, B. S. & STEWART, R. J. C. Transverse trabeculae and osteoporosis in bones in experimental protein-calorie deficiencies. *Brit. J. Nutr.*, 1962, **16**, 483–495.

QUAADE, F. *Obese children.* Copenhagen: Danish Science Press, 1955.

RIMOIN, D. L., MERIMEE, T. J., & McKUSICK, V. A. Growth-hormone deficiency in man: An isolated, recessively inherited defect. *Science*, 1966, **152**, 1635–1637.

SCRIMSHAW, N. S. & BÉHAR, M. Protein malnutrition in young children. *Science*, 1961, **133**, 2039–2047.

——, TAYLOR, C. E., & GORDON, J. E. Interactions of nutrition and infection. *Amer. J. Med. Sci.*, 1959, **237**, 367–403.

SHIMAGUCHI, S., ASHIZAWA, K., ENDO, B., & SAKURO, H. An anthropometrical approach to the Turner's syndrome. *Zinruigaku Zassi*, 1964, **72**, 29–50.

SMITH, C. A. Effect of wartime starvation in Holland upon pregnancy and its product. *Amer. J. Obst. & Gynec.*, 1947, **53**, 599–608 (a).

——. Effects of maternal undernutrition upon the newborn infant in Holland. *J. Pediat.*, 1947, **30**, 229–243 (b).

STOCH, M. B. & SMYTHE, P. M. Does undernutrition during infancy inhibit brain growth and subsequent intellectual development? *Arch. Dis. Child.*, 1963, **38**, 546–552.

STOUDT, H. W., DAMON, A., & MACFARLAND, R. A. Heights and weights of white Americans. *Hum. Biol.*, 1960, **32**, 331–341.

TANNER, J. M. (Ed.). *Human growth.* Oxford: Pergamon Press, 1960.

——. *Growth at adolescence.* (2nd ed.) Oxford: Blackwell Scientific Publications, 1962.

——, PRADER, A., HABICH, H., & FERGUSON-SMITH, M. A. Genes on the Y chromosome influencing rate of maturation in man: skeletal age studies in Klinefelter's (XXY) and Turner's (XO) syndromes. *Lancet*, 1959, **2**, 141–144.

WOLFF, O. H. Obesity in childhood: a study of the birth weight, the height, and the onset of puberty. *Quart. J. Med.*, 1955, **24**, 109–123.

Fundamental Motor Skills

Anna Espenschade
UNIVERSITY OF CALIFORNIA

Running, jumping, and throwing are common elements in active games. Throughout the growing years boys and girls have opportunities for frequent participation in these and so develop these capacities. Thus performance in running, jumping, and throwing may be used as an indication of motor ability, although it must be recognized that experience and training, interest and attitude play increasingly important parts in achievement. Since these are the same basic activities that are important indicators of motor development in early and middle childhood, it is possible to study age changes and sex differences over a wide age range. Two measures of jumping have been consistently used— the standing broad jump and the jump and reach. Although techniques have differed slightly in some cases, the number of comparable records is considerable. Running events have been given less frequently probably due to space limitations or safety factors. Then, too, the distances vary by age and sex. However, the number of yards per second can be computed from available records and

From pp. 430–437 (including figures and References) in "Motor Development" by Anna Espenschade from *Science and Medicine of Exercise and Sports* edited by Warren R. Johnson. Copyright © 1960 by Warren R. Johnson. Reprinted by permission of Harper & Row, Publishers, Inc.

so the data may be made roughly comparable. In throwing, the event commonly selected is a distance throw but the size and weight of ball and measurement of records differ somewhat from study to study. In so far as possible, comparable scores have been obtained. The results are presented in Table 1 and Figures 1, 2, 3, and 4. Norms in many cases are given according to classification by age, height, and weight, so the actual scores selected from these tables are those of the "average" boy or girl.

All studies agree in showing increase in scores by age for boys from the earliest measures made in childhood to those taken in the last year of high

TABLE 1
Age Changes in Motor Performance

AGE	RUN YARDS PER SEC	STANDING BROAD JUMP (INCHES)	JUMP AND REACH (INCHES)	BRACE (SCORE)	DISTANCE THROW (FEET)
			BOYS		
5	3.8	33.7	2.5		23.6
6	4.2	37.4	4.0	5.5	32.8
7	4.6	41.6	6.1	7.5	42.3
8	5.1	46.7	8.3	9.0	57.4
9		50.4	8.5	10.0	66.6
10	5.9	54.7	11.0	11.0	83.0
11	6.1	61.0	11.5	11.1	95.0
12	6.3	64.9	12.2	12.7	104.0
13	6.5	69.3	12.5	13.1	114.0
14	6.7	73.2	13.3	14.5	123.0
15	6.8	79.5	14.8	15.2	135.0
16	7.1	88.0	16.3	16.2	144.0
17	7.2	88.4	16.9	(15.9)	153.0
			GIRLS		
5	3.6	31.6	2.2		14.5
6	4.1	36.2	3.5	5.5	17.8
7	4.4	40.0	5.7	7.5	25.4
8	4.6	45.9	7.7	9.0	30.0
9		51.3	8.7	10.0	38.7
10	5.8		10.5	10.5	47.0
11	6.0	52.0	11.0	11.1	54.0
12	6.1		11.2	11.8	61.0
13	6.3	62.1	11.0	11.8	70.0
14	6.2	62.7	11.8	11.9	74.5
15	6.1	63.2	12.2	11.5	75.7
16	6.0	63.0	12.0	11.8	74.0
17	5.9				

SOURCE: References 2, 3, 4, 6, 7, 8, 9, 10, 12, 13, 14, 15, 17, 19, 20, 21, 25, 26. Scores presented are averages from available reports.

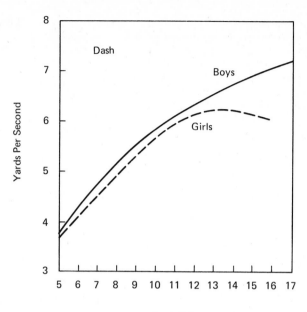

FIGURE 1.   *Running.*

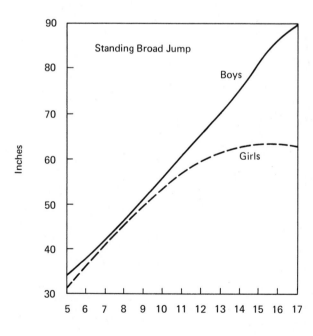

FIGURE 2.   *Standing broad jump.*

283

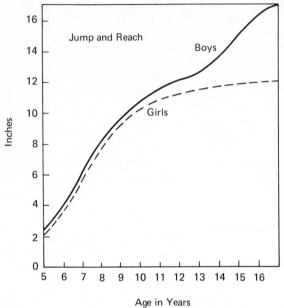

FIGURE 3.   *Jump and reach.*

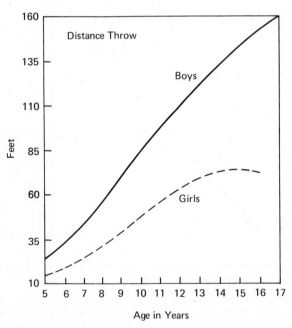

FIGURE 4.   *Distance throw.*

school. Girls show improvement throughout the early school years but scores reach their maximum as early as 13 years of age in running and jumping and show little change after 13 in distance throwing. Physical size and strength measures continue to increase well beyond this age level so this cessation of change cannot be due to attainment of physical maturity. Some authors have attributed it to adolescent changes in build and development of secondary sexual characteristics. However, there is considerable evidence of loss of interest due to cultural influences. An explanation in terms of capacity seems less tenable than one in terms of motivation.

Sex differences are present in all events at almost all age levels, but, due to the changing inflection of the curves for boys and for girls after 13 years, differences increase markedly after this time. Times in the 40- or 50-yard dash are quite close for boys and girls aged 11 and 12, but boys are consistently superior. In jumping and especially in throwing, the boys excel at every age level. The magnitude of the difference in throwing is remarkable and is out of proportion to those in any other physical measure. This difference is confined to distance throwing, however, and does not apply to target throwing at short distances. Differential practice seems insufficient to account for these results but certainly no other reasons have been advanced to date to throw light on these facts.

The relation between pubescence and performance in these basic activities has been studied on several occasions. In 1925, Atkinson (2) published an analysis of records from 9000 Philadelphia high school girls in six events. When the data were grouped according to those who had not yet reached the menarche, those who were one year beyond and so on up to seven years, no marked deviations in mean scores were found from those by chronological age. However, a study of the best performances showed that they were made by the developmental extremes. In jumping, throwing for distance, and basketball goal shooting, girls maturing very late excelled. In the running events, and in ropeclimbing, the early maturing girls excelled.

In the California Adolescent Study (8) it was possible to group the girls according to age deviation from menarche but there were very few cases studied as early as a year before this time. When chronological age was held constant, correlations between physiological maturity and performance in most events was negligible.

The picture for boys is different, however, and resembles more closely the findings in relation to strength. McCloy (15) investigated the influence of pubescence on performance and found it of some significance but discarded it as a factor in classification because of the difficulty in assessing stage of pubescence and the fact that its influence extends over a limited age range.

More recently Nevers (19) has shown the relationship between a combined score in five track events (running, jumping, shot put) and the McCloy classification index, for each of three pubescent groups. Pre- and postpubescent boys improve steadily at each class but pubescent boys of all classes seem to score approximately the same number of points. The rate of gain and the actual scores are greater for postpubescents at all overlapping indices. These results differ from those obtained by the same author in strength measures, especially in regard to performance of the pubescent group.

The determination of physiological maturity in the California Adolescent Study was on a different basis, and three phases or zones of pubescence were tentatively identified. When the several motor tests were correlated with this estimate of physiological maturity (chronological age held constant) the highest relationship was found to be with the distance throw, the lowest with the broad jump. Percentage change in performance according to zones of maturity was of especial interest as it appeared that boys in Zones II, III, and in early maturity each improved approximately equal amounts in the dash, whereas in both jumps, the largest proportion of change occurred in Zone II and in the distance throw in Zone III. Thus the pubescent boy gains steadily in running, rather abruptly and early in jumping and somewhat later in throwing (8). This is in accord with the physical growth sequence in which legs lengthen and hips widen earlier than shoulder girdle development occurs.

Each of these basic activities differs from the others not only in developmental pattern but in qualities required for performance. This is readily seen when test scores are intercorrelated. It is true, of course, that errors of measurement must be considered in studying relationships found. In running events, stop-watch timing even when carefully done is subject to considerable error. This is especially true in the case of records for young children when the distance run is only 35 or 40 yards. The additional problems in testing children—of simple, clear directions which the child surely understands, of attention span, of interest and effort, may all contribute to error. Experienced experimenters, however, have obtained reliabilities in running events of .88 (10) for 4–6-year-olds, and coefficients of the order of .9 are frequently reported for older children.

Jumping can be measured still more accurately, especially the broad jump. Reliability coefficients range from .82–.89 for elementary school children to .95 or above for senior high school boys. Throwing tends to be highly reliable when reasonable care in procedures is maintained. Coefficients of the order of .9 to .98 may be obtained.

It should be noted that measurement in these events is least consistent in young children and in girls and in the case of older boys is especially reliable. Quite possibly motivation is a factor here. Certainly reliability may be expected to influence the intercorrelations computed between the several events. Actually, very few studies are available on young children in which this interrelationship has been studied. Indeed, the literature does not yield many studies at any ages in which exactly the same events have been interrelated. Since standard track and field events for boys ordinarily include a shot-put and it has been considered easier to administer than a throw for distance, many studies on boys have selected this event. McCloy (15) has shown that either a distance throw or a shot-put may be used in combination with running and jumping to predict "total points" on a larger number of track and field events for boys. The majority of physical activity programs for girls do not include a shot-put, however. As the technique of performance must be learned, this event ordinarily cannot be used as a test for girls.

Intercorrelations between the dash, broad jump, jump and reach, and indoor baseball (softball) throw for distance as reported by a number of investigators are given in Table 2. Certainly no consistent trends are evidenced. There does seem to be a tendency for relationships between events for boys to be

TABLE 2
Intercorrelations Reported by Various Investigators

Age	Dash with Broad Jump		Ref.	Dash with Distance Throw	
	Boys	Girls		Boys	Girls
49–78 mo.	.53		(10)	.36	
1st 3 grades	.475	.576	(5)	.244	.442
10–14 yr.		.61	(16)		.43
10–13 yr.	.665		(unpub.)	.502	
Jr. H.S.	.642		(22)	.545	
	.787		(23)		
	.64	.61	(8)	.38	.51
	.67	.64	(8)	.48	.44
Sr. H.S.	.44		(15)		
	.76		(15)		
	.58	.60	(11)		
	.48	.45	(8)	.38	.41
	.49		(8)	.24	.23
		.57	(20)		

Age	Broad Jump and Distance Throw		Ref.	Broad Jump with Jump and Reach	
	Boys	Girls		Boys	Girls
49–78 mo.	.41		(10)	.53	
1st 3 grades	.311	.441	(5)	.401	.547
8 year	.58	.35	(24)	.63	.62
10–13 yr.	.53		(unpub.)		
10–14 yr.			(16)		.49
Jr. H.S.	.721		(22)		
	.39	.45	(8)	.42	.30
	.60	.51	(8)	.45	.37
Sr. H.S.	.46	.48	(8)	.65	.56
	.47	.42	(8)	.51	.64
			(1)	.604	

greater at the junior high school level than before or after this time. In the case of the girls, however, correlations are of approximately the same order at all age levels. Those between dash and broad jump are approximately .6 while those between dash and distance throw and between distance throw and broad jump average more nearly .4. More investigators have reported figures for boys and less consistency appears among these. It would certainly be premature in the light of the available evidence to draw conclusions in regard to the organization of motor abilities in children of 6–18 years.

Nor are factor analysis studies adequate to throw real light on this subject.

Analyses of this type have been made for the most part on data from college men. Selection of tests given and resulting emphasis in factors extracted has been different in the different studies. Although strength or power and speed or velocity are identified in practically all cases, these two factors are not adequate to account for all components underlying performances in running, jumping, and throwing. And the relative importance of even these factors is not firmly established.

In tracing the course of development of postural-locomotor control from infancy through adolescence, two basic concepts emerge. Structure and function are found to be closely interrelated at all times; there are wide individual differences in rate of maturation, but the over-all pattern of development is the same for all. In infancy, developing neural structures especially seem to bring about rapid changes in motor behavior. Sex differences in rate of maturation may be observed in childhood in the earlier age at which girls perform such activities as hopping and skipping in comparison to boys. At puberty, a marked change in rate of development is again evident. In boys, the postpubescent period is one of continuing development in motor performance; in girls little change appears after puberty. It must be recognized that the marked sex differences at adolescence are due in part to experience and training, interests and attitudes, as well as to capacity.

Motor performances dependent upon strength and power are closely related to size and build at all ages. Balance and coordination show little relationship to physique or strength at any one time but do increase with age. There is some evidence to show retardation in growth in balance during the period of most rapid physical growth, at puberty. In spite of these differing growth patterns, measures of coordination, of running, jumping, and throwing are substantially intercorrelated at all ages, 4–17. It is possible, that the cross-sectional data, including as they do a range of maturity levels, may obscure the true picture here as is true for the curves of growth. It may be that maturity itself operates as a factor to increase the size of the intercorrelations.

Extensive data on the same children over this entire age span are needed to answer fully the questions raised in this review, but a variety of investigations of smaller scope may make substantial contributions to this field.

References

1. ANDERSON, THERESA, & McCLOY, C. H. The measurement of sports ability in high school girls. *Res. quart.*, 1947, **18**, 2–11.
2. ATKINSON, R. K. A motor efficiency study of eight thousand New York City high school boys. *Amer. Phys. Educ. Rev.*, 1924, **29**, 56–59.
3. ———. A study of athletic ability of high school girls. *Amer. Phys. Educ. Rev.*, 1925, **30**, 389–399.
4. BLISS, J. G. A study of progression based on age, sex, and individual differences in strength and skill. *Amer. Phys. Educ. Rev.*, Jan & Feb. 1927, **32**, 11–21; **32**, 85–99.
5. CARPENTER, AILEEN. Tests of motor educability for the first three grades. *Child Develpm.*, 1940, **11**, 293–99.
6. COZENS, F. W., CUBBERLEY, HAZEL, & NEILSON, N. P. *Achievement scales in physical education activities for secondary school girls and college women.* New York: Barnes, 1937.

7. ———, TRIEB, M. H., & NEILSON, N. P. *Physical education achievement scales in activities for boys in secondary schools*. New York: Barnes, 1936.
8. ESPENSCHADE, ANNA. Motor performance in adolescence. *Soc. Res. in Child Develpm. Monogr.*, 1940, **5**, 1.
9. ———. Development of motor coordination in boys and girls. *Res. quart.*, 1947, **18**, 30–43.
10. HARTMAN, DORIS M. The hurdle jump as a measure of the motor proficiency of young children. *Child Develpm.*, 1943, **14**, 201–211.
11. HUTTO, L. E. Measurement of the velocity factor and of athletic power in high school boys. *Res. quart.*, 1938, **9**, 109–128.
12. JENKINS, L. M. *A comparative study of motor achievements of children five, six and seven years of age*. New York: Teachers College, Columbia University, Contribution to Education, no. 414, 1930.
13. KANE, R. J., & MEREDITH, H. V. Ability in the standing broad jump of elementary school children 7, 9, and 11 years of age. *Res. quart.*, 1952, **23**, 198–208.
14. LATCHAW, MARJORIE. Measuring selected motor skills in fourth, fifth and sixth grades. *Res. quart.*, 1954, **25**, 439–499.
15. McCLOY, C. H. *Measurement of athletic power*. New York: Barnes, 1932.
16. McCRAW, L. W. A factor analysis of motor learning. *Res. quart.*, 1949, **20**, 316–335.
17. NEILSON, N. P., & COZENS, F. W. *Achievement scales in physical education activities*. Sacramento: State Dept. of Education, 1934.
18. NELSON, CAROLINE E. The effect of motor ability and previous training upon the achievement and learning of sport skills in the ninth grade. Unpublished M.A. thesis, Univ. of California, 1950.
19. NEVERS, J. E. The effects of physiological age on motor achievement. *Res. quart.*, 1948, **19**, 103–110.
20. Physical performance levels for high school girls. *Education for Victory*, 1945, **3**, 1–4.
21. POOLE, MARGARET. Physical performance levels for high school girls. Unpublished M.A. thesis, Univer. of California, 1946.
22. POWELL, ELIZABETH, & HOWE, E. C. Motor ability tests for high school girls. *Res. quart.*, 1939, 10, 81–88.
23. RAGSDALE, C. E., & BRECHENFELD, I. J. The organization of physical and motor traits in junior high school boys. *Res. quart.*, 1934, **5**, 47–55.
24. SEASHORE, H. G. The development of a beam walking test and its use in measuring development of balance in children. *Res. quart.*, 1947, **18**, 246–259.
25. SEILS, L. G. The relationship between measures of physical growth and gross motor performance of primary-grade school children. *Res. quart.*, 1951, **22**, 244–260.
26. TEMPLE, ANDREE. Motor abilities of white and negro children of 7, 8, and 9 years of age. Unpublished M.A. thesis, Univer. of California, 1952.

Personality Characteristics of Converted Left Handers*

Harben Boutourline Young
HARVARD SCHOOL OF PUBLIC HEALTH

Robert Knapp
WESLEYAN UNIVERSITY

Summary.—Left-handed children in Italy are subjected to social opprobrium and in school are forced to forego their natural disposition in favor of right handedness. Italian-American children, on the other hand, are free from such coercion. In this study three samples of Italian children are compared with a sample of Italian-American children on personality source traits taken from Cattell's High School Personality Questionnaire. Left-handed Italian children show a consistent and statistically very secure elevation on Factor I of the Cattell scale, a finding unparalleled in the data from the American sample. While the interpretation of this particular finding is not entirely clear, it does suggest that left-handed children show a higher degree of sensitivity and self-centeredness in consequence of their forced lateral conversion.

The prevalence of left handedness has been estimated as varying from .5 to 13 per cent in different populations (Verhaegen & Ntumba, 1964; Belmont & Birch, 1963). The figure undoubtedly varies not only because of genetic influences but also according to the criteria used for determining left lateral dominance. For example, if writing with the left hand were used as the criterion, it might be that in the Northeastern United States the true figure would be somewhat raised whereas in Italy there would be apparently zero prevalence of left handers. In a cross-cultural study of young Americans of Southern Italian descent and Southern Italians in Italy we found for the United States resident population that all left handers wrote with the left hand and there was even one basic right hander who had joined them. In Italy although the true prevalence was the same as in America (about 10 per cent) not one S was a left-handed writer.

History demonstrates that considerable pains have been taken to show the inferiority of left handers. The Concise Oxford Dictionary gives among others the following meanings of left handed: "awkward, clumsy, ambiguous, double-edged, of doubtful sincerity or validity, ill-omened, sinister." Roget's Thesaurus adds for good measure, "gauche, gauchipawed, unskillful." The dominant note of pity becomes tinged with alarm as one examines further the meaning of "sinister:" of evil omen, ill-looking, of villainous aspect, wicked.

Reprinted with permission of author and publisher: Young, H. B., and Knapp, R. H. Personality characteristics of converted left handers. *Perceptual and Motor Skills*, 1965, 23, 35–40.

* The financial support of the Grant Foundation, 130 E. Fifty-ninth Street, New York, and the Wenner-Gren Foundation for Anthropological Research, 14 E. Seventy-first Street, New York, is gratefully acknowledged.

However, one by one the old ideas have had to yield. Left handers are neither less intelligent, nor lower achievers, nor more clumsy (Clark, 1957; Ihinger, 1963). There is not a higher proportion of left lateral dominants among children with reading disability (Belmont & Birch, 1965). The swing of the pendulum has presented some interesting hypotheses still to be tested, e.g., are left handers different in relation to originality and creativity? But it is an over-all impression that left lateral dominants do not differ from right handers, at least in tolerant cultures. This is a contrast to evidence that ambilaterality may be associated with poor ego strength and more maladjustment (Palmer, 1963).

The problem of the effects of forced change was presented to us by the situation described in the first paragraph of this paper where the entire population of Italian resident left handers (48 boys in a population of 724) were obliged to convert to the right side. In America no opprobrium attaches to left handedness, children are not required to "convert," and this quality is even often considered an advantage in various sports. The left-handed person in America suffers few penalties if any. In Italy, it is quite otherwise. Left handedness is considered both a moral and personal defect and regarded with widespread suspicion. The term "sinister" means both "left" and "dangerous" in Italian. As a result of this the left handed in Italy are subject to a peculiar and frequently painful personal experience not shared by their American counterparts. We were drawn to explore possible differential effects upon their development in their differing circumstances.

METHOD

SUBJECTS   Ss were all males in the age range 13 to 15. Each S from Boston, Rome, and Palermo had four grandparents from the South of Italy (defined as the regions comprising Mezzogiorno, excluding Sardegna). The Boston boys were second-generation born. The Florence boys were students at the junior and middle high schools. They were distributed as follows:

CITY	N_{tot}	LEFT LATERAL DOMINANT N	%
Boston	95	11	12
Rome	127	10	8
Palermo	108	11	10
Florence	489	27	6
Total	819	59	7

TESTS OF LATERAL DOMINANCE AND PERSONALITY SOURCE TRAITS   Clark's (1957) tests of laterality were employed.

(a) *Handedness* was determined from three tests. (1) *Clark No. 18, Throwing.* —A small box was placed on a chair. The boy stood at about 2 yards distance with the ball on the table in front of him. He was requested to pick up the ball and throw it into the box. (2) *Clark No. 12, Reaching.*—The boy was seated with his arms hanging down. The tester stood behind him holding a cylinder over his head almost out of reach but in an equally favorable position for either side. The boy was asked to reach up and take the tube. (3) *Clark No. 1, Manual rotation.*—Here a small screw-top bottle, filled with colored counters, was used. The task was to remove the top, take the counters, arrange them, put them back and then replace the top. The task was performed on three occasions and note was made of which hand was used for manipulation of the top and the counters.

(b) *Foot* preference was based on three tasks. (1) *Clark No. 5, Kicking.*—A rubber ball was placed three yards from a chair. The boy was asked to kick the ball between the legs of the chair. (2) *Clark No. 17, Hopping.*—The boy stood with his back against the wall and his feet together. He was instructed on command to commence hopping to the far side of the room. (3) *Clark No. 8, Stepping.* —The boy stood with his back against the wall and his heels touching it. On the command go he was to take two steps out from the wall.

Each of the above tests was performed three times. Ss were not informed that these were tests for lateral dominance and were left with the impression that the examiner was interested in motor skills and agility. Three tests for ear dominance and four for eye dominance were also performed, but these will not be reported here since eye and ear dimensions are not subject to coercive correction in Italy.

In order to adhere to Clark's findings as to the relative importance of these tests, a double weighting was accorded to throwing and kicking. Ss were then classified as marked right (R2), moderate right (R1), ambidextrous (0), moderate left (L1), and marked left (L2). In each of the four centers, Boston, Palermo, Rome, and Florence, a group of left handers was selected from the available samples. A control group of right handers, in every instance twice the number of left-handers, was selected from the remaining Ss in each city. In all three cities the right-handed control group was selected in such a fashion that their average Raven Progressive Matrix score (Raven, 1956; Tesi & Young, 1962) was equated with that of the left-handed Ss. The Ss then answered the High School Personality Questionnaire (Cattell & Beloff, 1957; Cattell, et al., 1961), a factor scaled instrument designed to measure personality source traits.

RESULTS

The composite score for lateral dimensions for the hand and foot tests yielded a Pearson correlation of .79 among the boys included in this study. Table 1 gives the mean raw scores for each factor of the High School Personality Questionnaire for right- and left-handed boys in each center. Between right and left handers there are no significant differences in Boston. A significant difference on Factor A (Schizothymia vs. Cyclothymia) for Palermo (left handers are more schizothymic) is not sustained in Rome or Florence. A significant difference on Factor C (ego strength) for Palermo (left handers have less ego strength) is not sustained in Rome or Florence. On Factor E (submissiveness vs. dominance) the Florence left handers are significantly more submissive but there is a reverse trend (neither significant) in Palermo and Rome. On Factor F (desurgency vs. surgency) the left-handed Palermo Ss are significantly less

TABLE 1

Raw Factor Scores on the HSPQ for Right and Left Handers in Four Cities

City		N	A	B	C	D	E	F	G	H	I	J	O	Q²	Q³	Q⁴
Boston	L	11	5.5	6.7	6.1	4.7	4.8	5.4	5.9	5.3	3.8	5.6	4.5	6.6	4.9	4.3
	R	22	5.8	6.6	5.2	5.0	5.2	5.5	6.0	5.7	4.0	5.3	4.2	5.9	5.0	4.1
					NS									NS		
Palermo	L	11	3.9	6.3	4.2	4.8	5.3	4.6	6.0	6.2	4.8	5.1	5.9	5.6	4.2	4.6
	R	22	4.9	6.4	5.8	5.1	4.5	6.2	6.1	6.2	3.4	5.2	4.9	6.0	4.5	4.9
			$p = .05$		$p < .01$			$p < .02$			$p = .02$		$p < .10$ $> .05$			
Rome	L	10	4.7	7.6	5.5	4.2	5.2	5.9	6.2	5.4	4.6	4.6	5.8	6.7	5.0	4.9
	R	20	5.2	6.7	5.8	4.5	4.7	5.6	6.4	6.1	3.3	4.9	5.3	6.6	5.0	4.8
											$p < .10$ $> .05$					
Florence	L	27	5.4	8.4	5.3	4.3	4.2	5.6	5.9	5.4	4.1	5.2	5.8	6.4	4.8	5.0
	R	49	5.5	7.6	5.5	5.1	5.3	5.4	5.5	5.2	3.0	5.1	5.9	6.2	4.3	4.9
							$p < .01$				$p < .02$					

enthusiastic and happy-go-lucky, but this is not sustained in the other two Italian centers. Only on Factor I (harria vs. premsia) is there a marked consistent trend in all three centers. The left handers are consistently more premsic, that is, more demanding, impatient, subjective, dependent, hypochondriacal. Accordingly, it will be seen that only Factor I yields consistent differences in all three Italian cities between right and left handers. The differences on Factors A, C, and F observed in the Palermo sample are not sustained in the other two cities. There is reason to believe that the cultures of Sicily and Southern Italy imposed greater penalties upon the left-handed child than those of Central, and especially of Northern Italy. But we shall not attempt here to advance any conclusive explanation of the special findings applying to the Palermo sample.

TABLE 2

Mean Scores on Cattell's Factor I for Right and Left Handers in Three Italian Cities

		ROME	PALERMO	FLORENCE
Left	N	10	11	27
	M	4.60	4.73	4.15
Right	N	20	22	49
	M	3.35	3.41	2.98

$$F_{\text{handedness}} = 14.88, \text{df} = 1/135, p = .01$$
$$F_{\text{cities}} = 1.13, \text{df} = 1/135, \text{n.s.}$$

Table 2 presents an analysis of variance which confirms the overall significant association of left lateral dominance with high score on Factor I, significant beyond the .001 level of confidence.

DISCUSSION

The results seem perfectly clear but not so the cause. It is tempting to attribute the difference to the forced conversion, but apart from such conversion there is still the relatively more hostile environment to assess.

It is our impression that since World War II much of the opprobrium associated with left handedness has dissolved, at least among upper social classes in Italy. On the other hand, it still remains the practice to require left-handed children to convert in school to right handedness in writing. Were opprobrium and not conversion the prime source of elevation on Factor I, we might expect this factor to be lower among Ss from high social classes. This proves on inspection not to be the case, suggesting that the duress of forced conversion in school may be the primary determinant of our finding.

Factor I is regarded by Cattell as having an association with neuroticism but not with anxiety. There is evidence that it is associated with over-protective treatment in early childhood. But there is also evidence of association with insecurity in the child (Cattell, personal communication, 1965). Cattell considers this factor as being strongly affected by the environment. It is clear, in any event, that the personal qualities associated with this factor must be related to hypersensitivity and heightened self-preoccupation. It was striking that the separation of right- and left-handed Ss on Factor I so incisive in Italy is not confirmed in our sample of Boston children.

Clark (1957) has presented suggestive evidence that Ss who had been forcibly converted from left to right did less well on achievement tests than right handers paired for intelligence. Sielicka, et al. (1963) have observed a high proportion of neurotic symptoms in 83 left-handed children who had been forcibly converted. It must be concluded that attention should be given to the psychological fate of left-handed children, especially in those cultures which, through opprobrium or forced conversion in school, force them to abandon their natural disposition or face the disadvantage of social penalties.

References

BELMONT, L., & BIRCH, H. G. Lateral dominance and right-left awareness in normal children. *Child Develpm.*, 1963, 34, 257–270.
———, & BIRCH, H. G. Lateral dominance, lateral awareness and reading disability. *Child Develpm.*, 1965, 36, 57–71.
CATTELL, R. B., & BELOFF, J. *The High School Personality Questionnaire.* Champaign, Ill.; Institute for Personality and Ability Testing, 1957.
———, BELOFF, J., & COAN, R. W. *The High School Personality Questionnaire.* (Translation and adaptation into Italian language and culture by the Harvard Florence Research Project in collaboration with the Psychological Division of the Italian National Research Center) Florence: Organizzazioni Speciali, 1961.
CLARK, M. M. *Left handedness.* London: Univer. of London Press, 1957.
IHINGER, R. F. Some relationships among laterality groups at three grade levels in performances on the California Achievement Tests. In California Association of School Psychologists and Psychometrists, *Towards a professional identity in school psychology.* Los Angeles: Author, 1963. Pp. 70–74.
PALMER, R. D. Hand differentiation and psychological functioning. *J. Pers.*, 1963, 31, 445–461.
RAVEN, J. C. *Guide to using Progressive Matrices 1938.* (Revised Order 1956). London: Lewis, 1956.
SIELICKA, M., BOGDANOWICZ, I., DILLING-OSTROWSKA, E., SZELOZYNSKA, K., & KACZENSKA, M. [Forced use of the right hand in lefthanded children as a cause of neurosis.] *Pediat. Polska*, 1963, 38, 405–408.
TESI, G., & YOUNG, B. H. [A standardization of Raven's Progressive Matrices 1938 (Revised Order 1956).] *Arch. Psicol. Neurol. Psichiat.*, 1962, 23, 455–464.
VERHAEGEN, P., & NTUMBA, A. Note on the frequency of left-handedness in African children. *J. educ. Psychol.*, 1964, 55, 89–90.

10

Intellectual Development

Thinking, reasoning, problem solving are obviously psychological processes. As contrasted with digestion and respiration, for instance, there are no substances or organs of which an adult is aware as the processes are going on. One of Piaget's great contributions to the understanding of human behavior is his demonstration of the fact that thinking begins with the manipulation of objects during what he calls, significantly in this connection, the sensorimotor period of the development of intelligence. The end of the sensorimotor period occurs when the child has internalized experiences and developed images of past occurrences.

Readers of this book of selections from the child development literature are by this time probably very aware of the fact that we insist on the importance of physical and physiological structures and processes in understanding children's behavior. The first article in this chapter is a paper in which Sylvia Farnham-Diggory reports psychological experiments she did with young children as a means toward understanding the neurological systems which are used by human beings in understanding complex material. In order to explain the differences she found between boys and girls in her experiments she points out the differences that exist in the life situations of the boys and girls. Sociological, psychological, and physical facts are interwoven, supplementing and explaining each other.

The second article is part of the report of a speech given by K. Lovell in which he summarized several studies done by him and under his direction in England. This part tells about a study of gifted children between the ages of three and ten. He compares his results with the conclusions reached by Lewis Terman in a study of similarly gifted children in California in the 1920's. His main interest, however, seems to have been to find out how gifted children perform on Piagetian intellectual tasks. Terman's book about gifted children was published in 1926, the year in which the first of Piaget's books appeared in English translation.

The concluding part of Lovell's paper is reprinted as a part of Chapter 14, pp. 429–434.

The test used in the search reported in the third article was devised to be a relatively nonverbal test measuring the ability of young children to solve classification problems. In this paper Herbert Zimiles and Harvey Asch compare the performance of two groups of children in Mexico City with two roughly similar groups of children in New York City. They offer explanations of the rankings of the four groups on the several abilities tapped by the Matrix Test. The test was first devised in New York to investigate cognitive processes of children in that city. There is some evidence in the Mexican results that objects represented in the test were unfamiliar to those children and that this influenced the results, even though the children did not have to talk to solve the problems. Even beyond this difference, however, there were differences between the two national samples in strategy.

The Growth of Symbolic Abilities in Black and White Children*

Sylvia Farnham-Diggory
CARNEGIE-MELLON UNIVERSITY

I am reporting here only a few findings from a three-year project on the development of symbolic operational abilities in Negro and white children from 4 to 10 years of age. (More detailed information is available in Farnham-Diggory, 1970.)

I use the term "operational" in a more general sense than Piaget's (1967). In fact I worry that Piaget's compelling arguments may blind us to the fact that there's a child there—within whom those intricate, interlocking sets of Piagetian functions may or may not actually exist.

I have always been impressed by the shielded conservation experiments—which Piaget himself invented—where, for example, beakers with beads or water in them are screened from the subject so that only their tops are visible. Under these conditions, it is alleged—by Piaget among others, most notably Bruner (1964)—that when the liquid is poured from a low fat beaker into a high thin one, preoperational children are likely to say—"Well of course it's still the same. You only poured it." But when the screen is removed, the child will then look sheepish and say, "Oh, I guess I was wrong. There's more in the high one."

Aside from the arguments about whether or not they elicit true conservation, these screened experiments may be providing an important clue to the possible neurological aspects of those interlocking Piagetian functions. If, because of the screen, the child is forced to handle the liquids–conservation problem on the basis of language, remembered images, and remembered actions, then he seems better able to put that information together logically. If—when the screen is removed—he must bring immediate visual stimulation into the integration process, his logic disintegrates. It's as if the addition of the visual system—involving direct occipital stimulation—was more than he could handle at that stage of his neurological development, probably because some critical associative areas are not yet physically quite finished.

Now, if we pursue that line of reasoning, we can come up with a tentative general theory that alternative neurological systems may be available for handling complex information—even when normative systems are underdeveloped or deficient. All we have to do is find out how to engage the alternative systems. Screening out some of the information may be one way. Changing the language of the instructions may be another. Luria (1966) gives the example of changing the instruction "Reach as high as you can," to "Try to touch that spot on the

A Report to the Society for Research in Child Development Santa Monica, 1969. By permission.

* This research was supported by Public Health Service Research Grant MH-0722, from the National Institute of Mental Health.

ceiling." This literally brings different parts of the brain into operation, although the overt behavior may superficially appear to be the same.

Still another way of engaging alternate neurological systems would be through pretraining procedures that, in effect, enrich certain associative systems so that they are more likely to be available for later problem solving. This is what we do when we supplement a picture book of animals with a trip to the zoo. We are enriching visual and motor and speech associative potential to the picture book.

We could of course vary these enrichment or pretraining experiences in countless ways. To take the famous sentence, "See Spot run," for example, we could take a child to a playground, introduce him to a dog named Spot, and have him watch Spot running. If he didn't talk about it, we might assume that the major enrichment concerned visual or visual-memory associative systems. If he talked about it—if he said, "I see Spot running!" we would assume that something has also happened to the speech associative systems. If he just listened to others saying, "See Spot run," then presumably the enrichment would have been limited to the auditory systems. Or we might introduce a variation of this sort: we could tell the child, "pretend you're a dog named Spot. Now run!" That of course would produce motoric associations.

Although this mostly illustrates the conceptual poverty of our early reading materials, it also illustrates a method of systematically comparing the effects of different kinds of pretraining experiences on later symbolic operational capacities. Because the point of all that playground business would be to affect the child's subsequent ability to meaningfully integrate particular word-symbols, after he got back to his book in the classroom.

Now, to return to the problem of development and to introduce the problem of race, my theoretical position has been that some intersensory associative systems (which may or may not be what Piaget means by schemata) may be more available, and more trainable in young children, in boys, in girls, in black

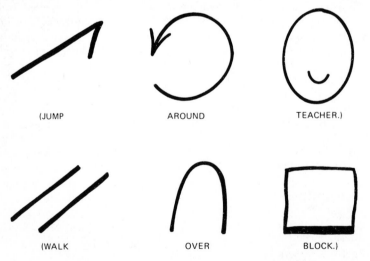

(JUMP   AROUND   TEACHER.)

(WALK   OVER   BLOCK.)

FIGURE 1.   *Sample logograph sentences. (Words were not printed on the stimulus cards.)*

children, and in lower class children—than in their counterparts. This theoretical supposition has generated a series of experiments testing the interaction of pretraining conditions with individual differences—as this interaction affects certain kinds of symbolic integrations.

Figure 1 shows a sample of the *verbal synthesis* task: the child reads simple logograph sentences—of course he learns the logographs first—and then acts out the instruction given in the sentence. If he is in fact synthesizing the information, this is clear from his behavior: he will jump around the teacher (who is the experimenter), for example. If he is not synthesizing the information, he may jump in the air, make a sign for around, and then point to the teacher. His behavior signifies mental dissociation, not mental integration, of the separate ideas represented by the logographs.

Figure 2 shows the *maplike synthesis* task: the child first learns to construct string patterns to match the card symbols, and then learns that the pattern on the left is supposed to be a bridge, the two-string pattern next to it is supposed to be a river, and the next two patterns are both roads. The child is then asked to "Make a bridge, going across a river, with a road on each side."

The correct answer would receive a score of 5, as shown in Figure 3: the bridge is going across the river, and there is a road on each side.

The most extreme incorrect answer, demonstrated in Figure 2, appears when the child lines up the string patterns, to match the cards, without relating the symbols to each other in accord with the instructions.

An additional important problem revealed by this task is illustrated by the fact that the child in Figure 2 has failed to discriminate (or to consider

FIGURE 2.   *Child performing maplike synthesis task.*

important) differences in the relative size of the strings. She made the bridge
out of 3 long strings, instead of 1 long and 2 short strings—which she has
actually used incorrectly to make the river. From 25 to 40 percent of the several
hundred children that I have tested—in lower class or ghetto districts, both
white and black—fail to make this simple discrimination. I think this is telling us
something very important about the extent to which visual cues may be neurologically registered. If they are not registered, the probability that they will connect with other ideas—for example, the idea of "across" or "on each side of"
—must be lower.

I have closely followed Pollack's (1969) exploration of similar perceptual
deficiencies—which he thinks may be related to retinal pigmentation. The
darker the retina—and of course in Negro children the retina is very dark—the
lower the perceptual sensitivity (to certain kinds of illusions, for example).

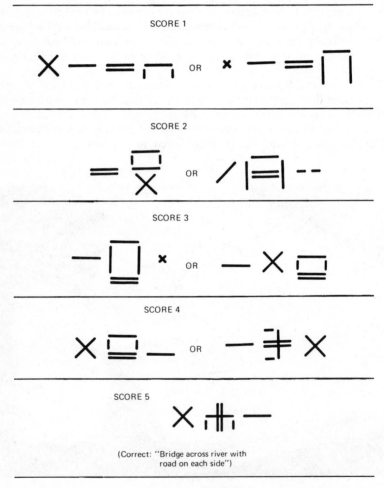

FIGURE 3.   *Score key for maplike synthesis task.*

But Pollack also concedes that social factors may intensify or compensate for a perceptual handicap of this type—just as social factors might intensify or compensate for a visual deficiency like near-sightedness. And I will be telling you shortly about some of the correlations I found which would suggest that certain aspects of lower class life may indeed produce heightened perceptual sensitivities—at least of the sort that I have been studying.

My third symbolic integration task (called *mathematical synthesis*) involves recognizing that an order in six dot-cards matches an order in six blocks—as illustrated in Figure 4. The child is shown a row of blocks which increase and then decrease in size. He is then given a scrambled pile of cards with one, two, or three inked dots on them, and instructed to "Put the dots with the blocks, the way they are supposed to go." The correct insight involves the recognition that the increasing and decreasing order in one set of materials can be coordinated with the increasing and decreasing order in the other set of materials.

Perceptual discrimination has something to do with this too. Children were tested on their ability to recognize differences between numbers of dots, and differences between sizes of blocks—and their scores on this discrimination task were significantly correlated with their scores on the final mathematical coordination task.

Now to report some of the research using these three tasks.

In the original normative study of these tasks, there were no differences between the black and white children on the verbal synthesis task. If anything the black children were better than the white ones in putting visual symbols, words, and actions together in this special way.

But there were significant racial differences on the maplike and mathematical tasks—which appear to require something more like a spatial factor. There is evidence other than Pollack's that the ability to integrate spatial or pictorial ideas may be somewhat defective in Negroes (compared to whites) whereas verbal integration abilities may not be defective (Tyler, 1956; Pettigrew, 1964). My findings would support that general view.

The second normative finding was that all three tasks improve with age, regardless of race or social class. But this could result from general growth of

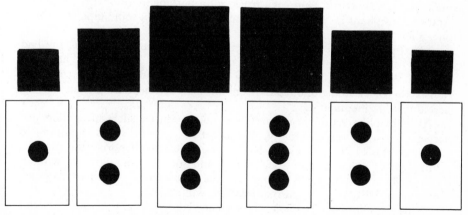

FIGURE 4.   *Correct placement of dot cards with blocks, in mathematical synthesis task.*

associative brain power. What we really need is information about specific intersensory systems that may be critical to this increased power. This is the theoretical value of attempting to accelerate symbolic integrations, by using different pretraining methods. If a verbal pretraining method does not accelerate a particular kind of synthesis, and a sensory-motor, non-verbal method does, then this may be telling us that sensory-motor networks are more involved than verbal networks, in the development of certain operational capacities. Of course arguments can be raised against this interpretation, but it is nevertheless the one I'm fondest of.

To test the acceleration potential of the verbal synthesis task, kindergarten children from a black ghetto were trained in one of the following ways: they were given practice on the reading portion of the task—actually training in visual speech coordinations. Or they were given practice on the behavior portion of the task—they practiced saying the sentences, and then acting them out, before they even saw the logographs. Or they were pretrained on both of the task components—they practiced the actions, and then they also practiced the reading.

The results were that the reading practice alone did not produce much sentence comprehension—as signalled by the child's ability to act out the synthesized sentences. A better way of producing this comprehension was letting the child practice the actions. However an even better way was to combine the pretraining procedures. Innercity kindergartners who received the combined training, produced synthesis scores which were equal to the scores of white suburban children in 4th grade. This tells us, presumably, that prior enrichment of a child's motoric associative systems may substantially assist his reading comprehension.

A similar effect was found for the mathematical task.

In a ghetto preschool, one group of children were verbally drilled in the inequalities represented by the blocks and dots. The children practiced saying "This is more than this," while pointing to different pairs of stimuli. That's a sort of visual-speech drill. Another group had a guided play experience. They had a big doll, a medium size doll, and a little doll. And each doll got a big, medium, or little truck. And each truck got a big, medium, or little elephant. And each elephant got a bubble pipe, and each pipe got some pipe cleaners— one, a few, or a lot, and so forth.

That pretraining condition enriched many sensory motor systems, but had nothing to do with the mathematical task materials, and didn't drill anything verbally. Nevertheless, the guided play pretraining produced better coordination of the block and dot materials on the final synthesis task, than did the verbal drill on inequalities.

The maplike synthesis research has not produced such straightforward acceleration functions. Actually, it's possible—among Negro children—to accelerate this ability simply by having the children memorize the maplike symbols first (which is quite easy to do), and then coordinate them without further reference to the cards—which are put out of sight. Then there is a much higher probability that the correct relations will appear.

This is similar in principle to the screened conservation task, but it doesn't solve the problem of how to get the children to do the standard maplike task rather than an altered version of it.

One aspect of the problem is that both sex and social class affect maplike synthesis capability. In lower class districts—not innercity ghettos—girls are generally better than boys on this task. In middle class districts, the black girls are also better than the black boys—but in the white group, the advantaged white boys soared above all the other groups in the sample, including the white girls.

Now this raises some interesting questions of mechanisms. We all know, of course, that advantaged white boys have fathers and tinker toys and erector sets, and various other kinds of opportunities to practice the symbolic operations of making bridges go across rivers with roads on each side.

But this comforting theoretical explanation doesn't stand us in such good stead when it comes to explaining why lower class black girls may be better than lower class black boys—not in the ghetto but in edgetown and milltown communities. I mean it's a bit silly to talk about more fathers and more tinker toys in this particular girl-boy comparison. But what about mothers and housekeeping chores? That ought to be another good way of practicing symbolic operations of this sort—you put knives and forks on each side of plates, for example, and you may have to learn to do this when the hands of the clock are lined up in a certain way. Housekeeping responsibilities generally seem to increase, for female children, as class declines—that is, lower class girls (especially older ones) presumably do more housekeeping than upper class girls. So, in one study, I separated the lower class and middle class 3rd and 4th grade girls of both races and compared them on maplike synthesis ability— and lo, the lower class girls were indeed significantly better than the middle class counterparts. But this effect was not found among the boys.

Now of course it's always interesting to find that lower class children can do anything better than middle class children, and the maplike task got even more interesting from this standpoint when I discovered that innercity boys, second graders, from a ghetto that was actually rioting during the testing period, were better than suburban black boys in 4th grade—on this maplike task. They were not better than suburban white boys, they couldn't even come close. But the ghetto boys were certainly not behaving, on this task, like the severely disadvantaged 2nd graders that they were supposed to be.

So again, casting about for ecological correlates—and father and tinker toys wouldn't do me any good here either—in fact fathers seemed to be really out of it: 40% of my boys in that experiment had fathers who were either unemployed or absent. That gave me the idea that possibly father-less, or father-weak boys, living in ghettos during these terribly dangerous periods, would have to develop perceptual acuities—in order to survive. You have to learn perceptual signals such as "soul brother" signs—which were bright orange in our city—to know which store to hide in, and which store to loot. (Many of my children were happy looters, much to the consternation of their teachers on "show-and-tell" days.) So I separated all the boys who had no fathers, or unemployed fathers, from boys whose fathers were employed and known to be in the home—and lo, the boys from the father-less or father-weak backgrounds were indeed significantly better on this maplike task, than were their strong-father counterparts. But this effect was not found among the girls.

Now, in this ghetto group, I also attempted to accelerate maplike synthesis ability in three ways: one group played with a large architects' model of bridges, rivers, and roads, for 10 minutes. A second group played with the model for 6 minutes, and spent 4 minutes being drilled, by me, in verbal statements about what they were doing—statements like, "A bridge goes across a river," and then putting the bridge across the river. A third group not only did everything the first two groups had done, but also drilled the instructions. They practiced saying, "I'm going to make a bridge, going across a river, with a road on each side," before they performed the task.

The results of this study were different for boys and girls. Among the girls, the verbalization pretraining improved their maplike synthesis capabilities. Among the boys, the verbalization training disrupted their synthesis capabilities.

So I have been formulating this kind of a conclusion about the intersensory significance of interactions between where you live, and what sex you are. Housekeeping experience may increase the verbal associative potential of girls. And this increased verbal potential may have assisted them in the performance of the maplike symbolic operations. Among boys, the factors associated with being on your own in a ghetto may sharpen non-verbal associative systems— perceptual systems, action systems—which may also help you perform maplike operations.

For the boys, the kind of pretraining that helps the girls may be disruptive. For the girls, the kind of pretraining that helps the boys may be disruptive. Presumably in both cases the disruption results from the intrusion of intersensory associative systems which the respective sexes do not normally use in performing mental operations of this type. The boys are negatively affected by verbal pretraining, and the girls are negatively affected by the ghetto life.

That, at the moment, is just a hunch. But it does suggest one way in which we could try to nail down some of the actual neurological mechanisms that may be associated with sociological differences affecting cognitive development.

References

BRUNER, J. S. The course of cognitive growth. *American Psychologist*, 1964, *19*, 1–16.

FARNHAM-DIGGORY, S. Cognitive synthesis in Negro and white children. *Monographs of the Society for Research in Child Development*, 1970, Serial No. 135.

LURIA, A. R. *Human brain and psychological processes.* New York: Harper & Row, 1966.

PETTIGREW, T. F. *A profile of the Negro American.* Princeton: D. Van Nostrand Co., 1964.

PIAGET, J. *Six psychological studies.* New York: Random House, 1967.

POLLACK, R. H. Some implications of ontogenetic changes in perception, in Elkind, D., & Flavell, J. H. (Eds.), *Studies in cognitive development.* New York: Oxford University Press, 1969. Pp. 365–408.

TYLER, L. E. *The psychology of human differences.* New York: Appleton-Century-Crofts, 1956.

Some Recent Studies in Cognitive and Language Development*

K. Lovell

UNIVERSITY OF LEEDS, ENGLAND

This paper deals with five of our more recent studies. The first concerns a study of fifty 3- to 10-year-olds, all of whom obtained a WISC Verbal Score of 140 or more. The group was in every way comparable with Terman's (1926) sample of gifted children. Five issues were studied: language, personality, mathematical attainment, logical thought, and the relationship between scores obtained on so called creativity tests and those obtained on WISC Scales and on tests of logical thinking. However, this paper does not deal with the language of these pupils, and it has little to say about their personalities; rather it concentrates on the other issues.

There are comparatively few studies of gifted children defined as those who obtain a score of 140 or more on an intelligence test, and what knowledge is available comes largely from Terman's monumental work begun more than 40 years ago. To-day, however, there are issues which did not enter into the thinking of the earlier investigators. For example, do gifted children move into Piaget's stage of formal thought much earlier than pupils of average ability as measured by I.Q. tests? . . .

In our study all the subjects were drawn from schools in two large cities. The Principals were asked to nominate pupils of outstanding intellectual ability. Over 100 pupils so nominated, were tested using WISC with the alterations suggested by the British Psychological Society. Verbal, Performance, and Full-Scale I.Q.'s were obtained. The first fifty pupils who obtained an I.Q. of 140 or more on the Verbal Scale formed the selected group; the numbers of children with I.Q.'s in the ranges of 140–144, 145–149, 150–154, and 155+ being respectively 30, 12, 4, and 4. There were thirty-five boys and fifteen girls. Twelve pupils were between 8.5 and 10.4 years, and seventeen between 10.5 and 11.7 years old. Using the British Registrar-General's Classification of Occupations it was found that nine pupils came from homes in Social Class I—major professional and managerial; twenty-two in Social Class 2—minor professional and managerial; fourteen in Social Class 3—skilled working; and four in Social Class 4—semi-skilled.

In addition to the WISC Scales the following groups of tests were used:

> 1. *Creativity Tests.* These comprised Hidden Shapes, Word Association, Uses for Things, Fables, and Make-up Arithmetic Problems (Getzels and Jackson, 1962).
>
> 2. *Tests of Logical Thinking.* In this group were Equilibrium in the Balance, Combinations of Colorless Liquids, Oscillation of a Pendulum

Excerpted from *Merrill-Palmer Quarterly*, 1968, *14*, 123–127. By permission.

* This is the substance of a lecture given at The Merrill-Palmer Institute in September, 1966.

(all from Inhelder and Piaget, 1958), and Concept of Volume (Lovell and Ogilvie, 1961).

3. *Mathematical Tests*. These included three tests of mathematical concepts and one of mathematical insight, all published by the National Foundation for Educational Research; Vernon's Graded Arithmetic-Mathematics Test; and a numerical series and a numerical analogies test.

All testing was performed in the pupils' schools and was on an individual basis, except that in the case of the mathematics tests up to three children were tested at the same time. In addition a Terman Personality Trait Rating Form was completed by a teacher, for each pupil, for each of the twenty-five personality traits. Thirteen grades were used for each trait.

An examination of the replies showed that only 15 out of the 150 responses to the Balance, Chemicals, and Pendulum experiments were at Piaget's stage of formal thought, while 11 of these replies were at the first stage of formal thought. Almost all the pupils understood internal volume, occupied volume, and simple displacement; but only 36 grasped that the amounts of water displaced by a single cube when immersed in a full-pint can and a full-gallon can (English gallon) were the same. Again, only 26 could understand that the amounts of water displaced by two cubes of the same size but different weights were equal. Overall, 48 per cent of the subjects answered all the questions concerning volume correctly. The proportion of younger children, 42 per cent, did not differ greatly from the proportion of older pupils, 53 per cent, passing all the tests.

Performance on the mathematics tests was as high as expected. For example, on Vernon's Graded Arithmetic-Mathematics Test the mean achievement age was 3 years 7 months in advance of the mean chronological age, with twelve pupils having attainment ages more than 4 years, and three pupils more than 5 years ahead of their chronological ages. At the same time, however, these gifted pupils had extreme difficulty with certain of the problems involving numerical series and numerical analogies, and in particular those that involved the schema of proportion. This involves the recognition of the equivalence of two ratios and depends upon the subject being able to elaborate second order relations—in the Piagetian sense. Although 48 pupils could continue the series 48, 24, 12, 6 . . . ; only 11 could continue the series 16, 24, 36, 54 . . . ; only 5 could answer the questions "3 is to 7 as 9 is to . . .," and "2 is to . . . is to 8 as 3 is to 9 is to. . . ."

It seems that while these gifted pupils do not generally attain the level of formal operational thought until 11 or 12 years of age at least, the flexibility of their first order schemas is much greater than in the case of ordinary pupils. It is as if they possess sub-schemas of much greater generality which permits transfer to new situations. Thus when gifted children reach the stage of concrete operational thought it tends to be available in a far greater variety of situations and tasks than in the case with ordinary pupils at first.

In order to look at the relationships between the responses obtained on the creativity tests and those on the other tasks, product moment intercorrelation coefficients for the cognitive measures were calculated, and a Principal Component Analysis and rotation of the principal axes by the Varimax method were carried out. Six components were extracted; the percentage variance contributed by these being respectively 39.3, 12.4, 9.7, 7.1, 6.3, and 5.6—or 80.4 per cent in all.

A large general component was found running through all these tasks even within this highly selective group; indeed it accounted for almost one-half of the identified variance. When the axes were rotated the first dimension clearly indicated an ability measured by the WISC scales, or as would be said in Britain, a general plus verbal-educational ability. The second reflected an ability to think logically in the Piagetian type situation; the summed scores of the logical tasks had a loading as high as .93 on it. The remaining dimensions suggest that divergent thinking cannot be accounted for by one dimension; rather the able pupil is "creative" in differing degrees according to the task that is set him. While the verbal creativity tests, Word Association and Uses for Things, loaded the third dimension to the extent of .76 and .82 respectively, the ability to make up numerical problems is clearly linked with the ability to work the mathematics tests as reflected in dimension 4. This study supports Burt when he wrote of divergent thinking tests (Burt, 1962, p. 295): ". . . these new tests have succeeded in eliciting supplementary activities that are rarely tapped by the usual brands of intelligence tests." On the other hand, it is clear that a great part of the identified variance of these tests is accounted for by a central intellective component which is common to a conventional test of intelligence, to tasks involving logical thinking, and to tests of mathematical attainment. Moreover, these "supplementary activities" seem to fragment in these able pupils. Wallach and Kogan (1965, p. 313) suggest that the emergence of combinatorial operations as reflected in the colorless chemicals experiment may depend on the emergence of associative (divergent) and evaluative (convergent) thinking. Our evidence does not support that if these tests of divergent thinking are regarded as adequate.

Little will be said of the findings in respect of personality. But it is of interest to note in passing that the mean scores obtained on the ratings were very close to those obtained by Terman's sample. Thus despite changes in education and life generally, both in America and in Britain between the 1920's and the 1960's, the gifted child seems to his teacher to be much the same kind of person. Further, the normalized scores on the cognitive variables were ranked and combined with twenty-one of the personality trait ratings, yielded some thirty-eight variables in all. A Principal Components Analysis of the intercorrelation matrix largely repeated the findings of our other analyses. But one point is of interest. The teachers' ratings of Originality loaded the same rotated axis (.84) as did the Logical Thinking summed scores (.63), yet Originality had a zero loading on the rotated axis which reflected the ability to answer the tests of divergent thinking on which Creativity summed scores had a loading of .82. It would seem that using Terman's personality Rating Scale, teachers think of Originality in these pupils more in terms of reasoning ability than they do in terms of inventiveness or unusual ideas. Or it may be that creativity as measured by the tests is rather too specific, or at times too trivial, to be noticed by teachers.

Gifted pupils have first order operational schemas of great flexibility, as was stated earlier. In the school situation this implies that they need suitable learning situations over a wide curriculum, with many imaginative and informative books on a wide variety of topics. But the failure of these pupils during the elementary school years to reach the level of formal operational thought, except occasionally, is a warning against the systematic provision of learning situations demanding formal thought. At the same time it is important that the pupils have access to teachers who understand their stage of cognitive development, and who can by questioning the interpretation put by these pupils on their data, persuade them to re-examine their arguments and conclusions whenever necessary in an endeavor to aid forward the onset of formal thinking. This study does not, however, give any grounds for believing that teaching procedures should be devised based upon a convergent-divergent dimension of the intellect entirely independent of I.Q.

The gifted child in Britain in the 1960's, like his counterpart in America in the 1920's, seems generally well endowed with personality traits highly regarded by Western society, and is popular with his school companions. Fears of ill-balanced personality development, and of unpopularity, are unfounded. The study confirms that the gifted child by reason of his more General Qualities and intelligence, is a most important figure in school life.

References

BURT, C. Critical notice: Creativity and intelligence, by J. W. Getzels & P. W. Jackson. *Brit. J. educ. Psychol.*, 1962, *32*, 292–98.

GETZELS, J. W., & JACKSON, P. N. *Creativity and intelligence.* London: Wiley, 1962.

INHELDER, B., & PIAGET, J. *The growth of logical thinking.* London: Routledge & Kegan Paul, 1958.

LOVELL, K., & OGILVIE, E. The growth of the concept of volume in Junior School children. *J. Child. Psychol. Psychiat.*, 1961, *2*, 118–26.

TERMAN, L. M. *Genetic Studies of Genius, Vol. 1. Mental and physical traits of a thousand gifted children.* Stanford University Press, 1926.

WALLACH, M. A., & KOGAN, N. *Modes of thinking in young children.* London: Holt, Rinehart & Winston, 1965.

A Cross-Cultural Comparison of Advantaged and Disadvantaged Children's Ability to Classify*

Herbert Zimiles and Harvey Asch
BANK STREET COLLEGE OF EDUCATION

This paper will present the results of a comparative study of classification behavior in middle-class and disadvantaged Mexican children selected from grades one to three and will examine these findings in conjunction with those

From a paper presented at Biennial Meeting of Society for Research in Child Development, Santa Monica, California, March 1969. By permission.

* This study was supported by Contract #OEO-1410 and OEO-4122 of the Office of Research and Evaluation of Project Head Start.

obtained in a previous study (Zimiles and Asch, 1967; Zimiles, 1968) which compared classification behavior of advantaged and disadvantaged of the same age range from New York. Data were gathered from Mexican children in order to extend the range of socio-cultural backgrounds of children performing the same non-verbal task and thereby to examine the impact of variation in cultural background on classification ability and related cognitive skills, and to observe whether differences in performance previously found between advantaged and disadvantaged United States children would be similarly found among Mexican children. The study also offered the opportunity to assess the usefulness of the Matrix Test as a method for studying aspects of cognition on a cross-cultural basis.

The Matrix Test was devised to measure classification ability and related skills in young children. Patterned after the work of Inhelder and Piaget (1964), each of the test's 44 items presents a matrix of 2 × 2 or 2 × 3 cells in which all but the lower right-hand cell, which is empty, contain figures which are related to each other. The subject must indicate which one of four alternative figures presented to him belongs in the empty cell by virtue of its relationship to the members of the matrix. The test is essentially non-verbal. Simple directions are given at the outset and the child need not utter a word; he needs only to point to the appropriate alternative figure.

Each item is presented individually on an 8″ × 15″ card in the form shown in Figure 1. Four classes of items have been distinguished. The first three items call for a Perceptual Matching response in that all members of the matrix are identical. To solve the problem, S must merely identify the figure among the alternatives that matches those in the matrix. These Perceptual Matching items are presented first because their simplicity makes it easy to communicate clearly to the child the basic requirements of the task, i.e., to find the member of the set of alternatives which belongs in the vacant cell of the matrix. After the first three Perceptual Matching items, 18 Class Membership items follow in which the figures in each cell of the matrix are different but are, nevertheless, members of the same class, e.g., they may all be birds or vehicles. Following the

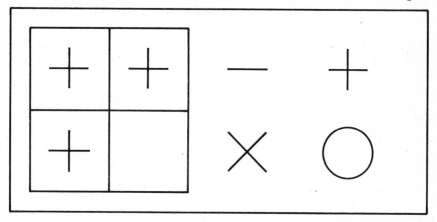

FIGURE 1.   Illustration of Matrix Test item format (example of a Perceptual Matching item).

Class Membership items are 11 One-Way Classification items in which it is the column or row membership of the vacant cell which determines the identity of the missing figure, since in these items, all members of the same column or row, as the case may be, are identical. Finally, there are 12 Two-Way Classification items in which it is the column and row membership of the vacant cell, in combination, which determines the correct response. Of the total of 44 items, 16 present geometric figures whose distinctive feature is their form or color and, in some instances, their number or order. The remaining 28 items contain representations of common objects mostly taken from illustrations in books for children.

METHOD

SUBJECTS   Subjects were selected from two schools in Mexico City. One school, located on a normal school campus, was attended by children who lived in relatively comfortable circumstances; their fathers were professionals or semi-professionals. In general, families living in the area of this school had a standard of living which corresponds approximately to that of a lower-middle-class family in the United States. The second school was located in an extremely impoverished area at the edge of the city occupied mostly by factory workers and migrant workers. In each of the two schools, the first of which we have designated as advantaged and the second as disadvantaged, slightly over 40 children were selected from each of the first three grades to serve as Ss. In those instances in which children were grouped by age or ability, the sample was determined by selecting at random from each of the strata. Approximately equal numbers of boys and girls were chosen. Unfortunately, reliable data regarding the age of the disadvantaged children were not available. However, it should be noted that the age range for this group was greater because many of the children began school later, and some were held back by the school. Therefore, portions of the samples from each of the grades were undoubtedly older than those in the advantaged school. It seemed inappropriate to exclude these children from the sample despite their older age; to do so would have introduced a clearcut bias of considerable proportion. In sum, 254 Mexican children approximately equally distributed in the first three grades from two schools, divided into a more and less privileged subgroup according to the school they attended, were studied.

The findings will be compared with those of a previous study involving groups of 40 children in each of the first three grades (kindergarten samples were also studied) selected from each of two schools in New York City.[1] One school was located in the slum of a black ghetto area; its children were for the most part from extremely deprived families. The other school was located in a very comfortable residential area made up of upper-middle-class, predominantly white families. It should be noted that the children from the New York advantage sample were living under much more privileged conditions than

---

[1] See Zimiles, H. "Classification and Inferential Thinking in Children of Varying Age and Social Class." Paper presented at symposium on Comparative Studies of Conceptual Functioning in Young Children, American Psychological Association meetings, San Francisco, California, September 1968.

those who constitute the advantaged group from Mexico. The pairs of groups from each country are similar in the contrast they present but not in the degree and nature of deprivation they have experienced.

PROCEDURE   All the children in both the Mexican and New York sample were administered the Matrix Test in a single session of individual testing. A single examiner, who lives in Mexico City,[2] gathered all the Mexican data. Two examiners, who tested equal numbers of children in both schools, collected the New York City data.[3] The test administration was the same in both countries, except for the identity of the examiners and the language in which the instructions were given.

RESULTS

As in the case of the findings previously obtained with the New York sample, the results from Mexico indicate consistent differences in performance between the social class groups and a steady rise as a function of age. However, the differences attributable to social class were of a smaller magnitude than those previously obtained with the New York City sample. The mean per cent of items answered correctly for each of the four item types is given in Table 1.

TABLE 1
Per Cent of Items Answered Correctly by Child Group and Grade

PERCEPTUAL MATCHING (3 ITEMS)	K	GRADES 1	2	3	ONE-WAY CLASSIFICATION (11 ITEMS)	K	GRADES 1	2	3
Mexican					Mexican				
Advantaged	–	82	90	92	Advantaged	–	55	65	67
Disadvantaged	–	87	72	90	Disadvantaged	–	44	45	53
New York					New York				
Advantaged	94	96	97	100	Advantaged	73	85	88	90
Disadvantaged	91	91	98	93	Disadvantaged	50	64	70	76

CLASS MEMBERSHIP (18 ITEMS)	K	GRADES 1	2	3	TWO-WAY CLASSIFICATION (12 ITEMS)	K	GRADES 1	2	3
Mexican					Mexican				
Advantaged	–	61	70	74	Advantaged	–	24	31	35
Disadvantaged	–	56	55	68	Disadvantaged	–	28	34	35
New York					New York				
Advantaged	73	82	84	85	Advantaged	25	41	48	48
Disadvantaged	62	73	76	80	Disadvantaged	24	24	24	27

[2] Deanne Marein gathered the data in Mexico City.
[3] Susan Lourenco and John Kaufman gathered the data in New York City.

It may be observed that almost all the children could cope effectively with the Perceptual Matching items, there was considerable success with the Class Membership, performance on the One-Way Classification items was somewhat lower, and the Two-Way Classification problems were almost consistently failed. The advantaged children almost invariably outperformed the disadvantaged, but only in the case of the One-Way Classification problems did these differences consistently achieve sizeable proportions.

When compared with the performance of the New York City sample, the Mexican children performed less well. Whereas it was the rare New York City child, even at age levels as low as five years, who failed the initial Perceptual Matching items, there were a handful of Mexican children at all age levels, from both of the schools, who failed this first item. Many of these children caught on to the demands of the test by the second item, but it remains clear that considerably more Mexican children did not understand the demands of the task upon first meeting it.

With the exception of the second-grade sample, in which the disadvantaged group performed consistently poorly, the children from the two Mexican schools performed equally well on the Perceptual Matching items and the first half of the Class Membership items—those involving categories of events of high salience to the children. As the Class Membership items became more difficult, as class membership was based on more remote characteristics of the figures, the advantaged group began to outperform the disadvantaged group by a substantial margin. The largest difference in performance between the two groups occurred in the One-Way Classification items. The groups were hardly distinguishable in their performance on the Two-Way Classification items.

Differences found between the advantaged and disadvantaged New York sample were of a somewhat greater magnitude but followed much of the same pattern except that group differences in performance on the Two-Way Classification items were as great and sometimes greater than those obtained with other item types, whereas differences between the Mexican groups on the Two-Way Classification items, because of the extreme difficulty of the items, were negligible.

Differences between the New York and Mexican groups, irrespective of social class background, were much larger and more pervasive than those differences between Mexican advantaged and disadvantaged groups. Both the advantaged and disadvantaged New York groups outperformed their Mexican counterparts at each age level by a large margin on virtually all the Class Membership and One-Way Classification items. But the most striking characteristic of these data is the wide margin by which the means of the advantaged New York group exceeded those of the other groups. A relatively consistent rank order of the four groups may be found at each of the three grade levels studied: the New York City advantaged, New York City disadvantaged, Mexican advantaged, Mexican disadvantaged. Whereas the means of the New York advantaged groups are consistently highest on all item types, the New York disadvantaged groups did not outperform either of the Mexican groups on the Two-Way Classification items.

The performance which most markedly distinguished the New York from the Mexico City groups involved items which required a change in strategy, a shift to a new basis for classification, in order to achieve solution. For example, the greatest difference between the groups was usually found on the initial item of the series of One-Way Classification problems. Apparently, the transition from Class Membership to One-Way Classification problems was particularly difficult for the disadvantaged groups. Another item which differentiated the New York and the Mexican groups presented a matrix of varying geometric figures all of which were the same color. Since the four preceding items called for a response in terms of form, relatively few children answered this item correctly.

Several kinds of items were too difficult for virtually all the children. Only substantial numbers of children from the New York advantaged group were able to solve those Class Membership problems which called for more remote categories of classification and One-Way Classification items which entailed categorization according to row membership, following a series of items which involved column membership. It was only in the New York advantaged group, too, that there were appreciable numbers of children who were able to solve the Two-Way Classification problems.

Another way of examining these data is to study the frequency distributions of scores on each of the item sets. This reveals something more about the nature of the distribution of scores than that indicated by indices of central tendency and variability. The distributions of the two Mexican school groups were often virtually identical, especially in their patterns of widespread failure on the Two-Way Classification problems. While there was very considerable overlap between these two school groups at each age level in Class Membership scores in the modal or central regions of the distribution, there were more advantaged than disadvantaged Mexican children who achieved the higher scores, and many more disadvantaged children in the lower tails of these distributions. The differences between these groups are most marked in the distribution of One-Way Classification scores. While there is considerable overlap among the higher scorers, there were many more disadvantaged children who simply were unable to solve these One-Way Classification problems.

The frequency distributions of the advantaged Mexican group bear a striking resemblance to the frequency distributions of the disadvantaged New York group. The major differences are: (1) there are more stragglers at the lower end of the distribution of Class Membership items among the Mexican advantaged group, (2) there are more perfect scores in One-Way Classification among the New York disadvantaged group, and (3) there were a few more children in the older age groups of the Mexican advantaged group who showed some signs of mastering the Two-Way Classification problem. In most respects, however, the distributions from these groups are dramatically alike.

The most striking characteristics of the frequency distributions of the New York advantaged group were the solidity of performance on the One-Way Classification problems by even the younger groups—virtually every first-grader and most kindergartners could handle most of these problems, and the appearance of small numbers of children at even the youngest age levels who could solve the Two-Way Classification problems.

Some Qualitative Features of Performance   Response latencies to each item were recorded. They indicate that the Mexican children consistently took more time to respond to each item than did the New York children. No substantial differences between the two Mexican school groups were found. Whereas the advantaged New York children were found to take more time to respond to the more difficult than to the easier items, no such relationship between response latency and item difficulty was found among the New York disadvantaged children or either of the two groups of Mexican children.

The tendency for positional response preferences to affect performance on multiple-choice problems is not uncommon. Examination of the position of incorrect alternatives chosen indicates that there was a slight preference for responding in terms of the alternative adjacent to the empty matrix cell. This pattern was found among young disadvantaged New York children, and observed to decline with increasing age. A similar preference of approximately the same magnitude was found among the Mexican children in both school groups. In the case of the Mexican children, however, this pattern was sustained among the older groups as well.

Perseveration in the face of failure or confusion frequently occurs in the response of young children to test situations. Employing a relatively harsh criterion of perseveration, i.e., five or more consecutive identical positional responses only one of which is correct, virtually none of the New York children were found to perseverate. There was one in all of the 120 New York advantaged group and two among the disadvantaged that responded in this fashion. Among the Mexican groups of comparable age, however, there were 11 children from the advantaged group and 21 from the disadvantaged group who showed this form of perseveration.

While the 12 Two-Way Classification problems were too difficult for virtually all the children to solve, it is possible, by studying the nature of the wrong alternatives selected, to observe whether a systematic approach, a strategy, though incorrect, was nevertheless applied in dealing with these problems. One such strategy was to choose an alternative identical to the cell member in the same row as the empty cell; in short, to impose, inappropriately, a One-Way Classification scheme upon the problem. This way of responding occurred to a substantial degree among the youngest children (even at kindergarten level) in the New York advantaged children but disappeared at the older levels when they began to solve the problem. A similar pattern of One-Way Classification is barely observable among the youngest groups of the New York disadvantaged groups and the two Mexican school groups, but occurred increasingly among their older children. This trend of using a One-Way Classification strategy with increasing age was stronger among the New York disadvantaged and weakest among the Mexican disadvantaged group. Thus, for these groups, the use of an inappropriate strategy on the Two-Way Classification problems mirrored the pattern of use of appropriate strategy on other, easier to solve items.

Finally, a flexibility index was devised by recording performance on those items that marked a transition from one set of items to another, and therefore required a shift in problem-solving strategy. The per cent of these problems answered correctly for each school group is given in Table 2.

TABLE 2
Flexibility Index: Per Cent of Transitional Items Answered Correctly

| | GRADES | | | | | GRADES | | | |
	K	1	2	3		K	1	2	3
Mexican					New York				
Advantaged	–	37	44	49	Advantaged	58	68	78	77
Disadvantaged	–	34	40	42	Disadvantaged	39	50	52	55

The data indicate that in each of the school groups, performance improved with age. The New York advantaged children were by far the most effective on these items, and the New York disadvantaged group substantially more effective than both of the Mexican groups. The Mexican disadvantaged group performed poorest on these transitional items.

DISCUSSION

This comparative study of advantaged and disadvantaged Mexican children revealed substantial differences between the two groups. More of the disadvantaged children floundered during the test, as evidenced by their greater tendency to perseverate and by their greater numbers at the bottom of distributions of scores.

Performance differences between the New York advantaged and disadvantaged groups were greater and extended over a wider range of item content, reflecting, perhaps, the greater difference in social-cultural background of the groups that were compared. It is of interest that the performance of the New York disadvantaged group surpassed that of the advantaged as well as the disadvantaged groups from Mexico. These differences were found in both the Class Membership and One-Way Classification series of items—those items on the test that were neither too easy nor too difficult for the age level studied.

The Mexican children took much longer to respond, but their more deliberate pace did not appear to enhance their performance. There was evidence of more confusion among them when first introduced to the task, more perseveration of response, their responses seemed more often to be affected by position preferences than by the inherent logic of the problem. These maladaptive response characteristics occurred more often and lasted longer, that is, they appeared in the older as well as the younger age groups. Even when responding incorrectly, as the New York disadvantaged usually did when presented with the Two-Way Classification problems, their incorrect response was based on a strategy. The Mexican children showed less systematic response patterns to these same items. In general, the performance of the Mexican children was like that of a slightly younger New York disadvantaged child and like a much younger advantaged child from New York.

In a previous analysis of the performance differences between the advantaged and disadvantaged children from New York, it was concluded that a major distinguishing characteristic between the groups was the ability of the advantaged children to respond to Class Membership problems in terms of attributes that were less immediately visible, or less salient among the criteria used when they typically order events. Their much greater success relative to the New York disadvantaged on the One-Way Classification problems was interpreted as further demonstration of their ability to recognize and deal effectively with a form of order that involves spatial organization, and that is not necessarily based on the high frequency with which the objects to be classified have occurred together in the past nor in their individual visually compelling quality. Among the older age groups, the performance of these children on the Two-Way Classification problems increasingly showed signs of the ability to order subjects according to two criteria of classification conjointly, that is, to engage in multi-dimensional thinking. These findings suggested further that the concept of a class or set was much more firmly rooted in the advantaged children.

In contrast, the New York disadvantaged children tended to perform effectively when the item called for an associative response. Success in classification appeared to depend much more on the degree to which the objects to be classified evoked common associations.

The data from Mexico help to identify still more primitive modes of dealing with the Matrix Test—from an inability to understand the demands of the test to a pattern of perseveration of response and positional responding. The New York disadvantaged group, while able to respond less abstractly and flexibly than their advantaged peers, were much more able to understand the task, to respond to it consistently on an associative basis, and also were more flexible in their response than either of the Mexican groups. These findings permit us to view the cognitive functioning of urban disadvantaged children in the United States from a perspective other than one which compares them with their advantaged counterparts.

Finally, it should be noted that the data of this study are clearly insufficient to make a definitive comparison of Mexican and United States children. In addition to the gross inadequacies of sampling it may well be that the Matrix Test, by virtue of the familiarity of its content, evokes a more attentive and receptive response from United States children. While there is no evidence from the present study that Mexican children performed less well on the items which involved representational as opposed to more culturally neutral geometric figures, it is possible that their general level of functioning was inhibited by the comparative strangeness of the materials.

A final note relates to the changes in performance that have been observed with age among these cross-sectional data. While the rise is consistent and unmistakable, it is extremely gradual. There is very considerable overlap in performance between distributions of five-year-olds in the kindergarten groups studied and those of eight-year-olds; there were many five-year-olds, especially from the advantaged New York group, whose scores exceeded those of large numbers of eight-year-olds. This was particularly true of performance on the One-Way Classification items, the task which produced the greatest variability in performance in the age range that was studied. Eight-year-olds are so profoundly different from five-year-olds in so many basic psychological and physical parameters that the overlap in performance among the range of age groups found in this study is noteworthy. It suggests that more refined study of age changes in performance as a function of their cognitive content is needed, that longitudinal studies of cognitive functioning may be better suited to identify significant developmental patterns, and that expectations of children's cognitive functioning based upon their chronological age are likely to be unrealistic. Age appears to be a much less decisive determinant of Matrix Test performance than was anticipated.

Bibliography

INHELDER, B., and PIAGET, J. *The Early Growth of Logic in the Child*. New York: Harper & Row, 1964.

ZIMILES, H. "Classification and Inferential Thinking in Children of Varying Age and Social Class." Paper presented at symposium on Comparative Studies of Conceptual Functioning in Young Children, American Psychological Association meetings, San Francisco, California, September 1968.

————, and ASCH, H. "Development of the Matrix Test." Document 1 of Head Start Evaluation and Research Center Progress Report of Research Studies, 1966 to 1967, December 1967.

11

Increasing Competence As a Learner and Doer

The important aspects of development during the period from six to twelve have to do with the skills that are considered important by the groups of which children are members. Some of the skills are important to the child because of their meaning for him in the present; some are important for both the present and the future. Physical skills like playing baseball or playing a violin, and the coordinations necessary to such feats, mental skills like reading or memorizing, and social skills like cooperating or leading are among the ways in which children can become competent in all the skills of which human beings are capable.

Because learning plays a part in the acquisition of all skills, factors which make learning easy or difficult have been studied. In the first reading Robert Havighurst singles out one of Thorndike's laws of learning and shows how children of some minority groups have different sources of approval and disapproval than children of middle-class Americans. Freya Owen, in the next article, summarizes a study of the characteristics of educationally handicapped children and their siblings when compared with a matched group of academically successful children and their siblings.

For at least some aspects of living, Americans try to foster cooperation in children. Millard Madsen has engaged in a series of studies of cooperative and competitive behavior, using an ingenious game in which the players can behave in either way. The article by Madsen and Ariella Shapira summarizes the results of several of these studies.

The author of the final paper in this chapter, J. W. Croake, brings up to date the study of children's fears, a subject studied extensively in the 1930's but very little since then.

Minority Subcultures and the Law of Effect

*Robert J. Havighurst**
UNIVERSITY OF CHICAGO

Since the 1950s we in the United States have become more and more acutely aware of and concerned about the socially disadvantaged segment of our

Reprinted from *American Psychologist*, *25*, 313–322., by permission of the American Psychological Association.

* The Annual Edward L. Thorndike Award Lecture, presented to Division 15, at the meeting of the American Psychological Association, Washington, D.C., August 31, 1969.

society. We have joined a "war on poverty." We have declared racial segregation in the public schools to be illegal. We have passed a Civil Rights Act. These things we have done out of our conviction that democracy is morally right and can be made to work better in our society than it has in the past.

We have also defined rather accurately the "socially disadvantaged" group as consisting of the bottom 15% of our population in terms of income and educational achievement. Some people would argue that this is too small a proportion. They would add another 10% to make it a quarter of the population. Others would go as far as to define all manual workers and their families (about 60% of the population) as socially disadvantaged, but this kind of proposition could not be supported with data on inadequacy of income, educational achievement, stability of family, law observance, or any other major index of standard of living. While the stable working class (or upper working class), consisting of 40% of the population, is slightly below the white collar group in average income, educational level, and other socioeconomic indices, this group is not disadvantaged in an absolute sense, does not feel disadvantaged, and has an active interchange of membership with the white collar group between successive generations.

As for the truly disadvantaged group of 15–20% of the population, there is disturbing evidence that this group is in danger of becoming a permanent "underclass" characterized by absence of steady employment, low level of education and work skills, living on welfare payments, and social isolation from the remainder of society.

The presence of this social and human problem cannot be passed off in any of the ways that might have been possible a century ago, or might be possible today in the poor countries. It cannot be ascribed to inherited inferiority of the disadvantaged. It cannot be blamed on the country's poverty, since we are an affluent society. It cannot be passed off with the optimistic prediction that the current group of disadvantaged will soon become assimilated into the general society as most ethnic groups have done in the past—the Irish, Germans, Swedes, Poles, Italians, etc.

The problem is brought to a head by the clearly established fact that the children of this group are *not* doing as well in school or in the world of juvenile work as did the children of poor people 50 and 100 years ago.

Furthermore, most Americans believe that true democracy means equality of economic and educational opportunity. There is a growing conviction that the proof of the existence of equality of economic and educational *opportunity* is the achievement of economic and educational *equality* by the previously disadvantaged groups within a reasonable period of time, measured by decades and not by centuries or even by generations.

THE WAR ON POVERTY?

For the past 10 years our principal attack on the problem of social disadvantage has been through the "war on poverty." We have spent much talent and energy and a good deal of money without raising the educational or occupational achievement level of this group appreciably, except in a few unusual situations. These unusual situations, in which disadvantaged children and youth have made normal or even superior progress, do not provide us with any broad program ideas that can be applied widely. They seem to tell us that:

1. No mere quantitative changes in the school program are likely to work. It does not bring a widespread improvement to extend the school day by an hour, or the school year by a month, or to reduce class size, or to revise school attendance boundaries.

2. Close and minute attention to the process of teaching a particular subject at a particular age may be useful.

3. We should look closely at children and their particular learning behavior for clues to action.

A LOOK AT WHAT WE KNOW

Examination of known facts about school achievement of definable social groups in the United States shows that poor school achievement is not primarily a problem of ethnic subcultures, but rather is primarily a problem of the lowest socioeconomic group interacting to a limited degree with minority subcultures.

There are certain ethnic minorities that do very well—as well or better than the national average in school achievement. Outstanding among these are the Japanese, Chinese, and Jews. The adults of these groups have an average occupational status above the national average, and the children of these groups do better than the national average on tests of school achievement.

Other ethnic groups do poorly in these respects, but these groups also have substantial numbers who equal or exceed the national average. There is no single ethnic group of any size that can be said to be disadvantaged educationally and economically *as a whole group*. Negroes might be thought of as a disadvantaged group, and this would be true, historically. But at present there is a large and growing Negro middle class and a large and growing Negro upper working class whose occupational status is average or above and whose children do average or better work in school.

The same statement applies to Puerto Ricans, Mexican Americans, and American Indians. It is the least educated and the least work-trained members of these groups who do least well in American society. These groups all have substantial and growing numbers of people who perform at average or higher levels of occupational status and whose children do well in school.

Thus, when we speak of the group of socially disadvantaged people in America, we are speaking of some 15–20% of the population who are like each other in their poverty, their lack of education and work skills, but unlike each other in ethnic subculture. Crude estimates indicate that this group contains about 20 million English-speaking Caucasians, 8 million Negroes, 2 million Spanish-Americans, 700,000 Puerto Ricans, and 500,000 American Indians.

These people have poverty in common. Insofar as there is a definable "culture of poverty," they share that culture. Still, a small fraction of them, though poor, do not have the characteristics of the "culture of poverty."

It may be that their various ethnic subcultures have something to do with success or failure in school and in the labor market. If so, it must be the combination of poverty with the ethnic subculture that produces these effects. It may also be true that other ethnic subcultures, such as the Japanese and Chinese, serve to prevent poverty.

THE IMPLICIT CONTRACT

It may be useful to examine the educational problem of the socially disadvantaged in terms of the *implicit contract* that a family and a school accept when a child is entrusted by his family to a school. The parents contract to prepare their child for school entrance, both cognitively and affectively. They further contract to keep him in school and to make home conditions appropriate for his success in school. The school contracts to receive the child, teach him as well as it can, taking account of his strengths and weaknesses and the ways in which he can learn most effectively.

Very little of this contract is put into legal codes, but the education of the child is successful only when both parties carry out their obligations fully. Sometimes one or both parties fail to understand the nature of these obligations.

In the case of the socially disadvantaged parents of this country, nearly all of them fail to meet the terms of the contract. But the schools generally fail also by failing to understand how the children of these families can learn most successfully.

THE HUMAN REWARD–PUNISHMENT SYSTEM

The principal proposition of this article is that the job of educating socially disadvantaged children would be done much better if educators understood the nature of rewards and how they function in human learning, and applied this knowledge to their work with children and with parents of socially disadvantaged children.

Leads to this proposition exist in the literature of research on education, but do not force themselves on the educator. For example, Davis (1965) offered one of these clues in his paper "Cultural Factors in Remediation." He noted that his wife, then working as a substitute teacher in the Chicago public schools, made a discovery about the way disadvantaged children may learn arithmetic. In a second grade in a ghetto school she found several children, including one nine-year-old boy, who could not count beyond two or three. The following day was Valentine's Day, and she brought some candy hearts to school. She told the children they could have as many candy hearts as they could count. The *nine-year-old boy thereupon counted 14 candy hearts.* Davis goes on to say that teachers of "culturally low-status children" should learn how their children live, and then work out new materials and ways of teaching in order to *encourage* and *approve* those students who have experienced little except disapproval, stigma, and failure in the conventional school program.

In the years since 1960 a number of psychologists have studied the nature of rewards in human learning. Among others, the work of Zigler, Rotter, Katz, and Crandall has widened the field of research and has stimulated others to work in this field.

What these people have in common is the following proposition: Human learning is influenced by a variety of rewards, which are themselves arranged in a culturally based *reward-punishment system* which is learned.

This requires us to examine the nature of rewards. We cannot simply assume that "a reward is a reward and that is it," as we might be tempted to do if we were studying the learning behavior of cats, or pigeons, or rats. It was more or less obvious to researchers that reward systems might vary with social class, or with ethnic subculture. It seemed likely that a child learns his reward system mainly in the family, but also in the school, and the peer group, and the wider community.

ANALYSIS OF THE REWARD–PUNISHMENT CONCEPT

The reward-punishment concept, and its related reinforcement theory, has been developed rather differently by each of three groups of psychologists.

Learning theorists, starting with E. L. Thorndike, have tended to use the concept to refer to something done *to* the learner by an experimenter or observer that influences the behavior of the learner. On the other hand, social psychologists and personality theorists have included the subjective experience of the learner as a source of reward-punishment. Thus, a person may be rewarded or punished by his own feelings or by the attitudes of other people toward him.

Thorndike (1905) stated the law of effect as follows: "Any act which in a given situation produces satisfaction becomes associated with that situation, so that when the situation recurs the act is more likely to recur also [p. 203]."

Skinner's (1953) definition is, "We first define a positive reinforcer as any stimulus the presentation of which strengthens the behavior upon which it is made contingent [p. 84]."

These are broad enough to cover the other usages, though the social psychologists and personality theorists have stated them more fully. Thus, Hartley and Hartley (1952) say,

> Reward . . . must be very broadly defined when we consider human learning. Because human beings are capable of retaining the effects of their experiences for long periods of time and because they are capable of generalization and transfer, functional rewards . . . may be far removed from physical rewards. When we speak of rewards we mean anything that operates as a source of satisfaction for the individual . . . the attitudes other people display and the individual's own feelings may come to serve as rewards [p. 275].

Personality theorists make much of the distinction between external and internal sources of reward–punishment. Fenichel (1945) writes,

> The superego is the heir of the parents not only as a source of threats and punishments but also as a source of protection and a provider of reassuring love. . . . Complying with the superego's demands brings not only relief but also definite feelings of pleasure and security of the same type that children experience from external supplies of love [p. 105].

THEORY OF THE EVOLUTION OF REWARD–PUNISHMENT

It appears, then, that we can distinguish four major types of reward–punishments. The earliest, in terms of operation in human learning, is satisfaction or deprivation of physiological appetites—the physiological needs for food and pain avoidance. In this same category belong other material rewards that arise later in physiological development, either through the maturation of the organism or through experience—such rewards as release of sexual tensions, toys and play materials, money, and, perhaps, power over other people.

Next in order of appearance comes approval–disapproval from other persons, beginning with praise and reproof and expressions of affection and esteem from parents, and extending to approval–disapproval from others in the family and adults such as teachers, and from age-mates.

Next comes the self-rewarding and self-punishing action of the child's superego, or conscience. This is extremely important from the point of view of educational development, because it means that the child who has reached this level can become capable of pushing ahead with his own education without being stimulated and directed by his parents or his teachers or his peers.

Finally comes the rewarding and punishing action of the ego, the executive functions of the personality. This is more difficult to conceptualize as a source of reward or punishment, but it is essential for an adequate theory. It is essential as a means of *anticipation* of future reward or punishment, success or failure, which will result as a consequence of an action performed now, in the present.

Table 1 presents the theory of evolution of the human reward–punishment system, with additional considerations to be discussed in the following section of this paper.

There are six major propositions of educational significance that have received some research testing.

1. *Different subcultures carry their children along this evolutionary path at different rates and in different ways.*

Several researchers have tested this proposition using social class as the subcultural variable. Zigler and de Labry (1962) compared the performance of middle-class and lower-class six-year-old children on a task of classifying cards on the basis of color and shape, and using intangible reinforcement ("right" and "wrong") and tangible reinforcement (tokens to be cashed in for toys). They found middle-class children to be superior with intangible reinforcement, but this superiority vanished when lower-class children were given tangible rewards.

Lighthall and Cernius (1967) compared Caucasian middle-class and working-class five- and six-year-old boys on a concept-switching task using intangible and tangible reinforcers. The tangible reinforcers were metal washers that could be traded in for a toy, a ball-point pen, a piece of candy, or a dime. They did *not* find a social class difference.

Zigler and Kanzer (1962) compared white middle-class and working-class eight-year-old boys on a simple gamelike task, using two types of verbal reinforcers—praise, and knowledge of how they were succeeding. They found that middle-class boys did better when reinforced with "right" or "correct" than when reinforced with "good" or "fine," but lower-class boys were more responsive to the praise reinforcement than to the level of performance reinforcement. The conclusion from this experiment is that middle-class boys are more able to reward themselves by simple knowledge of how well they are doing than

TABLE 1

Evolution of the Human Reward-Punishment System

AGE LEVEL IN YEARS	NATURE OF THE REWARD-PUNISHMENT	GIVER OF THE REWARD-PUNISHMENT	ACTION AREA
0–4	Satisfaction or deprivation of physical-physiological appetites (food, sex, pain, toys, money, power)	Parents	Basic motor skills Basic mental skills
5–10	Praise-disapproval from outside persons	Teachers and other adults in a teaching role	Social skills—social personality
		Self	Special motor skills (games)
	Approval-disapproval from superego	Peers and peer groups	Special mental skills (reading, arithmetic, etc.)
10–15	Approval-disapproval from ego	Wider community	Excitement Danger, uncertain outcome, sex Knowledge
15–25			Beauty Experience and expression
Adult years			Work roles Family roles

lower-class boys, who are still at the stage where they depend mainly on external approval. However, a replication of this experiment by Rosenhan and Greenwald (1965) did not bear out these findings. McGrade (1966) made a similar study, using an administrator of the test game who was naive with respect to the purpose and hypotheses of the experiment. She failed to confirm the Zigler and Kanzer findings.

We know that this kind of experiment is complicated by side effects of the experimenter's sex in relation to the sex and age of the children, as was demonstrated by Stevenson (1961). It also seems likely that the social class variable was not sufficiently differentiated in some of these experiments. Probably there is very little difference between middle-class and stable or upper-working-class families in the ways they teach their children to move up the evolutionary reward scale. Probably the big difference is between the stable upper-working-class and the "underclass" or lower-working-class. But it appears that most of the experiments reporting on social class differences used working-class samples of the upper-working-class level.

Two studies have clearly differentiated between these working-class levels. Hess and Shipman (1965) differentiated Negro lower-class children into a group with stable upper-working-class characteristics and another group whose mothers were receiving Aid for Dependent Children. There was a substantial difference between the two groups in the mother–child relationship in a learning situation. Also, Davidson and Greenberg (1967) studied high achievers and underachievers among Harlem Negro lower-class children, and found large differences in the orderliness of the home life between the two working-class groups.

2. *There are differences between ethnic subcultures among disadvantaged groups in the reward system they teach their children.*

Although all of the severely disadvantaged families share some common characteristics of the "culture of poverty," they may also have different ethnic cultural traits which lead to different reward systems. There is evidence of such differences between Negro, Appalachian white, and some American Indian groups.

American Indians have a wide variety of tribal cultures, and therefore it is dangerous to generalize about "Indians." However, among contemporary Indian groups there appears to be a general virtue of cooperation and mutual support within an extended family and to a lesser degree within a tribal community. It might be inferred that praise–blame from family and from peer group is the most effective form of reward–punishment for Indian children living in Indian communities.

The hypothesis of peer-group rewarding power is supported by observations of school behavior in several different places. Wax (1969) reports that in both the Cherokee group in Eastern Oklahoma and the Sioux of South Dakota the children tend to form a close-knit group with its own system of control that baffles the teacher. An observer in an Oklahoma Cherokee school writes,

> Observing the upper-grade classroom, I concluded that the students regard it as their own place, the locus of their own society, in which the teacher is an unwelcome intruder, introducing irrelevant demands. It is rather as though a group of mutinous sailors had agreed to the efficient manning of "their" ship while ignoring the captain and the captain's navigational goals [p. 101].

The children do not tolerate an individual show of superior knowledge. Often a teacher cannot find any pupil who will volunteer an answer to a question that several of them know. In oral reading, the whole class tends to read together in audible whispers, so that the child who is supposed to be reciting can simply wait when he comes to a difficult word until he hears it said by his classmates. Generally, pupils like to work together, and to help each other. Consequently, the weak students are carried along by the stronger ones, and the stronger ones do not exert themselves to excel the weaker ones. This same kind of behavior was noted by Wolcott (1967) in his study of Kwakiutl children in British Columbia.

The peer group may be less effective as a source of reward–punishment for Appalachian disadvantaged children. They seem to get their rewards mainly within the family circle. Conceivably, the teacher may be a more potent source of reward for Appalachian than for Indian children, if the teacher develops a motherly or fatherly relation with them.

The Negro lower-class children may operate much more at the level of approval–disapproval from the teacher than the Indian or Appalachian children. They are less likely to have both parents in the home, and they probably get less parental approval–disapproval. They do not generally fall into the mutual help pattern of the Indian children. The peer group becomes a powerful influence on the Negro children probably after the age of 9 or 10, but its influence operates mainly in out-of-school contexts—on the playground or the street corner.

This proposition needs much more research before it can be pushed very far. But the contrasting school behavior and school success of the various minority groups argue for the existence of different systems of rewards and punishments, as well as different achievement goals to which these systems are directed.

3. *In general, external rewards (material or intangible) have positive values for disadvantaged or failing children.*

This proposition differs from the first in being valid for all social classes, leaving open the question of the relative effectiveness of these kinds of rewards in different social classes. There is a growing amount of solid, practical evidence for this proposition, growing out mainly from the *operant-conditioning* programs and experiments stimulated by Skinner. They all have in common the giving of a reward for every small step in the direction of the desired learning. Work with preschool children, such as that done by Bereiter and Engelmann (1966), is being studied widely and their practices repeated at primary grade levels.

It is not established whether material rewards, such as pieces of candy, are more effective than verbal praise. Intermediate between them is some kind of point system, whereby a child gets a point for every correct answer (sometimes a point is subtracted for errors), and the points may be "cashed in" later for material objects, or special favors such as a trip to the zoo.

Several school systems have established a "reinforcement technique" for working with children who have various kinds of school adjustment problems, academic and behavioral. This method seems to work equally well with middle-class and lower-working-class children, as long as the child is having a school problem. The procedure is to diagnose the child's problem carefully, to work out a series of small steps from where he is to where he should be, and to reward him for each step. For example, an 11-year-old boy with a third-grade reading level but otherwise average intelligence may refuse to read with his sixth-grade class, and thus make no progress. Rewarding him for reading with his class does no good, because he makes himself ridiculous in the eyes of his classmates. (The punishment is greater than the reward.) But if a counselor studies the boy, discovers his third-grade reading level, and then arranges for individual remedial work with rewards for each advance above the third-grade level, the boy may catch up with his age-mates within a few months.

Validity of a symbolic reinforcement program with underachieving children was indicated with a junior high school group in Chicago, in a situation in which one might expect social reinforcement to have relatively little value. Clark and Walberg (1968) experimented with a system of massive symbolic rewards in classes of sixth- and seventh-grade Negro children in a Chicago ghetto—all the children being in classes for after-school remedial reading, because they were from one to four years below grade level in their school work. The reward system consisted of tallies made by each child on a card containing numbered squares. Whenever a child made a correct response or showed some other sign of learning, the teacher praised him and asked him to circle the next number on his card with a special colored pencil that he was to use only for this purpose. The cards were collected at the end of the class period. No other rewards were given for the points gained.

Teachers of nine remedial classes were instructed to give praise rewards so that even the very slow ones would get several in a session. After six sessions of this sort, five of the nine teachers were selected at random, and confidentially asked to double or triple the number of rewards they gave, while the four control group teachers were told to "keep up the good work."

As a result, the experimental groups got many more tally numbers, while the control groups remained at the early levels. After five weeks a reading test was given, and the experimental groups exceeded the controls by a substantially and statistically significant amount.

4. *An effective reward system in a complex, changing society must be based on a strong ego.*

This crucial step in the reward–punishment theory being developed here conceives the ego as a source of reward–punishment, as well as the executive and planning function of the personality. To develop this set of ideas we may turn to a recent article by Bettelheim (1969) entitled "Psychoanalysis and Education." Bettelheim starts with the conventional dynamic personality theory of learning by young children through rewards given first by the id (the physiological appetites) and then by the superego (the internalized praising and blaming voice of the parents). Therefore, learning based on the pleasure principle is supplemented by learning based on the superego, which carries a child from learning for fun to learning even if it is hard work because his superego rewards him for this kind of learning and punishes him for failing to learn. We all recognize that much necessary learning is hard work, and will not take place under the pressure of the id.

Perhaps this last sentence is not quite accurate. There are a number of creative teachers and writers about teaching who in effect take the position that the way to teach children successfully (whether they are socially disadvantaged or socially advantaged) is to get the id behind their learning experience, that is, to give their "natural drive to learn," their "native curiosity," free play, and to count on their learning "creatively" in this way throughout their school experience.

For example, Kohl (1967), in his book *36 Children*, describes how he worked for a year with a class of 36 Negro slum children who were below average in academic skills. He did get results. There is no reason to doubt this. His method of encouraging them to write about their fears, their hates, and their likes, about the bad and good things they experience in their homes and streets, loosened their pens and their tongues, added to their vocabulary, and got them interested in school. It seems that Kohl was helping them marshal the forces of the id on behalf of learning. But how far can this go? How far can a slum child (or a middle-class child) go toward mastery of arithmetic, of English sentence style, of knowledge of science and history, if he is motivated only by his drive to express his feelings, or possibly also by his desire to please his friendly and permissive teacher?

We do not know how far this kind of reward will carry a child's learning. We might guess that it would carry children up to about the seventh-grade level. Therefore, we should ask Kohl and others of this school of thought to prove that their methods will carry children to the eighth-grade level. No such claims appear to have been substantiated, except in the case of socially advantaged children, such as those attending A. S. Neill's school at Summerhill, England. And some observers of this school argue that it can only work with children who have a strong British middle-class superego, and can profit from teaming their somewhat starved id with the superego in the pursuit of learning.

Bettelheim (1969) argues that the main function of education is to help the ego develop so that with the aid of the superego it controls the id, but at the same time it balances the superego by allowing reasonable satisfaction of the id. "The goal of education ought to be a well-balanced personality where both id and superego are subordinated to reality, to the ego [p. 83]." "Nothing automatically assures ego growth, neither punishment nor reward. The only thing that assures it is having the right experiences to stimulate and foster growth at the right time, in the right sequence, and in the right amount [p. 84]."

Thus, the ego becomes a source of reward and punishment through enabling the child to promise himself realistically a future reward for doing something unpleasant at the moment and through making the child take the blame for the future consequences of his mistakes of judgment or his mistakes of self-indulgence.

5. *A strongly developed ego gives a sense of personal control and personal responsibility for important events in one's life.*

The ego can only become an effective reward and punishment giver if the social environment is orderly enough to permit the ego to operate on the basis of a rational study of reality. This is substantially the case with the family and the community environment of the middle class and the stable working class in America. But the disadvantaged groups we have been considering do not experience this kind of orderliness in their environment, and do not transmit to their children a sense of confidence in an orderly environment.

Consider, for example, a child of a stable working-class home in which the family has supper at a regular time, the children have a time to play after supper, and a time to go to bed. A four-year-old child in this family has learned a routine for the evening. He finishes his supper and carries his dishes to the place where they will be washed. He then plays with toys for a while, and then goes to his bedroom, puts on his pajamas, and goes to his mother who has finished the supper dishes. He says, "I'm ready for bed. Now let's read." His mother gets out a picture book, and they "read" together for a while, he nestled against his mother's body. Then she says, "Bedtime," and they go to his bed, where she kisses him goodnight. This is an orderly environment, in which the child's ego is developing so that it can promise him satisfaction if he does his share to bring it about.

Now consider a child of a mother with six children receiving welfare payments to care for them, because she has no husband at home. Rarely is there much order in this home. Hardly can this child count on starting a train of events by doing some household chore which eventually brings him into his mother's lap to read with her. She is just too busy, too preoccupied with a hundred worries and a few desires: she may not be able to read beyond the third-grade level, and she may dislike reading. She is not likely to have learned about the necessity of her children having regular rewards and punishments given consistently by her as a means of teaching them.

A good deal of research has been done on the acquisition by children of a sense of control of rewards. Rotter (Rotter, Seeman, & Liverant, 1962) has studied the "sense of personal control of the environment." Crandall (Crandall, Katkovsky, & Crandall, 1965) studied a child's feelings about whether his own efforts determine the rewards he gets from school and from important people or whether this is a matter of luck or the whims of important people. Battle and Rotter (1963) found that middle class and white skin color tended to be associated with a sense of self-responsibility and control of the outer world's rewards and punishments. Coleman (1966) in the National Survey of Educational Opportunity asked students to agree or disagree with three statements such as "Good luck is more important than hard work for success." Negro students had a greater belief in luck as the disposer. Coleman says, "It appears that children from advantaged groups assume the environment will respond if they are able to affect it; children from disadvantaged groups do not make this assumption, but in many cases assume that nothing they will do can affect the environment—it will give benefits or withhold them but not as a consequence of their own action [p. 321]." Negro children who answered "hard work" scored higher on a test of verbal performance than did white pupils who chose the "good luck" response.

Hall (1968) studied a group of young Caucasian and Negro men aged 18–20, all from working-class families in a big city. He divided these young men into three categories according to their work adjustment—one group who had a record of stable employment or went back to school and succeeded there; one group called "rolling stones" who had a recent history of frequent job changes or of going back to school and dropping out again; and a third group whom he called "lookers" who just loafed around, neither working nor going to school. He used with them a questionnaire aimed to measure their sense of control of the environment through their efforts. There was a clear difference in scores between the three groups, the "stable performers" having the most belief in their ability to control their environment.

From these studies it can be inferred that the ego is a less powerful source of reward, and the ego is itself weaker, in the socially disadvantaged groups. The child who can predict the consequences of his behavior can maximize his rewards.

6. *People learn to operate at all of the several levels of reward by the time they reach adolescence, and the level at which they operate varies with the action area.*

This proposition directs our attention to an important set of facts that are indicated in the right-hand column of Table 1. It is possible for a person at adolescence and later to operate in terms of physiological appetite rewards in one area of action, in terms of praise–blame from peers in another area, in terms of ego reward or punishment in yet another action area.

For example, a 17-year-old boy may seek id rewards or satisfaction of physiological appetite in his relations with the opposite sex. He also may seek the id rewards of excitement in doing perilous things such as driving a fast car, diving from a high diving board, rock climbing in the mountains, gang fighting, stealing cars. Some of these things he may do alone, thus cutting off rewards from others, and it is hard to see how one can get ego rewards from doing dangerous things for no purpose other than the thrill or from matching one's wits against nature.

This same boy may play a good game of tennis or basketball partly to get the reward of approval from his peers. He may work long hours at night on a high school course in calculus for advanced standing in college, primarily because his ego tells him he will be rewarded in the future by a successful occupational career.

Probably a social class and an ethnic subculture teaches a person to choose certain areas for certain kinds of rewards. For instance, some American Indian cultures may teach their children to rely on praise–blame from peers for much of their school behavior. A big-city, Negro, lower-working-class culture may teach boys to learn to fight, to play basketball, to throw rocks at school windows, and to smoke "pot" through id rewards and peer group rewards, while it teaches them to expect punishment from teachers for their behavior and lack of achievement in school.

But a particular Negro boy may become so accurate at "shooting baskets" on the park playground that he no longer gets much feeling of reward from being the best in his neighborhood. He may happen on an older high school athlete who rewards him by playing with him, or a man in the neighborhood who tells him that he might become a second Cazzie Russell, if he keeps on. At this point his ego may become effective as a promiser of future reward if he stays in school and makes his grades and then makes the school basketball team.

The study by Gross (1967) of "Learning Readiness in Two Jewish Groups" provides a striking illustration of action areas apparently selected by the minority group subculture for differential rewards. Ninety Brooklyn Jewish boys aged about six years and all middle-class were given a set of tests of cognitive development. About half of the boys came from Sephardic families (immigrants from Arabic or Oriental countries) and half came from Ashkenazic families (immigrants from Europe). The mothers were all native-born, and English was the household language. The boys with European family background were decidedly superior in the cognitive measures to the boys with Arabic-Oriental family backgrounds. There was a 17-point IQ difference on the Peabody Picture Vocabulary Test. Yet the parents were all middle-class Jews living in the same big city. Intensive study of the family training and background experience of the two groups of boys revealed little difference except in the mothers' attitudes toward wealth. Twice as many Ashkenazic (European) mothers said that earnings were "unimportant" in their desires for their children, and three times as many Sephardic mothers said they wanted their sons to be "wealthy."

One may infer from this study that the reward systems in the two groups of families (which were very similar according to the sophisticated methods used to study them) were directed toward different areas of action.

EDUCATION OF DISADVANTAGED MINORITY GROUPS

What can we say from this partially confirmed theory about the education of disadvantaged minority groups?

First, we can say that teachers would teach better if they had a systematic theory of the working of reward and punishment in the learning of children, and if they put this theory into practice. Their theory should include the concept of a hierarchy of reward levels, and they should understand what levels of reward are operating in their classes.

Second, we can assume that most socially disadvantaged children are lower on the evolutionary reward scale, at a given age, than are the advantaged children. Therefore, the teachers of these children should reward them with a great deal of praise, and perhaps with a point system that produces material rewards.

Third, a major goal of all teachers at all levels should be to help the child strengthen his ego as a controller and rewarder of his behavior. This means that the teacher cannot be content with using praise and other forms of external reward, although these should be used when they are needed. The teacher should help the child move up the reward scale.

Progress toward strengthening the ego can only be made in school by putting order and consistency into the school situation, so that the child can learn how to control his environment on the basis of the reality principle. This can be done for individual children partly by individualized instruction which enables them to learn and to predict their own learning in relation to their effort to learn. This can be done for a school class by an orderly program in which students know what their responsibilities are, participate in making decisions about their work, and get accurate information on their progress.

Since the family of the disadvantaged child so often fails to perform its part of the implicit contract, there is bound to be dissatisfaction by school teachers and administrators with the situation, and critics will sometimes blame the school and other times the family subculture. Probably the educator will have to spend much of his energy working with parents and leaders in the local subculture, helping them and receiving help from them to create an environment in the home and neighborhood that supports the learning experience of the child and directs it along socially desirable lines.

References

BATTLE, E., & ROTTER, J. Children's feelings of personal control as related to social class and ethnic group. *Journal of Personality*, 1963, **31**, 482–490.

BEREITER, C., & ENGELMANN, A. *Teaching disadvantaged children*. Englewood Cliffs, N.J.: Prentice-Hall, 1966.

BETTELHEIM, B. Psychoanalysis and education. *School Review*, 1969, **77**, 73–86.

CLARK, C. A., & WALBURG, H. J. The influence of massive rewards on reading achievement in potential urban school dropouts. *American Educational Research Journal*, 1968, **5**, 305–310.

COLEMAN, J. S. *Equality of educational opportunity*. Washington, D.C.: United States Government Printing Office, 1966.

CRANDALL, V. C., KATKOVSKY, W., & CRANDALL, V. J. Children's beliefs in their own control of reinforcements in intellectual-academic achievement situations. *Child Development*, 1965, **36**, 91–109.

DAVIDSON, H. H., & GREENBERG, J. *Traits of school achievers from a deprived background.* (Cooperative Research Project No. 2805) Washington, D.C.: United States Office of Education, 1967.

DAVIS, A. Cultural factors in remediation. *Educational Horizons*, 1965, **43**, 231–251.

FENICHEL, O. *The psychoanalytic theory of neurosis*. New York: Norton, 1945.

GROSS, M. *Learning readiness in two Jewish groups*. New York: Center for Urban Education, 1967.

HALL, W. S. Levels of productive economic and educational involvement in the culture among lower class young men: A comparative study. Unpublished doctoral dissertation, Department of Education, University of Chicago, 1968.

HARTLEY, E. L., & HARTLEY, R. E. *Fundamentals of social psychology*. New York: Knopf, 1952.

HESS, R. D., & SHIPMAN, V. Early experience and the socialization of cognitive modes in children. *Child Development*, 1965, **36**, 869–886.

KATZ, I. Some motivational determinants of racial differences in intellectual achievement. *International Journal of Psychology*, 1967, **2**, 1–12.

KOHL, H. R. *36 children*. New York: New American Library, 1967.

LIGHTHALL, F. F., & CERNIUS, V. *Effects of certain rewards for task performance among lower-class boys*. (United States Office of Education & University of Chicago Cooperative Research Project No. S-283) Chicago: Department of Education, University of Chicago, 1967.

McGRADE, B. J. Effectiveness of verbal reinforcers in relation to age and social class. *Journal of Personality and Social Psychology*, 1966, **4**, 555–560.

MARSHALL, H. H. Learning as a function of task interest, reinforcement, and social class variables. *Journal of Educational Psychology*, 1969, **60**, 133–137.

ROSENHAN, D., & GREENWALD, J. A. The effects of age, sex, and socioeconomic class on responsiveness to two classes of verbal reinforcement. *Journal of Personality*, 1965, **33**, 108–121.

ROTTER, J., SEEMAN, M., & LIVERANT, S. Internal versus external control of reinforcement. A major variable in behavior theory. In N. F. Washburne (Ed.), *Decisions, values, and groups*. Vol. 2. London: Pergamon Press, 1962.

SKINNER, B. F. *Science and human behavior*. New York: Macmillan, 1953.

STEVENSON, H. W. Social reinforcement with children as a function of chronological age, sex of experimenter, and sex of subject. *Journal of Abnormal and Social Psychology*, 1961, **63**, 147–154.

THORNDIKE, E. L. *The elements of psychology*. New York: Seiler, 1905.

————. *The fundamentals of learning*. New York: Bureau of Publications, Teachers College, Columbia University, 1932.

WAX, M. L. *Indian education in eastern Oklahoma*. (Research Contract Report No. O. E. 6-10-260 and BIA No. 5-0565-2-12-1) Washington, D.C.: United States Office of Education, 1969.

WOLCOTT, H. F. *A Kwakiutl village and school*. New York: Holt, Rinehart & Winston, 1967.

ZIGLER, E., & KANZER, P. The effectiveness of two classes of verbal reinforcers on the performance of middle- and lower-class children. *Journal of Personality*, 1962, **30**, 157–163.

————, & DE LABRY, J. Concept-switching in middle-class, lower-class, and retarded children. *Journal of Abnormal and Social Psychology*, 1962, **65**, 267–273.

The Palo Alto Study of Educationally Handicapped Children

Freya W. Owen
PALO ALTO UNIFIED SCHOOL DISTRICT

INTRODUCTION

Preliminary reports of the Palo Alto research on Educationally Handicapped pupils were presented at the Society for Research in Child Development meetings in New York City in 1967 (Owen, 1968).[1] The purpose of this introductory paper is to briefly review the earlier papers; including the major goals of the research, the sample, the data collecting procedures and the significant intellectual, medical and perceptual–motor findings.[2]

The study is being made in the Palo Alto Unified School District here in California where there is a special remedial program for "educationally handicapped" pupils (hereafter referred to as EH) (Owen, 1968). The major criteria for identification as EH is a significant discrepancy between ability and school achievement (1.5 to 2 years retarded). Approximately 2% (or 300 out of 16,000) are selected for this remedial help; hence, the children represent a rather severely impaired group academically (Money, 1966).

Purpose of the Study   Our research has two major purposes:

1. To discover whether the characteristics of these academically handicapped children can be more precisely identified and described;
2. To further clarify the causes of learning disabilities.

The design consists *first* in comparing EH children (a) with their same sex siblings, and (b) with matched same sex children who are academically successful, and their siblings, and *second*, in comparing the parents of the EH children with the parents of the Successful Academic children on a number of items. This design makes it possible to explore the familial aspects of the abnormality.

SUBJECTS   The subjects are 304 elementary and junior high school children; 244 are boys and 60 are girls.

Table 1 describes the sample. There are 76 EH children, and their 76 same sex siblings (referred to as EH and EH sibs). The 76 EH children are matched on the basis of grade, sex, and intelligence (within 10 points on the WISC) with 76 children who are successful academically (referred to as SA), and who have 76 same sex siblings (referred to as SA sibs). The two sets of siblings are matched for grade and sex.

Reprinted from a paper presented at the Society for Research in Child Development Meetings, March 28, 1969, Santa Monica, California. By permission.

[1] This research has been supported by a grant (1 RO1 HD 01730-04) from the National Institute of Child Health and Development.
[2] The investigators responsible for this project are: Principal Investigator, Freya W. Owen; Co-Investigator, Pauline A. Adams; Co-Investigator, Thomas Forrest; Consultant, Lois Meek Stolz; and Research Associate, Sara Fisher.

TABLE 1
Sample

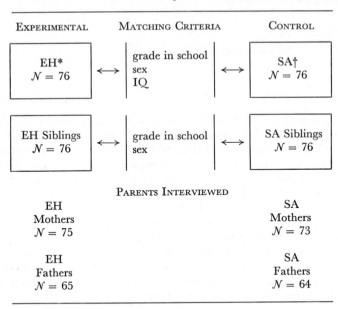

Experimental	Matching Criteria	Control
EH* $N = 76$	grade in school sex IQ	SA† $N = 76$
EH Siblings $N = 76$	grade in school sex	SA Siblings $N = 76$

PARENTS INTERVIEWED

EH Mothers $N = 75$	SA Mothers $N = 73$
EH Fathers $N = 65$	SA Fathers $N = 64$

* Educationally Handicapped.
† Successful Academic.

We first screened the remedial population to locate EH students with same sex siblings in our school district. After obtaining written permission from the parents for their children to participate (and with the understanding that the parents, too, would be involved), the EH children were given individual mental tests to see whether they would meet the criterion of normal ability (a full scale IQ of 90 or above).

Once having selected an appropriate EH–EH sib pair, we proceeded to locate a successful academic child with an appropriate sibling to match the EH pair. A clerical assistant combed the school district rosters in order to locate several potential matches. For example, let us suppose that we were searching for a successful academic student in the sixth grade, IQ ± 10 points from 120, who also had a male sibling in the third grade. After locating five or six possibilities, we sent out a simple rating form to the appropriate classroom teachers to obtain a teacher estimate of ability and academic performance. Previous test results available from school records were also considered. We then approached the families of children who appeared to be reasonable matches and, once having obtained parent cooperation, we proceeded to test the successful academic child to see whether or not he met our requirements. We tested 184 children in order to locate the 76 matched sets of EH and SA children included in the study. Of the 76 EH subjects, 64 were located from within the population of remedial children; 12 were recommended by school principals and guidance consultants.

The mean age of the experimental and control children is ten years.

The mean age of the sibling groups is nine years, eight months. The average age difference between the EH and EH sibs is two years, nine months; between the SA and SA sibs it is two years and ten months. There are no significant differences in the distribution of older and younger siblings between the experimental and control groups. The ordinal position within the family is not significantly related to learning disability in the sample.

Data obtained from parent interviews and school records indicate that our experimental and control groups do not differ significantly in social-economic background. Palo Alto is a university and scientific community with a primarily middle- to upper-middle-class population. The educational levels of the fathers of the two groups are practically identical. Furthermore, there are no significant differences between the groups on the occupational level of the fathers (Hollingshead, 1958).

Procedures   The data-collecting procedures employed in the study involved both individual interviews and evaluations with the children and their parents. All children in the study were given psychological and educational evaluations. A research assistant contacted the various schools and set up appointments. The psychologists, Dr. Pauline Adams and Dr. Sara Fisher, saw the children without knowing whether they were experimental or control subjects. The tests administered and the order of presentation are as follows: WISC, Bender, Draw-A-Person, and Wide Range Achievement Test. In addition, a brief child interview and a rating of his behavior during the testing interviews were completed.

The research assistant also set up appointments for Dr. Thomas Forrest, the pediatric neurologist, who also examined the children without knowing whether they were experimental or control subjects. He assessed the EH, EH sibs, and the SA children medically and neurologically. Following the medical examinations, Dr. Forrest and one other physician interviewed the children's mothers to obtain family medical histories, and signed releases for the hospital birth records on the children. In 1967–1968 EEG studies were made on 25 EH's and their siblings, and 25 SA's and their siblings (total $N = 100$).

Behavior ratings of the children were obtained in the following manner. A clerical worker was given a coded list of the participating children's names and schools. She was asked to go to the schools and to type information available in the cumulative records related to school adjustment and behavior. (In California there is a particular section of the cumulative record designated for this kind of information.) Code numbers were placed on the back of the cards. Thus, it was possible for three raters to work with these cards with no knowledge about the groups to which the children were assigned in the study.

Two psychiatrists and two clinical psychologists (two men and two women) interviewed separately the mothers and fathers of the children. These interviews were recorded on tape and were transcribed. At the end of the interview, we administered reading tests (WRAT) to both the mothers and fathers of the children and obtained releases from them in order to send for their high school records (Robbins, 1963).

Information regarding the speech and language development of the children was available from the Speech and Hearing Department in the Palo Alto

Unified School District.[3] All children entering kindergarten in Palo Alto receive speech and language evaluations from qualified therapists. When difficulties are present, they are diagnosed and appropriate therapeutic measures instituted. These data were available for the EH and their siblings, as well as for the SA's and their siblings.

REVIEW OF PRELIMINARY FINDINGS

Intellectual and Achievement Functioning   In 1967 Dr. Pauline Adams reported on the intellectual and achievement functioning of the children (Adams, 1968). As indicated earlier, the EH and SA subjects were matched within 10 points on the basis of their WISC full scale IQ's. The mean Verbal and Performance Scale IQ scores of all groups except the EH's are within one IQ point of each other, while there is a significant IQ difference of 5.73 points in favor of the Performance Scale for the EH children ($p < .01$). (The EH children with a positive performance discrepancy of 15 or more IQ points were analyzed as a special sub-group to be reported later.)

An analysis of the sub-test scaled scores on the WISC demonstrated impaired ability in numerical computation, sequencing, and fine-perceptual–motor hand-eye coordination and memory. Moreover, the siblings of the EH's showed similar weaknesses.

Achievement test (WRAT) findings indicated that both EH and EH sibs were significantly ($p < .01$) behind SA and SAS in reading and spelling.

As described earlier, data were collected related to the children's behavior in school. The educationally handicapped children were rated as significantly poorer in their classroom and playground behavior. Differences between EH versus SA and EHS versus SAS were highly significant ($p < .01$). Sibling similarities are also marked.

As reported, the parents' high school transcripts and adult reading skills were evaluated. As adults, EH fathers when compared with SA were less able readers ($p < .02$). High school English grades significantly differentiate both mothers and fathers in the experimental and control groups. The successful academic children's parents were significantly better ($p < .02$). Mathematics grades did not differentiate fathers. The EH mothers, however, were significantly poorer than the SA mothers ($p < .05$).

Neurological and Medical Factors   In 1967 Dr. Thomas Forrest discussed neurological and medical measures that differentiated EH from SA children. He also explored areas where strong similarities were apparent between EH and their siblings (Forrest, 1968).

His data indicated that EH compared with SA children were impaired in the following areas:

1. The ability to reproduce a tapped pattern $p < .01$.
2. Right-left discrimination $p < .01$ (Belmont, 1965; Silver & Hagen, 1960).

[3] Mrs. Ruth M. Jackson, Coordinator of this program, generously contributed these data for the project.

3. Double simultaneous touch $p < .05$ (Pollack, 1957).
4. Fast alternating finger movements $p < .05$ (Hertzig & Birch, 1966).
5. Fast alternating hand movements $p < .01$.

The following medical-history factors differentiated EH from SA:

1. Irritability during infancy $p < .05$.
2. Colic $p < .05$.
3. Decreased pre-lingual sound production $p < .05$.
4. Poor listening skills after age two $p < .01$.
5. Ease of mother–child communication $p < .01$.
6. Temper tantrums $p < .05$.

Perceptual-Motor Functioning   At the earlier symposium, Dr. Sara Fisher presented data on the perceptual–motor functioning of the EH and SA children (Fisher, 1968). The two assessment instruments utilized were the Draw-A-Person (Goodenough, 1926) and the Bender-Gestalt (Bender, 1938); both differentiated significantly between EH and SA as well as between sibling groups. The Koppitz Developmental Norms (Koppitz, 1964) were used to score the Bender-Gestalt (EH versus SA, $p < .01$; EHS versus SAS, $p < .01$).

The drawings (DAP) were evaluated with the Harris Point Scale (Harris, 1963) (EH versus SAS, $p < .05$).

This is a very brief summary of previous reports of the findings of this research. Analysis has now been made of additional medical data, of handwriting skills, of data from the parent interviews, and, in addition, a study has been made of five sub-groups within the educationally handicapped group. The complete study is being prepared for publication in 1970.

References

ADAMS, P. A. Patterns of intellectual functioning in learning disability children and their siblings compared with successful students and their siblings. *Bull. Orton Society,* 1968, 40–48.

BELMONT, L., and BIRCH, H. G. Lateral dominance, lateral awareness and reading disability. *Child Development.* March 1965, Vol. 36, #1.

BENDER, L. A visual motor Gestalt test and its clinical uses. *Research Monograph No. 3, American Ortho-psychiatric Association,* 1938.

FISHER, S. Two tests of perceptual-motor function; The Draw-A-Person and the Bender-Gestalt. *Bull. Orton Society,* 1968, 55–61.

FORREST, T. Neurological and medical factors discriminating between normal children and those with learning disability. *Bull. Orton Society,* 1968, 48–55.

GOODENOUGH, F. Measurement of intelligence by drawings. Chicago: World Book Co., 1926.

HARRIS, D. Children's drawings as measures of intellectual maturity. New York: Harcourt, Brace & World, 1963.

HOLLINGSHEAD, A. B., and F. C. REDLICH. *Social Class and Mental Illness.* New York: John Wiley and Sons, 1958.

KOPPITZ, E. *The Bender Test for Young Children.* New York: Grune and Stratton, 1964.

MONEY, J. The disabled reader. Baltimore: The Johns Hopkins Press, 1966.

OWEN, F. W. Learning disabilities: a familial study. *Bull. Orton Society,* 1968, 33–39.

Owen, F. W., and COMPTON, C. The learning centers in Palo Alto. *J. Learn. Dis.*, Nov. 1968, Vol. I, #11.

POLLACK, M., and GOLDFARB, W. The face hand test in schizophrenic children. *Arch. of Neurology and Psychiatry.* #77, 635–642, 1957.

ROBBINS, L. C. The accuracy of parental recall of aspects of child development and of child rearing practices. *J. Abnorm. Soc. Psychol.*, 1963, 66, 261–70.

SILVER, A., and HAGEN, R. Specific reading disability: delineation of the syndrome and its relationship to cerebral dominance. *Comprehensive Psychiatry*, 1960, *1* (2), 126–134.

URBAN, W. *The Draw-A-Person: Catalogue for Interpretive Analysis.* Beverly Hills, Calif: Western Psychological Services, 1963.

Cooperative and Competitive Behavior of Urban Afro-American, Anglo-American, Mexican-American, and Mexican Village Children*

Millard C. Madsen and Ariella Shapira
UNIVERSITY OF CALIFORNIA

Children of three ethnic groups in Los Angeles, California, ages 7–9, performed on the cooperation board developed by Madsen. In Experiment I, Mexican-American boys were less competitive than Mexican-American girls and Afro- and Anglo-Americans of both sexes. In Experiment II, all three ethnic groups behaved in a highly competitive manner. In Experiment III, the three ethnic groups in Los Angeles behaved in a non-adaptive competitive manner while a sample of village children in Mexico behaved co-operatively.

This study is the third in a series in which subcultural differences in cooperation and competition in children have been examined. In the initial study, Madsen (1967) found highly significant differences between children from different subcultural settings in Mexico. Rural village children and lower-class, urban children behaved in a much more cooperative manner on an experimental task than did urban, middle-class children. The aforementioned study was motivated by anthropological observations (Lewis, 1961; Romney & Romney, 1963) of child-rearing practices in different Mexican settings.

In a second study, Shapira and Madsen (1969) found children of Israeli kibbutzim (rural communal settlements) to be more cooperative than urban, middle-class Israeli children. In this study, the magnitude of the difference in cooperative behavior was greater for boys than for girls. That children of the kibbutz would be highly cooperative in an experimental task was predictable

Reprinted from *Developmental Psychology*, 1970, *3*, 16–20. By permission.

* This research was carried out with the support of the United States Office of Economic Opportunity, Contract No. 4117. The authors are indebted to Carolyn Stern, Director of the University of California, Los Angeles, Head Start Evaluation and Research Center, for her assistance in all phases of the study.

from observations of child-rearing practices and parental values in the kibbutz as reported by Spiro (1965).

In the first two studies reported here, children of three ethnic groups in the United States, all in the city of Los Angeles, California, were examined with the use of techniques identical to those used in Mexico and Israel. The ethnic groups were Mexican-American, Afro-American, and Anglo-American.

An important difference in the selection of subjects should be noted between the present study and the two earlier studies discussed in the preceding paragraphs. In the studies in Mexico and Israel the urban and rural groups were in physical isolation from one another. In addition, the social values and educational and child-rearing practices that might lead to the differential development of tendencies toward cooperative or competitive behavior are more readily distinguishable.

In the present study, however, the subcultural groups were all residents of the same urban center, and surely subject to numerous common social and educational influences. The question being asked, then, is whether or not the more subtle influences that characterize the developmental milieu in these ethnic subcultures in an area of the United States are sufficient to produce differential tendencies to cooperate or to compete as were found between subcultural groups in Mexico and Israel.

EXPERIMENT 1

METHOD

Subjects   One hundred and forty-four children who were all enrolled in the Los Angeles public school system served as subjects. All subjects were in either the second or third grade and ranged 7–9 years of age. The three ethnic groups were equally represented by 48 subjects, 24 of each sex. Each group was selected from a single elementary school in which over 90 per cent of the students were of one ethnic group. The areas served by each of the schools were judged to be lower-middle class or below by the school authorities and by the investigators.

Apparatus   The cooperation board developed by Madsen (1967) was used (see Figure 1). The cooperation board was 18 inches square with an eyelet fastened to each corner. Strings strung through these eyelets were connected to an object which served to hold a downward pointing ball-point pen. A sheet of white paper was placed on the board prior to each trial. When the subjects, who were seated at each of the four corners of the board, pulled the strings, responses were automatically recorded by the pen. Because of the eyelets, individual subjects were only able to pull the pen toward themselves. It was therefore necessary for the subjects to cooperate in order to draw a line over designated points which were not in a direct path from the starting point in the center of the board to any of the corners. In the first experiment, four circles were drawn on the recording sheets as illustrated in Figure 1.

Procedure   Four subjects of the same sex and ethnic group were seated at the four corners of the board which was on a small table. The subjects were then told that they were going to play a game in which they could get prizes. The experimenter then demonstrated that a line could be drawn on the paper by pulling on a string.

Reward was contingent on the performance of the group on the first three

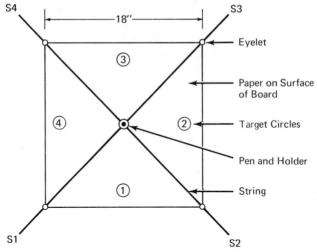

FIGURE 1.   *Cooperation board.*

trials. Prior to Trial 1, the experimenter drew numbers one through four in the circles and instructed the subjects that they were to draw a line through the circles in that order. The subjects were also told that each of them would receive a prize for each time that they crossed all four circles during a 1-minute period. On completion of a trial, the subjects were allowed to choose their prizes from an assortment of trinkets.

New instructions were given prior to Trial 4 by which reward was changed from a group to an individual basis. The experimenter wrote each subject's name in one of the circles and explained that each one now had a circle of his own, and that prizes would be given only to those whose name was in the circle that was crossed. The subjects thus received a prize for each time their designated circle was crossed. Trials 5 and 6 followed an identical procedure. It should be noted that no change was made in the task or procedure except for the change from group to individual reward.

RESULTS   The mean number of circles crossed per trial are presented in Table 1. A one-way analysis of variance of Trial 3 scores indicated that mean differences between groups did not approach significance. Thus the three ethnic groups were approximately equal in their ability to cooperate under group reward. In order to determine the relative change in the amount of cooperation with the introduction of individual reward, each group received a different score. This score was the number of circles crossed in Trial 3 minus the number of circles crossed in Trial 4.

A 2 × 3 (Sex × Ethnic Group) analysis of variance of these difference scores yielded no significant main effects. The Sex × Ethnic Group interaction approached significance ($F = 2.7$, df $= 2/30$, $p < .10$). An analysis of simple main effects of ethnic group yielded a significant effect for boys ($F = 3.88$, df $= 2/30$, $p < .05$) but not for girls. The mean decrease of 1.7 circles crossed from Trial 3 to Trial 4 by Mexican-American boys was significantly less than that of the combined Afro-American (mean drop of 6.8) and Anglo-American

TABLE 1
Mean Circles Crossed per Trial

| | TRIAL | | | | | |
| | GROUP REWARD | | | INDIVIDUAL REWARD | | |
GROUP	1	2	3	4	5	6
Anglo-American						
Boys	5.1	10.3	14.3	3.1	2.1	2.8
Girls	2.8	9.1	12.0	7.1	11.0	12.1
Mexican-American						
Boys	6.8	11.3	14.5	12.8	13.8	12.3
Girls	5.0	9.3	10.0	4.1	5.0	6.8
Afro-American						
Boys	5.5	8.0	11.5	4.7	6.0	6.1
Girls	4.5	4.8	10.7	1.5	2.5	4.1

(mean drop of 11.2) group ($F = 6.0$, df $= 1/30$, $p < .05$). The mean difference between the two latter groups did not approach significance.

The most striking result, then, was not the differential increase in competition with the introduction of individual reward, but rather the fact that all ethnic groups began to respond more competitively on Trial 4. Separate t tests comparing the mean number of circles crossed indicated a decrease from Trial 3 to Trial 4 that was significant at the .005 level for both Afro- and Anglo-Americans. A comparison of Trial 3 with Trial 6 scores indicated a significant difference at the .005 level for Afro-Americans, and the .05 level for Anglo-Americans, the latter being due to the boys. The mean of circles crossed by Mexican-Americans was lower on Trial 6 than on Trial 3, but fell short of the .05 level of significance. No ethnic group, therefore, improved performance over Trials 4–6 from that on Trial 3.

EXPERIMENT II

METHOD

Experiment II proceeded immediately after Experiment I with the same subjects participating in the same groups.

In Experiment I, competitive responses were nonadaptive in that they interfered with reward attainment. In Experiment II, circles were drawn on each of the four corners of the recording sheet. Competition was, therefore, somewhat more adaptive in that an individual child could pull the pen directly to his circle. The name of each child was written in the circle in front of him and they were then told that the first one to draw a line over his circle would receive a prize. The pen was placed at the center of the board at the beginning of four successive trials. A trial was terminated and no prizes were given if a circle was not crossed within 1 minute. Maximum cooperation, therefore, in terms of sharing of prizes, had to take place over trials, as opposed to within trials as in Experiment I.

RESULTS   If the line drawn by the pen deviated more than 1 inch in either direction from the direct path from the center of the board to a circle, or reversed directions within those limits, it was scored as a competitive response. Any less deviation indicated that subjects were not pulling against each other and was, therefore, scored as noncompetitive.

The results were that the majority of subjects in all ethnic groups responded competitively. Mexican-American subjects gave more noncompetitive responses ($M = 1.7$) than did the Afro-American ($M = .7$) or Anglo-American ($M = .7$) groups. The distributions were highly skewed in that the vast majority of groups gave four competitive responses and a few groups gave four noncompetitive responses. Comparisons between groups by Mann-Whitney U tests indicated no differences that reached the .05 level of significance.

While the results of Experiments I and II indicate a tendency for the Mexican-American group to be less competitive, the differences are not very substantial. These results, therefore, are of interest only when compared to the previous studies in other cultures in which the identical techniques were used. Such a comparison indicates that the responses of children of the three ethnic groups studied in the United States were more similar than were kibbutz versus nonkibbutz children in Israel and village versus urban children in Mexico.

EXPERIMENT III

In Experiment I, the initial three group reward trials were given in order to determine whether the three samples differed in their ability to perform the cooperative tasks when motivated to do so. This is the same procedure that was followed in the previous studies in Mexico and Israel. In all three studies, all subcultural groups of the age tested were able to substantially master the task under group reward. Subsequent differences in performance between groups under individual reward could, therefore, be interpreted as due to motivation rather than to the motor or cognitive ability necessary to perform the task. Another possibility, however, is that those groups that continued to cooperate after introduction of individual reward (kibbutz, Mexican village, and Mexican-American boys) do so because the initial group reward trials amount to an instructional cooperative set. It is quite possible that some subcultural groups are more sensitive to such a set than are others. In Experiment III, therefore, subjects performed on the cooperation board for individual reward without previous training under group reward. A sample of village children in Mexico was included in order to determine if the previously found tendency to cooperate under individual reward was due to an instructional set provided by the previous reward trials.

METHOD

Subjects   Children of the same age range, socioeconomic level, and ethnic groups as in Experiments I and II served as subjects. The experiment was conducted during summer vacation in the United States and subjects were enrolled in day care or summer school programs. The Mexican children, also ages 7–9, were enrolled in elementary school in the village of Nuevo San Vicente, located 54 miles south of Ensenada, Mexico, in the state of Mexicali. The village has approximately 800 inhabitants, the majority of whom are supported by an agriculture-based economy. Forty children, 20 of each sex, of each United States ethnic group and 36 children, 20 girls and 16 boys, from the Mexican village served as subjects.

Procedure   Four subjects of the same sex and ethnic group were seated at the four corners of the cooperation board. Each subject was allowed to pull his string to see that his action drew a line on the paper. A sheet with four circles in positions similar to Experiment I (Figure 1) was then placed on the board and the name of each subject was written in the circle to his right. The subjects were told that each time a line was drawn over their own circle they would receive a prize. Four 1-minute trials were given with prizes distributed after each trial.

RESULTS   The mean number of circles crossed by trial and ethnic group is presented in Table 2. The result is obvious without statistical test. The three

TABLE 2
Mean Circles Crossed per Trial

	TRIAL			
GROUP	1	2	3	4
Anglo-American	1.5	.4	.8	.4
Afro-American	.9	.6	.6	.5
Mexican-American	.2	.3	.5	1.0
Mexican village	1.8	3.6	5.4	6.5

United States ethnic groups responded in a nonadaptive competitive manner over the four trials with no differences between trials, groups, or sexes approaching statistical significance. This was in marked contrast with the cooperative performance of the Mexican village subjects. The data are, in fact, nonoverlapping by the second trial. There was not a single indication of competitive behavior on the part of any of the 36 village subjects and no instances of group cooperation in the three United States ethnic groups. The few circles crossed by the latter were made during active, sometimes almost violent, competition. The performance of the Mexican-American subjects, although competitive, was consistently less vigorous than the other two United States groups. For many of the Anglo- and Afro-American groups it was necessary for the experimenter to stand and press down on the cooperation board with both hands in order to keep it from flying through the air.

DISCUSSION

The results of the three experiments indicate a high degree of nonadaptive competitiveness among children of the three United States ethnic groups. This was less true for Mexican-American boys in Experiment I in that there was not a significant drop in the number of circles crossed with the introduction of individual reward. It should also be noted, however, that the mean circles crossed by this group on Trials 4, 5, and 6 was always below that achieved on Trial 3.

The results of Experiment III indicate a dramatic difference between the United States and Mexican village children. Even though the tabled results are nonoverlapping, they do not present the vividly contrasting behavior as observed by the experimenters. The often aggressive, wild, shouting matches among the children in the United States, who were desperately but unsuccessfully trying to cross their circles, was in total contrast to the rather slow, quiet, and deliberately cooperative behavior of the Mexican village children. It should be noted, however, that urban children in Mexico (Madsen, 1967) performed on the cooperation board in much the same manner as the competitive groups in the United States. The cooperative behavior of the Mexican village children, therefore, represents a specific subcultural, rather than a broad national characteristic.

References

LEWIS, O. *Life in a Mexican village: Tepoztlan restudied.* Urbana.: University of Illinois Press, 1961.

MADSEN, M. C. Cooperative and competitive motivation of children in three Mexican subcultures. *Psychological Reports,* 1967, **20**, 1307–1320.

ROMNEY, K., & ROMNEY, R. The Mixtecans of Juxtlahuaca, Mexico. In B. Whiting (Ed.), *Six cultures.* New York: Wiley, 1963.

SHAPIRA, A., & MADSEN, M. C. Cooperative and competitive behavior of kibbutz and urban children in Israel. *Child Development*, 1969, **40**, 609–617.

SPIRO, M. E. *Children of the kibbutz.* Cambridge: Harvard University Press, 1965.

Fears of Children

J. W. Croake

FLORIDA STATE UNIVERSITY

Previous to the thirties little had been done by way of extensive investigation into the fears of children. At this time Jersild and his associates conducted a number of studies. Since that time there have been relatively few studies reported, and there have been none in the last eleven years.

Child development and other texts, when reporting children's fears, most often refer to these studies conducted in the thirties. In recent years the world situation has altered appreciably, particularly in the political sphere. With this

Reprinted from *Human Development*, 1969, *12*, 239–247. Published by S. Karger AG Basel, New York. By permission.

alteration being transmitted through today's mass media, it is reasonable to suppose that what children of today fear may be vastly different from those fears of children 15, 20, and 30 years previous. This study was conducted to explore the nature of children's fears in a more current setting.

A comprehensive survey of the literature by the writer revealed that early studies were concerned with showing that at least some fears are innate (Kessen, 1965; Valentine, 1930). This was apparently substantiated (Watson, 1920). Later studies were more comprehensive and better controlled. These investigators disclosed that lower socioeconomic children tend to have more fears than upper socioeconomic children (Angelino, Dollins and Mech, 1956; Jersild and Holmes, 1933; Jersild, Markey and Jersild, 1933). Girls report more fears than boys and Negro children more than white children (Holmes, 1935; Jersild, Golman and Loftus, 1941; Jersild and Holmes, 1935; Lapouse and Monk, 1953; Pratt, 1943). There were inconsistent findings about the age of subjects and the number of fears. Dunlop (1951) and Lapouse and Monk (1953) found age to be an unimportant factor; whereas, Pratt (1943) and Hagman (1936) indicate that the number of fears increases with age. When working with "normal" children, there seemed to be little or no difference in the number of fears between intellectual levels (Gastwirth, 1943).

Children under four years of age were found to be most often afraid of noise and situations associated with noise (Holmes, 1936; Jersild and Holmes, 1933; Jersild and Holmes, 1935; Valentine, 1930). This was true for four-year-old girls as well, but four-year-old boys were more concerned with personal safety (Jersild, Markey and Jersild, 1933). Fear of animals was recorded as the most common fear in five and six year olds, as it was at age seven and eight, along with supernatural events and beings and safety (Dunlop, 1951; Ferguson, 1952; Holmes, 1935; Jersild, Markey and Jersild, 1933).

From age eight to adolescence, the various studies reviewed were not in unanimous agreement as to the most prevalent types of fears. Those most frequently mentioned were supernatural events and beings, school, bodily injury and punishment, and animals (Angelino and Shedd, 1953; Dunlop, 1951; Ferguson, 1952; Jersild, Markey and Jersild, 1933; Lapouse and Monk, 1953; Pintner and Levy, 1940).

METHOD

The present study which was carried out in three phases was designed to determine the number and type of fears peculiar to third and sixth grade pupils of low and high socioeconomic levels in the states of South Dakota and Nebraska. The sample was drawn from 12 schools of varying size including small town and large city systems. The subjects in all three phases were randomly selected from classroom enrolment sheets. Sex and socioeconomic level were controlled with the aim of obtaining approximately the same number of subjects in each of the categories. The socioeconomic level was determined by the Hatt-North Occupational Prestige Ratings scale.

In Phase I, 53 pupils were interviewed individually with respect to their fears. The sample in this phase included 10 upper and 16 lower socioeconomic males and 14 upper and 13 lower socioeconomic females. This was a total of 17 third, 18 sixth, and 18 ninth grade children. The responses given by these subjects were compiled to make a questionnaire which was administered to all of the Phase II population. The final questionnaire consisted of sixty-nine items including those fears which they held at present, three years previous, and those that they believed they would hold three years hence. Responses obtained from pupils in the ninth grade were used as possible stimuli for future fears and their responses appear only as a part of the questionnaire.

Illustrative items from the questionnaire and their ten categories appear below The categories were unanimously agreed upon by five professors of Educational Psychology at the University of South Dakota.[1]

Animals	*Personal Relations*
bugs	meeting new kids
wild animals	people I don't know
Future	*School*
getting married	school tests
college	getting bad grades
Supernatural Phenomena	*Home*
ghosts	afraid something will happen to mom or dad
the dark	mom or dad punishing me
Natural Phenomena	*Safety*
tornadoes	getting hurt while playing games
thunder and lightning	getting lost
Personal Appearance	*Political*
my hair style	communists taking over
my weight	war

The main purpose of Phase II was to determine the following: (1) What are the number and types of past fears? (2) What are the number and types of present fears? (3) What are the number and types of future fears?

The subjects in this phase were asked as classroom groups to respond to three administrations of the check list indicating those items which were like fears that they held at present, three years previously, and those which they believed they would hold three years hence.

Means for the various population groups are reported in table I. Also found in table I are the significance of the difference among the groups as determined by the Mann-Whitney U test. With the exception of one Catholic boarding school for lower socioeconomic Indian pupils, all but one of the 213 pupils in Phase II were white.

Phase III was concerned with interviewing a sample of children who participated in Phase II in order to gain some insight into the nature of the fears indicated in the questionnaires: (1) What sources are perceived as the genesis of fears? (2) What are the reasons for individual discrepancies between past, present, and future fears? (3) Which fears are the most intense?

The sample in this phase included: 1 upper socioeconomic third grade boy, 5 lower socioeconomic third grade boys, 2 upper socioeconomic third grade girls, 4 lower socioeconomic third grade girls, 1 upper socioeconomic sixth grade girl, 5 lower socioeconomic sixth grade girls.

RESULTS

As shown in Table 1 girls have more fears than boys, as do lower socioeconomic children in contrast to their upper socioeconomic peers. The subjects

[1] The complete list of items used in the questionnaire may be obtained by writing the author.

TABLE 1

Mean Number of Fears by Population Groups

	Past	Present	Future
GRADE THREE			
Boys ($N = 56$)	24.1†	23.1†	16.0*
Girls ($N = 51$)	30.2	28.2	22.1
Upper socioeconomic ($N = 38$)	20.4†	22.6†	16.0
Lower socioeconomic ($N = 69$)	30.7	27.2	20.5
GRADE SIX			
Boys ($N = 55$)	28.5†	23.1†	16.1†
Girls ($N = 51$)	26.2	28.6	26.8
Upper socioeconomic ($N = 32$)	28.4†	26.1†	20.7*
Lower socioeconomic ($N = 74$)	27.9	24.9	23.4
Total third ($N = 107$)	27.3	25.8	19.1
Total sixth ($N = 106$)	28.5	26.0	21.7

* $p < .05$.
† $p < .01$.

see themselves as having held more fears in the past then at present, and they see themselves as holding fewer fears in the future than at present. Statistical levels of significance are indicated between each of the population groups compared.

With the exception of third grade present tense, the most consistently held fears for all of the population group comparisons made in the present and future tenses were political. These data are presented in Tables 2 and 3. Natural phenomena were the most common past fears for all third grade subjects regardless of their sex and socioeconomic level; whereas, supernatural phenomena were the most frequently cited past fears of all sixth grade subjects with the exception of sixth grade girls who were most often fearful of natural phenomena and animals in the past.

In Phase III the twenty-four subjects were interviewed individually. When asked the genesis of each of the fears which they checked in Phase II group administration "don't know" received the majority of responses, about 75% of the total. This same order of response classes with approximately the same percentage appeared in attempting to account for fear discrepancies. A discrepancy occurred when a fear was indicated in one tense and not in another, i.e., fear of teachers was checked as being held three years previous and at present, but not anticipated as a fear three years hence.

The subjects in this phase were also given 3 × 5 cards indicating each of the fears which they had checked in Phase II. They were asked to place these cards in one of four titled piles: "I almost never worry about or am afraid of this fear," "I often worry about or am afraid of this fear," "I sometimes worry

TABLE 2

Percentage of Past, Present, and Future Fears by Reference Category for Upper and Lower Socio-economic Levels

CATEGORIES	PAST	PRESENT	FUTURE	PAST	PRESENT	FUTURE
	GRADE THREE					
	($N = 38$)			($N = 69$)		
Animals	13.3	14.6	7.8	11.4	9.2	6.6
Future	2.9	3.1	7.9	5.9	6.7	8.7
Supernatural	15.9	9.3	5.6	12.9	10.3	8.7
Natural	19.3	16.3	13.2	13.9	13.8	15.2
Personal appearance	2.1	4.4	8.6	3.6	4.8	6.7
Personal relations	6.8	5.9	7.9	7.0	7.0	7.7
School	8.3	10.1	11.4	9.2	10.1	11.3
Home	8.0	8.1	7.9	10.4	10.5	10.5
Safety	12.9	13.2	9.3	12.1	12.3	11.3
Political	10.0	14.5	19.9	12.1	14.8	13.4
	GRADE SIX					
	($N = 32$)			($N = 74$)		
Animals	13.1	9.6	3.2	12.6	9.6	3.2
Future	4.0	6.9	13.6	4.1	5.6	8.8
Supernatural	14.5	9.4	5.3	14.6	7.8	5.0
Natural	13.9	10.4	5.8	14.3	10.5	8.8
Personal appearance	2.5	4.6	9.8	2.0	5.7	11.3
Personal relations	9.2	8.7	11.0	7.2	8.0	9.3
School	10.2	12.3	14.0	10.2	12.4	13.6
Home	9.2	8.9	6.4	11.1	10.8	10.1
Safety	13.4	10.2	8.6	12.6	10.2	8.9
Political	9.5	18.5	21.6	10.9	19.0	20.5

about or am afraid of this fear," or "I am almost always worried about or am afraid of this fear."

The most common intensity response for the majority of fear groups was "sometimes worry about." This was particularly true for the category natural phenomena and other fears with which the child actually has had some contact such as strange noises, being late for school, people laughing at me, etc. The fear category which received the highest percentage of "almost always worry about" was political.

DISCUSSION

The results of this investigation indicate that girls and lower socioeconomic children hold more fears than do boys and upper socioeconomic children. These results are consistent in general with the findings of previous studies. The

TABLE 3

Percentage of Past, Present, and Future Fears by Reference Category for Boys and Girls

CATEGORIES	PAST	PRESENT	FUTURE	PAST	PRESENT	FUTURE
	BOYS			GIRLS		
	(N = 56)			(N = 51)		
Animals	12.4	10.7	6.6	11.5	11.2	7.3
Future	4.7	5.1	8.1	5.3	5.9	7.7
Supernatural	13.7	10.1	8.5	13.8	9.8	7.1
Natural	14.0	14.6	13.9	16.6	14.6	15.1
Personal appearance	2.8	5.0	5.3	3.4	4.4	9.1
Personal relations	6.8	6.6	8.5	7.1	6.6	7.6
School	8.8	9.7	10.9	9.2	10.5	11.7
Home	10.3	10.0	11.0	9.2	9.5	8.7
Safety	12.8	12.3	10.4	11.9	12.9	11.0
Political	13.1	15.4	16.8	11.6	14.1	14.3

GRADE SIX

	PAST	PRESENT	FUTURE	PAST	PRESENT	FUTURE
	(N = 55)			(N = 51)		
Animals	10.4	7.1	1.9	14.9	11.7	4.1
Future	4.7	7.4	11.1	13.6	4.8	9.9
Supernatural	15.1	8.3	5.6	14.1	8.2	4.8
Natural	13.3	9.6	7.3	14.9	11.2	8.1
Personal appearance	2.0	4.1	8.4	2.3	6.4	12.5
Personal relations	8.3	8.2	9.4	7.4	8.2	10.1
School	12.6	13.0	13.7	9.8	11.8	13.8
Home	9.8	10.4	8.7	11.2	10.0	9.0
Safety	12.6	10.2	9.4	13.0	10.3	9.4
Political	9.8	21.4	23.9	8.3	16.7	18.8

TABLE 4

Rank Order Correlations and Significance Levels

	CORRELATION	T*
Third Grade Past-Present	− .09	− .26
Third Grade Past-Future	.02	.05
Third Grade Future-Present	.35	1.04
Sixth Grade Past-Present	− .48	− 1.54
Sixth Grade Past-Future	.35	1.04
Sixth Grade Future-Present	.03	.09
Third Present-Sixth Past	.39	1.21
Third Future-Sixth Present	.62	2.66

* None of the T Values approached statistical significance.

apparent optimism of children is evident since all sample groups see themselves as having held more fears in the past than in the present, and they see themselves as holding fewer fears in the future than at present.

The extreme popularity and intensity of political fears was not so evident in previous research except with older adolescents (Angelino and Shedd, 1953). A comparison of the present results with those of earlier studies for comparably aged children are indicated in Table 5. Those studies which reported fears for this age group are illustrated in like categories to the present study.

Political and natural phenomena, the most common fears in this study, were not the most prominent for children of third grade age in the past. Supernatural phenomena and animals were most prevalent as found by Jersild, Markey and Jersild (1933) and Lapouse and Monk (1953).

TABLE 5

Comparison of Present Fears with Those of Previous Researchers

THIRD GRADE

	PRESENT	JERSILD, JERSILD AND MARKEY 1933	DUNLOP 1951	FERGUSON 1952	LAPOUSE AND MONK 1953
Political	1				
Animals		2			1
Supernatural phenomena		1	*		2
Natural phenomena	2				
Safety				1	

SIXTH GRADE

	PRESENT	JERSILD, JERSILD AND MARKEY 1933	PINTNER AND LEVY 1940	DUNLOP 1951	FERGUSON 1952	ANGELINO AND SHEDD 1953	LAPOUSE AND MONK 1953
Political	1						
Animals					2	1	
Supernatural phenomena		1					
Natural phenomena							
Safety		2		1	1		
School	2		1				1

* Where only the most frequently mentioned fear is cited, the second most common was not reported or was not classifiable in comparable categories to the present study.

Previous studies reporting fears for children of sixth grade age found school, safety, animals, and supernatural phenomena to be most prevalent. Only the most recent study, Angelino and Shedd (1953) mentioned political fears. That study found them to be the second most prominent behind fear of animals.

The Vietnam war, TV, and generally improved mass communication may account for the importance of political fears at an earlier age. TV and generally improved mass communication may also be the major reasons for the shift in fears away from animals and supernatural phenomena.

Since the attempt to account for the genesis of fears and the discrepancies in fears held from one tense to the next resulted in a majority of "don't know" responses, it was concluded that asking subjects to account for the origin and changes in fears was an inadequate source of information.

References

ANGELINO, H.; DOLLINS, J. and MECH, V.: Trends in the fears and worries of school children as related to socioeconomic status and age. J. of Genet. Psychol. *89*:263–276 (1956).

—— and SHEDD, C.: Shifts in content of fears and worries relative to chronological age. Proc. Oklahoma Acad. Sci., vol. 34, pp. 180–186 (1953).

DUNLOP, G.: Certain aspects of children's fears. Doctoral dissertation, Columbia University (New York 1951).

FERGUSON, R.: A study of children's fears; Master's thesis, University of North Carolina (Raleigh, NC 1952).

GASTWIRTH, F. and SILVERBLATT, J.: Reactions of junior high children to the war. High Points *25*:56–63 (1943).

HAGMAN, E. R.: A study of the fears of children of preschool age. J. exp. Educ. *1*:110–130 (1932).

HOLMES, F. B.: An experimental investigation of a method of overcoming children's fears. Child Develop. *7*:16–30 (1936).

——: Children's fears as observed in daily life by parents and other adults. Child. Fears *20*:1–106 (1935).

——: Fears recalled from childhood. Child. Fears *20*:107–164 (1935).

JERSILD, A.; GOLMAN, B. and LOFTUS, J.: A comparative study of the worries of children in two school situations. J. of exp. Educ. *9*:323–326 (1941).

—— and HOLMES, F.: Children's fears observed in daily life by parents and other adults. Children's Fears *20*:1–106 (1935).

—— and HOLMES, F.: A study of children's fears. J. of exp. Educ. *2*:109–118 (1933).

JERSILD, A. T. and HOLMES, F. B.: Children's fears. Child Develop. Monogr. *20*:358 (1935).

——; MARKEY, F. V. and JERSILD, C. L.: Children's fears, dreams, wishes, daydreams, likes, dislikes, pleasant, and unpleasant memories. Child Develop. Monogr. *12*:144–159 (1933).

JONES, H. E. and JONES, M. C.: A study of fear. Child. Educ. *5*:136–143 (1928).

KESSEN, W.: The child (Wiley and Sons, New York 1965).

LAPOUSE, R. and MONK, M. A.: Fears and worries in representative samples of children. Amer. J. Orthopsychiat. *24*:803–818 (1953).

MAHEN, V. B.: Some factors related to the expression of fear in a group of average and superior children; Master's thesis (Northhampton, MA, 1939).

PINTNER, R. and LEVY, J.: Worries of school children. J. genet. Psychol. *56*:67–76 (1940).

PRATT, K. C.: A study of the 'fears' of rural children. J. genet. Psychol. *67*:179–194 (1943).

VALENTINE, C.: The innate bases of fear. J. genet. Psychol. *37*:394–420 (1930).
WATSON, J.: Conditioned emotional reactions. J. of exp. Psychol. *3*:1–14 (1920).

SUMMARY

The present investigation attempted to determine the number and types of past, present, and projected future fears and the relationship among these fear tenses using a population of 290 school pupils. The subjects were also interviewed to determine the genesis and intensity of fears. The results indicate that girls have more fears than boys as do lower socioeconomic children in contrast to their upper socioeconomic peers. Children see themselves as having held more fears in the past than in the present, and they see themselves as holding fewer fears in the future than at present. Political were the most intense and most frequently mentioned present and projected fears.

12

Social Development and
Interpersonal Relationships

During the school years in America children get a great deal of experience with other people. During the school hours children see principally others of their own age; outside of school they see people who may be either related to them or unrelated and who may be of all ages. The development of motor and intellectual skills increases their modes of operation with others. As they develop cognitively they become able to understand principles of interaction with other people, both children and adults.

In the first article Ross Parke reviews research on the effects of punishment on children's behavior. He points out that until recently there was very little such research and makes it clear that he is not advocating the use of punishment in helping children learn. His last sentence is "punishment is only one technique which can be used in concert with other training tools such as positive reinforcement to shape, direct, and control the behavior of developing child."

The next article, by Wade Harrison and James and Donna Rawls, is a study of some of the characteristics of a sample of leaders among six- to eleven-year-olds as contrasted with a sample of nonleaders from the same population. Robert Krauss and Sam Glucksberg report a study of the development of the ability to communicate information. The aim here to is to understand better how accurate communication is achieved.

The final paper, by Carlfred Broderick and George Rowe, shows that in two large samples of American preadolescents most of the boys and girls went through a set of stages of interest in the company of the other sex. It thus substantiates through research an epigenetic development which has been discussed for some time in child development literature.

Some Effects of Punishment on Children's Behavior*

Ross D. Parke
UNIVERSITY OF WISCONSIN

Punishment is an effective way of controlling deviant behavior in children. Yet, there are many aspects to punishment which must be considered before it is used. Some of these are

Reprinted from *Young Children*, 24, 225–240. Copyright © 1969 National Association for the Education of Young Children. By permission.

* The preparation of this paper and some of the studies that are reported here were supported in part by Research Grant GS 1847, National Science Foundation.

timing, intensity, consistency, and the undesirable effects which punishment can cause when not administered properly.

A casual review of magazines, advice to parent columns or (until recently) the psychological journals quickly reveals that there is considerable controversy concerning the usefulness of punishment as a technique for controlling the behavior of young children. For many years the study of the impact of punishment on human behavior was restricted to armchair speculation and theorizing. In part, this paucity of information was due to the belief that punishment produced only a temporary suppression of behavior and that many undesirable side-effects were associated with its use. Moreover, ethical and practical considerations prohibited the employment of high intense punishment in research with human subjects—especially children—thus contributing to this information gap.

However, through both studies of childrearing and recent laboratory investigations, some of the effects of punishment on children's social behavior are being determined. It is the main aim of this paper to review these findings and assess the current status of our knowledge concerning the effects of punishment.

TIMING OF PUNISHMENT

A number of years ago at Harvard's Laboratory of Human Development, Black, Solomon and Whiting (1960) undertook a study of the effectiveness of punishment for producing "resistance to temptation" in a group of young puppies. Two training conditions were used. In one case the dogs were swatted with a rolled-up newspaper just *before* they touched a bowl of forbidden horsemeat. The remaining pups were punished only *after* eating a small amount of the taboo food. On subsequent tests—even though deprived of food—the animals punished as they approached the food showed greater avoidance of the prohibited meat than animals punished after committing the taboo act. This study is the prototype of a number of studies recently carried out with children; and it illustrates the importance of the *timing* of the punishment for producing effective control over children's behavior.

In recent studies of the effects of timing of punishment on children's behavior, the rolled-up newspaper has been replaced by a verbal rebuke or a loud noise, and an attractive toy stands in place of the horsemeat. For example, Walters, Parke and Cane (1965) presented subjects with pairs of toys—one attractive and one unattractive—on a series of nine trials; the 6–8 year-old boys were punished by a verbal rebuke, "No, that's for the other boy," when they chose the attractive toy. As in the dog study, one group of children was punished as they approached the attractive toy, but before they actually touched it. For the remaining boys, punishment was delivered only after they had picked up the critical toy and held it for two seconds. Following the punishment training session, the subjects were seated before a display of three rows of toys similar to those used in the training period and were reminded not to touch the toys. The resistance-to-deviation test consisted of a 15-minute period during which the boy was left alone with an unattractive German-English dictionary and, of course, the prohibited toys. The extent to which the subject touched the toys in the absence of the external agent was recorded by an observer located behind a one-way vision screen. The children's data paralleled the puppy results: the early punished children touched the taboo toys less than did the boys punished late in the response sequence. This timing of punishment effect has been replicated by a number of investigators (Aronfreed & Reber, 1965; Parke & Walters, 1967; Cheyne & Walters, 1968).

Recent extensions of this experimental model indicate that this finding is merely one aspect of a general relationship: *the longer the delay between the initiation of the act and the onset of punishment, the less effective the punishment for producing response inhibition.* This proposition is based on a study in which the effects of four delay-of-punishment positions were examined (Aronfreed, 1965). Using a design similar to Walters, Parke & Cane (1965), Aronfreed punished one group of children as they reached for the attractive toy; under a second condition, the subject was permitted to pick up the attractive toy and was punished at the apex of the lifting movement. Under a third condition, six seconds elapsed after picking the toy up before punishment was delivered. In the final group, six seconds after the child picked up the toy, he was asked to describe the toy and only then was punishment administered. The time elapsing between the experimenter's departure until the child made the first deviation steadily decreased as the time between the initiation of the act and the delivery of punishment increased.

Punishment also may be less effective in facilitating learning in young children if the punishment is delayed. Using a learning task in which errors were punished by the presentation of a loud noise combined with the loss of a token, Walters (1964) found that punishment delivered immediately after the error speeded learning more than did punishment which was delayed 10 seconds or 30 seconds.

Since it is often difficult to detect and punish a response in the approach phase of a transgression sequence, the practical implications of these studies may be questioned. However, Aronfreed (1968) has noted one feature of naturalistic socialization that may dilute the importance of punishing the act in the execution phase. "Parents frequently punish a child when he is about to repeat an act which they dislike" (p. 180). In this case, punishment may be delivered in the early stages of the next execution of the act, even though it is delayed in relation to the previously completed commission of this same deviant behavior.

In addition, the importance of timing of punishment may be contingent on a variety of other features of punishment administration, such as the intensity of the punishment, the nature of the agent–child relationship, and the kind of verbal rationale accompanying the punishment. The effects of these variables will be examined in the following sections.

INTENSITY OF PUNISHMENT

It is generally assumed that as the intensity of punishment increases the amount of inhibition will similarly increase. It is difficult to study severity of punishment in the laboratory due to the obvious ethical limitations against using potentially harmful stimuli in experimentation with children. Consequently, until recently most of the evidence concerning the relative effectiveness of different intensities of punishment derived either from animal studies or from child-rearing interview studies.

The animal studies (e.g., Church, 1963), in which electric shock is used as the punishing stimulus, have supported the conclusion that more complete suppression of the punished response results as the intensity of the punishment increases. On the other hand, the child-rearing data relating to the effects of intensity on children's behavior have not yielded clear cut conclusions. It is difficult, however, to assess the operation of specific punishment variables using rating scales of parent behavior because most of these scales confound several aspects of punishment, such as frequency, intensity and consistency (Walters & Parke, 1967). Differences between scale points may, therefore, be due to the impact of any of these variables, either alone or in combination.

Recent laboratory studies have avoided some of these short-comings and have yielded less equivocal conclusions concerning the effects of punishment intensity on children's behavior. Using the resistance-to-deviation model already described, Parke and Walters (1967) punished one group of boys with a soft tone (65 decibels) when they chose an attractive but prohibited toy. A second group heard a loud one (96 decibels) when they chose the attractive toy. In the subsequent temptation test, children who were exposed to the loud punisher were less likely to touch the prohibited toys in the experimenter's absence than were boys exposed to a less intense version of the tone. This finding has been confirmed using a noxious buzzer as the punishing stimulus (Cheyne & Walters, 1967; Parke, 1969).

The Parke study has also yielded some suggestive evidence concerning the impact of intensity variations on other aspects of punishment such as timing. Under conditions of high intensity punishment, the degree of inhibition produced by early and late punishment was similar. Under low intensity conditions, however, the early punished subjects showed significantly greater inhibition than subjects punished late in the response sequence. Thus, timing of punishment may be less important under conditions of high intensity punishment. However, the generality of this conclusion is limited by the narrow range of punishment intervals that have been investigated; perhaps when punishment is delayed over a number of hours, for example, this relationship would not hold. Further research is clearly required.

Other research has indicated, however, that high intensity punishment may not always lead to better inhibition or be more effective in controlling children's behavior than low intensity punishment. A study by Aronfreed and Leff (1963), who investigated the effects of intensity of punishment on response inhibition in a temptation situation, illustrates this possibility. Six- and seven-year-old boys were given a series of choice trials involving two toys roughly comparable in attractiveness, but which differed along certain stimulus dimensions that the child could use to distinguish between punished and non-punished choices. For two groups, a simple discrimination between red and yellow toys was required; the other groups of subjects were exposed to a complex discrimination between toys which represented passive containers and toys with active internal mechanisms. The punishment consisted of verbal disapproval (no); deprivation of candy, and a noise; the intensity and quality of the noise were varied in order to control the noxiousness of the punishment. Following training, each child was left alone with a pair of toys of which the more attractive one was similar in some respects to the toys that had been associated with punishment during the training procedure. Provided that the discrimination task was relatively simple, response inhibition was more frequently observed among children who received high intensity punishment. When the discrimination task was difficult, however, "transgression" was more frequent among children under the high intensity punishment than among children who received the milder punishment. As Aronfreed and Leff noted, the complex discrimination task combined with high intensity punishment, probably created a level of anxiety too high for adaptive learning to occur. When subtle discriminations are involved, or when the child is uncertain as to the appropriate response, high intensity punishment may create emotional levels that clearly interfere with learning and therefore retard inhibition of undesirable behaviors.

NATURE OF THE RELATIONSHIP BETWEEN THE AGENT AND RECIPIENT OF PUNISHMENT

The nature of the relationship between the socializing agent and the child is a significant determinant of the effectiveness of punishment. It is generally assumed that punishment will be a more effective means of controlling behavior when this relationship is close and affectional than when it is relatively impersonal. This argument assumes that any disciplinary act may involve in varying degrees at least two operations—the presentation of a negative reinforcer and the withdrawal or witholding of a positive reinforcer (Bandura & Walters, 1963). Physical punishment, may, in fact, achieve its effect partly because it symbolizes the withdrawal of approval or affection; hence punishment should be a more potent controlling technique when used by a nurturant parent or teacher.

Sears, Maccoby and Levin (1957) provided some evidence in favor of this proposition. Mothers who were rated as warm and affectionate and who made relatively frequent use of physical punishment were more likely to report that they found spanking to be an effective means of discipline. In contrast, cold, hostile mothers who made frequent use of physical punishment were more likely to report that spanking was ineffective. Moreover, according to the mothers' reports, spanking was more effective when it was administered by the warmer of the two parents.

A study by Parke and Walters (1967) confirmed these child-rearing findings in a controlled laboratory situation. In the investigation the nature of the experimenter-child relationship was varied in two interaction sessions prior to the administration of punishment. One group of boys experienced a 10-minute period of positive interaction with a female experimenter on two successive days. Attractive constructional materials were provided for the children and, as they played with them, the female experimenter provided encouragement and help and warmly expressed approval of their efforts. A second group of boys played, in two 10-minute sessions, with relatively unattractive materials while the experimenter sat in the room without interacting with the children. Following these interaction sessions, the children underwent punishment training involving verbal rebuke and a noxious noise for choosing incorrect toys. In the subsequent test for response inhibition, children who had experienced positive interaction with the agent of punishment showed significantly greater resistance to deviation than boys who had only impersonal contact.

It is difficult to determine whether this effect is due to an increase in the perceived noxiousness of the noise when delivered by a previously friendly agent or whether the result derives from the withdrawal of affection implied in the punitive operation. Probably it was the combination of these two sources of anxiety which contributes to our findings. A recent study by Parke (1967), while not directly concerned with the relative importance of these two components, found that nurturance-withdrawal alone, unaccompanied by noxious stimulation, can effectively increase resistance to deviation in young children. Two experimental treatments were employed. In one condition—the continuous nurturance group—the subjects, six- to eight-year-old boys and girls, experienced 10 minutes of friendly and nurturant interaction with either a male or female experimenter. Subjects in the nurturance-withdrawal group experienced five minutes of nurturant interaction, followed by five minutes of nurturance-withdrawal during which the experimenter turned away from the child, appeared busy, and refused to respond to any bid for attention. Following these manipulations, all subjects were placed in a resistance-to-deviation situation, involving a display of attractive, but forbidden, toys. In the instructions to the subject, it was made clear that if the subject conformed to the prohibition, the experimenter would play with him upon returning. In this way the link between resistance-to-deviation and nurturance was established. As in previous experiments, a hidden observer recorded the child's deviant activity during the 15-minute period that the adult was absent from the room. The results provided some support for the hypothesis, with subjects in the nurturance-withdrawal group deviating significantly less often than subjects in the continuous-nurturance condition. However, it was also found that nurturance withdrawal influenced girls to a greater degree than boys, and that the effect was most marked with girls experiencing withdrawal of a female agent's nurturance.

These data are consistent with previous studies of nurturance withdrawal, which have indicated that withdrawal of affection may motivate the previously nurtured child to engage in behavior that is likely to reinstate the affectional relationship (e.g., Hartup, 1958; Rosenblith, 1959, 1961). In the present study, the greater resistance to deviation of the subjects in the inconsistent nurturance condition may thus reflect an attempt to win back the experimenter's approval through conformity to his prohibition.

REASONING AND PUNISHMENT

In all of the studies discussed, punishment was presented in a relatively barren cognitive context. Very often, however, parents and teachers provide the child with a rationale for the punishment they administer. Is punishment more effective when accompanied by a set of reasons for nondeviation? The answer is clearly positive. For example, Sears, Maccoby and Levin (1957), in their interview study of child-rearing practices, found that mothers who combine physical punishment with extensive use of reasoning reported that punishment was more effective than mothers who tended to use punishment alone. Field investigations, however, have yielded little information concerning the relative effectiveness of different aspects of reasoning. In the child training literature, reasoning may include not only descriptions of untoward consequences that the child's behavior may have for others, but also the provision of examples of incompatible socially acceptable behaviors, explicit instructions on how to behave in specific situations, and explanations of motives for placing restraints on the child's behavior. Moreover, these child training studies do not indicate the manner in which the provision of reasons in combination with punishment can alter the operation of specific punishment parameters such as those already discussed—timing, intensity, and the nature of the agent–child relationship.

It is necessary to turn again to experimental studies for answer to these questions. Aronfreed (1965) has conducted a pioneering set of studies concerning the impact of reasoning procedures on the timing of punishment effect. In the earlier timing experiments, cognitive structure was minimized and no verbal rationale was given for the constraints placed on the child's behavior. In contrast, children in a second group of experiments were provided, in the initial instructions, with a brief explanation for not handling some of the toys. In one variation, for example, the cognitive structuring focused on the child's intentions. When punished, the child was told: "No, you should not have *wanted* to pick up that thing." The important finding here was that the addition of reasoning to a *late*-timed punishment markedly increased its effectiveness. In fact, when a verbal rationale accompanied the punishment the usual timing of punishment effect was absent; early- and late-timed punishments were equally effective inhibitors of the child's behavior. Other investigators have reported a similar relation between reasoning operations and timing of punishment (Cheyne & Walters, 1968; Parke, 1969). In these latter studies, the reasoning procedures presented in conjunction with punishment did not stress intentions, but focused on the consequences of violation of the experimenter's prohibition.

The delay periods used in all of these reasoning studies were relatively short. In everyday life, detection of a deviant act is often delayed many hours or the punishment may be postponed, for example, until the father returns home. An experiment reported by Walters and Andres (1967) addressed itself directly to this issue. Their aim was to determine the conditions under which a punishment delivered four hours after the commission of a deviant act could be made an effective inhibitor. By verbally describing the earlier deviation at the time that the punishment was administered, the effectiveness of the punishment was considerably increased in comparison to a punishment that was delivered without an accompanying restatement. An equally effective procedure involved exposing the children to a videotape recording of themselves committing the deviant act just prior to the long-delayed punishment. A partially analogous situation, not studied by these investigations, involves parental demonstration of the deviant behavior just before delivering the punishing blow. In any case, symbolic reinstatement of the deviant act, according to these data, seems to be a potent way of increasing the effectiveness of delayed punishment.

A question remains. Do reasoning manipulations alter the operation of any other parameters besides the timing of the punishment? Parke (1969) examined the modifying impact of reasoning on the intensity and nurturance variables. When no rationale was provided, the expected intensity of punishment effect was present: high intensity punishment produced significantly greater inhibition than low intensity punishment. However, when rationale accompanied the punisher, the difference between high and low intensity of punishment was not present.

As noted earlier, children who had experienced nurturant interaction with the punishing agent prior to punishment training deviated less often than subjects in the low nurturance condition. However, this effect was present in the Parke (1969) study only when no rationale accompanied the noxious buzzer. When the children were provided with a rationale for not touching certain toys, the children who had experienced the friendly interaction and children who had only impersonal contact with the agent were equally inhibited during the resistance-to-deviation test period.

Taken together, these experiments constitute impressive evidence of the important role played by cognitive variables in modifying the operation of punishment.

A common yardstick employed to gauge the success of a discrepancy procedure is the permanence of the inhibition produced. It is somewhat surprising, therefore, that little attention has been paid to the stability of inhibition over time as a consequence of various punishment training operations. One approach to this issue involves calculating changes in deviant activity occurring during the resistance-to-deviation test session in experimental studies. Does the amount of deviant behavior increase at different rates, for example, in response to different training procedures? As a first step in answering this question, Parke (1969) divided the 15-minute resistance-to-deviation test session into three

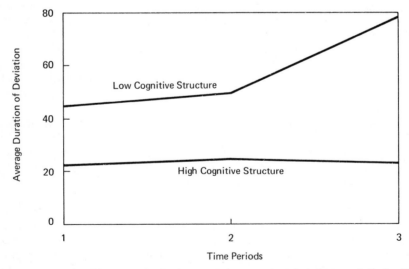

FIGURE 1.   *Stability of duration of deviation over three five-minute periods for high-cognitive and low-cognitive structure conditions.*

five-minute periods. As Figure 1 indicates, the low cognitive structure subjects (no rationale) increased their degree of illicit toy touching over the three time periods while the degree of deviation over the three intervals did not significantly change for the high cognitive structure (rationale provided) subjects. Cheyne and Walters (1968) have reported a similar finding. These data clearly indicate that the stability of inhibition over time was affected by the reasoning or cognitive structuring procedures. The interesting implication of this finding is that inhibition—or internalization—may *require* the use of cognitively-oriented training procedures. Punishment techniques that rely solely on anxiety induction, such as the noxious noises employed in many of the experiments discussed or the more extreme forms of physical punishment sometimes used by parents may be effective mainly in securing only short-term inhibition.

The type of research reviewed here does not provide us with any information concerning the relative effectiveness of reasoning procedures for producing behavioral control at different ages. It is likely that developmental trends will be discovered in light of recent Russian work (e.g., Luria, 1961) which indicates that the child's ability to use verbal behavior to control motor responses increases with age. Possibly with younger children response inhibition will be most successfully achieved by a reliance on physical punishment techniques which stress the production of anxiety. With older children, punishment techniques which diminish the role of anxiety and which stress the role of verbal control of motor behavior through the appeal to general rules, will be more effective in producing response inhibition (Parke, 1968).

CONSISTENCY OF PUNISHMENT

In naturalistic contexts, punishment is often intermittently and erratically employed; consequently, achieving an understanding of the effects of inconsistent punishment is a potentially important task. Data from field studies of delinquency have yielded a few clues concerning the consequences of inconsistency of discipline. Glueck and Glueck (1950) found that parents of delinquent boys were more "erratic" in their disciplinary practices than were parents of nondelinquent boys. Similarly, the McCords (e.g., McCord, McCord & Howard, 1961) have found that erratic disciplinary procedures were correlated with high degrees of criminality. Inconsistent patterns involving a combination of love, laxity and punitiveness, or a mixture of punitiveness and laxity alone were particularly likely to be found in the background of their delinquent sample. However, the definition of inconsistency has shifted from study to study in this delinquency research, making evaluation and meaningful conclusions difficult (Walters & Parke, 1967).

In a recently completed experiment, Deur and Parke (1968) examined the effects of inconsistent punishment on aggression in young children. Aggression was selected as the response measure in order to relate the findings to previous studies of inconsistent discipline and aggressive-delinquent behavior. An automated Bobo doll similar to that previously employed by Cowan and Walters (1963) was used to measure aggression. The child punches a large padded stomach of the clown-shaped doll and the frequency of hitting is automatically recorded. In principle, the apparatus is similar to the inflated punch toys commonly found in children's homes. To familiarize themselves with the doll, the six- to nine-year-old boys used in this study punched freely for two minutes. Following this warm-up or baseline session, the subjects underwent one of three training conditions. In one case the boys were rewarded with marbles each time they punched the Bobo doll for 18 trials. Subjects in the second training condition received marbles on nine trials, while on the remaining trials punching was neither rewarded nor punished. The final group of boys was rewarded on half of the trials, but heard a noxious buzzer on the other nine trials of the training session. The children were informed that they were playing the game "badly."

The aims of the study were to examine the effects of these training schedules on resistance to extinction—where both rewards and punishers were discontinued—and on resistance to continuous punishment—where every punch was punished. In the next part of the study, therefore, half of the children in each of the three groups were *neither* rewarded nor punished for hitting the Bobo doll. The remaining subjects heard the noxious buzzer each time they punched. The boys had been informed at the outset of the training session that they could terminate the punching game whenever they wished. The main index of persistence was the number of hitting responses before the child voluntarily ended the game. The results are shown in Figure 2. The punished subjects made fewer hitting responses than did subjects in the extinction conditions, which suggests that the punishment was effective in inhibiting the aggressive behavior. The training schedules produced particularly interesting results. The inconsistently punished subjects showed the greatest resistance to extinction. Moreover, these previously punished children tended to persist longer in the face of consistent punishment than the boys in the other training groups. The effects were most marked in comparison to the consistently rewarded sub-

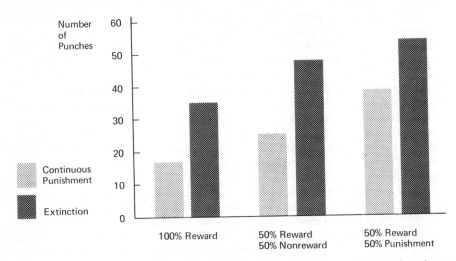

FIGURE 2.   *Mean number of punches in post-training period as a function of consistency of reward and punishment.*

jects. The implication is clear: the socializing agent using inconsistent punishment builds up resistance to future attempts to either extinguish it or suppress it by consistently administered punishment.

The particular form of inconsistency employed in this study represents only one of a variety of forms of inconsistency which occurs in naturalistic socialization. Consistency, as used in the present research, refers to the extent to which a single agent treats violations in the same manner each time such violations occur. Of equal importance would be studies of inter-agent inconsistency. For example, what effect will one parent rewarding aggressive behavior and the other parent punishing the same class of behaviors have on the persistence of aggressive response patterns? Similar inconsistencies between teacher and parental treatment of deviant behavior and the discrepancies between peer and teacher reactions to unacceptable behaviors require examination.

UNDESIRABLE CONSEQUENCES OF PUNISHMENT

The foregoing paragraphs indicate that punishment is effective in producing response suppression. Nevertheless, punishment may have undesirable side-effects which limit its usefulness as a socializing technique. In the first place, the teacher or parent who employs physical punishment to inhibit undesirable behaviors may also serve as an aggressive model. Bandura (1967) has summarized this viewpoint as follows: "When a parent punishes his child physically for having aggressed toward peers, for example, the intended outcome of this training is that the child should refrain from hitting others. The child, however, is also learning from parental demonstration how to aggress physically. And the imitative learning may provide the direction for the child's behavior when he is similarly frustrated in subsequent social interactions" (1967, p. 43).

Evidence supporting this position is, at best, indirect. There is a sizable body of data indicating a relationship between the frequent use of physical punishment by parents and aggressive behavior in their children (Becker, 1964). However, the increases in aggression could possibly be due to the *direct* encouragement that punitive parents often provide for behaving aggressively outside the home situation. Alternatively, highly aggressive children may require strong, physically punitive techniques to control them. Thus, even if it is assumed that the punitive parent acts as an aggressive model there is no evidence demonstrating that children imitate the aggressive behaviors the disciplinarian displays while punishing the child. It is recognized that exposure to aggressive models increases aggressive behavior in young children (Bandura, 1967); however, it is of questionable legitimacy to generalize from Bobo doll studies to children imitating a physically punitive adult who is often carrying out a justified spanking in line with his role as parent or teacher.

The results of a recent study by Slaby and Parke (1968) are relevant. Children were exposed to a film-mediated model who was disciplined for touching prohibited toys. In one case, the film agent "spanked" the child for touching the toys; in the second case, the adult on the film "reasoned" with the deviant model after detecting the violation of the prohibition. In addition to testing the child's resistance to deviation, the amount of aggression that a child would direct to a peer was assessed. Under the guise of helping the experimenter teach another child arithmetic problems, the subject was given the opportunity to punish the other child by "punching" him each time he made a mistake. A punch was administered by depressing a button on the subject's panel, which activated a punching machine in the adjacent room. Both the number and intensity of punches were recorded for each subject. The subjects who saw the physically punitive disciplinarian were more aggressive than the children exposed to the verbal reasoning sequence, although the differences were only of borderline statistical significance. Replication of this study is needed before a definite conclusion can clearly be drawn.

Another undesirable consequence of punishment is the effect on the agent-child relationship. As a result of punishment, the child may be motivated to avoid the punishing parent or teacher. Consequently, the socialization agent may no longer be able to direct or influence the child's behavior and encourage the development of appropriate behaviors. Conditions such as the classroom often prevent the child from physically escaping the presence of the agent. Continued use of punishment in an inescapable context, however, may lead to passivity and withdrawal (Seligman, Maier & Solomon, 1969) or adaptation to the punishing stimuli generally employed. In any case, whether escape is possible or not, the quality of the agent-child relationship may deteriorate if punishment is used with high frequency; punishment administered by such an agent will, therefore, be less effective in inhibiting the child.

The undesirable effects of punishment mentioned here may occur mainly in situations where the disciplinary agents are indiscriminatively punitive. In child-training contexts where the agent rewards and encourages a large proportion of the child's behavior, even though selectively and occasionally punishing certain kinds of behavior, these side effects are less likely to be found (Walters & Parke, 1967).

CONCLUSION

This review leaves little doubt that punishment can be an effective means of controlling children's behavior. The operation of punishment, however, is a complex process and its effects are quite varied and highly dependent on such parameters as timing, intensity, consistency, the affectional and/or status relationship between the agent and recipient of punishment, and the kind of cognitive structuring accompanying the punishing stimulus.

It is unlikely that a socialization program based solely on punishment would be very effective; the child needs to be taught new appropriate responses in addition to learning to suppress unacceptable forms of behavior. "In fact, in real-life situations the suppressive effect of punishment is usually only of value if alternative pro-social responses are elicited and strengthened while the undesirable behavior is held in check. The primary practical value of studies of parameters that influence the efficacy of punishment is . . . to determine the conditions under which suppression will most likely occur" (Walters & Parke, 1967, p. 217). From this viewpoint, punishment is only one technique which can be used in concert with other training tools such as positive reinforcement to shape, direct, and control the behavior of the developing child.

References

ARONFREED, J. Punishment learning and internationalization. Some parameters of reinforcement and cognition. Paper read at biennial meeting of Soc. for Research in Child Develm., Minneapolis, Mar., 1965.

———— Conduct and Conscience. New York: Academic Press, 1968.

———— & Leff, R. The effects of intensity of punishment and complexity of discrimination upon the learning of an internalized inhibition. Unpubl. mss. Univ. of Pennsylvania, 1963.

———— & Reber, A. Internalized behavioral suppression and the timing of social punishment. J. pers. soc. Psychol., 1965, 1, 3–16.

BANDURA, A. The role of modeling processes in personality development. In. W. W. Hartup & Nancy L. Smothergill (eds.), The Young Child. Washington: Natl. Assn. for the Education of Young Children, 1967, pp. 42–58.

———— & WALTERS, R. H. Social Learning and Personality Development. New York: Holt, Rinehart & Winston, 1963.

BECKER, W. C. Consequences of different kinds of parental discipline. In M. L. Hoffman & Lois W. Hoffman (eds.), Review of Child Development Research, Vol. 1. New York: Russell Sage Foundation, 1964, pp. 169–208.

BLACK, A. H., SOLOMON, R. L., & WHITING, J. W. M. Resistance to temptation in dogs. Cited by Mowrer, O. H., Learning Theory and the Symbolic Processes. New York: John Wiley, 1960.

CHEYNE, J. A. & WALTERS, R. H. Timing and intensity of punishment and cognitive structuring as determinants of response inhibition. Unpubl. mss., Univ. of Waterloo, 1968.

CHURCH, R. M. The varied effects of punishment on behavior. Psychol. Rev., 1963, 70, 369–402.

COWAN, P. A., & WALTERS, R. H. Studies of reinforcement of aggression: I. Effects of scheduling. Child Develm., 1963, 34, 543–551.

DEUR, J. L. & PARKE, R. D. The effects of inconsistent punishment on aggression in children. Unpubl. mss., Univ. of Wisconsin, 1968.

GLUECK, S. & GLUECK, ELEANOR. Unraveling Juvenile Delinquency. Cambridge: Harvard Univ. Press, 1950.

HARTUP, W. W. Nurturance and nurturance-withdrawal in relation to the dependency behavior of preschool children. Child Develm., 1958, 29, 191–201.

LURIA, A. R. The Role of Speech in the Regulation of Normal and Abnormal Behavior. New York: Liveright, 1961.

McCORD, W., McCORD, JOAN & HOWARD, A. Familial correlates of aggression in nondelinquent male children. J. abnorm. soc. Psychol., 1961, 62, 79–93.

PARKE, R. D. Nurturance, nurturance withdrawal and resistance to deviation. Child Develm., 1967, 38, 1101–1110.

————. The role of punishment in the socialization process. Paper read at Miami Symposium on Social Behavior, Miami, Ohio, Nov., 1968.

————. Effectiveness of punishment as an interaction of intensity, timing, agent nurturance and cognitive structuring. Child Develm., 1969, in press.

———— & WALTERS, R. H. Some factors determining the efficacy of punishment for inducing response inhibition. Monographs of the Soc. for Research in Child Develm., 1967, 32 (Serial No. 109).

ROSENBLITH, JUDY F. Learning by imitation in kindergarten children. Child Develm., 1959, 30, 69–80.

————. Imitative color choices in kindergarten children. Child Develm., 1961, 32, 211–223.

SEARS, R. R., MACCOBY, ELEANOR E. & LEVIN, H. *Patterns of Child Rearing.* Evanston, Ill.: Row, Peterson, 1957.

SELIGMAN, M. E. P., MAIER, S. F. & SOLOMON, R. L. Unpredictable and uncontrollable aversive events. In F. R. Brush (Ed.), *Aversive Conditioning and Learning.* New York: Academic Press, 1969.

SLABY, R. & PARKE, R. D. The influence of a punitive or reasoning model on resistance to deviation and aggression in children. Unpubl. mss., Univ. of Wisconsin, 1968.

WALTERS, R. H. Delay-of-reinforcement effects in children's learning. *Psychonom. Sci.,* 1964, 1, 307–308.

——— & ANDRES, D. Punishment procedures and self-control. Paper read at Annual Meeting of the Amer. Psychological Assn., Washington, D.C., Sept., 1967.

——— & PARKE, R. D. The influence of punishment and related disciplinary techniques on the social behavior of children: theory and empirical findings. In B. A. Maher (Ed.), *Progress in Experimental Personality Research,* Vol. 4, 1967, pp. 179–228.

——— PARKE, R. D., & CANE, VALERIE A. Timing of punishment and the observation of consequences to others as determinants of response inhibition. *J. exp. child Psychol.,* 1965, 2, 10–30.

Differences Between Leaders and Non-leaders in Six- to Eleven-Year-Old Children*

C. Wade Harrison
TEXAS CHRISTIAN UNIVERSITY

James R. Rawls and Donna J. Rawls
VANDERBILT UNIVERSITY

The present study was designed to investigate incidence of leadership ratings among 6 to 11 year old children as it is related to intellectual ability, academic performance, social interaction patterns, medical history, TAT responses, and scores on a number of other psychological tests. The leader sample consisted of 278 Ss rated by their teachers as being frequently chosen as leaders (143 boys and 135 girls), while non-leaders consisted of 416 Ss who were rated as seldom or never chosen (206 boys and 210 girls) Results indicated that children who were more frequently chosen as leaders were healthier, more intelligent, higher achievers in school, more socially adept, and better adjusted than those children who were infrequently chosen as leaders.

In the extensive literature of leadership research, there is surprisingly little data that is directly related to leadership behavior in young children. The

Reprinted from a paper presented at the Southwestern Psychological Association meetings, April 18–20, 1968, New Orleans, Louisiana. By permission. See also *Journal of Social Psychology,* 1971 (in press).

* Appreciation is expressed to the National Center for Health Statistics for permission to use the data upon which this study was based.

purpose of the present study was to investigate differences between children rated as leaders and non-leaders in a large sample of six- to eleven-year-old children.

Leadership among children has been found to be highly related to social participation (Parten, 1933), social acceptance, and popularity (Bonney, 1943; Tuddenham, 1951). As suggested by Pikunas and Albrecht (1961), the child who surpasses his peers in strength or achievement in preferred activities usually has a direct opportunity to assume leadership. If this child is aware of the likes and dislikes of other children and is friendly, enthusiastic, and daring, he is even more likely to assume a leadership role among his peers.

The present study was designed to investigate incidence of leadership among children as it is related to intellectual ability, academic performance, social interaction patterns, medical history, TAT responses, and scores on a number of other psychology tests.

METHOD

SUBJECTS   Ss were drawn from a national sample of 2,012 children included in the Health Examination Survey, conducted by the National Center for Health Statistics. The S population consisted of 694 children ranging in age from six to eleven years old. There were 349 boys and 345 girls.

The criterion for being considered as a leader or a non-leader was a teacher rating of the frequency with which each child was chosen a leader. Frequency of being chosen a leader was allotted three categories of response: (a) frequently chosen, (b) average incidence, (c) seldom or never chosen. Only those Ss who were frequently chosen or who were seldom or never chosen were included in the sample. The group of leaders selected included 278 Ss who were frequently chosen (143 boys and 135 girls), while the non-leaders consisted of 416 Ss who were seldom or never chosen (206 boys and 210 girls).

PROCEDURE   The communities from which the children were drawn were selected according to the field data collection locations of the National Center for Health Statistics. Ss were examined on site within each community in special examination trailers.

Data collected included medical and dental examinations, medical histories, teacher ratings, and ratings by mothers. Demographic data such as socio-economic status, income level, residential location, etc., were also gathered. Psychological tests included the WRAT reading and arithmetic subtests, the Draw-a-Man test and the WISC vocabulary and block design subtests. In addition, TAT protocols for cards 1, 2, 5, 8, and 16 were tape recorded and subsequently transcribed and scored. All psychological tests were administered and scored by psychologists holding a master's degree.

RESULTS

Results are presented in Table 1. A scale based upon S's medical history indicated that those Ss defined as leaders were significantly healthier than non-leaders ($p < .02$). A scale assessing present health also showed leaders to

TABLE 1
A Comparative Analysis of Leaders and Non-leaders

		DIRECTION OF SIGNIFICANCE	
VARIABLES	SIGNIFICANCE LEVEL	LEADERS	NON-LEADERS
General health	< .02	*	
Motor activity	< .001	*	
Aggression	< .01	*	
Frequency of disciplinary action	< .01	*	
Intellectual ability	< .001	*	
Academic performance	< .001	*	
Gifted	< .001	*	
Overall adjustment	< .001	*	
Chosen first	< .001	*	
Well liked	< .05	*	
Race	< .05	*	
WRAT reading	< .05	*	
WISC vocabulary	< .05	*	
WISC block design	< .05	*	
Emotionally disturbed	< .01		*
Sex	N.S.		
Residence location	N.S.		
Income level of parents	N.S.		
Incidence of childhood diseases	N.S.		
Incidence of asthma	N.S.		
Hayfever	N.S.		
Other allergies	N.S.		
Heart disease	N.S.		
Nursery school attendance	N.S.		
Kindergarten attendance	N.S.		
Tension level	N.S.		
Temper outbursts	N.S.		
WRAT arithmetic subtest	N.S.		

be healthier ($p < .01$). Teacher ratings indicated that leaders displayed significantly more motor activity ($p < .001$) and were more aggressive ($p < .01$).

With respect to school performance, *S*s identified as leaders showed a significantly greater frequency of disciplinary actions ($p < .01$), but also scored significantly higher on teacher ratings of intellectual ability ($p < .001$)and academic performance ($p < .001$). In a similar vein, teachers indicated that a greater number of gifted children were among those considered as leaders ($p < .001$).

Teacher ratings indicated that non-leaders were more frequently emotionally disturbed ($p < .01$). In contrast, leaders were rated significantly higher on overall adjustment ($p < .001$).

When choosing sides for games and activities, leaders were more often chosen toward the first ($p < .001$). Leaders were also rated as being well liked and more popular than non-leaders ($p < .05$).

Race was also found to differentiate leaders and non-leaders. Leaders were Caucasian significantly more often than not ($p < .05$). In other words, a significantly greater number of non-Caucasian Ss were found in the non-leader group than were in the leader group.

With regard to the intelligence test data, leaders scored significantly higher on the WRAT reading subtest ($p < .05$), the WISC vocabulary subtest ($p < .05$) and the WISC block design subtest ($p < .05$). Leaders also scored in the expected direction on the Draw-a-Man test, but this failed to reach significance.

An analysis of the protocols showed no identifiable patterns of language production or thematic expression discriminating leaders from non-leaders. However, a few isolated language and thematic variables did significantly differentiate the two groups. These differences are presently undergoing more extensive investigation.

The following variables showed no relationship with frequency of being chosen a leader: sex; residence location; income level of parents; incidence of childhood diseases; incidence of asthma, hay fever, and other allergies; heart disease or other serious illnesses; nursery school or kindergarten attendance; tension level; temper outbursts; incidence of early trauma and scores on the WRAT arithmetic subtests.

DISCUSSION

Results of the present study indicated that children who were more frequently chosen as leaders were healthier, more intelligent, higher achievers in school, more socially adept, and better adjusted than those children who were infrequently chosen as leaders. In short, leaders displayed greater potential to excel physically, mentally, and socially.

On the surface, these data are reminiscent of Terman's (1925) early findings with exceptional children, in that he found exceptionally bright children to be taller, heavier, and socially more poised than normal children. However, close scrutiny of these data disclosed that leaders taken as a group were not necessarily physically superior *and* mentally superior *and* socially superior. Instead, the data indicated that when taken individually, children who were frequently chosen as leaders excelled in at least one of these areas.

An earlier study by Chowdhry and Newcomb (1952) showed the ability to be sensitive to the needs of the group to be a necessary but not a sufficient condition for being chosen a leader. Several other investigators have shown the selection of a leader to be a function of his ability to satisfy the needs of the group. Bonney (1943) and Pikunas and Albrecht (1961) have suggested that those children who surpass their peers in strength or achievement have a direct opportunity to assume leadership. Findings of the present study lend strong support to these earlier suggestions. Because childhood leaders excelled mentally, physically, and socially, they were better equipped to assume positions of leadership in group activities.

References

BONNEY, M. E. The constancy of sociometric scores and their relationship to teacher judgments of social success, to personality self-ratings. *Sociometry*, 1943, *6*, 409–424.

CHOWDHRY, K., & NEWCOMB, T. M. The relative abilities of leaders and non-leaders to estimate opinions of their own groups. *Journal of Abnormal and Social Psychology*, 1952, *47*, 51–57.

PARTEN, M. B. Leadership among preschool children. *Journal of Abnormal and Social Psychology*, 1933, *27*, 430–440.

PIKUNAS, J., & ALBRECHT, E. J. *Psychology of human development*. New York: McGraw-Hill Book Co., 1961.

TERMAN, L. M., BALDWIN, B. T., & BRONSON, E. *Genetic studies of genius. The mental and physical traits of a thousand gifted children*, Vol. 1. Stanford, California: Stanford University Press, 1925.

Some Characteristics of Children's Messages

Robert M. Krauss

RUTGERS UNIVERSITY

Sam Glucksberg

PRINCETON UNIVERSITY

In previously reported research employing a two-person communication task, we have found that children display an increasing competence for accurate communication as a function of age. This effect has been shown to hold for matched-age pairs ranging from kindergarten to fifth grade (Krauss and Glucksberg, 1969) and below we will present some more recent data to show that the same effect is obtained when the age of speaker and listener are varied orthogonally. But today we would like to look beyond the issue of gross developmental differences in communicator accuracy and examine some of the age-differential characteristics of children's message which may underly differences in communicator accuracy.

Let us first describe the experimental communication task we have been employing and review in somewhat greater detail the results we have previously obtained. Then we will take a moment to speculate on the sorts of processes which might be responsible for these results and attempt to evaluate these speculations on some recently obtained data.

In most of our experiments, subjects are given the task of communicating about a set of novel graphic designs. The set of designs is illustrated in Figure 1. The property they have in common is their low codeability (Brown and Lenneberg, 1954). That is, they are difficult to name or characterize, each one eliciting

From a paper delivered at the meetings of the Society for Research in Child Development at Santa Monica, California, April, 1969. Reprinted by permission of the authors.

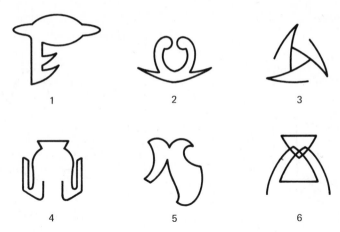

FIGURE 1.   *The graphic designs employed.*

from a group of speakers a wide variety of verbal labels. The designs are repro-
duced on the four vertical facets of a 2-inch wooden block, one design per
block. Each block has a hole drilled vertically through its center so that it can
be stacked on a wooden dowel. The experimental situation is illustrated in
Figure 2. There are two subjects, designated the speaker and the listener, each
of whom is given a duplicate set of blocks imprinted with the novel designs. The
speaker receives his blocks in a dispenser so constructed that the blocks must be
removed one at a time in a predetermined order. The listener receives the six
blocks spread out before her in random order. The subjects are separated by an
opaque screen placed so that they can neither see each other nor each other's
blocks.

The task is introduced to the subjects as a game called "Stack the Blocks."
The object of the game is to build two identical stacks of six blocks. The speaker
is instructed to remove the blocks from the dispenser one at a time and stack them
on his peg. At the same time, he is told, he must instruct his partner, the listener,
which block to stack on her peg. No restrictions are placed on either subject's
speech.

Before playing the game with the novel designs, subjects are given several
pretraining trials using a set of blocks imprinted with familiar objects (animals,
circus figures, etc.,). Since virtually all children can identify and name the
figures depicted on the pretraining blocks, this procedure greatly simplifies teaching the rules of the game. At the same time it ensures that defective performance
on the experimental task can be attributed to difficulties in dealing with the
novel designs and not simply to an inability to follow the rules of the game.

In our earliest study, done with nursery school age children, we observed
that the absurdly poor communicator performance of our subjects seemed to
derive from the idiosyncratic or egocentric nature of their messages. This
observation was reinforced by the finding that the same messages which communicated poorly or not at all to both young and adult listeners resulted in
extremely accurate choice behavior when they were addressed to the subjects
who initially had uttered them. Clearly the messages were in some sense

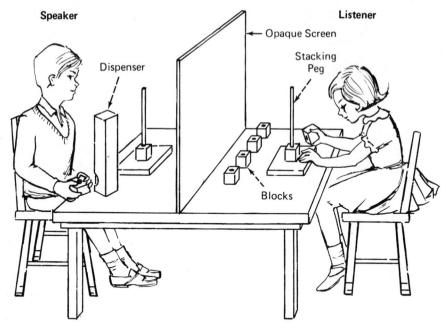

FIGURE 2.   *Experimental situation. Although a male speaker and female listener are shown, most of the studies employ same-sex pairs.*

"meaningful"; but their meaning was essentially private—which is simply another way of saying that they were not effective in an inter-personal communicative context.

But why should this be so? Let us look back for a moment at our communication task. How did our subjects go about communicating these rather exotic designs? If our stimuli had been representations of familiar objects (e.g., chairs, cups, horses) few children would have experienced difficulty; the simple strategy would have been to name the pictured objects. Indeed, this is precisely what subjects did in the pre-training phase of the experiment and all of our subjects can do it at least passably well. But our novel stimuli, by design, are not familiar. Hence, subjects have no well-formed names for them. The only viable strategy is for the subject to liken the designs to things for which he has names (a part of a figure may resemble a "snake" or a "saucer") and to use this resemblance with the necessary qualifications to guide his partner's identification. (There is, of course, another possibility—to give an exhaustive geometric description of the figure—but this is beyond our subject's capacity and, even if it were not, would probably be unproductive.)

So, at the very least, our subjects must have available in their repertoires a set of relevant concepts. They must be able to recognize elements of figures that look like snakes and saucers and, equally important, they must know the appropriate word-labels for these concepts.

But this alone is insufficient. The young subject in our early experiment who called a figure "mommy's hat" had obviously seen a resemblance between these two referents. The reason her message was uncommunicative was the small likelihood of some other person having any precise idea of what the latter referent looked like. Her message was perfectly adequate for herself, but not for anyone else.

This distinction, analogous to what Vygotsky (1962) has referred to as "inner" and "external speech," is one that is clearly reflected in adult usage. We are very much aware that the way we refer to things for our private use may communicate inadequately to another person. If I were to make up a list of "things to do" for my own use, it would be very different from the set of instructions I would provide for another person doing the same things. Indeed, competent adult communicators are careful to differentiate among the encodings appropriate for different listeners.

An experiment by Krauss, Vivekananthan and Weinheimer (1968) illustrates some of the differences between encoding for oneself and encoding for others. Subjects were asked to provide names for a set of color chips under one of two conditions. In the "Social Encoding Condition," subjects were told that the names they provided would, on some later occasion, be given to another person who would be asked to identify the color referred to. In the "Non-social Encoding Condition," subjects were told that they themselves would be called back in a few weeks and asked to make the color identifications from their own names. Actually, two weeks later all subjects were recalled and given three different types of names randomly intermixed. Some of the names were the ones the subject herself had given previously, some were names given by another subject under Social encoding instructions, and some were names given by another subject under Non-social encoding instructions. They were asked to identify for each name the color referred to. It was quite clear that subjects were best able to identify colors from names they themselves had provided, and this was independent of whether these names had been given under Social or Non-social instructions. They were somewhat less accurate in identifying colors from names provided by another person, under Social encoding instructions. For names encoded by others under Non-social instructions, identification accuracy was considerably poorer. A recent replication of this experiment, using male subjects and photographs of faces instead of color chips for stimuli, produced identical results.

In one sense, the behavior of our adult subjects in the Non-social encoding conditions was similar to that of the children in the experiment described above: they were providing messages which were privately (but not publicly) comprehensible. There was, however, an important difference: the adult behavior was task-appropriate; our subjects had no reason to believe that their messages would ever be transmitted to anyone else.

These results lead us to believe that, in addition to an adequate conceptual repertoire, a speaker must also have available some mechanism for determining which of the several possible alternative encodings present in his repertoire will communicate most effectively. The precise nature of such a mechanism we will leave open for the present. Let us, instead, turn to some relevant data.

It is fairly easy to demonstrate that the ability of children to communicate increases with age. Figure 3 indicates this, plotting the number of errors as a function of repetitive trials in our communication task for children in

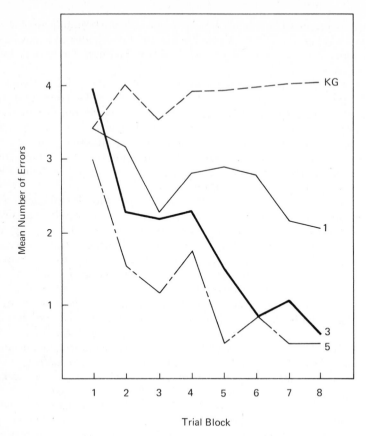

F IGURE 3.   *Mean errors over trials for matched-age pairs in the four grades.*

kindergarten, first, third, and fifth grades (Krauss and Glucksberg, 1969). A similar result is obtained when one varies the grade of speaker and listener independently. Figure 4 shows the mean number of errors for first, third, and fifth grade speakers who are communicating to first, third, or fifth grade listeners. Note that there is an effect for speaker's grade and for listener's grade, both effects in the direction of increased accuracy with increasing age.

But what is it our subjects are saying that gives rise to these results? In nearly all of these experiments we have transcribed our subjects' utterances verbatim for analysis. The data I will discuss was taken from a partial replication of the experiment discussed above using subjects in kindergarten, fifth and eighth grade. We chose these transcripts for analysis because it seemed more likely that the wide age range would maximize the possibility of detecting differences.

What we did was to count the number of conceptual responses for each speaker's message on the first trial. We chose the first trial because these messages are uncontaminated by contributions from the speaker's partner in a way that later messages may not be. By a conceptual response we mean the mention of a

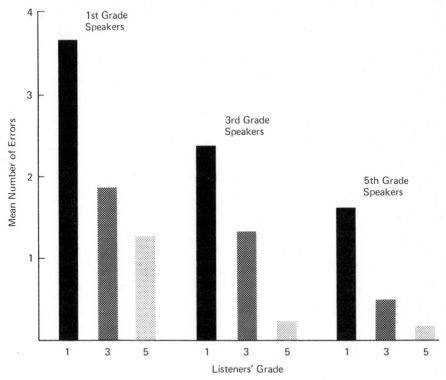

F I G U R E 4.   *Errors as a function of speaker and listener age.*

distinct descriptive element of a figure. So if a subject said that a figure looked like "snakes in a saucer" we would count two conceptual responses: snakes and saucer. A description like "a space-ship with points at either end and a wrench hanging down in back" would be coded as containing two conceptual responses, viz., space ship and wrench. The coding scheme is somewhat rough, but coders can use it with reasonably good reliability once they have some practice.

We would expect that the conceptual repertoires of our subjects would increase with age and that this would be reflected in the number of conceptual responses they gave in the communication task. The data are shown in Figure 5. The total number of conceptual responses are shown for kindergartners, fifth graders and eighth graders. Kindergartners on the average give only about two-thirds as many conceptual responses as fifth graders. And note that fifth graders and eighth graders give roughly the same number of conceptual responses—if anything the margin is trivially in favor of the younger group. We were somewhat surprised by this result but the wisdom of hindsight convinces us that it should not be too troubling. But if we look at the communication accuracy data for these same subjects, one fact is quite obvious: eighth grade speakers are more adequate communicators than fifth graders. The number of errors for fifth and eighth grade speakers communicating with their age peers are shown in Figure 6. The difference is clear. If one raises the objection that

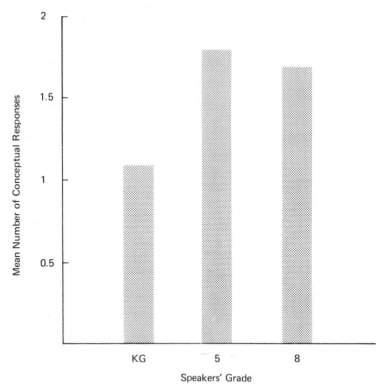

FIGURE 5.   *Mean number of conceptual responses per figure.*

this does not take into account the effect of the listener's age (and we know from previous work that the listener's age does have an effect), we can compare the performance of these two groups of subjects talking to listeners of the same age— namely kindergartners. This is shown in Figure 7. If anything, the difference is accentuated. Kindergartners are at best woefully inadequate partners but their performance when paired with eighth graders is vastly superior to what they do with fifth graders. Indeed, the performance of kindergarten listeners with fifth grade speakers shows relatively little improvement over trials.

Recall, however, that the conceptual repertoires of fifth and eighth grade speakers, to the extent that they are tapped by our measure, differ not at all. How, then, can we explain the increased effectiveness of the older subjects? Returning to our earlier argument, we hypothesized that a large repertoire was a necessary but insufficient condition for effective communication. In addition to the repertoire, it is necessary that a speaker have the ability to select out of that repertoire concepts that are at least potentially socially meaningful.

Unfortunately the communicative meaningfulness of a given conceptual response, although intuitively reasonably clear, is difficult to characterize operationally. If one who is familiar with the six stimulus figures simply reads the messages, it is obvious which are good ones (i.e., communicate effectively)

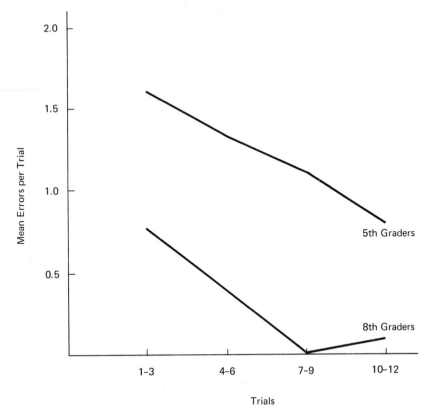

F I G U R E 6.   *Mean number of errors per trial (matched-age pairs).*

and which do not. But when one does this, he is simply taking the role of the listener in our experiment. What we need is a measure which we can apply to the messages themselves and which does not take into account the choice response of a real or role-playing listener. We know of no measure which does this precisely. But there are some which, it may be argued, are relevant to it.

The work of several sets of investigators (e.g., Brown and Lenneberg, 1954; Lantz and Stefflre, 1964; Krauss and Weinheimer, 1967; and Krauss, Vivekananthan and Weinheimer, 1968) provides some direct and indirect evidence for the proposition that the communality of names given to stimuli is a good index of how adequately the stimuli can be communicated. Brown and Lenneberg found that differences in the communality of names given to color chips was a good predictor of how accurately the colors could be identified on a delayed recognition task. Lantz and Stefflre showed that the same communality index was correlated with communication accuracy. Krauss and Weinheimer demonstrated that the communality index varied appropriately with the stimulus context in which the referent stimulus was set. And, in the experiment referred to above, Krauss, Vivekananthan and Weinheimer found that a rough analog of the communality index varied depending on whether a

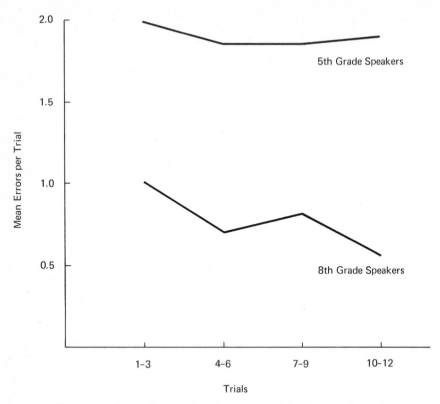

FIGURE 7.   *Mean number of errors per trial (kindergarten listeners).*

speaker's manipulated encoding condition was public or private. We would not argue that a communality index is the best measure imaginable to be applied to our data. Rather, it is the best one we could think of and there is at least some rationale for its use.

Therefore, we calculated from our transcripts the proportion of conceptual responses that were not unique—that is, were used by more than one speaker. We did this separately by grade and figure. This proportion will serve as our communality index. The results of this analysis are presented in Figure 8. Note that for kindergartners the proportion of conceptual responses given by more than one speaker was relatively low, less than one in five. And recall that this is so despite the fact that kindergartners as a group give a relatively small number of different conceptual responses to begin with. Clearly these responses, few in number though they may be, are a remarkably heterogeneous lot.

Now let us look at the data for fifth and eighth graders; bearing in mind the fact that the total number of conceptual responses given by subjects in these two groups is roughly the same. For eighth graders, about 35 percent of the conceptual responses given are used by more than one speaker; for fifth graders this figure drops to 28 percent. Not a very large difference perhaps, but nearly as large as the difference between fifth graders and kindergartners.

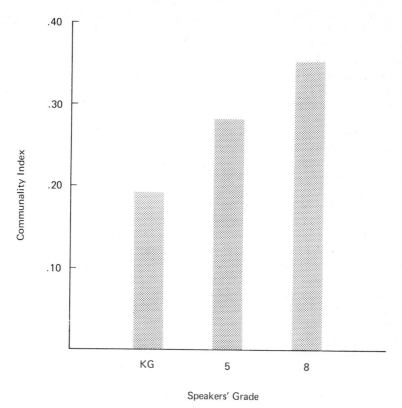

F IGURE 8.   *Proportion of conceptual responses used by more than one speaker.*

Sometimes qualitative data is more compelling than summary statistics. When eighth graders communicate with kindergartners, 80 percent of them use the conceptual response "flying saucer" in talking about Figure 1. Only 20 percent of the fifth graders do so. We know that "flying saucer" is a pretty good name for this figure and it is the modal response for adults. Another example: 70 percent of our eighth graders use the conceptual response "triangle" as part of their message for Figure 3, contrasted with 20 percent of the fifth graders. Across all figures the modal frequency is greater in five out of six cases for eighth graders compared to fifth graders.

We have previously (Glucksberg and Krauss, 1967) presented a model of communication process which postulates an editing process intervening between a speaker's selection of a conceptual response and his use of that response in a message. In editing, the speaker presumably takes into account relevant aspects of his listener, the likelihood that the conceptual responses might be applied to stimuli other than the referent stimulus, and so forth. In many respects this model is similar to a mathematical model proposed by Rosenberg and Cohen (1966). The Rosenberg-Cohen model postulates two stages in the speaker's formulation of a message. In the first stage, called sampling, the speaker samples from his repertoire of word associations to the target stimulus—the one he is trying to communicate. In the second stage, called comparison, the speaker evaluates the probable effectiveness of his message by comparing the associative value of the sampled word-message to both the target stimulus and to the non-referent stimuli. If the associative value is greater for the former than for the latter, the speaker will (with a certain probability) emit the word-message. Otherwise, he will reject it and sample another word, subjecting it to the comparison process, and so on until finally he emits a word message. The sampling is done with replacement so that the possibility exists of the speaker actually emitting a message he has previously rejected. Rosenberg and Cohen have used words as their stimuli, enabling them to use word association norms to estimate the speakers' repertoires, but this has been a matter of convenience and not an intrinsic limitation on the model.

Cohen and Klein (1968) have employed this model to explain differences in communicative effectiveness found among third, fifth and seventh grade subjects on their word association-communication task. Briefly stated, they interpret their finding as indicating that the lack of effectiveness of young speakers derives not from a deficiency in the comparison stage (comparable to our editing process), but rather from the paucity of the repertoire from which the speaker samples.

We would suggest that both factors may be at work. Clearly, the kindergartner's repertoire of conceptual responses is meager in comparison to that of the fifth and eighth grades. But even the fifth grader, whose task-relevant repertoire appears to be every bit as extensive as that of the eighth grader, seems at times to use available conceptual responses injudiciously.

It may be, of course, that the hierarchical organization or the associative structure of repertoires for the two grades differ. If that were the case, if the responses were present, but at a lower strength, this would fit with the explanation offered by Cohen and Klein. Alternatively, it may be the case that younger and older subjects differ in the adequacy of their editing-comparison process. It is this latter explanation that we prefer, but at present we have little more than our intuitions to support it.

References

BROWN, R., and LENNEBERG, E. H. A study in language and cognition. *Journal of Abnormal and Social Psychology*, 1954, *49*, 454–462.

COHEN, B. D., and KLEIN, J. F. Referent communication in school age children. *Child Development*, 1968, *39*, 597–609.

GLUCKSBERG, S., and KRAUSS, R. M. What do people say after they have learned how to talk? Studies of the development of referential communication. *Merrill-Palmer Quarterly*, 1967, *3*, 309–316.

KRAUSS, R. M., and GLUCKSBERG, S. The development of communication: Competence as a function of age. *Child Development*, 1969, *40*, 255–266.

———, VIVEKANANTHAN, P. S., and WEINHEIMER, S. "Inner speech" and "external speech": Characteristics and communication effectiveness of socially and non-socially encoded messages. *Journal of Personality and Social Psychology*, 1968, *9*, 295–300.

———, and WEINHEIMER, S. Effect of referent similarity and communication mode on verbal encoding. *Journal of Verbal Learning and Verbal Behavior*, 1967, *6*, 359–363.

LANTZ. D., and STEFFLRE, V. Language and cognition revisited. *Journal of Abnormal and Social Psychology*, 1964, *69*, 472–481.
ROSENBERG, S., and COHEN, B. D. Referential processes of speakers and listeners. *Psychological Review*, 1966, *73*, 208–231.

A Scale of Preadolescent Heterosexual Development*

Carlfred B. Broderick

PENNSYLVANIA STATE UNIVERSITY

George P. Rowe

UNIVERSITY OF MISSOURI

A five-item scale of social heterosexuality was developed in a sample of 1,029 ten-, eleven-, and twelve-year-olds in Pennsylvania. Since the theory of a sequence of developmental stages makes the same requirements of items as does a Guttman scale, it was suggested that these items represented a series of steps in the development of normal heterosexuality at these ages. The study was replicated with a sample of 610 children of the same age in Missouri, and the results supported the same conclusion.

In previous papers data have been reported to indicate that, far from being a period of heterosexual latency, preadolescence includes a number of important steps in the process of social heterosexual development.[1] The present paper addresses itself to the question of whether there is a sequence of stages during the 10-to-12 age span which build one upon the other like a pyramid, in such a way that each ascending step is dependent upon the successful completion of each earlier step. If such a series of steps could be firmly established, we would be approaching an empirically based addition to the current theories of heterosexual development which focus primarily on preschool familial factors.[2]

Reprinted from *Journal of Marriage and the Family*, February 1968, *30*, (1), 97–101. By permission.

* The Pennsylvania study was supported in part by a grant originally designated MH-04974 from the National Institute of Mental Health, but then transferred to the National Institute of Child Health and Human Development under the designation HD-00882. The data for the Pennsylvania part of the research were collected in the spring of 1962. The Missouri data were collected in the winter and spring of 1965.

[1] Carlfred B. Broderick and Stanley E. Fowler, "New Patterns of Relationships Between the Sexes Among Preadolescents," *Marriage and Family Living*, 23 (February, 1961), pp. 27–30; Carlfred B. Broderick, "Social Heterosexual Development Among Urban Negroes and Whites," *Journal of Marriage and the Family*, 27 (May, 1965), pp. 200–203; Carlfred B. Broderick, "Socio-Sexual Development in a Suburban Community," *Journal of Sex Research*, 2 (April, 1966), pp. 1–24; and Carlfred B. Broderick, "Sexual Behavior Among Preadolescents," *Journal of Social Issues*, 22 (April, 1966), pp. 6–21.
[2] See, for example, Jerome Kagan, "Acquisition and Significance of Sex Typing and Sex Role," in *Child Development Research*, ed. by Martin L. Hoffman and Lois W. Hoffman, New York: Russell Sage Foundation, 1964, pp. 137–167; Urie Bronfenbrenner, "Freudian Theories of Identification and Their Derivatives," *Child Development*, 31 (March, 1960), pp. 15–40; Robert Winch, *Identification and Its Familial Determinants*, Indianapolis: Bobbs-Merrill, 1962; Daniel G. Brown and David B. Lynn, "Human Sexual Development: An Outline of Components and Concepts," *Journal of Marriage and the Family*, 28 (May, 1966), pp. 155–162.

SAMPLES

The research strategy involved two phases. First the presence of developmental steps was documented in a sample of ten- to twelve-year-olds in Pennsylvania. Then, independently, the same items were administered to a sample of
ten- to twelve-year-olds in Missouri. The second study, coming after the
analysis of the first study was completed, served as a test of the generalizability
of the earlier findings.

The first sample included all of the ten- to twelve-year-olds in the fifth,
sixth, and seventh grades of ten central Pennsylvania schools. The districts
were chosen so as to encompass rural, suburban, and urban-industrial communities. In general, the rural and urban children came from the blue-collar
class, and the suburban children came from the upper-middle class. All of the
students from rural and suburban areas were white, but in the urban districts
about 25 percent were Negro. In all there were 1,029 subjects in the Pennsylvania samples, 530 boys and 499 girls.

The Missouri sample consisted of 312 boys and 298 girls about equally
divided among grades five, six, and seven in four localities within a radius of
75 miles from Kansas City. Subsamples included central Kansas City, an established contiguous suburb, a non-metropolitan city of about 25,000 population, and a rural county. Some general characteristics of this sample were that
all subjects were white, 93 percent were Protestant, and the majority of the
families were rated in the lower half on a modified McGuire-White Index of
Social Status.

DATA COLLECTION AND ANALYSIS

The schedules administered to the two samples were identical in most of
the items, although each included some questions omitted in the other. In
addition to background items, the questions were concerned with attitudes
toward marriage, kissing, dating, and romantic movies. There were, in addition,
questions on experience, if any, with kissing, dating, and being in "love."
Projective and sociometric items were also included. A descriptive analysis of
much of this information has been reported elsewhere.[3]

In working with the data from the first study, it became apparent that,
while the percentage of subjects answering positively to various items fluctuated
considerably from group to group, a number of items appeared to hold their
relative ranks for each age, sex, and locality group. This suggested the possibility
that they were related to each other in a sequential pattern. Since the theory of
a sequence of developmental stages makes the same requirements of items as does
a Guttman scale, Guttman-scale analysis was employed. This procedure tested
the proposition that the items were related to each other in such a way that a
positive response on a given item was indicative of a positive response on all
"easier" (or, in this case, "earlier") items.

Traditionally, Guttman-scale analysis provides a descriptive statistic, the

---

[3] Broderick, "Socio-Sexual Development in a Suburban Community," *op. cit.*; and George P.
Rowe, *Patterns of Interpersonal Relationships Among Youth Nine to Thirteen Years of Age*, unpublished
Ph.D. dissertation, The Florida State University, 1966.

coefficient of reproducibility, which indicates the extent to which the actual responses to the items correspond to the theoretical pyramidal model. A co-efficient of .90 is generally considered acceptable, particularly if an examination of the individual items reveals that none of them is contributing an undue share of the error.[4]

The coefficient of reproducibility has been correctly criticized, however, in that it gives no indication at all of the probability of getting a particular level of reproducibility by chance alone. In order to meet this objection, the number of exact scale-type responses expected by chance was computed and compared with the observed number of exact scale-type responses. The data were then submitted to Chi-square analysis.[5]

The five items which emerged from preliminary analysis as being most promising on empirical and logical grounds were the following, listed here in the same order in which they might hypothetically occur in the life of an individual: (1) desiring to marry someday, (2) having a current girlfriend (boyfriend for the girls), (3) having been in love, (4) preferring a companion of the opposite sex over a member of the same sex or no companion at all when going to a movie, and (5) having begun to date. The exact wording and coding of each of these items is recorded in Table 1.

TABLE 1
Five Items of the Social Heterosexuality Scale

1. "Would you like to get married someday?" *Yes* response was scored as positive, *No* and *Don't know* were scored as negative.
2. "Do you have a girlfriend now?" (or "Do you have a boyfriend now?" for the girls). *Yes* or *No*.
3. "Have you ever been in love?" *Yes* or *No*.
4. "Suppose you were in the pictures, place a number '1' by the picture which shows the situation you would like best . . ." One of the pictures showed a child, alone, at the ticket window of a moving picture theater, another showed him (her) in the same situation with a companion of the opposite sex and a third showed him (her) with a companion of the same sex. The item was scored positively if the opposite sex companion was rated first choice and negatively if it was not.
5. "Have you ever had a date?" *Yes* or *No*.

PENNSYLVANIA FINDINGS

As indicated in Table 2, these five items meet the criteria which have been established for scalability. The Guttman coefficient of reproducibility was .91 for the total group of boys and .93 for the girls. Both exceed the arbitrary .90

[4] For an excellent source on the evaluation of item error, see R. N. Ford, "A Rapid Scoring Procedure for Scaling Attitude Questions," *Public Opinion Quarterly*, 14 (1950), pp. 507–532.
[5] This technique was suggested first by Festinger but because of the complex computation involved has seldom been used. See Leon Festinger, "The Treatment of Quantitative Data by Scale Analysis," *Psychological Bulletin*, 44 (1947), pp. 149–161. Present computer technology renders the problem simple, however, and this feature has been built into a FORTRAN program for Guttman-Scale analysis written by the senior author. It is available through the Computation Center of Pennsylvania State University.

TABLE 2

Guttman-Scale Analysis of Five Items for Pennsylvania Boys and Girls
Ten to Twelve Years of Age

	TOTAL RESPONDING		PERCENT POSITIVE RESPONSE		PERCENT ERROR	
ITEM	GIRLS	BOYS	GIRLS	BOYS	GIRLS	BOYS
Want to marry	492	514	84	62	4	11
Have girlfriend/boyfriend	487	506	71	56	6	7
Have been in love	479	506	51	47	8	10
Prefer opposite sex for movies	476	483	39	39	10	11
Have had a date	495	525	22	24	5	8

	GIRLS	BOYS
Coefficient of reproducibility	.93	.91
Expected number of exact scale-type responses	234.8	176.6
Observed number of exact scale-type responses	324.0	317.0
Chi-square	64.0	167.3
p less than	.001	.001

level which most often is accepted. It can also be seen that none of the five individual items failed to fit into a perfect scale-type in more than 15 percent of the cases, thus meeting the criterion for items established by Ford.[6] Finally, the observed number of exact scale-type responses exceeded the expected number by a statistically significant margin. The Chi-square for the boys (1 degree of freedom) was 167.3 and for the girls 64.0, in each case far exceeding the criterion for significance at the .001 level.

These five items, then, meet all of the requirements for scalability, and by implication they constitute a series of pyramidally related developmental stages.

It should be noted that the items did not scale equally well in all of the subgroups. In general they scaled better with ten- and eleven-year-olds than with twelve-year-olds. When applied to a sample of older children from the same school districts (ages 13 to 17), the scale broke down altogether, indicating perhaps that in adolescence developmental factors may be overshadowed by other factors such as social pressures to date.

Of the eight residence-by-sex-and-race subgroupings, the items met all of the criteria for scaling among suburban boys and girls, urban white boys and girls, urban Negro girls, and rural boys. Rural girls just failed to meet the Chi-square criterion and probably do not call for an explanation. Among Negro boys, however, the items did not scale well at all, and this probably

[6] Ford, *op. cit.*

reflects the general atypicality of heterosexual social development in this sub-group as discussed in a previous article.[7]

MISSOURI FINDINGS

In order to test the applicability of this scale beyond the limits of the population in which it was first observed, the same five items were included in the Missouri study and analyzed for scalability.

It can be seen from Table 3 that the replicated Missouri study gives very nearly the same results as were found earlier in Pennsylvania. The coefficient of reproducibility, the percent error on each item, and the statistically significant differences between the observed and the expected scale-type responses suggest that all of the requirements for scalability have been met.

TABLE 3

Guttman-Scale Analysis of Five Items for Missouri Boys and Girls Ten to Twelve Years of Age

ITEM	TOTAL RESPONDING		PERCENT POSITIVE RESPONSE		PERCENT ERROR	
	GIRLS	BOYS	GIRLS	BOYS	GIRLS	BOYS
Want to marry	298	311	85	62	5	12
Have girlfriend/boyfriend	298	312	72	57	6	6
Have been in love	298	312	50	47	8	10
Prefer opposite sex for movies	269	275	35	34	7	8
Have had a date	298	310	11	19	2	6

	GIRLS	BOYS
Coefficient of reproducibility	.95	.91
Expected number of exact scale-type responses	159.7	114.2
Observed number of exact scale-type responses	217.0	194.0
Chi-square	44.3	88.0
p less than	.001	.001

When each age and sex group was scaled separately, the coefficients of reproducibility ranged from .90 to .96. Only in one instance did an individual item pass the level of acceptable error (ten-year-old boys on the dating item). In each case the observed number of exact scale-type responses exceeded the number expected by chance to a statistically significant degree.

DISCUSSION

The evidence is compelling that there does exist a pyramidally structured set of stages which most preadolescent boys and girls undergo in pursuit of

[7] Broderick, "Social Heterosexual Development Among Urban Negroes and Whites," *op. cit.*

social heterosexual maturation. These steps are represented in these studies by items which meet the criteria for a stable Guttman scale among preadolescents of various ages from a wide range of social and geographic backgrounds.

Work on the sociosexual awareness of preschool children has indicated that recognition of the heterosexual nature of marriage is one of the key conceptual tasks of the early years.[8] The present findings underscore the relevance of the next logical step, coming to view marriage as an attractive element in one's own projected future. From these data it would appear that, until this funda- mental step is achieved, further progress in relating socially to the opposite sex is inhibited during preadolescence.[9]

Commitment to the desirability of marriage, in turn, appears to lead, sooner or later, to singling out some member of the opposite sex as particularly attractive and placing him or her in the special category of "boyfriend" or "girlfriend." In an earlier analysis of these data,[10] it was noted that at this age the boyfriend-girlfriend relationship was quite likely to be nonreciprocal and that commonly the object of affection was unaware of his or her status. Despite the largely imaginary nature of these relationships, however, the children who feel these attachments apparently take them quite seriously. The majority described themselves as having been "in love"; and it seems probable that in most cases the reference was to the current relationships, since all but a few reported first being in love within the last year.

Having been in love, in turn, seems to be a prerequisite for appreciating the companionship of the opposite sex when going to the movies. Those who have never loved are likely, as a group, to prefer going alone or with a like-sex friend. Finally, it appears that some appreciation of the desirability of a cross-sex companion precedes the next big step, actually going out on a date.

The significant finding of these studies, of course, is not centered upon the importance of these particular items (other items could probably be found which would serve as well), but rather upon the existence of a heterosexual developmental continuum among adolescents.

The continuum itself might be speculatively described in terms of movement along two of Parsons' pattern variables. On the diffuse-specific axis it is clear that the movement is toward the specific. The rather global concept of being married someday shrinks first to the boundaries of a fantasied relationship with a real age mate and then even more as that fantasy is disciplined by experience. Finally it is focused upon a specific date with a specific girl on a specific occasion and with a quite limited range of behavior to choose from.

On the particularistic-universalistic axis, the course of development appears to move from the universalistic to the particularistic, at least for the first three steps. One moves from wanting to marry somebody, to having a particular girlfriend, to being in love with this particular girlfriend. The location of the next two steps on this continuum is less clear. It is not known whether the desire to take a girl to the movies is generic or particular. Our own tendency would be to assume that at this age wanting to go to the movies alone with a girl is

[8] Constance Bennifield Farrell, *Awareness and Attitudes of Preschool Children Towards Heterosexual Social Relationships*, unpublished master's thesis, The Pennsylvania State University, 1966.
[9] As noted earlier, there is some evidence that this prerequisite breaks down at later ages.
[10] Broderick, "Socio-Sexual Development in a Suburban Community," *op. cit.*; and Rowe, *op. cit.*

evidence of a desire to be with the particular girl and that the eventual date is more often than not the consummation of this rather focused wish. At later ages when dating itself becomes a goal, this could be expected to break down, but at this age it would be our interpretation that each step on the scale is in fact a step in the direction of greater particularism

In non-Parsonian terms the preadolescent child could be said to be involved in a process of differentiation along two axes. On the one hand, he progressively differentiates dating behavior from the much broader repertoire of heterosexual behavior involved in "being married," (i.e., division of labor, being together, etc.) Simultaneously, he progressively differentiates one particular girl from the pool of females in general. From what we know about development during adolescence, it would seem that ultimately he begins to reintegrate his behavior toward girls, bringing the various components together in a series of global relationships. At the same time he continues the process of differentiating out a particular girl from the whole field of eligibles, in the process we call court-ship.

Whether this analysis is correct or not, however, it does appear, based on these data, that an orderly pattern of progression is discernible during these preadolescent years and that success or failure in each step has consequences for more advanced stages of heterosexual development.

Part Four

THE ADOLESCENT

13

Physical Growth, Health, and Coordination

A physical event, puberty, divides childhood from adolescence. In girls this event is menarche, the first menstruation. In boys there is no similarly observable event, but is estimated to have occurred when changes in genital and hair growth have been observed.

The article by J. M. Tanner, taken from a book on human biology by Tanner and others, describes the facts of the spurt in growth which always precedes puberty. The timing of this growth spurt therefore varies from individual to individual in about the same way that puberty does. The intensity of the spurt also varies from individual to individual. The average girl and the average boy experience the spurt at different ages, earlier for the girl than for the boy. On the average, girls' spurts not only occur early, but are less intense and shorter from beginning to end than are those of boys. From these three sex differences in growth—age, intensity, and duration—follow the differences in physique between the average adult male and female. Tanner also summarizes the changes in physiological functioning that occur at the same time as the spurt in growth. In these too there are sex differences which result in differences between the average adult of each sex. Tanner points out that a measure of physiological maturity or developmental age is a more accurate measure of physical maturity than chronological age.

The article by Hopwood and Van Iden demonstrates with sophisticated design and statistics one of the main theses of this volume: There is a close relationship between physical and psychological functioning. The Wetzel Grid, the instrument used by Hopwood and Van Iden to assess the rate of physical growth of the boys in their study, is described in references cited at the end of the article, and also in many textbooks on child development. Although the title of the article mentions underachievement and subpar physical growth, the study also found that high achievement and above-average physical growth occurred together in some of their subjects.

The Adolescent Growth-Spurt and Developmental Age

J. M. Tanner

INSTITUTE OF CHILD HEALTH, UNIVERSITY OF LONDON

The adolescent growth-spurt is a constant phenomenon and occurs in all children, though it varies in intensity and duration from one child to another. The peak velocity of growth in height averages about 10 cm a year in boys, and slightly less in girls. In boys the spurt takes place on the average between 13 and 15½, and in girls some two years earlier.

The sex difference can be seen in Figure 1, which shows the velocity curves

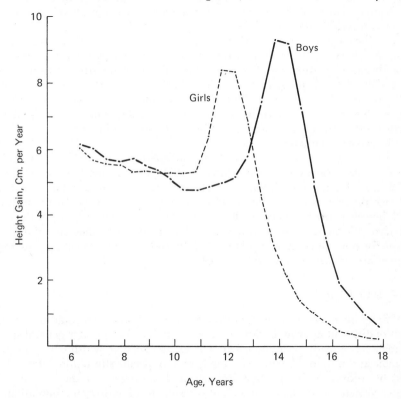

FIGURE 1.   *Adolescent spurt in height growth for girls and boys. The curves are from subjects who have their peak velocities during the modal years 12–13 for girls, and 14–15 for boys. Actual mean increments, each plotted at center of its ½-year period. Data from Shuttleworth (1939), tables 23 and 32.* (From Tanner, Growth at Adolescence, 2nd ed., Blackwell Scientific Publ., 1962.)

Reprinted from G. A. Harrison, J. S. Weiner, J. M. Tanner, and N. A. Barnicot. *Human Biology: An Introduction to Human Evolution, Variation and Growth*, 1964, pp. 321–339, by permission of Clarendon Press, Oxford.

for a group of boys who have their peak velocity between 14 and 15, and a group of girls with their peak between 12 and 13. These restricted groups have been taken so as to avoid as much as possible the time-spreading error referred to in [a previous figure]. The difference in size between men and women is to a large degree due to differences in timing and intensity of the adolescent spurt; before it boys and girls differ only by some 2 per cent in height; after it by an average of about 8 per cent. The difference partly comes about because of the later occurrence of the male spurt, allowing an extra period for growth, even at the slow prepubertal velocity; and partly because of the greater intensity of the spurt itself.

Practically all skeletal and muscular dimensions take part in the spurt, though not to an equal degree. Most of the spurt in height is due to trunk growth rather than growth of the legs. The muscles appear to have their spurt about three months after the height peak; and the weight peak velocity occurs about six months after the height peak.

The heart has a spurt in size no less than the other muscles, and other organs accelerate their growth also. Probably even the eye, the most advanced of any organ in maturity and thus the one with least growth still to undergo, has a slight spurt, to judge from the particularly rapid change towards myopia which occurs about this age. The degree of myopia increases continuously from age 6 or earlier till maturity, but this accelerated rate of change at puberty would be most simply accounted for by a fractionally greater spurt in axial than in vertical diameters.

It is not clear whether a spurt occurs in brain growth. In the bones of the face there is a spurt, though a relatively slight one. Individual variability is sufficient so that in some children no detectable spurt occurs at all in some head and face measurements, including those of the pituitary fossa. In the average child, however, the jaw becomes longer in relation to the front part of the face, and also thicker and more projecting. The profile becomes straighter, the incisors of both jaws more upright, and the nose more projecting. All these changes are greater in boys than in girls.

SEX DIFFERENCES

Many of the sex differences of body-size and shape seen in adults are the result of differential growth patterns at adolescence. The greater general size of the male has already been discussed. The greater relative width of shoulders in the male and hips in the female is largely due to specific stimulation of cartilage cells, by androgens in the first instance and oestrogens in the second. The greater growth of the male muscles also results from androgen stimulation, as do some other physiological differences mentioned below.

Not all sex differences develop in this way. The greater length of the male legs relative to the trunk comes about as a consequence of the longer prepubescent period of male growth, since the legs are growing faster than the trunk during this particular time. Other sex differences begin still earlier. The male forearm is longer, relative to the upper arm or the height, than the female forearm; and this difference is already established at birth, and increases gradually throughout the whole growing period. It is probably caused by the laying down in early foetal life of slightly more tissue in this area in the male, or of slightly more active tissue. It occurs in some other Primates, as well as in man.

A similar mechanism may be responsible for the sex difference in relative lengths of second and fourth fingers. The second finger is longer than the fourth more frequently in females than in males and this difference is also established before birth. The most striking of all the pre-pubertal sex differences, however, is the earlier maturation of the female. . . .

DEVELOPMENT OF THE REPRODUCTIVE SYSTEM

The adolescent spurt in skeletal and muscular dimensions is closely related to the rapid development of the reproductive system which takes place at this time. In Figure 2 the events of adolescence in the male are outlined diagrammatically. The solid areas marked *penis* and *testis* represent the period of accelerated growth of these organs, and the horizontal lines and rating numbers marked *pubic hair* stand for its advent and development. The sequences and timings represent in each case the average value. To give an idea of the individual departures from this, figures for the range of ages at which the spurts for height, penis, and testis growth begin and end are inserted under the first and last points of the curves or bars. The acceleration of penis growth, for example, begins on average at about 13, but sometimes occurs as early as 11 and sometimes as late as 14½. There are a few boys, be it noticed, who do not begin their

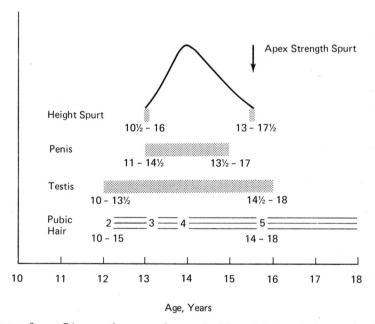

FIGURE 2.   *Diagram of sequence of events at adolescence in boys. An average boy is represented; the range of ages within which each event charted may begin and end is given by the figures placed directly below its start and finish.* (From Tanner, *Growth at Adolescence*, 2nd ed., Blackwell Scientific Publ., 1962.)

spurts in height or penis development until the earliest maturers have entirely completed theirs. At age 13 and 14 there is an enormous variability in development amongst any group of boys, who range practically all the way from complete maturity to absolute pre-adolescence. The fact raises difficult social and educational problems and is itself a contributory factor to the psychological maladjustment sometimes seen in adolescence. . . .

The *sequence* of events is much less variable than the age at which they take place. The first sign of puberty in boys is an accelerated growth of testes and scrotum. Slight growth of pubic hair may start at about the same time, but proceeds slowly until about the time the height and penis simultaneously accelerate, when it also grows faster. This is usually about a year after the first testicular acceleration. The testicular growth is mainly due to increase in size of the seminal tubules; the androgen-producing Leydig cells appear to lag somewhat behind and do not as a rule reach their full state of maturity until some time after active sperm are being produced.

Axillary hair usually first appears about two years after the beginning of pubic hair growth, though there is sufficient individual variability so that in a very few children axillary hair actually precedes pubic hair in appearance. Circumanal hair, which arises independently of the spread of pubic hair down the perineum, appears shortly before axillary hair. In boys *facial hair* begins at about the same time as axillary hair. An increase in length and pigmentation occurs first in the hair at the corners of the upper lip, then spreads medially. Hair next appears on the upper part of the cheeks and in the midline just below the lower lip, and finally along the sides and lower border of the chin. The remainder of the body-hair appears from about the time of first axillary hair development until a considerable period after puberty. The ultimate amount of body-hair an individual develops seems to depend largely on heredity, though whether because of the kinds and amounts of hormones secreted or because of the reactivity of the end-organs is not known.

The enlargement of the larynx in boys occurs at about the time the penis growth is nearing completion. The voice change is a gradual one and is often not complete until adolescence is practically over. In boys at adolescence there are frequently some changes seen in the breast; the areola enlarges in diameter and darkens. In some boys—about a third of most groups studied—there is a distinct enlargement with projection of the areola and the presence of firm subareolar mammary tissue. This occurs about midway through adolescence and lasts from a year to eighteen months, after which in the majority of the boys the mound and tissue disappear spontaneously.

A designation of how far a child has progressed through adolescence is frequently needed in clinical, anthropological, and educational work, and standards for rating the development of pubic hair, genitalia, and the breasts will be found in texts on adolescent development.

A diagram of the events of adolescence in girls is given in Figure 3. As in boys, there is a large variation in the time at which the spurt begins, though the sequence of events is fairly constant. The appearance of the breast-bud is as a rule the first sign of puberty, though the appearance of pubic hair may sometimes precede it. The uterus and vagina develop simultaneously with the breast. Menarche (the first menstrual period) occurs almost invariably after the peak of the height spurt has been passed. In Figure 4 is shown a Gompertz

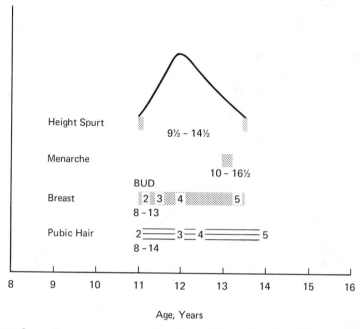

Age, Years

F I G U R E 3.   *Diagram of sequence of events at adolescence in girls. An average girl is repre-*
sented; the range of ages within which some of the events may occur is given by the figures placed
directly below them. (From Tanner, *Growth at Adolescence,* 2nd ed., Blackwell Scientific
Publ., 1962.)

curve fitted to the growth in height of an individual girl, differentiated to
give curves of velocity (above) and acceleration (below). The form of the acceleration curve is interesting and shows the gradually increasing acceleration, the
change to sharp deceleration, and gradual reduction of the deceleration. The
points marked *SS* and *M* stand for the first appearance of breast-bud and menarche respectively. It is striking how the one coincides with maximum acceleration and the other with maximum deceleration. This seems to be true of most
girls' acceleration curves so far studied, and makes the point that some hormonal forces may be better reflected in effects on acceleration than on velocity
or distance.

Menarche marks a definitive and probably mature stage of uterine development, but it does not usually signify the attainment of full reproductive function.
The early menstrual cycles frequently occur without an ovum being shed;
during the first year or more after menarche there is a period of relative infertility,
characteristic of apes and monkeys as well as the human.

CHANGES IN PHYSIOLOGICAL FUNCTION AND MOTOR DEVELOPMENT

Considerable changes in physiological function occur at the same time as
the adolescent growth-spurt. They are much more marked in boys than girls
and serve to confer on the male his greater strength and physical endurance.
Before adolescence boys are on average a little stronger than girls, there being

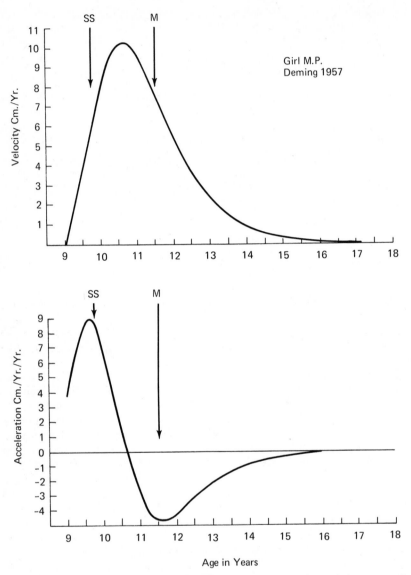

FIGURE 4.   *Velocity (above) and acceleration (below) curves of growth in stature of girl from age 9 to 18. Calculated from data of Deming (Human Biol. **29**, 83–122, 1957, appendix), using first and second derivatives of fitted Gompertz curve. SS represents the first appearance of breast development and M the menarche.* (From W. J. Israelsohn, in *Human Growth*, ed. J. M. Tanner, Pergamon Press, Oxford, 1960.)

more muscularly built or mesomorphic boys than girls in the population even then; but the difference is quite small. After adolescence boys are much stronger, chiefly by virtue of having larger muscles, and perhaps also by being able to develop more force per gramme of muscle present. They have larger hearts and lungs relative to their size, a greater capacity for carrying oxygen in the blood, and a greater power for neutralizing the chemical products of muscular exercise. In short, the male becomes at adolescence more adapted for the tasks of hunting, fighting, and manipulating all sorts of heavy objects, as is necessary in some forms of food-gathering.

In Figure 5 are plotted (as distance curves) data for two strength tests taken from a group of boys and girls followed longitudinally through adolescence. Arm pull refers to the movement of pulling apart clasped hands held up in front of the chest, the hands each holding a dynamometer handle; arm thrust refers to the reverse movement, of pushing the hands together. Each individual test represents the best of three trials made in competition with a classmate of similar ability and against the individual's own figure of six months before. Only with such precautions can reliable maximum values be obtained. There is a considerable spurt in the boys from about 13 to 16. Little spurt can be seen in the girls' data, though figures for hand grip taken from the same group show a slight acceleration at about 12 to $13\frac{1}{2}$ years.

The male increase in the number of red blood-cells at puberty, and consequently in the amount of haemoglobin in the blood, is shown in Figure 6. No sex difference exists before adolescence; hence the combining of data from both sexes up to this age in the lower portion of the figure. The systolic blood-pressure rises throughout childhood, but accelerates this process in boys at adolescence; the heart-rate falls. The alveolar carbon dioxide tension increases in boys and not in girls, giving rise to a sex difference also seen in the partial pressure of carbon dioxide in arterial blood. Coincidently the alkali reserve rises in boys. Thus the blood of an adult man can absorb during muscular exercise, without change of pH, greater quantities of lactic acid and other substances produced by the muscles than that of a woman—a necessity in view of the greater relative development of muscular bulk in the male. The efficiency of the response to exercise increases in several ways; the total ventilation required for each litre of oxygen actually utilized, for example, declines.

As a direct result of these anatomical and physiological changes the athletic ability of boys increases greatly at adolescence. The popular notion of a boy "outgrowing his strength" at this time has little scientific support. It is true that the peak velocity of strength increase occurs a year or so after the peak velocity of most of the skeletal measurements, so that a short period may exist when the adolescent, having completed his skeletal growth, still does not have the strength of a young adult of the same body-size and shape. But this is a temporary phase; considered absolutely, power, athletic skill, and physical endurance all increase progressively and rapidly throughout adolescence.

DEVELOPMENTAL AGE AND THE CONCEPT OF PHYSIOLOGICAL MATURITY

Though all the events of adolescence described above usually occur together, linked in a rather uniform sequence, the *age* at which they happen varies greatly

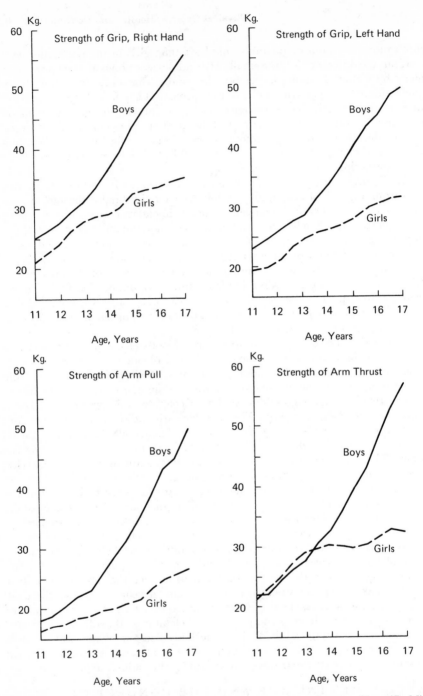

FIGURE 5.   *Strength of hand grip, arm pull, and arm thrust from age 11 to 17. Mixed longitudinal data, 65–93 boys and 66–93 girls in each group. Data from Jones, Motor Performance and Growth, Univ. Calif. Press, 1949.* (From Tanner, *Growth at Adolescence*, 2nd ed., Blackwell Scientific Publ., 1962.)

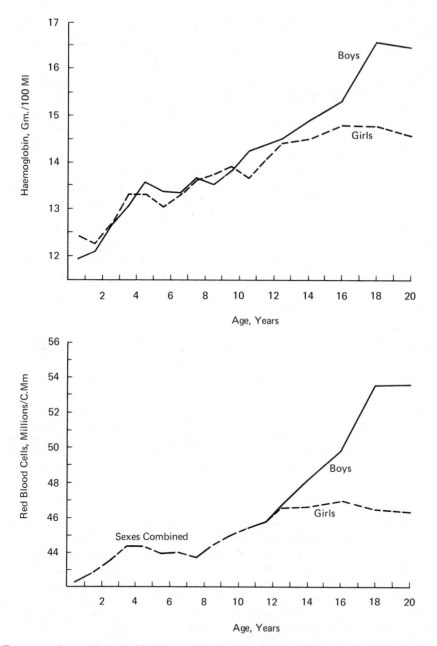

FIGURE 6.   *Change in blood haemoglobin (measured by Van Slyke manometric O_2 capacity)
and number of circulating red blood-corpuscles during childhood, showing the development of the
sex difference at adolescence. Distance curves. Mixed longitudinal data reported cross-sectionally.
(Redrawn from Mugrage and Andreson, 1936, 1938, Amer. J. Dis. Child.)* (From Tanner,
Growth at Adolescence, 2nd ed., Blackwell Scientific Publ., 1962.)

from one child to another. From a file of photographs of normally developing boys aged exactly 14 it is easy to select three examples which illustrate this. One boy is small, with childish muscles and no development of reproductive organs or body-hair; he could be mistaken for a 12-year-old. Another is practically a grown man, with broad shoulders, strong muscles, adult genitalia, and a bass voice. The third boy is in a stage intermediate between these two. It is manifestly ridiculous to consider all three as equally grown up physically, or, since much behaviour at this age is conditioned by physical status, in their social relations. The statement that a boy is 14 is in most contexts hopelessly vague; all depends, morphologically, physiologically, and sociologically on whether he is pre-adolescent, mid-adolescent, or post-adolescent.

Evidently some designation of physical maturity other than chronological age is needed, and in this instance the obvious one would be the degree of development of the reproductive system. But the same differences in *tempo of growth*, as its first describer, Franz Boas, called it, occur at all ages, though less spectacularly than at adolescence. Thus we need a measure of *developmental age* or *physiological maturity* applicable throughout the whole period of growth. Three possible measures exist at present; skeletal maturity, dental maturity, and shape age.

SKELETAL MATURITY

The most commonly used indicator of physiological maturity is the degree of development of the skeleton as shown by X-ray. Each bone begins as a primary center of ossification, passes through various stages of enlargement and shaping of the ossified area, acquires in some cases one or more epiphyses, that is, other centres where ossification begins independently of the main centre, and finally reaches adult form when these epiphyses fuse with the main body of the bone. All these changes can be easily seen in an X-ray, which distinguishes the ossified area, whose calcium content renders it opaque to the X-rays, from the areas of cartilage where ossification has not yet begun. The sequence of changes of shape through which each of the bone centres and epiphyses pass is constant from one person to another and skeletal maturity, or bone age, as it is often called, is judged both from the number of centres present and the stage of development of each.

In theory any or all parts of the skeleton could be used to give an assessment of skeletal maturity, but in practice the hand and wrist is the most convenient area and the one generally used. An X-ray of the hand is easily done without any radiation being delivered to other parts of the body, it requires only a minute dose of X-rays, and it demands only the minimum of X-ray equipment, such as a dental or a portable machine. Finally, the hand is an area where a large number of bones and epiphyses are developing. The left hand is used, placed flat on an X-ray film with the palm down and the tube placed 30 inches above the knuckle of the middle finger.

The figure for skeletal maturity is derived by comparing the given X-ray with a set of standards. There are two ways in which this may be done. In the older "atlas" method one matches the given X-ray successively with standards representing age 5, and 6, and so on, and sees with which age standard it most nearly coincides. The more recently developed method is to establish a series of standard stages through which each bone passes, and to match each bone of the given X-ray with these stages. Each bone is thus given a score, corresponding to the stage reached, and the whole X-ray scores a total of so many maturity points. This score is then compared with the range of scores of the standard group at the same age and a percentile status is then given to the child in skeletal maturity, that is, the percentage of normal children with lower scores at that age, perhaps 80 per cent, is read off. (The child would be in this case at the eightieth percentile.) A skeletal age may also be assigned, this being simply the age at which the given score lies at the fiftieth percentile.

DENTAL MATURITY

Dental maturity can be obtained by counting the number of teeth erupted and relating this to standard figures in much the same way as skeletal maturity. The deciduous dentition erupts from about 6 months to 2 years and can be used as a measure of physiological maturity during this period. The permanent or second dentition provides a measure from about 6 to 13 years. From 2 to 6 and from 13 onwards little information is obtainable from the teeth by simple counting, but recently new measures of dental maturity have been suggested which use the stages of calcification of teeth as seen in jaw X-rays in just the same way as the skeletal maturity assessment uses the stages of wrist ossification.

SHAPE AGE

As the child grows older his shape changes through the agency of the differential growth velocities described in Chapter 19 [of *Human Biology*]. In principle the degree of shape change achieved could be made a measure, and a practically very convenient one, of developmental maturity. But a difficulty enters here which does not arise in the skeletal and dental measures. The shape change is only useful if its measure is completely independent of the final shape reached (as skeletal and dental ages are, the final state being identical in everybody). This is the trouble which besets the "height age" and "weight age" once much used by pediatricians, and also the mental age or I.Q. used by psychologists. The height age of a given child is the age at which the average child achieves the height of the given one. Suppose the given child is tall for his age; this may be *either* because he is advanced developmentally (which is what we are trying to measure) or because he is simply going to be a taller-than-average adult and is already exhibiting the fact.

For shape age to be effective, therefore, a combination of body measurements must be found which would change with age, but independently of final size and shape. This is a mathematically complex and difficult proposition, but not an impossible one. Shape age is at present a research problem, not a practical method for use.

RELATIONS BETWEEN DIFFERENT MEASURES OF MATURITY

Skeletal maturity is closely related to the age at which adolescence occurs, that is, to maturity measured by secondary sex character development. Thus

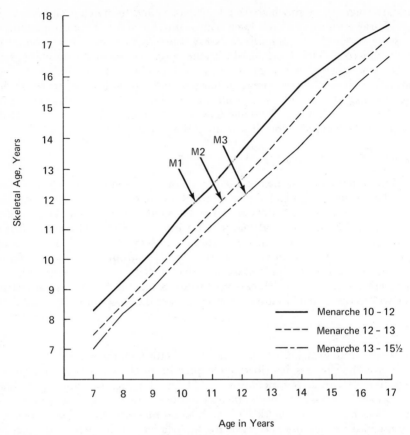

FIGURE 7.   *Relation of skeletal maturity and age at menarche. Skeletal development ages (Todd Standards) for early-, average-, and late-menarche groups of girls, from age 7 to maturity. M1, M2, M3, average time of menarche for each group. Mixed longitudinal data. Redrawn from Simmons and Greulich (1943).* (From Tanner, *Growth at Adolescence,* 2nd ed., Blackwell Scientific Publ., 1962.)

the range of *chronological* age within which menarche may normally fall is about 10 to 16½ but the corresponding range of *skeletal* age for menarche is only 12 to 14½. Evidently the physiological processes controlling progression of skeletal development are linked closely to those which initiate the events of adolescence.

Furthermore, as Figure 7 shows, children tend to be consistently advanced or retarded during their whole growth period, or at any rate after about age 3. In the figure three groups of girls are plotted separately; those with an early, those with a middling, and those with a late menarche. The early menarche girls are skeletally advanced not only at adolescence but at all ages back to 7; the late menarche girls have a skeletal age which is consistently retarded. The points *M1, M2,* and *M3* represent the average age of menarche in each group. To be quantitative, the correlation between age of menarche and skeletal age at 5 or 6 years old is between .5 and .6. The same figure applies to the correlation of menarche with per cent of mature height reached at 5 or 6 (another measure of maturity). The correlation gets less the farther back in growth one goes; the children's velocity curves are steeper then and they cross each other more, bringing reassortment of growth status. But by and large there is consistency in acceleration or retardation of skeletal and general bodily maturity.

Dental maturity partly shares in this general skeletal and bodily maturation, and at all ages from 6 to 13 children who are advanced skeletally have on average more erupted teeth than those who are skeletally retarded. Likewise those who have an early adolescence erupt their teeth earlier, as illustrated in Figure 8. But this relationship is not a very close one, as the figure also implies: even with only three maturity groups in each sex a certain amount of crossing of the lines takes place.

This relative independence of teeth and general bodily development is not altogether surprising. The teeth are part of the head end of the organism, and we have already seen in Chapter 19 [of *Human Biology*] how the growth of the head is advanced over the rest of the body and how for this reason its curve differs somewhat from the general growth curve.

The degree of independence of the teeth should not be over-emphasized, however. In fact, the correlation between skeletal age and dental age, as measured by third mandibular molar development in X-rays for children of the same chronological age (over the range 9–16) in one study was .45.

Evidently there is some general factor of bodily maturity throughout growth, creating a tendency for a child to be advanced or retarded as a whole; in his skeletal ossification, in the percentage attained of his eventual size, in his permanent dentition, doubtless in his physiological reactions, probably also in his intelligence test score, as described below, and perhaps in other psychological reactions also. Set under this general tendency are groups of more limited maturities, which vary independently of it and of each other. The teeth constitute two of these limited areas (primary and secondary dentition being largely independent of each other); the ossification centres another; probably the brain at least one more. Some of the mechanisms behind these relations can be dimly seen; in children who lack adequate thyroid gland secretion, for example, tooth eruption, skeletal development, and brain organization are all retarded; whereas in children with precocious puberty, whether due to a brain disorder or a disease of the adrenal gland, there is advancement of skeletal and genital maturity without any corresponding effect upon the teeth or, as far as we can tell, upon the progression of organization in the brain.

SEX DIFFERENCE IN DEVELOPMENTAL AGE

Girls are on the average ahead of boys in skeletal maturity from birth to adulthood, and in dental maturity also during the whole of the permanent dentition eruption (though not, curiously, in primary dentition). It would seem, therefore, that the sex difference lies in the general maturity factor (as well as in various more detailed specific factors), which prompts the question as to whether it may not exist in intelligence tests and social responses also.

The skeletal age difference begins during foetal life, the male retardation apparently being due, directly or indirectly, to the action of genes on the

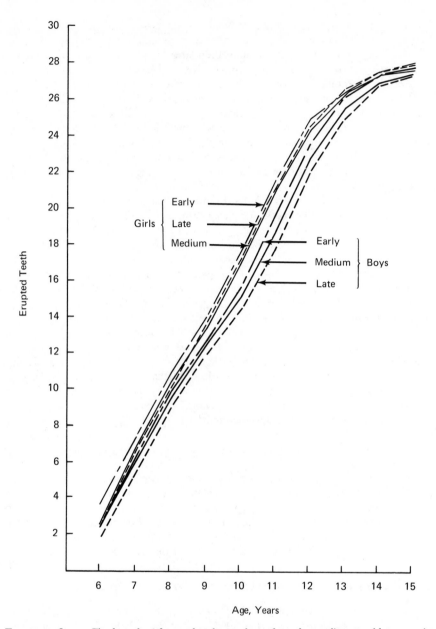

FIGURE 8.   *Total number of erupted teeth at each age for early-, medium-, and late-maturing girls and boys. Maturity groups defined by age at peak height velocity. Mixed longitudinal data, reported longitudinally. Redrawn from Shuttleworth (1939).* (From Tanner, *Growth at Adolescence*, 2nd ed., Blackwell Scientific Publ., 1962.)

Y-chromosome. The evidence for this is that children with the abnormal chromosome constitution XXY (Klinefelter's syndrome) have a skeletal maturity indistinguishable from the normal XY male, and children with the chromosome constitution XO (Turner's syndrome) have skeletal maturities closely approximating to the normal XX, at least up till puberty. In what manner these genes work we cannot say. Possibly this is as basic a difference as the differentiation of testis or ovary, and begins at about the same time, in the second intra-uterine month. Or it may be due to secretion by the foetal gonads or adrenals of sex-specific hormones. At birth, boys are about four weeks behind girls in skeletal age, and from then till adulthood they remain about 80 per cent of the skeletal age of girls of the same chronological age. It is for this reason that girls reach adolescence and their final mature size some two years before boys. The percentage difference in dental age is not so great, the boys being about 95 per cent of the dental age of girls of the same chronological age.

PHYSICAL MATURATION, MENTAL ABILITY, AND EMOTIONAL DEVELOPMENT

There is considerable evidence that intellectual and emotional advancement is to some extent linked to advancement in skeletal maturity. This may be most simply construed, at least so far as intellectual development goes, as evidence that the brain is affected by the general factor of developmental tempo, in the same manner as the teeth. Thus those advanced in physical development do better in mental tests than those retarded in physical development. [Tanner here refers to Chapter 22 of *Human Biology.*]

There is little doubt that being an early or late maturer has considerable repercussions on emotional development and social behaviour, particularly at adolescence. These problems are also discussed in Chapter 22. Clearly the occurrence of tempo differences in human development has profound implications for educational theory and practice.

Scholastic Underachievement As Related to Sub-par Physical Growth

A New Look and Some New Facts About an Old Problem Gathered in a 10-Year Study in the Shaker Heights School District

Howard H. Hopwood, and Starr S. Van Iden

SHAKER HEIGHTS SCHOOL DISTRICT, OHIO

INTRODUCTION

Modernized school plants, high quality teachers and enriched programs have not succeeded in preventing or in eliminating an old educational malady: *scholastic underachievement* (1). Indeed, the existence of this syndrome, even if its incidence is no greater, is definitely more noticeable and more thought-provoking than heretofore because today's operations have been accelerated to keep pace with space-age demands, not merely for the "new math" but, in fact, for innovations in all academic areas.[1] Virtually every department is involved, teaching, physical education, athletics and school health. The latter, indeed, has become more than ever the court of last resort when difficulties arise, to see whether "anything at all can be found" that is physically wrong with an under-achieving student and that might explain the trouble he has encountered.[2]

Unlike an acute appendix or tonsillitis, however, scholastic underachievement, at the time of its official discovery by the classroom teacher, has very likely been brewing for months and even for several years. As in other chronic disturbances, restitution can hardly be expected or accomplished over the ensuing week-end, much less overnight. This, in itself, adds materially to the compounded frustrations of all concerned as well as to the challenge to deal with such problems effectively. More often than not, the absence of frank physical signs of organic or metabolic disease leads, in the fashion of the day, either to the allergist or to psychiatric referral, but in neither case, with much promise of immediate solution or help. By this time, the affected boy or girl is removed from friendly guidance at the hands of school counsellors; except for a dutiful record entry, the school's attention must be turned to the next in line! By year's end, the pupil's report card shows—as a rule—another drop, fractional though it may be, in English, mathematics or some other major study, if not in all three. . . . As with the football team, there is always next year to look forward to in quest of a better standing.

This story is not overdrawn. We have new positive data. What is more, they are of a kind that any school in the country, besides our own, could equally well have reported, and we think, too, at an earlier date. Be this as it may,

---

Reprinted from the *Journal of School Health*, 1965, *35*, 337–349. By permission.

[1] See, for example, "Kids under Pressure," *The Wall Street Journal*, XLV, 117 (March 31, 1965), p. 1.

[2] Rogers and Reese (13) have presented a valuable, comprehensive 3-part discussion of school health objectives and procedures in high schools. Glaser and Clemmens, in a broad approach to school failure, touch on all aspects except that of physical growth. (14)

our more than 10-year study has assembled much of practical value for all school personnel who are concerned with the problem of under-achievement in their pursuit of "high quality" education.

We have in mind, first, those who are in the front line of daily operations, the teachers, themselves; second, the school health staff of nurses and physicians, not omitting school psychologists and psychiatrists whose special interests should not prevent them from paying due attention to pertinent physical events and especially to the character of physical growth; third, to be sure, our colleagues in physical education who, today, are far removed from being exponents of "muscle alone." But our new results should also have particular significance for administrators as well as for Boards of Education whose duty it is to provide the best schooling their budget allows. Yet, still others must be included on the list, since it cannot be said that parents or other taxpayers, even though removed from the immediate scene where under-achievement is developing, will forever accept, without inquiry or complaint, such extra costs as are invariably connected with the additional burden of scholastic under-achievement when outlays already run $400–$700 per pupil per year.

For, even in the schools of favored communities, the plain fact is that academic success, measured in terms of teachers' marks in major courses (English, mathematics, social studies, . . .) drops off, *on the average,* about 15% or more,[3] between the early elementary years and the time of graduation from Senior High School.

BACKGROUND

To prevent misunderstanding, let it be explained, at once, that the foregoing is *not* one of our "new facts," though we do contend that it must be given fresh attention, and, as we can show, a new meaning. Up to now, however, most educators, when confronted with this "15 + % decline" are apt to shrug it off as something long known among them. Such drop-off, they are quick to assert, is easily accounted for (a) by the "obviously" more difficult subject matter a pupil encounters as he progresses from elementary school to Junior and later to Senior High School; and (b) by the "necessarily" stiffer grading system which teachers in the two high schools are obliged to employ, as much as anything, to meet college entrance requirements for increasing numbers of students. A "B" in Junior or Senior High School, so the defense goes, is much more difficult to earn than is a "B" in the comparatively simpler and less strenuous life of the elementary years. Of course, there have also been other explanations, e.g., "adolescence," though (a) and (b), taken together, appeared sufficiently plausible to those of us who were not on the daily firing line of the classroom. We left the issue to the teaching personnel as a "natural fact" of school life that was outside of our own province and turned to concentrate on our counselling and medical problems of the day. But it would not go away.

Even as long as a decade or more ago we had the feeling that there was something not quite right about such a cavalier attitude toward a matter which reflected, if anything at all, considerably less efficiency in the two chief operations of schooling, namely, teaching and learning, than most administrators and

[3] Individual range: +19% to −78%.

few Boards of Education would willingly admit or privately be satisfied with. There appeared, in fact, to be sticky questions that kept recurring both in the school health clinic and at the counsellors' desks in the guidance office—vantage points, it seemed, from which the "whole child" and his performance are more readily evaluated than in the closer confines of the classroom. At both stations we were made aware of pupil's problems; in the one, those of physical and medical nature; in the other, the kind that arise from the "occupational stress" of being a school boy or girl, e.g., personality difficulties, social adjustment, competition complexes, home attitudes and a host of others. At both positions, moreover, we heard "about school,"—either spontaneously or upon casual inquiry. We learned, in fact, how good, but also how "bad" things could be at one and the same time! . . .

In the medical clinic, let it be emphasized, we saw something more than acne, an upset stomach, a headache or a broken leg. Through the foresight of earlier administrators, former Superintendent Slade, his able assistant Kuechle and the then Medical Director, Dr. Justin Garvin, the Board of Education had been persuaded—after several years of pilot study—to profit by some of the lessons that had been learned in the 1937 Depression, more particularly with respect to the prevalence of simple growth failure of the malnutritional type[4] (2). By Board action, systematic follow-up of physical growth was made mandatory in the Shaker medical and physical education programs. To implement this decision, they arranged to have the Wetzel Grid incorporated as the official health part of each child's cumulative school record (3).

Ever since, we have enjoyed the objective advantage of "seeing"—originally 3,500 and now about 8,000 youngsters—"step forward in growth" each semester as they trace out characteristic channel and auxodrome trends on their individual Grids. These charts have also been routinely available at the counsellor's desk where their full significance, however, has not always been realized—owing, no doubt, to the notion that information such as the Grid conveyed was primarily in the province of the Medical Department. Yet, it has been our observation that few guidance counsellors would fail to be impressed with various tell-tale patterns that kept recurring on individual pupil's Grids: e.g., steady progress in the case of pupils with minimum counselling needs as compared with bizarre effects in the Grid curves of those who had "high voltage" problems—some, to the point of literally throwing rocks through windows. To us, monitoring physical growth is an essential first step in pupil guidance.

On the other hand, while school principals had full access to, and often took great interest in, developments as shown on a pupil's Grid record, teachers, themselves, with multiple records of their own to keep, had little opportunity "to see the purely physical side of growing up." This, we think, is a mistake, though we wish to make it clear that, if so, it was more ours than anyone else's. Besides, the Grid record like a "tummy-ache" was supposed to be essentially our business, not theirs. In actual practice, then, classroom teachers were constrained by routine conventions to view their pupils primarily as a mind or

[4] In recent times also called "catch-up growth." Generally overlooked, however, is the fact that the Grid characteristics of this "entity" were first and extensively described by Wetzel many years ago. (2a)

intellect of given IQ and distinct personality, housed in a physical body whose presence was acknowledged, but whose physical attributes, height and weight, for example, had, in effect, been parked outside with the bicycles, so far as any meaning they might convey (as to growth) was concerned.

Such, then, were the traditional differences of approach that pervaded the daily operations of a leading Ohio school system which annually received its share of National Merit Awards but which also showed, on the record, a proportionate share of growth failure. Academic programs and performance were matters on the teachers' docket, whereas physical growth, health and fitness were the concern of other departments whose staffs were similarly restricted in official responsibility. But, if connections between the classroom and the clinic or to physical education and counselling were always open, it must be fairly said that communication over these lines was seldom utilized to its full potential. In theory, the organismic concept of the "whole child" was still in vogue; whereas, in practice, it must be recognized, a pupil wore two caps, the one in the classroom, and the other in the clinic. We believe he could do better with just one.

Impressions of this kind continued gradually to be assembled and to suggest that academic and physical troubles were somehow more intimately connected than was generally realized. The point was reached at which it seemed imperative to get more definitive information on such possibilities. As a result, the study just completed (1) was decided upon. At first, it was pursued quite casually, but later as evidence mounted, it was formally organized to determine to what extent good grades and good growth as well as poor grades and poor growth might be found to be associated.

REMARKS ON EARLIER STUDIES

We cannot, here, do justice to work that has preceded ours; it has been fully dealt with elsewhere (1). Nevertheless, a few very brief remarks would seem in order.

Galton, Terman, Paterson, Abernethy and Laycock among many others have made major contributions, although, it is important to note, all had quite different objectives from those we have pursued. Their interest in possible relations between academic and physical traits was limited to investigations that focussed almost entirely on correlations between intelligence test scores (IQ's) and stature, though weight and other body measurements were occasionally employed. There was general agreement that r's between IQ and stature, for example, were positive but low; that gifted children tended to be taller than average; and, that children of inferior intelligence were often shorter than normal children of the same age. Emphasis was clearly on *intellect* rather than on *learning* as measured by teacher's marks. Interestingly, however, Gray and Ayres, at Chicago, did investigate the use of teachers' marks in relation to IQ as a method of screening out behaviour problems (4). In any event, among educators, it has generally been thought that this whole matter of body measurements and intelligence had been adequately disposed of long ago. Thus, Paterson, himself, on the basis of work he had intensely reviewed, felt obliged to conclude with what must impress observers today as strange and most astonishing advice to the effect that, "physical measurements of school children should concern the school administrator and teacher . . . academically only in so far as physical size is a factor to be reckoned with in determining the size of desks and seats to be installed in the school room"! (5)

Thirty-five years later, in the face of our own 10-year findings, we cannot possibly agree; for what may well have seemed justified to him in regard to *IQ* and *stature* does not apply when one studies, instead, as we have done, the relations between the *quality of growth* and the *rate of learning*—not at a point, but over a 10-year span of school life.

GENERAL FEATURES OF THE STUDY

Our basic study was carried out in the Shaker Heights, Ohio, School District which has long held a reputation for high scholarship, first class faculties and a fine curriculum. The 9 Elementary, 2 Junior and 1 Senior High Schools have always been administered by a competent professional staff in conjunction with an elected Board of Education whose members are prominent citizens dedicated to excellence and to maintaining the highest pre-collegiate standards. Conditions in Shaker Heights are probably as nearly ideal as anywhere in the nation. It was here, in this high income, residential, prestige suburb of Cleveland that our original study was set up to ascertain to what extent a good scholarship record tends to accompany good physical growth, and, conversely, whether poor growth would predominate in cases of poor scholarship and under-achievement.

The entire class of 1962 was chosen as our original sample, in part, because its graduation coincided approximately with the formal initiation of the investigation and, in part, because its members would be within easy recall, if desired, for additional follow-up. Of the 474 students, 257 had long-term (10-year or more) continuous data on academic as well as growth progress in the official cumulative records. While preliminary analysis of all data was carried out, the present report applies only to the 134 boys with 10 or more years' continuing attendance in the Shaker Schools from grade III to XII.

THE DATA

Academic performance was documented in 3 ways: for each boy 60 teachers' marks summarizing 3 intra-semester reports or 180 marks in all; about 50 periodic IQ test-scores and profile ratings; 240 achievement test results; altogether some 470 data on each pupil, or a total of 62,000 scholastic entries in the cumulative records for the group of 134 boys. Main reliance was placed on the annual means of six summary teachers' marks (GPA) in English, mathematics and social studies for two semesters, with IQ's determined from 5–7 tests as co-variates.

Physical growth was evaluated semi-annually in terms of Wetzel Grid standards for body size, physique, direction and speed of development based on about 50 plotted points for each boy from kindergarten to grade XII that marked out his channel and auxodromic trends. Standard specifications and tolerances (6) were employed (Table 1) in classifying both the channel and the auxo-

TABLE 1

Ten-Year Career Performance of Growth Quality Groups in Terms of Wetzel Grid Channel Fluctuations and Speed of Development *

GROUP	DIRECTION MAINTAINED WITHIN	SPEED	
	CHANNELS	LEVELS PER MONTH	LEVELS PER YEAR
(NNN)—32	1.023 ± 0.071	$1.0248 + 0.0096$	12.30 ± 0.12
(NFF)—30	2.31 ± 0.17	0.878 ± 0.020	10.50 ± 0.24
(FFF)—13	2.08 ± 0.26	0.842 ± 0.015	10.10 ± 0.18
Other (F)'s	2.0	0.20–0.75	2.5–9.0
(AC)–19	2.0	$1.40+$	$16.8+$
(Ob)–14	$3.0+$	$1.25+$	$15.0+$

* Means $\pm$ s.e. based on individual linear trends for the age-interval, 5–16 years, and for the corresponding level-span from 20 to 180. Note approximation to Grid standard ($\frac{1}{4}$ channel per 10 levels and 1.0 *lev./mo.*) as growth quality improved from (FFF) to (NNN).

drome curves as satisfactory (N) or unsatisfactory (F) during elementary, junior and senior high school periods. This resulted in a factorial scheme consisting of 8 growth-quality groups: (NNN), (NNF), . . . (FFF) along with four additional sub-groups of (N) and (F)-types among obese (Ob) and highly advanced boys (AC). Thus, the designation (NFN) signified, for example, that a boy had "passed" his Grid-test of growth during his Elementary and Senior High School periods, but had shown growth failure (F) during Junior High.[5]

METHODS

Individual annual GPA means, variability (*s.d.*) and trend components were calculated for the boys in all 12 growth quality groups with further subclassification by schools and districts. Standard methods of multivariate analysis, with special reference to trend components, were employed whenever possible. Results were presented in (Chi)² summaries, distributions of 3045 Teachers' Marks in Elementary school, analysis of variance tables and some 43 graphs, a large number of which represented 10-year group trends and comparisons of academic progress.

RESULTS

For briefest possible presentation, the more important practical results have been set out in Tables 1, 2 and 3. Only a few additional remarks will be added.

The data in Table 1 clearly demonstrate that Grid appraisals of growth quality can be objectively and quantitatively evaluated with considerably

[5] An excellent account of how Wetzel Grid surveillance can be effectively carried out in school health programs has been given by Drs. Robert W., and Elizabeth Bryan Deisher in this *Journal.* (7) See also references (10), (11) and (12).

TABLE 2

Annual Grade-Point Averages, Career Means and Scholastic Gradients (Slopes) of Various Growth Quality Sub-groups, for Entire Sample of 134 Boys and for Randomly Chosen Sample in the Shaker Heights High School Class of '62

LINE	GROUP	n	IQ	III	IV	v	vi	VII	VIII	IX	x	XI	XII	MEAN	10-YR. SLOPE
1	NNN	32	122	3.92	4.06	4.12	4.09	3.76	3.84	3.87	3.84	3.95	3.92	3.94	−.016
2	NFF	30	118	3.86	3.77	3.83	3.81	3.45	3.46	3.39	3.02	3.08	3.82	3.50	−.094
3	FFF	13	113	3.27	3.33	3.55	3.58	2.68	2.93	2.91	2.26	2.34	2.72	2.95	−.122
4	Highly Advanced	19	122	3.98	3.99	4.18	3.94	3.53	3.81	3.91	3.61	3.52	3.56	3.80	−.059
5	Obese	14	115	3.76	3.74	3.75	3.44	2.99	3.16	3.22	3.14	2.93	3.11	3.38	−.091
6	Mean (1962–Boys)	134	121	3.74	3.77	3.83	3.75	3.30	3.44	3.43	3.18	3.15	3.30	3.49	−.075
7	Random Sample	30	120	3.83	3.84	3.94	3.82	3.42	3.56	3.61	3.31	3.30	3.41	3.60	−.068

greater precision than might ordinarily be needed. It is interesting to see how closely our groups approximate the original Grid standards of growth (deviations no more than ½ channel per 10 levels of advancement within a given year, and 1 level per month auxodromic progress, which were originally proposed some 3 to 5 years before most of our students were born) as quality improved from (FFF) to (NNN).

Attention is called, next, to the various comparisons of academic trends among the different sub-groups of Table 2, a number of which are shown graphically in Figure 1. A tendency for GPA to decline is evident in all sets although the drop-off slope for (NNN)–32 in line 1, namely, $-.016$, is the only gradient that is not significantly different from 0 (zero). From the standpoint of the classroom teacher as well as of educators in general, it should be emphasized that this 10-yr. GPA slope of the (NNN)–32 group, who showed the best combined growth and academic performance, was very significantly smaller ($p <$ .001) than the corresponding down-trend of any other subgroup observed in the study or listed in lines 2–7 of Table 2. Statistically speaking, these lads had a "flat" curve over their entire III–XII career. Contrariwise, as (F)-content increased, academic proficiency diminished year-by-year, as in lines 2, 3 and 5, despite altogether similar IQ's.

The differences in performance between the various sub-groups and the over-all mean curve for the 134 boys of the '62 class are all very significant and leave no doubt, even on the basis of visual inspection, that the (NNN) . . . (FFF) sets cannot possibly be regarded as ordinary sampling variations. Support for this conclusion, if any is really required, is offered by the results in line 7 which represent the GPA mean trend of 30 boys chosen strictly with the help of a table of random numbers from the original group of 134. Their averages (IQ, GPA and slope) were all but identical to those of the whole study group. It is evident that the probability of obtaining the (NNN) group by random chance alone is even less than that for a full hand of spades, $viz.$, 6.35×10^{-11}.

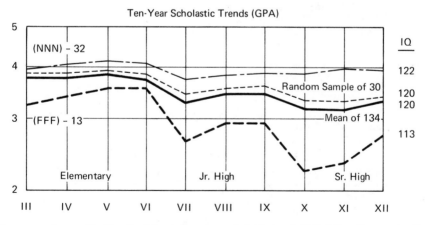

FIGURE 1.   *Significantly different, long-term scholastic trends plotted from the corresponding data in Table 2. Note: (1) the steady, high-level course of the (NNN)–32 boys; (2) how faithfully the random sample of 30 reflects the average downtrend and (3) how drop-off and negative gradients increase with increasing (F)-quality growth.*

Summary of Most Important Findings on Scholastic Achievement and Growth Quality

	n	IQ	GPA	TREND
A. *Academic:*				
Over-all	134	121	3.30	Significantly Negative
Mean				
(NNN)	32	122	3.94	0 (Flat)
(NFF)	30	118	3.50	Sig. Neg.
(FFF)	13	113	2.95	Sig. Neg.
Matched IQ				
(NNN)	15	118	3.60	0 (Flat)
(NFF)	15	118	3.40	Sig. Neg.

GPA Trends in (N) vs. (F) Growth Quality Groups consistently superior in (N)

GPA Variability (s.d.) increased with diminishing class rank and GPA; minimum value found in (NNN) $= \pm .33$

Correlations between Teachers' Marks (GPA) and Standardized Achievement Test Scores were uniformly high, i.e., $> .90$. See Text.

B. *Growth:*

1. $50/134 = 37\%$ showed solid Satisfactory (N) Growth throughout K-XII (El./Jr./Sr. H.S.)
2. $33/134 = 25\%$ showed continuously Unsatisfactory Growth (F) throughout K-XII (El./Jr./Sr. H.S.)
3. $30/96* = 31\%$ showed unsatisfactory trends in Jr. and Sr. H.S.—i.e., 60% of time.
4. $64/96* = 67\%$ had at least 1 major period in El., Jr. or Sr. H.S. rated (F).
5. Of a *possible* 288 (3 × 96) pupil periods of Satisfactory (N) Growth among 96 Non-obese and Non-accelerated boys, 125 or 43.4% showed demonstrable (F)-growth.
6. Prevalence of (N)-growth—even in an economically favored community —was slightly better than 1:2 in the Non-obese group.
7. Moderate to Serious Obesity: $14/134 = 10.5\%$.

C. *Academic vs. Growth Performance:*

1. Career GPA Trend in NNN–32 (i.e., Mean El. vs. Mean Sr. H.S.) showed only a 3.5% drop
2. Career GPA Trend for all 134 boys (i.e., Mean El. vs. Mean Sr. H.S.) showed a 15% drop
3. Career GPA Trend for (F) groups (NNF) . . . (FFF) showed a still larger drop from 3.6 to 2.4, i.e., a 33% loss despite comparable IQ's.

---

* 96 = 134 less the boys in Special groups, i.e., Obese, accelerated or extreme types (Dwarfism).

Before summarizing this phase of the study we wish also to stress two additional results of practical interest to educators. First, as had been expected, GPA and IQ were closely correlated, r_{13} ranging from .64 to .94 within the various growth quality groups of Table 2, whereas GPA and Slope ($r_{12} = .54$) and Slope vs. IQ ($r_{23} = .32$) yielded much lower values for the entire set of paired observations. Thus, while GPA-*trend* appeared to be somewhat influenced by IQ, in accordance with 0-order $r_{23} = .32$, such association was completely eliminated by the further demonstration that the partial correlations ($r_{23.1}$) in the primary and all subgroups turned out to be not significantly different from 0 (zero). In other words, the data of the present study clearly indicated that GPA *trends* were independent of IQ and the inference, then, was that the trend differences shown in Figure 1 and Table 2 could not be ascribed to concomitant differences in IQ.

Secondly, since standardized Achievement Tests of various kinds are widely used, it is important to point out that correlations in our study between GPA and available Achievement Test Scores were high, viz., $r = .96$, with fiducial limits ($p < .01$) of .90 and .98. This does not mean, of course, that achievement tests should be dispensed with, but it does indicate that the differences in academic trend we have reported for boys in the several growth quality groups would, in practice, be essentially the same regardless of whether GPA or Achievement Test Scores are used as the criterion of scholastic performance. The results of this long-term longitudinal study, accordingly, should go far in encouraging Educators to renew their original interest and to restore their confidence in teachers' marks (GPA) as valuable practical measures of academic progress and success.

On the other hand, in view of well known ambiguities and limitations in simple height or weight data, Educators would hardly choose to rely on these alone for appraisals of the *quality* of physical growth in place of the more definitive evaluations in terms of the size, shape, direction and speed standards provided by the Grid technique. For example, the concept of "developmental age" has long been rooted in the lay as well as in medical or scientific language. It has led to expressions such as "height-age," "skeletal age" and the corresponding assertions, "as big" or "as tall as a 10-year-old," and the like. When this concept of "relative advancement," however, is stretched, with serious intention, to include the notion of "physique age" (!) it indicates how unnecessarily confused the appraisal of physical growth has become. Happily, we and others, who apply the principles of the Grid technique in school or medical ratings of physical growth quality, are spared such conceptual misadventures. Similar considerations hold for the obese group of boys shortly to be described.

There are, accordingly, two clear conclusions that may be drawn from these findings: (1) that the "natural drop-off" in pupils' grade-point averages, presumptively associated with more difficult subject matter and stiffer grading systems as a child advances into the high schools, appears to be confirmed in the sample we have studied, but that such drop-off amounts to only about 3–5% in the case of boys who have shown satisfactory physical growth; and (2) that, in other groups *not* so advantaged, GPA decline between Elementary and Senior High years is from 3 to 8 times greater depending on the F-content of their growth quality. Scholastic achievement, in other words, as measured by teachers' marks in required courses, is directly associated with how successfully a pupil has maintained acceptable growth performance over his 10-year, grade III to XII career.[6]

ACADEMIC PROGRESS IN OBESE AND OBESITY-PRONE BOYS[7]

No less than 10.5% of the boys in the 1962 class were obese, i.e., with points at one period or another in Wetzel Grid channels A_4 and beyond. Most were moderately affected but a few were of extreme grade (A_8 at level 208) in grade XI. Only two of these boys had GPA's above 3.8 and both were comparatively mild and well controlled. As a group, their academic achievement was notably less than that of the standard (NNN)-32 boys and also than that of the group who were highly advanced in maturity.[8] These lads pose special problems for the Medical Service and they are frequently more difficult to deal with by guidance counsellors, owing, we believe, in large part, to their stubborn affliction. In all cases the Wetzel Grid is of great value not only in giving early warning signs that quite obvious obesity will emerge, unless the indicated trend is altered, but also, when the disorder is already established, in teaching these subjects to understand what their own curves signify as regards body composition and thus to cooperate more effectively with their physicians. Each, moreover, represents an extreme type of deviation in body composition, with densities as low as 1.01 and body fat of 40% or more. In this connection, it should be noted that one of the advantages of Grid ratings is that they yield very high correlations ($r = .995+$) with measurements of underwater weighing and also with K^{40} determinations obtained by means of whole body scintillation counters for the ultimate estimation of density and body fat (1).

RÉSUMÉ

In this 10-year longitudinal study of scholastic performance and physical growth of 134 boys who graduated from Shaker Heights High School in the Class of 1962 we have been able to show that unacceptable forms of growth (F) were characteristically accompanied by academic underachievement which grew worse as the years of poor growth continued to accumulate. Entry upon a period of poor growth was followed, not merely by a simple, temporary drop

[6] Susan Robertson of Cornell University working with R. H. Barnes, R. Z. Zimmerman and H. J. Simmons reported at the Federation Meetings in April 1965 that malnourished (growth failure) rats showed a significantly decreased ability to learn.
[7] Obesity, of course, is only one form of "nutritional problem" we encounter in our school health operations. Actually, every advance, whether (N) or (F), that a pupil displays on his Grid has *some* nutritional implication (2a). Recent efforts to check "nutritional status" in entire school populations with the help of Mobile Laboratories should provide information heretofore desirable, but unavailable, except in hospital or clinic referrals. However, unless such findings, when gathered in the mass, are appraised in conjunction with concurrent growth quality trends, it is doubtful whether their full value can be realized. Conversely, mobile tests, *made for cause*, for example, on the basis of (F)-type growth appearing on a child's Grid, should prove much more rewarding.
[8] In Seattle, Hammar (9) has likewise reported scholastic underachievement as a characteristic finding in obese students.

or diversion in a student's marks, but, more often than not, by a downward deflection that persisted to the end of secondary schooling. The academic aftermath of unsatisfactory physical growth was, very plainly, sub-par scholastic achievement—apparently for the quite plausible reason that a child too tired or weak to grow properly can hardly be expected to possess either the will or the strength to develop his physique or to improve his mind.

Another finding, in support of this general premise, was the all but perfectly constant and high-level GPA trend of the (NNN)-32 group which presented a splendid example of harmonious development with respect to academic success, physical fitness and good growth over a long 10-year span of school life that was, by no means entirely free from stress and strain in the world today.

All results, taken together, pointed to the single conclusion that steady scholastic achievement, consistent with capacity (IQ) cannot be expected from pupils whose physical growth is demonstrably underpar by Wetzel Grid standards.

To this conclusion, the data of the present study have provided, so far as the authors can see, no basis for an alternative view. Thus, other things being equal, physical fitness appears to be an important prerequisite for good scholastic achievement. Moreover, since there is much ado about physical fitness today, this finding is timely. Yet, so long as good growth is, in essence, the proper development of physique, it should come as no surprise that it has also turned out to be the common denominator of academic as well as of physical performance.

The broad implication of our results is simply that greater cooperation between all departments—academic, guidance, physical education and health— is needed to lay the groundwork for preventing scholastic underachievment that is associated with, and possibly induced by, sub-par physical growth. For we have seen that neither scholastic performance nor physical fitness can be casually regarded or taken for granted (8). They must both be worked for in all daily operations by cooperating staffs who are fully aware of the alternatives.[9]

Bibliography

1. VAN IDEN, STARR S. *Scholastic Progress of Boys Classified by the Wetzel Grid Technique* (*A 10-Year Longitudinal Study*). Doctoral dissertation, Western Reserve University, 1965.
2. WETZEL, N. C., HOPWOOD, H. H., KUECHLE, M. E., and GRUENINGER, R. M. Growth Failure in School Children—Further Studies of Vitamin B_{12} Dietary Supplements. *The J. of Clin. Nutrition* 1:17, 1952.
2a. WETZEL, N. C. Assessing the Physical Condition of Children II. Simple Malnutrition: A Problem of Failing Growth and Development. *J. Ped.* 22:208, 1943.
3. VAN IDEN, *op. cit.*
4. GRAY, HORACE and AYRES, J. G. *Growth in Private School Children.* Chicago: University of Chicago Press, 1931.
5. PATERSON, DONALD G. *Physique and Intellect.* New York: The Century Co., 1930.
6. WETZEL, N. C. *Instruction Manual in the Use of the Grid for Evaluating Physical Fitness.* New York, Chicago, San Francisco: N. E. A. Service, Inc., 1941, p. 3.

[9] Inquiries regarding the Grid or available literature should be addressed to Jean Mooney, Newspaper Enterprise Association, Inc., 1200 West Third Street, Cleveland, Ohio 44113.

7. DEISHER, ROBERT W. and DEISHER, ELIZABETH BRYAN. The Value of the Wetzel Grid in a School Health Program and Problems Related to Its Use. *The Journal of School Health*, XXII, No. 2, February, 1952.

8. GRUENINGER, ROBERT M. *Don't Take Growth for Granted*. N. E. A. Service, Inc., Cleveland, Ohio, 1961.

9. HAMMAR, S. L. The Obese Adolescent. *The Journal of School Health*, XXXV, No. 6, June, 1965, p. 246.

10. MARTIN, ETHEL A. *Roberts' Nutrition Work with Children*. The University of Chicago Press, Chicago, 1954, p. 118, 374.

11. OLIVER, J. N. Physical Growth and the Measurement of Height and Weight in the Schools; The Wetzel Grid. *J. Phys. Educ.* Mar. and July, 1952. (England).

12. RANDALL, M. W. and WAINE, W. K. *The Objectives of the Physical Education Lesson*, London, G. Bell and Sons, Ltd.

13. ROGERS, K. D. and GRACE REESE. Health Studies—Presumably Normal High School Students, I, II and III. *A. J. Dis. Child.*, 108 and 109, Dec. 1964 and Jan. 1965.

14. GLASER, K. and CLEMMONS, R. L. School Failure. *Pediatrics* 35:128, 1965.

14

Intellectual Development

In the first article in this chapter E. A. Peel discusses some of the noteworthy events in intellectual growth during adolescence. In line with current thinking, influenced by Piaget's stress on the importance of experience in the development of cognition, Peel shows that besides maturation of the organism experience is an important determiner of cognitive development in adolescence. Part of this experience has to do with objects and the knowledge abstracted from the objects. The other is derived from the actions of the adolescent and is related to his ability to think about his thinking. Both kinds of cognitive development are influenced by teaching through the use of language, if the teaching is geared to the readiness of the person taught.

K. Lovell's article, a continuation of the speech that is excerpted in Chapter 10 (pp. 305–308), gives examples of tasks which become possible to solve during adolescence. The first study dealt with proportions, the second with history.

In the third article, David Elkind discusses the egocentricity of adolescence. He shows how it differs from earlier egocentricity and how it leads to certain other characteristics of adolescents that are related to their social and personal functioning.

Intellectual Growth During Adolescence *

E. A. Peel
BIRMINGHAM UNIVERSITY

1. ADOLESCENT THINKING

In every respect but one the adolescent has received unstinted attention concerning his development and its so-called problems. Furthermore he appears to thrive on it. Almost monthly he creates new values in a subculture which grows more self-determined and self-defined. The peripheral signs of this sub-

Reprinted from *Educational Review*, 1965, *17*, 169–180. By permission.

* Being the substance of the 1965 Bartholomew Lecture—University of Keel.

culture, as seen in its sound and beat and clothes, assume an ascendancy that reaches into adult values. When I was young it was the late adolescent, nay the young adult, who gave the sartorial lead both to his juniors and seniors. But now it is the mid-adolescent who exercises such an influence on his elders. I'm not sure he always wishes it so—though what he wishes is often difficult to determine for his is a jealously guarded culture. It does not do for the adult to be a square but it is equally unwise to try to be too expert.

In their preoccupation with how he feels, plays, herds and adorns himself very few people have studied his intellectual growth systematically. This is not to say that educationists are insensitive to the problem. The central theme of the Newsom report is the intellectual difference between primary and secondary school experience. The difference is more than a matter of attainment. There is a change of quality as well. Such nouns as *self-awareness, imagination, judgment, insight* crop up throughout the report. We are told that

> The work in a secondary school becomes secondary in character whenever it is concerned, first, with selfconscious thought and judgment; secondly, with the relation of school and the work done there to the world outside of which the pupils form a part and of which they are increasingly aware.

and that

> the quality of selfconscious judgment . . . describes a mental process that involves the use of reason and imagination to bring order into the world of things perceived.

Awareness, however, is not explanation.

There may be several reasons for this lack of information about adolescent thinking. On the surface young children's thinking changes more dramatically and is capable of examination by simpler material. There is also a widespread belief that by mid-adolescence, thinking is more a function of the particular school subject—say science, mathematics or history—than of more general thought processes and psychological changes. But thinking is an interaction between pupil and subject and the adolescent has not ceased to be a pupil.

In this neglect we tend to forget that there are many formative years between 11 and 20. The intellectual changes are indeed both complex and significant. Any problem in a school subject, provided it is not too technically difficult to be given to a wide age range of pupils, will bring out these qualities of the change. Here are a few.

> Suppose there are 32 entrants to a knock-out championship in table tennis. How many games must be played to find the winner? What if there are 24, 17? Is there a general rule? Can you prove it?

Most lower and mid secondary school pupils can produce the general induction—but only sixth formers, and not all of them, are able to prove the rule deductively from the essential structure of the problem—one winner and each losing individual being immediately eliminated.

Again if we give pupils a new number system, say to base 6 or 7, to learn and use, we find younger adolescents can learn the number system and use it by simple correlation of new symbols with decimal symbols, translation and re-translation, without ever giving a hint that the change of base is understood.

Older pupils and students set about it quite differently by setting up possible rules, trying them out and accepting, modifying or rejecting as appropriate. In exercises they also give evidence of thinking in the novel system.

If you put colorless liquid samples of dilute acid, dilute alkali and pure water before a pupil and supply him with specimens of blue and red litmus paper after having shown him the reactions between the chemicals and indicator and then ask him to identify the three liquids you will find a failure before thirteen to act purposefully according to hypotheses. The power to eliminate alternatives appears later.

Lastly, turning to social studies, if we ask pupils to define such terms as *laws* (1), we are likely up to 13, to get such answers as *rules which should be obeyed, rules made for the good of the country* to 15 or 16, and a *system of rule imposed upon society in order to promote a freedom for the individual without encroaching on each other's freedom* from the most mature at 19.

These are pointers to what we may look for and how we may do it. Clearly the method of study requires a *guided* taxonomy, in which emphasis is laid on observing developmental changes as well as differences arising from learning various school subjects, followed by a more etiological analysis.

Our questions are

(i) What is changing during adolescence?

(ii) What is common, what different in the modes of thinking required in different subjects?

I shall be concerned mainly with the former.

The method of experiment is to use simple contrived situations, purified from school problems or nearly similar. The material shall not demand too high a level of subject matter knowledge but is designed at producing a problem situation testing thinking rather than attainment.

2. DESCRIPTION AND EXPLANATION

What are the lines to guide our empirical studies? Over the period of adolescence the most fundamental is that between what I call describer and explainer thinking. Description, as I am using the term, entails no more than a relating of the parts of a phenomenon with each other. Explanation involves referring the phenomenon to other previously experienced phenomena, and to generalizations and concepts independently formed. The familiar experiment from elementary physics of causing a tin to collapse by boiling a little water in it, stoppering it and immediately cooling it, illustrates well what I mean. A pupil may describe this sequence of events very adequately but he has not explained it unless he refers to the function of the steam in driving out the air, the subsequent cooling to condense the steam to produce a vacuum and the final collapse under atmospheric pressure. Here the concepts of boiling, gaseous state, condensation, vacuum and atmospheric pressure and strengths of material are all involved.

As in the case of the learners of the 6 base number system, who were able to apply their knowledge to simple tasks without understanding the base of the system, so the describer of the above phenomenon may well be able to predict what might happen in similar instances, but his power of prediction will be far more limited than that of the thinker who can explain the phenomenon. The latter would be able to predict outcomes in superficially quite different situations as, for example, to explain various physical and physiological phenomena associated with going high into the atmosphere or deep into the sea.

Analogy clearly lies at the basis of explanation but there is a spectrum of predictive effectiveness ranging from the powerful models of physics at one extreme (2) to the tempting analogies at the other which so often ensnare the politicians and historians. The 100 days analogy was long used against the intentions of its originator (3).

It is doubtful how far pure description is possible, that is, without any hint of explanation. We use the word *collapse* to account for the change in the shape of the tin. This implies analogy and explanation, which nevertheless are not very useful without the idea of air pressure.

If however we concede the point that pure description is at one end of an explanatory dimension, it would not invalidate the scheme of analysis to be outlined. The range of thought is wide during adolescent growth. The concession however does bear on naive positivistic assumptions in practical science and on the "unique event" theory of history teaching. According to it both would tend to be untenable.

3. THE IMAGINATION OF POSSIBLE EXPLANATIONS

The growth of explanatory thought involves several changes very noticeable in mid- and late adolescence. Let us look at three of them. First there is the growth from partial and circumstantial observations to comprehensive judgments involving the imagination and invocation of possibilities to explain the phenomenon.

We may set a short anecdote with questions.

> Only brave pilots are allowed to fly over high mountains. This summer a fighter pilot flying over the Alps collided with an aerial cable-way, and cut a main cable causing some cars to fall to the glacier below. Several people were killed and many others had to spend the night suspended above the glacier.

(1) Was the pilot a careful airman? (2) Why do you think so?

The questions evoke answers at four clearly marked levels:

1. Not sure. Maybe, invoking or imagining extenuating possibilities, vision, weather, state of the plane.
2. No, because if he was careful, he would not have cut the cable.
3. No, because he hit the cable, etc.
4. Yes or No, with irrelevant comment or denial of the premise. E.g., Yes, he was brave; Yes, the cable shouldn't be there.

The ages associated with these levels are respectively $13\frac{1}{2}$, $12\frac{1}{2}$, 12, and $10\frac{1}{2}$.

When instead of the above questions we posed the wholly nondirective question of "What do you think about the happening in the story?" we compel the child to identify his own problem and the replies indicate the level at which he is thinking. At $14\frac{1}{2}$ we got:

He was either not informed of the mountain railway on his route or he was flying too low also his flying compass may have been affected by something before or after take-off this setting him off course causing collision with the cable.

At 12:

I think that the pilot was not very good at flying and also not fit for doing it. He would have been far better off if he went on with fighting.

and at $11\frac{1}{2}$:

The people must also be brave to stay the night suspended above the glacier. The pilot must be not only brave but a good driver.

From this and other test passages conducted with statistically respectable numbers, the genesis of the pupil's thinking-comprehension seems to proceed as follows:

First there is a capacity to think propositionally by pupils at least as young as 11–12. A proposition is produced linking that implied in the question with the salient feature of the story related circumstantially to the question. Other possibilities do not enter. To this extent the judgment is partial and circumstantial and is essentially descriptive since no outside concept is invoked.

followed next by

a transformation of this judgment by forming its complement with the addition of no new inferences from the material but a change of language form and emphasis. This phase appears at ages from a half year older than that associated with the first category answers.

followed finally by

recognition that there might have been other elements outside the pilot's control which made it not possible for him to see the cable etc. The answers at this stage shift to invoked explanations and suggestions to account for the incident. Their plausibility reveals that they have been related to the data of the problem. Chronological ages of 13 + and mental ages of 14 + years seem to be associated with this phase.

School subject matter confirms the appearance of *imagined* possibilities, comprehensively related to the data of the problem at 13 +, but not frequently by younger pupils.

This was shown by Piaget and Inhelder (4) in their studies of pupils' understanding of fluid pressure and their discovery of Newton's First law. The invocation of imagined causes does not appear to be marked before 13 +.

4. INDUCTION AND DEDUCTION

Description turns on inductive methods, whereas explanation involves deduction from a basis of hypotheses. The contrasting roles of induction and deduction in mathematics need no underlining—we saw it in the table tennis problem. But a similar opposition is apparent between induction and hypothetico-deduction in material situations involving empirical data—such as those of science and geography. The successful use of imagined hypotheses to explain phenomena always contains a deductive element in the comparison of hypotheses with data to arrive at solutions or for the generalizations seen in so-called "thought experiments" in physics (5).

When does the adolescent begin to show signs of using hypothetico-deductive methods spontaneously?

Here is an experiment aimed at obtaining an answer to this question.

The problem concerned crofter-farming in the Isle of Lewis. No text was used but two maps showed the essential geographical features: mountains, deer forest, rough grazing, common pasture and croft areas and emphasised the generally poor nature of the land. Charts showed the proportion of crops and grass (good land) to common pasture (poor, ill-drained, rock-strewn land), the composition of the crops and grass (grass, oats and potatoes) and the proportion of sheep (many) and cattle (few). Monthly rainfall and temperature charts were also provided (6).

The central problem for the farmer lies in the natural restrictions placed on him by the poor quality of land and climate, even though there is plenty of land available. Only a minimum degree of geographical expertise is required that is not evident from the maps and charts, namely that sheep will graze on rough land but cattle not.

Rhys then asked the question:

> Are they making sensible use of their land by only growing a few crops on a very small area?

This may arouse a conflict between (i) the visual evidence of the large amount of land apparently available and the large number of sheep and (ii) the nature of the land and climate leading to a deductive process to arrive at a conclusion. Here are two answers, the first characteristic of 11–12 year olds:

> Yes. Because they only live in a small place and they only need a small number of crops. The rest of the land has to be kept to feed the animals.

and the second characteristic of older pupils of age $14\frac{1}{2}+$:

> The crofters are sensible in growing only a few crops over a little area because the ground is mainly mountains and very rough. It would be hard to get the necessary amount of crops needed to feed the crofters, the only crops which they have cultivated with a little success are the hardier, tougher crops, oats and potatoes. The land can be made of better use by rough grazing with sheep on the hills and mountains.

The first shows some deduction but solely in terms of area of land and numbers of sheep. The second starts from the quality of the land and deduces consequences which relate to the area and number features.

5. ELIMINATING ALTERNATIVES

The testing of hypotheses and the elimination of those less effective make up severe tests of adolescent and adult thinking. People are usually too ready to infer a particular belief from evidence which would also support another. In one test (7) students had to find the concept of *three numbers in increasing order* by putting up sets of three numbers for judgment by the experimenter, who of course knew the concept. The most frequent responses were positive instances enumerated to illustrate the concept chosen. Relatively few sets were chosen to eliminate alternative concepts, and also few negative instances deliberately chosen to test the assumed concept. Wason concluded: very few intelligent adults spontaneously test their beliefs in a situation which does not appear to be of a "scientific" nature.

These results found support from a research (8) on student nurses' ideas of correlation. They were presented with packs of cards, each card of which described a patient by giving a relationship between a *symptom* and a *diagnosis* Suppose the symptom was spots on the chest and the diagnosis measles. Four types of card are possible:

Presence of spots (positive)—diagnosis of measles (positive)
Presence of spots (positive)—measles *not* diagnosed (negative)
Absence of spots (negative—diagnosis of measles (positive)
Absence of spots (negative)—measles *not* diagnosed (negative)

They thumbed through the packs and were asked to judge to what extent each pack revealed a correlation between symptom and diagnosis. The worker concluded that

Their strategies and inferences reveal a particularistic, nonstatistical approach, or an exclusive dependence on the frequency of + + instances.

When secondary school pupils are given simple chemical experiments requiring identification of substances and the elimination of alternative possibilities, they are rarely capable spontaneously of successful elimination procedures until they are 14, 15 and older.

What are the main features of intellectual growth between eleven and twenty?

In the growth from a largely descriptive type of thinking to explanation we see a change from particularistic, perceptual, circumstantial and largely inductive ways of thinking to modes of thought revealing the invocation of imagined possibilities which gradually become more articulate in form to warrant the use of the terms hypotheses and propositions. This articulateness is shown in the increased use of deduction and in the power to eliminate unsupported alternatives.

6. THE ETIOLOGY OF CHANGES IN THINKING

The generalizations about the ages at which significant changes take place are of course statistical and assume fairly normal conditions of schooling and intelligence. I have deliberately avoided any reference to the influence of schooling and instruction. We need, however, to raise these questions when we turn now to the etiology of the changes.

The factors which enter into the changes we have described are *maturation, experience, communication* and *instruction* and the urge in every individual *to come to intellectual terms* with his environment.

We may pass over maturation fairly quickly. If cognitive maturation means anything it must reflect neurological maturation. We know little about the latter after the first few years of life. But we know nothing about maturation during adolescence—it is likely that there is little neurological maturation over this period. Lastly, the statement that development is maturation is largely unfalsifiable, particularly over later years, as during adolescence.

Turning to the role of experience there appear to be two aspects which count for much in the child's intellectual development. First there is physical experience which "consists of acting upon objects and drawing some knowledge about the objects by abstraction from the objects" (9). This is concept formation, the kind of experience that everyone recognizes and uses to shape his behavior. But there is also another kind of experience where knowledge is drawn from the *actions* effected by the persons. This knowledge consists of the discovery of the properties of the set of actions used by the person in abstracting from and ordering the physical phenomena of his environment and constitutes "logico-mathematical experience." The laws of mathematical operations, associativity and commutativity and the like, are examples, as are those of the logical structure of classes, relations and propositions.

We have then two fundamental kinds of experience leading to recognition of the properties (a) of objects and material, and (b) of the actions carried out on the objects.

The two experiences develop hand in hand and attempts to teach a person to carry out certain abstractions about his environment will be fruitless unless he possesses also the related "structure of action." The growth of thinking, in fact, consists of the movement from structure of prior and lower order to those at a higher plane.

The third factor concerns formal and informal teaching by the use of language. It is fundamental and necessary and is very powerful in adolescence, when language is well developed, but like the other elements not by itself sufficient. As will be appreciated from the comments of the previous paragraphs the child can receive real information by such means "only if he is in a state where he can understand this information." The state requires that the new information is presented in a form demanding not more than the structure of action which the child has already formed. The child will make of the information what he can by virtue of his particular level of development—but this may not be what the adult intends. Hence the so-called discrepancy between language and thought.

The urge to come to intellectual terms with one's world provides the mainspring of intellectual development. It involves the child in a combined process of assimilation of and accommodation to the material world and his fellow creatures.

In the act of knowing the person is faced with a need to resolve a discrepancy basically between him and his environment which constitutes to him an external disturbance. Consequently he seeks equilibrium by active resolution and compensation. The most obvious and general action of this kind in adolescence is the need for and the process of explanation. When a person explains a phenomenon he effects an equilibrium. Such an equilibrium is not stable in that better explanations may be forthcoming with more knowledge etc., but explanation is far more stable than description, which is relatively unstable tending to pass into explanation. Description, as I have defined it, does not relate an event or phenomenon to the wider context of knowledge. The equilibrium of description will always lead to that of explanation.

The above refers to equilibrium between person and environment, but the process of finding equilibrium also refers to parts within the phenomenon. All natural and contrived situations involve the idea of equilibrium—disequilibrium. Behind this interaction there are the ideas of cancelling an operation or a state and compensating for such a change to re-establish equilibria.

The principle is seen operating in all the dynamic problems in science as in heat–energy change, and the law of moments. The geographical environment is in a continuously changing state of dynamic equilibrium where forces of climate, terrain, organic life and the intervention of men are constantly operating on each other.

When we give problems from geography in which the balance of nature is upset by farming, mining and building we find that an awareness of equilibrium as a combination of cancellation and compensation is only fully apparent in the mid- and late adolescent. The same is true of his understanding of history. Most events in history seen in treaties, declarations of war, concessions to groups, etc., contain the same principles of balance. Such material may be used to test thinking (10) as I did by using extracts from medieval European history. Often a balanced judgment is not forthcoming until 14–15 years of age.

But our world does not only consist of equilibria and disequilibria patterns. There is both balance and change. Changes with time are important. The human adapts himself to these changes by a *sensitivity to sequential phenomena*. This shows itself in two types of concepts which are complementary to each other (a) those of no change, of conservation and invariance seen in the invariants of physics: matter, weight, momentum . . . , mass energy . . . , nuclear properties, and (b) those of directional changes: order–chaos, development–degeneration, integration–disintegration, cause–effect.

The former have been well investigated but some of the latter particularly of order–disorder as seen in the thermo-dynamic changes have yet to be investigated in the adolescent range of thinking.

If the idea of structure of thought finds its origin in the equilibria of the physical world of science, of the geographical environment, and of men's interactions as in history and the social sciences, the idea of sequential and temporal order springs from the change of phenomena with time.

I could hardly conclude this discussion of adolescent thinking and its investigation without saying something about its implications for education. This must have been apparent at several places. The main change in adolescent thinking is the use of imagined explanations, carrying with it the capacity to manipulate and eliminate possibilities and is to some extent educable. I gave a similar test to the Pilot passage to two groups of eleven-year-olds, matched for conventional intelligence. One of the groups came from middle-class academic homes where ideas would be tossed about, the other from working-class homes. The first group was markedly superior in ideas and their manipulation.

But although teaching aids intellectual growth its effect is limited as we saw when we looked at the etiology of the process. The pupil and student can only take what he is ready for. If he is given too advanced material he'll make of it what he can. The key to progress is in insuring that he has had the two kinds of experience required, that is, of the properties of his environment, constructed by him, and of the properties of his actions, seen in mathematics and logic, used to define the material properties. These two go hand in glove, mathematics and logic need to be based on material experience but they then become necessities for further progress. Mathematics is often not well taught and symbolic logic scarcely at all in secondary schools. Just as mathematics forms the cognitive structure of science thinking so logic provides the structure of the humanities and the language subjects. A lot can be done by giving language teaching a new look and by teaching all pupils and students some logic, not necessarily over-symbolic but linked with use.

What we hope ensues from learning mathematics, physics or history, or any other subject is not merely data collection but the power to think in the way inherent in these disciplines, so that long later, although particular theorems, laws or changes are half or almost wholly forgotten, they can be resuscitated and used in the proper manner and the new circumstance, and fresh information and problems can be dealt with constructively. This is learning to think.

Notes and References

1. Wood, D. M. (1964). *The development of some concepts of social relations in childhood and adolescence investigated by means of the analysis of their definitions*, M. Ed. Thesis, University of Nottingham.
2. Hesse, M. B. (1963). *Models and Analogies in Science*. Sheed and Ward.
3. See Cummings' cartoon "The first hundred days", *Daily Express*, 30th October 1964.
4. Inhelder, B. and Piaget, I. (1958). *The growth of logical thinking*, London, Routledge.
5. Miller, F. (1959). *College Physics*, p. 132, to "prove" the relativity of time with respect to the motion of the frame of reference. Harcourt, Brace.
6. Rhys, W. T. (1965). The development of logical thought in the adolescent with reference to the teaching of geography in the secondary school. Unpublished research, Birmingham University Education Department.
7. Wason, P. C. (1960). On the failure to eliminate hypotheses in a conceptual task. *Qu. J. Exp. Psy.*, 12, 129.
8. Smedslund, J. (1963). The concept of correlation in adults. *Scand. J. Psy.*, 4, 165.
9. Piaget, J. in *Piaget Rediscovered* (1964). Conf. Cognit. Studies and Curric. Det., Berkeley and Cornell.
10. Peel, E. A., *The Pupil's Thinking* (1960). Oldbourne Press, pp. 122–125. Use of passage from *The Sicilian Vespers* by S. Runciman.

Growth of Schema of Proportion

K. Lovell

UNIVERSITY OF LEEDS

GROWTH OF SCHEMA OF PROPORTION

The second study to be discussed, very briefly, is concerned with the growth of the schema of proportion itself. Far fewer studies have been carried out into the growth of schemas at the level of formal thought than at the level of concrete operational thought, yet the former are vital in every area of school work and of life generally. Some of the studies that have been made, outside Geneva, are those of Lovell (1961), Hannam (1963), Hughes (1965), Jackson (1965), and Peluffo (1964). In addition, Lunzer (1965) has given details of studies relating to the growth of the ability to solve problems involving verbal and numerical analogies, and numerical series. All these studies reveal the slow growth of the proportionality schema in pupils of high school age. The aim of the present study was to test, within the same group of pupils, and using a number of different types of problems and settings, the following hypotheses:

a. The schema of proportion depends on some central intellective ability which underpins performance on all tasks involving proportion.

b. In addition to some central intellective ability, specific abilities contribute to the ability to use proportionality in particular tasks.

c. Tasks involving ratio will depend less on the ability indicated under (a) than in the case of the tasks involving proportion.

Twenty tasks were given, many of which involved more than one problem. Some of the tasks did not involve the schema of proportion; they involved, say, the schema of ratio or arithmetic series or geometric series that could be solved by multiplication or division by a whole number. The tasks were:

1. Calculation of the corresponding sides of similar triangles and rectangles. Easy examples of proportion were involved.

2. Calculation of the ratio of areas of rectangles displayed as in form of a fraction board. The task involved harder examples of ratio but not the schema of proportion.

3. Completion of numerical series. Six problems only one of which involved the schema of proportion and this was extremely easy.

4. The series 1^2, 2^2, 3^2, etc. illustrated by means of nesting equilateral triangles. Calculation of the ratio of the xth term to the $(x + 1)$th term. No proportion involved.

5. Calculation of the ratio of the volume of cuboids from given dimensions.

6. Rate and time problems in written form involving direct and inverse proportion.

Excerpted from *Merrill-Palmer Quarterly*, 1968, *14*, 127–138. By permission.

7. Money problems in written form involving proportion.

8. Calculation of the missing numbers:

5	1	5	15
8	4	4	12
15	11	3	9
7	?	?	18

9. Calculation of the missing numbers:

5	13	2	5
7	17	7	20
4	11	5	14
6	?	?	26

10. Calculation of the missing numbers:

3	9	2	8
5	25	4	64
2	4	3	27
7	?	5	?

11. Calculation of the missing numbers:

16	12
8	6
10	$7\frac{1}{2}$
?	9

12. Further numerical analogies.

13. Ratio of the areas of similar triangles given the dimensions of one pair of corresponding sides.

14. Relation between the size of the external angle of a regular polygon and the number of sides of the polygon. Using apparatus, the subject had to establish the relationship in the case of 3-, 4-, 5-, and 6-sided polygons and then predict the size of the angle in the case of 8-, 9-, 12-, 15-, and 18-sided figures. The schema of proportion is clearly involved.

15. Balance experiment (Inhelder and Piaget, 1958; Lovell, 1961; Lunzer and Pumfrey, 1966).

16. Rings and Shadow experiment (Inhelder and Piaget, 1958; Lovell, 1961; Lunzer and Pumfrey, 1966).

17. Ratio of speeds of toy cars moving across a track marked out in units.

18. Ratio of times taken by the toy cars in moving along the track in 17.

19. Verbal analogies.

20. Non-verbal reasoning test not all of which involved the schema of proportion.

Tasks 19 and 20 were administered to groups of three or four pupils and the answers written by them on paper. All the other tasks were worked individually by the subject in the presence of the experimenter. Not only had the subject to supply the solution but he had to justify through question and answer, his answers and working. Supplementary questions were asked when there was any doubt about the degree of understanding that he revealed in his replies. In short, a Piagetian-type approach was used throughout.

The tasks were given to 60 pupils of average ability or better. Six children were selected at each of the ages 9, 10, and 11, and twelve at each of the ages 13, 14, and 15.

In order to evaluate the findings the responses were graded, the tasks ranked for order of difficulty, and the rankings converted to a normal distribution. An intercorrelation matrix was calculated and a Principal Component analysis carried out. This revealed a large general component accounting for a little over 44 per cent of the variance and which reflected some central intellectual ability embracing the schema of proportion. Tasks 11, 16, 15, 14, 13, and 19 all had loadings greater than .7 on this component and so may be said to involve this ability to a considerable degree. It is not surprising that task 11 should have the highest loading since it is the clearest type of exercise involving the equivalence of two ratios. The presence of three bipolar components all with eigen values greater than unity confirmed our second hypotheses, and supports the now known fact that the schemas of proportion and ratio are not available in all situations and tasks at the same time. Contents of the question and the nature of the apparatus are important in situations where formal thought is concerned. Furthermore, tasks which require the schema of ratio had, overall, lower loadings on the first general component than tasks involving proportion. In task No. 5 where the subject had only to calculate the ratio of the volumes of cuboids from their given dimensions, the loading was only .47. The third hypothesis was thus generally confirmed.

The move towards understanding proportionality is slow until well on into high school. Even at 15 years of age the number of responses at or near the stage of formal thought in tasks 11, 16, 15, 14, 13, and 19, is still a little under 50 per cent.

It is not possible, at present, to say what school experiences can help forward the growth of formal thought except in general terms. But cross-cultural studies clearly indicate that the culture together with the forms of thinking practised and valued by a society are of great importance. The study of Peluffo (1964) which compared children born in Sardinia but who had been in Genoa for varying lengths of time, with children born and bred in Genoa, shows a clear effect of the culture pattern on the onset of combinatorial operations.

MEASUREMENT OF INFERENTIAL THOUGHT IN HISTORY

The third study employed Piaget's stages of intellectual development as a criterion against which inferential thought in history could be measured.

The subjects consisted of 100 volunteers, twenty from each of the first five years of a co-educational high school. Their ages thus ranged from 11 + to 16 + years of age. The children agreed to work with the experimenter after school hours; their attitude towards history should, therefore, have been sympathetic. The mean I.Q. of the group was a little above average with a range from

76 to 131. Boys and girls were not found in equal numbers—there were usually about 12 boys to 8 girls in each age group—but this was not regarded as important since no previous studies involving thinking in relation to historical problems have shown sex differences. All the subjects came from small country towns or villages, but they could not have been unaffected by the urban life of two cities which stood on either side of the school's catchment area.

Three passages from English history were read silently by each of the subjects. After each passage had been read silently, it was read aloud by the experimenter and any difficult words, phrases or ideas discussed. The testee was then asked a set of standard questions and the replies recorded verbatim. After the first passage had been dealt with, the second and third passages were similarly dealt with in turn. Subjects' answers to all the questions on each story were assessed globally; in addition, five questions were each assessed individually. Here it will be necessary to confine the discussion to the results of the global assessments and it will not be possible to say anything of the questions set to assess moral judgment. The assessments were made in terms of nine stages; viz., Piaget's stages 1, 1/2a, 2a, 2a/b, 2b, 2b/3a, 3a, 3a/b, 3b.

The subjects' level of thinking remained fairly steady across the three passages for Kendall's Coefficient of Concordance was .87. When numerical values were substituted for stages, the product moment correlation coefficient between total score obtained on the three passages and chronological age was .54, and that between total score and the mental age .70. Using Guttman's scalogram analysis to establish if the results could be scaled trichotomously into pre-operational, concrete and formal stages, it was found that a coefficient of reproducibility of at least 85 could be obtained when grades obtained on each passage were scaled against total score for all three passages. Further, when the highest of the three scores obtained on the passages was scaled against the mental age the coefficient of reproducibility was .77. True, the latter figure is below Guttman's figure of 85, but his figure is regarded by some as too stringent. It is suggested then that Piaget's (1950) sequence of stages *can* be discerned in historical thinking.

One of the passages involved William the Conqueror and the invasion of 1066. After studying the passage one of the questions asked was "Why did William destroy Northern England?" A reply at the pre-operational level of thought was illustrated by: "Many were robbers and killers of some sort. They didn't have the right to live."

Another question asked on this passage was "Do you think William was a cruel man?" A reply at the level of concrete operational thought was: "At the beginning of the battle he showed a certain amount of leniency to the kinsfolk of the dead and I thought he wasn't so bad. Then he came to the north of England, and his measures there made me think he was a cruel sort of person determined to take England from them whether they wanted him or not."

A reply at the level of formal operational thought to the same question was:

It depends on what you call cruel. If the definition of cruel is to kill and ravish and burn for any purpose whatever, William was cruel. On the other hand, if one is prepared to accept political necessity, William's cruelty was justified. Compared with many other feudatories, knights etc., he was essentially a kind man. They ravaged for their own advantage and without care for the common folk of their land. Duke William, if the common people went with him, seems to have been prepared to protect the common people from ravages. If, however, they went against him he seems to have treated it as a deliberate breaking of faith and acted accordingly. So, by the standards of his own day, for we cannot really judge him by our standards, he was probably not a cruel man. [I.Q. of 127.]

There is however, one serious issue that must be mentioned. Formal thinking in history comes late. Ignoring extreme instances, it is about the 16th birthday at which formal thought begins to be in evidence. It seems that a mental age of between 16 and 16½ years is also required as a minimum. All the pupils in this study who answered at the stage of formal thought scored above average on the intelligence test. This late age for the onset of formal thought is consonant with our findings in respect of formal thought in other fields, although if anything it is a little later in history. The subject can be a particularly adult one. Not only is the action far removed from the child's immediate world but he is faced with inferences and moral dilemmas which perplex the most intelligent of adults. As Piaget (1950) has pointed out, the hierarchy of response patterns may be represented as a matter of progressively extending the distances and of progressively complicating the paths of interaction between the organism and the environment. In history, the usually immature pupil is confronted with an environment which envelops the inner moves of adults living in an age different from that of the twentieth century. Other British studies (Bassett, 1940; Coltham, 1960), although not quite of this type, have also shown the late development of mature thinking in history.

It is necessary in this paper to confine the discussion to the global assessments of total responses to each passage. But it also needs to be said that such assessments are a more reliable guide to the level of a child's thought than are his responses to particular questions. Our experience is in line with the view of Inhelder and Piaget (1958) when they write that it is very difficult to differentiate between concrete and formal thought when a particular statement is taken as a point of reference. Such differentiation can only be made when the subject's entire reasoning or a sufficiently systematic series of inferences are taken as a context. It is thus better to compare all the statements made by a single subject.

References

BASSETT, G. W. The comprehension of historical narrative. Unpublished Ph.D. Thesis, University of London, 1940.

COLTHAM, J. Junior School Children's understanding of some terms commonly used in the teaching of history. Unpublished Ph.D. Thesis, University of Manchester, 1960.

HANNAM, R. Concept formation in relation to the study of landforms among training college students. M.Ed. Thesis, University of Leeds, 1963.

HUGHES, M. M. A four-year longitudinal study of the growth of logical thinking in a group of secondary modern school boys. M.Ed. Thesis, University of Leeds, 1965.

INHELDER, B. and PIAGET, J. *The growth of logical thinking*. London: Routledge and Kegan Paul, 1958.

JACKSON, S. The growth of logical thinking in normal and sub-normal children. *Brit. J. educ. Psychol.*, 1965, *35*, 255–258.

LOVELL, K., and OGILVIE, E. The growth of the concept of volume in Junior School children. *J. Child Psychol. Psychiat.*, 1961, *2*, 118–126.

LUNZER, E. A. Problems of formal reasoning in test situations. In P. Mussen (Ed.) European research in cognitive development. *Monogr. Soc. Res. Child Develpm.*, 1965, *30*, No. 2, 19–46.

—— and PUMFREY, P. D. Understanding proportionality. *Mathematics Teaching*, 1966, *34*, 7–13.

PELUFFO, N. La nozioni di conservazione del volume e le operazioni di combinazione come induce di sviluppo del pensuro operatorio in soggetti appartenenti ad ambienti fisici e socioculturali diversi. *Rivista di Psicolozia Sociale*, 1964, *2–3*, 99–132.

PIAGET, J. *The psychology of intelligence.* London: Routledge & Kegan Paul, 1950.

Egocentrism in Adolescence *

David Elkind

UNIVERSITY OF ROCHESTER

This paper describes the different forms of egocentrism characteristic of each of the major stages of cognitive growth outlined by Piaget. Particular attention is paid to the egocentrism of adolescence which is here described as the failure to differentiate between the cognitive concerns of others and those of the self. This adolescent egocentrism is said to give rise to 2 mental constructions, the imaginary audience and the personal fable, which help to account for certain forms of adolescent behavior and experience. These considerations suggest, it is concluded, that the cognitive structures peculiar to a given age period can provide insights with respect to the personality characteristics of that age level.

Within the Piagetian theory of intellectual growth, the concept of egocentrism generally refers to a lack of differentiation in some area of subject-object interaction (Piaget, 1962). At each stage of mental development, this lack of differentiation takes a unique form and is manifested in a unique set of behaviors. The transition from one form of egocentrism to another takes place in a dialectic fashion such that the mental structures which free the child from a lower form of egocentrism are the same structures which ensnare him in a higher form of egocentrism. From the developmental point of view, therefore, egocentrism can be regarded as a negative by-product of any emergent mental system in the sense that it corresponds to the fresh cognitive problems engendered by that system.

Although in recent years Piaget has focused his attention more on the positive than on the negative products of mental structures, egocentrism continues to be of interest because of its relation to the affective aspects of child thought and behavior. Indeed, it is possible that the study of egocentrism may provide a bridge between the study of cognitive structure, on the one hand, and

Reprinted from *Child Development*, *38*, 1025–1034. Copyright © 1967 by the Society for Research in Child Development, Inc. By permission.

* Preparation of this paper was supported in part by grant No. 6881 from the Office of Education.

the exploration of personality dynamics, on the other (Cowan, 1966; Gourevitch & Feffer, 1962). The purpose of the present paper is to describe, in greater detail than Inhelder and Piaget (1958), what seems to me to be the nature of egocentrism in adolescence and some of its behavioral and experiential correlates. Before doing that, however, it might be well to set the stage for the discussion with a brief review of the forms of egocentrism which precede this mode of thought in adolescence.

FORMS OF EGOCENTRISM IN INFANCY AND CHILDHOOD

In presenting the childhood forms of egocentrism, it is useful to treat each of Piaget's major stages as if it were primarily concerned with resolving one major cognitive task. The egocentrism of a particular stage can then be described with reference to this special problem of cognition. It must be stressed, however, that while the cognitive task characteristic of a particular stage seems to attract the major share of the child's mental energies, it is not the only cognitive problem with which the child is attempting to cope. In mental development there are major battles and minor skirmishes, and if I here ignore the lesser engagements it is for purposes of economy of presentation rather than because I assume that such engagements are insignificant.

SENSORI-MOTOR EGOCENTRISM (0–2 YEARS)   The major cognitive task of infancy might be regarded as *the conquest of the object.* In the early months of life, the infant deals with objects as if their existence were dependent upon their being present in immediate perception (Charlesworth, 1966; Piaget, 1954). The egocentrism of this stage corresponds, therefore, to a lack of differentiation between the object and the sense impressions occasioned by it. Toward the end of the first year, however, the infant begins to seek the object even when it is hidden, and thus shows that he can now differentiate between the object and the "experience of the object." This breakdown of egocentrism with respect to objects is brought about by mental representation of the absent object.[1] An internal representation of the absent object is the earliest manifestation of the symbolic function which develops gradually during the second year of life and whose activities dominate the next stage of mental growth.

PRE-OPERATIONAL EGOCENTRISM (2–6 YEARS)   During the preschool period, the child's major cognitive task can be regarded as *the conquest of the symbol.* It is during the preschool period that the symbolic function becomes fully active, as evidenced by the rapid growth in the acquisition and utilization of language, by the appearance of symbolic play, and by the first reports of dreams. Yet this new capacity for representation, which loosed the infant from his egocentrism with respect to objects, now ensnares the preschool child in a new egocentrism with regard to symbols. At the beginning of this period, the child fails to differentiate between words and their referents (Piaget, 1952b) and between his self-created play and dream symbols and reality (Kohlberg,

---

[1] It is characteristic of the dialectic of mental growth that the capacity to represent internally the absent object also enables the infant to cognize the object as externally existent.

1966; Piaget, 1951). Children at this stage believe that the name inheres in the thing and that an object cannot have more than one name (Elkind, 1961a, 1962, 1963).

The egocentrism of this period is particularly evident in children's linguistic behavior. When explaining a piece of apparatus to another child, for example, the youngster at this stage uses many indefinite terms and leaves out important information (Piaget, 1952b). Although this observation is sometimes explained by saying that the child fails to take the other person's point of view, it can also be explained by saying that the child assumes words carry much more information than they actually do. This results from his belief that even the indefinite "thing" somehow conveys the properties of the object which it is used to represent. In short, the egocentrism of this period consists in a lack of clear differentiation between symbols and their referents.

Toward the end of the pre-operational period, the differentiation between symbols and their referents is gradually brought about by the emergence of concrete operations (internalized actions which are roughly comparable in their activity to the elementary operations of arithmetic). One consequence of concrete operational thought is that it enables the child to deal with two elements, properties, or relations at the same time. A child with concrete operations can, for example, take account of both the height and width of a glass of colored liquid and recognize that, when the liquid is poured into a differently shaped container, the changes in height and width of the liquid compensate one another so that the total quantity of liquid is conserved (Elkind, 1961b; Piaget, 1952a). This ability, to hold two dimensions in mind at the same time, also enables the child to hold both symbol and referent in mind simultaneously, and thus distinguish between them. Concrete operations are, therefore, instrumental in overcoming the egocentrism of the preoperational stage.

CONCRETE OPERATIONAL EGOCENTRISM (7–11 YEARS)   With the emergence of concrete operations, the major cognitive task of the school-age child becomes that of *mastering classes, relations, and quantities*. While the preschool child forms global notions of classes, relations, and quantities, such notions are imprecise and cannot be combined one with the other. The child with concrete operations, on the other hand, can nest classes, seriate relations, and conserve quantities. In addition, concrete operations enable the school-age child to perform elementary syllogistic reasoning and to formulate hypotheses and explanations about concrete matters. This system of concrete operations, however, which lifts the school-age child to new heights of thought, nonetheless lowers him to new depths of egocentrism.

Operations are essentially mental tools whose products, series, class hierarchies, conservations, etc., are not directly derived from experience. At this stage, however, the child nonetheless regards these mental products as being on a par with perceptual phenomena. It is the inability to differentiate clearly between mental constructions and perceptual givens which constitutes the egocentrism of the school-age child. An example may help to clarify the form which egocentrism takes during the concrete operational stage.

In a study reported by Peel (1960), children and adolescents were read a passage about Stonehenge and then asked questions about it. One of the questions had to do with whether Stonehenge was a place for religious worship or a fort. The children (ages 7–10) answered the question with flat statements, as if they were stating a fact. When they were given evidence that contradicted their statements, they rationalized the evidence to make it conform with their initial position. Adolescents, on the other hand, phrased their replies in probabilistic terms and supported their judgments with material gleaned from the passage. Similar differences between children and adolescents have been found by Elkind (1966) and Weir (1964).

What these studies show is that, when a child constructs a hypothesis or formulates a strategy, he assumes that this product is imposed by the data rather than derived from his own mental activity. When his position is challenged, he does not change his stance but, on the contrary, reinterprets the data to fit with his assumption. This observation, however, raises a puzzling question. Why, if the child regards both his thought products and the givens of perception as coming from the environment, does he nonetheless give preference to his own mental constructions? The answer probably lies in the fact that the child's mental constructions are the product of reasoning, and hence are experienced as imbued with a (logical) necessity. This "felt" necessity is absent when the child experiences the products of perception. It is not surprising, then, that the child should give priority to what seems permanent and necessary in perception (the products of his own thought, such as conservation) rather than to what seems transitory and arbitrary in perception (products of environmental stimulation). Only in adolescence do young people differentiate their own mental constructions and the givens of perception. For the child, there are no problems of epistemology.

Toward the end of childhood, the emergence of formal operational thought (which is analogous to propositional logic) gradually frees the child from his egocentrism with respect to his own mental constructions. As Inhelder and Piaget (1958) have shown, formal operational thought enables the young person to deal with all of the possible combinations and permutations of elements within a given set. Provided with four differently colored pieces of plastic, for example, the adolescent can work out all the possible combinations of colors by taking the pieces one, two, three, and four, and none, at a time. Children, on the other hand, cannot formulate these combinations in any systematic way. The ability to conceptualize all of the possible combinations in a system allows the adolescent to construct contrary-to-fact hypotheses and to reason about such propositions "as if" they were true. The adolescent, for example, can accept the statement, "Let's suppose coal is white," whereas the child would reply, "But coal is black." This ability to formulate contrary-to-fact hypotheses is crucial to the overcoming of the egocentrism of the concrete operational period. Through the formulation of such contrary-to-fact hypotheses, the young person discovers the arbitrariness of his own mental constructions and learns to differentiate them from perceptual reality.

ADOLESCENT EGOCENTRISM

From the strictly cognitive point of view (as opposed to the psychoanalytic point of view as represented by Blos [1962] and A. Freud [1946] or the ego psychological point of view as represented by Erikson [1959]), the major task of early adolescence can be regarded as having to do with *the conquest of thought.* Formal operations not only permit the young person to construct all the possibilities in a system and construct contrary-to-fact propositions (Inhelder & Piaget, 1958); they also enable him to conceptualize his own thought, to take his mental constructions as objects and reason about them. Only at about the ages of 11–12, for example, do children spontaneously introduce concepts of belief, intelligence, and faith into their definitions of their religious denomination (Elkind, 1961a; 1962; 1963). Once more, however, this new mental system which frees the young person from the egocentrism of childhood entangles him in a new form of egocentrism characteristic of adolescence.

Formal operational thought not only enables the adolescent to conceptualize his thought, it also permits him to conceptualize the thought of other people. It is this capacity to take account of other people's thought, however, which is the crux of adolescent egocentrism. This egocentrism emerges because, while the adolescent can now cognize the thoughts of others, he fails to differentiate between the objects toward which the thoughts of others are directed and those which are the focus of his own concern. Now, it is well known that the young adolescent, because of the physiological metamorphosis he is undergoing, is primarily concerned with himself. Accordingly, since he fails to differentiate between what others are thinking about and his own mental preoccupations, he assumes that other people are as obsessed with his behavior and appearance as he is himself. *It is this belief that others are preoccupied with his appearance and behavior that constitutes the egocentrism of the adolescent.*

One consequence of adolescent egocentrism is that, in actual or impending social situations, the young person anticipates the reactions of other people to himself. These anticipations, however, are based on the premise that others are as admiring or as critical of him as he is of himself. In a sense, then, the adolescent is continually constructing, or reacting to, *an imaginary audience.* It is an audience because the adolescent believes that he will be the focus of attention; and it is imaginary because, in actual social situations, this is not usually the case (unless he contrives to make it so). The construction of imaginary audiences would seem to account, in part at least, for a wide variety of typical adolescent behaviors and experiences.

The imaginary audience, for example, probably plays a role in the self-consciousness which is so characteristic of early adolescence. When the young person is feeling critical of himself, he anticipates that the audience—of which he is necessarily a part—will be critical too. And, since the audience is his own construction and privy to his own knowledge of himself, it knows just what to look for in the way of cosmetic and behavioral sensitivities. The adolescent's wish for privacy and his reluctance to reveal himself may, to some extent, be a reaction to the feeling of being under the constant critical scrutiny of other people. The notion of an imaginary audience also helps to explain the observation that the affect which most concerns adolescents is not guilt but, rather, shame, that is, the reaction to an audience (Lynd, 1961).

While the adolescent is often self-critical, he is frequently self-admiring too. At such times, the audience takes on the same affective coloration. A good deal of adolescent boorishness, loudness, and faddish dress is probably provoked, partially in any case, by a failure to differentiate between what the young person believes to be attractive and what others admire. It is for this reason that the young person frequently fails to understand why adults disapprove of the way he dresses and behaves. The same sort of egocentrism is often seen in behavior directed toward the opposite sex. The boy who stands in front of the mirror for 2 hours combing his hair is probably imagining the swooning reactions he will produce in the girls. Likewise, the girl applying her makeup is more likely than not imagining the admiring glances that will come her way. When these young people actually meet, each is more concerned with being the observed than with being the observer. Gatherings of young adolescents are unique in the sense that each young person is simultaneously an actor to himself and an audience to others.

One of the most common admiring audience constructions, in the adolescent, is the anticipation of how others will react to his own demise. A certain bittersweet pleasure is derived from anticipating the belated recognition by others of his positive qualities. As often happens with such universal fantasies, the imaginary anticipation of one's own demise has been realized in fiction. Below, for example, is the passage in *Tom Sawyer* where Tom sneaks back to his home, after having run away with Joe and Huck, to discover that he and his friends are thought to have been drowned:

> But this memory was too much for the old lady, and she broke entirely down. Tom was snuffling, now, himself—and more in pity of himself than anybody else. He could hear Mary crying and putting in a kindly word for him from time to time. He began to have a nobler opinion of himself than ever before. Still, he was sufficiently touched by his aunt's grief to long to rush out from under the bed and overwhelm her with joy—and the theatrical gorgeousness of the thing appealed strongly to his nature too—but he resisted and lay still.

Corresponding to the imaginary audience is another mental construction which is its complement. While the adolescent fails to differentiate the concerns of his own thought from those of others, he at the same time overdifferentiates his feelings. Perhaps because he believes he is of importance to so many people, the imaginary audience, he comes to regard himself, and particularly his feelings, as something special and unique. Only he can suffer with such agonized intensity, or experience such exquisite rapture. How many parents have been confronted with the typically adolescent phrase, "But you don't know how it feels. . . ." The emotional torments undergone by Goethe's young Werther and by Salinger's Holden Caulfield exemplify the adolescent's belief in the uniqueness of his own emotional experience. At a somewhat different level, this belief in personal uniqueness becomes a conviction that he will not die, that death will happen to others but not to him. This complex of beliefs in the uniqueness of his feelings and of his immortality might be called *a personal fable*, a story which he tells himself and which is not true.

Evidences of the personal fable are particularly prominent in adolescent diaries. Such diaries are often written for posterity in the conviction that the young person's experiences, crushes, and frustrations are of universal significance and importance. Another kind of evidence for the personal fable during this period is the tendency to confide in a personal God. The search for privacy and the belief in personal uniqueness leads to the establishment of an I-Thou relationship with God as a personal confidant to whom one no longer looks for gifts but rather for guidance and support (Long, Elkind, & Spilka, 1967).

The concepts of an imaginary audience and a personal fable have proved useful at least to the writer, in the understanding and treatment of troubled adolescents. The imaginary audience, for example, seems often to play a role in middle-class delinquency (Elkind, 1967). As a case in point, one young man took $1,000 from a golf tournament purse, hid the money, and then promptly revealed himself. It turned out that much of the motivation for this act was derived from the anticipated response of "the audience" to the guttiness of his action. In a similar vein, many young girls become pregnant because, in part at least, their personal fable convinces them that pregnancy will happen to others but never to them and so they need not take precautions. Such examples could be multiplied but will perhaps suffice to illustrate how adolescent egocentrism, as manifested in the imaginary audience and in the personal fable, can help provide a rationale for some adolescent behavior. These concepts can, moreover, be utilized in the treatment of adolescent offenders. It is often helpful to these young people if they can learn to differentiate between the real and the imaginary audience, which often boils down to a discrimination between the real and the imaginary parents.

THE PASSING OF ADOLESCENT EGOCENTRISM

After the appearance of formal operational thought, no new mental systems develop and the mental structures of adolescence must serve for the rest of the life span. The egocentrism of early adolescence nonetheless tends to diminish by the age of 15 or 16, the age at which formal operations become firmly established. What appears to happen is that the imaginary audience, which is primarily an anticipatory audience, is progressively modified in the direction of the reactions of the real audience. In a way, the imaginary audience can be regarded as hypothesis—or better, as a series of hypotheses—which the young person tests against reality. As a consequence of this testing, he gradually comes to recognize the difference between his own preoccupations and the interests and concerns of others.

The personal fable, on the other hand, is probably overcome (although probably never in its entirety) by the gradual establishment of what Erikson (1959) has called "intimacy." Once the young person sees himself in a more realistic light as a function of having adjusted his imaginary audience to the real one, he can establish true rather than self-interested interpersonal relations. Once relations of mutuality are established and confidences are shared, the young person discovers that others have feelings similar to his own and have suffered and been enraptured in the same way.

Adolescent egocentrism is thus overcome by a twofold transformation. On the cognitive plane, it is overcome by the gradual differentiation between his own preoccupations and the thoughts of others; while on the plane of affectivity it is overcome by a gradual integration of the feelings of others with his own emotions.

SUMMARY AND CONCLUSIONS

In this paper I have tried to describe the forms which egocentrism takes and the mechanisms by which it is overcome, in the course of mental development. In infancy, egocentrism corresponds to the impression that objects are identical with the perception of them, and this form of egocentrism is overcome with the appearance of representation. During the preschool period, egocentrism appears in the guise of a belief that symbols contain the same information as is provided by the objects which they represent. With the emergence of concrete operations, the child is able to discriminate between symbol and referent, and so overcome this type of egocentrism. The egocentrism of the school-age period can be characterized as the belief that one's own mental constructions correspond to a superior form of perceptual reality. With the advent of formal operations and the ability to construct contrary-to-fact hypotheses, this kind of egocentrism is dissolved because the young person can now recognize the arbitrariness of his own mental constructions. Finally, during early adolescence, egocentrism appears as the belief that the thoughts of others are directed toward the self. This variety of egocentrism is overcome as a consequence of the conflict between the reactions which the young person anticipates and those which actually occur.

Although egocentrism corresponds to a negative product of mental growth, its usefulness would seem to lie in the light which it throws upon the affective reactions characteristic of any particular stage of mental development. In this paper I have dealt primarily with the affective reactions associated with the egocentrism of adolescence. Much of the material, particularly the discussion of the *imaginary audience* and the *personal fable* is speculative in the sense that it is based as much upon my clinical experience with young people as it is upon research data. These constructions are offered, not as the final word on adolescent egocentrism, but rather to illustrate how the cognitive structures peculiar to a particular level of development can be related to the affective experience and behavior characteristic of that stage. Although I have here only considered the correspondence between mental structure and affect in adolescence, it is possible that similar correspondences can be found at the earlier levels of development as well. A consideration of egocentrism, then, would seem to be a useful starting point for any attempt to reconcile cognitive structure and the dynamics of personality.

References

BLOS, P. *On adolescence.* New York: Free Press, 1962.

CHARLESWORTH, W. R. Development of the object concept in infancy: methodological study. *American Psychologist*, 1966, **21**, 623. (Abstract)

COWAN, P. A. Cognitive egocentrism and social interaction in children. *American Psychologist*, 1966, **21**, 623. (Abstract)

ELKIND, D. The child's conception of his religious denomination, I: The Jewish child. *Journal of genetic Psychology*, 1961, **99**, 209–225. (a)

———. The development of quantitative thinking. *Journal of genetic Psychology*, 1961, **98**, 37–46. (b)

———. The child's conception of his religious denomination, II: The Catholic child. *Journal of genetic Psychology*, 1962, **111**, 185–193.

ELKIND, D. The child's conception of his religious denomination, III: The Protestant child. *Journal of genetic Psychology*, 1963, **113**, 291–304.

———. Conceptual orientation shifts in children and adolescents. *Child Development*, 1966, **37**, 493–498.

———. Middle-class delinquency. *Mental Hygiene*, 1967, **51**, 80–84.

ERIKSON, E. H. Identity and the life cycle. *Psychological issues*. Vol. **1**, No. 1, New York: International Universities Press, 1959.

FREUD, ANNA. *The ego and the mechanisms of defense*. New York: International Universities Press, 1946.

GOUREVITCH, VIVIAN, & FEFFER, M. H. A study of motivational development. *Journal of genetic Psychology*, 1962, **100**, 361–375.

INHELDER, BÄRBEL, & PIAGET, J. *The growth of logical thinking from childhood to adolescence*. New York: Basic Books, 1958.

KOHLBERG, L. Cognitive stages and preschool education. *Human Development*, 1966, **9**, 5–17.

LONG, DIANE, ELKIND, D., & SPILKA, B. The child's conception of prayer. *Journal for the scientific Study of Religion*, 1967, **6**, 101–109.

LYND, HELEN M. *On shame and the search for identity*. New York: Science Editions, 1961.

PEEL, E. A. *The pupil's thinking*. London: Oldbourne, 1960.

PIAGET, J. *The child's conception of the world*. London: Routledge & Kegan Paul, 1951.

———. *The child's conception of number*. New York: Humanities Press, 1952. (a)

———. *The language and thought of the child*. London: Routledge & Kegan Paul, 1952. (b)

———. *The construction of reality in the child*. New York: Basic Books, 1954.

———. *Comments on Vygotsky's critical remarks concerning " The language and thought of the child" and "Judgment and reasoning in the child."* Cambridge, Mass.: M.I.T. Press, 1962.

WEIR, M. W. Development changes in problem solving strategies. *Psychological Review*, 1964, **71**, 473–490.

15

Parents, Peers, and the Quest for Identity

Relationships between parents and adolescents can be described from the points of view of the parents, the adolescent, or a person outside the family. The latter point of view may be called the "objective" one, particularly if two outsiders agree as to what they see. But the "objective" view may be quite unimportant as far as the functioning of the family is concerned. If a parent sees his child as ungrateful and if the child sees his parent as domineering, they will act in accordance with their perceptions of events, even though outsiders disagree completely as to how things are.

The first article, by Karl King, uses adolescent males and females to investigate the power structure of a sample of Negro families. The individuals who make decisions either singly or with other people define the power structure. As King points out in the article, some have stated that the modal Negro family is matriarchal; that is, the main source of power is the mother, or the grandmother in a three-generation family. Others have indicated that there may be a difference in power structure between rural and urban families and between socioeconomic levels, and that a change is taking place as time goes by. In the larger study, of which this report is a part, King compared the power structure, as reported by adolescents, in Negro and white families.

The second article, the summary of a research monograph, combines data obtained from two views within families with some objectively determined facts. The main emphasis, however, is on how life looks to a group of seemingly advantaged adolescents who by their behavior showed that they were dissatisfied with things as they were. Robert Shellow and his co-workers say that the dissatisfaction may have been with family life, with friends, or with school, but that most often it was dissatisfaction with school that caused their subjects to run away. They make recommendations for changes in the schools and other community facilities for adolescents which they think would improve present deficiencies.

The third article presents a view of a part of the world, abstracted by Elizabeth Douvan and Joseph Adelson, as seen by over 3,000 adolescents in the mid-1950's. The technical aspects of the study are described in The Adolescent Experience. *In summary, the adolescents were carefully selected to represent their age group; the interviewers were trained; the responses were coded. This selection has to do with adolescents' ideas about what the future held for them. The typical boy and the typical girl saw themselves in different settings and with different clarity.*

Adolescent Perception of Power Structure in the Negro Family *

Karl King

UNIVERSITY OF GEORGIA

The purpose of this study was to assess the perception of the Negro adolescents concerning the power structure within the Negro family. The sample was divided by the father's occupation into three levels: white collar, blue collar, and unskilled. The results indicated the male and female adolescents viewed the power structure to be mainly syncratic. Males reported stronger father participation than did the females, and females reported stronger mother participation than did the males. Both males and females indicated stronger father participation in decision-making than has been historically presented.

The urbanization of the Negro family has "affected the most momentous change in the life of the Negro since his emancipation."[1] Not only has this resulted in the "disorganization of the family . . . but in the reorganization according to middle-class patterns, thus reflecting the new class structure in urban communities."[2] In this reorganization from a rural to an urban way of life, the "new class structure" has become more complex and has been classified into "three fairly well-defined socioeconomic classes."[3] These have been identified as being the lower class, which comprises the vast majority of urban Negroes; the middle class, where there seems to be a stabilization of the family life; the upper class, which is a life style comparable to the white upper class.[4]

In the transition from rural to urban, the family power structure has also been subjected to change. While most of the previous studies in this area have been impressionistic and somewhat contradictory, they have afforded many insights into the present situation. For example, in her study of the Negro in "Cottonville," Powdermaker noted: "in the upper class . . . the patriarchal family structure predominates, with the man assuming chief economic responsibility and also chief authority."[5] Burgess and Locke supported this description when they said "in the south . . . families of 'Black Puritans' have the father as head [and also] have a high economic status."[6] In their Detroit study, Blood and Wolfe found the "husband's power is correlated with occupa-

Reprinted from *Journal of Marriage and the Family*, 1969, *31*, 751–755. By permission.

* The data were gathered under the sponsorship of the Rockefeller Foundation through the Institute for Social Research, Florida State University.

1 E. Franklin Frazier, "The Impact of Urban Civilization Upon Negro Family Life," *American Sociological Review*, 2 (1937), p. 609.
2 E. Franklin Frazier, *The Negro in the United States*, New York: The Macmillan Company, 1957, p. 333.
3 E. Franklin Frazier, "Ethnic Family Patterns: The Negro Family in the United States," *American Journal of Sociology*, 53 (1948), p. 437.
4 *Ibid*, pp. 437–438.
5 Hortense Powdermaker, *After Freedom*, New York: The Viking Press, 1939, p. 148.
6 Ernest W. Burgess and Harvey J. Locke, *The Family: From Institution to Companionship*, New York: American Book Company, 2nd ed., 1953, p. 141.

tional status"[7] with the husband evidencing more power as his occupational status increases.

For the middle class Frazier noted: "A large proportion of the middle class are salaried persons and the relations between husband and wife, especially where both are employed, tend to be equalitarian."[8] Other researchers have supported this observation.[9]

On the other hand, Powdermaker found there was very little, if any, difference between the lower and middle class, when she reported: "Among the middle- and lower-class Negroes . . . the woman is usually the head of the house in importance and authority and is frequently the chief economic supporter."[10] Some 20 years later Middleton and Putney tested the dominance pattern in the decisions of a Negro sample, and they found no differences existed between socioeconomic classes.[11] More recently, Hilda O. Fortune indicated decision-making in all areas of the lower-class Negro family rather equally divided by male and female heads.[12] Additionally, Frumkin has noted a tendency for a change within the classes: "A change in Negro family organization, although slow, is taking place in the direction of white norms and ideals . . . the equalitarian family."[13]

The somewhat contradictory findings of the relatively few studies dealing with the locus of the Negro family power structure seem to call for additional research. It was felt an attempt to locate the present position of the Negro family power structure on a continuum from matriarchy to patriarchy would provide an additional step in trying to arrive at an accurate appraisal of the urban Negro family.

METHOD

Adolescent respondents were used in the conduct of the study. It was believed ninth-grade students would afford a better representation in the lower socioeconomic class than might be found at the tenth, eleventh, or twelfth grades.

All of the ninth-grade Negro students attending school on the particular day the school was visited were asked to complete a questionnaire. The data were gathered in April, 1963, in a metropolitan area of Florida in four junior high schools as part of a larger project.[14]

[7] Robert O. Blood and Donald M. Wolfe, *Husbands and Wives: The Dynamics of Married Living,* Glencoe: The Free Press, 1960, p. 30.
[8] Frazier, *The Negro in the United States, op. cit.,* p. 439.
[9] A. Davis, B. B. Gardiner, and M. R. Gardner, *Deep South,* Chicago: The University of Chicago Press, 1941; Frazier, "Ethnic Family Patterns: The Negro Family in the United States," *op. cit.,* p. 438.
[10] Powdermaker, *op. cit.,* p. 141.
[11] Russell Middleton and Snell Putney, "Dominance in Decision in the Family, Race and Class Differences," *American Journal of Sociology,* 65 (1960), p. 607.
[12] Hilda O. Fortune, *A Study of the Power Position of Mothers in Contemporary Negro Family Life in New York City,* unpublished Ph.D. dissertation, New York University, 1963.
[13] Robert M. Frumkin, "Attitudes of Negro College Students Toward Intrafamily Leadership and Control," *Journal of Marriage and the Family,* 16 (1954), pp. 252–253.
[14] Karl B. King, Jr., *Comparison of the Power Structure of the Negro and White Family by Socioeconomic Class,* unpublished Ph.D. dissertation, Florida State University, 1964.

The instrument used was adopted from one used by Herbst[15] to study intrafamilial roles in Australia. Items which did not have wide cultural acceptance in America were deleted. Research reported in the present study is based on data from selected items in the areas of behavior which were at least potentially capable of being decided by both father and mother. The respondents were asked to indicate who made the decisions in their family concerning the items in question.

The possible response categories were as follows:

1. *Father Autonomous Power:* the degree to which the father alone made the decision.

2. *Mother Autonomous Power:* the degree to which the mother alone made the decision.

3. *Adolescent Power:* the degree to which the respondent alone made the decisions.

4. *Father-shared Power:* the degree to which the father and the respondent or other siblings shared in the decision-making.

5. *Mother-shared Power:* the degree to which the mother and the respondent or other siblings shared in the decision-making.

6. *Syncratic Power:* the degree to which the father and the mother, with or without the adolescent or other siblings, shared in the decision-making.

Since it is virtually impossible to obtain a complete record of the decisions a family makes, it was decided a sample of the decisions would provide one indication of the power structure of the urban Negro family. The items used were in the general areas of family decisions and child-rearing. For the area of family decisions, the following were used:

Who decides what television programs the family will watch?
Who decides on large purchases such as furniture, car, television set?

The items in the area of child-rearing were:

Who decides what your punishment will be when you have done something you were not supposed to have done?
Who decides what jobs you should do around the house?
Who decides how late you may stay out at night?

The family power structure was based on the family situations. It was felt the comments of the items were of such a nature as to minimize the possibility of subjective reporting by the respondent. This approach has been questioned by Heer on the basis "that the child's perception of the decisions his parents make may be incomplete and one-sided."[16] Yet, Gordon Allport declared that any bias reported is the subject's evaluation of the situation as he perceives it.[17]

---

[15] P. G. Herbst, "Conceptual Framework for Studying the Family," in *Social Structure and Personality in a City*, ed. by O. A. Oeser and S. B. Hammond, London: Routledge and Kegan Paul, Ltd., 1954, p. 322.
[16] David M. Heer, "The Measurement and Basis of Family Power: An Overview," *Journal of Marriage and the Family*, 25 (1963), p. 134.
[17] Gordon Allport, "The Use of Personal Documents in Psychological Science," *Social Science Research Council*, Bulletin 49 (1942), p. 170.

It has also been noted by Ingersoll that the subject "responds to the situation as it affects him on the basis of his conception of it and in terms of his pattern meaning."[18]

The families were grouped on the basis of the father's occupation, which was determined by the use of the occupational categories employed by the United States Census Bureau. The occupations were further divided into white collar, comprised of professional, sales, manager, or proprietor; blue collar, which included craftsman, foreman, and operatives; and unskilled, which was made up of service, household, military, and laborer categories.

Because of a difference in the way males and females perceive the power structure,[19] the respondents were separated by sex. This resulted in 226 Negro males and 313 Negro females. The modal age category was 14.

A frequency count of the number of participants who responded to a particular item was computed for Negro males and females within the white-collar, blue-collar, and unskilled categories. Percentages were used to indicate the degree of power prevalent for each item. A Chi-square statistical test was made to determine the differences between white-collar, blue-collar, and un-skilled categories for the males and females. This statistic was used under the assumption that "a χ^2 test . . . may be used if fewer than 20 percent of the cells have an expected frequency of less than 5 and if no cell has an expected frequency of less than 1."[20] Where possible, the category of "Adolescent Power" and that of "Syncratic" were collapsed for the purposes of statistical analysis.

RESULTS

For the item, "Who makes the decisions concerning large purchases like furniture, car, television set?" there were no significant differences for occupations among the male respondents (see Table 1). The males and females for the blue collar and unskilled viewed it as mainly syncratic with strong participation by the father, while the females whose father had a white-collar occupation reported overwhelming syncratic power (see Tables 1 and 2). The males at the white collar level reported more father autonomous participation with syncratic decision-making second.

In the other item pertaining to the family decision, "Who decides what television programs the family will watch?" there were significant differences among the occupations for the females. The white-collar and blue-collar occupations reported predominantly a syncratic pattern with the unskilled viewing it as adolescent first and syncratic (see Table 2). For the males syncratic power was characteristic of the white-collar group; while adolescent power was reported most prevalent, with syncratic second, for the blue-collar and unskilled (see Table 1).

In the area of child-rearing practices, the item, "Who decides what your

---

[18] Hazel L. Ingersoll, "A Study of the Transmission of Authority Patterns in the Family," *Genetic Psychology Monographs*, 38 (1948), p. 233.

[19] Urie Bronfenbrenner, "Toward A Theoretical Model for the Analysis of Parent-child Relationships in a Social Context," in *Parental Attitudes and Child Behavior*, ed. by J. C. Glidewell, Springfield, Illinois: Charles C Thomas, 1951, pp. 90–109.

[20] Sidney Siegel, *Nonparametric Statistics for the Behavioral Sciences*, New York: McGraw-Hill Book Company, Inc.,

TABLE 1

Perception of Family Power Structure by Male Adolescents for Area of Family Decisions by Father's Occupations

POWER STRUCTURE	WHO DECIDES ON LARGE PURCHASES FAMILY WILL MAKE?*							WHO DECIDES TELEVISION PROGRAMS FAMILY WILL WATCH?					
	WHITE COLLAR		BLUE-COLLAR		UNSKILLED		χ^2	WHITE-COLLAR		BLUE-COLLAR		UNSKILLED	
	%	N	%	N	%	N		%	N	%	N	%	N
Father autonomous	45.6	21	39.3	44	38.6	27		11.9	5	15.7	17	15.7	11
Father shared								7.1	3	2.8	3	2.8	2
Syncratic*	43.5	20	46.4	52	41.4	29	2.90	40.5	17	30.6	33	30.0	21
Mother shared								2.4	1	4.6	5	2.8	2
Mother autonomous	10.9	5	14.3	16	20.0	14		14.3	6	11.1	12	18.6	13
Adolescent*								23.8	10	35.2	38	30.0	21
Total	100.0		100.0		100.0			100.0		100.0		99.9	
Total N		46		112		70			42		108		70

* Syncratic and Adolescent Categories combined for statistical analysis.

TABLE 2

Perception of Family Power Structure by Female Adolescents for Area Decisions by Father's Occupation

POWER STRUCTURE	Who Decides on Large Purchases Family Will Make?						Who Decides Television Programs Family Will Watch?						
	White-Collar		Blue-Collar		Unskilled		White-Collar		Blue-Collar		Unskilled		χ^2
	%	N	%	N	%	N	%	N	%	N	%	N	
Father autonomous	13.2	7	28.6	42	31.8	35	5.5	3	23.1	33	14.4	14	
Father shared							1.9	1	2.1	3	8.2	8	46.16*
Syncratic	79.2	42	53.7	79	56.4	62	55.6	30	38.5	55	26.8	26	
Mother shared			1.4	2			3.7	2	2.8	4	7.2	7	
Mother autonomous	7.5	4	16.3	24	11.8	13	12.9	7	23.1	33	12.4	12	
Adolescent							20.4	11	10.4	15	30.9	30	
Total	99.9		100.0		100.0		100.0		100.0		99.9		
Total N		53		147		110		54		143		97	

* Significant at .001 level.

TABLE 3

Perception of Power Structure by Male Adolescents for Area of Child-rearing by Father's Occupation

| POWER STRUCTURE | WHO DECIDES ON PUNISHMENT?* | | | | | | | WHO DECIDES JOBS TO DO AROUND HOUSE? | | | | | | WHO DECIDES HOW LATE TO STAY OUT AT NIGHT? | | | | | |
| | WHITE-COLLAR | | BLUE-COLLAR | | UNSKILLED | | χ^2 | WHITE-COLLAR | | BLUE-COLLAR | | UNSKILLED | | WHITE-COLLAR | | BLUE-COLLAR | | UNSKILLED | |
	%	N	%	N	%	N		%	N	%	N	%	N	%	N	%	N	%	N
Father autonomous	33.3	15	32.4	36	30.9	21		24.4	11	27.1	29	13.0	9	20.0	9	28.8	32	18.6	13
Father shared							2.23			1.9	2			2.2	1			1.4	1
Syncratic	48.9	22	40.5	45	39.7	27		40.0	18	38.3	41	34.8	24	44.4	20	36.9	41	40.0	28
Mother shared												26.1	18	2.2	1	1.8	2		
Mother autonomous	17.8	8	27.0	30	29.4	20		28.9	13	30.8	33	26.1	18	20.0	9	24.3	27	30.0	21
Adolescent								6.7	3	1.9	2			11.1	5	8.1	9	10.0	7
Total Total N	100.0 45		99.9 111		100.0 68			100.0 45		100.0 107		100.0 69		99.9 45		99.9 111		100.0 70	

* Syncratic and Adolescent Categories combined for statistical analysis.

Perception of Power Structure by Female Adolescents for Area of Child-rearing by Father's Occupation

POWER STRUCTURE	WHO DECIDES ON PUNISHMENT?						WHO DECIDES JOBS TO DO AROUND HOUSE?						WHO DECIDES HOW LATE TO STAY OUT AT NIGHT?					
	WHITE-COLLAR		BLUE-COLLAR		UNSKILLED		WHITE-COLLAR		BLUE-COLLAR		UNSKILLED		WHITE-COLLAR		BLUE-COLLAR		UNSKILLED	
	%	N	%	N	%	N	%	N	%	N	%	N	%	N	%	N	%	N
Father autonomous	13.7	7	13.6	6	8.2	9			4.1	6	3.7	4	7.7	4	11.3	16	11.1	12
Father shared													1.9	1			1.9	2
Syncratic	52.9	27	43.5	20	41.3	45	35.8	19	25.5	37	21.1	23	55.8	29	47.2	67	43.5	47
Mother shared			2.2	1	.9	1	1.9	1	11.0	16	11.9	13			2.1	3	1.9	2
Mother autonomous	29.4	15	41.3	19	48.6	53	56.6	30	51.7	75	56.0	61	32.7	17	34.5	49	37.0	40
Adolescent	3.9	2			.9	1	5.7	3	7.6	1	7.3	8	1.9	11	4.9	7	4.6	5
Total	99.9		100.0		99.9		100.0		99.9		100.0		100.0		100.0		100.0	
Total N		51		46		109		53		145		109		52		142		108

punishment will be when you have done something that you were not supposed to have done?" showed no significant differences for males by occupational groups (see Table 3). Both males and females indicated syncratic power at most occupational levels (Tables 3 and 4). The females whose fathers' occupations were unskilled reported more mother autonomous power. On the other hand, the Negro males at all occupational levels reported more father participation than the females.

With the item, "Who decides what jobs you should do around the house?" there were differences reported by sex. Negro males at all occupational levels reported a syncratic power with mother autonomous second. The Negro females viewed this as predominantly mother autonomous with syncratic power second at all occupational levels (Tables 3 and 4).

For the item, "Who decides how late you may stay out at night?" males and females at all occupation levels indicated primarily syncratic power. However, females at all occupational levels showed a stronger participation by the mother than did the males who reported stronger father participation (Tables 3 and 4).

SUMMARY

The purpose of this study was to compare the power structure of the Negro family between occupational levels as determined by the father's occupation and by the sex of the respondent. It was decided the power structure could best be defined as to who makes the decisions, as reported by the ninth-grade student in the family, on questions related to the family decisions and to child-rearing practices.

The instrument used to determine the power structure was derived from one constructed by Herbst. The items selected were those wherein both parents could potentially make the decisions. The questionnaire was administered to ninth-grade Negro students from a metropolitan area in Florida in April, 1963.

A typology of parental power in decision-making was made: father autonomous, father shared, syncratic, mother shared, mother autonomous, and adolescent. A frequency count of the number of participants who responded to a particular item was made for each of the three occupational levels, and a percentage was computed to provide an indication of the power structure in the Negro family by sex for each of the three occupational levels. Where possible, categories were combined for statistical analysis and a Chi-square statistic was made to determine the differences between occupational levels for male and female respondents.

The occupational levels were determined on the basis of the father's occupation with the white-collar level made up of professional, manager or proprietor, and sales. The blue-collar level included craftsman, foreman, and operatives; and the unskilled was comprised of service, household, military, and laborer categories.

As a whole, the data indicated males and females viewed the power structure in their families to be mainly syncratic in most of the occupational levels. However, the males reported stronger father participation than did the females, while the females reported stronger mother participation than did the males. It can be said, for this sample, that participation by the Negro father in the decision-making process in the family was more frequent than has been historically presented.

Excerpt from
Suburban Runaways of the 1960's

Robert Shellow, Juliana R. Schamp, Elliott Liebow and Elizabeth Unger
MENTAL HEALTH STUDY CENTER, NATIONAL INSTITUTE OF HEALTH

The selection which follows is the authors' conclusions of the study reported in "Suburban Runaways of the 1960's" by Robert Shellow, Juliana F. Schamp, Elliott Liebow and Elizabeth Unger. A summary of the research plan follows:

The research was done by members of the Adolescent Process Section of the Mental Health Study Center, a part of the National Institute of Mental Health, located in Maryland. The study was carried out in Prince Georges County, Maryland, which borders on the District of Columbia. The county police and school departments, as well as various judicial institutions, cooperated in the study.

The subjects of the study were 731 adolescents aged 10 to 17 whose parents notified the county police between August, 1963, and July, 1964, that the adolescents were missing from home, and who it later turned out had left home voluntarily with the knowledge that they would be missed. One or both parents were seen by trained interviewers who obtained background material about the youngsters and the families, as well as information about events leading to the running away. Ninety-six of the adolescents were subjects of an intensive interview, which was tape-recorded and later coded. School, police, and court records for the adolescents were sought out, and various kinds of materials were taken from them. As a control group, 1,327 students in the appropriate Saint Georges County school grades filled out a questionnaire which asked for information about the pupils' homes and backgrounds, as well as for information about their having run away or having thought about running away at any time in the past.

CONCLUSIONS

Research on children who run away from home has a history of some 40 years or more. This past research does not present a single sharp image of the runaway child but rather a blurred and shifting configuration. Why children run away from home and the meaning of running away to the child, to his family, and

Reprinted from *Monographs of the Society for Research in Child Development* 1967, 32, #3, 28–33, Copyright © 1967 by the Society for Research in Child Development, Inc. By permission.

to society seem not to be constants but everchanging functions of time and place.

Since our study was carried out during a period of unprecedented national affluence, it is not surprising that our runaway children bear only slight resemblance to the children set to wandering during periods of social and economic upheaval. Nor do most children in our study look much like the clinic-captured runaways of, say, the Worcester Center, although both groups were drawn from comparable suburban metropolitan areas.

\It was only when we looked at the relatively small minority who ran away repeatedly that we were able to identify runaways who more nearly conformed both to the picture so consistently drawn by clinic investigations and to the popular stereotype of the runaway. Here, among the repeaters, and especially the frequent repeaters, we did run across evidence of personal and family disorganization, serious difficulties in school, and consistent involvement with law-enforcement agencies. However, it is not so much the repeated running away which attracts the concern of controlling and helping agencies but the fact that it is coupled with more threatening and destructive behavior. It is as if the frequent repeater appears in the runaway population by accident; perhaps he would more appropriately be located in the clinic population with those in need of special and professional help with many aspects of their lives. For the most part, however, the majority of runaways we encountered showed little evidence of severe personal or family disorganization. In many respects, they looked very much like their nonrunaway counterparts.

We found, then, two analytically separable groups of children who knowingly and purposefully removed themselves from the effective control and surveillance of their parents. One was a relatively small group for whom running away was intimately bound up with individual or family pathology. This group appeared almost exclusively among frequent runaways. The second and much larger group consisted mainly of those who ran away only once, but included many repeaters as well. This second group, though distinguishable from non-runaways in many respects, resemble more closely the nonrunaways than they do the seriously disturbed minority.

Attempts to understand and deal with the problem of running away from home must take these two distinct populations into account. Though the overt act may be the same for both groups, what lies behind it, the social and psychological meaning for it, is different for the two groups, and each group must be considered separately.

Had we considered only the seriously disturbed minority, we would have arrived at essentially the same conclusion as those previous studies which attacked the problem through clinical and agency populations—that is, runaways are damaged children badly in need of individual and expert care. Such a conclusion would be entirely inappropriate for children in the other, larger group, however. These, too, are troubled children, but they are troubled in much the same way that other adolescents are troubled. Unlike the pathologically driven frequent repeater, the others need no custodial care and have no special need for individualized professional services.

In part, their difficulties lie outside themselves, in the different social systems in which they move, in their relations with their parents, with the school system, and with their peers. For them, running away may be a calculated maneuver in their dealings with parents, ultimately designed to change the relationship rather than to deny it. It may be a way to break free from a long-standing conflict with an unyielding and profitless educational system. Or it may be simply a desire to step back, take stock, and rest before engaging again with parents, teachers, or friends. Running away may be any one of a number of things ranging from a cry of despair to a victory yell. Most frequently, perhaps, it is something in the middle: a plain, forthright expression of dissatisfaction at home or school. The problems facing most runaway adolescents are the same as those facing many other young people; in this sense, running away from home can be seen as one way of dealing with these problems. Other adolescents deal with these problems differently but not necessarily in ways that are better either for themselves or for the community.

From the very beginning of this study, our collaboration with the juvenile court, the county commissioners, the police, the schools, and other county agencies oriented us toward community action. Since we believe that the vast majority of runaways are adolescents responding in a particular way to problems common to adolescents generally, the remainder of this section will be devoted to recommendations centered on those problem areas which confront all adolescents and which we believe to be susceptible to community action.

School, for example, is a problem for a major part of the general adolescent population. Our own data show clearly the connection between school as a problem area and running away. Runaways tended to perform poorly at school. Not only was this poor performance frequently a direct source of trouble for the child, but it was also an important indirect one, causing conflict between him and his parents. Parental dissatisfaction with the child's school performance often led to nagging and disciplinary measures that, over a period of time, became conflicts in their own right. Although school problems appeared more marked among the runaways, the school questionnaire and our knowledge of other nonrunaway adolescents suggested a widespread dissatisfaction with school.

There were indications, never tested in our data, that children, whether runaway or not, generally appeared to meet increasing difficulty as they moved through the secondary school system. The diminishing holding power of schools throughout the entire country, as seen in the high rates of absenteeism, truancy, and dropouts, may well be symptomatic of this progressive difficulty encountered by students. Not so easily observed are the psychological dropouts, those who are present in body but whose thoughts are regularly elsewhere. Truancy and dropping out psychologically, which appear on the surface to be a child's rejection of school, might, in many instances, better be seen as the school's rejection of the child, especially the one who does not accept academic values.

The major problem appears to lie with those students—and they are in the majority—who will *not* go on to college. A way must be found to increase the ability of the school system to tolerate students who are not academically oriented. The prevailing sink-or-swim philosophy is a wasteful one. There is a need to make the daily 6 hours of school more meaningful to more students. For many students, the school experience might be improved by broader, better vocational programs. Work-study programs which allow for a split schedule of employment and studies are promising on several counts: they offer students firsthand acquaintance with skills and attitudes necessary for employment, and they draw representatives of industry, business, professions, and labor directly into the development of vocational training, which serves to keep the planners of school curricula abreast of the actual job market. It may be that much of the responsibility for vocational training can be assumed by industry and business, where equipment and methods of training are more likely to be up to date than they are in the schools. The investment of public funds in expensive, quickly obsolete equipment often has limited the utility of vocational programs in the past. In a world which has seen in a 10-year period the creation and elimination of actual job skills—for example, the clerical phase in preparing data for computers—such a shift of responsibility would help avoid the costly mistake of training students for nonexistent jobs. Vocational programs of this scope might go a long way toward helping these students make sense of school for their present lives as well as their future goals.

The present lives of adolescents require that schools provide other kinds of education as well. Our interviews with adolescents and our post-questionnaire discussions led us to recognize once again the imperative need of adolescents to make a place for themselves among those of their own age. Neither parents nor schools seem to be able to answer basic questions that adolescents sometimes hesitate or fear to ask adults. We therefore suggest the establishment of *peer-relations education* programs on a voluntary basis to discuss dating, associations and pressures in peer groups, sex facts and practices, early marriage, and the responsibilities of parenthood. Though peer-relations education would be the responsibility of the school and would be offered during school hours, this program could succeed only if the discussions were led by group leaders and professionals not in a formal evaluative relation to the students.

Another recommendation has to do directly with runaways and their families. The disruption of family life occasioned by running away may leave both parents and child in need of first aid. Police officers can provide sound advice and offer comfort to parents whose children have run off, but they do not have the time nor are they equipped to provide family counseling. Our interviews with parents pointed up the need for such counseling. Families frequently asked for help, and even those who did not explicitly do so welcomed the opportunity to talk about their recent troubles. Since most people are more willing to seek help when they are hurting, a lot can be accomplished during the runaway crisis. Once the child has returned, however, the crisis is considered to be over, and the families comfort themselves with the belief that everything is all right. In many cases, however, it is not. The runaway crisis offers an opportunity to give assistance to families when they most want it, and to wait at all may be to wait too long. We recommend that communities set up an around-the-clock, on-the-spot *emergency aid service*. This emergency service of aid and referral would be a unit of professionally trained counselors supervised by a member of the mental health professions. It could operate as a special group of consultants attached to the juvenile bureau of the police department.

There is evidence from interviews with parents and intensive interviews with children that adolescents encounter constant criticism from impatient adults. Parents consistently complain about misbehavior and school performance, and teachers register their disapproval through the medium of grades. Adolescents sometimes respond to this disapproval by fighting it, ignoring it, or running away from it, any one of which may alienate them further from the adult world.

As long as an adolescent is able to obtain satisfaction in peer relations, he may be able to compensate for loss of self-esteem in his relations with teachers and parents. Perhaps the adolescent who runs away only once does so because of a momentary breakdown of satisfactions in all spheres at once. In the school questionnaire, many of those who seriously considered running away but did not do so reported that their change of mind occurred after reflecting on what they might lose in being away from their friends. It is likely that the repeater's peer-group ties are not so strong, and he is therefore less restrained by such considerations. With virtually nothing to lose, of all adolescents he is most prone to act on the fantasy that life can be better outside his home territory.

Though public policy cannot easily and directly improve the quality of family life, it can greatly influence the way other institutions meet the needs of adolescents. In most communities, for example, there is no single agency that concerns itself with all areas in the lives of adolescents. There is a fragmentation of concern among existing agencies—secondary schools, juvenile court, police department, recreation board, and a host of voluntary organizations. Most communities could benefit from the establishment of a central *youth board* to develop an overall picture of the needs of youth, to plan programs beyond those already under way, and to coordinate and balance efforts in the community. The youth board would not only survey and study but would be empowered to take positive action through a permanent staff working with a budget of its own. The primary function of the youth board would be to assess and respond to the needs of youth—to have its staff constantly working with youth and to use young people themselves as advisors and program staff.

One such need is in the area of recreation, which we define as going beyond team sports. In the helter-skelter suburbias with their minimal or nonexistent systems of public transportation, recreational facilities typically are lacking, and what few exist are inaccessible to large numbers of adolescents. Recreational facilities need to be distributed throughout the community for ready access. The youth board would develop and operate a network of youth centers staffed by full-time professionals, each youth center offering a wide range of activities from performing arts to automotive repair. Since school property has always been used as a site for recreational activities, schools offer a ready-made base on which to build such a program. School plants could be kept open afternoons, evenings, weekends, and all summer, too.[1]

The range of these recommendations—only one of which deals directly with running away—reflects the shift in our concerns as the study progressed. Our initial concern with runaway adolescents steadily pressed us toward a concern with adolescents generally. More and more, running away came to appear as a reaction to the ambiguities and problems associated with the social role of the adolescent in the modern world. Runaways are frequently among those

---

[1] To do this, additional paid help would have to be provided, and in suburban areas the school bus system would need to be revised and perhaps expanded to provide adolescents with easy access to activities.

adolescents who are too shrewd, too questioning to accept comfortably the mere promise of adulthood in the indefinite future while pacified with privilege in the present.

Increasingly, school has become the only agent of meaningful initiation into full and valued participation in the community. The academic, career-oriented young person finds it relatively easy to accept his dependency status because he knows it leads directly to such participation. At the peak of his physical and sexual energy, he expends this energy in ways that support his goals. He sees his teachers and other adults as trainers whose task it is to assist him in reaching these goals. He submits more easily to their discipline and is eager for their approval.

But for many others, school is not a means to an end. For the adolescent unprepared or unwilling to pursue the career curriculum prescribed by the school system, school is a sort of deep freeze designed to preserve him in childhood or child status. Nor does society offer him any real alternatives. Child labor laws, compulsory school attendance, and the growing indiscriminate demand for formal educational credentials conspire to shut off the possibility of direct entrance into the full participation of earning a living and raising a family. Socially approved and self-promoting outlets for his energy typically are unavailable to him. He must contain this energy or get rid of it in ways that are socially unacceptable; he must spend it in the meaningless exercises of academic life or dissipate it in self-defeating irritation, impatience, and hostility with the system. For him, teachers and parents are not trainers, preparing and leading him to his goals, but keepers who stand between him and a valued place in society.

Clearly, current methods of preparing adolescents for adult life are simply not suitable for all young people. In a recent year, there were several thousand who ran away in a fairly typical suburban county, and there were many times more who considered doing so. In a sense, these runaways have taken the initiative; their usually inept attempts to escape from the nowhere of adolescence into the somewhere of adult status are a comment on our lack of inventiveness when it comes to youth. Whether we respond with our usual reflex of worry and criticism or whether we act to provide for the real needs of the adolescent generation will be a measure of our society.

Orientation Toward the Future

Elizabeth Douvan and Joseph Adelson
UNIVERSITY OF MICHIGAN

The metaphor commonly chosen for discussion of adolescent development has the bridge as its central image. The child at this period is pictured between two worlds, closer to childhood, but with his back turned to it, facing the adult status that lies ahead, on the other side of the adolescent pass. The conception is clear, simple, and apt in some ways. But we would suggest that the adolescent's relationship to these two worlds is less simple than the picture implies. There is, first of all, the fact that the passage between the two worlds is not simple and unidirectional. There is a great deal of wavering, backtracking, and even simultaneous movement in both directions (as though the youngster were trying to encompass the whole transitional span by widening his step, avoiding complete commitment to either side). In addition to these complexities of pace, we would add another condition about the child's relation to the future adulthood which makes the metaphor even less descriptive. The fact is that adulthood is not just a prospect that the child sees ahead of him. It is also a crucial component of his activities and life as he makes the adolescent transition. The outlines of his personal future are roughly established, although they are not filled in or realized. The future enters adolescent identity like a crucial piece omitted from a picture puzzle. The color and content of the piece are missing, but the shape is established, and bears an intimate relationship to bordering pieces. If the piece is really crucial—as the future *is* in adolescent identity, the whole puzzle depends for its interpretation and meaning on what the piece will look like. To make any meaningful assessment of adolescent personality, we must look at the shape of the future as it enters and conditions the formulation.

We can think offhand of a number of alternative ways in which adolescents in our culture orient toward the future, making use of it or managing to avoid it. Some youngsters hold a general conception of their future life, or an element of it, which they invest with some importance and use as a guide in current decisions, interests, and activities insofar as these bear on it. In such cases, one has the feeling that the future is managed with some sense of proportion—there is neither a denial of its importance nor an overinvestment in it at the expense of appropriate adolescent interests. The future concept in these cases is more often general than specific, more often partial than complete and detailed. It is a recognition that the future is important within the present, but not a denial or exaggeration of either aspect of time.

Contrast this use of the future with other postures: the child who has no operating concept of future time but is totally absorbed in the adolescent present, and the child whose concept of the future is so concrete and elaborate, so highly invested that it effectively insulates him against *any* involvement in

Reprinted from *The Adolescent Experience* (New York: Wiley, 1966), pp. 22–26, 48–52. By permission.

the problems and pressures of his own age group. One adolescent may have a clear notion of the immediate future and a blank beyond that point, another may be vague about the immediate future and have a detailed picture of some later period. The degree of detail he supplies for one period or aspect of the future may be only slightly related to the degree of emotional investment or color the adolescent places in that phase.

The normal adolescent holds, we think, two conceptions of himself—what he is and what he will be—and the way in which he integrates the future image into his current life will indicate a good deal about his current adolescent integration.

To explore adolescent conceptions of future time and of adulthood, we used two general types of questions. One type consisted of direct questions about plans and expectations for the future. We asked boys and girls what kinds of decisions they think they will have to make in the next few years, what kind of life plan they hold, whether they plan to finish high school and what other educational plans they have, what kind of work they think they will go into and why. In all these questions we asked specifically about the youngster's conception of his future life and about the most articulated aspects of this conception—the verbalizable, intelligible plans and expectations. In all of them we asked about the future within a clear reality context.

The second set of questions approached the future concept somewhat less directly. Here our effort was to pose questions that would give us some insight into the less formulated and intellectual aspects of the youngster's image of the future, the visual and emotional qualities of that image. We asked about day-dreams and about adults whom our subjects admired and would like to be like. We asked them to tell us what they found exemplary about these particular adults. We asked them to tell us the most wonderful thing they could imagine happening to them, and the worst thing that had ever happened to them. And we asked what they would like to change about themselves or their lives if they had the power of their wishes. These questions deal with hopes and dreams rather than expectations, and they ask for visual and concrete references rather than intellectual and abstract ones. They approach the child's future concept in a context of fantasy rather than asking him to discuss it realistically.[1]

We expected that boys and girls would differ in their handling of future time. The identity problems posed for the two sexes differ sharply, and since the use of the future is guided by identity considerations, this too, we thought, would differ. For the boy, identity revolves around the questions, "Who am I? What do I do?" The nature of his occupation plays a crucial defining role in a man's identity. The girl, on the other hand, depends on marriage for her critical defining element; she will take her self-definition, by and large, from the man she marries and the children she raises.

[1] These two levels, the fantastic and the realistic, are not always clearly distinguishable. Some children, we shall see, have vocational aims that the hard-headed outsider must feel are fantasy-based. And in talking with girls about their ideas of marriage, we can hardly expect that they will not present fantasy; since, except for very few girls, they have no real experience from which to discuss the future reality of their married lives. We can, on the other hand, differentiate most of the questions we asked into those that refer to hopes and dreams and those that ask about plans and expectations. It is useful to maintain this distinction where we can, and consider other questions frankly ambiguous, falling, as they seem to, somewhere between the two levels of discourse.

This difference has critical implications for the adolescent work of identity formation. The occupational issue which forms the core of masculine identity is to a large extent an issue of individual choice and action; it arises during or shortly after the adolescent era, and preparation for the choice starts during adolescence itself. The boy in adolescence can begin to choose and prepare for work, and this activity can focus and stabilize many of the problems and conflicts that arise for the child in transition. The girl faces a more ambiguous task. Marriage is not a matter of simple individual choice, and for most girls it lies not in the immediate future but beyond in some relatively undefined time. It lends itself neither to rational planning nor specific preparation since it involves the decision and initiative of another person. A girl who plans and prepares explicitly for marriage may be thought aggressive and ungraceful, and she may also be courting disappointment and embarrassment since there is always the possibility, however slight, that she will not marry. There is also the fact that the identity task of the girl, tied as it is to marriage, revolves directly about her sexual identity. Far from relieving the anxieties and conflicts of adolescence by providing them focus and outlet in some neutral ground (as occupational choice and preparation may), this issue very likely intensifies the normal problems of the era.

We expected, then, that boys and girls would assume quite different postures toward the future and toward the work of integrating a concept of adult identity. We expected the boy to have a relatively extended time perspective, to have some concept of his adult role, and to connect that concept to the present by a more or less coherent and developed notion of intervening steps, of choices and actions instrumental to achieving his ultimate goal. We thought that some boys might overuse the future, that is, might use a highly concrete and specified concept of adulthood to avoid some of the more unsettling aspects of adolescence (for example, the erotic fantasies that their psychosexual status stimulates). We did not expect avoidance of the future to be a common pattern among boys.

Our notions about girls' use of future time were much less specific than this. They might, on the one hand, have no clear concept of the future—absorbing themselves, rather, in current adolescent activities and concerns. Or they might turn their interest in the future to a relatively immediate future—the period of education and work that commonly precedes marriage for girls in our culture. In this case we might find a displacement of emotional energy from the central issue of marriage to these more immediate but secondary interests. What we find, in fact, is a variation of this pattern.

The clearest form in which the sex difference appears in our interviews is in the degree of coherence between fantasy and reality conceptions of future adulthood. In the boys we find that dreams and plans are either similar in focus or at least appropriate to each other. Girls, on the other hand, show a marked discontinuity between fantasy and reality planning. When girls discuss their plans, they concentrate on events in their lives before marriage. They talk of educational decisions, occupational plans, and so forth. When they describe their daydreams and hopes, or when they describe ways in which they would like to change themselves, they do not emphasize individual achievement or seek changes relevant to a future work. Fantasy for them revolves around other interests. Marriage, which is surprisingly absent from their plans, does appear in dreams. Glamour and physical beauty assert an influence in daydreams which is not expressed in any realistic efforts toward change.

Boys stress education and work in their plans, and in line with this focus, they dream of outstanding achievement, choose adult ideals on the basis of their talents and work skills or the success they have achieved. When they imagine changes in themselves, the changes reflect their dominant reality interests; they wish for more of the qualities and characteristics which they relate to success in the adult role they hope to achieve. . . .[2]

A look at answers from two sample interviews may clarify some of the differences in the way boys and girls approach and conceive the future. These are not to be construed as typical interviews. They are in many respects quite unusual. The boy whose interview we quote is softer and more passive in his stance toward reality than most boys. The girl we look at is among the small minority of girls who choose traditional professions in their job aspirations (although, in our case, the girl names this relatively masculine goal along with other occupations that represent extensions of the traditional feminine role). But the interviews, for all their uniqueness, do serve to illustrate and concretize some of the contrasts we have discussed as general trends: the unifying thread between boys' plans and fantasies, the discontinuity between these two levels in girls; girls' larger, more direct investment in fantasies, and the fact that boys' fantasies, even when they are rather well developed, borrow structure and language from the reality problem of occupational choice.

Both of these interviews are with middle-class youngsters. Both respondents intend to go to college, and they both clearly expect to live the middle-class pattern that is currently theirs by virtue of the parents' status.

The boy is a 14-year-old who lives in the northeast. His father is a personnel manager in industry; his family consists of mother, father, and three sons. This boy is the youngest.

The young man wants to be an ornithologist some day. His answer to the question "What kind of work would you like to do as an adult?" reveals a taste for the field and some indication of the source of his interest: "I'd just love ornithology work. It seems to be in my family."

This boy is young, and he does not have much information about the field of his choice yet: "I don't know exactly what they do though—whether migration work with birds or what." He thinks that other fields may claim his interest in the future. When asked how sure he is of his choice, and whether he would like to learn more about various occupations, he shows a degree of objectivity and self-awareness. "That's what I can't tell. I'm sure of it now, but you know how teenagers are. But I think I'll stick on it." ("Like to know about other jobs?") "Well, yes. I don't know which is which. There may be something I don't know about which would be very interesting."

Despite his youth and his awareness of the limitations of his knowledge of the field, his ideas about preparing for a career in ornithology are fairly detailed and not inaccurate except, perhaps, in emphasis. He plans to go to college, to

---

[2] In the pages omitted here, Douvan and Adelson describe in some detail the boys' and girls' plans and future expectations and fantasies about the future. They conclude the chapter by exemplifying the differences between the boys and girls with one boy's responses and one girl's. —Eds.

forestry school, and he thinks he will need to study "Latin—for bird names—zoology, biology, and, of course, ornithology. Sciences of all kinds." He assesses his chances of becoming an ornithologist: "That depends upon whether I can get a job in the field; and if the job suits me. With what my determination is now, I think my chances are pretty good. I know I'm going to college, and I'll just go along these lines."

These work goals and educational plans are supported by a strong achievement drive that comes up at several points in the interview. When asked what job characteristics would be most and least important to him, he chooses "interesting work" and "good chance for promotion" as most important, and "job in home town" and "leader of other people" as least important. He is attracted to a job with risk and opportunity more than one which provides security but less opportunity for individual achievement. He thinks boys worry about success and achievement, and the self-changes he would like to effect are work-relevant: "I'd like to have better study habits and get more done in less time. I'm working on this, and I'll have to get better at it before I get to college."

We have seen up to this point that this youngster is visualizing a future job, and is judging it in relation to his taste and aptitudes, mechanisms for moving into the field, and his limited knowledge about it. The job idea concretizes his concept of future time. The particular job choice links his future back into the present. He states the linkage when he tells us why he has chosen ornithology as a job aspiration: "I've always liked the study of birds. I just like to get outdoors and hear them sing; find a new bird and find out what it is. It's fun to find rare birds where they don't belong—[at this point in the interview he told about two mockingbirds which nested in his yard the previous summer]—I keep a bird chart—name, date seen, where, who saw it."

He knows an ornithologist: "One of the Scout leaders at summer camp. He's almost blind; identifies them by sound and tells how far away they are." At the outset of the interview when asked to suggest activities for a new club, he had already introduced us to his vocational interest in a set of remarkably egocentric suggestions: "Me, I like the outdoors very much. My hobby is birds. Go on hikes. Most boys like nature. *Some* like mechanics—but I don't especially."

We find the same theme dominating answers which are closely tied to reality. The first answer is to the question "Are there any other things [in addition to the thirty-one listed leisure activities] you enjoy doing in your spare time?" He says, in response to this: "Yes, hiking—and just plain sitting out on nice afternoons and listening to sounds. You see more birds just sitting still than looking around for them." The second is his choice of an adult ideal, and his justification of the choice: "Audubon." (Question: "Why?") "How he painted pictures of birds. How he carried on when down and out and became famous that way."

The girl whose interview we have chosen is from a middle-sized midwestern city. Her family has upper-middle-class status (the father is an executive in a large industrial organization) and consists of father, mother, our respondent (15 years old), and a younger sister (13 years old). This girl wants to be a "doctor or a nurse"; she chooses these jobs because she is interested in medicine, and "[I] would like to help people, especially children." The criteria she thinks would be most crucial in judging a job are its social setting ("nice people to work with") and job content ("interesting work"). She would least desire a job in which she would be "a leader of other people" or her own boss. She would rather have a secure job than one offering less security but an opportunity for individual success.

Her plans and decisions regarding the future revolve around school and vocational plans: When asked what decisions she will make in the next few years, she answers "I have to decide whether I'll go into medicine or teaching. I'll definitely go to college, but I don't know whether I'll go to junior college or go away. My parents would like me to go away for at least one year. If I definitely decide to be a doctor, I'll go away, or I may go to the University for nurses training." Her "plan or picture of the way [she would] like life to work out for [her]" includes an allusion to marriage, but does not focus strongly on marriage or motherhood: "I'll finish school and go to college. I'd like to become a doctor or teach, and have a nice job helping people and getting to know different kinds of people. I'd like to get married, but I think I'll work anyway, at least for a while."

When we look at other parts of this girl's interview—at her less reality-tied conceptions of the future, at her current interests and preoccupations, at her ideals and attitudes toward herself, we find little to support these professional aspirations. Within the plan itself we can note some discrepancies, but this might be explained by the fact that she is young and has not yet settled on a single occupational goal. The more significant discontinuity occurs between the discussion of future plans and the rest of her interview: nowhere do we find evidence of the kind of commitment or motivation toward individual goals which her plan would seem to imply and require. She shows none of the personal ambition we might expect; individual achievement is neither a source of concern nor a focus of current interests.

In these regards she looks like girls in our modal category: she is concerned with personal attractiveness and a feminine social facility, she is interested in popularity and particularly popularity with boys. She thinks the most wonderful thing that could happen to her is "to be really popular, be asked out a lot, and have a steady boyfriend I really like." What would she like to change about herself? She would like to be "a better conversationalist, . . . be able to talk to everyone easily . . . [and] not have to wear braces." When asked what girls worry about, she says "Boys mostly. Some kids worry about their families—kids whose parents don't get along or fight. But I don't have to worry about anything like that. Sometimes a friend gets mad at you, and then you worry."

She chooses her mother as an adult ideal because "she's fun and understands young people. She jokes with us and doesn't think everything we do is juvenile or silly. She always looks real nice too." Her major sources of self-esteem revolve around acceptance by others and feminine helpfulness. She feels important "doing something with my club, especially when I know they wouldn't have as much fun without me. And I feel important when I do something for my girlfriend—help her with her work or talk to her when she's worried." (Probe: "Worried?") "About her boyfriend or her school work."

The theme of achievement occurs once in this interview, when the girl is talking about the kind of man she would like to marry. She thinks of high occupational aspirations for her future husband, just as she does for herself, but in connection with *his* work she alludes to the kind of motive base in achievement that we miss in her own plans. "I've always thought I'd like to marry a doctor, but mostly I'd want him to do the kind of work he likes and is best at. I'd like him to have some aim in life like medicine, and the ambition to make good." She also wants to marry someone "with a sense of humor, someone who enjoys the same things, not tired and grouchy." (Probe: "What kind of things?") "Play with the children, help me, go out in the evening after the work is done."

To reiterate the central differences between boys and girls in their posture toward future time: the feminine stance is characterized by a sharp break between fantasy and reality conceptions, and by a concentration of affect and color in the fantasy realm. Girls' reality plans for the future slight and disguise the feminine goals which are crucial to them, and they fail to integrate present and future time. Girls' adolescent preoccupations with personal attractiveness and popularity as well as their fantasies about themselves and their future lives feed into and support feminine fulfillment, but are discontinuous with at least the manifest content of their reality plans.

The boy's future conceptions are more likely to be all of one piece and heavily infused with the rhetoric of reality. He plans for a vocation; his fantasy conception of himself and of future time feed into and support his plans. He may use reality planning to escape the dangers of fantasy (by evasion or by restructuring fantasy in the less dangerous terms of reality). But he does not, as the girl does, invest directly in fantasy and cover the investment by a detached second bet, a conventional gesture. He either avoids fantasy through concentration on reality or recognizes fantasy in the terms of his real plans. The girl can maintain the two systems independently—the reality plans clear and articulate but uninvested, fantasy carrying her emotional investment and establishing continuity with her current preoccupations.

16

Growth in Self-direction

The stages of development of the human being are arbitrary divisions of a continuous process. In this book we have used four stages—infancy, preschool, childhood, and adolescence. The adolescence we have visualized stops at the usual time for graduation from high school in the United States, a definition which we chose because it fitted our plans for the book. Recently Kenneth Keniston has suggested that for at least some Americans there is another stage, which he calls youth, between adolescence and adulthood; and there is growing evidence that adulthood is a stage of development which should be subdivided. Certainly, as two people in our fifties, we are aware that we have been changing during the last thirty years. We think we are not fooling ourselves when we think that not all those changes have been deteriorations.

The first paper in this chapter, by Adah Maurer, used as subjects individuals ranging in age from five years to adulthood. The adults' ages are not specified, and all adults are grouped together in Dr. Maurer's discussion of the results. Evidently no division of the adults into subgroups was advisable, because Dr. Maurer expresses mild surprise that the adults' responses were remarkably similar to the younger people's. The questions asked of the subjects had to do with the characteristics of living things and the differences between living and nonliving. We suggest that after you read the questions posed by Dr. Maurer you stop to answer them yourself before continuing to read the article. You might find it interesting also to give the questions to your friends for comparison with this study's results.

The oldest subjects in the paper by Adelson, Green, and O'Neil fall within our definition of adolescence. The youngest subjects (average age 10.9 years) come just at the end of childhood. The authors found a turning point in ideas about law at around the age of 15. They link this change with adolescents' capacity for formal thought which is the important cognitive difference between children and adolescents.

Just as Adah Maurer discovered that some adults gave answers to her questions similar to those given by children, so Constance Holstein reports (as other investigators on the topic of moral judgment have) that some adults exhibit a level of moral judgment which is less mature than that of some adolescents. Dr. Holstein used Kohlberg's moral judgment stories with a group of adolescents and their parents. She hypothesized that parents who themselves were at a high level of moral judgment and who maintained good communication with their adolescents would have children who were also at a high level. Such children live in a culture, within their families, which fosters mature moral judgments.

Maturation of Concepts of Life *

Adah Maurer

A. INTRODUCTION

Computer-phobics think of erudite machinery as a fearsome invasion into the human realm. Since the danger is symbolic rather than real, such fearfulness must stem from a deeply embedded irrationality. But what? Newness or strangeness *per se* does not explain it; other inventions have been accepted without a quiver. Edison's light bulbs were greeted with wonder and delight; we couldn't get automobiles, truly a murderous toy, fast enough.

The problem is bound up with our definitions of life (11). A computer acts like a brain and a competent brain is man's sole survival weapon, the factor that has made him fittest. Jealous concern for our uniqueness is aroused by the idea that a piece of hardware is partly human. But more than jealousy is involved. The overlap of inanimate things that have some of the characteristics of life and living things that lack some of the abilities usually associated with aliveness confuses and frightens us. Certainly this is true in childhood as will be shown and, to a certain extent, remains true even among the scientifically sophisticated. At the Waxworks, Renee Spitz reminds us (10), an attendant posed as a display creates a squealing havoc by suddenly stepping out toward a susceptible customer. Such a joke gives the calmest of adults a primordial jolt, however briefly.

Practical decisions of the utmost gravity turn upon this quirk of the human mind. For example: Is early abortion murder or a sanitary service? Those who think of life as having a moment of beginning are unalterably opposed to the presumed murder; those who are aware that sperm and ova consist of living cells before, as well as after, they unite can consider the question by more relevant criteria. The moment of death, no longer a simple certitude, poses legal, medical, and moral dilemmas because of our lack of an agreed definition of life. Our ancestor's simple belief in animism in which everything was alive: the angry volcano, the vengeful storm, the loving mother earth, the watching stars, must of necessity give way before new definitions usable in the quest for signs of life in outer space, as well as in determining the ethics of organ transplants.

To define and redefine life is the task of the biologist (1, 2, 11), but to trace the origin of concepts of life, how these originate in infancy and develop through childhood, and to discover how the various working definitions defend against anxiety becomes a legitimate field of inquiry for the psychologist. We shall make a beginning.

Reprinted from *The Journal of Genetic Psychology*, 1970, *116*, 101–111. By permission.

* A research project undertaken originally to counterbalance the effect of researching a comparable study: Maturation of concepts of death (8). Special thanks are due to Dr. Don R. Shupe, University of Utah College of Nursing, and to Prof. Ellis D. Evans, University of Washington, Department of Educational Psychology, for their enthusiastic cooperation in collecting questionnaires from their students and in making many helpful suggestions in regard to the implications of the research.

In *Life and the Dialogue* (10, pp. 166, 177–172), we read

> The child begins to distinguish the animate from the inanimate toward the end of the first year of life. . . . The failure to achieve this discrimination is one of the factors which perforce leads to a misinterpretation of reality with resulting developmental maladaptation. Adaptive measures are taken . . . against non-existent perils. The usual defenses of the ego are aimed at the wrong targets. Extravagant demands for protection against imaginary adversaries are made on the surround. The normally available supplies of constructive energy . . . are drained by the misdirection of defensive measures. The consequences of such processes [include] anxiety readiness, insomnia, night terrors, dereistic thinking, magical ritual, denial, withdrawal . . . [and] irrational, aggressive, destructive violence.

This is a serious indictment. A number of clinical examples may be pertinent: A disturbed four-year-old screamed in unremitting horror, not at the puppet show which she enjoyed, but at the sight of the dismantled puppets being packed away in their storage box. A child in his third year would not permit his mother to use the telephone in peace; the disembodied voice was a source of irrational fright. Another refused to permit the removal of a wart because its location was similar to that of the valve of his inflatable clown, and he confessed the fear that he would "go all down to nothing" (6). Spitz photographed infants rejecting dolls with exaggerated signs of terror. Bettelheim's Joey, the mechanical boy, who preferred machinery to human beings because it protected him better is also a case in point.

To add a longer perspective to Spitz' studies of this phenomenon in the first year of life, to determine if there is indeed considerable confusion surrounding ideas of aliveness and to discover what factors may be involved, this investigation was undertaken. Preliminary questioning of a random sample of people, age five to adult, consisted of inserting the word "life" in vocabulary lists in intelligence tests. The first results were not especially enlightening. Definitions tended to be noncommittal, as "not dead" or "how long you live." When questioning was separated from formal testing situations and the form of the question changed, maturational factors were immediately conspicuous. Consider these replies to the query; "How can you tell if something is alive?"

> *A kindergartner:* Well, if it's alive it'd wiggle and make some kind of noise, open its eyes at you. If it was in the bushes it'd jump out at you and eat you up.
> *A boyscout:* It's breathing and the heart is beating. You can't always tell just by looking at it. If you cut it open and it doesn't have any blood, it's not real.
> *A high school girl:* It moves of its own free will. It feels or has feelings. It has to have air to survive. It gets babies and sometimes has a mind of its own.
> *A primary teacher:* It moves and emits sounds. It needs nourishment and it responds to its environment. It learns.
> *An associate professor of nursing:* It has metabolic processes, has reproductive potential, matures, requires a certain environment to maintain itself. Individuals die, but the species lives on.
> *A biologist (3):* Life—macromolecular, hierarchically organized and characterized by replication, metabolic turnover, and exquisite regulation of energy flow—constitutes a spreading center of order in a less ordered universe.

From the malevolence of "eat you up" to the beneficence of "a spreading center of order" is a long way. From these samples it would appear that among the very young aliveness inspires anxious thoughts about an external agent fraught with danger, a finding that correlates with the nearly universal fear of animals at these ages (7). The boyscout has studied first aid, but he remains haunted by the bloodless zombie, a classic example of mixed animate and inanimate characteristics, the living dead that is distinctly menacing. By adolescence, life is epitomized by freedom and strange, new feelings; definitions of life at this age project the newly developing desires for autonomy and the joy of procreation. The primary teacher projects also; but, rather than her personal feelings, a more mature social conscience directs her attention to the characteristics of her students as prototypes of aliveness. Medical and allied professionals are even more other-centered in that their statements stem from professional responsibility for their patients with an added philosophic concern for life's continuity. To the biologist, life, abstracted from self and from other humans, reveals itself as ordered and exquisite, a phenomenon to be studied with fascinated commitment.

Illustrations, however, are insufficient to demonstrate an ordered progression in the maturation of concepts of life.

B. METHODS OF INVESTIGATION

Setting aside metaphorical uses of the word life (the life of the party; the half life of an atomic particle), we find that in English the word "living" has not one but four or more opposites. "Not living" includes (a) the once but no longer living—a dead body, (b) the inorganic—a granite rock, (c) the imaginary—a fairy godmother, and (d) the simulated—a graven image or a photograph. Perhaps there are others. Preliminary questioning discovered a lack of clarity on the part of some subjects between the living and the life-necessary, as well as between alive and awake. Thus there are semantic, scientific, and superstitious reasons for the human inability to agree from the beginning as to what are the characteristics of living things and what things exhibit those characteristics.

Within the areas of overlapping characteristics, 20 common objects were chosen as being representative of a variety of possible confusions. Ten of them are living things that lack some of the characteristics of mammalian life, being rooted, dormant, microscopic, or lacking limbs. The other 10 items are non-living things that share some characteristics of mammals, such as motion, sound, or shape. The list as presented: an airplane flying, an apple tree in an orchard, a wind and rain storm, the sun that shines, a tiny fish swimming, an old cat asleep, a crying doll, the telephone ringing, a bug crawling, germs that make you sick, a ghost in the night, a worm in the garden, seeds that you plant, a statue of a man on a horse, monsters from outer space, a bird's egg in its nest, T.V. cartoons, a Halloween skeleton, seaweed in the ocean, a dandelion in the lawn.

Other objects might have been equally suitable but some were deliberately avoided: words unknown to children, those that might stir religious controversy, and items temporarily in that limbo between life and death, such as recently plucked or amputated parts. Some few of the included items are possibly subject to nit-picking: an apple tree in an untended orchard might remain after it had died of disease, a certain percent of planted seeds are likely to be infertile; but to have specified more exactly in these cases would have indicated too clearly the expected response or have been unintelligible to children.

In all, 672 subjects supplied responses first to the question, "How can you tell if something is alive?" and second to the list of 20 objects which they were requested to designate as alive or not alive.[1] The children were randomly chosen from seven elementary schools and three high schools. Consisting of equal numbers of boys and girls, they represent middle- and lower-middle-class families with a sprinkling of minority groups. The adults were drawn from extension classes at the University of California, Davis, from the faculty of the College of Nursing at the University of Utah, from classes in Child Development at the University of Washington, and from psychiatrists, members of the Society for Phenomenology and Existential Psychotherapy. No adults from under-educated groups were included because their responses, it was assumed, would have provided less contrast to those of the children and they would, thus, function less well as a control group.

C. RESULTS

How can you tell if something is alive? "It moves," was the all but unanimous first response. Of the 131 children in the five- and six-year-old group, 18 were unable to respond; but, of the remainder, 72 used the word "move" and another 30 implied motion by such descriptions as *walk, play, run, work, dance, move their hands, pick up things, stomp their foot, jump, bounce a ball, hop, climb, stand up, exercise, kick, swim, bend over, pull a wagon, shake their head, do tricks, roll, slide, dig,* and *throw things.* Only 11 responders failed to impute motion to alive things and most of these merely gave examples: "A birdie and a fishie," "Like me," or generalized: "God made them alive." One misunderstood "alive" as "a lie." Thus, for 90 percent of the youngest, their own ability to be in motion seemed to epitomize aliveness; but, since there was opportunity for five responses, most took the next step of thinking in terms of some other. "We dig holes and we find things alive," said one. Motion words, such as, *crawl, wiggle, fly, swim away, chase, jump at you, rustle in the bushes,* seem to reflect experiences with pets, observation of garden and pond animals, and, perhaps, participation in the killing of household vermin. Motion conspicuously sets these apart from toys and dead insects or pets and, thus, the young child's limited experience and lack of learning could account for the emphasis upon motion as the essential quality of aliveness.

Motion, however, continues to be the first thought of older children, of 75 percent of adolescents, and of a majority of educated adults. Lack of opportunity to learn of the aliveness of plants cannot be blamed for this strange misinformation. Among those adults who replied orally, there was a tendency to respond impulsively, "It moves," and then to withdraw the judgment with laughter or embarrassment as second thoughts arose. The first response seemed

[1] For copies of the original questionnaire and instructions to teachers, as well as a résumé as presented to the Western Psychological Association Conference, San Diego, California, March 1968, order NAPS Document 00685 from ASIS National Auxiliary Publications Service, c/o CCM Information Sciences, Inc., 22 West 34th Street, New York, New York 10001; remitting $1.00 for microfiche or $3.00 for photocopies.

more in the nature of an association than a judgment and, as in associative thinking generally, to rely upon a residual impression formed long before and unexamined since. Associative thinking is also more likely to be emotional rather than cognitive and, thus, we have a first hint that this topic is indeed tinged with regressive, irrational uncertainty.

Motion in an unknown other induces wariness under primitive conditions. In jungle warfare patrols are instructed, "If it moves, kill it." The assumption is that if it moves, it is alive and if it is alive, it is an enemy. Observations of two-year-olds confirm the impression that tentativeness, wariness, and a wavering between fear and fascination characterize the first approaches to moving, living things. For some 14 percent of our youngest subjects the request to define aliveness immediately aroused thoughts of danger and death. "A monster is alive because he eats branches and he eats people up." Several mentioned killing: "He reaches for his gun." "If you kill somebody and take them to the doctors, they will be alive." One Air Force child whose father had just returned from a tour of duty opened her eyes wide, took a deep breath, and announced: "Everything is alive except if it got burned up," and her teacher could not shake her from this conviction. Some 16 kindergartners and two first graders were too taken aback to be able to respond at all; they simply stared open mouthed or shook their heads in defensive negativism. With some the suspicion of danger remains dominant for many years. A slow learner at 15 wrote, "If a skunk stinks on you, it's alive; if a bee stings you, it's alive; and if a dog bites you, it's alive."

Another evidence of the anxiety-arousing effect of questioning about life was in a subset of action responses that reflected parental injunctions coupled to ideas of growing up, becoming adept, and keeping healthy: "They can put on their own shoes." "They eat up all their vegetables." "They brush their teeth nicely." "They do what their mother tells them." The mothers would probably be surprised to learn that these injunctions are close in the child's mind to ideas of aliveness; since, by implication, failure to obey means nonaliveness. Concealed death threat seems too strong a phrase to apply to insistence upon health rules for the very young, but it may be that some children so hear them.

Next to motion, sound is the chief identifying characteristic of life to children. *Talking, buzzing, barking, singing, making noise* were listed as typical of human life, of pet bird and insect life, and also as warning signals given by hazardous wildlife: "It rattles before it strikes." Attention to sound increases in middle childhood, but never becomes as important as sight.

Middle childhood gives evidence of instruction, but not in the life sciences. Physiology, yes, with emphasis upon proper nutrition and cleanliness and a modicum of first aid useful, presumably, to cope with carnage on the highways and battlefields. Boys trained to resuscitate the drowned and to tourniquet the amputated (skills which none of them will be permitted to practice without genuine training as soldiers, police, or interns) have learned little to increase their understanding of themselves or their fellows. Primordial fears remain untouched; acceptance of life in its fullness and variety, compassion for the crippled in body or mind are bypassed as though they did not matter. Sex education has either been nonexistent or has fallen on deaf ears because, before puberty, only a scattering of little girls are aware that reproduction is an essential characteristic of life on this planet. Less than a third of adolescents and just under a half of adults thought of the continuity of life from one generation to the next, although surely all of them "knew" the facts.

The adults in the study proved to be amazingly untutored. The professor and instructors of nursing and the high school teachers of science excepted, few had any organized conception of the elements of biology. Semantic niceties seemed laughingly unimportant to the five who checked as alive, an airplane flying. "Well, I meant the pilot," defended one. Some of the 20 percent who claimed to believe in ghosts or monsters from outer space shook their heads ominously, "You never can tell!" These were college graduates with teaching credentials. Seeds and bird's eggs confused 17 and 22 percent respectively, many of whom followed their choice of "not alive" with a row of "?'s" or comments, such as "not yet." One who was questioned afterward admitted that it had set her to worrying about abortions. Often what they wrote was pertinent, but incomplete, redundant, or qualified with "sometimes." To say that living things are animate or that they are self-propelled, that they sparkle, see, think, respond to pain, are warm, smell, contribute to society, communicate, have a central nervous system, and the like is not to have given much thought to a problem that has such universal significance.

Turning next to the second part of the problem, we find that no one had any difficulty discarding the criteria he had listed and checking the various objects as alive or not alive on empirical grounds. In this there is a clear-cut and steady gain in correctness. From an average of 8.95 errors at age five, there was a sharp drop to 5.23 errors at age seven, and slower but consistent drops to 2.45 during adolescence, and 1.15 for educated adults. All five- and six-year-olds made more than two mistakes. Among the seven- to 11-year-olds, a few in each age group made none and 20 percent had only one error. Adolescents, all in junior or senior high schools and presumably exposed to elementary biology, did a little better, but very little. Only a fifth were able to distinguish correctly between things animate and inanimate, and less than half made but one error. All this becomes less startling when we look at the figures for their mentors. Less than half of their teachers, nurses, and of *their* instructors, professors, and psychiatrists fully understood what constitutes aliveness, and only 73 percent made less than two errors. It should be noted, also, that while motion is a feature of 14 of the listed objects, not one of the 672 subjects checked those and only those as alive. Alas for deductive thinking; it does not come naturally.

The youngest subjects with an average of almost nine errors each would seem to have answered randomly, since 10 errors equals pure chance. Such a conclusion is not justified for several reasons: They showed a propensity to prefer things to be alive in that 77 percent of their errors were in the direction of thinking the inanimate alive and only 22 percent the obverse. Two shy kindergartners nodded agreement "alive" for all 20 objects. Their motto seemed to be, "When in doubt, it's alive." (This tendency remained, but shrank steadily until adulthood when errors fell equally in either direction.) Then, too, more than 90 percent of them knew that fish and bugs were alive and almost as many knew about worms. Eighty percent distinguished correctly between asleep and not alive and 65 percent had learned about germs. Seeds and eggs were correctly identified as alive by 70 and 85 percent respectively, considerably better judgment than their older siblings and indeed about as astute as their teachers.

On the other hand, television cartoons are adamantly alive to the amusement and sometimes despair of their teachers. One kindergarten teacher who utilized this testing as the basis for a nature study lesson explained carefully that cartoons are only pictures, puppets are only dolls moved by hand, but that the beans and avocado plants on the nature table and the greenery in the fish tank are alive because they grow. Dutifully they agreed with her. The next day they saw a nature study cartoon. Asked what was alive in the film, the same 60 percent chose the dancing stick figures over the placid vegetables.

The conviction of a similar majority of the fives and sixes that the sun is alive matches the universal propensity of the child artist to draw a sun with smiling features in his outdoor scenes. Students of children's drawings (5) have found this representation of a living sun to be common to children, primitives, and prehistoric man. Drawn, it is called a mandala defined as a "graphic mystic symbol of the universe." Spoken of, it may similarly have primitive roots. The seven percent of the adults who also checked the sun as alive may have made the simple mistake of confusing "is alive" with "is necessary to life on earth," since it is true that the "energetic foundation of all life is converted solar energy—the radiated output of thermonuclear fusion in the core of the sun" (3). But children could hardly have been taught this especially since the facts of life in a broad sense have proven very difficult to teach before the age of seven. In all, one third of the subjects thought of the sun as alive including one psychiatrist who insisted that this was true in a poetical sense.

The remaining items could give rise to considerable speculation. For example, it may be that many of the youngest subjects, because of their pervasive egocentrism, responded "alive" to those items that they liked or that they conceived of as safeguarding or enhancing their own lives, and "not alive" to those items they thought of as dangerous to themselves. The sharp drop in errors at age seven, especially in regard to cartoons, statues, dolls, airplanes, and Halloween skeletons, and the rise in the "monster" syndrome (which many confused with the scientific search for extraterrestrial life) would seem to indicate a sudden sophistication of discernment that may parallel Piaget's findings in regard to cognitive development. The change in ideas about life is far more marked at seven than at adolescence or between adolescence and adulthood.

The question as to education vs. maturation is not resolved by these figures. The 17 percent of seven-year-olds who made not more than one error in the 20 items could hardly have been either more mature or better educated than the 27 percent of adults who did less well. And of course there is no guarantee but that they too might change their minds about monsters when they become nine. Part of the original design had been to judge the effect of IQ on responses; but this proved to be not feasible, since only a variety of group intelligence scores were available and these are not sufficiently reliable in the earliest years. Teacher's reports on the handful of high scorers on this survey leads one to the impression that a carefully designed experiment would indeed find interesting correlations.

D. CONCLUSIONS

Spitz' postulates definitely are borne out by this extension of his studies. He surmised that "distinguishing the animate from the inanimate is an achievement of major importance and, as such, fraught with conflict" and further that such discrimination is important from the viewpoint of survival. Such a statement is consonant with the current findings. He listed (10, p. 167) appearance (especially the face), motion, and sound in the inanimate as most productive of anxiety in the infant. Our data demonstrate that motion, sound, and having eyes were the prime criteria by which young children judge something to be alive. We also found that a fairly large group confessed directly that aliveness in an unknown other was fearsome. Spitz found that the animate was preferred; these data indicate a preference for aliveness, since far more errors of judgment were made in the direction of assigning aliveness to inanimates than in denying aliveness to animates.

Piaget's pinpointing of ages seven to nine as the years when logical thinking begins would also seem to be verified by the sharp reduction in inaccuracies in regard to living things shown to be typical of this age.

The occurrence of adult inaccuracies in so simple a series of questions about the animate *vs.* the inanimate seems little short of disastrous, especially as the most inaccurate were the primary teachers. The most immediate response to this situation would seem to be additional training in biology or at least elementary nature study as part of the teacher training curriculum.

E. DISCUSSION

Biologists generally agree that man's actions are intimately tied to his genetic past but that the theory that his beliefs and ideas should be similarly tied to the history of the species runs counter to the current reliance on teaching and learning as the dominant influences in man's development. Of the major theorists of the human mind only Jung (4) considered the possibility of there being preprinted in the untutored brain traces of the beliefs of our primitive ancestors. This approach is seldom honored even by serious debate and the rare negotiations usually depend upon the stopper: "not one iota of proof." This is, of course, true. Lack of proof, accusations of heresy, and unpopularity would be insufficient to explain the dearth of interest and investigation along the lines that Jung opened for speculation unless there were social and personal preferences for avoiding what are thought of as the unacceptable corollaries. It is a credit to the decency of scientists, generally, and biological psychologists, in particular, that they cling so fervently to the *tabula rasa* theory. If this were true, then indeed have all people been created equal and the task of implementing equality is the comparatively simple one of providing each with an education. This simplistic plan of social action is idealistic but inadequate, if only for the stubborn fact that massively rewarded recitations that cartoons are only pictures of puppets fades before the untaught conviction that whatever moves is alive, an erroneous notion that moulds the decisions of 60 percent of educated adults.

Smiling suns on primary pictures, beliefs in ghosts, monsters, and living storms, regressive associations between an unknown in motion and an enemy attack, fearfulness or distaste for uncertainties connected with overlapping characteristics of the animate and the inanimate do not in any way constitute a "proof" that man's instincts function rather more pervasively than we would like to believe. They do, however, need a better explanation than the rather feeble suggestion of the *tabula rasa* behaviorists that the child "must have learned them (12) perhaps from overhearing adults talk in these terms." If such firmly entrenched notions, and "wrong" ones at that, are learned so casually, the very least that we can conclude is that inadvertent eavesdropping is a more effective learning procedure than anything that goes on in school. More likely it points to the fact that untaught beliefs of such universality are a gold mine of research possibilities.

If we become aware of what must be unlearned before logical manipulations of reality can begin, if we become aware of a heritage of our past as a species moulded even dimly into our genes, a whole new terrain is opened in which to hunt for an increasingly accurate understanding of ourselves. We would, thus, forge another link in the chain of scientific ideas underlying a philosophic naturalism: the study of man's irrationalities without recourse to supernatural or occult forces (9).

References

1. BERNAL, J. D. The Origins of Life. New York: World, 1967.
2. DOBZHANSKY, T. Evolution, Genetics and Man. New York: Wiley, 1963.
3. GROBSTEIN, C. The Strategy of Life. San Francisco, Calif.: W. H. Freeman, 1964.
4. JUNG, J. C. Basic Writings (*Ed.*, V. S. deLaszlo). New York: Modern Library, 1959.
5. KELLOG, R. The Psychology of Children's Art. San Diego, Calif.: Communications/Research/Machines, Inc., 1967.
6. MAURER, A. The child's knowledge of non-existence. *J. Exist. Psychiat.*, 1961, **2**, No. 6.
7. ———. What children fear. *J. Genet. Psychol.*, 1965, **106**, 265–277.
8. ———. Maturation of concepts of death. *Brit. J. Med. Psychol.*, 1966, **39**, 35.
9. PITTENDRIGH, C. S. The biologist in the solar system. *Bull. Atom. Sci.*, 1967, **23**, No. 3.
10. SPITZ, R. A. Life and the dialogue. In *Counterpoint: Libidinal Object and Subject.*, H. S. Gaskill, Ed. New York: Internat. Univ. Press, 1963.
11. WADDINGTON, C. H. The Nature of Life. London, England: Allen & Unwin, 1961.
12. WOLPE, J. Personal communication, 1965.

Growth of the Idea of Law in Adolescence *

Joseph Adelson
UNIVERSITY OF MICHIGAN

Bernard Green
UNIVERSITY OF OKLAHOMA MEDICAL SCHOOL

Robert O'Neil
UNIVERSITY OF DETROIT

This paper traced the growth of the idea of law during adolescence. Depth interviews were conducted with 120 subjects, 30 each at the ages of 11, 13, 15, and 18. Significant changes in the view of law take place between 13 and 15. Level of discourse shifts from concrete to abstract; a restrictive emphasis is replaced by a stress on the positive aims of law; a conception of amendment is increasingly present in the later years, as is an emphasis on the intrapsychic effects of law. In general, law loses its absolutistic meanings, and is seen as functional, as a tool for achieving community ends.

The adolescent years see sweeping changes in the comprehension of the political order. The preadolescent youngster has only a dim recognition of politics and government; his understanding of these topics is diffuse, personalized, and concrete. By the end of adolescence he has invariably achieved an abstract, differentiated, and functional view of the political domain.

How does this transition take place? In an earlier paper (Adelson & O'Neil, 1966) the growth of the sense of community was examined. In the early years of adolescence—roughly between the ages of 13 and 15—the youngster cannot easily imagine an abstract collectivity; hence, his formulations of political processes cannot take into account the present or future needs of government and community. At best he understands government in the persons of its visible deputies—teachers, the police, the mayor, the President—but does not grasp the institutions they act for and represent. In the later years of adolescence the youngster attains a sense of the structure and processes of community, and in doing so can sort out and make sense of previously mysterious happenings in the political realm. He can recognize that the social order has purposes of its own, that the visible agents of the government are servants of these purposes, that politics involves the interacting legitimacies of citizen and community.

In this paper the authors will explore the growth of the idea of law. Its relevance to politics and government is plain enough. Since law is the principal medium of government, the enactment of law is the goal toward which politics moves. If we are to grasp the changes in political thought taking place during

Reprinted from *Developmental Psychology*, 1969, *1*, 327–332. By permission of The American Psychological Association.

* The research was supported by grants to the first author from the H. H. Rackham Fund of the University of Michigan and from the Social Science Research Council. The authors thank Lynnette Beall and Ruthellen Lefkowitz for their help in data analysis.

this period, we must look into the adolescent's emerging sense of law—his view of its scope and limits, his idea of its place in the total political process.

METHOD

INTERVIEW

The data were obtained through an interview schedule which offered the following premise:

> Imagine that a thousand people move to an island in the Pacific, and set about building a community de novo. They are confronted by the tasks of forming a government and of developing laws and other modes of communal regulation.

Given this framework the schedule, largely open ended in character, asked the subject to make political and social decisions, to justify them, and to respond to opposing opinions. The scope of the interview included, inter alia, such topics as the nature of political authority, the mutual obligations of state and citizen, ideology and idealism, crime and justice, and the process of politics. The interviews were conducted in school and were tape-recorded and transcribed verbatim. They were generally completed in 60 to 90 minutes. There were six interviewers, all of whom had had graduate training in clinical psychology.

SAMPLE

One hundred and twenty adolescents in a suburban community were interviewed. The sample was divided into four age-groups: fifth grade, average age = 10.9; seventh grade, average age = 12.6; ninth grade, average age = 14.7; and twelfth grade, average age = 17.7. There were 30 subjects at each grade, and within each there was an equal number of boys and girls. The sample was further divided by intelligence, two-thirds with scores between 95 and 110 on the California Test of Mental Maturity, and one-third 125 and over. Thus, within each of the age groups, there were 10 boys and 10 girls of average intelligence, and 5 of each sex with superior intelligence. These criteria were established beforehand, and students meeting them were selected randomly until the quota for each cell was met. Two students with histories of serious emotional disorders were excluded. To reduce incomparability of age samples due to differential dropout rates, the authors decided beforehand not to include Negroes; had they done so, however, only two would have been selected. Interviews were conducted at schools representing the socioeconomic "middle" of the community. Given the nature of that community, and of the criteria employed in choosing the sample, the subjects were from families of above average income and education.

The findings are reported by age alone (to the next nearest age) and without reference to sex or intelligence level. For all the findings herein reported, tests were carried out for sex and IQ differences, and none of a significant order was obtained.

RELIABILITY

To establish the lower limits of reliability, only the more complex or ambiguous items were examined. For five of this type, intercoder reliabilities ranged from .79 to .84.

RESULTS

When the authors spoke to adolescents about their understanding of law, age changes were immediately visible in two directions: First, younger adolescents were usually unable to respond abstractly; their discourse was concrete, almost literal. Second, they emphasized the constraining, coercing side of the law. Taken together these tendencies resulted in the younger adolescent's speaking of law largely in terms of specific acts of wickedness which society must curb and punish. Older adolescents were more likely to use an abstract language, and more often adverted to the beneficial functions of law. The differences between younger and older subjects may be made more graphic if one examines some representative interview excerpts. The subjects were all boys, all of average intelligence, who were asked, "What is the purpose of laws?" The responses were the following:

> *Eleven years old.* Well, so everybody won't fight and they have certain laws so they won't go around breaking windows and stuff and getting away with it.
> *Thirteen years old.* To keep the people from doing things they're not supposed to like killing people and like. . . . if you're in the city, like speeding in the car and things like that.
> *Fifteen years old.* To help keep us safe and free.
> *Eighteen years old.* Well, the main purpose would be just to set up a standard of behavior for people, for society living together so that they can live peacefully and in harmony with each other.

Table 1 reports the change from concrete to abstract discourse on law during the years from 11 to 18. In this analysis "abstractness" was coded generously; any evidence of a generalizing or synthesizing tendency, however diffuse or thinly detailed, was counted as abstract. The authors noted a sharp shift between the ages of 13 and 15.

A similar pattern is found in Table 2, which describes the change from a restrictive to a beneficial view of the purpose of laws. Again, the period between 13 and 15 appeared to be the watershed mark. At 15 most of the subjects looked beyond the merely constraining functions of laws, to recognize that they may aim to promote the general good and to achieve moral or social benefits.

LAW AND THE LARGER COMMUNITY   How are we to understand this shift in emphasis, from a constraining to an enhancing view of law's purpose? For one thing, the young adolescent is locked, matter of factly, into benignly authoritarian relationships to his milieu, both at home and at school. He takes

TABLE 1
Concrete and Abstract Views of Law

VIEW OF LAW	AGE			
	11*	13†	15†	18*
Concrete	.72	.69	.19	.07
Abstract	.28	.31	.81	.93

Note.—$\chi^2 = 48.45$, df $= 3$, $p < .001$.
* $N = 30$.
† $N = 29$.

TABLE 2
Restrictive and Beneficial Views of Law

VIEW OF LAW	AGE			
	11	13	15	18
Restrictive	.76	.73	.31	.17
Restrictive & beneficial	.10	.17	.27	.21
Beneficial	.14	.10	.42	.62

Note—$\chi^2 = 34.01$, df $= 6, p < .001$: $N = 29$ in each age group.

it for granted that authority exercises its dominion over its subjects—teacher over student, parent over child—and almost casually he generalizes this direction of ordinance to the domain of government. With the easing of control that accompanies adolescence, with the adolescent's sharp surge toward autonomy, there is a gradual yielding of this way of looking at the politics of household and schoolroom, and ultimately of politics at large.

Concurrently the youngster begins to achieve an articulated sense of the community. Before the age of 15 (or thereabouts) the adolescent, lacking a differentiated view of the social order, cannot grasp the needs, present and future, of the total community; when the child thinks of law, he refers it only to individual conduct, and, more specifically, to the constraint of antisocial conduct. Once a sense of the community has been established, it penetrates all phases of political and social thought. The adolescent can now relate law to the needs of the polity. He understands, first, that the law inhibits for the sake of the common good; later, he can recognize that the constraining side of the law is not necessarily central, but only one of a number of social functions that the law must fulfill.

LAW'S MUTABILITY   At the threshold of adolescence the child does not know—or cannot grasp—the concept of *amendment*. Law is viewed in an either-or fashion. If it is suggested that for one reason or another a law is ineffective in achieving its aims, the youngster may suggest strengthening it, or—though less commonly—abolishing it altogether. Only rarely will he spontaneously imagine that the law can be revised, its strengths retained, its weaknesses eliminated.

Later in adolescence—again, 15 years seems to be the turning point—the youngster begins to adopt a functional view of law. Law is an experiment, a rehearsal. We try out the law and consult the common experience. If that tells us that the law is ineffectual, we may then abandon it. But we may choose instead to revise it in seeking to improve it. This is a pragmatic manner of reasoning about the law; in all likelihood it reflects the older adolescent's enhanced capacity for formal operations (Inhelder & Piaget, 1958). The younger adolescent more commonly imagines a law as either present or absent; the authors' older subjects could more easily conceive that what exists in the present can exist in an altered form in the future.

Table 3 reports some findings to illustrate the growth of the idea of

TABLE 3

Responses to the Question: Should Laws Be Permanent or Changeable?

| | AGE | | | |
RESPONSE	11	13	15	18
Mentions amendment solution	.00	.00	.30	.23

Note—$\chi^2 = 16.50$, df $= 3$, $p < .001$; $N = 30$ in each age group.

amendment. Subjects were asked to imagine whether, as members of the island community, they would prefer that some laws be deemed irrevocable. A full analysis of responses to this question would take us beyond the present concern; the interest here is in observing the sudden appearance, at age 15, of responses which propose the possibility of an amendment procedure to bypass the either-or alternatives suggested in the question. Additional data bearing on this issue will be shown later.

EFFECTS OF LAW: INNER AND OUTER   As they grow older, the subjects increasingly see beyond the external effects of law to recognize its impact on internal states of being. Younger subjects connect law exclusively to external conduct, more specifically to the inhibition of action—they are, if you will, naive behaviorists—and rarely sense the subtle, indirect influences of the law in changing the spirit and motivation of the citizenry.

The most telling evidence came from the question: "What would happen if there were no laws?" The authors expected that the answers would evoke visions of Armageddon, and so they do. Almost without exception, the subjects anticipated pillage, chaos, and the rule of the strong and evil; only a few dared to imagine that good will might survive in a world without law. What is pertinent in this context is the difference in how younger and older adolescents conceived of this anarchic cataclysm. For the younger the loss of law would produce a loss of regulation; the conduct of persons *toward each other* would be chaotic. Older adolescents also mentioned this side of the matter, but many of

TABLE 4

External and Internal Effects of a Lawless Society

| | AGE | | | |
EFFECTS	11*	13†	15†	18‡
External	.87	.97	.55	.56
Internal	.13	.03	.45	.44

Note—$\chi^2 = 20.24$, df $= 3$, $p < .001$.
* $N = 30$.
† $N = 29$.
‡ $N = 27$.

them went on to stress the *inner* corruption which would follow a state of lawlessness—personal confusion, anomie, and ultimately a dwindling of moral sense and capacity. Table 4 has the findings.

AN ILLUSTRATION: THE CONTROL OF CIGARETTE SMOKING   Some of the developmental trends so far discussed may be illuminated if one observes them at work as the child considers a concrete, though hypothetical, problem a government might confront: How to regulate cigarette smoking once it is determined to be a public health hazard. The authors developed a sequence of questions on this issue, designed to offer some way of comparing responses concerning concrete problems to those elicited by more abstract and general questions on the nature of law. The issue chosen was (and is) much in the news, and it is one which engages contrasting philosophies on the question of public authority and personal freedom.

The first item in the series posed the problem directly:

> A majority [of the Council] felt that cigarette smoking was undesirable because of the effect on health. The question they asked themselves was what, if anything, the government ought to do about it. Should the government forbid smoking or not? What do you think?

One finds in Table 5 that only a minority of subjects at any age favor forbidding smoking, but that the number doing so falls sharply at 15. Older adolescents are wary of the restrictive powers of government, here as elsewhere. In their spontaneous comments to the question they often point out that to forbid smoking would be to infringe upon personal rights; and they may go on to argue such a law would be unenforceable.

A later question in the series carried the problem a step further:

> Now here's what happened. A majority of the Council voted for a law to forbid smoking with a fine for those caught selling or smoking cigarettes. But the law didn't seem to work. Cigarettes were smuggled into the island and people smoked secretly. A majority of the Council still believed in forbidding cigarette smoking and the problem they had was how to enforce the law. What do you think they should do in this case?

TABLE 5
Responses to the Question: Should Government Forbid Smoking?

	AGE			
RESPONSE	11*	13†	15‡	18†
Forbid	.39	.45	.12	.14
Don't forbid	.61	.55	.88	.86

Note.—$\chi^2 = 11.94$, df = 3. $p < .01$.
* $N = 28$.
† $N = 29$.
‡ $N = 25$.

TABLE 6
Government's Response to Violations of Smoking Law

GOVERNMENT'S RESPONSE	AGE			
	11*	13†	15‡	18‡
Revise or repeal	.07	.24	.40	.47
Increase enforcement	.93	.76	.60	.53

Note.—χ^2 = 12.39, df = 3, $p < .01$.
* $N = 27$.
† $N = 29$.
‡ $N = 30$.

Table 6 makes it quite clear that older subjects were far more willing to disavow an apparently unworkable law. These data in fact underestimated considerably the cleavage between younger and older adolescents. Many older subjects had predicted just the outcome mentioned in the question, and now offered their "solutions" to the Council sardonically, tongue in cheek. If you pass a foolish law, you are stuck with foolish ways of enforcing it. So when some of them proposed searching homes, or the use of spies or informers, they did so in the spirit of black humor. But those of the younger subjects who suggested police-state methods did so quite solemnly.

The final question was the following:

> Two different points of view emerged in the discussion of the Council. Some said that a law that didn't work was no good and ought to be voted down. Others felt the law should be made to work and thought there should be even heavier fines to make the law work. What are the arguments you can think of on both sides? Which do you prefer?

The authors noted again a decided reduction, with age, in the number of adolescents who would retain an unpopular and ineffective law (Table 7). It is of particular interest to note the sharp increase, at age 15, in the proportion

TABLE 7
Government's Response to Law Difficult to Enforce

GOVERNMENT'S RESPONSE	AGE			
	11*	13†	15†	18†
Repeal	.38	.53	.53	.53
Enforce more strictly	.62	.43	.20	.10
Revise law	.00	.03	.27	.37

Note.—χ^2 = 32.40, $p < .001$.
* $N = 29$.
† $N = 30$.

of subjects who resisted the either-or alternative of the question to suggest a revision of the law to make it workable. This finding would seem to support the results reported earlier in this paper, on the availability of an amendment concept during the later years of adolescence.

DISCUSSION

It is one of the commonplaces of the study of adolescence that one finds during this period a sudden accession of political idealism. Perhaps so, but what was far more striking in the interviews was the unusually quick growth, in the years between 13 and 15, of political realism. That was the most telling difference between younger and older subjects: The former made their judgments without much concern for the social needs that the law serves. Neither did they think much about issues of feasibility—whether, for example, a law can in practical terms be enforced, or whether the gains brought by the law warrant the costs of enforcement.

Older adolescents are less likely to lose sight of these considerations. As the child enters more completely into adolescence, one sees a steady accretion of worldliness: He grows in his knowledge of political institutions and functions, of recent political history, of current political rhetoric. As he understands more of what is and what has been in the political domain, he can extrapolate more easily to what might and should be.

Yet is would be misleading to attribute the youngster's growth in sophistication solely to his increased knowledge, or to his greater capacity in handling the abstractions inherent in political thought. The authors also noted a fundamental change in outlook, in the temper and quality of discourse. The younger students were brusquely judgmental. A narrow moralism dominated their appraisals of law. It was as though law emerged from the empyrean; once it has arrived, man's sole duty is to obey it. If he does not, the authorities are right to coerce him, using whatever means ingenuity will allow.

Younger adolescents rarely imagined on their own—that is, unless the interview item suggested it—that a law is absurd, mistaken, or unfair. They assumed authority to be omniscient and benign, hence law to be enacted only for good and sufficient reasons. But if they were conservative with regard to the maintenance of existing law, they were radical with respect to enforcement. In a mood of serene omnipotence they proposed baroque methods for the detection and punishment of "crime," giving little apparent heed to the gap between the possible triviality of the violation and the Orwellian apparatus needed to control, enforce, and punish.

By the time a child is 15—in some cases earlier—a very different tone of discourse is evident. Now it is understood that law is a human product, and that men are fallible; hence, law is to be treated in the same skeptical spirit we treat other human artifacts. Though the *institution* of law may be deemed sacred, specific laws are very much in the realm of the secular, subject to disinterested scrutiny. Law invites tempering and tampering, all to the greater good, that good either social or spiritual. Law is a tool of the spirit, not spirit itself.

The critical, pragmatic mood of the older adolescent leads him to wonder, when confronting a proposal for law, whether there is more to it than meets the eye. What are its latent effects? Whose interests are served, whose are damaged? He asks these questions not out of a reflexive suspiciousness, but because he weighs heavily, as the younger adolescent does not, the obstacles between the will and the act. The younger subjects imagine history, tradition, social convention, and human nature as infinitely tractable to the will of law. By the age of 15 the youngster recognizes that the law must reckon with the dead hand of the past, entrenched privilege, human recalcitrance.

When weighing the merits of a proposed or established law, the older adolescent has available to him a number of understandings that influence his decision: that law must accommodate competing interests and values; that ends must be balanced against means; that the short-term good of the law must be appraised against its latent or long-term or indirect effects. Until a law meets this scrutiny, the older subject does not easily assent to it.

References

ADELSON, J., & O'NEIL, R. The growth of political ideas in adolescence: The sense of community. *Journal of Personality and Social Psychology*, 1966, **4**, 295–306.

INHELDER, B., & PIAGET, J. *The growth of logical thinking from childhood to adolescence*. New York: Basic Books, 1958.

The Relation of Children's Moral Judgment Level to That of Their Parents and to Communication Patterns in the Family

Constance E. Holstein
UNIVERSITY OF CALIFORNIA, BERKELEY

While increasing maturity in moral judgment tends to follow an age developmental pattern, considerable variation within age levels still exists and has not been explained. This study was designed to test the effects of parental influence on such development within one age group and one social class. The research centered on two basic questions: Does it make any difference to the child's rate of development if his parents are advanced, and if it does, *how* does it? What, specifically, are the linkages between the two?

The six stages of moral judgment on Kohlberg's scheme can be differentiated from each other and ordered sequentially on the basis of how "well" they make moral judgments, i.e., how closely they are governed by the criteria of consistency, universality, inclusiveness, and justice. A brief description of each stage is given below.

Presented March 28, 1969 at the Biennial Meeting of the Society for Research in Child Development, Santa Monica, California. Reprinted by permission.

I. Preconventional level

At this level the child is responsive to cultural rules and labels of good and bad, right and wrong, but interprets these labels in terms of either the physical or the hedonistic consequences of action (punishment, reward, exchange of favors) or in terms of the physical power of those who enunciate the rules and labels. The level is divided into the following two stages:

Stage 1: *The Punishment and Obedience Orientation.* The physical consequences of action determine its goodness or badness regardless of the human meaning or value of these consequences. Avoidance of punishment and unquestioning deference to power are valued in their own right, not in terms of respect for an underlying moral order supported by punishment and authority (the latter being Stage 4).

Stage 2: *The Instrumental Relativist Orientation.* Right action consists of that which instrumentally satisfies one's own needs and occasionally the needs of others. Human relations are viewed in terms like those of the market place. Elements of fairness, of reciprocity and equal sharing are present, but they are always interpreted in a physical pragmatic way. Reciprocity is a matter of "you scratch my back and I'll scratch yours," not of loyalty, gratitude or justice.

II. Conventional level

At this level, maintaining the expectations of the individual's family, group, or nation is perceived as valuable in its own right, regardless of immediate and obvious consequences. The attitude is not only one of *conformity* to personal expectations and social order, but of loyalty to it, of actively *maintaining*, supporting and justifying the order and of identifying with the persons or group involved in it. At this level, there are the following two stages:

Stage 3: *The Interpersonal Concordance or "Good Boy—Nice Girl" Orientation.* Good behavior is that which pleases or helps others and is approved by them. There is much conformity to stereotypical images of what is majority or "natural" behavior. Behavior is frequently judged by intention—"he means well" becomes important for the first time. One earns approval by being "nice."

Stage 4: *The "Law and Order" Orientation.* There is orientation toward authority, fixed rules, and the maintenance of the social order. Right behavior consists of doing one's duty, showing respect for authority and maintaining the given social order for its own sake.

III. Post-conventional, Autonomous, or Principled Level.

At this level, there is a clear effort to define moral values and principles which have validity and application apart from the authority of the groups or persons holding these principles and apart from the individual's own identification with these groups. This level again has two stages:

Stage 5: *The Social-Contract Legalistic Orientation* generally with utilitarian overtones. Right action tends to be defined in terms of general individual rights and in terms of standards which have been critically examined and agreed upon by the whole society. There is a clear awareness of the relativism of personal values and opinions and a corresponding emphasis upon procedural rules for reaching consensus. Aside from what is constitutionally and democratically agreed upon, the right is a matter of personal "values" and "opinion." The result is an emphasis upon changing law in terms of rational considerations of social utility, (rather than freezing it in terms of Stage 4 "law and order"). Outside the legal realm, free agreement, and contract is the binding element of obligation. This is the "official" morality of the American government and Constitution.

Stage 6: *The Universal Ethical Principle Orientation.* Right is defined by the decision of conscience in accord with self-chosen *ethical principles* appealing to logical comprehensiveness, universality, and consistency. These principles are abstract and ethical, (the Golden Rule, the categorical imperative)—they are not concrete moral rules like the Ten Commandments. At heart, these are universal principles of justice, of the *reciprocity* and *equality* of human *rights*, and of respect for the dignity of human beings as *individual persons*.

From Kohlberg's discussion of these criteria in a number of publications (1963, 1964, 1968) and his conception of moral development as a successive restructuring of modes of role-taking, three major research hypotheses were formulated. It was hypothesized that advanced judgment in young adolescents is encouraged: (1) when parents themselves operate on more advanced stages of moral judgment, (2) when they provide opportunities for stimulating the child's own cognitive resources by encouraging his greater participation and decision-making, and (3) when they encourage greater exploration of the structural properties of a moral problem by allocating more time for this purpose. Our major operational measures of parental influence were parents' level of moral judgment as measured by the Kohlberg moral judgment stories, and parent–child quality of communication in a family discussion of differences over prior moral choices in the Kohlberg stories.

METHOD

The population frame from which the fifty-three families were recruited consisted of the eighth-grade class from a small upper-middle and upper class community in the San Francisco Bay area. Of the one-hundred seventy-three families contacted, fifty-three (about one-third) were willing to participate. In order to determine how representative these families were of the families contacted as a whole, the two groups were compared on a variety of variables taken from the school records. The overall picture for the fifty-three participating families is one of better educated parents in the professions who had lived in the community for a shorter length of time and whose children fit a "well-socialized" pattern of compliant and good performer in school.

Interviews were generally conducted in the evenings when father, mother, and eighth grader could be home at the same time. Parents were interviewed in separate rooms on a variety of parental practices and the Kohlberg moral judgment stories, mothers by the researcher and fathers by the male interviewer. Children filled out their questionnaires regarding parental practices and the moral judgment stories by themselves in a separate room. When this phase of the interview was completed, the three family members were asked to discuss two moral judgment stories in which they had made different moral choices. A tape recorder was turned on and the families were asked to discuss their differences and try to resolve them, with the option that final agreement was not necessary. The interviewers then left the room and returned after both stories had been discussed.

Five of the ten original moral judgment stories by Kohlberg, which had been used in a recent study by Haan, Block and Smith (1968) were used in the present study. Scoring of the one hundred fifty-nine protocols obtained from the fifty-three families was performed by a judge trained by Kohlberg for employment in the Haan, Smith and Block study. She had had no previous access to the study sample and did not know which protocols belonged to which families.

Scoring was based on sentence responses which could be assigned to a stage as described in coding forms for each of the five moral judgment stories used. Coding was done on a story-by-story basis rather than subject-by-subject. Each subject received a major code which represented his preferred stage usage, defined as 50 percent or greater of the moral statements made, and a minor code, which represented the next most frequently used stage. A twenty percent random sub-sample of cases was selected in order to make an estimate of inter-coder reliability. The estimate of reliability was based upon percentage of agreement between two judges, the second judge being the researcher. As in the Haan, Smith and Block study, agreement was defined as complete agreement on both major and minor code, major code only, or reversals of major and minor code. The percent of agreement between the two judges was eighty-one.

Significance testing: Probabilities of .05 using χ^2 or Student's t are considered significant, although we recognize that the self-selected nature of the sample is such that tests of significance do not strictly apply.

RESULTS

The distribution of moral judgment types for the study sample is given in Table 1.

TABLE 1

Distribution of Moral Judgment Types for Parents and Children, by Sex
(Total $\mathcal{N} = 159$)

	N	MORAL JUDGMENT STAGES (MODAL TYPES)					
		PO 1	IR 2	PC 3	LO 4	SC 5	IP 6
Parents							
Men	53	0	0	3	33	14	3
Women	53	0	0	24	17	11	1
Children							
Boys	24	1	8	9	5	1	0
Girls	29	1	10	12	6	0	0

Abbreviations for each moral judgment type are as follows:
  Level 1: Pre-conventional
        Stage 1: Punishment and Obedience (PO).
        Stage 2: Instrumental Relativists (IR).
  Level 2: Conventional
        Stage 3: Personal Concordance (PC).
        Stage 4: Law-Order (LO).
  Level 3: Post-Conventional, or Principled
        Stage 5: Social Contract (SC).
        Stage 6: Individual Principles (IP).

The vast majority of parents employ a conventional level of moral reasoning. Stage 4 is the modal type for fathers, with 62 percent of the cases accounted for, and stage 3 is the modal type for mothers, with 45 percent accounted for. When we look at the children we find that it is more difficult to talk in terms of mode. They are almost equally split between the preconventional and conventional of moral judgment. Forty percent of them employ stage 3 reasoning dominantly and 34 percent employ stage 2 reasoning.

HYPOTHESIS 1: THE PARENT–CHILD MORAL JUDGMENT RELATION-SHIP   Hypothesis 1 predicts that the child's moral judgment will be positively related to parental moral judgment. This hypothesis is derived from the assumption that types of formal operations found by Kohlberg (1969) in higher stage reasoning should facilitate upward movement through the stages. Such operations include the ability to take the role of the other, the ability to deal with every aspect of a moral conflict situation, and the ability to keep one category or aspect of moral judgment separate from another, thus avoiding contradictions in reasoning common at the lower stages. Such formal operations can be distinguished from actual moral arguments or messages characteristic of each stage even though they function as criteria for those arguments. Children may be able to comprehend and paraphrase moral arguments best which are no more than one stage higher than their own, as we have seen from the work of Turiel (1966, 1968) and Rest (1968). But the formal operations employed at two or even three stages higher than their own could still have an effect on the *rate* at which they develop over time in the family setting. Thus, if we assume that the child learns from his parent through covert role playing, he should be learning those kinds of formal operations which will expedite upward movement in his own moral reasoning. If the child's parent is operating on an advanced level of reasoning, his development should proceed more rapidly than a child whose parent operates on a lower level.

We were interested originally in the effect which both parents jointly had on their child's development. Principled moral reasoning, represented by stages 5 and 6, is rare enough in the general population to warrant the assumption that when it is present in the home it should make a difference to the child regardless of the parent who employs it. We can look first at the general relationship between parents' combined moral judgment level and their child's in Table 2.

For purposes of looking at the relationship, the children were divided into the two most meaningful moral judgment levels suggested by the distribution in Table 1: the preconventional and the conventional. The fifty-three parental pairs were categorized into three groups, the first, one in which both parents exhibited conventional moral reasoning, the second, or intermediate group,

TABLE 2
Child's Moral Judgment Level by Parents' Combined Moral Judgment Level

PARENTS' MORAL JUDGMENT	N 53	CHILD'S MORAL JUDGMENT LEVEL	
		PRECONVENTIONAL (STAGES 1, 2)	CONVENTIONAL* (STAGES 3, 4)
Both conventional	30	14 (49%)	16 (51%)
One conventional, one principled	17	6· (35%)	11 (65%)
Both principled	6	0	6 (100%)

df = 2 $\chi^2 = 4.72$ $p < .10.$

* The one principled child was included in this category for computational purposes. Both his parents were principled.

comprised those cases in which at least one of the parents was operating on a principled level of reasoning, and the third comprised those cases in which both parents were principled.

Parents' combined level of moral reasoning is a fairly good predictor of the child's level of reasoning. Modal stage usage for the child tends to rise as parental level rises. The association does not reach the .05 level of probability which we have adopted as significant for the analysis, but the probability is still low ($p < .10$) and is in the expected direction.

When fathers and mothers were looked at separately we found that the mother–child relationship was very significant ($p < .001$). This did not vary by sex of the child when that was held constant. One of the reasons why the relationship is so significant is that *none* of the principled mothers had children operating on a preconventional level of moral judgment. When we looked at the fathers separately, we found no relationship between their moral judgment and the child's. This result did not vary by sex of the child either.

Why should there be a difference? When we looked more closely at the data we found that one group of fathers provided an answer. They were all principled and had children operating on a preconventional level of moral judgment. These were our "deviant" cases, since none of the principled mothers had preconventional children. These fathers all had conventional level wives. There was another group of principled fathers with conventional wives whose children employed conventional level reasoning. These comprised our "successful" cases. We decided to compare these two groups on several relevant variables to see whether they differed systematically.

It has been suggested repeatedly in the socialization literature that degree of influence is proportional to degree of exposure, and that the influence of a socialization model is increased when he is perceived as nurturant or warm. Maccoby (1968) has suggested that if warmth promotes the socialization process it may be because the child wishes to remain in the parent's presence, thus increasing the chance for learning to occur. Our main tool for measuring parental warmth and involvement with the child was adopted from Hoffman and Saltzstein's work (1967) on parental antecedents of conscience types in young adolescents. The 19-item measure requires the child to rate how often his parent either expresses his affection openly or indulges in a number of child-centered activities when he is with the child. When this measure was related independently to the child's moral judgment level, no relationship emerged. Parental warmth and involvement did not differentiate more advanced children from less advanced.[1] But when parental warmth and involvement was treated as an intervening variable in the parent–child relationship, it strengthened that relationship. The greater the degree of affectionate involvement, the stronger the relationship between the two. Where no relationship between father and child's moral judgment existed before a significant one emerged now. When we looked at our deviant fathers' scores on this measure, we found that they fell into the lower half of the sample distribution. In contrast, our group of successful fathers fell into the upper half.

The wives of our deviant group also had interesting things to say regarding

[1] This was also true for a number of other standard socialization variables dealing with discipline techniques, parental control and supportiveness.

their husbands. In response to a question about differences between themselves and their spouses over the handling of the child, all but one complained that their husbands were overly demanding and strict. At the same time they felt that parents should agree over the handling of their child, while recognizing that their husbands and themselves did not agree. In contrast, only one of the wives of the successful fathers described him as strict and did not present the difference in the form of a complaint.

While the total number of cases for this analysis was small ($N = 11$), we did find meaningful differences between the two groups of principled fathers. Not only do the children of the deviant fathers regard them as relatively low on affectionate involvement, their wives do not approve of their demanding and strict attitude. As parents they do not seem to offer conditions which would facilitate the learning process.

HYPOTHESIS 2: ENCOURAGEMENT OF CHILD PARTICIPATION AND DECISION-MAKING   If the higher stages involve the capacity to deal with many aspects of a moral conflict situation and differentiate categories of moral judgment from each other, then parents operating on those stages should be able to clarify contradictions and fusion of moral aspects present in a child's lower stage reasoning. But lecturing to the child, even with superior conceptual tools at one's disposal, is not enough. Cognitive developmental theory suggests that advances in development require activity on the part of the individual. In the realm of moral development, the process of making principles of judgment one's own requires active structuring and restructuring of one's perceived social environment. But the activity and effort need not be without the help of catalytic agents such as the parents. If movement from one stage to another is best facilitated by the encouragement of the child's own cognitive resources, it should be the case that higher level parents encourage their child more than lower level parents. One strategy for discovering whether they do was to obtain a sample of family discussion of moral issues, using a revealed difference technique. Our second hypothesis predicts that parental encouragement of child participation and decision-making over moral issues will be positively related both to parents' combined moral judgment level and to the child's.

Parental encouragement was scored for both parents jointly. A twenty-percent random sub-sample of cases was scored independently by a second judge for an estimate of reliability. Agreement on this measure was 100%.

We found that conventional parents are much more likely to be low encouragers than are principled parents ($p < .05$) and that children with low encouraging parents are much more likely to employ preconventional reasoning than are children with high encouraging parents ($p < .001$). Table 3 presents parental moral judgment, parental encouragement, and the child's moral judgment simultaneously. By treating encouragement as an intervening variable in the parent–child relationship we can better evaluate what role it plays in linking the parents' moral judgment to the child's. When we look at the marginal distribution, we find so few principled parents who are low encouragers ($N = 3$) that it is meaningless to compare them with the more numerous, low encouraging conventional parents ($N = 12$). But this fact is significant in itself, since principled parents have more advanced children, as we have already

TABLE 3

*Child's Moral Judgment Level by Parental Encouragement by Parents'
Combined Moral Judgment Level*

PARENTS' MORAL JUDGMENT LEVEL	PARENTAL ENCOURAGE-MENT*	N 52†	CHILD'S MORAL JUDGMENT LEVEL	
			PRECONVENTIONAL	CONVENTIONAL
Both conventional	Low	12	9 (75%)	3 (25%)
	High	19	6 (32%)	13 (68%)
One or both principled	Low	3	1	2
	High	18	5 (28%)	13 (72%)

df = 3 $\chi^2 = 9.91$ $p = .02$

* Low encouragement was based on cases in which the child was expected to agree with his parents but was given some reasons why their position was right, and cases in which the child's expression of his own opinion was tolerated but not related to decision-making. High encouragement was based on those cases in which the child's opinion was taken seriously and related to decision-making.
† Due to mechanical failure the contents of one taped discussion were lost, reducing our N from 53 to 52.

seen. Encouragement may well be the link between the two. When we look at high encouragers for both conventional and principled parents we find that over two-thirds of their children are relatively advanced.

If encouragement leads to the stimulation of the child's own cognitive resources we need a more direct measure of this. It is one thing to encourage a child's serious participation, but doing so does not prove that he actually participates. We related parental encouragement to the percent of family discussion time used by the child and found that the two were significantly related ($p < .001$). The percentage distribution of discussion time used by the children ranged from 1 to 40 percent. As we can see from Table 4, not a single

TABLE 4

Percent of Total Discussion Time Used by Child by Parental Encouragement

PARENTAL ENCOURAGEMENT	N 52	PERCENT OF TOTAL DISCUSSION TIME USED BY CHILD*	
		LESS THAN 20%	20–40%
Low	14	14	0
High	38	16	22

df = 1 $\chi^2 = 41.06$ $p < .001$

* Range in total discussion time used by children was 1–40 per cent.

child of low encouraging parents used more than twenty percent of the discussion time. In contrast, more than half of the children of high encouraging parents used up to 40 percent of the family discussion time.

HYPOTHESIS 3: EXPLORATION OF THE STRUCTURAL PROPERTIES OF A MORAL PROBLEM　Those advanced in moral reasoning see the issues involved in moral conflict in a complex way. The individual caught in a moral dilemma is viewed not simply as a violator or upholder of law or custom, but as a moral agent involved in a network of human rights and obligations, and faced with decisions of principle that must do justice to the uniqueness of the situation. As moral reasoning becomes more advanced it becomes more differentiated. Because the issues are seen more complexly, more time is needed to resolve them.

If parents at advanced stages discuss the issues in moral dilemmas at greater length, does this process in turn stimulate the child's own thinking? Cognitive conflict as a factor causing developmental change has been defined by Turiel (1967) as "an active concern with and thinking through of a problem." He suggests that it is induced when the existing cognitive equilibrium is upset, as it would be when discussants at various stages of reasoning differ over moral

TABLE 5

Mean Discussion Time for Family Triads by Parents' Moral Judgment Level and Child's Moral Judgment Level

Summary of Data:
$N = 53$
Units of Z = minutes

PARENTS' MORAL JUDGMENT LEVEL	CHILD'S MORAL JUDGMENT LEVEL			ROW MEANS:
	PRECONVENT.	CONVENT.	PRINCIPLED	
Both conventional	$N = 14$ $Z = 168$ $\bar{A}_1 = 12.0$	$N = 16$ $Z = 226$ $\bar{A}_2 = 14.1$	$N = 0$	$\bar{A}_r = 13.1$
One conventional One principled	$N = 6$ $Z = 94$ $\bar{B}_1 = 15.7$	$N = 11$ $Z = 163$ $\bar{B}_2 = 14.8$	$N = 0$	$\bar{B}_r = 15.1$
Both principled	$N = 0$	$N = 5$ $Z = 5$ $\bar{C}_2 = 16.2$	$N = 1$ $Z = 21$ $\bar{C}_3 = 21.0$	$\bar{C}_r = 17.0$

Column Means:
$$\bar{A}_c = 13.1 \qquad \bar{B}_c = 14.7 \qquad \bar{C}_c = 21.0$$

Analysis of Data:
Hypotheses:
H_0: Parental moral judgment level has no effect on length of discussion. $\bar{A}_r = 13.1$ deviation is purely due to chance.
H_1: Parental moral judgment level has an effect.
Accept H_1 if $p < .05$ (Corresponds to $t \geqslant 1.69$ for degrees of freedom $N - 1 = 29$)
$t = 2.8$ ∴ Accept H_1

choice. Turiel also suggests that it would be induced by presenting opportunity to explore the structural properties of the problem. Greater exposure, then, to the many facets of a complex moral situation should stimulate the child's cognitive resources and expedite the reorganization needed to move upward in the stage sequence. If this is the case, we should find significant differences between moral judgment groups in the amount of time they require for discussion of moral issues. Hypothesis 3 predicts that discussion time for family triads will be significantly longer when parents independently show advanced moral reasoning.

The data in Table 5 support this prediction at the .01 level of significance. There is a linear relationship between parents' combined moral judgment level and mean time of discussion over moral issues.

Since we have already seen that parents' and child's moral judgment levels are moderately related, and that more advanced parents are more encouraging of their child, we would expect more advanced children to make a greater contribution to the discussion. When we control parents' moral judgment and inspect the data in Table 5 by columns only, we can see that mean discussion time increases somewhat by moral judgment level of the child.

If we think of moral reasoning as a progression from a simpler, undifferentiated mode of thought to one of greater complexity, we can see that the more principled the reasoning of the parents the more the child contributes to the discussion as his own moral judgment level increases. So the effect on discussion time is a joint product and the stimulation comes from both sides of the family coin. As the moral reasoning of both parents and child becomes more differentiated and complex, the suggestions and counter-suggestions for resolution of a moral dilemma increase and hence, discussion time increases.

SUMMARY AND SUGGESTIONS FOR FUTURE RESEARCH

When we examined the parent–child moral judgment relationship we found it to be affected by family conditions which promote modeling in general, such as amount of involvement and warmth. We saw that children of principled but remote fathers have not yet reached a conventional level of reasoning. We then tried to chalk out the more dynamic links in the parent–child relationship by looking at encouragement of the child's participation, and allocation of time. When we looked at parental encouragement we saw that the more advanced the parents, the more likely they encouraged their child, regardless of what moral judgment level he had already attained. Our analysis of discussion time does not rule out the possibility that parents provide the moral atmosphere and if the child can learn from it, he in turn becomes a contributing member to it. Thus, movement upward in the sequence of moral stages is a dynamic interchange when it is viewed in the family context.

Our results have given us two rather gross dimensions to investigate in more detail. If exploring the structural properties of a moral problem is important for upward movement, how exactly do principled parents accomplish it besides encouraging their child and providing more time for that purpose? How well, for example, do they clarify disagreements in modes of thinking? Do they talk conventional morality to the child or not? Do they distinguish disagreement of fact from disagreement of moral structure? More microscopic analyses of family discussion will help to clarify and isolate specific components of discussions which lead to upward movement.

References

HAAN, N., SMITH M. B., and BLOCK, J. "The Moral Reasoning of Young Adults: Political-Social Behavior, Family Background and Personality Correlates," *Journal of Personality and Social Psychology*. 1969. (In press.)

HOFFMAN, M. L. and SALTZSTEIN, H. D. "Parent Discipline and the Child's Moral Development," *Journal of Personality and Social Psychology*," 1967, Vol. 5, 45–57.

KOHLBERG, L. "The Development of Children's Orientations Toward a Moral Order: I. Sequence in the Development of Moral Thought," *Vita Humana*. 1963, Vol. 6, 11–33.

———. "Moral Development," *International Encyclopedia of the Social Sciences*. New York: The Macmillan Company and the Free Press, 1968, 483–94.

———. *Stages in the Development of Moral Thought and Action*. New York: Holt, Rinehart, and Winston, 1969.

MACCOBY, E. "The Development of Moral Values and Behavior in Childhood," In J. A. Clausen (Ed.), *Socialization and Society*. Boston: Little, Brown and Company, 1968.

REST, O. "Developmental Hierarchy in Preference and Comprehension of Moral Judgment." Unpublished doctoral dissertation. University of Chicago, 1968.

TURIEL, E. "An Experimental Test of the Sequentiality of Developmental Stages in the Child's Moral Judgments," *Journal of Personality and Social Psychology*. 1966, Vol. 3, 611–18.

———. "Developmental Processes in the Child's Moral Thinking," In P. Mussen, J. Langer, and M. Covington (eds.), *New Directions in Developmental Psychology*. New York: Holt, Rinehart and Winston, 1969.

Part Five

SUMMARY

17

An Overview of Human Life and Growth

In an earlier and possibly in some ways happier time, man was considered the final and triumphant item of creation, the master and user of other living things. Even the early evolutionary biologists considered that man stood at the apex of evolution; they did not seem aware of the possibility that the process of evolution might continue, resulting in the appearance of new species. They seemed even less aware of the possibility that the evolutionary process of man resulted in a creature who had within him the seeds of his own destruction, like the sabre-toothed tiger, whose overdeveloped canine teeth prevented him from ingesting his prey.

Ecology is the branch of biology which studies the relationship of living things to their environment, including other living things. Recently ecologists have included man as the subject of their study. In general the results of their investigations have been frightening. Especially in North America man is seen as a fouler of his environment—air, water, and soil—to such an extent that ecologists say that if present trends go unchecked, man may make his continued existence impossible.

In the first article in this chapter William W. Ballard, a biologist, describes some of the facts about man's evolutionary development and speculates about the future. He makes the important distinction between man as a species and men as individuals who together make up the species. Each individual has characteristics of the species which have arisen during the course of evolution, but each individual has his own personal history, during which he has learned some ways of behaving that may be, in the long run, maladaptive for the species.

Lawrence K. Frank, the author of the second article, gave form, direction, and impetus to the field of child development. Frank's genius provided a flow of ideas for research, education, and theory. He was responsible for establishing child development centers, the parent education movement, and interdisciplinary research. In the article presented here, Frank shows his characteristic warmth and wonder while analyzing the growth processes at work in infants. He shows how the child elaborates his individuality through interaction. In the terms used by Ballard in the first article, Frank shows how the "second computer" begins, based on the beginnings of the "first computer."

Erikson and Piaget, the authors of the third and fourth selections, are also primarily concerned with the development of the "second computer." But both are explicit in their statement that their theories are based on biology. Although both are dealing with psychological material, they start from biological characteristics of man.

The epigenetic theory of Erik H. Erikson is represented by the next essay, taken from his book Identity, Youth and Crisis. An artist, teacher, and philosopher thoroughly trained in Freudian psychoanalysis, Erikson has made enormous contributions to the field of child development. His theory is built upon Freudian theory, which he extends and develops into a way of understanding and describing the healthy personality throughout life. Erikson describes stages of personality growth, showing for each one a relation of personality to bodily development and to interaction with the culture. Each stage is derived from and built upon the one preceding it. The organization of this book is shaped by Erikson's stages in childhood and adolescence. The content is influenced by his thinking.

Jean Piaget, the world-famous Swiss psychologist, is the author of the fourth piece in this section. Piaget is primarily a genetic epistemologist, a scientist-philosopher who investigates the production of knowledge. He has developed a comprehensive theory of the mental structures through which human beings build their concept of reality and deal with it. Piaget has stimulated psychological research all over the world. Americans have produced hundreds of studies in response to his theories and findings. Like Erikson's theory of personality development, Piaget's account of the growth of intelligence is epigenetic and interactional. Piaget's theory is very compatible with a child development point of view, because the child's mind is seen as resulting from biologically given beginnings, actively engaged with the environment.

In the concluding selection in this chapter, Myrtle McGraw admonishes students of child development, particularly students of the development of very young children, that those who study growth need to be aware of the complexity and interrelatedness of their subject matter. To those who make applications of research knowledge about children she makes a plea for the careful consideration of terms, the continuous viewing of the child as a multifaceted organism, and the importance of adult guidance which changes synchronously with the child's development.

The Rise and Fall of Humanity

William W. Ballard

The reading which follows is the last part of a lecture titled " The Rise and Fall of Humanity." In the first part Ballard summarizes the development of living things during the course of 4 billion years of earth history, the accelerating growth of knowledge in the last few thousand years, and the serious threats to man's continued existence which have stemmed from this knowledge. Basically, Ballard says, the present crisis has arisen because there are too many people on the earth and they are demanding more than the earth can provide. These things have happened because man as a species of animal is composed of men as individuals.

To maximize the amount of life that can be supported in a given ecosystem, a large number of species of plants, animals and decomposers are brought into

Reprinted from *Dartmouth Alumni Magazine*, 1970, 62 (6), 60–64. By permission of the author, the Dartmouth Alumni College, and the *Dartmouth Alumni Magazine*.

balance, each occupying its own niche and following its own instructions to make the best of the things available to it while contributing to the flow of energy and the recycling of materials. If one species in the ecosystem gets out of balance the whole community develops an instability that may either result in an irreversible change in its character, or in the control or rejection of the destabilizing element.

The human species has been manipulating its environment since the invention of agriculture, favoring the plants and animals that serve it for food, repressing or even exterminating others. Where this was overdone—e.g., Mesopotamia, the Near East, Yucatan—ghost cities and records of dead cultures remain to show how powerfully nature can strike back. Quite recently we have begun to use the treasure trove of fossil fuels to grow the food to satisfy the multiplying demands of our own population, and we congratulate ourselves on having temporarily freed ourselves from the normal restrictions of the natural world. It is a dangerous game we are playing.

No good asking why the human *species* takes these risks. A species is an invention of the mind, a generalization. Only human *individuals* actually walk and breathe and make decisions and it is the collection of individuals who have been doing what I say the species has been doing. What went wrong with human individuals, that they have gotten their species and their environment into such a mess? The other face of this question is, what is an individual supposed to be doing, and within what limits is he supposed to be held?

The Primary Computer   To simplify, I shall restrict the latter question to animals rather than plants or decomposers. I shall pick animals that are not on a rampage, animals that have (so far as we can tell) no conscious reasoning ability, no thoughts, loyalties, hopes or faiths. Some kind of earthworm or some frog will do. I assume that whatever one of these animals does, any choice that it makes, is determined by its inherited computer system. It receives from its ancestors a scanning mechanism which reports what all the circumstances around and inside it are at the moment. This information is checked against an inherited memory encoded in its central nervous system. The computer then not only orders up the strategy and tactics that had met that sort of situation successfully before, but directs what every cell, what every organ, what the whole earthworm or frog must be doing to contribute to that response. (Directions for unsuccessful responses are not encoded in this primary computer, because they simply are not inherited.)

To see what this genetic computer requires the individual worm or frog to do, let us follow his life history, watching him obey and reconstructing from what he does the nature of the commands.

1. As a member of a bisexual species he (or she) starts as a fertilized egg, a single diploid individual with unique heterozygous genic individuality. First, *he develops*. Since the fertilized egg is insulated to a degree from the outside world, his computer works at first mostly on internal information. It refers to the inherited memory in the chromosomes and brings out instructions of various intricate sorts to the ultrastructures of the cell, programmed so that the cell divides into two, then four, then eight cells . . . until the word gets back to the multiplied computers in the multiplied cells that it is time to activate their

inherited instructions for differentiation. Tissues and organs are formed, in such sorts and such patterns as have enabled the species to survive so far. The new individual acquires the sensory and neural apparatus for bringing in more and more information from the outside, and this is referred to the more and more specialized computer developing out of the inherited instructions, in a central nervous system (in the case of a frog, a brain and spinal cord). He begins to move about, respire, feed, excrete, defend himself, in directions and at rates calculated to be appropriate to the sensed state of affairs from moment to moment. This is quite a trick for a self-built computer to bring off, and as an embryologist I wish I understood more of how it is done.

2. The young earthworm or pollywog, having broken loose from its protective envelopes and used up its dowry of yolk, is next under orders to *reach adulthood*. He recognizes dangers and opportunities by continually referring the information flowing in from his sensory apparatus to his inherited memory. He certainly has not learned his behavioral responses from his parents, never having met them. It is the inherited computer which tells him what to do from one millisecond to the next. He survives or not, partly by luck but also partly according to whether his own inherited variant of the species-specific computer will deliver the right answers to the problems of his own day and place. (The *species* survives by offering up enough varieties so that some individuals will have what the new situations demand, the wastage of the other individuals being a necessary part of the cost. No other way has yet been discovered for meeting the demands of an unpredictable future, i.e. winning a game the rules for which have not yet been written.)

3. Our earthworm or frog, if lucky, finds himself a sexually mature individual, with his instructions to reproduce now turned on. These instructions, activated by seasonal or other environmental signals, operate upon particular genes, particular cells, particular organs, and particular behavioral mechanisms set off through the nervous system. Without knowing it, much less knowing why, the animal seeks out a mate, copulates, and shares in the production of fertilized eggs that bring us again to phase 1 of the cycle.

4. Having blindly and without thought followed his instructions to (1) develop, (2) make do, survive, gain strength, and (3) reproduce, our earthworm or frog subsequently (4) *dies*. It is the ancient law. So far as the interests of the individual are concerned, it is absurd.

But now how about man? How unique is he? Does he not learn by experience and education, manage his own life, consciously determine what jobs he shall tackle, what ends he shall serve? My argument that he too is run by an inherited computer program rests partly on the observed fact that (1) he develops, (2) he makes every effort to reach maturity, (3) if lucky enough he sets the cycle going again, and (4) he dies. There is nothing unique about that. Experience, learning, individual preferences serve only for minor embellishments.

I select one case to illustrate that an animal's program is mostly inherited. Four to six weeks after fertilization (depending on temperature) a salamander embryo will have used up its yolk and must by then have acquired an elaborate repertoire of locomotor, hunting-sensory, food-grabbing and swallowing behavior to keep itself fed and growing. Does the individual learn this behavior by trial and error? No. Starting a day before any of his muscles were mature enough to contract, you can rear him in a dilute anesthetic solution until he has reached the feeding stage. Put him back into pond water, and in twenty minutes the anesthetic will have worn off and he is swimming, hunting, grabbing and swallowing like a normal tadpole. One is seeing here the computer-controlled maturation of a computer-controlled behavior. No practice, no learning. The individual within which this remarkable apparatus matures is an expendable pawn, and the apparatus is not for his enjoyment of life, it is to keep the species going.

The Secondary Computer   There is such an inherited program in the human individual, but there is much more. The baby does not so much learn to walk as to develop the inherited capacity to walk; but then he can learn a dance that no man has ever danced before, he can paint a picture with a brush clasped between his toes. During late fetal life and his first six or eight years he gradually matures a second computer system superimposed on, controlling and almost completely masking the ancient frog-type computer. The evolutionary history of this new device is traceable back to, and in some respects beyond, the time of origin of the modern mammals 70 million or more years ago. It has progressed farthest in particular mammalian orders—the carnivores, hoofed animals, bats, whales and primates, and least in the egg-laying mammals and marsupials.

The new trend has worked certain real advantages, and has been kept under reasonable control, in the higher mammals, but it is my strong suspicion that its over-development in man is the root of our trouble. Like the dinosaurs, we contain in our own structure the reason why we will have to go. Robinson Jeffers[1] said it: "We have minds like the fangs of those forgotten tigers, hypertrophied and terrible."

Up to a point, the development of brain and spinal cord follows the same course in frog and man. Sense organs, cranial and spinal nerves, principal subdivisions of the brain, basic fiber tract systems, all form in strictly comparable fashion in both. But the adult human brain is a far different thing from the adult frog brain. It continues the multiplication and interconnection of neurons during a far longer growth period, and adds to the elementary or frog-type apparatus two principal complicating tissues that far overshadow the earlier developments. One is often called reticular substance, the other is the cerebral cortex.

The reticular substance is so called because it is an interweaving of small centers of gray substance with short bundles and interspersed mats of axons (the white substance), quite different from the simple contrast between gray and white substance seen in primitive animals and in early embryos. The frog brain is not without this sort of tissue, but in the brains of advanced vertebrates like the teleost fishes, the reptiles and the birds, it becomes indescribably complex. The modern mammals push this development to still higher orders of magnitude.

Although neurological science is not yet ready with answers to most specific questions about what happens where in the central nervous system, the

---

[1] R. Jeffers, "Passenger Pigeons," in *The Beginning and the End*.

new techniques of exploration within the brain suggest that in and through the reticular substance the connections for integrating sensory information with the devices for evaluation and for making decisions and coordinated responses are multiplied exponentially.

Thus, an electrode planted within a single neuron in the reticular substance of the hindbrain can give startling evidence that this one cell is receiving and reacting to sensations reported from widely scattered parts of the body, and sending out coded pulses as a calculated response. Your own brain contains hundreds of millions, probably billions of such cells, every one individually a computer.

The neurologists can now stimulate chosen localized areas through implanted electrodes, either hooked up to wires dangling from the cage ceiling or activated through miniaturized transmitters healed in under the scalp and controlled by radio transmission. In such experiments, stimuli delivered to many parts of the reticular substance cause the animal to react as though he were flooded with agreeable sensation. If the cat or rat or monkey learns how to deliver the stimulus to himself by pressing a pedal, he will do so repeatedly and rapidly, until he falls asleep exhausted. As soon as he wakes up, he goes to pounding the pedal again.

There are other reticular areas which have the reverse effect. If the stimulus comes at rhythmical intervals and the animal discovers that he can forestall it by pressing the pedal, he quickly learns to regulate his life so as to be there and step on it just in time. What kind of sensation such a stimulus produces in him can only be guessed by the experimenter. One might suppose that these areas of reticular substance which have such opposite effects are there to add into the computer's analysis of the situation at the moment a go signal or a stop signal for particular alternative choices, or a sense of goodness or badness, satisfaction or distress, urgency or caution, danger or relaxation. A value judgment, in other words.

It is not difficult to see the survival value of such a device. No doubt the basic mechanism exists in the brains of fishes and frogs, though I am not aware that experiments have been done to locate it. In the reticular substance of mammals, however, we see it hugely developed. The result of overdoing this might produce an awareness of the good and bad features of so very many facets of a situation as to delay and perplex the individual in calculating his single coordinated response.

Mammals are also conspicuously good at remembering experiences from their own lives as individuals, and these memories are loaded with value judgments. There is still no clear answer as to where or in what coded form these new personal memories are stored. But an animal with all this added to the ancestral memory, enhanced with perhaps casually acquired and unwisely generalized connotations of goodness and badness, might predictably be endowed with excessive individuality, prone to unnecessarily variable behavior, chosen more often for self-satisfaction than in the interest of species survival.

The other evolutionary development, the formation of the cerebral cortex, is almost unknown in vertebrates other than mammals, and is feeble in some of these. Cerebral cortex is a tissue of awesome complexity, and our techniques for analyzing what happens in it are still highly inadequate. Stimulation of willing human subjects, in chosen spots exposed surgically, or radio stimulation of these areas through permanently installed electrodes operated by healed-in transistor devices, evoke feelings referred to a particular part of the body, or cause normal-appearing localized movements, e.g. the flexion of an arm or a finger, time and again, upon repetition of the signal. Other areas produce more generalized sensory or motor or emotional or physiologic effects. The patient, his brain exposed under local anesthesia, does not know when the stimulus is applied. When the electrode touches a particular spot of his cortex he may report that he is suddenly remembering a scene identifiable as to time and place, but the memory blacks out when the current is off. Stimulation of other areas may elicit emotions of sexual attraction or anxiety or rage graded according to the intensity of the signal.

More wide-ranging experiments with cats, monkeys or barnyard stock, singly or in groups, free to move in large caged areas, show the possibility of turning on and off a great range of complex emotions, behavior, and even personality traits, by local stimulation.[2] The effect produced through a permanently planted electrode is area specific. Though not predictable before the first stimulus is given, the response is repeated with each stimulus, many times a day or over periods of months or years.

In subjective comparison of mammals with greater or less personal individuality one gets the impression that the degrees of freedom of choice, of imaginative recognition of possible ways to react to situations, of storage capacity and retentiveness of memory, and the richness of association, are correlated with the intricacy and amount of the cerebral cortex and reticular substance. Animals highest on both scales include porpoises, elephants, cats and dogs, apes, and people.

One cannot underestimate the effects on the human species of other evolutionary trends that came to a climax in us, for instance the development of upright posture that frees the hands, the reshaping of the fingers for grasping and manipulating, the perfection of binocular vision that can bring into focus either the hands or the far distance at will. Far more significant than these was the development of speech, made possible by and controlled in a particular small area of the new cerebral cortex. This expanded the powers of the human secondary computer by orders of magnitude, even in comparison with that of close relatives like apes.

We no longer communicate with each other by baring teeth, raising hackles and flaunting rumps, but in symbolic language. We can make abstractions and generalizations and artificial associations. Through speech we can feed into the recording apparatus of each other's secondary computers not only the vast and rather accidental store of individually acquired and long-lasting memories of our own experience, but also the loads of approval or disapproval which we deliberately or unwittingly put upon them. We increasingly remove ourselves into created worlds of our own, calculating our choices by reference to a memory bank of second-hand ghosts of other people's experiences and feelings, prettied up or uglified with value judgments picked up who knows where, by whom, for what reason.

[2] J. M. R. Delgado, 1969, *Physical Control of the Mind.*

Language gave a fourth dimension to the powers of the secondary computer, and writing a fifth dimension. We can now convince each other that things are good or bad, acceptable or intolerable, merely by agreeing with each other, or by reciting catechisms. With writing we can color the judgments of people unborn, just as our judgments are tailored to the whim of influential teachers in the past.

Symbols have given us the means to attach a value judgment to some abstract noun, some shibboleth, and transfer this by association to any person or situation at will. We invent, we practice, we delight in tricks for saying things indirectly by poetry and figures of speech, that might sound false or trite or slanderous or nonsensical if we said them directly. A more normally constructed animal, a porpoise or an elephant, mercifully spared such subtleties, might well look at human beings and see that each one of us has become to some degree insane, out of touch with the actual world, pursuing a mad course of options in the imagined interest of self rather than of species.

The primary computer is still there, programmed in the interest of species survival. With his new powers, man should do better than any other animal at understanding the present crisis and generating an appropriate strategy and tactics. Instead, the effort is drowned out in the noise, the flicker-bicker, the chattering flood of directives from the personalized secondary computer. In pursuit of his own comfort and his own pleasure, man wars against his fellows and against the good earth.

The frame of each person is like a racing shell with two oarsmen in it, back to back, rowing in opposite directions. The one represents the ancient computer system, comparing the personal situation of the moment with an inherited value system and driving the person to perform in such a way that the species will survive, irrespective of how absurd his own expendable life may be. The other represents the secondary computer system, probably located in reticular substance and cerebral cortex, surveying chiefly the memories of childhood and adult life, and deciding how to act according to the value-loaded store of personal experience.

It is this runaway evolutionary development of our superimposed second computer that has produced our inventors, our artists, our saints and heroes, our poets, our thinkers. Our love and hate, ecstasy and despair. The infinite variety of human personalities. It has also atomized the species into a cloud of ungovernable individuals. We split our elections 48 to 52, make laws to break them, and either ignore community priorities or establish them by political blind-man's-buff in frivolous disregard of real emergencies. Six experts will come violently to six different decisions on how to meet a crisis because their personal histories lead them to weight the same data differently. Each of us can see bad logic and conflicts of interest affecting the judgment of most of our associates; it is more difficult to detect them in ourselves. Our individually acquired prejudices have been built into our secondary computers.

Yet it is a glorious thing to feel the uniqueness, the power of decision, the freedom of being human. Who would prefer to be even so wonderful a creature as a dog, an elephant, a horse, a porpoise? I believe nevertheless that just this ungovernable power of the human individual, the essence of our humanity, is the root of our trouble.

The California biologist Garrett Hardin, in a famous essay called "The Tragedy of the Commons," showed that this accounts for practically all the facets of our apocalyptic crisis, from the population explosion to runaway technology.[3] He is referring to the community pasture where anyone may feed his animals. Overgrazing will bring erosion and irreversible deterioration in it. Each herdsman, calculating the advantage and disadvantage to himself of putting out one more animal to graze, balancing his small share of the possible damage against his sole ownership of the extra income, adds another animal in his own interest, and another, and another. All do, and all lose together. The tragedy is the inescapable disaster when each herdsman pursues his own advantage without limit, in a limited commons. This is the tragedy that leaves us with too many human mouths to feed, soil impoverished and washed or blown away, forests skinned off, lakes ruined, plastic bottles and aluminum cans scattered over the countryside, rivers clogged with dead fish, bilge oil spreading on public waters, streets and highways made obscene with advertisements. It is what gives us choking smog, the stink and corruption below paper mills and slaughter houses, the draining of one well by another in a falling water table, the sneaking of radioactive wastes into the air and the oceans.

All these, Hardin makes clear, are problems with *no technological solution*. To be sure, the technology stands ready, but the trouble starts with some individual, you, me, whose response to a situation is to give highest priority to his personal chance of profit, or his family's, or his country's. He has a vivid sense of the value to himself of his own freedom, but the total effects of all such freedoms on the species and on the natural world which supports it is invisible or far out of focus. The technology might just as well not exist.

Some of these problems that will not be solved by technology alone can indeed be brought under control by compacts, treaties, and other agreements between willing groups, or by laws imposed by the majority upon a minority in the common interest. Hardin, however, puts the finger on the population problem as the worst example of the worst class of problems, in which all of us must restrict the freedom of all of us, when none of us want to. He is properly skeptical of conscience or altruism as forces for uniting the community when nearly all of us are still daring to gamble on the continued capacity of the commons to withstand collapse. What is needed, he says, is a fundamental extension of morality.

My way of agreeing with him is to say that human nature is our chief enemy because the species-preserving function of our primary computer has not yet been built into the secondary computer which generates our human nature. It is by now clear that our nature as individuals is not so much inherited as learned by babies as they grow into people, in and from their individual, accidental and culture-bound experiences. We need to incorporate into the decision-making apparatus that will really control them a new survival morality, a system of values the principal axiom of which is that anything which threatens the welfare of the species is bad, anything that serves to bring the species into harmony with its environment is good. We must, each of us, because of this inner drive, regulate our numbers and our selfish wants as rigorously as the

[3] G. Hardin, 1968, *Science* 162: 1243. The Tragedy of the Commons.

forces of natural selection would have done had we not learned how to set them aside.

Do we know how to create a human nature that can keep the species going without undue sacrifice of the privilege and joy of being human? How much freedom must we give up? Do we want to? Is there time?

Basic Processes in Organisms

Lawrence K. Frank

If we are to understand the infant as a persistent, but ever changing, organism, we need to think in terms that are dynamic, which calls for a recognition of the ongoing processes by which the infant grows, develops, matures and ages while continually functioning and behaving. As a young mammalian organism, the human infant lives by much the same basic physiological processes as other mammals.

The recognition of process has come with the acceptance of such recently formulated conceptions as that of self-organization, self-stabilization, self-repair and self-direction which are characteristic not only of organisms but of various man-made machines such as computers and systems designed to operate a planned sequence of activities with the use of positive and negative feedbacks. (Wiener 1961; Von Foerster and Zopf 1962). The organism may be said to be "programmed" by its heredity but capable of flexible functioning through the life cycle.

Moreover, it must be re-emphasized that each infant differs to a greater or lesser extent from all other infants, exhibiting not only individual variation but also displaying a considerable range of intra-individual variability, or continually changing functioning and physiological states, especially during the early months of life when the infant is not yet fully organized or capable of adequate self-stabilization.

Since most of our knowledge of infancy and childhood is derived from observations and measurements of selected variables, responses to stimuli, at a given time or a succession of times, we do not gain an adequate conception of the continuous, dynamic processes of living organisms, especially since we tend to focus upon the outcomes, without recognizing the processes which produce them. Accordingly, some account of these basic processes and how they operate may provide a conceptual model for understanding the multidimensional development of infants during the first year of life. Whatever is done to and for the infant, what privations, frustrations and deprivations he may suffer, what demands and coercions he must accept, what spontaneous activity and learning he displays, may be viewed as expressions of his basic functioning processes.

Every experience in the life of an infant evokes some alteration in these organic processes whereby he manages not only to survive but to grow and develop, to learn while carrying on his incessant intercourse with the surrounding world. Thus, by focusing on the organic processes we may discover what is taking place when we speak of adjustment, learning, adaptation, and the transitions encountered at critical stages in his development.

The concept of mechanism indicates or implies a deterministic relationship between antecedent and consequent, usually as a *linear* relationship in which the consequent is proportional to the antecedent. The concept of *process* involves a dynamic, *non-linear* operation, whereby the same process, depending upon where, when, how, and in what quantities or intensities it operates, may produce different products which may be all out of proportion to that which initiates or touches off the process. For example the process of fertilization and gestation operates in all mammals to produce the immense variety of mammalian young. But different processes may produce similar or equivalent products, an operation which has been called "equifinality" by Bertalanffy (1950).

A brief discussion of the six basic processes operating in organisms will indicate how the infant organism is able to persist and survive by continually changing and is thereby able to cope with the particular version of infant care and rearing to which he is subjected.

These six processes are: The Growth Process, The Organizing Process, The Communicating Process, The Stabilizing Process, The Directive or Purposive Process and The Creative Process. (Frank 1963.)

The Growth Process   The infant who has been growing since conception continues, with a brief interruption and often some loss of weight, to grow incrementally, adding gradually to his size and weight. His growth may be slowed down by inadequate or inappropriate feeding, by some difficulties in digesting and assimilating whatever foodstuff he be given, or by a variety of disturbances and dysfunctions. A continuing upward trend in weight is expected as an expression of normal development, although recent cautions have been expressed on the undesirability of too rapid increase in weight and the vulnerability of a fat, waterlogged infant.

This incremental growth in size and weight indicates that the infant is maintaining an excess of growth over the daily losses through elimination of urine and feces, through skin and lungs, and also in the replacement of many cells that are discarded. Thus, millions of blood corpuscles are destroyed and replaced each day, the iron of those destroyed being salvaged and reused. Likewise, cells of the skin and lining of the gastrointestinal tract, of the lungs, kidneys, liver, indeed of almost all organ systems, except the central nervous system and brain, are continually being replaced at different rates.

Probably more vitally significant but less clearly recognized is the continual replacement of the chemical constituents of cells, tissues and bony structures, like the skeleton and the teeth in which different chemicals are discarded and new materials are selected out of the blood stream to replace them. Here we see a dramatic illustration of the statement that an organism is a configuration which must continually change in order to survive, a conception which is wholly congruous with the recently formulated assumption of the world as an aggregate of highly organized complexes of energy transformations.

Growth, incremental and replacement, is a major functioning process, gradually producing an enlarging infant as the growing cells differentiate, specialize and organize to give rise to the varied tissues and organ systems in the developing embryo and fetus. In this prenatal development the creative process is also operating to produce the unique, unduplicated human infant along with the operation of the organizing process.

The Organizing Process   Only recently has the process of self-organization been recognized in scientific thinking as basic to all organisms which start with some kind of genetic inheritance and undergo multiplication and duplication of cells with differentiation and specialization of components that become organized into a living organism. (Von Foerster and Zopf 1962.) Thus the initial development of an infant takes place through the operation of the growth and the organizing processes which continue to operate throughout its life, maintaining the organism as it undergoes various transitions and transformations and copes with the many discontinuities encountered in its life cycle.

Since the normal infant arrives fully equipped with all the essential bodily components and organ systems, the growth process and the organizing process operate to incorporate the intakes of food, water and air into its ever changing structure-functioning. Most of the highly organized foodstuffs, proteins, fats and carbohydrates, are progressively broken down, disorganized and randomized, and the products of these digestive operations are then circulated through the blood stream from which the constituent cells, tissues and fluids select out what they need for metabolism and organize these into their specialized structure-functioning components. The recent dramatic findings in molecular biology show how this organizing process operates within the cell as the DNA (the carrier of the genetic information) of the genes directs the production of the various proteins and the utilization of the minerals and vitamins for the growth and multiplication of cells and the maintenance of their functioning.

Also of large significance for the understanding of organic processes are the sequential steps in the utilization of food stuffs for metabolism involving many steps and numerous specialized enzymes and catalysts. Unfortunately some infants suffer from so-called metabolic errors when one or more of these steps in the metabolic sequence is missing or inadequate and therefore his growth and development and healthy functioning are jeopardized.

In the self-organizing organism we encounter circular and reciprocal operations in which every component of the organism by its specialized functioning, gives rise to, and maintains, the total organism of which it is a participant; concurrently, the total organism reciprocally governs when, what and how each of these components must function and operate to maintain the organized whole. This capacity for self-organizing arises from the autonomy of each component of an organism which over millions of years of evolution has developed its own highly individualized and specialized functioning within the total organic complex but functions according to the requirements of the organism in which it operates.

Communication Process   Obviously, these autonomous components which give rise to growth and organization must continually communicate, internally and with the external "surround." The infant has an inherited communication network in his nervous system, his circulatory system, and his lymphatic system. Through these several channels every constituent of an organism continually communicates with all others, directly or indirectly, and with different degrees of speed in communication. Each component continually sends and receives messages whereby its functioning operations are regulated, synchronized, articulated and related to all others, with greater or less immediacy. The infant is born with most of these internal communications already functioning, having been in operation for varying periods of its prenatal development but with the central nervous system still immature. The infant also has the sensory apparatus for various inputs, of light, of sound, touch, taste and smell, also for pain, heat and cold, and for gravity and for atmospheric pressure changes. But the infant is also initially prepared for dealing with the varying intensities and durations of these intakes and impacts, gradually increasing his capacity for filtering, buffering, mingling and transducing these inputs whereby he may monitor these sensory communications according to his ever changing internal, physiological states and the kinesthetic and proprioceptive messages by which he continually orients himself and gradually achieves an equilibrium in space.

The infant must carry on this incessant intercourse with the world more or less protected by adults from too severe or hazardous impacts and provided with the food and care required by his helpless dependency. But the infant often must try to defend himself from what his caretakers try to impose on him or compel him to accept, as in feeding, toilet training, etc. Under this treatment much of the infant's energies may be expended in these efforts to maintain his stability and integrity against unwelcomed and uncongenial treatment which may interfere with his normal functioning and compromise his growth and development and learning as a unique organism. Thus we may say that the growth and organizing processes contribute to and are dependent upon the communication process, which operates through the inherited receptors of the infant which may become progressively altered, refined, and increasingly sensitized through learning. Quite early the infant may become receptive to nonverbal communications such as tones of voice, smiling, tactile comforting, or painful treatment.

Stabilizing Process   Since the world presents so many different and continually varying messages and impacts, organisms must be able to cope with the ever changing flux of experience and maintain their integrity and functional capacities by monitoring all their organic functions. While all other organisms have evolved with their species-specific range of sensory awareness and capacity for perception and for living in their ancestral life zones, the human infant, and a few other mammals are able to live in a wide variety of climates and habitations and maintain their internal world within fairly close limitations upon intra-organic variability. This becomes possible through the operation of the stabilizing process.

The stabilizing process operates through a network of physiological feedbacks, both negative and positive, to maintain a dynamic equilibrium and is not limited to the concept of homeostasis which Cannon used to describe the maintenance of the fluid internal environment. The stabilizing process maintains continually changing physiological states. At birth it is not fully developed or operationally effective and hence the infant needs continual care, protection, and appropriate nutrition. But as he grows and develops he increasingly regulates his internal functioning by responding appropriately to the various inputs and outputs, intakes, and outlets. Obviously an infant who must grow, both incrementally and by replacement, cannot tolerate too stable an internal environment which might prevent or limit such growth and adaptive functioning. With his increasing exposure to the world the infant learns to calibrate all his sensory inputs and increasingly to "equalize his thresholds," as Kurt Goldstein (1939) has pointed out.

Not the least significant and often stressful experience under which an infant must maintain his internal stability are the varying practices of child care and feeding, the efforts of parents to regularize his functioning and compel him to conform to whatever regimen of living they wish to establish. Clearly the stabilizing process is essential to the infant's survival and to his continuing growth and development and the variety of learning which he must master. Happily, most infants achieve a progressive enlargement of their capacity for living and for self-regulation and self-stabilization to assume an autonomy expressing their integrity in the face of often uncongenial treatment and surroundings.

The Directive or Purposive Process   With the achievement of motor co-ordination and locomotion, by creeping and crawling, and then assuming an erect posture and learning to walk, the infant enlarges the purposive or goal seeking process which involves continual scanning, probing and exploring the world and developing his selective awareness and patterned perception, and especially the ability to ignore or to reject what may interfere or distract him in his endeavor to attain remote or deferred goals. Obviously, the purposive process cannot operate effectively until the infant has achieved a considerable degree of internal stabilization and of neuro-muscular coordination, and the ability to cope with a three dimensional, spatial world.

Since the child initially is attracted or impelled by whatever he may become aware of or has an impulse to seek, to handle, to put into his mouth, or otherwise to manipulate, the purposive process is frequently blocked and the child may be severely punished in his attempts to develop his autonomous mastery of his small world. Thus the purposive process operates differentially in each infant who is likely to be attracted by and responsive to different dimensions of his environment at different times; these early explorations provide an endless sequence of learning experiences which involve, not only the actual world of nature, but the wide range of artifacts and of highly individuated personalities with whom he is in contact. With language the infant learns to deal with people and verbal symbols of language for goal seeking.

The Creative Process   As noted earlier, the creative process begins to operate early in gestation to produce a unique infant as a human organism with the same basic organic functions and similar or equivalent components which, however, are different in each infant. From birth on, therefore, each infant is engaged in creating a highly selective environment or a "life space" that is as congenial and appropriate for his individualized organism, with its peculiar needs and capacities, as is possible under the constraints and coercions imposed by others upon his growth, development, functioning, and learning. In infancy and childhood the individual is more creative than in any other period in his life cycle, but this creativity may be either ignored or discouraged by those who are intent upon making the child conform as nearly as possible to their image or ideal of attainment.

Within recent years the purposive and creative processes have become major foci in the studies of early child growth, development and education, but it must be remembered that the purposive and creative processes cannot operate independently because they are inextricably related to and dependent upon the other four basic processes which reciprocally contribute to the operation of these two processes.

Most of the training and education of the infant and young child involves curbing, regulating, focusing, and patterning, and also evoking the communicating and stabilizing and directive processes which are more amenable to intervention and control by others. Through supervision and regulation of these processes the child is largely molded, patterned, and oriented into the kind of organism-personality favored by his parents and appropriately prepared for living in his cultural and social order. As he grows older the infant is expected to learn the required conduct for group living and to master the various symbol systems by which he can relate cognitively to the world and negotiate with other people. It appears that learning as an expression of the purposive and the creative processes may be compromised and sometimes severely distorted or blocked when the child is expected or compelled to alter the organizing, communicating, and stabilizing processes, as required by his parents and other more experienced persons.

In the discussion of humanization we will see how the young mammalian organism is transformed into a personality for living in a symbolic cultural world and for participating in a social order, through the various practices of infant care and rearing that are focused upon, and directly intervene in, the operation of these six basic organic processes. But each infant is a highly individualized organism who develops his own idiosyncratic personality through the development and utilization of his basic organic processes.

Bibliography

BERTALANFFY, L. VON, "Theory of Open Systems in Physics and Biology," *Science*, CXI, 1950, pp. 27–29. See also Yearbooks of Society for General Systems Research.

FRANK, L. K., "Human Development—An Emerging Discipline," in *Modern Perspectives in Child Development*, In honor of Milton J. E. Senn, Eds. Albert J. Solnit and Sally Provence, New York: International Universities Press, 1963.

———. "Potentiality: Its Definition and Development," in *Insights and the Curriculum*, Yearbook, Association for Supervision and Curriculum Development, Washington, D.C.: National Education Association, 1963.

GOLDSTEIN, KURT, *The Organism*, New York: American Book Company, 1939.

VON FOERSTER, HEINZ, and ZOPF, JR., GEORGE W., Eds., *Principles of Self Organizing Systems*, London: Pergamon Press, 1962.

WIENER, NORBERT, *Cybernetics*, Cambridge and New York: M.I.T. Press and John Wiley and Sons, Inc., 1961.

The Life Cycle: Epigenesis of Identity

Erik H. Erikson
HARVARD UNIVERSITY

Whenever we try to understand growth, it is well to remember the *epigenetic principle* which is derived from the growth of organisms *in utero*. Somewhat generalized, this principle states that anything that grows has a ground plan, and that out of this ground plan the parts arise, each part having its time of special ascendancy, until all parts have arisen to form a functioning whole. This, obviously, is true for fetal development where each part of the organism has its critical time of ascendance or danger of defect. At birth the baby leaves the chemical exchange of the womb for the social exchange system of his society, where his gradually increasing capacities meet the opportunities and limitations of his culture. How the maturing organism continues to unfold, not by developing new organs but by means of a prescribed sequence of locomotor, sensory, and social capacities, is described in the child-development literature. As pointed out, psychoanalysis has given us an understanding of the more idiosyncratic experiences, and especially the inner conflicts, which constitute the manner in which an individual becomes a distinct personality. But here, too, it is important to realize that in the sequence of his most personal experiences the healthy child, given a reasonable amount of proper guidance, can be trusted to obey inner laws of development, laws which create a succession of potentialities for significant interaction with those persons who tend and respond to him and those institutions which are ready for him. While such interaction varies from culture to culture, it must remain within "the proper rate and the proper sequence" which governs all epigenesis. Personality, therefore, can be said to develop according to steps predetermined in the human organism's readiness to be driven toward, to be aware of, and to interact with a widening radius of significant individuals and institutions.

It is for this reason that, in the presentation of stages in the development of the personality, we employ an epigenetic diagram analogous to the one employed in *Childhood and Society* for an analysis of Freud's psychosexual stages.[1] It is, in fact, an implicit purpose of this presentation to bridge the theory of infantile sexuality (without repeating it here in detail) and our knowledge of the child's physical and social growth.

In Diagram 1 the double-lined squares signify both a sequence of stages and a gradual development of component parts. In other words, the diagram formalizes a progression through time of a differentiation of parts. This indicates (1) that each item of the vital personality to be discussed is systematically related to all others, and that they all depend on the proper development in the proper sequence of each item; and (2) that each item exists in some form before "its" decisive and critical time normally arrives.

Reprinted from *Identity, Youth and Crisis*, Copyright © 1968 by W. W. Norton & Company, Inc., pp. 92–96. By permission.

[1] See Erik H. Erikson, *Childhood and Society*, 2nd ed., New York: W. W. Norton, 1963, Part I.

DIAGRAM 1

	1	2	3	4	5	6	7	8
VIII								INTEGRITY vs. DESPAIR
VII							GENERATIVITY vs. STAGNATION	
VI						INTIMACY vs. ISOLATION		
V	Temporal Perspective vs. Time Confusion	Self-Certainty vs. Self-Consciousness	Role Experimentation vs. Role Fixation	Apprenticeship vs. Work Paralysis	IDENTITY vs. IDENTITY CONFUSION	Sexual Polarization vs. Bisexual Confusion	Leader- and Followership vs. Authority Confusion	Ideological Commitment vs. Confusion of Values
IV				INDUSTRY vs. INFERIORITY	Task Identification vs. Sense of Futility			
III			INITIATIVE vs. GUILT		Anticipation of Roles vs. Role Inhibition			
II		AUTONOMY vs. SHAME, DOUBT			Will to Be Oneself vs. Self-Doubt			
I	TRUST vs. MISTRUST				Mutual Recognition vs. Autistic Isolation			

If I say, for example, that a sense of basic trust is the first component of mental vitality to develop in life, a sense of autonomous will the second, and a sense of initiative the third, the diagram expresses a number of fundamental relations that exist among the three components, as well as a few fundamental facts for each.

Each comes to its ascendance, meets its crisis, and finds its lasting solution in ways to be described here, toward the end of the stages mentioned. All of them exist in the beginning in some form, although we do not make a point of this fact, and we shall not confuse things by calling these components different names at earlier or later stages. A baby may show something like "autonomy" from the beginning, for example, in the particular way in which he angrily tries to wriggle his hand free when tightly held. However, under normal conditions, it is not until the second year that he begins to experience the whole critical alternative between being an autonomous creature and being a dependent one, and it is not until then that he is ready for a specifically new encounter with his environment. The environment, in turn, now feels called upon to convey to him its particular ideas and concepts of autonomy in ways decisively contributing to his personal character, his relative efficiency, and the strength of his vitality.

It is this encounter, together with the resulting crisis, which is to be described for each stage. Each stage becomes a crisis because incipient growth and awareness in a new part function go together with a shift in instinctual energy and yet also cause a specific vulnerability in that part. One of the most difficult questions to decide, therefore, is whether or not a child at a given stage is weak or strong. Perhaps it would be best to say that he is always vulnerable in some respects and completely oblivious and insensitive in others, but that at the same time he is unbelievably persistent in the same respects in which he is vulnerable. It must be added that the baby's weakness gives him power; out of his very dependence and weakness he makes signs to which his environment, if it is guided well by a responsiveness combining "instinctive" and traditional patterns, is peculiarly sensitive. A baby's presence exerts a consistent and persistent domination over the outer and inner lives of every member of a household. Because these members must reorient themselves to accommodate his presence, they must also grow as individuals and as a group. It is as true to say that babies control and bring up their families as it is to say the converse. A family can bring up a baby only by being brought up by him. His growth consists of a series of challenges to them to serve his newly developing potentialities for social interaction.

Each successive step, then, is a potential crisis because of a radical change in perspective. Crisis is used here in a developmental sense to connote not a threat of catastrophe, but a turning point, a crucial period of increased vulnerability and heightened potential, and therefore, the ontogenetic source of generational strength and maladjustment. The most radical change of all, from intrauterine to extrauterine life, comes at the very beginning of life. But in postnatal existence, too, such radical adjustments of perspective as lying relaxed, sitting firmly, and running fast must all be accomplished in their own good time. With them, the interpersonal perspective also changes rapidly and often radically, as is testified by the proximity in time of such opposites as "not letting mother out of sight" and "wanting to be independent." Thus, different capacities use different opportunities to become full-grown components of the ever-new configuration that is the growing personality.

Equilibrium

Jean Piaget
UNIVERSITY OF GENEVA

The psychological development that starts at birth and terminates in adulthood is comparable to organic growth. Like the latter, it consists essentially of activity directed toward equilibrium. Just as the body evolves toward a relatively stable level characterized by the completion of the growth process and by organ maturity, so mental life can be conceived as evolving toward a final form of equilibrium represented by the adult mind. In a sense, development is a progressive equilibration from a lesser to a higher state of equilibrium. From the point of view of intelligence, it is easy to contrast the relative instability and incoherence of childhood ideas with the systematization of adult reason. With respect to the affective life, it has frequently been noted how extensively emotional equilibrium increases with age. Social relations also obey the same law of gradual stabilization.

An essential difference between the life of the body and that of the mind must nonetheless be stressed if the dynamism inherent in the reality of the mind is to be respected. The final form of equilibrium reached through organic growth is more static and, above all, more unstable than the equilibrium toward which mental development strives, so that no sooner has ascending evolution terminated than a regressive evolution automatically starts, leading to old age. Certain psychological functions that depend closely on the physical condition of the body follow an analogous curve. Visual acuity, for example, is at a maximum toward the end of childhood, only to diminish subsequently; and many other perceptual processes are regulated by the same law. By contrast, the higher functions of intelligence and affectivity tend toward a "mobile equilibrium." The more mobile it is, the more stable it is, so that the termination of growth, in healthy minds, by no means marks the beginning of decline but rather permits progress that in no sense contradicts inner equilibrium.

It is thus in terms of equilibrium that we shall try to describe the evolution of the child and the adolescent. From this point of view, mental development is a continuous construction comparable to the erection of a vast building that becomes more solid with each addition. Alternatively, and perhaps more appropriately, it may be likened to the assembly of a subtle mechanism that goes through gradual phases of adjustment in which the individual pieces become more supple and mobile as the equilibrium of the mechanism as a whole becomes more stable. We must, however, introduce an important distinction between two complementary aspects of the process of equilibration. This is the distinction between the variable structures that define the successive states of equilibrium and a certain constant functioning that assures the transition from any one state to the following one.

There is sometimes a striking similarity between the reactions of the child and the adult, as, for example, when the child is sure of what he wants and acts as adults do with respect to their own special interests. At other times there is a world of difference—in games, for example, or in the manner of reasoning. From a functional point of view, i.e., if we take into consideration the general motives of behavior and thought, there are constant functions common to all ages. At all levels of development, action presupposes a precipitating factor: a physiological, affective, or intellectual need. (In the latter case, the need appears in the guise of a question or a problem.) At all levels, intelligence seeks to understand or explain, etc. However, while the functions of interest, explanation, etc., are common to all developmental stages, that is to say, are "invariable" as far as the functions themselves are concerned, it is nonetheless true that "interests" (as opposed to "interest") vary considerably from one mental level to another, and that the particular explanations (as opposed to the function of explaining) are of a very different nature, depending on the degree of intellectual development. In addition to the constant functions, there are the variable structures. An analysis of these progressive forms of successive equilibrium highlights the differences from one behavioral level to another, all the way from the elementary behavior of the neonate through adolescence.

The variable structures—motor or intellectual on the one hand and affective on the other—are the organizational forms of mental activity. They are organized along two dimensions—intrapersonal and social (interpersonal). For greater clarity we shall distinguish six stages or periods of development which mark the appearance of these successively constructed structures:

1. The reflex or hereditary stage, at which the first instinctual nutritional drives and the first emotions appear.

2. The stage of the first motor habits and of the first organized percepts, as well as of the first differentiated emotions.

3. The stage of sensorimotor or practical intelligence (prior to language), of elementary affective organization, and of the first external affective fixations. These first three stages constitute the infancy period—from birth till the age of one and a half to two years—i.e., the period prior to the development of language and thought as such.

4. The stage of intuitive intelligence, of spontaneous interpersonal feelings, and of social relationships in which the child is subordinate to the adult (ages two to seven years, or "early childhood").

5. The stage of concrete intellectual operations (the beginning of logic) and of moral and social feelings of cooperation (ages seven to eleven or twelve, or "middle childhood").

6. The stage of abstract intellectual operations, of the formation of the personality, and of affective and intellectual entry into the society of adults (adolescence).

Each of these stages is characterized by the appearance of original structures whose construction distinguishes it from previous stages. The essentials of these successive constructions exist at subsequent stages in the form of substructures onto which new characteristics have been built. It follows that in the adult each stage through which he has passed corresponds to a given level in the total hierarchy of behavior. But at each stage there are also temporary and secondary characteristics that are modified by subsequent development as a function of the need for better organization. Each stage thus constitutes a particular form of equilibrium as a function of its characteristic structures, and mental evolution is effectuated in the direction of an ever-increasing equilibrium.

We know which functional mechanisms are common to all stages. In an absolutely general way (not only in comparing one stage with the following but also in comparing each item of behavior that is part of that stage with ensuing behavior), one can say that all action—that is to say, all movement, all thought, or all emotion—responds to a need. Neither the child nor the adult executes any external or even entirely internal act unless impelled by a motive; this motive can always be translated into a need (an elementary need, an interest, a question, etc.).

As Claparède (1951) has shown, a need is always a manifestation of disequilibrium: there is need when something either outside ourselves or within us (physically or mentally) is changed and behavior has to be adjusted as a function of this change. For example, hunger or fatigue will provoke a search for nourishment or rest; encountering an external object will lead to a need to play, which in turn has practical ends, or it leads to a question or a theoretical problem. A casual word will excite the need to imitate, to sympathize, or will engender reserve or opposition if it conflicts with some interest of our own. Conversely, action terminates when a need is satisfied, that is to say, when equilibrium is re-established between the new factor that has provoked the need and the mental organization that existed prior to the introduction of this factor. Eating or sleeping, playing or reaching a goal, replying to a question or resolving a problem, imitating successfully, establishing an affective tie, or maintaining one's point of view are all satisfactions that, in the preceding examples, will put an end to the particular behavior aroused by the need. At any given moment, one can thus say, action is disequilibrated by the transformations that arise in the external or internal world, and each new behavior consists not only in re-establishing equilibrium but also in moving toward a more stable equilibrium than that which preceded the disturbance.

Human action consists of a continuous and perpetual mechanism of readjustment or equilibration. For this reason, in these initial phases of construction, the successive mental structures that engender development can be considered as so many progressive forms of equilibrium, each of which is an advance upon its predecessor. It must be understood, however, that this functional mechanism, general though it may be, does not explain the content or the structure of the various needs, since each of them is related to the organization of the particular stage that is being considered. For example, the sight of the same object will occasion very different questions in the small child who is still incapable of classification from those of the older child whose ideas are more extensive and systematic. The interests of a child at any given moment depend on the system of ideas he has acquired plus his affective inclinations, and he tends to fulfill his interests in the direction of greater equilibrium.

Before examining the details of development we must try to find that which is common to the needs and interests present at all ages. One can say, in regard to this, that all needs tend first of all to incorporate things and people into the subject's own activity, i.e., to "assimilate" the external world into the structures that have already been constructed, and secondly to readjust these structures as a function of subtle transformations, i.e., to "accommodate" them to external objects. From this point of view, all mental life, as indeed all organic life, tends progressively to assimilate the surrounding environment. This incorporation is effected thanks to the structures or psychic organs whose scope of action becomes more and more extended. Initially, perception and elementary movement (prehension, etc.) are concerned with objects that are close and viewed statically; then later, memory and practical intelligence permit the representation of earlier states of the object as well as the anticipation of their future states resulting from as yet unrealized transformations. Still later intuitive thought reinforces these two abilities. Logical intelligence in the guise of concrete operations and ultimately of abstract deduction terminates this evolution by making the subject master of events that are far distant in space and time. At each of these levels the mind fulfills the same function, which is to incorporate the universe to itself, but the nature of assimilation varies, i.e., the successive modes of incorporation evolve from those of perception and movement to those of the higher mental operations.

In assimilating objects, action and thought must accommodate to these objects; they must adjust to external variation. The balancing of the processes of assimilation and accommodation may be called "adaptation." Such is the general form of psychological equilibrium, and the progressive organization of mental development appears to be simply an ever more precise adaptation to reality.

Reference

CLAPARÈDE, E. *Le développement mental.* Neuchâtel: Delachaux et Niestlé, 1951.

Major Challenges for Students of Infancy and Early Childhood

Myrtle B. McGraw
BRIARCLIFF COLLEGE

It is not possible to pinpoint any particular ideologies or theories that have given rise to the present interest in early childhood development. The forces were many; they were complex and intertwined. Sputnik shocked the nation out of a state of educational complacency. The disparity of educational opportunities and achievements of children from differing socioeconomic and ethnic groups was brought to light. Then it was determined that children from less favorable environments entered school with their educational handicaps already established. To alleviate this situation, the federal government set up Head Start programs. The outcome of the Head Start programs has led to the claim that even the pre-kindergarten period is too late—education begins in the cradle. Furthermore, since the body of knowledge doubles every 10 years, the amount of knowledge one must master favors an early beginning.

Clearly, the goal of this current wave of concern is to develop the optimum potentials of all children. The pressure is on learning, early learning. It seems clear that the infant and toddler are capable of learning a great deal, *if* the opportunities for learning are properly presented. It also seems evident that the principles of learning derived from laboratory studies of animals or college students are inadequate when it comes to dealing with rapid behavior development of the human infant. The prevailing notion is that these goals can be achieved by manipulation of the environments in which the child lives. To some extent these ideas are reinforced by experiments of the effects of "sensory deprivation," "prolonged isolation," and the comparative effects of "enriched and impoverished" environments. Such studies have been conducted on animals, children, and adults. Once again, the emphasis seems to be shifting to the environmental side of the scale, but it is not locked in with the old heredity-environment dichotomy. It is generally recognized now that nature-nurture are interdependent forces, and to try to separate them clouds inquiry. A few studies (Fowler, 1962; McGraw, 1935; Moore, 1960) have demonstrated that the performances of the young *in particular activities* can be advanced beyond normal expectancy. But we have not as yet learned how to develop to the maximum *all potentials of the growing child.* To do this we shall need new theories or concepts of development that transcend the established principles of learning.

1. *Challenge for the Researchers of Growth*   The present corps of growth scientists are the legatees of a vast body of concepts, theories, and research strategies inherited from the "psychological establishment." Of course, the growth scientists will be drawn from many disciplines and from diverse areas of psychology, other than developmental. Already it is apparent that some

Reprinted from *American Psychologist*, August 1970, *25*, 754–756 by permission of the American Psychological Association.

dyed-in-the-wool experimentalists are selecting the human infant in preference to animals for special investigations. The challenge for all the students of growth —regardless of their scientific expertise and theoretical orientation—is to scan their legacy of knowledge and skills and to have the courage to rule out those theories and techniques that are not applicable to the study of a complex, ever-changing phenomenon, such as growth. Many experimentalists fail to take into account that their own preconceptions may operate as uncontrolled variables within a particular situation. Will the experimentalist, skillful in the manipulation of the variables and instruments of measurement, become able to recognize that the way the infant is held or positioned may also be a factor in the results obtained? Will the examiner be so focused on the toddler's response to the items set before him that he fails to detect that the child's wiggling and climbing off the chair and running toward the door is his way of saying that there is pressure on his bladder? Will researchers trained to use the IQ or just chronological age be able to devise strategies to evaluate a multiplicity of systems constantly in flux, each system influencing another and in different degrees? All growth and development is not in the form of accretion. The growth scientists will need to design methods that reveal the rises and falls, the pulsations and rhythms manifest in the growth of a given function. An understanding of these pulsations and rhythms may become promising guidelines for the development of optimum potentials of the growing child. Strategies developed in other disciplines (e.g., communication theories) may provide suggestive models for evaluating constantly changing phenomena, such as rapid growth during the early years. There is evidence that many of the current investigators (Endler, Boulter, & Osser, 1968) are alert to the problem, and that is the first step to improving methodologies.

2. *The Challenge of Cultural Acceptance of Scientific Theories*   In the past, it has been traditional for scientists, especially those dealing with basic sciences, to be removed from the applied aspects of their findings. They were searching for fundamental truths, and whatever society did with it was none of their concern. On the other hand, many atomic physicists have begun to voice a sense of responsibility for the way society makes use of their knowledge. During this century we have been able to see how many psychological theories have been applied and misapplied to the matter of child rearing and education. If the periods of infancy and the early years are as important for total development as generally contended, then it is reasonable to expect the behavioral scientists to take some responsibility for the way in which their thoughts and theories are adopted into the cultural patterns of child management. Just how this can be done is not clear because it has never been systematically undertaken by any scientific discipline. The general public has faith in science and mass media and is quick to announce, "Science proves thus and so." Sometimes the misapplication of a theory may be ascribed to the use of a particular word, perhaps a word that was originally drawn from another discipline.

Let us consider for a moment some current thoughts that have the potential for creating parental anxiety. Take the question of "critical periods" as applied to learning. The concept was first used by embryologists. It was reinforced by Lorenz's (1935) study of imprinting. Recently, it has been emphasized in connection with studies of the effects of an impoverished environment. It has been asserted that if the impoverishment occurs at critical periods in development, then the damage done may be irreversible. Back in 1935, the writer applied the term "critical periods" to the acquisition of motor skills during infancy. If the agreed meaning of "critical periods" carries the idea that whatever is attained in development or learning must be achieved during a specified period, then the term should not be applied to normal behavioral growth. In the aforementioned instance, it was intended to signify that there are *opportune* times when specific activities can most economically be learned. If one misses that opportune time, then the methods of instruction should be altered for later learning of the same function. It is the irreversibility of damage done that adds emotion and fear to the "critical period" concept.

Just the amount of emphasis attached to certain concepts can also distort their meaning when adopted into the culture. Take, for example, the current emphasis on cognition. No investigator would contend that cognition operates independently of other aspects of learning. Yet, merely because it is the focus of investigative activity, cognition, like personality adjustment of old, is a kind of umbrella for all other goals: expose the child to the right knowledge, in the right way, and at the right time—then the job would be well done.

Perhaps most urgently of all, the growth scientists need to review the accepted principles of learning as they have been articulated and generally accepted. These principles of learning were determined largely by studies of animal subjects in laboratory situations and studies of children in the classroom. As stated above, there is every reason to suspect that they are not applicable to the process of growth taking place during infancy and during the early years. There is a pressing need for totally new guidelines for the benefit of those persons responsible for the management and socialization of the child from birth to three years of age. Obviously the most dominant force is change, change in the organism and change in behavior from day to day. Consistency in parental management does not mean setting up a pattern or rule and sticking to it. It means, rather, dealing with a child in a manner consistent with his developmental changes. To do this effectively requires knowledge, sensitivity, intuition, and flexibility. So the challenge is to orient mothers and teachers toward the concept of change, not toward stability in the ordinary sense. Parents should be taught to observe, to scan, and to detect the nonverbal as well as verbal signals of growth within the child and to design methods of instruction accordingly.

The United States may well be at the threshold of institutional reorganization for the care and education of the young. To develop maximum potentials of children of this age will require special preparation on the part of those responsible for this age group. They need to be not only knowledgeable but intuitive and observant. We have long adhered to the tradition that the biological parents are the ones best qualified to bring up young children. Whether we continue to follow that tradition or turn the education of the young over to specialists—kibbutz fashion—the personnel will require special preparation quite unlike that offered to elementary school teachers or even mothers of today.

The growth scientists are challenged to provide a theoretical frame of reference for the education of this crucial age group. And they are advised also to take account of the way in which their theories and pronouncements are adopted into the culture so that the growing child of today can confidently meet the social changes of the twenty-first century.

References

ENDLER, N. S., BOULTER, L. R., & OSSER, H. *Contemporary issues in developmental psychology*, New York: Holt, Rinehart and Winston, 1968.

FOWLER, W. Teaching a two-year-old to read: An experiment in early childhood reading. *Genetic Psychology Monographs*, 1962, 66, 181–283.

LORENZ, K. J. Der Kumpan in der Umwelt des Vogels. Der Artgenosse als auslösendes Moment sozialer Verhaltungsweisen. *Journal of Ornithology (Leipzig)*, 1935, 83, 137–213.

McGRAW, M. B. *Growth, a study of Johnny and Jimmy*. New York: Appleton-Century, 1935.

MOORE, O. K. *Automated responsive environments*. Hamden, Conn.: Basic Education, Inc., 1960. (Film)

Author Index

Italic numbers indicate that the author is mentioned in the *References* section that follows the reading. **Boldface** numbers indicate that the author is the author of a reading.

Abernethy, E. M., 266, *279*
Acheson, R. M., 274, *279*
Achs, R., 146, *154*
Adams, P. A., 336, *337*
Adelson, J., **459–465, 476–484**
Ainsworth, M. D. S., **84–100**
Aitken, F. C., 36, 40, 41, *42*
Akiyama, Y., 46, *49*
Albert, J., 173, 179, *180*
Albrecht, E. J., 367, 369, *370*
Aldrich, C. A., 40, *42*
Alexander, B. K., 107, *109*
Allen, L., 115, *121*, 150, *154*
Allport, G., *446*
Almy, M., 165, *172*
Amatruda, C. S., 69, *71*
Anderson, T., 287, *288*
Andres, D., 359, *366*
Angelino, H., 345, 350, *351*
Antonov, A. N., 274, *279*
Aronfreed, J., 226, 230, *237*, 355, 356, 359, *365*
Arsenian, J. M., 86, 94, *98*
Asch, H., **308–317**
Aserinsky, E., 46, *49*
Ashizawa, K., 272, *281*
Atkinson, R. K., 282, 285, *288*
Ayres, J. G., 409, *417*

Bain, K., 36, *42*
Bakwin, H., 33, 34, 38, *42*

Baldwin, B. T., 369, *370*
Ballard, W. W., **497–505**
Bandura, A., 231, *237*, 357, 363, *365*
Barclay, A., 243, *244*
Barker, R., *62*
Barnes, G. R., Jr., 37, *42*
Barnes, R. H., 276, *280*
Bartsch, G. E., 41, *44*
Bassett, G. W., *433*
Battle, E., 329, *331*
Bayer, L., 139, *144*
Bayley, N., 139, *144*, 157, *163*, 174, *180*
Beach, D. R., *179*
Beaglehole, E., 12, *13*
Beaglehole, P., 12, *13*
Becenti, M., **189–190**
Becker, W. C., 363, *265*
Beg, M. A., 86, **100**
Béhar, M., 275, 276, *281*
Bell, R. Q., *109*, 146, *155*
Bell, S. M., **84–100**
Beller, E. K., 256, *261*
Bellugi, U., 68, *71*
Belmont, L., 290, 291, *295*, 336, *337*
Beloff, J., 292, *295*
Benda, C. E., 146, *154*
Bender, L., *337*
Bendix, R., 7, *9*
Bereiter, C., 192, 196, *199*, 326, *331*
Berko, J., 183, *188*
Berkowitz, L., 228, *237*
Berkson, J., 31, *33*

Subject Index